INSIDERS' GUIDE® TO
Connecticut

SECOND EDITION

ERIC D. LEHMAN

gPP®

Guilford, Connecticut

An imprint of Rowman & Littlefield

Distributed by NATIONAL BOOK NETWORK

Copyright © 2015 by Rowman & Littlefield
Maps: Design Maps Inc. © Rowman & Littlefield

British Library Cataloguing in Publication Information available

Library of Congress Cataloging-in-Publication Data available

ISBN 978-1-4930-1284-8 (paperback)
ISBN 978-1-4930-1618-1 (e-book)

∞™ The paper used in this publication meets the minimum requirements of American National Standard for Information Sciences—Permanence of Paper for Printed Library Materials, ANSI/NISO Z39.48-1992.

All the information in this guidebook is subject to change. We recommend that you call ahead to obtain current information before traveling.

CONTENTS

Directory of Maps

ABOUT THE AUTHOR

Eric D. Lehman teaches literature and creative writing at the University of Bridgeport, and his essays, articles, and stories have appeared in dozens of journals, newspapers, and magazines. He is the author of nine other books about Connecticut, including *Becoming Tom Thumb: Charles Stratton, P. T. Barnum, and the Dawn of American Celebrity; Homegrown Terror: Benedict Arnold and the Burning of New London; Literary Connecticut, A History of Connecticut Wine;* and *A History of Connecticut Food.* He lives in Hamden with his wife, poet and author Amy Nawrocki, and their two cats.

ACKNOWLEDGMENTS

I would like to thank my editor, Amy Lyons, and my mother, Trena Lehman, for all their help assembling this project. I am also grateful to David Lehman, Michael and Elizabeth Nawrocki, Kris Nawrocki, J. Timothy Quirk, Eddie Podbielski, Hans van der Geissen, Ann Nyberg, Francois Steichen, David Leff, Winter Caplanson, and all the other friends and family who made sure I didn't forget their favorite places to eat, play, and stay.

Most of all, I would like to thank my wife, poet Amy Nawrocki. Her compassion and courage are beacons of hope in a world too often dark, and she continues to light the way as we explore Connecticut together. I could not ask for a better traveling companion.

INTRODUCTION

What is home? This is a question that often troubles our nomadic society. Home is certainly more than the place we lay our head to sleep each night, or labor at in the day. Maybe it is a feeling, a spirit, a state of being. We might even think it is just an illusion. Whatever it is, we search for it, traveling the gray back roads of the world, wondering what we are missing. In the words of native son and playwright Eugene O'Neill: "Obsessed by a fairy tale, we spend our lives searching for a magic door and a lost kingdom of peace."

There are many places in this world that promise you that fairy tale, easy to imagine and in reality hard to live with. Connecticut is a doorway to the truth.

Here you can walk through some of the oldest buildings in America and feel moss on the stone walls of colonial farmers. You can taste a fried oyster in a seaside restaurant or the first sip of this year's Chardonnay in a local vineyard. You can fish the small, stony rivers or hike the edge of traprock ridges. The loamy smell of deep forests might call, or the salty tang of long golden beaches.

One thing becomes abundantly clear: There is no one path to knowing the truth Connecticut offers. You may find it on the green grass of a hill, on the porch of a clapboard inn, or at the top of a roller coaster. It is waiting for you at a farm stand, at an antiques store, and at the curve of the next country road. You can find truth through our paintings, our architecture, and our music. And hopefully you will find it in the people you meet, in their sparkling eyes and firm handshakes.

Literary giant Wallace Stevens once said, "There is nothing that gives the feel of Connecticut like coming home to it." He found that feeling in the ground beneath his feet each day on the way to work. "Going back to Connecticut is a return to an origin . . . an origin of hardihood, good faith and good will." Long before Stevens composed poems on the streets of the state capital, ardent patriot of the American Revolution Nathan Hale found his own truth here before the United States of America officially existed. He loved Connecticut so much that he died for it, sneaking into British-controlled New York City, not in the pursuit of some abstract freedom but to save the home he loved. "Home"—Hale understood what that word meant, and though he died before he could tell us more in words, his actions speak to us over two centuries later.

Connecticut offers visitors and residents alike glimpses of that unspoken truth. What is it, you ask? I can only tell you what I found in the years since I made my home here, something that Nathan Hale might have echoed had he lived. We must first become patriots of a small plot of earth, then a watershed, then a township, a county, a state. We must love, and love deeply, the people around us and the earth we stand on. Only then can we be in the real and truest sense patriots of a nation, and hopefully of the human race.

Is that what you will learn here in Connecticut? It's time to find out.

HOW TO USE THIS BOOK

Whether you are just visiting the varied landscapes of Connecticut or are here to stay, this book will guide you well. Vital facts and insiders' insights are organized in a way that minimizes your time spent searching the book, which does not require sequential reading. This guide is chock-full of special places that insiders know, and with it firmly in hand as you travel the state, you will soon be one of us.

The first few sections are designed to make you comfortable with both Connecticut and this book. **Welcome to Connecticut** lays out the structural and cultural map of the state, which can seem small at first glance but soon reveals layer after layer of possibilities. It also details the state's transportation grid in a clear way. No doubt you will have an easier time than the early pioneers who hacked their own paths through dense forest and swamp. Still, it helps to get a feel for the options we have to move around freely in our densely woven state.

The **History** chapter cannot hope to contain the rich tapestry of times gone by, but I have highlighted some of the most exciting and relevant incidents. It will hopefully whet your appetite for the many historical attractions we have to offer.

Throughout the book you will find **Insider's Tips** (ℹ️) that will guide you to an important resource, illuminate a special point, or reveal a local secret. These tips are also built into the listings themselves, and it is my hope that you'll find your own special place as you use this book to explore. Larger **Close-ups** highlight a particularly rich subject for discovery. Be sure to use a pen and highlighter to annotate the listings as you experience them for yourself. Also be on the lookout for our **Insiders' Choice** icons (✳), which highlight this insider's favorites and recommendations.

The greater part of the book is divided into the eight Connecticut counties: **Fairfield, Litchfield, New Haven, Middlesex, Hartford, Tolland, New London,** and **Windham.** This will allow you to zoom in on a particular region for exploration. These chapters are broken down into sections of Attractions, Events & Activities, Shopping, Accommodations, and Restaurants. For example, under Attractions you'll find sections on art museums, historical sites, kidstuff, landmarks, etc. There are certain overlaps and cross-references, such as an old inn that also boasts a fine restaurant.

The listings in each section are further broken into alphabetically ordered subsections by type of restaurant, activity, etc. For example, looking for Mystic Pizza, you would find it in the restaurants section of New London County under the subheading Pizza. And of course this works the other way around. If you're in the mood for sushi while driving past New Haven on I-95, you can search through the guide under New Haven County, Restaurants, and Asian & Indian, finding local options like Midori or Miya's. The descriptions will then steer you to the best option.

Each county's chapter also includes a suggested day trip. However, I am confident you will soon find your own favorite places and pathways. A day well spent in our enchanting state presents endless possibilities.

The final **Living Here** section is for those of you who are in the process of moving to the state, or moving within to another town or region. Options for real estate, health care, and education are detailed. I can't help but think how lucky we are to live in Connecticut, and how we owe it to our home to all become "insiders."

Every effort has been made to provide the freshest and most accurate information possible, but details always change no matter where we travel and live. If you discover an element that needs updating or something you feel has been missed, please don't hesitate to contact us at editorial@globepequot.com.

ACCOMMODATIONS PRICE CODE

The following price code for hotels, motels, campgrounds, and bed-and-breakfasts is based on double occupancy during high season (usually Memorial Day through October). Most accommodations offer a range of rooms; this is the average.

$ . . . . **Less than $90**
$$ . . . . **$90 to $140**
$$$ . . . . **$140 to $200**
$$$$ . . . . **More than $200**

RESTAURANT PRICE CODE

Most restaurants have offerings at a range of prices. The following price code represents the average price of a single dinner entree, excluding drinks, hors d'oeuvres, side dishes, tax, and tip. Occasionally, when warranted, a restaurant will be given a range.

$ . . . . **Less than $10**
$$ . . . . **$10 to $20**
$$$ . . . . **$20 to $30**
$$$$ . . . . **More than $30**

WELCOME TO CONNECTICUT

Welcome to the Constitution State! When I first began exploring Connecticut, I found out very quickly that it was not known for any one thing. Instead, the state is a like a multilayered book or painting: There are many ways to know it. As a teacher, I met thousands of Connecticut residents, young and old, and talked to them about their experiences here. "Peaceful" to one and "exciting" to another, Connecticut often seems more the fluid opinion of the viewer than a hard reality.

However, there are some facts you can grab hold of. You should probably be on the lookout for Connecticut's state flower, the mountain laurel, which can be seen blooming in the traprock highlands every spring. Connecticut's state song is the timeless classic of the American Revolution, "Yankee Doodle Dandy," and, yes, the correct lyrics do include "stuck a feather in his cap and called it macaroni." Connecticut boasts America's first public library, hamburger, telephone book, helicopter, pull-cord light switch, friction matches, and nuclear submarine, and the oldest stone building in colonial America, the Henry Whitfield House in Guilford, built in 1639.

But these are facts you can learn by looking at the state from the outside. It's time to explore from the inside out.

LANDSCAPE

If you were so inclined, you could divide inland Connecticut into three sections, nearly equal in size: the western highlands, the rich river valley, and the eastern uplands. These are accompanied by the thin strip of low, alluvial plain created by the many rivers flowing into Long Island Sound. The state is only 60 miles north to south, and 100 miles across. Driving from the northwest corner in Salisbury to the southeast corner in Stonington can take less than three hours. This is a great bonus for the traveler, and allows any point in the state to be used as a home base for exploration.

Though Connecticut's cities at first seem small, this is an illusion created by the early incorporation of the region, so with 169 small communities, assessing the metropolitan areas rather than individual towns is a better indicator of size. Hartford has a contiguous metro area bigger than any in New England except, of course, Boston, and possibly Providence, depending on how they are judged. Fairfield County's gold coast from Stratford to Greenwich is technically a contiguous metropolis as well, and if considered such, is easily the second-largest city after Boston. And yet, despite being so full of busy life, Connecticut rarely feels crowded, and a quiet stream or stone-walled farm is only a few steps away.

Connecticut is a driving culture, so unless you are located at the heart of one of the larger cities, you will need a car. However, there is a lot of public transportation compared to some areas of the country, and the distances are short. Of course you may be one of those intrepid bicyclists who

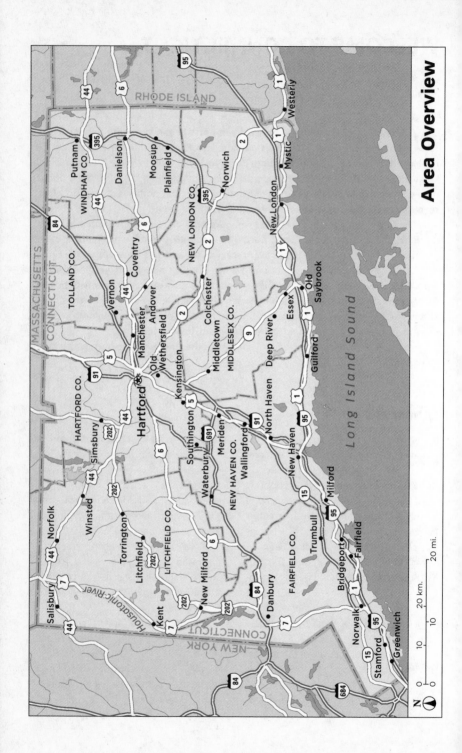

Area Overview

travel the back roads of the state each summer, riding from village to village. If so, more power to you.

GEOLOGY

When the glaciers receded from Long Island across Connecticut at the end of the last ice age, they left innumerable stones and glacial "erratics," large boulders often of a different rock type than the surrounding landscape. Later these stones would cause settlers to complain mightily as they cleared their fields for tilling. The glaciers also carved the ancient volcanic and sedimentary rock, leaving cliffs and notches in a general north–south direction, especially in the lower middle part of the state. The glaciers have carved and pressed this land into its present form, and the evidence of their passing is everywhere you look.

The Connecticut River is the longest in New England, stretching up to the Canadian border in a series of lakes. Once, it most likely came directly south to present-day New Haven, in what is now the Quinnipiac River valley, but it was diverted either by a giant stone spirit named Hobbomock (who was later transformed into the Sleeping Giant mountain north of New Haven) or by accumulated sand and gravel deposits near the town of Rocky Hill, depending on the source you prefer to believe. It splits the state neatly into two parts, and has provided a conduit for people and goods for thousands of years.

The northern part of the river valley in the state spreads out, since it was part of a geologically recent glacial pool that we call Lake Hitchcock. The silts left behind in this low river-bottom land are rich and have supported farming for hundreds of years. Today there are still numerous tobacco farms in this part of the state, benefiting from these rich silty soils.

The rocky western hills are part of the Appalachian uplands, rising to 2,316 feet on the peak of Bear Mountain in Salisbury. The eastern hills are smaller, but no less rocky, and both ranges are covered in forests today, though during the first 300 years of European colonization they were denuded several times. For most of its modern history, Connecticut looked more like the green, hilly farmland of present-day England than the ocean of trees you will see from high points like Bear Mountain today.

ℹ **Make sure you use the area codes 203 or 860 even when making local calls in Connecticut, with 203 covering the southwest corner. Recently the codes 475 and 959 overlaid the other two areas for new phone numbers.**

PEOPLE

Who lives in Connecticut? Because of the state's ports and its proximity to New York, it tends to be more diverse than the rest of New England, though its demographics match the national averages fairly well. Its population is somewhere between 3.5 and 4 million people, and immigration brings in about 75,000 new residents each decade. It is the 29th most populous state, although it is the 3rd smallest. Two hundred years ago, the population was 97 percent rural, but now that number is about 10 percent. Despite being called the "land of steady habits," it has been considered one of the more progressive states politically since the time of the Civil War, and is also one of the wealthiest. According to an aggregate of various statistics and surveys, only Vermont ranks ahead of Connecticut as far as education.

The Connecticut accent is more subtle than some, but you'll hear it on words with a *t* in the middle. For example, the towns of Clinton and Shelton are often pronounced "Clin-en" and "Shel-en." This accent seems to develop almost immediately, and you can hear it in the speech of Connecticut residents originally from countries as diverse as Poland, Vietnam, and Jamaica.

We are sometimes called the "Nutmeg State" and our inhabitants "nutmeggers." This designation actually comes from a long-ago insult. Connecticut Yankees were accused of replacing nutmegs with wooden replicas and selling them to unwitting buyers. Historians remain divided on whether this was the work of those Yankees or the sailors who brought the nutmeg from the Caribbean, but they agree on the fact that it probably only happened once or twice. So, since this appellation is not complimentary, and "Yankees" has been reserved since the early 20th century by our neighboring baseball team, what does that leave? In recent years "Connecticutians" has made great strides but has yet to catch on, perhaps because of its numerous syllables. My favorite is "Connectors," a rare but apt name, not too long, and brimming with symbolism and strength.

THE ARTS

The arts have a long and storied history in the state. Literary giants like Harriet Beecher Stowe, Mark Twain, Eugene O'Neill, and Arthur Miller all had homes in Connecticut and included its foibles and glories in their many writings. Poets like Wallace Stevens and James Merrill wrote their complex poems here, and the Hill-Stead Museum's Sunken Garden Poetry Festival is nationally famous. You'll find the hills and shores simply swarming with Pulitzer Prize winners, who might make their reputations in New York but live here.

Visual artists have also found success in Connecticut. Sculptor Alexander Calder, architect Frederick Law Olmsted, and experimental painter Sol LeWitt lived and worked here, and the art scene has remained vital on its own. The Connecticut Impressionists represented a seminal moment in American art history, and many of the state's museums feature not only the paintings of masters such as Childe Hassam but their homes and artifacts as well.

Theaters are everywhere in the state, and often feature the famous actors who live here. Actors such as Paul Newman, Katharine Hepburn, and Meryl Streep have not only resided in the state, but actively participated in improving the theater here. Many actors were born in Connecticut and got their starts at one of the wonderful theaters or summer stock companies throughout the state. Musicians from Dave Brubeck to Moby have also lived here, and the music scene is often intensely competitive, with garage bands and DJs fighting it out on the stages of famous venues like Toad's Place before hitting the big time in New York.

Despite having no huge central city to focus the arts scene, Connecticut boasts a number of quality venues for art, theater, music, and literary expression, helped of course by the wealthy culturistas who live here and by the many quality colleges and universities packed into the small area. That means that no matter what area of the state you visit, you can find and enjoy whatever type of art you like, in a wide variety of venues.

OUTDOOR ACTIVITIES

Connecticut's shoreline is the first place to come to people's minds when they think of outdoor activities. The access to the protected waters of Long Island Sound makes the state's countless harbors and marinas home to yachts, sailboats, and speedboats of all sorts. A quiet day out on the Sound is the dream of everyone in coastal Connecticut, and cruising the charming Thimble Islands or fishing for muscular striped bass brings locals and tourists alike out on the water.

The many rivers, lakes, and streams are havens for anglers, canoers, kayakers, and more. The Connecticut River itself is huge—a half-mile across in some sections—and provides ample room for sailing and fishing. The Farmington River is a world-class fly-fishing destination, and the Housatonic River is the summer home for kayakers and rafters of all ages. The state is riddled with small lakes, many of which are fun swimming destinations, and all of which lure canoes and powerboats out on any summer weekend.

Golf is a popular way to get outdoors here, and there are dozens of public courses, some of which are nationally known. In winter, cross-country and downhill skiing are both available in the state; snowshoeing and snowmobiling are rarer activities, seen only in the northeast and northwest areas.

Though the mountains of Connecticut are not high, these rolling hills broken by rivers and streams provide great hiking opportunities, and the state's blue trail system (officially called Blue-Blazed Hiking Trail System) and greenways have networked the entire state for anyone interested in a lifetime of walking. Many of these trails go through forests that have grown over farms or even villages, and finding the ruins of colonial farmers is only one of many exciting outcomes of a day's walk. Public and private campgrounds dot the landscape, and some even allow winter camping.

The greenways and many seldom-traveled back roads are also havens for thousands of bicyclists during the warmer months, and there are new places to explore around every corner. In fact, the state seems made for this activity, being just the right size for cycling expeditions along the coast or among the hills. There are also those, like me, who have walked the state from end to end.

CUISINE

As with Connecticut's other offerings, this is a land of multiplicity, with a variety of options and flavors. Italian restaurants became omnipresent in the mid-20th century, but today you can get almost any sort of global cuisine here. If there are fewer Chinese and Mexican restaurants than other nearby states, it is only because there are so many other varieties: Mongolian, Vietnamese, Thai, Peruvian, Jamaican, Ethiopian . . . the list goes on. You will find that Japanese sushi restaurants are everywhere, even in the depths of suburbia. And if you're interested in drinks as well as food, you will find plenty of Irish-style pubs, martini bars, wine bars, and colonial taverns.

"Shore food" is common in Connecticut, and steamers, mussels, lobster rolls, and all sorts of fried fish make an appearance. Abraham Lincoln's favorite dish, fried oysters, is a local invention, and bluefish is a common local catch, although few seafood restaurants seem to carry it. New England is of course known for its clam chowder, and though you can get all kinds here, the Connecticut version is often a briny broth brimming with potatoes and onions. In the past, corn, turkeys, dairy, chickens, apples, and peaches were all local crops. Pigs were raised for salt pork, and maple trees were tapped for syrup. Other historical delicacies are pumpkin pie, planked shad, and Indian pudding—a mix of cornmeal, molasses, and spices that has been slow-cooked to a sweet perfection. You can still find most of these items here today, especially at the surviving colonial inns and taverns.

Though Connecticut does not boast a major city like Boston or Philadelphia, it has more fine restaurants than any comparable area of small cities in the country. This is no doubt due to the wealth and education of many of its inhabitants. Villages that elsewhere in America would be too small even for chain restaurants, here have at least one five-star dining establishment. Many restaurants are following the national trend toward experimentation, with both global delicacies and local specialties making more frequent appearances.

However, fine dining is not the only way to eat your way across the state. There are numerous famous "road food" joints dotting the landscape as well, including remarkably preserved drive-ins, hot dog stands, and lobster shacks from the early 20th century. The hot lobster roll and New Haven–style apizza are two local inventions that remain popular everywhere. The hamburger made its first appearance in a restaurant here in Connecticut, and dozens of traditional diners still serve their down-home dishes.

i **Connecticut has recently passed a law making it legal to cork a bottle of wine and take it home from a restaurant. That's a relief to all of us who don't want to finish a full bottle with dinner but don't want any to go to waste.**

WITH CHILDREN

Like any area worth its salt, Connecticut has plenty of activities and amusements for children, and as with adult adventures, there is a wide variety from which to choose. From Quassy to Lake Compounce, the fun parks are varied and never fail to entertain. Exploring Mystic Seaport, playing miniature golf among giant dinosaurs, river tubing through Satan's Kingdom, and riding the Essex Steam Train are all kid-friendly activities that adults will not have to pretend to enjoy. For those who want to teach their children while also amusing them, there are a number of science centers, planetariums, and fun kids' museums.

Events like fairs and festivals are nearly constant during the summer months, and many have activities geared toward children, with some, like the Renaissance Faires, designed with children in mind. Petting farms, wildlife preserves, and nature centers are around every corner for those children (and adults) who enjoy our animal brethren. If those aren't enough, there are beaches, carousels, cider mills, ski slopes, and horseback riding.

Of course you could always turn on the video games or download a movie. But this is not what Connecticut is made for. Our roots in true family values run deep, and those are reflected in the active ways we engage our children.

WHEN TO GO

Autumn in New England? Christmas in Connecticut? Or perhaps summer on the shore? Ah, yes, there are so many seasons to enjoy the Constitution State, and it is difficult to say when a bad time would be. That is not a partisan statement; it is merely a fact of the generally mild climate and diverse attractions that draw visitors throughout the year. Of course Connecticut can occasionally get very hot in July or August, but since it is 10 degrees cooler in the forests (the state is covered in them) and 15 degrees cooler on the shore, these temperatures never stop visitors or locals from enjoying the outdoor activities and events of the summer season. A stormy winter like 2014's can occasionally bring a deluge of heavy snow, but usually it is just enough to make the landscape look idyllic. And there is rarely a problem getting somewhere the next morning on the well-plowed streets and roads.

So, really it is a matter of deciding what you want to do here when deciding when to visit the state. The delights of the shore such as the beaches and historic seaports are obviously most popular in summer. Many of the historic homes are only open in summer as well, due to the need for preservation. There are numerous events and festivals on many of the town greens, wharfs, and fairgrounds throughout the warmer months, and if you're coming for the amusement parks, that is the time to go as well.

Autumn is legendary in Connecticut, and rightfully so. The trees have had more time to grow here than in some other parts of the country, and the species of temperate trees and rainfall averages are just right for the kind of display that makes people from desert states or European countries shake their heads in amazement. Cynical locals try to take the beautiful leaf colors for granted, but usually fail. Fall is also a great time to get outdoors to hike or bike the endless network of trails, or go antiquing in the small village shops. It is also the perfect time to visit the northwest and northeast parts of the state, but don't try to book a bed-and-breakfast the night before.

If you're looking for a peaceful country inn without gaggles of tourists, try December, especially if you can catch an early snow. Christmas is a lovely time in New England, and many towns and villages sponsor events leading up to it throughout December, as well as First Night celebrations at New Year's. Downhill and cross-country skiing, snowshoeing, and other outdoor winter activities tend to peak in February here, while April sees the first stirrings of life in the forests and rivers, bringing out anglers and hikers. For couples and single travelers, May is also a wonderfully quiet time, especially if you can catch an early warm spell, with all the attractions open but without so many children (who are in school until mid-June).

i **Connecticut's state animal is the sperm whale, once the source of precious whale oil for New London merchants and now a source of delight and wonder to us all.**

Some attractions, like the two huge casinos, the art museums, and the theaters, bring people year-round. There is never a bad time to visit Connecticut. Native son and world-famous entertainer P. T. Barnum said, "The noblest art is that of making others happy," and the people here live by that motto. If you are searching for happiness, this may just be the place you will find it.

TRAVEL INFORMATION & RESOURCES

Connecticut's small size is a benefit for travelers and gives both newcomers and locals the opportunity to easily access a variety of conveniences and attractions. Travel into the state is easy by plane, train, and even ferry. Inevitably, though, travel within and through the state is largely dependent on the automobile, despite access to public transportation in the major urban areas. Indeed, the best way to see those out-of-the-way charms and get to know much of the Connecticut character is by car.

Much of Connecticut remains rural, and the roads less traveled present an accessible network for sightseers and cyclists. Back roads and country avenues weave throughout the state, and hiking trails provide the chance to wander around lakes and into the woodlands on foot. For many, getting around is a self-propelled activity or one that lends itself best to two wheels rather than four. It's not uncommon during spring, summer, and autumn months for cyclists to be seen pedaling through the Litchfield Hills or the Quiet Corner, or for a lone bicycle to take its place in the scenery along the Long Island shore. If traveling by car, watch out for cyclists, give them a wide berth as you pass, and don't be surprised if you happen upon a road race.

STATE OF CONNECTICUT DEPARTMENT OF TRANSPORTATION
2800 Berlin Tpke.
Newington, CT 06111
(860) 594-2000
ct.gov/dot

DEPARTMENT OF MOTOR VEHICLES
60 State St.
Wethersfield, CT 06161
(860) 263-5700 (within Hartford area or outside Connecticut)
(800) 842-8222
ct.gov/DMV
Open Mon through Fri 8 a.m. to 4 p.m.

GETTING HERE

Airports

BRADLEY INTERNATIONAL AIRPORT
Schoephoester Rd.
Windsor Locks, CT 06096
(860) 292-2000
bradleyairport.com
Bradley International Airport (BDL) is Connecticut's primary airport. Located in Windsor Locks—11 miles northwest of Hartford via I-91 (exit 40) and the Airport Connector, Route 20—this airport is easy to get to, making the first or last legs of your trip relatively comfortable and hopefully hassle-free. The complex is smaller than its counterparts in New York City or Boston, so it is a good alternative, especially for Fairfield County travelers who might otherwise choose the

city's airports. As you arrive near the terminal, look for signage to direct you to arrivals and departures. Outside, a pergola-type structure of tinted glass curves high above the entranceway to departing flights. Ticket counters, security, and departures are located on the main floor, while arrivals come in on the lower level, where you'll find baggage claim. The interior is spacious, bright, and welcoming, with high ceilings and glass facades.

Business as well as leisure travelers find nonstop and regional connection service to all major US markets, Canada, and San Juan, Puerto Rico. Charter service to Mexico and the Caribbean is also offered. Seven major airlines and their subsidiaries operate out of Bradley, including Air Canada (888-247-2262), American (800-433-7300), Delta (800-221-1212), Jet Blue (800-538-2583), Southwest (800-435-9792), United (800-241-6522), and US Airways (800-428-4322).

Services at the airport include customs, wireless Internet, executive clubs, ADA-accessible passenger drop-off and pickup, wheelchairs, a Commuter Carrier Lift, telecommunication devices for the speech and hearing impaired, luggage carts, and of course shoe shines. Restrooms are wheelchair accessible and located throughout the terminal. Within, you'll find a number of gift shops, various eateries, and a food court.

Accommodations

Newly renovated, the Sheraton Bradley (860-627-5311), located between terminals A and B, is the closest and most convenient lodging option. The Sheraton offers 237 guest rooms, Internet access, and a health and fitness center, as well as meeting space. The Concord Restaurant is on-site, and there are 2 additional eating options at the Sheraton. The surrounding towns and the larger region offer a number of additional accommodation options.

Parking

Short-term parking spaces are available directly across from the terminal and in one other lot on the other side of the hotel. Some long-term spots are also available near the terminal; otherwise, long-term parking is available in 6 other lots with shuttle service to the terminal. For more information and rates go to ParkBradley.com or call (877) 735-9280.

Ground Travel

All major car rental agencies offer service at Bradley, and all rental companies provide shuttle service to and from the terminal. They are located near Long Term Parking Lot 3. Eight national companies serve the airport, with 5 hosting on-airport locations: Alamo (800-GO-ALAMO), Avis (800-331-1212), Budget (800-527-0700), Hertz (800-654-3131), and National (800-CAR-RENT).

A number of limousine and car service companies provide transportation to and from the airport, including Connecticut Limo (800-472-LIMO). See the main airport website for a full list. GO Airport Shuttle services Bradley and can carry up to 10 passengers (866-284-3247; 2theairport.com). Bus service connects to Hartford; see the Bradley Flyer Route, and call CT Transit at (860) 525-9181 or visit cttransit.com. Taxi service to or from the airport can be expensive and would be reasonable only within the Hartford area. One-way fare from Hartford will be about $45.

The New England Air Museum, a fun trip for the whole family, is located only minutes from the airport. Plan a few hours here before picking up the relatives.

Other Airports

TWEED NEW HAVEN REGIONAL
AIRPORT
155 Burr St.
New Haven, CT 06512
(203) 466-8833
flytweed.com

With service to Philadelphia (and then the world), Tweed New Haven Regional Airport (HVN) offers a smart alternative for travelers in Connecticut to avoid the long lines and tiresome delays of bigger airports. Easily accessible from I-95 or I-91, Tweed is just 3 miles from downtown New Haven.

A number of major airlines and their subsidiaries operate out of Tweed, providing service to over 330 domestic destinations and 130 worldwide, including London-Heathrow. There are hourly, short-term, and long-term parking lots. Four major car rental companies (Avis, National, Budget, and Hertz) operate directly at the terminal. Taxi service is available outside the terminal as well: Metro Taxi (203-777-7777) or Heritage Taxi (203-466-6666). Taxis and buses make it an easy trip to new Haven's train stations. Buses operated by CT Transit (203-624-0151) stop at the main entrance. Robinson Aviation's Corporate Aviation Center, located at Tweed, offers on-demand charter service and flight training (203-467-9555; robinso-naviation.com).

In addition to Tweed and Bradley, Connecticut has a number of small airports with charter service, including regional service through Groton/New London Airport (860-445-8549). Also operated by the Connecticut Department of Transportation, Hartford Brainard Airport, Waterbury-Oxford Airport, Danielson Airport, and Windham Airport in Willimantic are general aviation airports and offer charter service, hangar space, and instruction. Other public airports, like the Danbury Municipal Airport and Robertson Field in Plainville, which is the oldest airport in the US, are designed to relieve airline congestion at larger airports. Airports like the Igor I. Sikorsky Memorial Airport in Bridgeport, named for the first man to fly a helicopter in the Western Hemisphere, have heliports. A number of other public use and general aviation airports operate. Among the 19 small airports in the state, the Goodspeed Airport in East Haddam is the only one that has a water runway.

GETTING AROUND

Highways

The Nutmeg State is cradled by three major interstates: I-95 hugs the coast; I-84 traverses west to east and crosses I-91, which bisects the state and then begins to tag along the Connecticut River near Wethersfield, as it will do as it heads to northern New England. Spidering from these major thruways and crisscrossing the state are other important highways—Routes 15, 8, 9, and 2—and a host of other regionally significant byways. Depending on your departure and destination sites, the major thruways provide standard transit into and out of the state and between Connecticut's major cities. But you'd be hard-pressed to see the real Connecticut with these major highways alone.

I-95 & I-395

Officially named the Governor John Davis Lodge Turnpike, I-95 enters Greenwich from New York and continues across the state for 128 miles. It is also identified as the Connecticut Turnpike, the name it was originally given when it opened in 1958. Coming from New York, look for the New England Thruway. All of these different names can cause some confusion, especially when entering the state. Plus, though the interstate highway system usually uses odd numbers to denote north–south routes and even numbers for east–west routes, I-95 actually takes on a distinct easterly direction through the state as it parallels Long Island Sound.

The bulk of volume flows through Fairfield County, with commuters and commerce going to and coming from New York, and rush hour can be a tedious experience. As the main commercial route through the state, tractor-trailers will be omnipresent on I-95. From Greenwich to New Haven, volume can load between 120,000 and 200,000 cars per day. Expect heavy traffic from 6 to 9 a.m. and 4 to 7 p.m. on weekdays, and tune in for local traffic reports, as congestion is likely to hit at any time.

I-95, I-91, and Route 34 converge in New Haven. Despite recent improvements to I-95 between Long Wharf at Sargent Drive (exit 46) in New Haven and exit 54 in Branford, delays and congestion still occur. Part of the New Haven Harbor Crossing (NHHC) Corridor Improvement Program included remodeling, reinforcing, and expanding (to 10 lanes) the Pearl Harbor Memorial Bridge, also called the "Q" bridge, as it crosses over the Quinnipiac River and overlooks the busy harbor. For the 140,000 cars that travel the bridge daily, the drive is smoother, but construction on Route 34 continues, so take care when merging and moving in from downtown exits. For traffic information and updates visit i95newhaven.com.

Technically, the designated turnpike becomes I-395 and spurs in a more northerly direction from East Lyme (at 76, a left-side exit ramp). This leg connects to Plainfield, finally ending in Killingly, where it becomes US 6 into Rhode Island. Technically, I-395 continues into Massachusetts, but not as the Governor Lodge Pike. Traffic is relatively light on I-395 once you pass the exit for Mohegan Sun Casino, and the scenery becomes more rural through the eastern part of the Quiet Corner.

However, many continue on I-95 proper through New London to the exits of Mystic and Stonington, heading to Rhode Island or Cape Cod. Volume is less, officially, on the eastern part of the highway, but watch for pockets of heavy traffic in this section, especially on summer weekends, when vacationers head toward and return from the destinations of our sister states.

Once a toll road, fares were discontinued at the end of 1985. Thirteen service plazas are available, as is a rest area between exits 65 and 66 in Westbrook. Plan your stops accordingly, as once past Madison (between exits 61 and 62) another plaza won't appear again until Plainfield between exits 89 and 90. Westbound only there's respite between 79A and 79. Facilities, however, are never far from the exits, and reentry is usually easy. Note: By the end of 2015, exits on I-395 will be numbered according to road miles rather than consecutively. Signs will carry both numbers for at least two years.

i Connecticut Welcome Centers are located on I-95 in North Stonington (southbound), Westbrook (northbound), and Darien (northbound); on I-84 in Danbury (eastbound) and West Willington (westbound); and on the Merritt Parkway in Greenwich (northbound).

I-91

Connecting the state to its neighbors in the north, I-91 is the main north–south passageway through eastern New England and will take you through Massachusetts, eventually snuggling the border between Vermont and New Hampshire all the way to the Canada border. As the longest of the three interstates whose entire route is located within New England, it is also the only one to intersect all five of the others (I-84 and I-95 in Connecticut, I-90 in Massachusetts, and

I-89 and I-93 in Vermont). Fifty-eight of these miles travel through Connecticut from New Haven to Enfield.

Northeast through the suburbs of New Haven, the interstate enters Meriden, which is about halfway between the Elm City and the capital. In Meriden it connects with I-691, a spur that follows west and offers an alternate connection to I-84. Heading toward Hartford, it passes the towns of Middletown, Cromwell, Rocky Hill, and Wethersfield. Arriving at Hartford you'll see the Connecticut River, which the highway will piggyback into the northern states.

Just before the city limits of Hartford, the interchange to I-84 will come in at exit 29A for westbound and 30 for eastbound, a potential trouble spot, as merging traffic in either direction is likely to get backed up. Exit 29A will also take you into the capital area. HOV (High Occupancy Vehicle), or carpool, lanes are available on I-91 northbound past Hartford (exits 33–40). These lanes are separate from regular lanes, marked as "Restricted Lanes" with a white diamond on a black background, and have their own exit and entrance ramps. Designed for buses, vans, and cars with two or more passengers, HOV lanes allow vehicles to avoid slow or stalled traffic.

Bradley International Airport is accessible from exit 40 via Brainard Road, while I-291 heads off from exit 34 to Manchester.

I-84

Weaving 97.9 miles northeast from Danbury, I-84, which originates in Pennsylvania, scrolls through Waterbury, Hartford, and Tolland County on its way to the Massachusetts border by Sturbridge Village. The 1961 General Assembly designated the line from the New York border to the Connecticut River as the Yankee Expressway, though few if any locals refer to it as such. I-84 claims the widest highway expanse as 12 lanes spread

out between exits 57 and 59, including HOV lanes.

Over the New York border in Danbury, connections to Routes 6, 202, 7, 25, and 34 are available. Crossing the Rochambeau Bridge, which spans the Housatonic River at exit 11, I-84 ascends into Southbury and Middlebury, where connections are available to Route 8. Through the double-decked interchange into Waterbury, the city's vintage brick architecture stands out through exits 19 to 23, with access to downtown at exit 22. Through Cheshire, where you'll find access to I-691 and the towns to the south and west of Hartford, I-84 begins to take on a slightly more congested look; construction delays, seemingly frequent accidents, and commuter traffic frequently clog the route for this stretch. Through West Hartford and Hartford the highway curves quite a bit, and look out for a number of left exits.

At exits 51 and 52, the highway intersects I-91 (northbound and southbound, respectively) and then crosses the Bulkeley Bridge, the oldest bridge on the interstate system, over the Connecticut River. East of Hartford, I-84 takes on a more rural character. Exit 53 links to US 44, which will take you west or farther east across the northern half of the state, while Route 2 at exit 55 heads east. Spurs for I-384 (exit 59) and I-291 (exit 61) provide convenient access for the towns of Windsor, South Windsor, and Manchester. HOV lanes are accessible on I-84 east of Hartford with westbound exits at 64 and eastbound entrances at exit 58. Access to the Founders Bridge from Route 2 westbound will bring you toward downtown Hartford.

Route 15—Merritt Parkway & Wilbur Cross Parkway

The longest continuous stretch of scenic highway (almost 38 miles) is the Merritt Parkway (Route 15) traversing lower Fairfield County from the New York border to the Housatonic River Bridge in Stratford. Named for congressman Schuyler Merritt, who helped put legislation together to build it, the parkway is one of the oldest in the US (built between 1934 and 1940) and has been designated a National Scenic Route. The Merritt offers pleasant respite after tackling the bridges or tunnels of New York City. Architecturally, overpasses were originally designed by George L. Dunkelberger so that no two were alike, though newer overpasses do not necessarily have this quality. With trees all around—thin forests on both sides and a single line of trees through much of the divide—it's particularly beautiful in mid-spring and autumn. More recently, trees have been cut or removed, mostly as maintenance, but debate continues as to whether this has changed, or will change, the unique character of this road. Still, there's plenty of green to be enjoyed. Watch out for deer, as they enjoy grazing along the sides of the route, despite the traffic.

Commercial vehicles—those with more than four wheels, over 8 feet high, or more than four tons—are prohibited. No towed trailers are allowed either, so consider alternate routes if you plan to tow your boat. Tolls were eliminated in 1988. On-ramps can be short or sloped, so observe speed limits. Rest areas include parking and gas stations with convenience stores and are located on both sides near exit 46 and at the visitor center in Greenwich. Service stations are available in Orange and North Haven.

Once across the Sikorsky Bridge over the Housatonic River, the Merritt becomes the Wilbur Cross Parkway in Milford and continues to Meriden. Travelers can pick up the I-95 connector (Milford Parkway) here and head north or south on that interstate. Named for a former governor, the Wilbur Cross may not be as scenic as its counterpart, but it does have its charms, namely the Heroes' Tunnel (formerly the West Rock

Tunnel), the only thruway in Connecticut to cut through a natural obstacle. Also interesting is that the tunnel is lit by sodium vapor lamps. The parkway ends after connecting with I-91/I-691, the main east–west corridor in Meriden, and merging with Route 5 (US 5) and becoming the Berlin Turnpike.

Now a utilitarian byway, the Berlin Turnpike officially connects the Wilbur Cross Parkway with the Wilbur Cross Highway (the alias for the highway through Wethersfield, Hartford, and Manchester all the way to the Mass Pike). Look for signage designating Routes 15/5. It spans about 11 miles through Berlin, Newington, and Wethersfield. Frequent traffic lights make travel on this arterial four- to six-lane highway a bit of a chore. You're likely to see more than a fair share of dubious motels and auto repair shops, but also a number of popular shopping destinations and eateries.

Route 8

Running north–south, Route 8 begins in Bridgeport from I-95 by way of an interchange of the Colonel Henry Mucci Highway that also connects to Route 15 and Route 25. The highway splits in Trumbull, with Route 8 winding north through the Naugatuck Valley and into Waterbury, through the Litchfield Hills, and eventually continuing to Winchester, where the freeway portion ends and a rural arterial route continues past the Massachusetts border.

One of the more scenic highways in the state (though not officially designated as such), Route 8 was planned and constructed over several decades but was originally meant to improve the Waterbury Turnpike, which was chartered way back in 1801. The towns of the Naugatuck River valley, including Derby, Ansonia, Seymour, Beacon Falls, and Naugatuck, were once industrial centers, and you'll get a glimpse of that history as you twist past old brick factory buildings and the rust-colored tracks of the Naugatuck Railroad.

The southern section twists a little more, but through Waterbury and north to Watertown and Thomaston some of that bygone industrial character is still quite visible. Onward to Litchfield, Harwington, Torrington, and Winchester, the hills seem to blend in with the road, making travel especially pleasant. Though a major highway, Route 8 often feels solitary; for much of the journey through the Litchfield Hills, the opposing traffic is invisible through a thick barrier of trees. Whether the leaves are full of summer or blazing toward autumn, Route 8's scenery will not disappoint.

Access to I-84 comes in at exits 31 (eastbound) and 33 (westbound). Route 6 enters in Watertown, US 202/Route 4 picks up in Torrington, and junctions for US 44 begin in Winchester. Route 20 begins in Winchester after Route 8 ceases to be a highway and winds through Hartland and Windsor Locks, passing Bradley International Airport and reaching I-91.

Route 9

Beginning just west of the mouth of the Connecticut River in Old Saybrook, Route 9 takes off from exit 69 on I-95 (at the junction of US 1) and continues northwesterly through Essex, Deep River, Chester, Haddam, and Middletown to Cromwell. Along much of this passage you'll see geological evidence of the past as exposed layers of rock color the way. At exit 20 in Cromwell, Route 9 bisects I-91 and continues through Berlin, New Britain, and Newington until reaching I-84 in Farmington.

Forty-one miles in length, Route 9 is a great alternative to the often more congested interstates, especially if you're headed south from Harford or east from Waterbury toward the casinos or other coastal destinations. Through Middletown, the highway is interrupted and becomes a town thruway with stoplights and a speed limit of 45 mph. Once through Middletown, Route 9 again becomes an expressway.

Interestingly, during its proposed construction, building was halted when archaeological evidence of the Wangunk tribe was uncovered.

Route 2

Following the path of the historic Hartford–New London and Colchester–Norwich turnpikes, Route 2 now forges through 53 miles from the state capital to Stonington. It is a state route with expressway from Hartford to Norwich, then two lanes afterwards through the towns of New London County. The route crosses the Connecticut River over the Founder's Bridge in Hartford and provides interchanges with I-91 and shortly after with I-84 in East Hartford. As it continues in a southeasterly direction through Glastonbury, Marlborough, Colchester, Lebanon, and Bozrah, there are connections to several local routes. In Norwich, connection to I-395 and Route 2A provides an easy link to Mohegan Sun Casino. For those traveling on to Foxwoods, continue along the Thames River on the surface road to Ledyard, past the Mashantucket Pequot Reservation, and then conveniently to the casino. Volume on Route 2 has increased significantly in the past 20 years due to the popularity of the casinos. When Route 2 terminates in Stonington, there is access to US 1 and the Rhode Island border.

Other Major Roads

US 1

Route 1 (officially known as US 1) runs for 117.37 miles across the state from Greenwich to Stonington. Like the more brawny I-95 that it parallels, US 1 is designated a north–south highway, though it is actually oriented east–west. It may in fact be signed as either, and so can be confusing for travelers. Before the interstate was built, Route 1 was the main traverse along the coast. Now an arterial road with traffic lights and four lanes (in some spots just two), it is utilized principally for local commercial access, offering gas, food, strip malls, and the occasional hot spot.

Built on the old Boston Post Road, one of the original highways in the country, US 1 was first used as a postal route that connected New York City to Boston. In fact, the entire span of Route 1 connects Key West, Florida, to the Canadian border. Route 1 is still locally known by the old highway's name, and sometimes as just the Post Road. I-95 offers frequent access to Route I, and from it major junctions are available to Route 7 in Norwalk, Route 8 in Bridgeport, Route 34 in New Haven, Route 9 in Old Saybrook, and Route 32 in New London.

Travel on Route 1 is certainly not as quick as it is on the interstate or larger roads, but it does offer a close-up look at the shoreline towns of Fairfield, New Haven, Middlesex, and New London Counties, as well as the convenience of a bounty of amenities. For a few miles in Madison, Route 1 is designated as a Scenic Road.

Route 44

Route 44 (US 44), a road that passes through four northeastern states, travels 106 miles east–west across the northern counties. Most of the road is designated the Jonathan Trumbull Highway. It is a rural, two-lane road through upper Litchfield County, with four lanes in Winchester. When it joins US 202 in Canton, it provides access to the Hartford area as a four-lane highway. For a while in Hartford, via Albany Avenue, Route 44 joins I-84/US 6 across the Bulkeley Bridge and the Connecticut River. With two lanes through Tolland County (where it is known as the Boston Pike) and Windham County (called

the Providence Pike until Putnam), the road becomes more rural, coinciding with US 6 in Manchester and Bolton.

The route was constructed over an early system of turnpikes, which date from the 19th century. Through Salisbury it's designated a Scenic Road. In addition to the I-84 connection, major junctions are found to US 7 in Canaan and I-91 in Hartford.

ℹ **Even with the availability of GPS devices, a good map (and a copy of this Insiders' Guide) will serve you well as you travel around the state. Pick up a free copy of the Official State Tourism Map, available at most information areas or wherever brochures are found.**

Route 7

Officially known as US 7, and also known as the Ethan Allen Highway (and sometimes Super 7), Route 7 travels north–south from the junction at I-95 in Norwalk to Canaan, where it continues all the way to Vermont. Mostly a two-lane roadway, Route 7 has two expressway sections in Norwalk (with access to the business district) and in Danbury. There is access to US 1 and Route 15 through the Norwalk expressway.

In Danbury the Route 7 expressway joins I-84 for 4 miles and shares signage with I-84, US 6, and US 202. After Danbury Route 7 and US 202 split off and continue as a dual route until New Milford, where US 202 heads northeast and Route 7 continues until Canaan as a two-lane roadway. In Sharon, Kent, and Cornwall (from the Cornwall Bridge to the border of North Canaan), Route 7 is designated as a Scenic Road.

Route 6

Route 6 (US 6) traverses the state east to west for 116 miles. In the western part of the state, Route 6 lines up with I-84 and shares that highway for 3 miles in Danbury. It enters the state as US 6/202, briefly joins US 7, and the four highways converge until exit 8, when it again becomes a two-lane surface road through Bethel, Newtown, and Southbury. There it connects again with I-84. Afterward, it is again a two-lane local route, taking on a slightly more northern trajectory through Southbury, Woodbury, and Watertown, running into Route 8 briefly in Thomaston. Through Plymouth, Bristol, and Farmington, it is again two lanes until it catches up again with I-84 for 13 miles through the Hartford area to Manchester.

As a triple-signed passage, US 6/I-84 joins US 44 over the Connecticut River. I-84 exits at Manchester and US 6/44 continue for almost 7 miles to Bolton at the end of I-384. In Bolton, US 44 jets slightly north as it continues east, and Route 6 goes slightly south. The two routes frame the Natchaug State Forest. At this point Route 6 is known as the Willimantic Bypass. It passes over the Hop River State Park Trail and crosses the Natchaug River in Windham and continues through Hampton, Brooklyn, and into Killingly, where it crosses the Rhode Island border.

Scenic Roads & Highways

In all, almost 300 miles of scenic roadway crisscross the state, providing incentives for sightseers and a means to preserve the picturesque, rural quality of the state, where forests and farmland, meadows and marshes can be experienced and enjoyed. A different way to go "off-roading," scenic routes occur frequently enough to not only get travelers to and from less populated places but also show off some of the state's most beautiful landscape.

There are two distinctions: State Scenic Highways and local Scenic Roads. The designation helps to promote tourism and to safeguard the roads, ensuring their attractive appearance is maintained. To gain the

designation as a distinct route, the road must lie alongside naturally maintained land, like farmland; provide ample views of shoreland, marshes, forests, or other geologic features; or highlight cultural features such as buildings located on the National or State Register of Historic Places. Any development must blend in with the surroundings and cannot take away from the beauty of the area.

Two routes—169 and 15 (the Merritt Parkway)—have been singled out as National Historic Roads. Route 169 covers 32.1 miles from Lisbon to Woodstock at the Massachusetts border. Maples and majestic pines line the roadway as the route winds through one of the last unspoiled areas in the US—the Quiet Corner. The quintessential landscape includes views of colonial churches, homes, and meetinghouses near well-kept stone walls. Also in the eastern part of the state in New London County is Route 49 through Stonington and Voluntown and almost 3 miles in Preston on Route 164.

In Middlesex County, Route 154 runs from the Chester/Haddam line to Middlefield, with a 6-mile spur in Old Saybrook beginning at Route 1. In Haddam, the mighty Connecticut River shoulders the view. In New Haven County, 12 miles of Route 146 meander between Guilford and Branford, into the Indian Neck portion of town along the Long Island shore. Connect to Route 77 in Guilford at the Town Green and travel north for about 13 miles along the Coginchaug River and Quonnipaug Lake to Durham and the Durham Meadows Wildlife Area.

In Fairfield County, besides the Merritt, there are Scenic Roads along Route 58, which overlooks the Hemlock Reservoir through Easton and winds under stunning, majestic pines into Redding. Route 33 in Wilton will take you to Weir Farm, and you'll understand why Connecticut Impressionist painters so loved that area of the state. In

Litchfield County, Route 41 through Sharon and Salisbury as well as Routes 44 and 7 showcase the hilly, forested landscape of the northwest corner. Route 45 circles Lake Waramaug, and Route 272 passes Dennis Hill State Park and Haystack Mountain State Park. Route 202, which runs from New Milford all the way to the Massachusetts border at Granby, has designated Scenic Roads in New Hartford along the Nepaug State Forest. Routes 20 and 219 in Barkhamsted offer views of the Farmington River, where you're likely to see an angler out for a morning catch. Moose have been spotted skirting along the forested roads, so always be on the lookout for wildlife, and take care, especially on the twisting byways.

These are just a few mentions of the many Scenic Roads across the state, and the actual signed Scenic Roads may run for only a few miles. Indeed, a fluid array of beautiful traverses and landscapes inhabit most of the state's rural roads. As you might guess, these quiet countryside passages are especially beautiful in autumn, but they are also blossom-rich in spring, well shaded through summer's full growth, and pristinely crystal in winter. Set your GPS for "Least Amount of Highways" and see where the exploration leads you.

Trains

CONNECTICUT DEPARTMENT OF TRANSPORTATION
Office of Rail
ct.gov/dot/cwp/view.asp?a=1386&q=316722

Trains offer a significant means of transportation, especially for commuters traveling to New York City. There are 50 rail stations in Connecticut, providing a convenient means of travel between major cities within the state. Major railways are the New Haven and Shore Line East Lines. Interstate travel and service to major cities is provided by Amtrak.

AMTRAK
(800) USA-RAIL (872-7245)
amtrak.com

With stations in 13 cities or towns in Connecticut, Amtrak brings visitors into every county except Tolland and Windham, where rural access is best acquired by car. You'll find service in Bridgeport, Hartford, Berlin (Kensington), Ledyard (stopping at Foxwoods Casino), Meriden, Mystic, New Haven, New London, Stamford, Wallingford, Windsor, and Windsor Locks. With Amtrak service throughout the Northeast and from coast-to-coast destinations, travelers and commuters have alternatives to flying and driving. Amtrak operates the Acela Express, which stops in New Haven's Union Station and offers high-speed service between Boston, New York, Philadelphia, and Washington, DC.

NEW HAVEN LINE
(212) 532-4900
mta.info/mnr

The major rail route through Connecticut parallels I-95 along the coast. The New Haven Line, operated by Metro North, runs the service between Grand Central Station in New York City and New Haven. With stations in virtually all townships along the I-95 corridor, the New Haven Line offers commuters respite from the often-clogged interstate. This line has branches that connect to New Canaan, Danbury, and Waterbury. Ridership is consistently increasing, with over 37 million travelers in 2010. As gas prices continue to fluctuate, no doubt those numbers will rise.

New Haven's Union Station is the main hub between the two Connecticut lines. Renovations and repairs to the station's exterior, windows, and sidewalks are scheduled to be completed by the end of 2014 and should improve the historic building and help reinstate its grandeur. Commuter Connection shuttles, buses, and taxi service are available

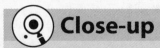

Close-up

The Golden Age of Rail

Connecticut's train stations—whether in operation, converted for other use, or abandoned altogether—are a major link to the state's past. Rail travel was an essential part of Connecticut's industrial growth, and tracks (as well as museums honoring these old workhorses) carry the remnants of this history.

New Haven's Union Station, designed in the Beaux Arts (neoclassical) style by American architect Cass Gilbert and built in 1920, is listed on the National Register of Historic Places. Located right next to the Danbury Station, the Danbury Railway Museum entered film history when Alfred Hitchcock filmed *Strangers on a Train* on the platform. Waterbury Station's distinctive clock tower provides the focus of that city's skyline and pays homage to that part of the state's innovations in the clock industry.

Architect George Keller designed Hartford's Union Station, an 1887 Romanesque brownstone building. Amtrak's Northeast Corridor trains run out of this transportation center, which also offers connections to buses, cabs, and airport limousines.

New London's Union Station is a grand brick structure with a pentagon-shaped entranceway. As the endpoint of the North East Corridor system, the New London stop has the distinction of offering the longest continuous commuter rail journey. It's possible to get to Newark, New Jersey, using public transit from here.

Victorian architecture is featured in the Windsor Train Station, where you'll find connections to Springfield, Massachusetts. Built in 1871, it is another of the historic stations listed on the National Register of Historic Places. It is the busiest of the 12 Connecticut Amtrak stations.

The station in Canaan had been the oldest operating union station in the country until fire destroyed most of it in 2001, though passenger service was stopped in 1974. It's been rebuilt to resemble the original structure, in the Victorian style, but transformed into a pleasantly bright structure with two main levels and a tower formation at the center.

Some stations, like the Cannondale station in Wilton, have only a depot building, and these are often small and charming reminders of the whistle-stops of old. Others seem notably modern, like the Stamford Transportation Center with its glass skywalk, which is used by 7,900 passengers daily. But regardless of where you pick up or get off the train, the romance of the rails is not a lost pleasure in Connecticut.

outside the main entrance. Parking can be tricky, as the attached lot fills quickly, but additional parking is available at the Temple Street Garage or near Sargent Street, where shuttles to the station are available. If you're picking someone up, coordinate your arrival time, as street parking is limited and the driveway directly in front of the station fills up quickly and is meant for quick drop-offs and pickups.

Select Shore Line East and Metro North trains depart or arrive at the State Street Station, so check schedules. State Street Station is located just 2 blocks from New Haven Green, and free shuttles are available to Union Station.

Save on parking and transportation at the station by purchasing a UniTicket, which offers discount monthly tickets and combines monthly bus on CTTransit and rail fares. Uni-Tickets can be purchased at any Metro North ticket office or by mail. For information call (212) 340-2020 or (800) METRO INFO.

SHORE LINE EAST (SLE)
(800) ALL-RIDE (255-7433)
shorelineeast.com

Shore Line East is operated by the Connecticut Department of Transportation, with service between New Haven and Old Saybrook 7 days a week. Service from New Haven to New London operates Mon through Fri. A few Shore Line East connections are available to Bridgeport and Stamford.

The stations along the Shore Line East route are varied and inviting. There are 9 in all, located in New Haven (Union and State Street Stations), Branford, Guilford, Madison, Clinton, Westbrook, Old Saybrook, and New London. All are wheelchair accessible (at Westbrook there's a lift), and free parking is available everywhere except New Haven and New London. Ticket windows are located at the New Haven Union Station, Old Saybrook, and New London stations. Otherwise, tickets are sold on the train and exact fare is helpful, as credit cards are not accepted on board. If connecting to the New Haven Line, separate tickets are needed, although UniRail tickets are available and combine Shore Line East and New Haven Line travel. These are available for one-way or weekly purchase. Also available are UniTicket rail tickets, which combine the two lines with local bus service on stops on the New Haven Line. For more information call (212) 532-4900 or visit mta.info/mnr.

Those commuting west of New Haven can purchase a UniRail ticket, which allows for discounted commutes on both the New Haven Line and Shore Line East. UniRail tickets can help you save up to $51 a month and help ease the hassle of traffic if you work east of New Haven. UniRail tickets are available at Union Station in New Haven and through Metro North's Mail & Ride program (mailandride.com). Monthly tickets can be mailed to you.

Buses & Shuttles

CONNECTICUT DEPARTMENT OF TRANSPORTATION
Office of Transit and Ride Sharing
ct.gov/dot/cwp/view.asp?a=1386&Q=414754

The Office of Transit and Ride Sharing provides information about busses and commuting through three programs: CTTransit, CTRides, and CTFastrack

GREYHOUND
(800) 231-2222
greyhound.com

Greyhound buses reach terminals and bus stops across the state. Terminals are the best for long-distance connections, since they offer more scheduling and ticketing options. You'll find terminals in Bridgeport, Danbury, Canaan, Enfield, Hartford, New Britain, New Haven, New London, Southbury, Stamford, Waterbury, Willimantic, and Winsted. A terminal is also conveniently located in Foxwoods Casino, where a host of other commercial bus lines bring visitors to play slots or check out shows, shopping, and eateries. Though service amenities are limited at connections designated simply as Bus Stops (no ticketing, baggage, or package express service), these still offer additional connections in Brooklyn, Farmington, Manchester, Mystic, Torrington, the University of Connecticut campus in Storrs, and Mohegan Sun Casino.

LOCAL BUS SERVICE
CTTransit
100 Leibert Rd.
PO Box 66
Hartford, CT 06141
(860) 522-8101
cttransit.com

Despite the driving culture, Connecticut offers quite a large network of bus routes. Most service self-contained regions, making border-to-border travel less accessible and unlikely. Therefore, for interstate crossings, Greyhound is really the only option. But it is possible to get around cities and travel within individual regions and towns without a car. No doubt, most bus transit is utilized by busy commuters and by locals who use bus service for access to shopping. Many local operators offer door-to-door service and free pickup for the elderly and those with disabilities.

CTTransit operates the state's bus system, with divisions in Hartford, New Haven, Stamford, Waterbury, New Britain and Bristol, and Meriden and Wallingford. Tickets are available for purchase online. Regular fare is $1.50, and exact change is needed. All day unlimited passes ($3) are available, as well as 3-day ($7.50), 5-day ($12), 7-day ($16.50) and 31-day ($54) tickets. Buy online and use a credit card. If you spend more than $100 a month on bus transportation, you may qualify for a tax benefit. (See commutertax-benefit.org). Thirty-one-day passes for local and express routes are also available, as are 10-ride fare tickets with no expiration dates.

CT Transit operates the 30 Bradley Flyer, which offers quick transport (30 minutes) to and from downtown Hartford to Bradley International Airport for the cost of a local bus fare ($1.50). Service is also available to the Connecticut Connection Center and to Hartford's Union Station. Also available in downtown Hartford is "Dash" transit—free shuttle service between the Convention Center, the Riverfront, and the Science Center, as well as select restaurants and attractions. The Dash shuttle runs regularly on weekdays from 7 a.m. to 7 p.m., with enhanced service during special events.

In Hartford and towns in the capital region, connections can be made to the Middletown area and New Britain Division (860-525-9181). The New Haven Division can connect with service in Meriden, Wallingford, and the lower Naugatuck Valley.

Meriden and Wallingford also have their own fixed routes (800-704-3113). New Haven Division routes also connect travelers to the New Haven and Shore Line East rail lines (203-624-0151). With Stamford's connections, service is available to Norwalk and to the New Haven and Harlem lines on Metro North as well as buses in Westchester County, New York. The I-BUS offers express service between Stamford and White Plains (203-327-7433). Each of these divisions offers service 7 days a week.

In the Waterbury area, ADA (Americans with Disabilities Act) paratransit offers service to Waterbury, Watertown, Middlebury, Wolcott, Prospect, and Naugatuck and is available Mon through Sat (203-753-2538). The New Britain Transportation Company (NBT) operates routes in Berlin, New Britain, Cromwell, Newington, Plainville, Bristol, and Meriden, operating Mon through Sat, including complimentary ADA service (860-828-0511).

Besides state-operated divisions, local bus lines are available in most other major metro areas. As each is independently operated, check out websites for complete information. The Greater Bridgeport Transit Authority (203-333-3031; gogbt.com) oversees service to Bridgeport, Fairfield, Stratford, and Trumbull.

Servicing 9 towns in Middlesex County is the Estuary Transit District (860-510-0429; estuarytransit.org). Housatonic Area Regional Transit (HART; hartct.com) brings mass transportation to Danbury and the towns in the Housatonic River valley as well as connections to Brewster, New York. Seniors and disabled commuters benefit from the Dial-a-Ride service (203-744-4070).

The Middletown Transit District (MAT; 860-346-0212; middletownareatransit.org) connects the towns of Portland, East Hampton, Cromwell, Durham, and Middletown. The Milford Transit District (203-874-4507;

milfordtransit.com) operates fixed service in the town and a Route 1 Coastal Link to Norwalk. The Norwalk Transit District (203-852-0000; norwalktransit.com) aligns other Fairfield County towns, including Westport, Wilton, and Greenwich, as well as Fairfield, Bridgeport, Stratford, and Milford through the Coastal link. Local door-to-door service is available in 7 towns. The northern towns of Litchfield County are connected by the Northwestern Connecticut Transit District (860-489-2535; nwctransit.com).

The Northeastern Connecticut Transit District (860-774-3902; nectd.org) operates routes through Brooklyn, Killingly, Putnam, and Thompson. The Windham Region Transit District (WRTD; wrtd.net) operates in Mansfield and Windham; other service is on-demand.

The Southeast Area Transit District (SEAT; 860-886-2631; seatbus.com) brings service to 9 towns of New London Country, with service to Mohegan Sun and Foxwoods.

Commuter Connection shuttles offer service out of New Haven from both train stations, and serve downtown and Sargent Drive. The Yale University shuttle (203-432-9790) also operates to Union Station. Local buses connect to other cities where further shuttle service is available. Shuttle service is available from Milford to Orange. In lower Fairfield County, shuttle service is available from the Stratford Commuter Connection (203-333-3031) or through the Greater Bridgeport Transit Authority (203-330-0657). Elsewhere the Commuter Connection shuttle takes passengers around Norwalk (203-852-0000), Stamford (203-327-7433), and Greenwich (800-982-8420).

COMMUTER SERVICES
Department of Transportation
CTrides.com
Whether you're traveling by car, train, bus or bike, CTrides provides information and links and connects commuters to discount programs. There is even a page devoted to helping employers and employees connect through telecommuting. Link up with others to carpool and earn Commuter Rewards. For more information see nuride.com or call (877) CTrides (287-4337).

Ferries
Out-of-State Connections
With Long Island and the Sound to the south of the coastline, ferry service is a great way to get across "the pond," as it's sometimes humorously called, or commute directly to Long Island without the hassle of going through the New York City. Ocean travel can be breathtaking, and thanks to the ship's size, the voyage shouldn't churn your stomach.

PORT JEFFERSON FERRY
Bridgeport and Port Jefferson
Steamboat Ferry Company
330 Water St.
Bridgeport, CT 06604
(888) 44-FERRY
88844ferry.com
The Port Jefferson Ferry connects Bridgeport to Port Jefferson, New York, and operates year-round, with departures about every hour and a half. Transit takes about an hour and 15 minutes. One-way fare for a car (with driver) is $56; additional car passengers are $16 for adults, with children 12 and under riding free. Higher rates apply for oversize vehicles and on weekends. Foot passengers ride for $27. Discounts are given for seniors. Watch the darting cormorants and gulls, feel the cooling ocean breeze, or cuddle up in the lounge with a good book and a cup of hot chocolate. Refreshments and concessions are available in The Galley. For a more sophisticated atmosphere, try the Steamboat Lounge, where you'll enjoy the bar. The ferry can also be a fun means of recreation, with special cruises like the Summer Music Cruises. For those looking to escape from the

North Fork, take one of the Casino Ferries, which dock in Bridgeport and then offer bus service to either Mohegan Sun or Foxwoods.

NEW LONDON FERRIES

Cross Sound Ferry
New London Ferry Dock
2 Ferry St.
New London, CT 06320
(860) 443-5281
longislandferry.com
goblockisland.com

From New London, ferry service is available to Orient Point, Long Island, or Block Island, Rhode Island (For Block Island call 860-444-4624.) From May through December take a standard ferry or the Sea Jet for high-speed service and arrive in Orient Point, New York, in 40 minutes. One-way fares for autos (with driver) are $51 (including surcharges); adult foot passengers, $14.50; $25 round-trip (Sea Jet, $20.25; $32.50 round-trip); children under 12 ride for $6 one way, $9 round-trip. Casino service to Mohegan and Foxwoods is also available, with bus connection for arriving travelers. The Block Island Express also departs from the Ferry Street dock May through September. One-way fares are $25 for adults and $12.50 for children. There are charges for bicycles, bike trailers, carts, wagons, and surfboards. Crossing takes approximately an hour and 40 minutes. For foot passengers only, service between New London and Montauk, New York, runs from Memorial Day to Labor Day by way of Viking Fleet Voyage (vikingfleet.com).

In-State Connections

Chester–Hadlyme Ferry
Route 148
Chester, CT 06412
(860) 443-3856
ct.gov/dot

A wonderful way to reach Gillette Castle State Park, this ferry crosses the Connecticut River and connects the towns of Chester and Hadlyme at Route 148, where salt and freshwater meet. Ferry service along this passage began in 1769, and the ferry was used to transport goods during the Revolutionary War. Steam-powered barge service began in 1879, and the name was changed to Chester–Hadlyme in 1882 when it was operated by the town of Chester. The ferry slip on the east side, a small red barn, is listed on the National Register of Historic Places. Visitors can ride the *Selden III* Apr through Nov (closed Thanksgiving), Mon through Fri from 7 a.m. to 6:45 p.m., weekends from 10:30 a.m. to 5 p.m. Fares are $5 per car ($6 weekends) and $2 for walk-ons and bicycles. There is a special commuter rate of $3, but pre-purchased coupons are required. Discount books are also available for frequent users.

ROCKY HILL–GLASTONBURY FERRY

Route 160
Rocky Hill, CT 06067
(860) 443-3856
wethersfield.org

Also crossing the Connecticut River is the Rocky Hill–Glastonbury Ferry, connecting those two towns at Route 160. It is the oldest continuously operating ferry in the US. Dating back to 1655, the original ferry service was operated by local families and served as an important transportation route for the state. At one point the ferry was driven by true horsepower—a horse on a treadmill, which gave enough power for a crossing. Today the *Holister III* is steam-driven. The ferry operates Apr 1 to Nov 30 7 days a week, 7 a.m. to 6:45 p.m. Mon through Fri and 10:30 a.m. to 5 p.m. on weekends. Fares are the same as they are for the Chester–Hadlyme Ferry. Note that this and the Chester–Hadlyme ferry have been under recent threats of closure, so always call ahead.

HISTORY

Designated the Constitution State in 1959, Connecticut has the honor of having what is likely the first Constitution in history, the Fundamental Orders of 1638–1639. As chief justice of the State Supreme Court Simeon Baldwin said, "Never had a company of men deliberately met to frame a social compact for immediate use, constituting a new and independent commonwealth, with definite officers, executive and legislative, and prescribed rules and modes of government, until the first planters of Connecticut came together for their great work." The independent spirit of this amazing document's writers has lived on throughout the centuries, and the state's rich history grows from that proud tradition.

PRECOLONIAL PERIOD

Connecticut's history begins with the arrival of nomadic peoples from the northwest at the end of the last ice age. At that time the area was treeless tundra, inhabited by mastodons, caribou, and giant beavers. For thousands of years these peoples lived a hunter-gatherer existence, with tribes of about 50 people following the seasons and animals. Tribes moved out of the region, and others moved in. Then, about a millennia ago, the tribes began to change their agricultural practices, from a more casual cultivation of the wild plants to a more focused cultivation of maize and winter squash. This caused a population boom, with villages of hundreds, and a more static population of Algonquian-speaking tribes.

This is the society that the Europeans first encountered on their arrival in New England, with at least a dozen culturally distinctive groups. However, it was not to last for long, as diseases from the traders and explorers soon reduced the numbers of natives by at least a third, and perhaps as much as 9 out of 10. Many of the weakened tribes made alliances with the powerful newcomers, rather than submit to their historical enemies.

In 1614 a Dutchman working for the East India Company, Adriaen Block, may have been the first European to sail up the Connecticut River. By 1633 the Dutch had established a trading post far inland. But it was short-lived. A few months later English settlers led by Thomas Hooker arrived from Massachusetts and soon became the dominant traders and explorers. Many of these colonists were Puritans, fleeing England to establish a new social and moral order based on their own beliefs. They quickly established Congregational parishes that would define the boundaries of Connecticut life until at least the Revolution.

THE INDIAN WARS

While the European settlers arrived in the 1630s, the Pequot tribe was aggressively expanding its control of the fur trade, filling the power vacuum left by the smallpox outbreaks. After the murder of one of their chieftains, they gathered their Dutch and

Indian allies and attacked, besieging Fort Saybrook and raiding Wethersfield in 1636. Then, as the Pequot sachem Sassacus took a force of his warriors to attack Hartford, Captain John Mason took a band of 400 men and attacked the Pequots' main town of Misistuck (modern-day Mystic) by surprise. Most of the 700 people left inside were women, children, and elderly men. Mason burned the palisade town to the ground while his men surrounded it and shot anyone who attempted to leave. Only 14 people escaped the massacre, which effectively ended resistance from the horrified Pequot.

The English settlers were now firmly at the top of the social hierarchy. Three separate colonies were initially established: the Connecticut Colony, the Saybrook Colony, and the New Haven Colony. The Saybrook Colony was sold relatively quickly to Connecticut in 1644, but the New Haven Colony merged with the other two in 1665, partly as punishment for having harbored the fugitive regicides of Charles I, and partly to prevent the English crown from levying further punishment.

King Philip's War in 1675 was the last gasp of Native American resistance in the state. Started by the head of the Wampanoag Confederacy, Metacom (King Philip), it may have been proportionally the bloodiest war in North American history. More than half the 90 towns in New England were attacked, and over 15 percent of the Native Americans lost their lives. Though many of the towns in the Connecticut Colony escaped burning, Simsbury, Suffield, and what is today Plainville were all attacked. The numbers of Native Americans dwindled from this point forward, as many fled west and others joined the English navies and armies to continue their warrior traditions. The war also gave New Englanders a sense of common purpose, and a sense of their own struggle as separate from England's.

This new sense of autonomy was helped by the degree of freedom given Connecticut by King Charles II in 1662 when he combined the 500 small settlements into one official colony. However, the next king, James II, took a firmer hand and sent his governor-general, Sir Edmund Andros, to collect the colonies' charters and reclaim more authority. When Andros reached Hartford in 1687, according to the sources of the day, he demanded the document but was refused in a unique manner. The candles were put out, and someone, possibly Captain Joseph Wadsworth, took the charter out a window and hid it in a nearby oak tree, thereafter called the Charter Oak. This act of defiance was an early precursor to the independent tradition that arose over the next century in Connecticut.

INDEPENDENCE REALIZED

The second century of recorded history in Connecticut was a period of rapid expansion. Immigrants continued to flood in, and a period of relative peace spurred the growth of both governmental and private institutions. In 1701 the Collegiate School was founded in Saybrook to prepare men for leadership in the ministry and politics. Moving down the coast to New Haven 15 years later, they renamed the school Yale. The Congregationalist ministers began to lose some control over the aspects of everyday life, and the mushrooming population lost some of its Puritan rigidity. By mid-century, the tax to support local churches could even be paid to other, non-Congregationalist churches.

Since the state had been largely self-governing from the beginning, rebellion against England became very popular. In fact, the General Assembly declared their independence from the crown 16 days before the Continental Congress in Philadelphia. Residents Nathan Hale and Benedict Arnold rode eagerly to fight for independence, though one would become the country's first patriotic martyr and the other its first traitor.

The British troops invaded Connecticut several times, and were repulsed. An invasion force landed in Westport and marched inland to Danbury, which they burnt in 1777. On their return, they were attacked by generals Benedict Arnold and David Wooster at the Battle of Ridgefield. In 1779 New Haven, Norwalk, and Fairfield were all attacked, and Fairfield was burnt to the ground. In 1781 New London and Groton were raided by the traitorous Benedict Arnold.

Connecticut became known as the Provisions State, due to Governor Jonathan Trumbull's effective marshalling of supplies, like food and ammunition, for the Continental Army. Lebanon's mile-long town green became a center for operations in the Northeast, hosting Generals Rochambeau and George Washington. Washington credited Trumbull's efforts as paramount in the new nation's victory.

i Connecticut settlers founded the town of Wilkes-Barre in 1769, following the original charter that claimed a portion of northeast Pennsylvania for their own. Open warfare broke out between the states; 150 settlers were killed and thousands fled. Finally, the new United States Congress settled the matter by giving Connecticut part of present-day Ohio, and releasing it from its war debt.

THE INDUSTRIAL REVOLUTION

The Industrial Revolution came to Connecticut first in the form of armaments. In 1797 Eli Whitney began to make firearms at his factory in Hamden, using the new methods of cost accounting, interchangeable parts, machine tools, and the assembly line. Others quickly followed, like Middletown's Oliver Bidwell, Nathan Starr, and Simeon North,

who built rival pistol and arms factories. In 1836 Samuel Colt invented the revolver and began to produce pistols with interchangeable parts in Hartford. Then, Horace Smith and Daniel B. Wesson created the first repeating rifle in Norwich in the 1850s, and produced these in Whitney's old factory, soon to become the Winchester Repeating Arms Company. Christian Sharps invented the breech-loading rifle in 1854 in Hartford, and Christopher Spencer invented the Spencer repeating rifle, which would help the North win the Civil War.

But arms were not the only area in which Connecticut became prominent. Precision clocks, watches, and other timepieces were made by dozens of manufacturers, including the New England Clock Company, the Ansonia Clock Company, the New Haven Clock Company, the Forestville Manufacturing Company, and the Waterbury Clock Company, which eventually became Timex.

Milling machines, vertical borers, lathe chucks, drop hammers, screw machines, and other machine tools were all invented and produced in the state. Waterbury became a world center of brass production, Danbury of hats, and Bridgeport of sewing machines. By the end of the 19th century the state also led the world in innovative silverware production, bicycle manufacturing, textile fabrication, and submarine construction. The first military submarine was actually built by David Bushnell as far back as 1775, and inventors Simon Lake and John P. Holland took up the work in the 20th century.

The city of Bridgeport alone contained 500 factories in the early 1900s. Invention itself was the prime mover of these industries, with Connecticut issuing more patents per capita than any other state from 1790 to 1930. For example, a lone Colt engineer named William Mason patented 125 inventions and improvements himself.

ROLES IN THE CIVIL WAR & THE TWO WORLD WARS

Many Connecticut residents were strong abolitionists, such as Leonard Bacon, Simeon Baldwin, Horace Bushnell, Prudence Crandall, and showman P. T. Barnum. Author Harriet Beecher Stowe wrote *Uncle Tom's Cabin*, the most popular and influential antislavery book of the day. When Abraham Lincoln met her, he said, "So you're the little woman whose book started this great war." He was only exaggerating slightly. Connecticut's own laws concerning emancipation were also challenged in the famous Amistad trial, which became a rallying point for the antislavery movement.

When Fort Sumter was attacked by rebel troops in 1861, Connecticut soldiers answered President Lincoln's call immediately. Governor William Buckingham was a strong supporter of Lincoln and rallied the state's citizens to join the war effort. Thirty Connecticut foot regiments fought in every major encounter in the Civil War. The 29th and 30th regiments were composed of free African Americans from the state, and they became among the first Northern soldiers to enter the Southern capital of Richmond, clearing the way for President Lincoln's arrival.

But as in the Revolution so many years before, the state would provide the most support for the Union through supplies. The weapons companies in New Haven and Hartford provided the army with the Henry rifle and the Colt sidearm. The yards in Mystic produced ships for the Union Navy. The uniforms were tailored by Bridgeport's sewing machines and fitted with brass from Waterbury.

Connecticut would provide the same support in the two World Wars. Along with the arms factories already present in Hartford, New Haven, and New London, Bridgeport became the leader in US munitions production when the Remington factory was built, at the time the largest building in the world. They also provided the Riker staff cars, built in the Locomobile Factory. Connecticut produced over two-thirds of all Allied ammunition during World War I. Thousands of citizens volunteered to fight in Europe and as Home Guards, protecting this "arsenal of democracy." They also purchased the largest amount of liberty bonds of any state in America, for a total of $437 million.

Although the Great Depression hurt manufacturing in Connecticut, World War II revived the munitions industry. Airplane engines, rifles, parachutes, submarines, helicopters, uniforms, artillery, and more all left the state to help American soldiers. However, this dependence on the arms industry would prove a challenge to the state as the Cold War wound down. The new interstate highway system relegated Connecticut's proximity to rail and shipping unnecessary, and many industries left the state as the 20th century transformed the old patterns of the world.

i Find out more about Connecticut history at cthistory.org.

THE 20TH CENTURY & BEYOND

The 20th century was in part defined by the influx of immigrants into the state from all over the world. At first Polish, Hungarian, Portuguese, Jewish, and Italian immigrants arrived in the major cities, looking for work at factories. African Americans came to the state from the South, especially following World War I. As the century progressed, large numbers of Latino and Eastern European immigrants also arrived.

The challenge of decreasing manufacturing in the state was exacerbated by natural disasters: the hurricane of 1938 and the flood of 1955. The hole in the economy led to the increased prominence of the insurance companies and financial services centered in Hartford. The state constitution was redrafted in 1965, giving cities fairer representation, and an income tax was finally established to make up for the loss of business revenue. The Foxwoods Casino was finished in 1992, making the Mashantucket Pequot Reservation incredibly wealthy. The nearby Mohegan Reservation followed with their own casino in 1994, and the success of these gambling and entertainment centers helped solidify the state's economy. Pharmaceutical firms like Pfizer and media companies like ESPN built their own empires here. And the influx of wealth into the southwest part of the state has made Connecticut one of the wealthiest per capita states in the nation by the turn of the 21st century.

Connecticut's history is all around us, in every stone wall and clapboard house. It is built into the way we live and the things we love. And best of all, it is being written every day. What part will you play?

FAIRFIELD COUNTY

Fairfield County is the most densely populated area of Connecticut, and the richest. Often called the "Gold Coast" or the "bedroom of New York," this is one of the most exclusive counties in the entire nation. Named for its most prosperous colonial town, the county now boasts a string of cities along the Old Post Road and a hilly interior of prosperous suburbs. Though swamped with wealth, the county surprisingly retains much of its charming character, and we can thank our fussy Yankee values for not allowing it to become a haven of ostentatious excess.

The exclusive addresses of Greenwich, New Canaan, Darien, and Westport give the county its reputation, filled with celebrities and entrepreneurs who have settled here for a quick commute to New York City. Greenwich boasts some of the best restaurants in the county and the finest stores in the world. Darien has been a retreat for New Yorkers since the Civil War, and Westport has been called Beverly Hills East.

Anchoring these communities is Stamford, a large city that has recently become a vital center of corporate business, with its motto "The City that Works." The city of Norwalk has also been revitalized, with the restaurant district of SoNo, which jumps with small bistros, galleries, and shops, and an arty, grit-and-polish feel and WPA murals.

Farther up the coast, Bridgeport has not experienced the revivification that Norwalk and Stamford have, but it boasts some of the county's biggest attractions, including Fairfield County's largest music and sports venue, Bluefish Stadium and the Arena at Harbor Yard. A hundred years ago this was the richest and most powerful city between Boston and New York, and vestiges of its former glory linger in its parks and downtown and along some of the tree-lined avenues. Surrounding Bridgeport are Stratford and Fairfield, two colonial towns that have risen again to prominence. The nexus of universities in the area recently earned it a nod from the American Institute for Economic Research as one of the best college "metro areas" in the nation.

The interior of the county is mostly a string of wealthy suburbs: Wilton, Weston, Easton, and Trumbull. Unlike tract-housing suburbs in some other areas of the country, however, they are heavily forested and feature diverse homes. The former "hat city" of Danbury is the western gateway to the state, benefiting from the influx of wealth as the New York metro area expands. And the charming towns of Ridgefield, Newtown, Redding, and Bethel grant a quaint, clapboard feel that everyone expects of Connecticut.

Fairfield County contains amazing attractions, from wildlife encounters to historical homes. If you are a foodie, this is heaven, full of fascinating restaurants, from the fanciest French gourmets to the yummiest hot dog joints. And the shopping is by far the glitziest and most glamorous in the state. Keep an open mind and an open wallet as you explore this gateway to the pleasures of Connecticut.

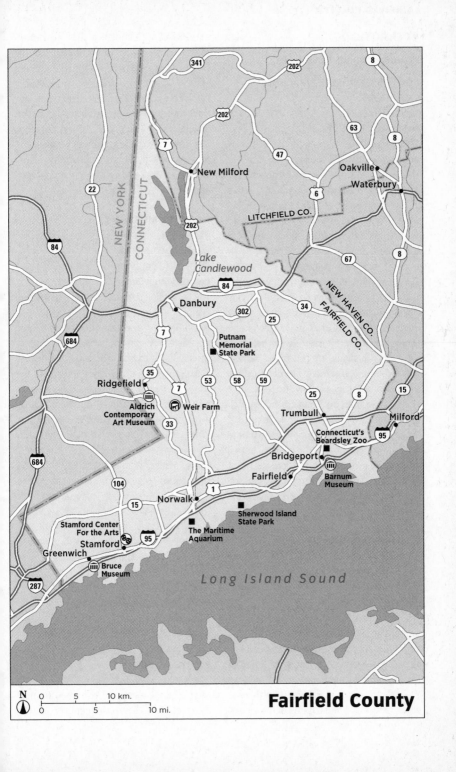

Fairfield County

ATTRACTIONS

Historical Sites & Landmarks

BOOTHE MEMORIAL PARK AND GARDENS

5800 Main St.
Stratford, CT 06614
(203) 381-2046
boothememorialpark.org

This small, 32-acre park just off the Merritt Parkway in Stratford was once the estate of the Boothe family, including the site of what is often called the oldest homestead in America, built on the foundation of a 1663 house and continuously occupied ever since (though remodeled several times). In 1949 the park was willed to the town, and it is listed on the National Register of Historic Places. What makes this museum and park unique is that two brothers in the Boothe family, David and Stephen, were avid collectors of buildings. Yes, buildings. As you stroll around, you'll find a blacksmith shop, icehouse, miniature windmill, trolley station, clock tower museum, carriage house, tollbooth plaza, aviary, a redwood building, and more. Children walk around thinking they're in some sort of Disneyland exhibit, but all these buildings are real. Stratford also runs events like Shakespearean plays and the Great Pumpkin Festival here, so check the schedule.

BUSH-HOLLEY HOUSE

39 Strickland Rd.
Cos Cob, CT 06807
(203) 869-6899
hstg.org/visit_bh

This 1732 central-chimney saltbox house is a treasure of colonial America that also played an important part in the American Impressionist movement at the turn of the 20th century. Artists Childe Hassam and J. Alden Weir stayed and painted here when this was a boardinghouse, and it is one of three great sites in Connecticut dedicated to this movement, including Weir Farm in Wilton and the Florence Griswold House in Lyme. The Bush-Holley House is the home of the Greenwich Historical Society, and as you might imagine, they have the money to sponsor all sorts of fun programs, like hearth cooking, painting, and ice-cream making, throughout the summer. Farmers' markets are usually held here weekly as well. Call to check the calendar, and bring your paintbrushes.

DANBURY MUSEUMS

43 Main St.
Danbury, CT 06810
(203) 743-5200
danburymuseum.org

This collection of buildings in downtown Danbury includes the John Dodd Hat Shop, the 1785 John and Mary Rider House, and the Marian Anderson Studio. The studio is probably the most moving—it's the actual place where the opera singer rehearsed for 50 years. Her struggle for racial equality as a singer is inspiring to all. Less than a mile away, or a 15-minute walk if you like, at 120 White St. (danbury.org/DRM) is the Danbury Railway Museum, built in the restored Union Station that was featured in Alfred Hitchcock's *Strangers on a Train*. It's full of memorabilia and model train layouts, and the yard contains 70 vintage railcars. There are very short rail rides in the yard daily, but the daylong trips to the Hudson Valley are the ticket to buy. Call for a schedule.

KEELER TAVERN MUSEUM AND CASS GILBERT GARDEN HOUSE

132 Main St.
Ridgefield, CT 06877
(203) 431-0815
keelertavernmuseum.org

The Keeler Tavern started its life in 1713 as a farm and became the home of noted architect Cass Gilbert. In between it was

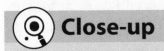

Close-up

Our World of Books

The human being is a reading animal. We have language, and moreover we like to make that language permanent. We put long strings of words together and create stories with that language. It is a remarkable process, and one too often taken for granted. It is no exaggeration to say that we live in a world of books.

In Connecticut we can observe this phenomenon more acutely, since our hills and dales are filled with authors and writers of every sort: poets, playwrights, novelists, historians, journalists, screenwriters, and more. We are unfailingly rated one of the most educated states in America, with a surfeit of advanced-degree earners, colleges per citizen, and library visits per capita. Despite our small population and size, we have an astonishing 183 public libraries, where you will find ordinary citizens stretching their minds without stretching their wallets. Like everyone else, I often grumble about property taxes, but every time I visit the huge Miller Memorial Library in Hamden, I have at least one concrete result to smile about.

Compared with some other states, our libraries have bigger collections and better librarians. Even more surprisingly, every library in the state looks different, with Gothic Revival, Greek Revival, Victorian, Romanesque, Prairie School, Federalist, modernist, and postmodernist architectures all taking their turns next to unclassifiable, unique masterpieces of marble or glass. And each of these unique buildings has its own story.

The Scoville Library in Salisbury is probably the oldest free lender in the country, and its story may stand in for the rest. In 1771 Richard Smith brought 200 books to town with the help of 39 subscribers. Why? "For the Encouragement of true religion; for the Promoting of Virtue, Education, and Learning; for the Discouragement of Vice and Immorality." This collection was added to over the years, and in 1890 Jonathan Scoville left money in his will for a new granite building, with a tower clock that has chimed the quarter hours with 4, 8, 12, and 16 notes from *Parsifal* ever since. Many visitors think it is the town church rather than the library, and inside you will in fact find a piece of the legendary Salisbury Cathedral in England.

Many other Connecticut libraries began far back in history as "free libraries" or were donated later by prominent citizens. The Mark Twain Library in Redding was gifted by America's most famous novelist himself when he lived in town at the end of his life. Some of his most pithy quotes grace the walls, and you can even find some of his own annotated books there.

Our academic libraries are nothing to sniff at, either, with some of the best, most technologically advanced high school libraries in the nation. And of course we have some of the greatest archives in the world at repositories like Yale's Beinecke Library. When you add in our dozens of historical society and other private archives, it's a surprise that we don't sink into the Sound under the weight of all these books.

These libraries are more than just a place to collect dusty old tomes read by historians like myself. They are community centers, providing hubs for activities and events, bringing in a cultural jumble of authors, musicians, and artists into every small town. You can learn art at the Avon Free Public Library or watch a radio play at the Ansonia Public Library. You can get your own books at the Pequot Library of Southport's annual book sale. There is even a passport system, much like the one for our wine trail. So whether you are a resident or a visitor, don't forget to stop at the local library, even if it is just to wonder at the world of books.

a stagecoach stop and a summer hotel from 1772 to 1907, as well as serving as the town post office. The beautiful garden house, designed and built in 1915 by Gilbert, the architect of the Woolworth Building and the Supreme Court Building, is a popular place for weddings. Walk in the brick-walled garden with its reflecting pool, fountain, and flower beds and you'll find an oasis of peace. When touring this fascinating house, don't miss the cannonball fired by the British during the Battle of Ridgefield in 1777, embedded in a corner post.

LOCKWOOD-MATHEWS MANSION
295 West Ave.
Norwalk, CT 06850
(203) 838-9799
lockwoodmathewsmansion.com

This gigantic eight-pointed-star chateau was built between 1864 and 1868 by LeGrand Lockwood, a native of Norwalk who made his fortune in the stock market, married a hometown girl, and brought his family back from New York City to this "summer home." It is considered the first great (surviving) mansion in the US, predating the Newport mansions by 20 years. In 1878 the Mathews family moved in and lived here until the city purchased the property, turning it into a museum in 1966. It is also available for other events and activities (both the original and remake of *The Stepford Wives* were filmed here). It is certainly the largest and most opulent house open to the public in Connecticut. Inside, walk the multicolored marble and parquet floors, staring at the paintings and marble sculptures and up into the huge central rotunda, 42 feet high. Look for hidden treasures like the silver vault in the dining room, the rare book closet in the library, and the wonderful bathroom sinks throughout the house. Behind the mansion is Pine Island Cemetery, which predates the house and has some very old graves.

NEW CANAAN HISTORICAL SOCIETY
13 Oenoke Ridge
New Canaan, CT 06840
(203) 966-1776
nchistory.org

Unlike many historical societies, this one is housed in not just one building but five, and boasts seven museums and a library. There is an old-time drugstore and ice-cream parlor, a costume museum, a 1799 schoolhouse, a 19th-century printing press office, and a tool museum. The 1764 Hanford-Silliman House has doll, toy, and quilt collections; the 1868 John Rogers Studio and Museum includes a collection of Rogers's work in the studio it was sculpted in. Close by is the Gores Pavilion, a museum of modern architecture that gives a great overview of the area's many modernist houses. If it sounds like a lot to see, it is. If you are interested in history, the New Canaan museums make a great afternoon.

*PHILIP JOHNSON GLASS HOUSE
199 Elm St., #11
New Canaan, CT 06840
(203) 594-9884
theglasshouse.org

Part of the National Trust for Historic Preservation, the Glass House is really a 47-acre park in New Canaan dedicated to 20th-century architecture. The glass house itself was the modernist architect's residence, but the park contains more than just one house. Architectural "follies" and other buildings are scattered around the landscape, and the art collection on-site includes giants like Frank Stella and Andy Warhol. Open from May to Nov, the site offers a variety of guided tours. You can talk to the many architecture students who seem to come on the tours and get their opinions on the unique buildings and landscape. This is one of the most fascinating sites in Connecticut, a stone-walled farmland that has been transformed by one of the most creative minds of his age. My wife and I discussed the ideas sparked by this wonderful place all evening and the next day.

PUTNAM COTTAGE
243 E. Putnam Ave.
Greenwich, CT 06830
(203) 869-9697
putnamcottage.org

This unusual fish-scale-shingle house was built in 1692 and later became a meeting place during the Revolution, when it was known as Knapp's Tavern. George Washington's second-in-command, Connecticut's Israel Putnam, used it often. During an attack, General Putnam supposedly rode his horse down the steep cliff near the cottage, a skirmish that is reenacted here the last Sunday in February every year. Relics include Putnam's desk, Bible, military uniform, glasses, and hat (with bullet hole!). It was opened to the public on the centennial of Putnam's ride, and in 1906 it became an official museum. The cottage has been restored to its 18th-century appearance but has kept the more modern (if 150 years old can be called modern) name.

PUTNAM MEMORIAL STATE PARK
492 Black Rock Tpke.
West Redding, CT 06896
(203) 938-2285
putnampark.org

Up the gorgeous Black Rock Turnpike from the Merritt, past some well-kept old houses and a Congregational church, is Connecticut's oldest state park, actually an archaeological preserve worth your time and your respect. This is the site of the 1778–79 winter encampment of part of the Continental Army watching New York City, Connecticut's own Valley Forge. General Israel Putnam, Washington's second-in-command, sheltered his troops in over 100 small cabins here that winter, and the evidence of the crumbled chimneys still exists in two long rows in the park. There are also reconstructions of a camp guardhouse, an officer's cabin, two blockhouses, and a huge memorial, all of them already 120 years old themselves. The visitor center and a small museum contain relics like pipes, fifes, and cannonballs picked up from the site, as well as a bronze cannon and Putnam's own plow and horse bridle.

WEIR FARM
735 Nod Hill Rd.
Wilton, CT 06897
(203) 834-1896
nps.gov/wefa

Though Connecticut is full of National Historic Landmarks, Weir Farm is the only one run by the National Park Service. On a narrow road in the hamlet of Branchville, this is a monument to J. Alden Weir's home, a center for American Impressionism for 40 years. In the visitor center, one of Weir's landscapes will draw your attention before you step into a room with changing displays of today's Weir Farm artists. Take a walk to the pond and try to see it through Impressionist eyes. The park service actually provides sketch paper and colored pencils for you to try to capture the yellow finches, the shagbark hickories, and the sunken garden. The historic site connects to Weir Preserve, run by The Nature Conservancy, where grassy trails lead into forests, a great opportunity to see the trees growing around old farm walls and glacial boulders. If you want to see inside the Weir studio and home, though, you'll need a guided tour. Call ahead to schedule one.

Museums

*ALDRICH CONTEMPORARY ART MUSEUM
258 Main St.
Ridgefield, CT 06877
(203) 438-4519
aldrichart.org

The Aldrich is one of the only noncollecting contemporary art museums in the country, which means it brings in changing exhibitions of surprising sculpture, painting, and unclassifiable experimental work. The building itself is a strange abstraction of New England architecture, a granite and clapboard structure containing a screening room for films, a sound gallery, a 100-seat performance area, and a 2-acre outdoor sculpture garden. Inside the galleries you'll find an open feel that suits the contemporary art well. Check out the museum store and purchase some strange and wonderful toys (for adults and children). The administrative offices are housed next door in the original Aldrich, a grocery and hardware store called the "Old Hundred," built in 1783. Someone asked me recently why we go so often to contemporary art museums. I told her for the discussions we have about them afterward of course. Whether the exhibit is "good" or "bad," it never fails to get my wife and me talking.

BARNUM MUSEUM
820 Main St.
Bridgeport, CT 06604
(203) 331-1104
barnum-museum.org

When P. T. Barnum died in 1891, he was by a wide margin the most famous man in the entire world. He granted this unique building to the city he loved as a museum of science and industry. Today it houses a history of Barnum's exploits, as well as those of his protégés, singer Jenny Lind and Bridgeport's own Charles Stratton, better known as Tom Thumb. The new centaur display always delights children and adults alike. In 2011 the Barnum Museum was hit by a tornado, and currently the exhibits are in one giant room (which makes for an interesting mix-up). For now go on Thursday and Friday from 11 a.m. to 3 p.m. They have just redesigned the place and will hopefully start renovations on the main building soon.

BRUCE MUSEUM
1 Museum Dr.
Greenwich, CT 06830
(203) 869-0376
brucemuseum.org

This museum was once the home of textile baron Robert Moffat Bruce, though it has expanded significantly beyond that into all-purpose museum of art and natural history, including both the work of American Impressionists like Childe Hassam and displays of fossils and local animals. The focus is on the land, which serves as a great primer to learning the geology, biology, and history of Connecticut. They also have a nice selection of rotating exhibits, including some to bring in the kids. The Bruce also runs the Seaside Center in Greenwich Point Park, about 6 miles down the road, where they teach you about the ecology of Long Island Sound. If you get a chance, make sure to catch a talk in their lecture series: They bring in some of the top names in art, science, and history to brush us up on the latest developments. I learned about Jean-Pierre Houdin's Great Pyramid internal ramp theory here days before the rest of the world did.

FAIRFIELD MUSEUM AND HISTORY CENTER
370 Beach Rd.
Fairfield, CT 06824
(203) 259-1598
fairfieldhs.org

Located on the old town green, south of the Post Road, the Fairfield Museum features two temporary exhibits at any one time, along with the main history room. Unlike many small-town museums, this has a professionally curated exhibit room, with fascinating displays on precolonial Fairfield, children's education in the 19th century, and the burning of the town in 1779. There's also a large space for conferences and parties, but you'll probably be more interested in the 1780 Sun Tavern across the green. Built after Fairfield was burned in the Revolutionary War by the British, the new tavern was the site of a much-celebrated visit from President George Washington. Walk or bike the deserted streets toward the beaches, and don't miss the cemetery nestled onto Beach Road right next to the museum driveway, with its wonderful old graves. Head the other way up to the Old Post Road, where you can shop and eat at one of Fairfield's great restaurants.

MILITARY MUSEUM OF SOUTHERN NEW ENGLAND
125 Park Ave.
Danbury, CT 06810
(203) 790-9277
usmilitarymuseum.org
This is the largest private collection of 20th-century military vehicles in America. There are vehicles from all branches of the military, from staff cars to tanks, and they range from World War I through Vietnam to the present. The biggest (not literally) attraction here is the 1917 Renault tank, the first made in the US. They have an "open turret weekend" once every month during summer when you can climb into the tanks yourself. Along with the numerous vehicles, they have 10,000 artifacts like mess kits, uniforms, and weapons.

Parks & Beaches

COVE ISLAND PARK
1281 Cove Rd.
Stamford, CT 06902
(203) 977-5214
stamfordct.gov/city-parks
If you're in far southwest Connecticut and want to beat the heat, come to Cove Island's large open beaches, which are now open to nonresidents. One of the two beaches here is actually on the island, right at the mouth of a large inlet called Holly Pond. This is a jogger's

paradise, complete with a sign-posted loop. The park has areas for picnicking, biking, and in-line skating, along with a summer food court, a playground, a harbor for small boats, and fishing hot spots. In one corner a scenic rocky area faces Long Island, a favorite for photographers, and a small salt marsh is a great place for spotting birds. There is also an interpretive trail on which you'll learn all about Long Island Sound.

SEASIDE PARK
1 Barnum Dyke
Bridgeport, CT 06604
(203) 367-7917
bridgeportct.gov
This park, designed by Frederick Law Olmsted (who also did Central Park in Manhattan), boasts the longest stretch of public shoreline in Fairfield County, and its long, thin beach is certainly busy during the summer months. However, the eastern side of the park is perhaps more interesting, with its historic carriageways and odd, subtropical trees. There are statues here in honor of showman P. T. Barnum and Elias Howe, whose sewing machines sparked Bridgeport as an industrial powerhouse. The huge, distinctive 1916 arch at the entrance on Park Avenue was built by Henry Bacon, who designed the Lincoln Memorial in DC the same year. Drive to the very end of the beach and walk out along the jetty to Fayerweather Island, which features an 1823 lighthouse that was kept by local hero Catherine Moore for nearly the entire 19th century. You can watch the oyster boats out in the harbor or fish from the seawall. Look for the green parrots that live here year-round in huge, refrigerator-size nests. How they got here is a mystery, and every local will tell you a different story.

*SHERWOOD ISLAND
1 Sherwood Island Rd.
Westport, CT 06880
(203) 226-6983
friendsofsherwoodisland.org

This gorgeous island in Westport is one of the few public-access beach areas in Fairfield County, and luckily for us it is one of the best. In fact, this was Connecticut's first recreational state park, purchased in 1914. These days Sherwood Island is no longer an island but a peninsula, and along with its gorgeous beachfront, it offers some great, if short, hiking in a variety of ecosystems. There is a beach pavilion that serves food, and a nature center, both open in summer. But this is an even better place to come in fall or winter, to walk the shore and watch the ships go by on their way to New York. In any season this is a great place for birding, with its salt marsh and millpond areas, as well as the scattered thickets among the fields. Don't miss the oak-and-beech forest at the west end of the park.

STAMFORD MUSEUM & NATURE
CENTER AND BARTLETT
ARBORETUM & GARDENS
39 Scofieldtown Rd.
Stamford, CT 06903
(203) 322-1646
stamfordmuseum.org
151 Brookdale Rd.
Stamford, CT 06903
(203) 322-6971
bartlettarboretum.org

Technically these side-by-side attractions are run by different entities, but what do you care about that? They are adjacent to each other just north of the Merritt Parkway, and both have fine nature trails that connect across Brookdale Road. In fact, this combined attraction could take you all day to see. The arboretum has, as you might imagine, a fine collection of trees and contains the home of noted dendrologist Dr. Francis Bartlett, now the visitor center. This living museum of trees is supplemented by a herbarium, with 3,500 specimens. The lush green landscapes, streams, and small rest areas provide a calm ambience allowing the adventurer's escape. The Stamford Museum also has some amazing beeches and birches, as well as ponds full of amphibians, an educational farm with a 1750 barn, a maple sugar house, a planetarium, an observatory with a 22-inch telescope, changing museum exhibits, and an interactive area called Nature's Playground, which kids go crazy for. The Bendel Mansion on the grounds has fine art and Americana exhibits.

TARRYWILE PARK AND MANSION
70 Southern Blvd.
Danbury, CT 06810
(203) 744-3130
tarrywile.com

Danbury has kept this little gem a secret from the rest of us, and no wonder—it might be the nicest city park in the state. A former dairy farm just south of the center of Danbury, it is known by outsiders mostly as a place for weddings and events (at "the Mansion"). But insiders know it as a place to jog, hike, walk their dogs, and picnic in the mix of meadows and forests. There are gardens, hiking trails, and the ruins of Hearthstone Castle. Yes, it is a castle; better yet, it looks straight out of a gothic tale. I noticed a lot of poison ivy nearby, which is appropriate for a ruined castle, but be careful.

Wildlife & Zoos

AUDUBON CENTER AT FAIRFIELD AND
LARSEN SANCTUARY
2325 Burr St.
Fairfield, CT 06824
(203) 259-6305
ctaudubon.org/center-at-fairfield

This wildlife sanctuary is a true pleasure for any walker or lover of nature. The Fairfield

Audubon Center by the parking lot includes a rehabilitation center for birds of prey, a butterfly garden, a farm pond full of frogs and turtles, and a greenhouse. But take a few steps north onto the trails of the Roy and Margot Larsen Wildlife Sanctuary, and you will see much more. A network of pleasant farm trails snake through the 155 acres deep in the suburbs of Westport and Fairfield. This is a birder's and botanist's paradise, with hundreds of species of birds and plants. Bring binoculars and a steady camera hand for rare bluebirds nesting here, flocks of turkeys, and several herds of deer. Try to walk quietly on the easy sanctuary paths and you will see and hear more; a rowdy group of teens is unlikely to see much of anything.

BIRDCRAFT MUSEUM AND SANCTUARY
314 Unquowa Rd.
Fairfield, CT 06824
(203) 259-0416
ctaudubon.org/birdcraft-museum
This was the first songbird sanctuary in the US, and it will appeal to anyone who loves birds. Set aside in 1914 by Mabel Osgood Wright, one of the pioneers of the American conservation movement, this small gem in Fairfield will make you love birds, and appreciate people like Mabel who protected them. At the time this sanctuary was created, it was still common practice to kill random birds in your backyard without provocation, and it's sometimes hard for us today to wrap our minds around that. Come on a quiet weekday when the kids are in school and see one of the rare songbirds without needing a pair of binoculars. Or bring the kids to one of their summer camps with hands-on programs. The bridge over the pond and the vintage cottage are charming, and there are guided tours by appointment.

CONNECTICUT'S BEARDSLEY ZOO
1875 Noble Ave.
Bridgeport, CT 06610
(203) 394-6565
beardsleyzoo.org
Connecticut's only zoo is set in beautiful Beardsley Park in the north of Bridgeport. For 50 years when the Ringling Bros. and Barnum & Bailey Circus wintered here, the animals were taken for walks in this park. When the zoo was started, some of its first animals came from the circus. Now, almost 100 years later, the zoo features North and South American animals of all sorts, like ocelots, peccaries, red wolves, buffalo, and otters. The Amur tigers, which are part of an endangered species breeding program at the zoo, are spectacular. But the kids seem to love the monkeys and prairie dogs the most, as well as the working indoor carousel. The zoo also runs programs, including the very popular Connecticut Free Shakespeare performances every July.

*THE MARITIME AQUARIUM
10 N. Water St.
Norwalk, CT 06854
(203) 852-0700
maritimeaquarium.org
In the heart of historic "SoNo" is one of two great aquariums in the state—this one once an old warehouse in disrepair and now a prime destination for families from all 50 states. The harbor seals are a big attraction, but don't miss the otters and sea turtles, kid-friendly favorites, although some children seem to gravitate toward the sharks and jellyfish instead. You can touch live stingrays, a unique experience when they begin to call out and flap their winglike fins. There is a section dedicated to local fish, so this is a great place to learn about Connecticut as well. The aquarium also features the best IMAX theater in the state; it shows not only current hits but also wonderful nature and science films that

never fail to blow children and adults out of the water (so to speak). Afterwards, walk up Washington Street for a bite to eat at one of the dozen great restaurants only a block away from the aquarium.

Wineries and Breweries

DIGRAZIA VINEYARDS
131 Tower Rd.
Brookfield, CT 06804
(203) 775-1616
digraziavineyards.com

Founded in 1978, this winery offers a unique array of wines. Founder and winemaker Dr. Paul DiGrazia pioneered the production of wines rich in antioxidants (try the Wild Blue—made with blueberries) and has created some of the most interesting blends on the Connecticut Wine Trail. In the tasting room you find whites featuring grapes like Traminette, Seyval Blanc, and Vidal Blanc. Red blends, blush-style, and dessert wines are also featured, including a spectacularly smooth port-style wine and another that blends pear, black walnut, and brandy. Local honey can be found along with wine, pumpkin cinnamon, ginger, nutmeg, and cloves in Autumn Spice or the slightly sweeter Harvest Spice.

*JONES FAMILY FARM AND WINERY
605 Israel Hill Rd.
Shelton, CT 06484
(203) 929-8425
jonesfamilyfarms.com

The Jones family has farmed their land among the White Hills of Shelton for more than 150 years. More than 400 acres, the farm is a local favorite in any season, where visitors can discover first-hand the family's commitment to the land. Christmas trees were planted on the dairy farm in the 1940s by fourth-generation son Philip. A few decades later, his son Terry added strawberries and blueberries. Now the sixth generation has created the winery, opened

in 2004. Bring the family and pick your own berries in June and July, or enjoy the autumn leaves or a light snowfall as you pick out your perfect pumpkin or select the best tree. But save time for a visit to the tasting room, with its beautiful handcrafted bar. Whites like Pinot Gris and Stonewall Chardonnay are crisp, so they pair well with foods. Red offerings include Cabernet Franc—one of the best examples in the state—and Jones's signature blend, Ripton Red, that has notes of vanilla and spice.

MCLAUGHLIN VINEYARDS
14 Albert's Hill Rd.
Sandy Hook, CT 06482
(203) 426-1533
mclaughlinvineyards.com

In the heart of Sandy Hook, not far from the Housatonic River, you'll find McLaughlin Vineyards. Established in 1979, it is one of the oldest vineyards in the state. The winery and tasting room are nestled among 160 acres of picturesque property, where you'll find hiking trails and even a bald eagle sanctuary. The winery's 15 acres spread out as you travel the gravel road to the tasting room, where stone steps ascend to a patio and tables full of tasters or a band strumming away on a summer evening. You'll sample whites like Blue Coyote, made with estate-grown Vidal Blanc and Aurora grapes, and reds like Vista Reposa, a complex blend that provides three distinct notes—earth, vanilla, and chocolate on the finish. In the front area of the tasting building is the Country Store, and don't miss the maple sugar produced on-site.

TWO ROADS BREWING
1700 Stratford Ave.
Stratford, CT 06615
(203) 335-2010
tworoadsbrewing.com

I had tried the beer from Two Roads Brewing before, and although it was good, I mistakenly assumed they had a small operation. Boy, was I wrong. This place is a destination, not just a brewery. Right off the I-95 exit, Two Roads fills an old factory and has over a dozen large tanks. It is a huge operation for Connecticut, and the impressive layout inside must have cost a lot. Of course I like the Robert Frost quote inside (from where the brewery gets its name) and the idea of Igor Sikorsky Russian Stout beer (being a Connecticut inventor from Stratford). My wife and I tried 11 beers currently on tap, and I was particularly taken with the Maibock. Two Roads is larger than any of the wineries currently operating in the state, and its product is consistent and strong. This is quite simply one of Connecticut's newest and best attractions, especially for those of us who enjoy a pint of good beer.

WHITE SILO FARM AND WINERY
32 Route 37 East
Sherman, CT 06784
(860) 355-0271
whitesilowinery.com
White Silo Farm and Winery specializes in wine made from fruit grown on the property. The winery and tasting room are found in an old barn; and, yes, it features a white silo and also a gallery that showcases local artists. The rhubarb wine will surprise you, and you'll fall in love with the raspberry, blackberry, and black currant wines. If you thought fruit wine was always sugary and powerfully sweet, try these made in the dry style. If sweeter is your style, and even if it's not, White Silo offers dessert versions as well. Try the black currant Cassis, or savor the puckering goodness of Raspberry and compare it to the dry version. Pick raspberries and blackberries on-site, and enjoy the picturesque family-run farm.

ACTIVITIES & EVENTS

Adventure Sports

CHELSEA PIERS
1 Blachley Rd.
Stamford, CT 06902
(203) 989-1000
chelseapiersct.com
This is the largest amateur sports complex in the state of Connecticut. They run camps and clinics, sponsor competitive teams, and run tournaments and meets. You can buy a membership for more privileges and options, or you can go for the day. Members can join leagues in soccer, basketball, volleyball, and more. Ice-skating, squash, tennis . . . this place is enormous. A number of my national champion gymnastics students from the University of Bridgeport teach there too—all their trainers are professionals. Call ahead to get private lessons. You can rent sections for birthday parties or corporate retreats, and you can join their leagues and clubs if you live in the area. Most day users will want to try the adventure center, specifically the batting cages, parkour, trampolines, foam pits, or rock climbing. Literally any age can use the adventure center, with an indoor gym for the "youngest athletes."

SPORTSCENTER OF CONNECTICUT
784 River Rd. (Route 110)
Shelton, CT 06484
(203) 929-6500
sportscenterct.com
This sizable recreation complex along the Housatonic River on Route 110 in Shelton is a great place to bring the family or a date. There are 2 year-round, NHL-size ice rinks here, one on top of the other. If that doesn't make sense to you, you'll have to skate it to believe it. The 18-hole miniature golf course is challenging, and the laser tag in a 5,000-square-foot indoor forest is fantastic fun for children ages 8 to 80. There's a food

court, basketball courts, and video arcade; and unlike some amusement parks, this is pay-as-you-play. Maybe you'll even see one of the famous ghost squirrels of Shelton while you're here; they look like albinos but have black eyes. If you're wondering what happened to all those great parks with their batting cages and golf driving ranges, the SportsCenter of Connecticut is open for business. The business of play, that is.

i From 1892 until 1958 the island of Pleasure Beach off Bridgeport and Stratford was home to a popular amusement park. During summer you can now take a free water taxi from downtown Bridgeport and visit this deserted beach (bridgeportct.gov/pleasurebeach).

Arts Venues

*CHARLES IVES CONCERT PARK
Western Connecticut State University
Westside Campus
43 Lake Ave. Ext.
Danbury, CT 06813
(203) 837-9226
ivesconcertpark.com

Danbury's own composer Charles Ives was the father of what in the 20th century would become known as "American music." This Pulitzer Prize winner loved open-air instrumentation, and that's just what you'll get here at the Ives Concert Park in his hometown. There are essentially two levels of seating—the seats and a general admission area where you can bring a picnic (beverages must be purchased there) and sit on blankets or chairs on the lawn. If you just care about the music and not seeing the performers up close, this is the way to do it. Singers know this is the place to play, and the park's summer schedule is packed with big names. They have a winter schedule too, with concerts and plays at Western's Berkshire Theatre or the Ives Concert Hall.

KLEIN MEMORIAL AUDITORIUM
910 Fairfield Ave.
Bridgeport, CT 06605
(203) 319-1404, ext. 309
theklein.org

Opening in 1940, this 1,400-seat theater in Bridgeport has seen performances and speeches by people like Leonard Bernstein, Eleanor Roosevelt, and Martin Luther King Jr. These days the Art Deco building is run by the nonprofit Fairfield Theater Company and hosts comedy acts, pop bands, and theater performances. These marble halls are also the home of the Greater Bridgeport Symphony, headed by conductor Eric Jacobsen. Their performances of classics like Handel's Messiah and Orff's Carmina Burana are simply magical. There's also free parking—often a rarity at city theaters. Try to get a seat about 10 to 15 rows back; those are the best, except for the first row of the balcony.

LEVITT PAVILION FOR THE
PERFORMING ARTS
40 Jesup Rd.
Westport, CT 06880
(203) 226-7600
levittpavilion.com

Westport's free summer venue takes the typical town summer concert series and supersizes it. They've been running for over 40 years, and in summer 2014, this summer entertainment venue opened a new performance stage and landscaped walks along the Saugatuck River. This is the place to bring a blanket and picnic to enjoy a band. Unlike some town pavilions that feature one performance a week at most during the summer, the Levitt has more than 50 every summer, mixing theater, music, magic, and family entertainment. It also serves as a venue for numerous fund-raising events and is able to bring in big names. One of their best events is Blues, Views, and BBQs, with a contest for best barbecue that causes the end of many diets at the end of every summer.

QUICK CENTER FOR THE ARTS
Fairfield University
1073 N. Benson Rd.
Fairfield, CT 06824
(203) 254-4010
quickcenter.com

This multipurpose venue at Fairfield University features concerts, plays, comedy performances, lectures, readings by popular authors, and dance. If that isn't enough, they also do simulcasts from the live Metropolitan Opera here too. The high ceilings in the entryway give a feeling of grandness, even though this is a more intimate venue, and the adjoining art gallery is worth your time as you sip wine before the show. This is one of four or five university-run performance venues in the state that consistently bring in big names, from Dar Williams to the Russian National Ballet. While you're here, you might want to stop at Fairfield's Bellarmine Museum of Art to check out the Kress Collection of Italian Paintings or the Asian art collection.

THE PALACE THEATRE
307 Atlantic St.
Stamford, CT 06901
(203) 325-4466
palacestamford.org

With almost 800 seats, the Palace Theatre has been a center for music and theater since 1927, and these days also provides education programs to the public. It is the home of the Stamford Symphony Orchestra, the Connecticut Grand Opera, the City Ballet, and the Connecticut Ballet, all of which put on moving performances. If classical is not your style, this is also where big-name pop music stars and comedians play in Stamford,

so check the schedule. There's bound to be something playing at this diverse performance venue for you.

RIDGEFIELD PLAYHOUSE
80 East Ridge Rd.
Ridgefield, CT 06877
(203) 438-5795
ridgefieldplayhouse.org

This restored Cass Gilbert Jr.–designed theater in Ridgefield hosts musical acts from Diana Krall to Clint Black, question-and-answer sessions with film industry people like Ron Howard and Harvey Keitel, stand-up comedy from the likes of Dana Carvey and Kathy Griffin, speakers like David Sedaris and Stephen Sondheim, and more. Nearly every (brand-new) seat in the 500-seat theater is a good one, and everything is state of the art. Chow down on some of the real-butter popcorn and enjoy your favorite entertainment. Oh, I forgot to mention, they also feature plays.

Cruises

SHEFFIELD ISLAND LIGHTHOUSE CRUISE
Norwalk Seaport Association
132 Water St.
South Norwalk, CT 06854
(203) 838-9444
seaport.org

This is one of two standout island cruises in the state (the other is the Thimbles in New Haven County), and it should be on everyone's list of activities. The catamaran cruise leaves from Norwalk Harbor, right next to the Maritime Aquarium, and holds up to 49 passengers. The captain and crew will tell you facts and legends on your way out past harbor seals to the island. The large 1868 stone lighthouse is the big attraction on the island, and you should certainly take the tour of its 10 rooms and the view from the top. There is also a nice picnic grove, and some folks choose to go swimming out here in the Sound. A small nature trail is located in the part of the island run by the Stewart B. McKinney National Wildlife Refuge; you can walk out to a nice observation deck or even circumnavigate the island. Keep your eye on the time, though. You don't want to get left out here. Or do you?

SOUNDWATERS CENTER AND SCHOONER CENTER AT COVE ISLAND PARK

1281 Cove Rd.
Stamford, CT 06902
(203) 323-1978
Schooner docked at Brewer Yacht Haven Marina, Dock S-1
1 Bateman Way
Stamford, CT 06902
(203) 406-3335
soundwaters.org

Take a ride on the 80-foot *SoundWaters,* a replica of an old three-masted schooner. The tours are 2.5 hours and include lectures by trained naturalists. You might not pay too much attention, though, while you're raising the sails, hauling in the net, and examining the day's catch. Children under 5 are unfortunately not permitted on the boat. The schooner is attached to the Coastal Education Center in Cove Island Park (see entry), and here you can learn about the history and science of Long Island Sound. There are aquarium tanks too, and if you're there on Saturday at 1 p.m., you'll see the fish get fed.

Festivals & Annual Events

BARNUM FESTIVAL

1070 Main St.
Bridgeport, CT 06604
(203) 367-8495
barnumfestival.com

Since 1948 this festival has been lifting the spirits of the people of Bridgeport. It is really not one event but many throughout early summer: a car show, comedy night, road races, the Jenny Lind voice competition (since long before *American Idol*), fireworks, and more, all leading up to the Fourth of July. On or close to the Fourth, Bridgeport hosts the Street Day Parade. Once this was second in size only to Macy's Thanksgiving Day Parade, and though it has since been surpassed, it is still a huge deal. Along with the usual marching bands and floats, people from across the region dress up in outrageous costumes, and they are a sight to behold.

GATHERING OF THE VIBES

Soundview Drive
Bridgeport, CT 06604
(203) 908-3030
gatheringofthevibes.com

This annual music festival has been going and growing for almost 2 decades and is now a 4-day wonderland. Its primary residence is in Bridgeport's Seaside Park, though it has also set up shop in other locations. You can camp right in the park (the only time during the year you're allowed to do that), stay nearby, or just come for a single day. Expect to find kids and families, as well as tripped-out teenagers. This is a music festival as it should be: friendly chaos among the tunes of amazing artists like the Grateful Dead, George Clinton, and P-Funk. Various craft and food vendors serve the 20,000 people who attend every year. This is the biggest music festival in the Northeast and a once-in-a-lifetime experience—unless you go every year of course.

GREATEST BLUEFISH TOURNAMENT ON EARTH

2 Lafayette Sq.
Bridgeport, CT 06604
(203) 366-6000
wicc600.com

This annual competition offers a $25,000 prize for the largest bluefish caught. That is a lot of money for any angler, and the runner-up prizes aren't too shabby either. Though it is sponsored and run by the WICC radio station in Bridgeport, the contest takes place all along the coast of Connecticut (and Long Island), so wherever you are the last weekend of August, you can sign up and head out into the Sound to fish. There are weigh-in stations from Greenwich to Old Saybrook that will measure your catch. Recently they have also offered a prize of $50,000 for the capture of a specific tagged fish swimming somewhere in the Sound. You're still better off trying for it than playing the lottery.

i Check out visitfairfieldcountyct .com for updated information about the area's events.

NORWALK OYSTER FESTIVAL
Veteran's Memorial State Park
Fort Point Street and Seaview Avenue
East Norwalk, CT 06855
(203) 838-9444
seaport.org
Since 1978 people have been coming to Norwalk the weekend after Labor Day to celebrate (and eat) the mighty oyster. Among the clams, soft-shell crabs, and lobsters, you can prove your oyster-eating prowess in a "slurp-off" contest, or just try your first one. Run by the Norwalk Seaport Association, this festival is more than just food, with a focus on maritime heritage that includes old oyster boats, a shucking contest, marching bands, harbor cruises, arts and crafts exhibitions, and more. And of course this is a great time to take the ferry out to Sheffield Island, to visit the Maritime Aquarium, or simply to wander around the streets of South Norwalk, just across the bridge from Veteran's Memorial State Park, where the festival is held.

WESTPORT FINE ARTS FESTIVAL
159 Main St.
Westport, CT 06880
(203) 505-8716
westportfineartsfestival.com
There are a number of fine arts festivals throughout Connecticut in summer, but this is one of the standouts. Perhaps it is Westport's reputation as a home for both the rich and artistic, but this arts festival brings out real talent every year. Sponsored by the local merchants' association, the festival is an annual highlight for collectors from all over New England and Manhattan. It's been around for over 40 years, and usually features around 150 artists displaying their work along the Westport River and in the squares of this lovely town. The event is juried, and you can try to guess which artist will win. This is also a great chance to check out the visually stunning contemporary art at the unrelated Westport Arts Center (westport artscenter.org), which also brings in some exciting new work.

Fishing

SAUGATUCK FALLS NATURAL AREA
Route 53, opposite John Read Middle School
mianustu.org/areafishing/saugatuckriver .html
Fishing in Fairfield County can often be a frustrating experience: Both parking and river frontage are limited by the endless suburbs. But once you get north of the Merritt Parkway, things open up. The Saugatuck Falls Natural Area is a nice woodland park with 312 acres of colonial stone walls and glacier-formed landscape. There is parking for a couple cars in a gravel lot on the side of the road, or you can park in the school lot across the street (when school's out). You can walk along the Saugatuck River, which is really a stream by the time it gets here, fish under the falls or in shady wooded glades, and

never see another person. I suggest waders and a fly rod as the best way to stay along the stream if you want to do more than just the falls. The Trout Unlimited website above has other options for fishing in Fairfield County as well, including farther down the Saugatuck watershed in Westport. I caught a nice-size bluefish in the tidal estuary there.

Golf

*RICHTER PARK GOLF COURSE
100 Aunt Hack Rd.
Danbury, CT 06811
(203) 792-2550
richterpark.com

Built in 1970, this is one of the country's top golf courses, as consistently rated and listed in numerous magazines. That's top courses, not just top public ones; though in that case it is one of the nation's top 25. It has challenging holes with deceptive greens, and there's a lot of water here, coming into play on 14 holes. In 2008 they redesigned and renovated all their bunkers, and they have implemented an online reservation system. Try going early in the season, when the rates are half what they are during prime time. The clubhouse and restaurant serve solid, consistent food, better than you'll find at most other courses and clubs. Richter Park is not only golf; it offers hiking trails and tennis, as well as concerts in the summer.

RIDGEFIELD GOLF COURSE
545 Ridgebury Rd.
Ridgefield, CT 06877
(203) 748-7008
ridgefieldct.org

This par 71 public course plays like a private club but is open to residents and nonresidents alike. Designed by George Fazio and opened in 1975, it is managed by Frank Sergiovanni, PGA. It is well maintained and has a very challenging back 9. You can tune up your skills in the practice area, eat and drink

at the restaurant, and visit the full-service pro shop for all your needs. You can get season or 10-day passes if you're visiting the area; these reduced-rate passes give preferential weekend tee times that you might not otherwise get as a nonresident. On the website they have maps with the pros' tips on how to conquer the course; I suggest you follow their advice.

Health & Wellness

ADAM BRODERICK SALON AND SPA
89 Danbury Rd.
Ridgefield, CT 06877
(203) 431-3994
adambroderick.com

Adam Broderick's combination of hair salon and spa is not unique, but few do it better. The salon has surprisingly reasonable prices for Fairfield County, considering how chic the place is. Adam himself is available for a consultation on the best style for you. The spa has all the usual treatments to relax and rejuvenate you, but they also have more unusual ones, like their bodicure cocoon that uses a cooling or warming gel, a seaweed wrap, and a Mylar wrap, and finishes with hydrating body mist and silk. They also offer services like teeth whitening and reflexology. Broderick boasts a satellite salon in Southbury (New Haven County), but this is the original and most say the best.

AETHERIA RELAXATION SPA
121 Cherry St.
New Canaan, CT 06840
(203) 966-6650
aetheriaspa.com

Aetheria means "heavenly" in Latin, and this spa set in a Victorian house in New Canaan may get you close. They pride themselves on their calm, soothing atmosphere, and the plush robes and acupressure sandals immediately begin the process of relaxation as you sit under a skylight before the

treatment. Don't worry about tips here—
they are included in the price. Aetheria has
packages for brides and expecting mothers,
as well as seasonal specials, and they only
use organic products. Their philosophy is
that if it isn't edible, it isn't good enough for
your skin. However, what sets this spa apart
might be the health and wellness options like
acupuncture and their support for healthy
community eating and local business. They
feature "wellness packages" that are simply
priced by time; the guest, with the help of
wellness experts, can decide how that is best
used for specific problems. Aetheria really
seems to care for the whole person they treat
and not just the surface. That's real heaven.

SALTANA CAVE
590 Danbury Rd.
Ridgefield, CT 06877
(203) 969-4327
saltanacave.com

Saltana Cave is not a spelunking expedition in Fairfield County, it's a unique spa.
Sit in gravity chairs, listen to meditative
music, and breathe in the salt air of this
man-made cave. Using a halogenerator and
a more natural method, Saltana gives you
the benefits of salt therapy, which more
and more is becoming accepted—especially
for people with respiratory problems like
me—as naturally anti-inflammatory, anti-
bacterial, antiviral, and antifungal. The space
itself is beautiful—white and glowing with
low light. Sessions last 45 minutes and start
every hour on the hour. Wear loose clothing
and white socks, because you will be asked
to take off your shoes.

Hiking, Biking & Walking

GREENWICH AUDUBON CENTER
613 Riversville Rd.
Greenwich, CT 06831
(203) 869-5272
greenwich.audubon.org

Opening in 1942, this was the first environmental education center in the US initiated
by the Audubon Society. There are 15 miles
of trails in and around this large park, a testament to the appeal of open green spaces
even here in what is essentially a suburb of
New York. The Kimberlin Nature Education
Center has a nice little exhibit gallery. This is
a great place to hike with children, who will
marvel at the huge trees and the waterfall
along the edge of Mead Lake. Every autumn,
hawks migrate through here, and the Quaker
Ridge Hawk Watch Site is a great spot for the
patient to see these majestic creatures on
their way through Greenwich. If it's difficult
to imagine densely populated Greenwich as
a "big city" in the same way as Stamford or
Norwalk, it's because of its commitment to
places like this.

NEWTOWN TRAILWAYS
Newtown, CT 06470
(203) 270-3650
newtownforestassociation.org

Many towns in Connecticut have their own
elaborate trail system, often attached to but
not part of nearby state parks, greenways, and
blue trails. Newtown's land trust association
is the oldest in Connecticut, and one of their
"town forests" is thought to be the first of its
kind in America. Multiuse biking, walking, and
cross-country skiing trails stretch throughout
the town. Al's Trail forms an 11-mile backbone, and the bald eagles that nest by the
Shepaug Dam in winter make it a destination.
From Dec 15 to Mar 15 this section is closed
to protect them, but there is a designated
observatory. There is also a beaver lodge near
the old rail bed in this section. The trail passes
through Rocky Glen State Park, where Charles
Goodyear discovered the process for vulca-
nizing rubber. North of McLaughlin Vineyards,
Upper Paugussett State Forest has a network
of trails, including the blue-blazed Lillinoah
Trail, which heads along the huge man-made

lake and is the only trail in the park designated for foot travel only.

SHELTON LAKES RECREATION PATH
Shelton Ave. and Meadow St.
Shelton, CT 06484
sheltonconservation.org/recreation/
shelton_trails

The Shelton Lakes multiuse path can be used for walking or cross-country skiing in winter, but it is one of the most fun to bike in the state. The mostly gravel trail goes from Route 108 right outside downtown Shelton, all the way to Huntington Village over 5 miles away. Since it pretty much goes right over the White Hills, it is more challenging than canal or railroad bike paths, so don't do this first thing in the season. Along the reservoirs near the north end you'll find white pines; farther on you'll see oaks, hickories, birches, and maples in what is one of the nicest forest rides I've been on. The path shown on the online map connects to another 1-mile path, creating a full 10-mile round-trip, which you can access at several points. At the southern end, stop at the Huntington Street Café for a nice lunch—maybe a steamed cheeseburger or salad—and head back over the hills.

Kidstuff

DISCOVERY MUSEUM, BRIDGEPORT
4450 Park Ave.
Bridgeport, CT 06604
(203) 372-3521
discoverymuseum.org

This is a great museum to bring children if you want them to learn something while having fun. Besides the solar trail and disc golf outside, this museum features a small planetarium and mostly interactive exhibits, like an echo tube to clap into or "moon base" activities. There is also a preschool workshop for kids ages 0 to 3. Behind the museum is a 180-platform "adventure park" with ropes and zip lines, combining a day of knowledge

with a day of action. Though the permanent exhibits are for children, there are some temporary traveling exhibits for adults. And you'll marvel at the model of Gustave Whitehead's revolutionary 1901 airplane hanging in the lobby. Check the website for current events; the science demonstrations for the general public are a lot of fun, featuring lightning and fireballs. The best thing about the museum is the summer camp program, with 28 different classes in subjects like CSI forensics and model rocketry. If you're in the area in summer, send your budding scientists here.

EARTHPLACE
10 Woodside Ln.
PO Box 165
Westport, CT 06881
(203) 227-7253
earthplace.org

This nature discovery center for kids has been around since 1958 and manages 2 miles of trails in the largest open space in Westport. It is more than just a 20,000-square-foot nature museum filled with fun activities, though. It's got a live animal hall from which you can hear the oohs and aahs of children checking out the snakes and ferrets. A favorite among the parents is the birds of prey area, which includes a pair of bald eagles. However, just bringing your children to Earthplace on a random day does not get the full effect. Their genius is in their workshops, like maple sugaring, bird banding, and family campfires. It's a chance for your kids to connect to nature, yes, but also to connect with you.

✳STEPPING STONES MUSEUM FOR CHILDREN
303 West Ave.
Norwalk, CT 06850
(203) 899-0606
steppingstonesmuseum.org

First of all, this eclectic and colorful building is not a museum; it is a science-based amusement park that parents will have to hold themselves back from playing in. Certainly your children will learn things here, from both the hands-on activities and the colorful information on the walls. There is a story room, an art studio, a science lab, a multimedia gallery, and several stages for performance, all welded into an organic whole by color and design. Kids move excitedly through the activities, changing hard hats for scientist jackets, while volunteers and parents supervise the action. Westport's wonderful Age of Reason store runs the gift shop, and a cafe serves lunches for everyone. Across the parking lot is a wonderful, wheelchair-accessible playground that some kids like even better than the museum. Stepping Stones is for younger children (under 10); they even have a special "tot town" area for those under 3.

Nightlife

ACOUSTIC CAFE
2926 Fairfield Ave., #3
Bridgeport, CT 06605
(203) 335-3655
theacoustic.rocks

This chill, funky venue is the prime place to hear local music in Fairfield County. Located in the Black Rock section of Bridgeport, the Acoustic focuses on folk and contemporary alternative music but often breaks out into different styles like metal, jazz, bluegrass, electronic, hip-hop, and zydeco. More of a bar or nightclub with a stage, they have open-mike nights and a great selection of local bands. The cafe's walls are covered with hippie art, they have a great sound system, and they're always packed with music fans. If you get a chance to peek in the green room, you'll see photos of thousands of performers who have rocked this stage. Have dinner at nearby Bloodroot and then see one of these intimate shows.

GRAND
15 Bank St.
Stamford, CT 06901
(203) 323-3232
stamfordgrand.com/press

Technically called g/r/a/n/d, this high-ceilinged nightclub in the center of downtown Stamford features cocktail hours at a sleek bar with glass panels that change colors, curved steel stairs and glass railings, and unusual serving trays. Upstairs you can eat at a quieter table or head up to the lounge. The New American food here is a cut above most nightclubs, with "little plates" like Wagyu beef sliders and crispy artichoke hearts taking center stage. The macaroni and cheese in particular is fantastic. That makes this fascinating bar/restaurant/club the perfect place to take a date and spend all night. Just be careful about spilling the chocolate fondue on your clothes.

LUSH
18 S. Main St.
South Norwalk, CT 06854
(203) 854-9116
stratatech.net/lush

In SoNo this is your best bet for a night out on the town, with very professionally designed and executed decor. Plush chairs and small tables are perfect for just having drinks, and the atmosphere is chill but festive. As far as music, DJs usually spin hip-hop and house music at Lush, and people are not shy about getting on the floor to dance. The popular DJ Newberry, a tristate legend since the 1990s, spins here on Saturday nights. There's a VIP lounge where you can relax with a bottle of champagne, and the bar makes great martinis. Lush does have a strictly enforced dress code, so dress to impress.

Spectator Sports

ARENA AT HARBOR YARD AND BRIDGEPORT SOUND TIGERS

600 Main St.
Bridgeport, CT 06604
(203)-345-2300
websterbankarena.com
soundtigers.com

Now sponsored by Webster Bank, this beautifully designed venue off I-95 in Bridgeport is directly next to the Bridgeport Bluefish stadium and provides a huge sports and entertainment destination for Fairfield County. The 10,000-seat arena brings in concerts, comedy performances, and the Ringling Bros. and Barnum & Bailey Circus, and hosts Fairfield University's NCAA basketball season. But the biggest draw (other than when hometown guitar legend John Mayer plays here) is the Bridgeport Sound Tigers. The Sound Tigers (as in Long Island Sound) play in the AHL hockey league every winter, and seats right on the ice are reasonably priced for the board-slamming action. It's worth the couple extra bucks to get right up front and watch your kids (and probably yourself) pound on the glass as the players slide by. There are food concessions throughout the concourse, or you can walk underneath I-95 to Ralph and Rich's excellent Italian restaurant (see entry).

BLUEFISH BASEBALL

500 Main St.
Bridgeport, CT 06604
(203) 345-4800
bridgeportbluefish.com

Founded in 1998, the Bridgeport Bluefish baseball team is one of the few professional sports teams left in Connecticut, whose sports fans usually gravitate toward the larger New York or Boston franchises. However, local pride comes out every spring when these Atlantic League players suit up (they have won the most games in the history of the league). One of the early major-league heroes, James O'Rourke, came from Bridgeport; he also signed the first African American to play professional baseball in 1895. A statue of this legend stands outside the gates of the Ballpark at Harbor Yard baseball stadium, with its backdrop of the giant power plant and train tracks. It has been called one of the best urban fields in America, and watching a game here is a fascinating experience. Many stadiums endeavor to block out the outside world, but not this one. Look for the local parrot flock (seriously) to fly over the games at sunset, making their distinctive calls. One might even call out "home run."

Theater

CURTAIN CALL THEATER

1349 Newfield Ave., #E
Stamford, CT 06905
(203) 329-8207
curtaincallinc.com

This theater company was founded in 1990 as part of Stamford's great cultural and business renaissance. The performances they put on are mostly musicals like *1776* or *Annie*, including some fun interactive murder mysteries. There are actually two stages here, the main one and the Dressing Room Theatre, to which you may bring your own dinner and drinks. The name of this venue is technically the Sterling Farms Theatre Complex, so don't get confused if you see that name being used. Students pay half price, although the ticket prices are incredibly low for Connecticut, period. I recently enjoyed a terrifying performance of *Wait Until Dark* here.

SHERMAN PLAYHOUSE

5 Route 39 North
Sherman, CT 06784
(860) 354-3622
shermanplayers.org

At the north end of Candlewood Lake in the tiny hamlet of Sherman, this playhouse continues the tradition begun in 1923. From Apr to Nov the Sherman Players put on gritty and moving performances in a renovated 19th-century church. They also sometimes include lighter fare, like fun musicals and kids' productions. This is local theater at its best, something you'll find brings as much pride as local sports in Connecticut. You're so far out here, it seems more like Litchfield County than Fairfield, and there's easier access if you're in that area. Stop by White Silo Winery, just up Route 37, and the 1829 Federal-style Northrop House Museum on Saturday or Sunday afternoon from 2 to 4 p.m. (sherman historicalsociety.org).

✳WESTPORT COUNTRY PLAYHOUSE
25 Powers Ct.
Westport, CT 06880
(203) 227-4177
westportplayhouse.org

Putting on plays since 1931, the Westport Country Playhouse is a local tradition and a national institution all at once. Set in a restored 1835 cow barn (thus the "Country"), this playhouse has debuted many plays of note before they went to New York, but more appealing to us might be the list of actors who have graced its stage, sometimes before they hit the screen in Hollywood: Helen Hayes, Ethel Barrymore, José Ferrer, Henry Fonda, Alan Alda, Cicely Tyson, Liza Minnelli, et cetera. It was here that Hamden resident Thornton Wilder made his debut as the stage manager in his own play, *Our Town*, in 1946. When the playhouse ran into trouble a few years back, Westport's own Joanne Woodward took the reins, bringing in a list of Oscar winners (including her late husband, Paul Newman) to act here. You'll see new talent and veterans alike on these boards, in an intimate setting that you'll seldom find elsewhere in America.

Water Sports

CANDLEWOOD LAKE
178 Shortwoods Rd.
New Fairfield, CT 06812
(203) 797-4165
ct.gov/dep [search "Squantz Pond State Park"]

This is not a natural lake, but it is Connecticut's largest. There are some local access points, but most of the lake's edge is lined with private residences (of New York's elite). The biggest exception is Squantz Pond State Park, which is set on one of the long arms of the lake. You can launch your boat here from two different coves and pass under the Route 39 causeway into the main lake. You'll find a swimming and picnic area here as well, and a few short hiking trails, one of which leads to "Council Rock," where native tribes held meetings in centuries past. In summer a concession stand is usually open, and pedal boats and canoes are available to rent. This "pond" is great for that sort of activity, unlike some other areas of Candlewood, which have large boat wakes. Candlewood also happens to be a popular place to scuba dive, despite low visibility, because intrepid divers have found old Model-T Fords, farm buildings, and covered bridges, completely submerged when the lake was dammed in 1926.

CAPTAIN'S COVE SEAPORT
1 Bostwick Ave.
Bridgeport, CT 06605
(203) 335-1433
captainscoveseaport.com

This marina and amusement center in historic Black Rock Harbor helped begin the reimagining of Bridgeport back in 1982, and it has expanded almost every year. "The Cove" is seasonal, from May to Sept, and centers around the large 400-seat (or 500, depending on how many squeeze in on a summer night) restaurant, with its wonderful deck overlooking the harbor and the marina. Upstairs, the bar area is built in a tugboat wheelhouse, and a 40-foot model of the *Titanic* hangs from the ceiling. Outside, a row of adorable shops line the wharf, with new vendors every summer. The Victorian Dundon House has been moved here and turned into a maritime museum as well, but call for an appointment. There are also several charter boats, tours in a US Navy launch boat, and a sailing school (teamsailaway .com) here. Check the Captain's Cove website for special events, which seem to bring all of Bridgeport every weekend.

i If you'd like to charter a saltwater fishing boat, check out ctsport fishing.com, which has a list of captains and boats for you to choose from.

DOWNUNDER KAYAKING
157 Rowayton Ave.
Rowayton, CT 06583
(203) 642-3660
downunderkayaking.com

The owner, Kim Beaumont, comes to us from New Zealand, and seems to have been born on a kayak. Like many who come to our shores, she brings optimistic energy, as well as skills to impart, and she is joined by a young and enthusiastic staff of experts. Downunder has paddleboard and kayak rentals, classes, and even more challenging kayak fitness options. They also sponsor races and corporate team-building exercises and offer overnight camping trips to the Norwalk Islands. Whether you already know how to kayak or want to try it for the first time, go to Downunder. There's a second location in Westport on the Saugatuck River, which is more protected and is open year-round. So if you want to kayak in February (and more power to you if you do), you can.

LAKE LILLINONAH
Hanover Road
Newtown, CT 06470
(203) 364-4002
lakelillinonahauthority.org [search "Lake Lillinonah Park"]

"The Lilly" is one of the prime boating lakes in Connecticut, formed by the damming of the Housatonic River in Sandy Hook. It's deep, long, and thin, to the point where a few bridges cross it high above you on cliffs. However, there's enough space for you to crank up the speed in your powerboat and head down the pleasantly curved lake without having to worry. Most of it is great for waterskiing and personal watercraft. Fishing tournaments are held on the lake, and despite the boat noise, there are plenty of quiet spots to reel in a large bass. Pull up and dock the boat at the steak and seafood restaurant Down the Hatch in Brookfield. There are several state and town parks along the shores, including Lovers Leap State Park at the north end. The crimson 1895 Berlin Iron Bridge crosses the river, one of only five such bridges left in Connecticut. Nearby is the rock formation where Chief Waramaug's daughter Lillinonah and her lover jumped to their death.

SHOPPING

Antiques

✳**ANTIQUE AND ARTISAN CENTER**
69 Jefferson St.
Stamford, CT 06902
(203) 327-6022
stamfordantiques.com

This has been called the best antiques center in the country, and when you walk into the huge, 22,000-square-foot store, it's easy to see why. The choices are varied among the 85 or so booths, but all are quite solid because the owners, Mark Candido and Ronald Louis, handpick respected antiques dealers. American furniture and home goods seem to dominant the aisles, and you'll find period lamps, benches, bars, tables, desks, chairs, and architectural elements to complete your dream house. You will also find jewelry and vintage couture scattered throughout. The inventory changes quite often here, so every trip to the Antique and Artisan Center is a brand-new experience. You have to love a place that has buttons to press for assistance, along with free notepads and pens to take notes as you walk around the store.

HARBOR VIEW CENTER FOR ANTIQUES
121 Jefferson St.
Stamford, CT 06902
(203) 325-8070
harborviewantiques.com
With dozens of premier dealers from places as far away as England and Japan, Harbor View Center for Antiques carefully vets its merchandise for quality. The selection of fine art on any given day will remind you of the high-end auctions you've seen only in movies, and the period furnishings and decorative accessories (all the way back to the 18th century) are hard to beat. Wealthy New Yorkers take the train out of Manhattan to decorate their homes with items from Harbor View. Some dealers here also specialize in ceramics, silver, clocks, jewelry, and textiles. Both Harbor View and the nearby Antique and Artisan Center were established in 1999 and have made Stamford a destination for antiques collectors.

SILVER LINING CONSIGNMENTS
470 Main St.
Ridgefield, CT 06877
(203) 431-0132
mysilverliningboutique.com
This is not a clothing consignment store, but rather an antiques store that buys and sells frequently and displays consigned articles

in its shop. It is a fine store with items, from giant plant urns to china, priced for many different budgets. The staff at Silver Lining is friendly and welcoming and will help you pick a gift or a piece of furniture from their large selection. They are located in the heart of downtown Ridgefield, and there are plenty of other shopping opportunities here as well. Check out Touch of Sedona two doors down if you're interested in the American Southwest, or the Toy Chest across the street for the children in your life.

STRATFORD ANTIQUE CENTER
400 Honeyspot Rd.
Stratford, CT 06615
(203) 378-7754
stratfordantique.com
Driving north, you cannot miss the huge warehouse off I-95 labeled Stratford Antique Center. You might think this is just an advertisement, rather than the place itself, but this enormous multidealer antiques depot needs this huge warehouse. With its endless stalls full of ancient signs, paintings, and furniture, the Stratford equivalent of a "mall" of antiques is worth a stop. Of course a short stop may turn into a few hours of browsing, as you try to take in the volume and density of fascinating relics of yesteryear. Because of all the competition, the prices are a little better too. Dig around and you'll find a fine set of silverware or a vintage movie poster to decorate your office.

UNITED HOUSE WRECKING
535 Hope St.
Stamford, CT 06906
(203) 348-5371
unitedhousewrecking.com
This unique store in northern Stamford has 40,000 square feet of showroom space, and they need it because they specialize in large elements like corbels, full vintage bars, mantels, and doors. But they also have mirrors,

rugs, lamps, and wonderful reclaimed pine furniture for sale. Outside, you'll immediately see what has brought random people off Hope Street and into the store for the last 60 years: the antique and reproduction statues, fountains, and urns. If you want a weathervane for your new house or a gazebo for your backyard, this is the place to come. And considering the prices for new gazebos built from scratch, you'll probably get a better deal here. I picked up a beautiful Chinese water bucket here for only $90.

Books

BARNES & NOBLE BOOKSELLERS
Multiple Locations
barnesandnoble.com
This familiar franchise has many convenient locations throughout the state. Although this is a nationwide chain, they always include local books and adapt each store slightly to their local clientele. You can find Fairfield County locations in Danbury (Danbury Square, 15 Backus Ave., Danbury, CT 06810; 203-730-2733), Westport (Post Plaza Shopping Center, 1076 Post Rd. East, Westport, CT 06880; 203-221-7955), Norwalk (360 Connecticut Ave., Norwalk, CT 06854; 203-866-2213), and Stamford (100 Greyrock Place Suite H009, Stamford, CT 06901; 203-323-1248). There's a reason you can find these stores throughout America: They provide a quality selection with great service. And let's not forget the great coffee and pastries.

BYRD'S BOOKS
126 Greenwood Avenue
Bethel, CT 06801
(203) 730-2973
byrdsbooks.com
Alice Hutchinson of Byrd's Books is one of those community leaders who make our state's cultural landscape better for the rest of us. With experience in the field of bookselling and business, she runs a professional but homelike bookstore that carries only new titles, with a special focus on Bethel authors, Connecticut authors, poets, publishers, and illustrators. The children's books section is huge, and you can also find greeting cards, gifts, and puzzles. You can find a healthy selection of local authors here, and many stop by for the frequent readings and events. The store fronts the main street of Bethel, but there is plenty of parking in the back. Head in through the rear entrance Tues through Sun, get a cup of coffee, and browse to your heart's content.

PEQUOT LIBRARY BOOK SALE
720 Pequot Ave.
Southport, CT 06890
(203) 259-0346
pequotlibrary.org
You might be thinking that this should be in the events section (if that) rather than in shopping, but this is not like any other library book sale you've ever been to. Founded in 1961, it has become one of the largest in the country, with an average of 140,000 books. You can find literally anything here in any genre, as well as collectible LPs and 45s, CDs, and DVDs. Some collectors just come for the comic books, which are numerous and rare. The summer sale lasts almost a week (check the website for exact dates in a given year), and the library has instituted one in midwinter as well. On normal days a thematic selection is available for sale in the lobby. While you're here, take some time to drive around beautiful residential Southport and marvel at the huge houses, well-kept lawns, and ancient beech trees.

WRITTEN WORDS BOOKSTORE
482 River Rd.
Shelton, CT 06484
(203) 944-0400
writtenwordsbookstore.com
Dorothy Sim-Broder's little independent bookstore in the White Hills of Shelton is

hidden in a fairly common shopping center. But her selection and friendly, do-anything-for-you service is anything but common. This is a community bookstore in the best sense of the word, supporting other local independent businesses and featuring community services like discussion groups, language classes, educator and senior discounts, knitting classes, and complimentary gift wrapping. When you step into the sunlit reading room, you can serve yourself free coffee or tea and sit in a comfortable chair to browse through the latest offerings from the book world. The latest opinion is that small bookstores will be making a comeback in the 21st century. That's good news for everyone, and Written Words will be at the head of the pack.

Clothing

GROOVE
420 Post Rd. West
Westport, CT 06880
(203) 557-8112
grooveforkids.com

Groove is a recent addition to Westport, carrying California-style apparel and accessories for toddlers, tweens, and teens. I'm told this is the perfect place to shop for your younger teens (thank God I don't have to worry about one of those right now), with laid-back "cool" clothing that will give them the edge they need to maintain their fragile self-confidence. They have popular brands named for animals, like Flying Monkey and Wildfox, and others that sound like band names, like Flow Society and Appaman. You don't have to keep track of them—your kids already know which one they want. And it's not just clothing—you can pick up one of those faux-spiky back packs from Madpax they all seem to be wearing these days. Or better yet, go in, sit on the yellow couch, and wait while they browse.

HELEN AINSON DARIEN
1078 Post Rd., #A
Darien, CT 06820
(203) 655-9841
helenainson.com

Helen Ainson opened an independent clothing store in NYC in 1948, and her daughter Erica opened this one in Darien in 1977. Since then Erica's store has won recognition for having the best women's clothing in Connecticut. The longevity of a boutique like this is a testament to great service and great taste, as well as to the expertise of the carefully hired staff. They carry cocktail dresses, evening separates, designer sportswear, and other special-occasion attire. This is a community store too, and Erica gives back to the Darien community as a sponsor of various local charities. If you have an event you need to look good for, Helen Ainson Darien has something for you; best of all, they have it in sizes 2 to 24.

Farm Stores/Pick Your Own

BLUE JAY ORCHARDS
125 Plumtrees Rd.
Bethel, CT 06801
(203) 748-0119
bluejayorchardsct.com

In the 18th and 19th centuries, Connecticut was absolutely blanketed in apple orchards, from which people made a delightful, mildly alcoholic cider drunk by adults and children alike. Today there are only a few farms left in the state (and especially in Fairfield County) with large apple orchards, and Blue Jay in Bethel is one of them. In 1934 the Josephy family bought this farm from the Weeds and expanded it to its current size of 140 acres, now owned by the Pattersons. In fact, it was the first farmland preserved by selling development rights to the state. That means it must always stay a working farm. From Aug to Oct you can enjoy this treasure through pick-your-own apples, of which they have dozens of varieties. Their gift store is open until Dec, with gifts and baked goods, including, of course, apple pie.

SILVERMAN'S FARM
451 Sport Hill Rd.
Easton, CT 06612
(203) 261-3306
silvermansfarm.com
From July to Oct Silverman's Farm is abuzz with pick-your-own fans, all grabbing peaches, apples, and plums to eat fresh or can to enjoy over the long winter. However, the real draw here is the animal farm, which attracts countless children to its petting zoo every year. Silverman's has animals you'd expect to find on a farm: sheep, pigs, and goats (which walk across a fascinating raised boardwalk). But what delights the kids most are the buffalo, the emus, and the llamas. Silverman's also has a year-round farm market with 18 different kinds of homemade pies, as well as jams, flowers, produce, and salsas. Come here for a picnic or a tractor ride to the pumpkin patch.

Grocery

✳STEW LEONARD'S
100 Westport Ave.
Norwalk, CT 06851
(203) 847-7214
stewleonards.com
With its humble beginnings as a small dairy store, Stew Leonard started a grocery with the farmers' market approach back in the 1960s. He envisioned a place where kids could watch the milk get pasteurized and bottled while their mothers shopped. Far outgrowing his initial idea, Stew's has grown into the World's Largest Dairy Store, complete with interactive farm animal–themed automatons for children; a real farm with cows, goats, chickens, and geese in the front; and a very welcoming atmosphere. Today there are new locations, including Danbury and Newington, but this is the original. Including a grocery in this Insiders' Guide is rare, so you know this is something special—like an amusement park where you happen to buy groceries.

Kids

AGE OF REASON
19 Post Rd. West
Westport, CT 06880
(203) 226-8199
ageofreasonct.com
Children are like sponges and will absorb whatever we expose them to. That's why independent stores like Age of Reason are so vital. Walking inside this shop just up the hill from the Westport River, you'll find toys and games you won't find in a chain store. There are multifunctional easels for budding artists, language blocks, and tool technology kits. Age of Reason has toys for all age groups, but you won't find video games here; these toys engage both body and mind. Of course they do have brand names like LEGO, Buckyballs, and other toys that stimulate creativity. "The important thing is not to stop questioning," said Albert Einstein, who had a summer home in Connecticut. A few games and toys from Age of Reason will start everyone out on the right foot.

Home & Crafts

BROOKFIELD CRAFT CENTER
286 Whisconier Rd.
Brookfield, CT 06804
(203) 775-4526
brookfieldcraft.org
This is not strictly a store, but first and foremost the campus of a professional school, where creative craftspeople learn to make ceramics, jewelry, and pottery. In six historic buildings off Route 25 on the banks of the Still River, the students and faculty use a blacksmith forge, a wood-turning shop, and

a weaving studio to create some of the finest handicrafts in Connecticut. You can check out their exhibition gallery and gift shop to purchase these amazing crafts. Most of these are so-called dying arts, but you'll see no evidence of death here, only a firm commitment to creation. If you get a chance to take classes here at Brookfield, it is a unique opportunity to improve your craft under some of the finest masters available.

DOVECOTE
56 Post Rd. East
Westport, CT 06880
(203) 222-7500
dovecote-westport.com

Domestic visionary Sarah Kaplan has created this unique home goods store in Westport, full of "mid-to-the-19th-and-beyond century furniture and furnishings." To do so, she travels to France six times a year and scours the countryside for antiques of worth and beauty. The merchandise here is divided into apothecary, furniture, and fabric and wallpaper, but those distinctions don't really do the store justice. The interior might remind you a little of one of those big chain furniture stores, but a hundred times classier and cooler. Yes, cooler. Kaplan's eye for the old that can become new again is flawless, and her thousands of satisfied customers agree.

MEEKER'S HARDWARE
90 White St.
Danbury, CT 06810
(203) 748-8017
No website

In the downtown area of Danbury, you'll find this huge brick building next to the train station and an old-fashioned Pepsi-Cola mural. It is the only hardware store in America that is also on the National Register of Historic Places. It's been here since 1889, and was originally four stories. The top two burned down in 1896, and they've kept it

the present appearance since then. If you've only been in giant warehouse hardware stores, this will be an experience (it has great prices too). Meeker's is still a family business after over a century; it's a great place to go, not just for your hardware needs but also to browse the shelves of history.

Malls & Outlets

CANNONDALE VILLAGE
30 Cannon Rd.
Wilton, CT 06897
(203) 762-8617
schoolhouseatcannondale.com

All right, this isn't exactly a mall, other than the fact that it features several different stores. But Cannondale Village is otherwise unclassifiable—a unique treat for anyone passing through Wilton. Set in a historic group of charming buildings by the old Cannondale station on the Danbury line, as you pull into the parking lot you'll see old Mobil gas pumps and then the stores of Bella and Company (jewelry), Penny Ha'Penny (gifts), and Annabel Green (flowers and finery). The Schoolhouse restaurant ($$$) is in an 1872 chapel-like one-room schoolhouse with a "class schedule" posted out front. A waterfall on the Norwalk River splashes behind the patio. The Schoolhouse serves mostly dinner, with delights like parsnip soup and Berkshire pork belly, but their Sunday brunches are legendary. Why isn't this in the restaurant section? Because Cannondale Village is a total experience, not just a place to eat.

DANBURY FAIR MALL
7 Backus Ave.
Danbury, CT 06810
(203) 743-3247
danburyfairmall.com

In 1821 a small agricultural fair began on this spot in Danbury as a venue for farmers to show off crops, cooking, and animal husbandry skills. Then in 1932 a stock car racetrack began here as well, operating until 1986, when this mall was built. We can sigh at the lost past but should also rejoice at present opportunities. The Danbury Fair is the fifth-largest mall in New England, with 200 retailers and restaurants, and is located right off I-84. The stores include all the big and small ones you'd expect to find, as well as ones like Teavana, Yankee Candle, and White House/Black Market. Best of all, you can still ride the carousel here, and you should.

STAMFORD TOWN CENTER MALL
100 Greyrock Place
Stamford, CT 06901
(203) 324-0935
shopstamfordtowncenter.com

Like most states in America, Connecticut is full of malls, but most are built around the suburban experience. You drive to a big parking lot and spend the day wandering a gigantic building out in the burbs. Stamford Town Center is Connecticut's best urban mall, with over 100 stores on different floors in a glass-and-neon building right at the heart of this thriving city. The mall was certainly a part of the revivification of this town, and it provides everything everyone living downtown could possibly want within easy walking distance. But if you're coming from elsewhere, you can enjoy it too. Shops, restaurants, and services include Barnes & Noble, Forever 21, Ross-Simons, J. Crew, The Capital Grille, Mitchell's Fish Market, P.F. Chang's China Bistro, Kona Grill, Saks Fifth Avenue, and Macy's. If you're there with kids, don't forget to take them to the Looney Tunes Children's Play Area on Level 7.

Outdoors

RANKIN SPORTING GOODS
7 Newtown Rd.
Danbury, CT 06810
(203) 743-7601
rankinsports.com

Most sporting goods stores are terrible. Let's face it—they change their clothing inventory too often, and they only have the most expensive (or at least only one brand of) equipment. And getting sporting goods at the nearest superstore guarantees you'll get the cheapest, and thus probably the worst, stuff. So you should shop at Rankin, a family-owned-and-operated business since 1971. They have an absolute ton of stuff, for baseball, softball, basketball, badminton, croquet, horseshoes, bocce, football, and tetherball. Tetherball! I used to love that at camp, but was unaware that it was a real sport. My mistake. They have training and coaching equipment, and their clothing is available year-round for all sports. Their custom-made apparel is high quality, and even fire departments get their work shirts done in their in-house print shop.

Specialty Foods

DARIEN CHEESE AND FINE FOODS
25-10 Old Kings Hwy. North
Darien, CT 06820
(203) 655-4344
facebook.com/dariencheesefinefoods

Established in 1967, long before cheese shops were a common sight in America, this Darien shop focuses on artisanal cheeses. Carrying 200 varieties from around the world at any given time, proprietors Ken and Tori Skovron keep their shop between 58 and 62 degrees to maintain the cheese aging process. Best of all, Darien Cheese and Fine Foods carries a number of the great Connecticut cheeses from local farms, like Cato Corner in Colchester, Beltane Farm in Lebanon, and Sankow Beaver Brook Farm in Lyme. Try Cato Corner's beautifully marbled Black Ledge Blue or their Drunken Hooligan cheese, washed in red wine from Connecticut's Priam Vineyards. Sankow makes a raw sheep's milk cheese, the only one in the state.

HAUSER CHOCOLATIER
137 Greenwood Ave.
Bethel, CT 06801
(203) 794-1861
hauserchocolates.com

These are chocolates made by a real Swiss chocolatier (Ruedi Hauser) right here in America since 1983. Recently, Hauser Chocolates became so popular that they had to expand to a factory in Rhode Island and boast a sizable online business, but the Bethel location is the original, and some of the chocolate goodies (including fudge) are made in a factory right behind this little shop. There are truffles, sauces, and chocolate-covered nuts and coffee beans. With Ruedi's son now firmly at the helm, Hauser was the first father-and-son team to win Emeritus Awards from Confectioners International. This looks to be one of the great success stories of American artisanal creation. Check out the vintage ceiling in the charming shop, and pick up one of their boxed assortments for the chocoholic in your life.

KAAS AND COMPANY
83 Washington St.
Norwalk, CT 06854
(203) 838-6161
kaasnco.com

This blue storefront that declares "A Taste of Holland" is a destination for locals in SoNo and for homesick Dutch immigrants, who come for hundreds of miles to get the items they can only get here. This family business, founded in 1983, has the usual teas, cookies, jams, spices, candies, and cakes from the Netherlands, but they also have 85 flavors of Dutch licorice and dozens of cheeses, like Edam, Friese Nagel, and Rookvlees. The herring and mackerel here is the best you can find anywhere. Kaas also has souvenirs of various sorts, including Dutch tiles. If you're not a homesick Dutch tourist, this is still a great stop while walking the streets of SoNo after viewing the aquarium or before eating across the street at Match (see entry).

VERSAILLES
339 Greenwich Ave.
Greenwich, CT 06830
(203) 661-6634
versaillesgreenwich.com

Founded in 1980, Versailles (actually the original owner's last name) is a patisserie, boulangerie, and bistro. People come here for the boules and baguettes in the morning, the same way they do in Paris. The bistro part of the store serves all three meals, with delights such as crepes and brioche for breakfast, *croque monsieur* and quiche for lunch, and arctic char and roast beef fillet for dinner. Internationally acclaimed chef Jean-Pierre Bagnato offers authentic food in gorgeous presentations. This is also a popular patisserie, where you can stop just to pick up dessert. Versailles makes éclairs, napoleons, cakes, pies, and tarts—all the finest French pastries, except they're not French. They're from Connecticut.

WAVE HILL BREADS
30 High St.
Norwalk, CT 06851
(203) 762-9595
wavehillbreads.com

Called by some the best bread in America, or at least between Boston and New York, Wave Hill started in Wilton in a tiny shop and has now moved into a larger place in Norwalk. That means you'll find Wave Hill at farmers' markets, restaurants, and retail stores throughout the state. But why not visit their cafe attached to the bakery? They are open 8 a.m. to 3 p.m. weekdays, until 2 p.m. on the weekends, with a full menu of sandwiches, salads, and soups, as well as iced coffee, soda, and more. But don't just get brunch. Take some (or all) of their bread home: a baguette, a spelt and rye loaf, a crusty country boule—whatever smells good.

ACCOMMODATIONS

All lodgings listed have both smoking and nonsmoking rooms unless otherwise noted, or have a designated smoking area, and do not accept pets unless noted. Hotels, motels, and resorts are wheelchair accessible unless otherwise noted. Bed-and-breakfasts and inns are not wheelchair accessible unless otherwise noted, since many are in historic buildings exempt from the Americans with Disabilities Act. Call to make sure if there's any question. We do not list specific credit cards in either this section or the restaurants section.

Bed-and-Breakfasts

GREEN ROCKS INN   **$$$$**
415 Danbury Rd.
Ridgefield, CT 06877
(203) 894-8944
greenrocksinn.com

This "eco-friendly" bed-and-breakfast in Ridgefield gets rave reviews from everyone who stays here. The air is filtered, the water is filtered, life is filtered down to its essence. They serve natural and organic foods, but this is not a back-to-nature experience— they feature an iPod docking station in each room, along with flat-screen HD satellite TV, DVD players, and wireless Internet. There are 4 rooms with private baths to choose from in this modern (non-antique-filled) home. You'll get a quiet stay with magnetic, far-infrared sleep systems and organic bedding, and after a satisfying sleep you can maybe use the eco-yoga mats before enjoying fresh juice and french toast in the morning.

HARBOR HOUSE INN   **$$$**
165 Shore Rd.
Old Greenwich, CT 06870
(203) 637-0145
hhinn.com

This large Victorian mansion has 23 rooms with 3 suites, and is a 10-minute walk to the beach along Shore Road in Greenwich. All rooms have private baths, but ask for one with a whirlpool. The lobby with its throne, knight, and grand piano lets you know that you are in for an evening of luxury. The rooms are more simply appointed, but simple in a very good way. The four-poster beds and comfortable chairs throughout the inn ooze relaxation. The inn offers an afternoon tea to guests and bicycles to ride around the flat, tree-lined streets. This is probably your best bet in Greenwich if you have children, but it also contains a modern conference room for business travelers.

STANTON HOUSE INN   **$$$**
76 Maple Ave.
Greenwich, CT 06830
(203) 869-2110
www.stantonhouseinn.com

This beautiful inn was built in its present form by famous architect Stanford White and was named for the owner's grandmother, Elizabeth Cady Stanton, renowned pioneer for women's right to vote. Today this bed-and-breakfast has 22 rooms and 2 suites, all with private baths. There's a very relaxing patio next to the pool, and afternoon tea and beach passes (expensive to get otherwise) are available. You can walk from the inn to all the fine restaurants and shops of Greenwich, as well as to historic Putnam Cottage. This is a comfortable, reasonably priced house that will become your own, for a little while.

*WEST LANE INN $$$
22 West Ln.
Ridgefield, CT 06877
(203) 438-7323
westlaneinn.com

This elegant, pale yellow 1849 Victorian house is a model of convenience and charming village appeal. There are 18 nonsmoking rooms with either queen or king beds and full private baths, and each will make you feel the comforts of a home away from home. Some even come with fireplaces, and the vintage wallpapers are something to see. Next door is the long green awning of Bernard's, one of the state's best restaurants (see entry), and you can walk the sidewalks into town quite easily, passing the beautiful old homes and churches of Ridgefield. In the morning, though, West Lane will take care of you with their terrace breakfast, either continental or a la carte. Sit on the wide Victorian porch and reminisce, or plan for a bright future.

Hotels & Motels

*DELAMAR $$$$
275 Old Post Rd.
Southport, CT 06890
(203) 259-2800
delamarsouthport.com

On the Old Post Road in historic Southport, the white-clapboard Delamar makes for a lovely rest in one of America's most exclusive communities. When you walk past the gold-lettered sign into the lobby, with its antique marble floors and museum-quality art, you'll immediately feel like royalty. There are 44 rooms in this boutique hotel, some of which are suites. Each is different and features marble-floored baths, Italian linens, and all the amenities you could possibly want. Make sure to drive or, better yet, walk around Southport, with its enormous homes and old beech trees. You can also use the fitness room at the Delamar. Afterwards you should splurge for the on-site spa, which is a private suite complete with steam shower, couples massage room, and fireplace. You can now dine at the Delamar too, in the new restaurant and bar that opened in 2011 (and features produce from local farms on its menu).

ETHAN ALLEN HOTEL $$
21 Lake Ave. Ext.
Danbury, CT 06811
(203) 744-1776
ethanallenhotel.com

This large hotel just off I-84 is the place to stay in Danbury. There are 193 rooms and suites, at a variety of prices for all budgets. It's actually owned by the Ethan Allen Corporation and is on their campus here in Connecticut (patriot and founder of Vermont, Ethan Allen was born nearby in Litchfield). So you can imagine they have done a good job of decorating their own hotel. The rooms all come with tons of amenities, more than your standard hotel, with great extras like robes, newspapers, and coffeemakers. The adjoining Fairfields Restaurant has been serving patrons since 1974, and the lounge is a great place for a nightcap. There's an outdoor pool in summer, and though this is technically in Fairfield County, the Ethan Allen is a great place to stay as a gateway to the Litchfield Hills.

J HOUSE $$–$$$
1114 E. Putnam Ave.
Riverside, CT 06878
(203) 698-6980
jhousegreenwich.com

The outside of the J House looks like a strange mixture of stone, glass, and steel. And then you walk inside and find one of the most interesting and spectacular hotels in Connecticut. Though it looks like a museum, it is comfortable and relaxing, with 85 "high-tech" rooms. When you get to your lodging, you'll find that the whole room (lighting, temperature, shades, etc.) is controllable by iPad. The toilet seat is heated, and the televisions are embedded in the mirrors. Along with these modern miracles of technology, they have a car service that will take you anywhere in town. Ask for a room away from the parking lot. Pets are allowed for an additional fee. The restaurant here is excellent for cocktails and appetizers.

STAMFORD PLAZA $$
2701 Summer St.
Stamford, CT 06905
(203) 359-1300
stamfordplazahotel.com

This enormous hotel and conference center about a mile from Stamford Town Center is a reasonable deal with all the posh amenities of a more expensive hotel. With 448 rooms, they have the space to be pet friendly, and offer both smoking and nonsmoking options. There's a pool, a gym, a restaurant, and a very nice bar area. The club lounge and the atrium are particularly attractive, and from the look of the non-room areas, you would think this would be a much more expensive hotel. Instead, it offers nice rooms for reasonable prices, especially for Fairfield County. They probably make all their money on the many conferences held here, and you can reap the benefits of this. If you're staying in the far southwest of the state and looking for a bargain, don't look any farther.

STAMFORD SUITES $$$$
720 Bedford St.
Stamford, CT 06901
(203) 359-7300
stamfordsuites.com

The Stamford Suites is an all-efficiency hotel with 750 square feet of living space in each of the 45 suites. This is the place to stay if you're relocating to Connecticut or staying a long time as a business traveler, because your room is actually a small apartment, with kitchen, bedroom, living room, and bath (with either king, queen, or 2 double beds). All the suites are nonsmoking, though there is a designated area for smoking in the hotel. There's a laundry service and a gym, and hot tubs in the rooms. The Suites are located right downtown in Stamford, so if you don't have a car here, you can walk to everything you need.

Inns

HOMESTEAD INN $$$$
420 Field Point Rd.
Greenwich, CT 06830
(203) 869-7500
homesteadinn.com

The Homestead Inn in Greenwich will be one of the nicer (or possibly the nicest, period) places you'll likely stay in this lifetime. Each of the 18 rooms is full of art and artifacts, and the bold use of color in each fits a carefully designed theme. All come with comfortable linens, bathrobes, and heated bathroom floors—do you need to know more? Okay, how about carved wood four-poster beds, cherry furniture, and Bulgari amenities. You can relax on the beautiful porches or in one of the "relaxation rooms" (calling them public areas really doesn't do them justice). The Homestead is attached to the Thomas Henkelmann restaurant (see entry), one of the best in Connecticut and, in fact, the country. This is a great escape from New York (or anywhere else), and if you can afford it, the experience is well worth it.

INN AT FAIRFIELD BEACH $$$
1160 Reef Rd.
Fairfield, CT 06824
(203) 255-6808
innatfairfieldbeach.com

This landmark hotel has been recently renovated, and it shows. Each of the 8 suites and 6 studios comes with a kitchenette and is uniquely decorated with a theme:

the Lighthouse, the Safari Suite, the Greek Studio, et cetera. Next door is the Seagrape Cafe, open daily, where you can catch your own lobster from the tank and try 30 different beers. Or you can order their food up to your room. You can also order from a mobile spa service that comes to your room, but make an appointment at least 24 hours in advance. The real bonus of staying here is that almost no one uses this beach on the majority of summer days, and you can walk or swim here. You can also walk or bike around this beautiful area of Fairfield, up to the museum and Old Burying Ground, or even a few blocks farther to the shopping and restaurants along the Post Road.

INN AT LONGSHORE $$$
260 Compo Rd. South
Westport, CT 06880
(203) 226-3316
innatlongshore.com

This elegant inn was once a private estate until it was turned into a country club that hosted President Roosevelt, J. D. Rockefeller, and F. Scott and Zelda Fitzgerald. Today it is a large hotel and conference center, complete with an enormous ballroom. The inn is often used for conferences, and its 18-hole golf course is a destination in itself. The view of Long Island Sound from the Longshore is excellent, and the "great lawn" between the inn and the water is a place for clambakes and barbecues, as well as receptions and weddings. The "drawing room" is a great place to relax in the winter months. Although the facility itself is huge, there are only 12 guest rooms, so expect to be treated well.

THE NORWALK INN AND
CONFERENCE CENTER $$$
99 East Ave.
Norwalk, CT 06851
(800) 303-0808
norwalkinn.com

Located at the heart of Norwalk's many attractions, the Inn and Conference Center was originally built by the citizens of the town. Right next to the town green in a residential area, the inn is a quiet and relaxed setting from which to set forth in exploration. There are 72 rooms, some of which are deluxe suites. They also have huge banquet spaces, a swimming pool, and the sorts of amenities that make modern travel so pleasant. Adam's Rib, the 50-year-old restaurant attached to the inn, is best known for its premium steaks and fish, providing an intimate dining experience for the guests here. However, it is good enough to bring in many locals and features a cocktail hour with complimentary hors d'oeuvres.

ROGER SHERMAN INN $$
195 Oenoke Ridge
New Canaan, CT 06840
(203) 966-4541
rogershermaninn.com

Built by Rev. Justus Mitchell in the 1700s, this historic house was revamped in 1868 by financier William Bond and turned into a rambling inn in 1925. Named for patriot and Connecticut politician Roger Sherman, the present inn has been renovated and remastered into one of the finest lodgings in the state, with 17 rooms at 3 different rates. The restaurant here offers fine, modern dining as well. Try the cognac-scented lobster bisque and the homemade ricotta gnocchi. Note the mural wallpaper hanging in the main dining room, done in the 1850s by Jean Zuber, whose wallpaper you'll also find in the White House. There's also a smaller dining room with Tiffany windows and a Dutch-tiled fireplace. This is a country inn as close to the hustle and bustle of New York as you can get.

STONEHENGE INN AND
RESTAURANT $$
35 Stonehenge Rd.
Ridgefield, CT 06877
(203) 438-6511
stonehengeinn-ct.com

Since the 1940s the Stonehenge Inn has welcomed guests traveling along Route 7 from Norwalk to Danbury. It combines charming guest rooms with fine dining about 2.5 miles (a perfect bike ride) from Fairfield County's most beautiful village. There are 16 rooms throughout the 3 buildings on the property. The rates for most of the rooms are very reasonable for Fairfield County, with 2 fancier suites if you'd like to spend a little more. The on-site restaurant serves traditional American cuisine, with a prix-fixe menu, and is considered one of the best in the state. The menu is full of French-American classics like grilled filet mignon, rack of lamb, and seared duck breast. Stay here and visit Weir Farm, Putnam Memorial State Park, and all the rural delights between the great cities of the southwest part of the state.

RESTAURANTS

Please note that all Connecticut restaurants are smoke free, and all are required to be wheelchair accessible. Pets are not allowed inside most restaurants, but during the warmer months, there are plenty of restaurants with patio areas just right for your canine friend. Call ahead to make sure it's okay.

American & Modern

*BERNARD'S $$$$
20 West Ln.
Ridgefield, CT 06877
(203) 438-8282
bernardsridgefield.com

This old clapboard inn renovated by Bernard and Sarah Bouissou is a four-star foodie destination far beyond our borders. Bernard worked at Le Cirque in New York and creates a seasonal menu here based on French cooking, but pushes the boundaries in the way of the best restaurants. This is the perfect place for a romantic dinner; you can get an ounce of caviar as an appetizer and pair your braised lamb shank with one of the 1,300 world's best wines. Upstairs is Sarah's Wine Bar, which has a more relaxed, casual atmosphere and serves some lighter dishes like a ground sirloin burger with a bottle of fine Bordeaux or lighter Beaujolais. Last time I stopped there, I tried the crispy pig's knuckles and quail in rich risotto. This restaurant lures people from New York through its long green awning, so you know it must be something special.

THE INN AT NEWTOWN $$
19 Main St.
Newtown, CT 06470
(203) 270-1876
theinnatnewtown.com

Just south of the famous Flagpole, the Inn at Newtown is housed in one of the historic homes that grace Main Street. Featuring a fine selection of food and wine, this spot is great for lunch or dinner in either of the 2 dining rooms or just a cocktail downstairs at Proud Mary's bar, on the site of an old roadhouse. The front taproom is casual, and the larger dining area is elegant. With a diverse selection of New American–style soups, salads, appetizers, and entrees, you'll have a hard time choosing. Main dishes include grilled hanger steak, expertly seasoned and served with a Syrah demi-glace; braised lamb shank; and a selection of fine pasta dishes. For lighter fare, the salmon BLT or one of the flatbread pizzettes are good choices. Spend some time perusing the wine list; it's one of the best in the state. There are 3 beautifully appointed rooms upstairs at the inn. You'll be transported back in time in the charm-filled accommodations that feature gaslit fireplaces, hand-painted dressers, and oil paintings from the 19th and early 20th centuries.

JOSEPH'S STEAKHOUSE $$$$
360 Fairfield Ave., #2
Bridgeport, CT 06604
(203) 337-9944
josephssteakhouse.com

Joseph Kustra worked at world-famous Peter Luger Steak House in Brooklyn before opening this restaurant in Bridgeport, and you can immediately see the influence in its USDA prime dry-aged beef. The cuts are expensive but huge, with the smallest at 20 ounces. If you're there with a group, get the 88-ounce behemoth and divide it, unless you have a very, very big appetite. I did see someone finish (barely) the 44-ounce himself, but the key here is the taste of these dry-aged, hand-selected pieces of beef, so try to enjoy every bite. The extra-thick bacon appetizer and creamed spinach are classic keepers from Luger's as well, and are just as good here. Note that parking can be a challenge here—you should probably park in the garage farther east on Fairfield Avenue and walk 2 blocks to the restaurant rather than try to squeeze into Joseph's lot.

*MATCH $$$
98 Washington St.
Norwalk, CT 06854
(203) 852-1088
matchsono.com

Serving only dinner, Match has high-quality service and a cool industrial ambience that makes SoNo a destination for foodies as well as families. Of course they also come for exquisite dishes like handmade ravioli and designer thin-crust pizza. Little details, like the delicious sliced potatoes that accompany the wood-fired chicken dish, make Match the classic it has become. Save room for dessert, because there's a selection that will have your mouth ready, if your stomach is not. In summer, sit in the sidewalk seating area and people-watch as the sun goes down and the elevated train rumbles by the old Switch Tower.

*REBECCAS $$$$
265 Glenville Rd.
Greenwich, CT 06831
(203) 532-9270
rebeccas.moonfruit.com

Across from the firehouse in Greenwich, Rebeccas is run by two chefs with outstanding pedigrees: Rebecca Kirhoffer and her husband, Reza Khorshidi. Kirhoffer also has a degree in design, and that eye for detail has gone into the impeccable trendy design here. The creative menu draws from all sorts of global cuisines, with dishes like eggs scrambled in their shells with caviar, and roasted California squab with morel mushrooms. This being Connecticut, seafood takes up a good portion of the menu, with sashimi appetizers and various fillets for entrees. The two soups in one bowl special (yellow and red gazpacho or butternut and acorn squash with roasted chestnuts, depending on the season) is a new classic, the roasted breast of wild pheasant is a rare joy, and the roasted suckling pig will make you fall in love with pork all over again. Don't miss the cheese selection and the beautifully made and designed desserts.

RED BARN RESTAURANT $$$
292 Wilton Rd.
Westport, CT 06880
(203) 222-9549
redbarnrestaurant.com

Right off exit 41 of the Merritt Parkway is a huge red barn, one of the most popular and long-lasting restaurants in the area. The Red Barn has been a Westport landmark for over 50 years and has been lovingly restored.

Inside, polished wood and roaring fireplaces welcome you, but the spotless tablecloths are certainly not rustic, nor is the food. It has an impressive raw bar and serves a mostly continental and American menu, full of classics. If you need a fancy restaurant you can take your kids to, they have options for children and a kid-friendly atmosphere. The Red Barn is also popular with the afternoon business crowd. If it's nice outside, definitely sit on the stone porch amid the gardens.

Asian & Indian

BANGKOK $$
72 Newtown Rd.
Danbury, CT 06810
(203) 791-0640
bangkokrestaurant.com

Bangkok was the first Thai restaurant in Connecticut, and Chef Taew has continued to maintain her exalted position many years later. The waitresses serve you at the wooden booths in traditional costumes, but this is not so much a gimmick as a reflection of the authentic food. They keep the genuine ingredients like coriander and lemongrass, which have strangely dropped off the menus of other Thai restaurants. Coconut milk, spicy shrimp, bamboo shoots, bean sprouts, basil, hot chilis, noodles, rice, beef, galangal leaves, and more are all cooked freshly on the spot. The price is right here too. Bangkok's reputation and longevity have not caused Taew to raise the prices. If you like things really spicy, make sure to tell the waitress. They'll be happy to oblige.

COROMANDEL $$
25 Old Kings Hwy. North, #11
Darien, CT 06820
(203) 662-1213
coromandelcuisine.com

This is one of the best Indian restaurants in the state, with a great decor of murals and mirrors, and delicious food. The buffet lunch here is a bargain, with great choices of half a dozen or more main dishes, along with naan bread, a variety of chutneys, and tandoori chicken. The dinner menu is also reasonably priced; try the *lasi gobi*, a fried cauliflower, and the Indian lamb chops. Everything can be ordered at a comfortable level of spice (the moderate one is the best in my opinion). This is the original, and some say the best, Coromandel, but now there are two other locations in Fairfield County, one in Stamford (68 Broad St.; 203-964-1010) and one in SoNo (86 Washington St., Norwalk; 203-852-1213). There is also a Coromandel in New Haven County (185 Boston Post Rd., Orange; 203-795-9055) that is just as good as the Darien location, though in a less-impressive location in a shopping center.

MECHA NOODLE BAR $$
1215 Post Rd.
Fairfield, CT 06824
(203) 292-8222
mechanoodlebar.com

This is one of my favorite new restaurants in the state, with a menu that encourages me to try new things every time I go. As you might guess from the name, it is primarily a Japanese ramen joint, of which we have only a few here. Getting good, fresh, homemade ramen noodles is a revelation if you've just been eating those instant packets all these years. They also serve Vietnamese pho, doing several authentic versions of each kind of soup. But although their soups are amazing, it is the rest of the menu that earns Mecha Noodle a place in my heart. They have steamed pork buns with Korean fried chicken or roasted duck, pork jowl ssam, corn dumplings, fiery rice cakes, and many more—a pan-Asian fusion with modern American twists. Wash down your meal with one of their interesting cocktails or flavored sakes. If you really have an appetite, try to break the ramen noodle slurping record while you're there.

SAKURA $$$
680 Post Rd. East
Westport, CT 06880
(203) 222-0802
sakurarestaurant.com

It's difficult to know which way to head when you're here, the sushi bar or the hibachi grill. Both are outstanding. The grill is the place to be gregarious, and the sushi bar is the place to be quiet and alone, but of course your taste buds might be crying for the opposite. Sakura has serious longevity in this here-today-gone-tomorrow area, having been around since the 1980s. That means it has some quality going for it, especially at Westport prices (try the lunchtime half price). Sakura fills up consistently on the weekends, so make reservations if you can, especially if you want the hibachi. Try any of the rolls and the steak or shrimp hibachi, or just pretty much have anything. This is some delicious Japanese food, some of the best in the state. Don't forget to tip the sushi chef if he does a good job with your rolls or sashimi.

TENGDA ASIAN BISTRO $$$
21 Field Point Rd.
Greenwich, CT 06830
(203) 625-5338
tengdaasianbistrogroup.com

Naming your restaurant "prosperity" is a chancy idea, but it seems to be working for this local restaurant group, which is finding great success throughout the state, especially here in Fairfield County. The curries showcase a too-little-seen specialty of Japanese cuisine (in America), and they do them well. At the back of the restaurant is a classic sushi bar, great for an after-work plate of spicy tuna rolls or salmon sashimi. There are also Tengdas in Westport (1330 Post Rd. East; 203-255-6115) and Darien (25 Old Kings Hwy. North; 203-656-1688), as well as a few others throughout the state. The Greenwich one uses perhaps the greatest mixture of European and Asian traditions, but you'll find these to be some of the most reliable pan-Asian restaurants in Connecticut.

TORO $$
28 Church Hill Rd.
Newtown, CT 06470
(203) 364-0099
toronewtown.com

Toro may have a Japanese name, but it wanders all over Asia with its flavorful dishes. The Indian pancake with curry dipping sauce is done just right, and the Shanghai duck is excellent. There's even a nod to Connecticut with the fried oyster roll. The presentation of many of the dishes is astounding—how do they get the food into those colorful contortions? But the taste is why people come back time and time again. The hot and sour soup is to die for, probably the best of its kind in the state, with a perfect combination of flavors. You'll want a second bowl instead of your entree.

Breakfast & Lunch

AMERICAN PIE COMPANY $$
29 Route 37
Sherman, CT 06784
(860) 350-0662
americanpiecompany.com

Although this is primarily a bakery, the American Pie Company serves so many other dishes for breakfast, lunch, and dinner that it qualifies as at least a cafe, if not a large home-style restaurant. The eggs Benedict is the breakfast to go for here, and of course for any meal, get one of the pies. All are made from scratch with hand-rolled pie dough and come in flavors like peach, pecan, mince, apple crumb, cherry, Key lime, coconut custard, lemon meringue, pumpkin mousse, and black-bottom banana. The breads, muffins, cookies, cakes, and tarts are all made on the premises too, fresh every day. This is home cooking in the tiny village of Sherman by Candlewood Lake—a welcome change from the big-city atmosphere of many Fairfield County restaurants.

CHEF'S TABLE $$
1561 Post Rd.
Fairfield, CT 06824
(203) 255-1779
chefstable.com

The focus at the Chef's Table is on freshness and variety. Great for breakfast, lunch, or dinner, this restaurant located in downtown Fairfield offers a wide selection of wraps, paninis, burgers, and even breakfast sandwiches. Build your own salad, try the classic Reuben as a grilled flatbread panini, or enjoy the tomato, basil, and mozzarella focaccia. The smoothies are fresh and healthy, and there's a full-service coffee bar as well as wine and beer. Live music entertains lunch crowds, and vintage rock-and-roll posters don the walls. The posters are actually for sale, but you probably can't afford the proud owner's prices.

CHOCOPOLOGIE $$
12 S. Main St.
Norwalk, CT 06854
(203) 854-4754
knipschildt.com/flash.html

In the heart of SoNo, this cafe and retail shop is actually run by Knipschildt Chocolatier, which has created one of the world's top-rated chocolate truffles. The little cafe serves sandwiches, salads, crepes, and tea, as well as the amazing chocolates for which it is named. If you like mochas, try the eponymous Chocopologie drink—one-half espresso and one-half rich chocolate, topped with a lavender foam. Knipschildt chocolates all have female names, like Hannah or Helena, and usually are sold at high-end markets and shops. But you can get them here at Chocopologie without the markup. In fact, you can walk to the "gallery" next to the cafe and peek into the factory through a window to watch the chocolatiers in action.

COFFEE AN' DONUT SHOP $
343 Main St.
Westport, CT 06880
(203) 227-3808
No website

Former president Bill Clinton put this place on the map when he declared their donuts to be the best in the land. The donuts here are made from scratch, crunchy on the outside and cakelike inside, with flavors like honey-glazed, coconut twist, cinnamon, chocolate-frosted, old-fashioned, and more. Watch them bring the donuts out of the bakery on a rod and slide them onto the trays. Or you can just hold out your hands and grab them and stuff them into your mouth. They also have hot and cold sandwiches for lunch, including a delicious pastrami. But even if you aren't here for breakfast, get the donuts for Keats' sake. You'll never go back to . . . what is that other donut place called?

HUNTINGTON STREET CAFÉ $$
90 Huntington St.
Shelton, CT 06484
(203) 925-9064
huntingtonstrcafe.com

The Huntington Street Café in Shelton masquerades as a coffee shop but is so much more. Yes, it's got breakfast, and it's got lunch sandwiches. But like a caramelized onion, you keep peeling layers of amazing flavor: salads and wraps, pizza and mahimahi, along with fair-trade coffee that will keep you awake all day long. If you want something more substantial, they also serve pork sliders and steamed cheeseburgers. Friday and Saturday nights they have live music from local bands. Or stop by for a French toast breakfast and stay all day working on that novel you've been meaning to write, but never seem to find time for.

LIQUID LUNCH $
434 Howe Ave.
Shelton, CT 06484
(203) 924-0200
liquidlunchrestaurant.com

A husband-and-wife chef team who have lived their whole lives in the Naugatuck Valley wanted a better and healthier place for everyone to come and eat breakfast and lunch. They opened a restaurant in downtown Shelton and began to produce a huge selection of tasty sandwiches and breakfast frittatas. And of course that restaurant is named Liquid Lunch, and that liquid is soup. They have 6 staples that are always offered: chicken noodle, beef barley, vegetarian lentil, tomato basil, French onion, and split pea with ham. Then there are 4 to 6 new and unique soups every day, such as Ben's BBQ soup or bacon-potato-Gorgonzola. You can get them in 4 different sizes too. They have been so successful that they've opened a couple more locations, including one at 84 S. Broad St. in Milford (203-877-7687).

SONO BAKING COMPANY AND
   CAFE $$
101 Water St.
Norwalk, CT 06854
(203) 847-7666
sonobaking.com

The SoNo Baking Company makes some of the most delightful pastries in the state, as well as some outstanding breads. Pick up a loaf of sourdough here for a trip out to Sheffield Island. What they really do well, and something many bakeries ignore, is their tarts, which are varied and delicious, from plum to pecan, and from coconut cream to chocolate ganache. Of course this is also a cafe where you can get lunch and breakfast. For the latter, their stuffed brioche french toast with vanilla pastry cream and mixed berries is almost too good to eat. Their

Sunday brunch is becoming famous; go for the quiches—the Baking Company knows how to do crust.

SOUP THYME $$
450 Monroe Tpke.
Monroe, CT 06468
(203) 268-0214
soupthyme.com

The best lunch spot in Monroe, Soup Thyme insists that it is more than just soup. But the soup is so ridiculously good that you probably won't notice. Sure, you can order yummy salads and tasty paninis made with local ingredients—but the soups! So many varieties, and with 9 to 12 made fresh each day. Soups like chicken potpie, macaroni and cheese, lentil and sweet sausage, and chicken-spinach-Gorgonzola are all original and delicious. Chef Ronald Lee's takes on traditional soups like lobster bisque and chicken noodle will have you reevaluating your whole relationship with this underappreciated food. Long relegated to a small section not even related to appetizers on most menus, it's time to get back to this basic but wonderful food. Long live soup!

French

LUC'S CAFÉ $$$
3 Big Shop Ln.
Ridgefield, CT 06877
(203) 894-8522
lucscafe.com

This charming French bistro located in one of Ridgefield's oldest buildings can be difficult to find; it's in a shopping center behind the main street, east through one of the small alleys. Once you find the cavelike cafe, though, you'll be pleased by all the small touches that make it a new classic, like the blackboard of specials, the flour-sack dish towels for napkins, and the authentic wood-beam ceiling. Order lemonade and get it the French way: lemon juice in a glass with ice, to which you add your own sugar and water. Escargots au Pernod is a nice change from the usual, and the cassoulet is excellent. Luc's is not cheap, but they certainly don't skimp on the portions: The croque madame is hard to finish just by itself. As you enjoy your Sancerre wine while listening to crazy French pop music, sitting at a marble-topped bar table in the sun or at a black leather booth in the stone-walled cellar, you'll be transported. Is it Paris? No, it's Connecticut.

ONDINE $$$$
69 Pembroke Rd.
Danbury, CT 06811
(203) 746-4900
ondinerestaurant.com

Ondine looks like a French country inn, right in the old "hat city" of Danbury. Inside, the Staffordshire china and comfortable chairs will put you in the mood for some creamy French goodness. Chef Dieter Thiel has done his surroundings justice. The *potage billi bi* is a saffron cream-of-mussels soup that will at first astonish you, and then make you fall in love. Try the sea scallops poached in white wine; few do it better. The fixed-price menu gives you a startling number of choices among the five courses, for a more reasonable price than the rest of the a la carte menu by far. If you want fine dining in Danbury, this is a clear choice.

✳THOMAS HENKELMANN $$$$
420 Field Point Rd.
Greenwich, CT 06830
(203) 869-7500
thomashenkelmann.com

Set in the 1799 Homestead Inn in Greenwich, this restaurant draws out jaded diners from New York City to be born again. Thomas Henkelmann himself brings a pedigree few chefs in the world can match, and brings creativity and precise touches

to the menu. The tomato soup, with semolina dumplings, is remarkable for its simple taste and beauty. If you like to walk on the wild side, Henkelmann does amazing sweetbreads and loin of rabbit. But the more approachable dishes (for Americans) like lobster fricassee or whole roasted baby chicken are absolutely delectable, moist and rich, with touches of surprise. For dessert, try the crisp cherry purses filled with almond cream, cherry sauce, and cherry ice cream—unless you don't like cherry, that is. In summer, sit on the glass-enclosed porch, where you can enjoy the gardens while sampling from the exceptional wine list.

Ice Cream

DOCTOR MIKE'S ICE CREAM $
158 Greenwood Ave.
Bethel, CT 06801
(203) 792-4388
No website

Named for Dr. Michael Burnham by his daughter, this Bethel ice-cream parlor has been run by Robert Allison since 1975. At first you might be confused: The parlor is around the back of an old house. Once inside you'll find 4 rotating flavors (50 total) and 4 standards (chocolate, strawberry, vanilla, and chocolate lace and cream made with hard candy), all of which are made fresh. The ice cream here is unbelievably rich, with an average 16 percent butterfat; the rich chocolate uses 24 percent cocoa butter and Bensdorf chocolate. Even though there are only a few tables, the parking lot is huge. There is another location at 444 Main St. in Monroe if you're coming off the Merritt Parkway and can't wait to eat.

✳FERRIS ACRES CREAMERY $
144 Sugar St.
Newtown, CT 06470
(203) 426-8803
ferrisacrescreamery.com

Unlike many ice-cream shops, this is a real farm, where you can relax and "watch the cows come home." In fact, this is the last dairy farm in Fairfield County, started in 1864 by William Ferris and still owned by the family today. The small red ice-cream shop in front of the silo and barn in Newtown is a local favorite, and it has better hours than most summer ice-cream shops. Along with dozens of flavors of ice cream, they have milk shakes, floats, sundaes, and frozen yogurt. They'll also custom-make ice-cream cakes and pies for you. Try the "campfire" ice cream (vanilla with fudge swirls, graham cracker pieces, and mini marshmallows) in a waffle bowl. That's right, not a waffle cone, a waffle bowl. Yum.

TIMOTHY'S ICE CREAM $$
2974 Fairfield Ave.
Bridgeport, CT 06605
(203) 366-7496
No website

The handmade ice cream from Timothy's in the Black Rock section of Bridgeport is another local secret that has exploded into fame. Family run and simply decorated, the shop focuses entirely on making the best possible ice cream in a cadre of changing flavors. You can actually smell the cream as you come in the front door. The hot fudge is also homemade, and the milk shakes are to die for. They even have a Black Rock flavor: almonds, cream, and chocolate. They do "mixins" where they spread ice cream on the counter and mash toppings into it, invented before the chains started doing that. Bring cash or a check, grab a cone to go, and head down to Black Rock's seawall (Capozzi Park) for an evening walk by the large mansions on the harbor.

Italian

ACQUA RESTAURANT $$$
43 Main St.
Westport, CT 06880
(203) 222-8899
zhospitalitygroup.com/acqua

This villa-like Mediterranean restaurant in downtown Westport has a frescoed ceiling that will have you leaning back in your chair to get a better look. With a number of different French and Italian dishes, you can try seafood, steak, pasta, and crisp thin-crust pizzas. The American dishes like Maryland crab cakes are tempting too. If you've never had a dessert soufflé before, this is certainly the place to get one; the chefs here have mastered the art. While shopping this chic district of celebrity sightings, you'll find Acqua is a great place to stop in for a dinner, except on Sunday, when it's closed. Try getting a seat in the upstairs bar, where there's a view of the Saugatuck River.

CAFE SYLVIUM $$
371 Shippan Ave.
Stamford, CT 06902
(203) 324-1651
cafesilvium.com

This family Italian restaurant in a working-class neighborhood is among the best of its kind, with handmade pasta and other fresh ingredients. The two brothers who own it specialize in recipes from their hometown in Italy: Gravina Di Puglia, Bari. Some of the best dishes include the best fried calamari I've had and the tender and flavorful veal Gorgonzola. The Italian cheesecake is light and fluffy, a real treat if you are used to the heavy ones served at those chain restaurants. I suggest reservations on weeknights; otherwise you might be waiting in line. On Friday and Saturday only parties of 5 or more can make reservations. (The cafe is closed on Sunday.) So get yourself a cocktail and wait with all the other foodies who have found Cafe Silvium.

MARIO'S PLACE $$
36 Railroad Place
Westport, CT 06880
(203) 226-0308
No website

Located right by the train station in Westport, this local legend serves big portions for low prices and has the friendliest bar in town. People come back here like to an old friend. Mario's serves American and Italian food, with the prime rib a standout for many. This is also a place for old-school cocktails, and the drinks are even better (and stronger) than the food. Some people get off the train for a drink at Mario's and then get back on to head to New York or Boston. That should tell you something. This has been an institution in Westport since 1967, and it's a great place to find the many celebrities who live in the area throwing a drink back with the rest of us.

RALPH 'N' RICH'S $$$
815 Main St.
Bridgeport, CT 06604
(203) 366-3597
ralphnrichsct.com

This Italian restaurant was practically the only higher-end restaurant in Bridgeport during the lean years of the late 20th century, and though there are many more now, Ralph 'n' Rich's is still near or at the top. Located between Housatonic Community College and the People's Bank headquarters, their well-kept bar is an after-work hangout for many of Bridgeport's white-collar workers and features a very nice raw bar. Get a sampler of crab, oysters, and littleneck clams. The restaurant has a huge selection of salads, pastas, and classic Italian entrees. Try the Eggplant Gelsomina, a cheesy delight drenched in marinara. This is a great place

to go after an afternoon at the Barnum Museum (across the street) or the ballpark (a block away just under I-95).

Latin American

BODEGA TACO BAR $$
980 Post Rd.
Darien, CT 06820
(203) 655-8500
bodegatacobar.com

Chef Michael Young mixes cuisines with creative care at Bodega Taco Bar in an "urban beach vibe" atmosphere. The menu is full of delightful treats, but they are all for your second visit. Try the tacos first: panko-crusted mahimahi, crispy Korean chicken, slow-cooked pork, and on and on. Mix and match your tacos, or get a big house-smoked brisket, torta, or camarones enchiladas. Then you can move on to the fantastic hoison-glazed pork belly arepas, bodega grilled corn, moles, and more. Specials like lobster nachos or Yucatan chicken will draw you back for another go. Along with good beer and sangria, sample the full selection of tequilas and single-estate mescals: blanco, reposado, and anejos. There is a second location in a cramped plaza at 1700 Post Rd. in Fairfield (203-292-9590), but don't worry—there is more parking behind. You will have more problems fitting all this food in your stomach.

MEZÓN TAPAS $$
56 Mill Plain Rd.
Danbury, CT 06810
(203) 748-0875
mezonct.com

Mezón, or mesón, means "inn" or "tavern"—a place where families gather, friends meet, and travelers rest. The best new mezon in Danbury has some of the best Spanish tapas in the state, though many of their dishes are technically not tapas but rather a variety of delicious, reasonably portioned and priced

Latin American or Spanish dishes. Get yourself some 18-month dry-cured Spanish ham, Ecuadorian shrimp ceviche, Cubano sliders, and more of the classics. But they have more interesting dishes too, like octopus tacos and quinoa fritters. Wash it down with their fantastic sangria or a crema mescal.

PALOMA $$$
15 Harbor Point Rd.
Stamford, CT 06902
(203) 998-7500
palomagrill.com
One of the stars of Food Network, Aarón Sánchez, opened Paloma in Stamford, and we all rejoiced. Whenever one of the country's leading chefs comes here, great things happen. Paloma is right on the new boardwalk along the newly built Harbor Point, with views of the water and a roof deck. As for the food, you will find traditional dishes alongside cactus fritters, sweetbreads, grilled octopus salad, braised pork cheeks, chicken in pumpkin seed mole, and much, much more. You can also share large plates like a whole roasted chicken or tomahawk steak.

VALENCIA LUNCHERIA $$
172 Main St.
Norwalk, CT 06851
(203) 846-8009
valencialuncheria.com
Often jammed before noon, this small, bright yellow luncheonette offers Venezuelan food at the north end of Norwalk. The portions here are huge, and the prices are head-scratchingly low, considering the creativity and craft that goes into the menu. Both the breakfast and lunch corn-cake arepas are excellent, and there are a couple dozen different interesting juices to try. The selection of empanadas is remarkable, with unusual ingredients available such as Nutella and chicken liver (not in the same one), as well as more traditional fillings. For dinner,

the pernil, Venezuelan roasted pork, and the plantain-crusted tilapia are standouts. The success of Valencia Luncheria and the newer Taste of Brazil restaurant across the street bodes well for this little North Norwalk district.

Pizza

COLONY GRILL $
172 Myrtle St.
Stamford, CT 06902
(203) 359-2184
colonygrill.com
In its utilitarian brick building in Stamford, the Colony Grill has been serving pizza since 1935. That's it. Just pizza. Well, okay, they have beer or soda to go along with it, but basically you get a pie for less than $10, and each topping is $1.50, including sausage, pepperoni, meatballs, mushrooms, onions, black olives, cherry peppers, stingers, hot oil, anchovies, or bacon. It's a great deal, and way better than any chain pizza shop will ever come up with. The pizza here is different than the kind you might get elsewhere, especially if you choose the hot oil topping. Maybe you'd rather go with the meatball and onion combo. But locals swear up and down by this place, and you might find yourself addicted soon as well. There is a new location at 1520 Post Rd., Fairfield (203-259-1989), that some say is as good as the original.

Pubs & Taverns

BARNUM PUBLICK HOUSE $$
1020 Broad St.
Bridgeport, CT 06604
(203) 690-1044
barnumpublickhouse.com
This new pub restaurant in downtown Bridgeport has bucked the trend, and its loyal and extensive fan base has kept people in the city on weeknights and summer afternoons.

Try the braised short rib sandwich, fried chicken and waffles, or the butternut squash ravioli. I suggest one of the fun cocktails before or after the meal: Circus Peanut, Cotton Candy, Sideshow, or my favorite, The Flying Trapeze. They also have a Sunday brunch, but make sure to make reservations, because the restaurant fills up. The chef also owns the fancier Bistro B just a few doors down (1006 Broad St.; 203-908-4224; bistrob.net) and another location in Westport. Go there if you prefer a wine bar with excellent small plates.

BOBBY Q'S BARBEQUE AND GRILLE $$
42 Main St.
Westport, CT 06880
(203) 454-7800
bobbyqsrestaurant.com

Bobby Q's seems like a typical pub, with a huge selection of bourbons and draft beers, family nights, and live music. Even their menu looks like something from a chain restaurant. But the food is a few steps above—at least—and you can find little gems among the cheese nachos and (excellent) wings. First of all, the barbecue is real pit-smoked stuff, with a sauce that has won awards against the best in Kansas City (available in bottled form), and they have genuine additions like sweet and smoky pit beans, succotash, and burnt ends. Beer-can chicken, fish tacos, and a huge selection of burgers mean that even if you don't like barbecue (?), you'll enjoy a meal at Bobby Q's. This is not the sort of place you might expect to find in chic Westport, or maybe you just have the wrong idea about the people there. In summer, go to the rooftop deck where the live music is; maybe you'll even dance the night away.

DONOVAN'S $$
138 Washington St.
Norwalk, CT 06854
(203) 354-9451
donovanssono.com

If you're in South Norwalk (SoNo) and looking for something not so pricey, Donovan's is a good bet. This bar, with its huge windows and mirrors, has been serving Norwalk's public since 1889 (under different names) with its "tables for ladies." On their menus you can see the old photo with the still-surviving moose head and long, smooth bar. Photos of old-time boxers hang on the walls above the new flat-screen televisions. Try the amazing macaroni-and-cheese balls, un-shellfish pizza, lobster sliders, or a seasonal dish like the soft-shell crabs. SoNo has regrown around Donovan's in some ways, and stepping into it will take you back. if you ask, the old-timers at the bar will be sure to tell you what the neighborhood was like only a few decades ago.

ROSY TOMORROW'S $$
15 Old Mill Plain Rd., #1
Danbury, CT 06811
(203) 743-5845
rosytomorrows.com

When a place advertises itself as a "historic eatery" and was founded in 1980, you might get suspicious, especially in a state with taverns hundreds of years old. However, on the menu you can read the history of "Rosy," who by all accounts grew from an orphan into an amazing woman and patriot. Her victuals booth at the Danbury Fair ran from 1915 to 1981 and was the inspiration for this restaurant. Inside the fairly priced and nicely decorated restaurant, you'll find amazing burgers, including their "garbage burger," which is a thousand times more appetizing than it sounds. Sit upstairs to look down over the bar (if you can—the place is always packed) and try a pint of Rosy's Ale. And perhaps ask the old fortune-teller at the entrance if you're in for a lifetime of happiness.

THE WALRUS AND THE CARPENTER $$
2895 Fairfield Ave.
Bridgeport, CT 06605
(203) 333-2733
walruscarpenterct.com

The Walrus and the Carpenter is the best new high-end barbecue place in the state, and you can smell the scent of their wonderful smoker as you walk up Fairfield Avenue in the Black Rock section of Bridgeport. Try their Canadian comfort food, poutine, or their smoked wings as appetizers, and then chow down on their maple-bourbon baby back ribs or their pit-smoked pork shoulder. You'll find a pub atmosphere, complete with dark wood and craft beers on tap. The beef brisket will melt in your mouth, the maple pork belly will slide into your stomach, and their deviled eggs will make you wonder if the owners did not make some sort of deal with that fallen angel of smoke and fire.

Road Food

BURGERS, SHAKES, AND FRIES $
302 Delavan Ave.
Greenwich, CT 06830
(203) 531-7433
burgersshakesnfries.com

The postmodern name of this fast-food restaurant in Greenwich nearly says it all. They also have excellent hot dogs and chicken sandwiches. The black-and-white milk shake is something special, and the fixings are a must (try the fried egg). The burgers come on toast, just like the originals in New Haven's Louis' Lunch did more than a century ago (and still do). If you want cheap eats in upper-crust Greenwich, this always-crowded little joint is it. There's also a new location at 800 Post Rd., Darien (203-202-9401). Oh, and the Darien location of Burgers, Shakes, and Fries serves beer and wine. That's fast food that we can all get behind.

CITY LIMITS DINER $–$$$
135 Harvard Ave.
Stamford, CT 06902
(203) 348-7000
citylimitsdiner.com

This joint right off I-95 looks like an Art Deco 1950s diner, but its food tastes like a four-star restaurant. The prices vary from very cheap to moderate on the huge menu, so what you order can vary according to your budget. The dishes vary in origin too. You could try the fried chicken or the crispy crab wontons, depending on your mood. But be sure to sample something from the on-site bakery, like the sweet rolls. You can also get a number of good beers here, proving once again that this isn't a greasy-spoon diner, but rather a cleverly conceived restaurant that has satisfied our need for nostalgia while capturing our present taste buds.

DANNY'S DRIVE-IN $
940 Ferry Blvd.
Stratford, CT 06614
(203) 378-6728
dannysdrive-in.com

This road-food classic in its small brick building has been around since 1935 and offers a selection of hot dogs like the Bull Dog, the Devil Dog, the Mad Dog, and the Super Dog, all with different fixings. The hamburger menu is the same, and even the regular burger comes with the works. What do all the others come with? You'll have to check out the Crazy Horse Burger or the Triple Piggy and find out. There's also pulled pork, lobster rolls, clam strips, and more. The "crazy fries" are messy fun, and be sure to get a peanut butter and chocolate milk shake or root beer float to go along with your meal.

LAKE ZOAR DRIVE-IN $
14 Roosevelt Dr.
Stevenson, CT 06491
(203) 268-8137
lakezoardrivein.com

A quintessential road-food joint, the Lake Zoar Drive-In is the only place to stop (literally and figuratively) on Route 34 between the Stevenson Dam and Sandy Hook. The menu is extensive at this small shack located next to the Lake Zoar boat launch, and you'll find something you like any time of day. Open at 7 a.m., the tiny shack is a favorite breakfast stop for locals. The best option, if you're not pressed for time, is to go for the sampler—pancakes, toast, sausage, eggs, and home fries. For lunch or dinner, you'll find everything from fried chicken and seafood to all-beef hot dogs and specialty sandwiches, like the rib-eye steak and cheese. The basic quarter-pounder is a standout, but you might not be able to resist "That Dam Burger" with chipotle mayonnaise and onion rings. If you have room for dessert, choose from 24 flavors of soft-serve and a hearty selection of malts and shakes.

MERRITT CANTEEN $
4355 Main St.
Bridgeport, CT 06606
(203) 372-1416
merrittcanteen.com

The Merritt Canteen is a "beloved Bridgeport dive" that has been serving incredibly fast food (which also tastes incredible) since 1942. Expect solid chili dogs, burgers, and seafood at fast-food prices that have not changed much for decades. Owner Jay Rodriguez has changed a few things, though, adding some modern delights like bison burgers and sweet potato fries to the menu. The Canteen was featured on the Food Network recently, although they missed a timeless classic on the menu: the little triangular deep-fried cheesecake bites

with strawberry dipping sauce. They are just as good as they sound. And did I mention the service is incredibly fast?

SUPER DUPER WEENIE $
306 Black Rock Tpke.
Fairfield, CT 06825
(203) 334-DOGS
superduperweenie.com

This Fairfield hot dog shop has garnered a huge customer base in the last two decades, with its fresh-baked bread from local sources delivered each morning and its custom relishes made from homemade pickled vegetables. They also use barrel-style sauerkraut, spiked with toasted caraway and bacon. As you can tell, Super Duper Weenie has a funny name but takes its hot dogs seriously. Note that they are only open for dinner on Friday and Saturday, and otherwise close at 4 p.m., so this is primarily a lunch stop. Try the New Englander—a dog with sauerkraut, onion, bacon, mustard, and relish. The french fries at Super Duper Weenie are made from local potatoes and consistently win "Best of Connecticut" awards. After you try them, you'll never go back to McDonald's.

*SYCAMORE DRIVE-IN $
282 Greenwood Ave.
Bethel, CT 06801
(203) 748-2716
sycamoredrivein.com

The Sycamore has been a locals' secret since 1948, and it's far enough from the highway system to remain that way. Its white, red, and green sign greets you from the road and invites you to drive up, roll down your window, and blink your lights for in-car dining. They have a full breakfast menu, and many locals come just for that. However, what made the Sycamore famous was its selection of classic road food, like the "French-style steakburgers" on buttered rolls. The Dagwood Burger is also a classic—hard to get into your mouth but delicious when you finally do. Get a Pot 'o' Beans on the side, made the way the trail cooks made it during pioneer days. And try the homemade (secret recipe) root beer, served in frosty mugs. During summer they have "cruise nights" every Saturday, with classic cars and music to accompany your delicious food.

Seafood

KNAPP'S LANDING $$
520 Sniffens Ln.
Stratford, CT 06511
(203) 378-5999
knappslanding.com

After driving through the concrete flats of the Sikorsky Airport, you'll turn off Route 113 and suddenly find yourself at the mouth of the Housatonic River at Knapp's Landing. With a deck that looks across to the salt marsh wildlife preserve in Milford, this charming, friendly place has a great view and great service. They have lots of traditional seafood dishes, like lightly buttered lobster rolls and a crispy calamari. Though it is primarily a seafood restaurant, there are also Italian dishes like chicken Florentine and penne a la vodka. This is a great place to take the kids, or to relax on the open deck on a summer day after going to the beach or seeing the sights of Bridgeport and Stratford. This was once (many years ago) a Japanese restaurant, and the koi pond is still there. There's also a ramp here for taking your boat out onto the river and into the wide blue seas of the Sound.

1020 POST $$$
1020 Post Rd.
Darien, CT 06820
(203) 655-1020
tentwentypost.com

Like a brasserie from the turn of the 20th century, 1020 (or Ten-Twenty) Post has so many items on its menu you'll like, it's tough to choose. Calling themselves an oyster bar/bistro, it's clear that the folks at 1020 can't decide either. That's okay, because everything is great. From their two-tiered seafood platters of raw and pan-fried oysters and clams to the braised barbecue ribs, this French-inspired American seafood cafe restaurant is many things to many people. The most interesting thing on the menu might be the "simple fish"—a selection of haddock, trout, salmon, and many more, done, as they say, simply, with beurre blanc, soy-ginger jus, or 1020's own chutney for accompaniment. The beautiful dark wood furniture, the old-fashioned bar stools, and the light coming in the long row of windows all combine to make this a comfortable, friendly place, with a sense of old and new, French and American, fish and feast, that will keep you and your stomach happy.

THE WHELK $$$
575 Riverside Ave.
Westport, CT 06880
(203) 557-0902
thewhelkwestport.com

Right on the water in a seldom-traveled area of upmarket Westport, The Whelk is one of a new breed of Connecticut restaurants that focus on farm-to-table fare and inventive menus, all at reasonable prices. The Whelk's focus is clearly on the sea, with salt-cod fritters, barbecued clams, and oyster shooters constants among blackened catfish and griddled sardines. They do wonderful things with pork too, with crispy pig tails and fried bacon-rice balls. Many of the tables are shared communally, a popular new method of getting more diners into restaurants, not to mention getting people to talk to one another. Their menu changes often, with lots of specials and changing seasonal dishes, depending on the catch of the day and the crop of the month. One popular special involves an entire griddled octopus to share among your friends if you like. Yes, you read that correctly.

Vegetarian

BLOODROOT $$
85 Ferris St.
Bridgeport, CT 06605
(203) 576-9168
bloodroot.com

Nearly hidden at the end of a suburban street that opens up to Black Rock Harbor, this vegetarian enclave brings in fans from as far away as New York. Bloodroot calls itself a "feminist restaurant and bookstore with a seasonal vegetarian menu," and they live up to it. Sunday brunch includes all locally sourced food. Connecticut cheeses, rhubarb cakes, spinach and potato gnocchi, and oatmeal/sunflower seed bread all make appearances, though since the menu changes often, you never know what you'll get. You can be sure that it will be good, however, and even meat lovers will enjoy these hearty and often taste-bud-baffling dishes. In business for over three decades, this is considered one of the top vegetarian restaurants in America. Don't be fooled by its humble appearance; Bloodroot continues to do great things within the vegetable kingdom.

LIME $$
168 Main St., #2
Norwalk, CT 06851
(203) 846-9240
limerestaurant.com

This small restaurant in Norwalk has been serving natural foods since 1979, and has been voted the best vegetarian restaurant by *Connecticut Magazine* for the last two decades. They make their own breads, soups, and sauces so that they are sure everything is natural, organic, and, when appropriate, meat free. Just the brown rice alone that comes with every meal is delicious and healthy. Any of the steamed vegetables are worthwhile as well, but the more complex dishes like the black bean chili and veggie phyllo are perfect lunchtime munchies. Lime also serves fish, chicken, and beef, however, which makes it a great family place to go if you have a vegetarian or two in your midst. They also serve organic beer, soda, and wine to go along with your meals, so there's something for everyone here.

DAY TRIP IN FAIRFIELD COUNTY

This trip through Fairfield County starts you off in the bustle of cities and seashore and then takes you inland to rural luxury. If you haven't had breakfast, start just off I-95 at the City Limits Diner (see entry). Then head north on Harvard to Baxter Avenue, taking a right, and then a left onto I-95 North. Get off at exit 14, then take a right at the bottom of the ramp onto Fairfield Avenue. This veers to the left, transforming into Washington Street. There is parking here, or on North Water Street, where you'll turn left and see the Maritime Aquarium (see entry), your morning destination.

See the shows, watch the otters, and pet the stingrays. Skip the IMAX theater here; while it's a fun thing to do, you've got a lot to accomplish today. If you'd rather do something outdoors than spend time inside the glass walls of the aquarium, make a reservation for a ✳Sheffield Island Lighthouse Cruise (see entry) and head out to the wonderful island lighthouse on a catamaran. They don't leave until 11 a.m.

When you're done at the aquarium, walk back up Washington Street and turn left on South Main Street to have a light lunch at Chocopologie (see entry). Be sure to walk back to the adjacent gallery and peek through the interior windows at their chocolatiers hard at work.

When you're done, walk back to your car and drive north on North Water Street 1

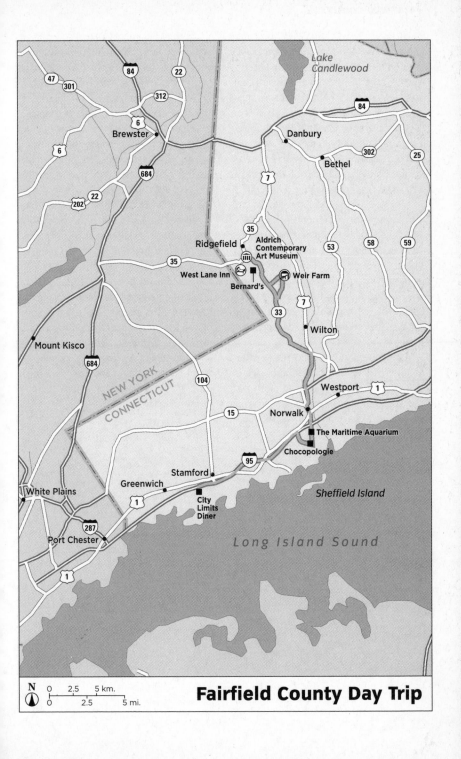

Fairfield County Day Trip

block to Ann Street, taking a left. You'll make a right onto North Main, and another right onto Martin Luther King Jr., which becomes West Avenue. In less than a mile you'll come to the ramp for US 7 North and take this all the way north through Norwalk and Wilton. If you're interested in a little light shopping, take a right at the sign for the Cannondale Railroad Station; right across the tracks is Cannondale Village, a quaint historic area of tiny shops (see entry).

Taking a left onto Mountain Road in Wilton, you'll make the first right onto Indian Hill Road, then another right onto Nod Hill. Weir Farm (see entry) will be a few hundred yards ahead on your right; parking is across from it on the left. Stop in the visitor center and then wander the beautiful, untouched fields, seeing them through American Impressionist eyes, before heading to the charming village of Ridgefield.

Continue north on Nod Hill Road just to the next intersection, then take a left on Pelham Lane. These back roads with their old stone walls are charming but narrow, so be careful. Take a right onto Whipstick Road, which merges into Nod Road, and then Branchville Road (Route 102). This will take you into the center of town. Turn right onto Main Street and the Aldrich Contemporary Art Museum (see entry) will be right there. This fascinating museum with its changing exhibitions of nationally famous artists will be sure to spark your imagination.

If you still have time, or if art is unappealing to you today, then walk along the beautiful sidewalks of Ridgefield to do some shopping downtown. There are a few good restaurants in town, but if dinner tonight is special, you should eat at Bernard's, just south of the museum on West Lane (see entry). If you are planning to stay the night, you couldn't do better than the bed-and-breakfast right next door, the West Lane Inn (see entry). This is a busy day full of all sorts of wonders, and you'll probably want a good night's rest. If you're really exhausted, make an appointment for the next morning at Adam Broderick Salon and Spa (see entry). Exploring the wonders of Fairfield County can be tough work.

LITCHFIELD COUNTY

When people think of the charming country life of Connecticut, they are usually thinking of Litchfield County. Forested hills and dales punctuated by idyllic farms and delightful villages make up most of this area. Bounded by I-84 on the south and Route 8 on the east, the Litchfield Hills have called people from the nearby cities for over a century. At one time this area was a hot spot for logging and mining, but no longer. Tourism is the county's main business today, despite some small population centers in Torrington, New Milford, and the northern suburbs of Waterbury. For visitors seeking beauty of both land and culture, search no farther.

Woodbury and Kent are antiquers' dreams, and a great introduction to the joys of shopping without the pressure or prices of the bigger cities to the south. Litchfield itself is a charming hill town; its town green has shops and restaurants along one side and the state's most photographed Congregational church on the other. Due to its accessibility off Route 8, it can be the busiest of the county's towns on a weekend morning, but you simply can't miss it. Nearby Bantam and Goshen are "blink-and-you-missed-it" small towns, but they have hidden rewards if you know where to look. In the far northwest corner, Sharon, Lakeville, and Salisbury are so far away from metropolitan centers that sometimes it seems they have remained in another, older and slower time. That is, until the cars at Lime Rock's NASCAR track speed things up on summer weekends.

Roxbury was once home to sculptor Alexander Calder and playwright Arthur Miller, and has more famous residents today. Don't expect the residents to point the way to their houses, though; privacy is considered a cardinal virtue in New England. Towns like Washington, New Preston, and Cornwall hide their own treasures, with charming bookstores and covered bridges, wineries and waterfalls. You'll need an insider, or at least an insiders' guide, to find them.

The Housatonic River is a fly-fishing paradise, and the white blazes of the Appalachian Trail guide thousands of hikers through the county every summer. In autumn, this is one of the best leaf-peeping areas in the entire world, and the many inns and B&Bs can be booked months in advance. However, Connecticut is so easily accessed that a day's drive in the Hills is no problem from any of the nearby counties. Drive or walk through displays of red and yellow and orange that you've only seen in photographs.

Norfolk, Canaan, Goshen, Riverton . . . the list of charming towns with country inns waiting for you to relax on their porches can seem endless. But time itself doesn't seem to move slower in Litchfield County, it actually *does* move slower. Visit and find out how they do it.

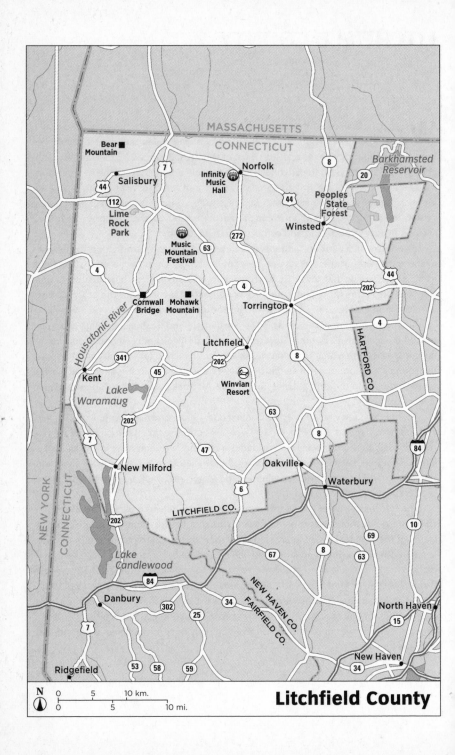

Litchfield County

ATTRACTIONS

Historical Sites & Landmarks

BELLAMY-FERRIDAY HOUSE AND GARDEN

9 Main St. North
PO Box 181
Bethlehem, CT 06751
(203) 266-7596
ctlandmarks.org

This 1754 homestead with its wonderful art and lilac-haunted gardens makes a great tour from May to Oct. The house was added to in 1767 and again in the 1790s, and a formal garden was added in the early 20th century by Caroline Ferriday, an actress and philanthropist involved in the civil rights movement. The gardens connect to 2 miles of trails run by the Bethlehem Land Trust called the Bellamy Preserve, with the entrance a few yards away on Munger Lane. At the far end of the preserve (just take the center trail to its conclusion) is the quaint Old Bethlehem Cemetery; you'll see old orchards and meadows along the way. The Bellamy-Ferriday House also runs painting workshops at the house throughout the summer, and you could not have a better subject for your brush.

BULL'S BRIDGE

Bull's Bridge Road
Kent, CT 06757
No phone
berkshirehiking.com/hikes/bulls_bridge .html

One of two covered bridges in the state open to vehicular traffic, this bridge was a community fixture as early as 1760, when originally built by Isaac Bull. In 1811 his son Jacob built this one, and it was refurbished in 1842. George Washington made this crossing famous in 1781 when a horse (probably his) slipped into the waterfall here (the bridge was undergoing repairs) and cost him $215 to get out, a princely sum at that time. The whitewater falls are just a few feet upstream from the bridge today.

THE GLEBE HOUSE MUSEUM AND GERTRUDE JECKLL GARDEN

49 Hollow Rd.
Woodbury, CT 06798
(203) 263-2855
theglebehouse.org

This 1745 minister's house was the birthplace of the Episcopal Church in America, when the first bishop was elected here in 1783 at a secret meeting that separated it from the Anglican Church of England. In 1923 it was restored by the Metropolitan Museum of Art as it was during those turbulent times of American Independence, one of the first restorations of a historic house in the whole country. The garden is the only one remaining in America designed by Gertrude Jekyll, England's premier garden landscape designer. Explore the streets of Woodbury and find the many other historic homes here, including the 1660 Hurd House, run by the Old Woodbury Historical Society, and the 1745 Bull Homestead, now Country Loft Antiques (countryloftantiques.com).

HOTCHKISS-FYLER HOUSE

192 Main St.
Torrington, CT 06790
(860) 482-8260
torringtonhistoricalsociety.org

There are dozens of historical houses in Connecticut, and all are worth a visit. However, a few stand out for their preservation, their collections, or their location. The Hotchkiss-Flyer has all three. This remarkable Queen Anne home was completed in 1900 and was bequeathed to the Torrington Historical Society 56 years later. Though not one of the older houses in the state, its beautiful millwork is second to none, with mahogany, bird's-eye maple, red birch, and quarter-sawn oak. Next door to the showpiece house is the historical museum. The collection of glass, porcelain, and paintings is impressive, with Limoges crystal and paintings by Connecticut Impressionist Winfield Scott Clime. While you're here, you probably should visit the site of controversial abolitionist John Brown, whose raid on Harper's Ferry helped spark the Civil War. Follow Route 4 west, turn right on University Drive, and 1 mile farther turn left onto John Brown Road. The birthplace site is 0.5 mile on the right.

*TAPPING REEVE HOUSE AND HISTORIC LITCHFIELD
82 South St.
Litchfield, CT 06759
(860) 567-4501
litchfieldhistoricalsociety.org
This large taupe house rambles back to a barn, with a small building the size of a one-room schoolhouse on the side. And in a way, that is what it is. In 1773 Tapping Reeve and his new wife, Sally Burr, settled in Litchfield, where Reeve began practicing law. He instructed several men from town, established a reputation, and soon began America's first formal law school. You can "attend" the school as a young student from Revolutionary times, a fun experience in living history. From here, walk the streets of this 1720 hill town on the great old-fashioned sidewalks that sit well back from the road. Check out the Oliver Wolcott Library just to the south of Tapping Reeve, marvel at the huge sycamores and beeches, and don't forget to take a picture of the huge Congregational church on the green. It's the most frequently photographed church in Connecticut, and one of the most photographed in America. Stop by the Litchfield Historical Society on the opposite corner, then walk north of the green on the west side of Route 3, past Revolutionary spymaster Benjamin Tallmadge's mansion, up to the place where

Lyman Beecher's house stood. Here he wrote his criticisms of slavery that helped spark the abolition movement.

WEST CORNWALL BRIDGE
Route 128
West Cornwall, CT 06753
No phone
No website
Ironically, perhaps, the Cornwall Bridge is not in the town of the same name but slightly north in West Cornwall, if that makes sense. It is one of the most distinctive covered bridges in the state, and one of only two you can drive over. It crosses the Housatonic River along Route 128, just where it meets Route 7. The covered bridge was invented here in Connecticut by New Haven architect Ithiel Town, who wanted to design a bridge that could be made by people without engineering experience in small towns around America. His friend, inventor Eli Whitney, suggested covering it. Town actually designed this particular bridge as well, and you can see the architect's work on his home turf.

Museums

INSTITUTE OF AMERICAN INDIAN STUDIES
38 Curtis Rd.
PO Box 1260
Washington, CT 06793
(860) 868-0518
iaismuseum.org
This rural museum focuses on Native Americans from the Northeast, especially the Algonquian peoples, and features tools and art. A re-creation of a longhouse and a Children's Discovery Room are both inside; outside, a 17th-century settlement allows you to walk through a life-size exhibit. Check their schedule, because the programs they run, like dances and craft workshops, are the best part of this museum. Literally right next door is the Steep Rock Reservation

(steeprockassoc.org), a nature preserve with hiking trails along the rivers and up to the summit of Steep Rock, where there are views of the Shepaug River below. There are old carriage roads in here too, which served a hotel, and other vestiges of the past. Nearby, at 626 Washington Rd. in Woodbury, the Schaghticoke Indian Reservation Cemetery is definitely worth a stop as well.

Parks & Beaches

*KENT FALLS
462 Kent-Cornwall Rd. (Route 7)
Kent, CT 06757
(860) 927-3238
ct.gov/dep [search "Kent Falls"]
If you pull off Route 7 north of Kent into the parking lot, you'll see a waterfall right away across a green meadow and think this was all very easy. But that is only the bottom falls; there is an entire series of different and equally picturesque drops, which you'll see as you hike up the side of the ridge more than 200 feet vertically from the Housatonic River valley where you parked. The top waterfall is the largest, dropping 70 feet in a fantastic cascade, and worth the climb, especially since the path has been reconstructed with well-made little wooden platforms that I like to call "excuse for stopping platforms." There's also a 1-mile loop trail on the north side of the stream, if you're looking for more exercise. And if you're into fishing, this is a designated trout park, barely used, where my father caught 12 small trout on a fly, one after the other in the space of an hour below the bottom falls.

SOUTHFORD FALLS
175 Quaker Farms Rd.
Southbury, CT 06488
(203) 264-5169
ct.gov/dep [search "Southford Falls"]

This is a great, free, short stop off the side of Route 188 in Southbury. Over a hundred years ago, the Diamond Match Company made its revolutionary friction matches here, and it was turned into a state park in 1932. There are several scenic waterfalls here; just park and walk down the hill, following the red trail along Eight Mile Brook. However, if you have a little more time, take the red trail for a loop back into the woods. This is also a designated trout park, so you can throw a line into Papermill Pond. People bring their lunches here and picnic by the roar of the falls, and you'll see painters and poets lining the rocky outcrops in the summertime.

TOPSMEAD STATE FOREST
Buell Road
Litchfield, CT 06759
(860) 567-5694
ct.gov/dep [search "Topsmead State Forest"]
Formerly the summer estate of Edith Morton Chase, this gorgeous park features a network of trails and gravel roads through forest and fields, all surrounding one of the most fantastic houses in the state. There is a fine pond and a wildlife-viewing blind. Definitely take a tour of the strange Tudorlike house if you're there June through Oct on the second and fourth weekends of each month from noon to 5 p.m. Check out the slate roof; they don't make them like that anymore. This is a pleasant place for a walk, like many of the estates in Great Britain where the public is allowed to walk freely. Make sure you leave before the posted gate-closing time; they are serious about that. Despite the park's proximity to nearby attractions, the hilltop fields and frog-haunted pond just off Route 118 on the way to Litchfield are somehow missed by most casual travelers. Don't be one of them.

Wildlife

SHEPAUG BALD EAGLE OBSERVATION AREA

2299 River Rd.
Southbury, CT 06488
(800) 368-8954
shepaugeagles.com

Right next to the Shepaug Dam along the Housatonic River is one of the great places to view nesting bald eagles in Connecticut during Jan, Feb, and Mar. Run by three organizations—Northeast Utilities, the Department of Environmental Protection, and the Connecticut Audubon Society—this observation area with its blind and spotting scopes is staffed by volunteers. Bring your binoculars and your patience; watching for eagles can take a while. In the meantime, you'll probably see goshawks and great blue herons. There is a nice nature trail that takes you past the dam along the shores of Lake Lillinoah. This is a completely free activity, but you need to make reservations to do it. Its open the third week of Dec to the first week of Mar on Wed, Sat, and Sun. Give them a call and take a day to appreciate and maybe even fall in love with our national bird.

Wineries

CONNECTICUT VALLEY WINERY

1480 Litchfield Tpke. (Route 202)
New Hartford, CT 06057
(860) 489-9463
ctvalleywinery.com

This is a perfect short stop on Route 202 between Hartford and Torrington. Standouts at Connecticut Valley Winery include Deep Purple, made with Chambourcin grapes, and Midnight, featuring Frontenac. Both estate bottled, as is Dolce Vita, a lovely sweet white. The Italian heritage of the winemaking Ferraro family is evident in their Chianti and Spumonte Muscato, a sparkling white. Try Chardonel for a sample of another hybrid. Specialty wines include Black Bear dessert wine, named for a bear that helped itself to the harvest and found the grapes as inviting as you will. The tasting room's wood ambience and hearty fireplace offer respite on a late autumn day, and the patio umbrellas will shield your glass from the sun if you're out in the summer heat.

HAIGHT-BROWN VINEYARD

Chestnut Hill
Litchfield, CT 06759
(860) 567-4054
haightvineyards.com

Connecticut's oldest winery was opened by Sherman Haight as soon as the Farm Winery Act was passed, making commercial winemaking legal in the state for the first time since Prohibition. The winery changed hands in 2008, and with 16 planted acres and 2,500 cases of wines produced annually, the tradition continues. Selections are varied, and the beautiful tasting room loft is located upstairs in a barn. Wines include Coverside, a white blend of Chardonnay and Seyval Blanc, and Riesling, which is light and semisweet. The Marechal Foch grape, one of many grown in the vineyard, is showcased in Nouveau Foch, a Beaujolais-style red that is light and fruity, and Picnic Red, which offers a little more bite. As the name implies, Big Red offers bold flavor to those who like full-bodied wines. With additional selections including apple wine blends and dessert wines, there's something for everyone.

✳HOPKINS VINEYARD

23 Hopkins Rd.
New Preston, CT 06777
(860) 868-7954
hopkinsvineyard.com

Developed on land that has been farmed for over 200 years, Hopkins Vineyard lies just above Lake Waramaug. Visit the winery's 19th-century red barn, where you'll find the tasting room, wine loft, and gift store. Tour the facilities and vines and witness the pride of the winemakers and the beauty of the land. Standouts include estate bottled Chardonnay; Duet, a blend of Chardonnay and Vidal Blanc; and Lady Rosé, a lovely dry rosé with tobacco on the nose and strawberry notes on the palate. Hopkins's Cabernet Franc may be the best in the state. Try Red Barn Red, a dry red with black currant overtones, and Sachem's Picnic, a red blend, served cool, which is a little sweeter and perfect for summer barbecues. Hopkins also offers peach wine, apple cider, a dessert wine, and an exquisite ice wine, made from Vidal Blanc picked when the grapes are frozen. Estate-picked Pinot Noir and Chardonnay are blended for the sparkling wine, made in the champagne style.

JERRAM WINERY
535 Town Hill Rd.
New Hartford, CT 06057
(860) 379-8749
jerramwinery.com

The tasting room at Jerram Winery is small, located down the gravel drive between two barns. But inside, the yellow brightness is inviting, especially on spring or summer days when the light hits just right. Jerram grows several varieties, including Marechal Foch, Vignoles, and Seyval Blanc. The wines offer tasters the chance to try these and sample unique blends, including S'il Vous Plait, made with Cabernet Franc grapes, and Vespers, a late-harvest dessert wine. You'll also find Aurora, the goddess of dawn, donning the frosted bottle of the wine (and the grape) that takes her name. This makes a great stop if you're up seeing the sights in Riverton or hiking Peoples State Forest.

LAND OF NOD WINERY
99 Lower Rd.
East Canaan, CT 06024
(860) 824-5225
landofnodwinery.com

History is rich at Land of Nod Winery. It is a nationally recognized bicentennial farm, and the family has farmed the land for nine generations. Named for a Robert Louis Stevenson poem, Land of Nod offers an intriguing selection of fruit wines made from berries grown on-site. Their offerings include raspberry wine, a blend of blueberry and raspberry, peach wine, and a delicious chocolate-raspberry dessert wine. They now produce grape wines, including Bianca, a lovely white, and Corot Noir, a deep red with hints of spice. Located up the road (you'll see it as you drive in) is the Historic Beckley Furnace. Built in 1837, the structure is listed on the National Register of Historic Places and stands as a reminder of the importance of the iron industry.

MIRANDA VINEYARD
42 Ives Rd.
Goshen, CT 06756
(860) 491-9906
mirandavineyard.com

Miranda Vineyards, another fine winery nestled in the Litchfield Hills, features wines made in the old-world traditions that owner and winemaker Manny Miranda learned from his parents in Portugal. The tasting room is located in a refurbished wood building that overlooks the vines; the rooster weathervane atop the building lends itself to the logo. Award-winning selections include single varietals—Chardonnay, Seyval Blanc—as well as Woodridge White, a blend of these two. Red offerings include Merlot and Woodridge Red, which has a pleasant earthiness along with notes of berry. Events like music, dinners, and fund-raisers are frequent throughout the summer months and offer a chance for young and old to enjoy the scenic winery. Go to their pig roast in the fall and perhaps win a bottle of wine to take home.

*SUNSET MEADOW VINEYARDS
599 Old Middle St. (Route 63)
Goshen, CT 06756
(860) 201-4654
sunsetmeadowvineyards.com

Sunset Meadow Vineyards has a perfect location for growing grapes—about 1,300 feet above sea level—and 21 acres of vines are planted on a western-facing slope, which you'll see as you drive up to the tasting room. The winery specializes in estate-bottled and Western Connecticut Highlands appellation selections featuring 14 grape varieties, including Cayuga White, Seyval Blanc, Riesling, and St. Croix. The Riesling has notes of lemon and a touch of sweetness. St. Croix is a beautiful red with notes of mocha and smoky spice. Twisted Red, a blend of four grapes, is medium-bodied and rich, and is another among Sunset Meadow's award winners. The tasting room, open year-round, is a converted barn with rustic rafters and a long, wood tasting bar. Watch swallows nest under the porch roof, or sit on the patio and look out over the vines.

ACTIVITIES & EVENTS

Arts Venues

*INFINITY MUSIC HALL
20 Greenwoods Rd.
PO Box 58
Norfolk, CT 06058
(860) 542-5531
infinityhall.com

Once the Norfolk Opera House, this remarkable green building along Route 44 has been turned into a classic venue, with concerts every couple of days in an intimate, 320-seat space. It is a musician's dream—a historic Victorian hall with stained-glass windows, wood floors, and a vaulted ceiling. There are really no bad seats at Infinity; everyone has a great view of the stage. You can order cocktails from your seat (there are convenient counters to set them on) and eat dinner in the mezzanine or go to the separate downstairs restaurant, the Infinity Bistro (see entry). They also have magic and comedy shows, but come here for the musical performances. It is a magical place with both a sense of history and a bright future. The town of Norfolk is charming and remote, and there are plenty of bed-and-breakfasts around where you can rest your head after a show. If Norfolk is too remote for you, Infinity has just opened a venue in Hartford as well (32 Front St.; 860-560-7757).

PLEASANT VALLEY DRIVE-IN
47 River Rd.
Barkhamsted, CT 06063
(860) 379-6102
driveinmovie.com/CT/PleasantValley/
schedule

This old-fashioned drive-in off Route 181 in the northeast corner of Litchfield County is a welcome sight for those who remember this unique way of watching films, and for those who have never done so. They usually have two showings a night, one at about 9 p.m. and one later, and of course you can stay for the double feature. They take cash only, and you should get there early if you want a "seat," because people drive out from Hartford on Route 44 all summer, rain or shine, for this treat. There's a snack bar, but unlike most theaters, you can bring your own snacks. Wash your windshield beforehand or bring some chairs to sit in front of your car. Drive-ins are superior to traditional theaters in many ways, and if you don't know why, you should come to Pleasant Valley and find out.

WARNER THEATRE
68 Main St.
Torrington, CT 06790
(860) 489-7180
warnertheatre.org

The Warner Theatre was built in 1931 as a movie theater when plays were supposedly going out of style; now ironically it has turned back to dramatic productions, leaving films to the big chain multiplexes. It's been restored and refitted and has become (again) one of the best venues in Connecticut, with over 2,500 seats and a unique star-shaped chandelier ceiling. There's also a smaller, 300-seat black box theater and an on-site school for the arts. All kinds of different events are presented throughout the year, including plays, discussions, comedy, classical music, country music, rock-and-roll concerts, operas, ballets, and more. In other words, the Warner is booked solid, and you should take advantage of this amazing theater, no matter what you enjoy.

Festivals & Annual Events

CANAAN RAILROAD DAYS
1 Railroad St.
PO Box 1146
Canaan, CT 06018
(860) 824-0850
canaanchamber.com/events
Part of the Housatonic and Connecticut Western Railroad systems in the 19th century, Canaan's Union Depot was the oldest operating station in the US until it was devastated by fire in 2001. Today it is being renovated, and at the famous Canaan Railroad Days you can honor the tradition while having some good family fun. Every business in town and the larger area participates in this weeklong festival, which includes car shows, craft fairs, a treasure hunt, gold panning, a parade, and fireworks. And of course you can ride the old trains up to Great Barrington, Massachusetts (and back if you like). Check the schedule for the days (usually in July); this is a great time to visit northwest Connecticut.

CONNECTICUT ANTIQUE MACHINERY ASSOCIATION'S FALL FESTIVAL
1 Kent Cornwall Rd.
Kent, CT 06757
(860) 927-0050
ctamachinery.com
This annual festival takes place at the Connecticut Antique Machinery Museum, usually a quiet little collection of history museums in some restored buildings in Kent. But every autumn the antique machines here start running, and things get very, very exciting. Old trains, engines, tractors, and other mining and agricultural machines chug away to the great delight of all attending. The festival also features wood splitting, blacksmithing, broom making, and cider making. Antique cars and trucks fill the fields, and food is available from a variety of vendors. Also on-site are the Cream Hill Agricultural School, with its original desks and library, and the Connecticut Museum of Mining and Mineral Science, full of native rocks and mining equipment. Literally next door is the separately run Sloane-Stanley Museum, featuring a wonderful collection of colonial American tools and the partially restored ruins of the Kent Iron Furnace.

CHRISTMAS IN RIVERTON
Riverton, CT 06065
(860) 738-9958
rivertonct.com/events
Picture the quintessential image of New England charm and it's likely you'll find it in Riverton during the Christmas festival. Usually held during the first weekend in December, the event transforms the small village into a winter wonderland. While shops in the center of town are open all day, the real draw is nighttime, when luminarias line the street and visitors tour the establishments. Especially appealing is the Peter Greenwood Glassworks studio, located in the historic Union Church. Adults can sample wine and

gourmet food, and kids of all ages can enjoy wagon rides and puppet shows, take a photo with Father Christmas, and wonder at ice sculptures. Stop at the Old Riverton Inn (see entry) for dinner, then head up the street for Charles Dickens's *A Christmas Carol* performed by the Riverton Theatre Group. Afterwards, you might mingle around a bonfire and watch sparks crisp into the winter sky.

HARWINTON FAIR
80 Locust Rd.
Harwinton, CT 06791
(860) 485-0464
harwintonfair.com

Connecticut has many town fairs, but not many that have been going steadily since 1853. The Harwinton Fair is one of the largest fairs as well, with hundreds of attractions, exhibits, vendors, and more. There are displays, like a blacksmith shop and working shingle mill; demonstrations of pioneer and Civil War living; and competitions, such as baking and wood chopping. The fair hosts a large traveling carnival with rides, a high-wire act by circus performers, and dozens and dozens of craft and food vendors. They have entertainment for kids, like magic shows, and music entertainment for adults. Skillet tossing, pig racing, oxen teamster challenges, and an antique tractor show . . . what more do you want from a country fair that has been going for more than 160 years?

LITCHFIELD JAZZ FESTIVAL
30 S. Main St.
Kent, CT 06757
(860) 361-6285
litchfieldjazzfest.com

In 1996 Litchfield began this festival on the third weekend in Aug, on the grounds of the White Memorial Foundation. Today it happens at different venues throughout the hills, and lasts all day Saturday and Sunday. Usually there are over a thousand seats, but thousands more eager listeners sprawl on picnic blankets and lawn chairs throughout the meadows. Performers like Diana Krall, Dave Brubeck, and Sonny Rollins have played here. You can bring food, beer, and wine or buy from the many vendors serving everything from pizza to oysters. There are a couple dozen craft vendors too, and you'll have plenty of time to browse; the concerts last from midday through the evening hours. That's a lot of jazz.

MUSIC MOUNTAIN SUMMER MUSIC FESTIVAL CONCERTS
225 Music Mountain Rd.
Falls Village, CT 06031
(860) 824-7126
musicmountain.org

Founded in 1930, the acoustically magical wooden concert hall at Music Mountain annually features 16 chamber music concerts and is now America's oldest continuous chamber music festival. But Music Mountain does not only have chamber music, they also feature jazz, blues, and folk. In 2011 they added a silent-movie night with live accompaniment. There is seating for 335 on cushioned pews, but you can picnic on the 132 acres of lawn under trees or in the sun if you like. You can also dance on the outdoor dance floor. This is a series of concerts throughout the summer rather than a single event, on Friday and Saturday evenings and Sunday afternoons. The concerts are listened to on 125 radio stations nationwide and in 35 other countries. But you can listen to them live, right here, amid the picturesque surroundings of the Litchfield Hills.

NORFOLK CHAMBER MUSIC FESTIVAL
18 Litchfield Rd.
Norfolk, CT 06058
(860) 542-3000 (June through Aug)
(203) 432-1966 (Sept through May)
norfolk.yale.edu

Just off the town green at the Ellen Battell Stoeckel Estate, this redwood and cedar music barn is the summer home of the Yale Music School and consistently features some of the best chamber music in America. Nationally and internationally famous quartets and quintets play here every summer on Friday and Saturday nights. On Tuesday and Thursday evenings and Saturday mornings, free concerts are given by the Fellows of the Norfolk Summer School. The Norfolk "Shed" also features lectures, usually on Wednesday nights, by some of the finest music teachers and critics in the country. If you have children, rejoice, because they get in free. Bring a picnic or eat at the nearby Infinity Bistro (see entry) before the evening concerts.

Fishing

BANTAM LAKE
East Shore Road
Morris, CT 06763
No phone
bantamlakect.com

The largest natural lake in Connecticut (though much smaller than the dammed ones), Bantam Lake has been a popular fishing and boating destination since the Pootatuck tribe summered here centuries ago. The culture is mostly motorboating, and to launch, drive west on Route 202 from Litchfield, take a left on Alain White Road, then a right on East Shore Road; just before the bend you'll see the entrance to Sandy Beach. If you like freshwater fishing, this lake has northern pike and largemouth bass, as well as the more common perch. The northern end of the lake is a protected

area, full of rare birds, part of the White Memorial Foundation (see entry). In winter Bantam Lake is one of the prime ice-fishing and ice-boating spots in the state, and since 1958 it has been home to the Bantam Lake Ski Club (bantamskiclub.com); you might see them practicing their amazing tricks on the water.

✳HOUSATONIC RIVER
Along Route 7
(860) 485-0226
ct.gov/dep/fishing

Fishing the Housatonic is a lot like fishing a river out west. It's large and full of fish, and since the PCB level from factories upriver has waned, it has become one of the state's three or four great fishing areas. If you're looking for trout, the 10-mile Management Area by Cornwall Bridge is your best bet, though it's fly fishing only (use the always reliable Blue-Winged Olives or Muddler Minnows; no need for tricks here). The state stocks large brown trout here, and during lower-flow months, this section is wadeable. Expect smallmouth bass to hit your line hard and often too. Most months this river can be fished from a canoe or float, and there are sections available to fish all the way from its mouth in Milford to the Massachusetts state line. In autumn, stand in the river or sit by the shore and watch barn swallows catch bugs high above, shaded by trees with leaves of gorgeous red, yellow, and orange.

i If you want to fish in Connecticut, get the *Connecticut Angler's Guide,* published annually by the DEP. This booklet gives opportunities and rules for everyone. Available wherever fishing licenses are sold (you'll need one!), you can also call (860) 424-FISH for a copy.

LAKE MCDONOUGH

Route 219
Barkhamsted, CT 06063
(860) 379-3036 (in-season)
(860) 278-7850
themdc.com

Looking like a lake from far north Quebec, Lake McDonough is surrounded by piney hills. This is a great fishing lake for all species of trout or for smallmouth bass. Try right below Saville Dam, above which is the even larger Barkhamsted Reservoir (off-limits to boating or fishing)—in fact, don't miss driving across it, with its little stone tower straight out of France. Launch from East Beach for a small fee, or just pull off on the side of Route 219 and walk to the pine-clad shore to fish from there. You can also swim from 3 different beaches here or rent rowboats or paddleboats. Near Goose Green Beach, a self-guided nature trail, with Braille signs and a system of ramps and railings for the blind, features about 80 natural landmarks such as trees and rocks to read about and touch.

RIVERTON FISHING DERBY

Riverton, CT 06065
(860) 379-0811
rivertonct.com/events

This is a great introduction to one of the best rivers in the country, a National Wild and Scenic River winding through the heart of Connecticut. Unlike some derbies, there is no entry fee, and kids under 12 have a special designated area. The contest starts at 6 a.m., so you might want to lodge the night before in the Old Riverton Inn (see entry) or a nearby motel. The Riverton Firehouse is the center of activity, so get the famous "fisherman's breakfast" here and walk the charming town. People waiting for their fishing family or friends can poke their heads into Peter Greenwood's nationally famous glass-blowing studio

(petergreenwood.com). Later in the day, take a hike in the Peoples State Forest or raft the river farther downstream at Satan's Kingdom.

Golf

CRESTBROOK PARK GOLF COURSE

834 Northfield Rd.
Watertown, CT 06795
(860) 945-5249
crestbrookpark.com

This public course in Watertown is also considered the best 18-hole course in the county. Once a 9-hole course, Crestbrook was expanded in 1980 after the town bought the course from a private club. From the back tees, the length is 6,930 yards (though there are 4 sets of tees for all abilities), and its fast-sloping greens are considered to be challenging. Carts will cost you extra at Crestbrook (as usual), and you need special permission to use a caddy. There's a pro shop and a restaurant at the course called Cavallo's Crestbrook Inn, open for lunch. It's a popular-enough course that it is self-supporting and costs Watertown nothing, so it must be doing something right.

Health & Wellness

CHARYM TEMPLE, SPA AND YOGA STUDIO

174 West St.
Litchfield, CT 06759
(860) 567-7795
charym.com

Don't be put off by the "temple" in the title—this is a temple to health, taking a full-person approach to changing our stressed-out lifestyles. Some people don't want to mix their yoga and fitness with their massages and facials, but it makes so much sense that you'll be surprised everyone isn't doing it. After all, your strength and flexibility are part of your ability to recover and relax from the daily vicissitudes and struggles. Along with their spa and yoga classes, they offer ayurvedic and holistic healing. Charym tries to integrate all these treatments and "good medicine" into making your body and mind the best they can be. It's hard to argue with that philosophy, and after one of their hot stone massages or a holistic treatment using raw herbs and virgin oils, you won't want to.

WISDOMHOUSE RETREAT CENTER
229 E. Litchfield Rd.
Litchfield, CT 06759
(860) 567-3163
wisdomhouse.org

The *New York Times* called this 54-acre retreat a "resort for the spirit," and if you're in need of a little rejuvenation, the WisdomHouse Retreat Center is the place for it. Once an old farm, it was purchased in 1949 by the Daughters of Wisdom, an inclusive group of Catholic sisters, and is now an interfaith center that welcomes all women and men seeking their own spiritual health. Sanctuary areas for meditation, prayer, and creative thinking abound, like the classic labyrinth, and there's even a swimming pool. Throughout the year you can sign up for a full program of different spiritual programs, lectures, interactive workshops, and retreats. This is also a frequent retreat for creative artists and writers, and they run a number of programs to that end. WisdomHouse has overnight space for about 140 people, although unless the Dalai Lama is making an appearance, you're unlikely to find that many visitors. This is a place for quiet reflection (you can even visit on "quiet days," when everyone speaks softly or not at all). Whatever your faith, we all need a little help on our spiritual journeys. This is the perfect place to get some.

Hiking, Biking & Walking

AMERICAN LEGION AND PEOPLES STATE FORESTS
East River Road
Barkhamsted, CT 06063
(860) 379-0922 (campground office, May through Sept)
(860) 379-2469 (forest office, year-round)
ct.gov/dep [search "Peoples State Forest"]

Right along the west branch of the Farmington River, these twin parks in Barkhamsted offer some of the state's most remote and interesting hiking. In the Peoples State Forest, the Stone Museum has nature exhibits to delight young and old. From there, head along the blue-and-yellow-blazed trail (Beaver Swamp Loop), where an old wagon trail leads up to a glacial hill where the remains of 18 ancient village sites have been discovered. There are also colonial house foundations in the park, and the westernmost yellow-blazed trail skirts the edge of a very steep drop to the Farmington River. This is also a great place to cross-country ski in winter; though you're high up, only a few trails are steep enough to prove difficult on skis. You'll also see lots of animal tracks in the snow at this time of year, including those of moose and bear. The Henry Buck Trail on the American Legion side of the river passes old mill sites on its way up the side of the mountain. On the western bank of the river, a small, 30-site camping area, with cabins for those who don't have tents, makes for a perfect rustic resting place after a difficult hike. Last time I was there I spent 7 hours relaxing by a roaring campfire, roasting potatoes, kielbasa, hot dogs, and marshmallows. There are worse ways to spend a summer night.

✳BEAR MOUNTAIN
Salisbury, CT 06068
(860) 485-0226
berkshirehiking.com

The highest peak in Connecticut is not exactly the Matterhorn. But the views from the giant, 20-foot-high cairn of stones on top (built in 1885) are fantastic, and this is the hiking gateway to the entire Taconic Range. Park on the side of Route 41 (Undermountain Road) just north of Salisbury and hike up the Undermountain Trail until you reach the white blazes of the Appalachian Trail. South is the Lion's Head, a promontory with another great view. In spring, look for lady's slippers. North of Bear Mountain's peak, just steps across the border in Massachusetts, is Sage's Ravine, full of old-growth trees. The Appalachian Mountain Club maintains a cabin on the west side of the mountain, and it is available by reservation to both members and nonmembers (ct-amc.org/nwcamp). It's probably the most isolated spot to spend a night in Connecticut. I must admit I have not seen a bear on the 6 hikes I've taken over Bear Mountain, but I have seen them elsewhere!

MOHAWK MOUNTAIN STATE FOREST
20 Mohawk Mountain Rd.
Goshen, CT 06756
(860) 491-3620
ct.gov/dep [search "Mohawk Mountain State Forest"]

During the warmer months, this state forest is one of the prime hiking areas in the state. The Appalachian Trail used to go through here, but now the huge loop of the Mohawk Trail meets it down in the Housatonic River valley. (If you stay at Cathedral Pines Farm, you can hike the whole loop in one day if you're quick about it.) Be sure to hike up to the 1,683-foot summit of Mohawk Mountain (it's not that hard because you're starting fairly high already),

where a wooden observation tower affords one of the best views in the entire state. Follow the blue trail just west of the ski area onto Essex Hill Road, where it dives into the woods again. This is the historic Cathedral Pines area, where one of the few old-growth remnants of white pines in New England exists. A tornado smashed through here in 1980, knocking down many of the trees, but some remain. It's a lovely little reminder of what the forests in Connecticut looked like 1,000 years ago.

ROXBURY LAND TRUST TRAILS
7 South St.
Roxbury, CT 06783
(860) 350-4148
roxburylandtrust.org

Roxbury Land Trust has created one of the best "private" sets of trails in a state with many secret trail systems. Few outside each town pay attention to these wonderful networks, which sometimes connect to our larger blue trail system and sometimes create their own little world. One of my favorites in Roxbury is Mine Hill, which should be a state park at least—the remnants of a huge foundry, roasting ovens, and other ruins, as well as donkey paths up the mountain to abandoned mine shafts full of bats. Don't go in them, though—they are dangerous. The Land Trust offices are open at the address above during weekday mornings, but the trail maps can all be found online. You probably wouldn't have found these trails on your own; few in Roxbury or any of these other Connecticut villages want the rest of us to know about them. Secret's out now.

WHITE MEMORIAL FOUNDATION TRAILS
80 Whitehall Rd.
Litchfield, CT 06759
(860) 567-0857
whitememorialcc.org

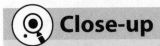

Close-up

Blue Trails and Greenways

Though many hikers stick to the family-friendly parks that dot the state, insiders who like to walk know there are alternatives. Connecticut's blue trails and greenways will lead you through hidden summer glens, along sparkling autumn rivers, and to the first spring flowers.

Connecticut's blue trail system crisscrosses the state, linking communities over old Indian trails and colonial byways. Founded in 1929 by the Connecticut Forest & Park Association (CFPA), this statewide forest trail system was built and continues to be maintained by volunteers. Today 825 miles of these blue-blazed trails wind through the suburbs and wilderness areas of every county. The CFPA publishes maps of these trails if you wish to go exploring.

These trails were an attempt to preserve the walking culture that was rapidly fading due to the rise of the automobile. Many of the early trails fell victim to the spread of suburbanization, but more were added to compensate. Find out more at ctwoodlands.org.

A parallel movement grew in the late 20th century to convert old unused rail and canal trails to multiuse paths. These "greenways" added a new overlapping web of trails. In winter they become havens for cross-country skiers, the long, flat rail beds and towpaths lending themselves to this pursuit. Find maps and more at ct.gov/dep under "Outdoor Recreation."

Both the blue trails and greenways often meet and interact with local trail systems, crossing state parks like Sleeping Giant or privately owned reserves like the White Memorial Foundation, providing walkers with seemingly endless variations for a day's hike. If you need some suggestions, you'll find a variety of excellent hikes in a number of books published by Globe Pequot, such as *50 Hikes in Connecticut,* or the AMC's *Best Day Hikes in Connecticut.* Some of the most interesting areas are highlighted in this Insiders' Guide, but no doubt you will find more.

Using these trails you can literally walk around the state of Connecticut in a way not possible in most of the country. Europeans used to the shorter distances and accessible walking paths immediately feel at home, often taking advantage of this unique opportunity here in America. In the Litchfield Hills, a savvy insider can walk these paths from town to town, staying at charming inns and bed-and-breakfasts.

For those who like backpack camping, Connecticut has more than you'd think. Of course it is legal to camp along the Appalachian Trail in Litchfield County, but the DEP has a number of other backpack and lean-to sites throughout the northern and eastern parts of the state. You'll need a reservation; go to ct.gov/dep and click your way to "Backpack Camping."

You will share some greenways with bicyclists and, on paved sections, in-line skaters and baby strollers, so be careful. Much of the blue trail system also cuts through private property, so please be respectful. Take only pictures and leave only footprints.

The sign and road off the side of Route 202 look like they might lead to some sort of charitable corporation. But actually this is one of the largest networks of trails in the state, a perfect place to bring beginning hikers or walkers. The foundation was formed in 1913, and in 1964 a conservation center was established in the home of Alain and May White. Today there is a nature museum here, as well as other facilities.

Within the 4,000 acres of the foundation, the trails maintain their generally flat and easy-walking nature, and this is a perfect place to introduce children to the joys of the outdoors. For longer hikes, the blue-blazed Mattatuck Trail connects to the foundation trails, and many of these flat, doubletrack dirt roads are open to bicyclists. Along with Bantam Lake, there are several ponds and even a cranberry swamp, as well as pine and deciduous forests. This is a great place for birders to spend all day watching in the various habitats. In spring and summer, the many flowering plants along these trails and ponds burst into pure beauty.

Horseback Riding

LEE'S RIDING STABLE
57 E. Litchfield Rd.
Litchfield, CT 06759
(860) 309-1654
windfieldmorganfarm.com
The Windfield Morgan Farm, set on 100 beautiful acres adjacent to Topsmead State Forest in Litchfield, has been raising primarily Morgan horses (thus the name) since 1976. Many show champions have come from here, and their breeding program is well respected. But unless you're looking to buy a horse, the adjunct Lee's Riding Stable at the farm is probably what you're interested in. The friendly horses are perfect for riding in the rolling hills of Litchfield, and guided riding tours are available from 9 a.m. to 5 p.m. 7 days a week. Call and make a reservation for up to 8 riders. Lee's also offers a variety of lessons for riders of all ages, including pony rides for very young horse lovers. The people and horses here are some of the friendliest you'll find in the state.

LOON MEADOW FARM
41 Loon Meadow Dr.
Norfolk, CT 06058
(860) 542-6085
loonmeadowfarm.com

On one of the back roads of Norfolk (all right, they are all back roads), you'll find a 19th-century farmhouse with draft horses in the pastures. However, this is not your traditional horse-riding farm. Loon Meadow is an appointed livery and provides a wide selection of horses and carriages for weddings, funerals, and parades. The farm offers hayrides in summer and sleigh rides in winter, with mulled cider and a bonfire afterwards. You can also take one of their historical horse-and-carriage rides through Norfolk, while a living-history interpreter tells you about her life in Civil War America.

RUSTLING WIND STABLES
164 Canaan Mountain Rd.
Falls Village, CT 06031
(860) 824-7634
rustlingwind.com
This 200-acre farm has been in the Lamothe family since the 1800s, and today the fourth generation is on the land. Since 1965 Rustling Wind has been a horse farm and today has 30 horses, an indoor and outdoor arena, a jumping field, and miles of trails. If you are 8 or older, you can take guided English or Western saddle rides for 1 to 2 hours through the forests of this picturesque area, though they do have pony rides for smaller children. The farm is also a creamery, and they offer 10 different delectable cheeses at their store, as well as jams, pickles, maple products, goat's milk soap, and hand knits from their own sheep wool. When you're done exploring the trails on horseback and sampling the cheese, be sure to stop at the Great Falls of the Housatonic, for which the village is named.

Pick Your Own/Farms

AVERILL FARM
250 Calhoun St.
Washington, CT 06794
(860) 868-2777
averillfarm.com

This farm dates back to colonial days, and the Averill family has been farming the land since 1746. The 200 acres boast structures that date to the early 1800s, including the huge old stone homestead. Ten generations of Averills have worked the land, and they continue to grow 100 varieties of apples and pears, which are available for picking. The farm stand is open Labor Day to Thanksgiving, and in addition to their own fruit, they sell cider, donuts, maple syrup, honey, cheese, and cut flowers. You'll drive back along the dirt road through the orchards and immediately be transported to the rural life we all once lived, and lived happily.

HUNT HILL FARM AND THE SILO
44 Upland Rd.
New Milford, CT 06776
(860) 355-0300
hunthillfarmtrust.org

The Hunt Hill Farm, known historically as the Bostwick Farm, has been used continuously since the 1700s. On the farm preserve you'll find 2 houses from the 1830s, an 1860 cottage, 2 barns with silos, a low tobacco barn, and several other buildings. It is not just a farm but also part of an attraction called the Henderson Cultural Center, run by the Hunt Hill Farm Trust, which includes an art gallery founded in 1975, the 130-acre farm preserve, and a cooking school called the Silo, which brings in instructors from around the country to teach. They also feature concerts, literary readings, and other events. If you're in the area, check their schedule, and take a cooking class if you can. There is also a store to stop at if you're passing through, which carries gourmet foods, cooking supplies, and autographed cookbooks. I recently attended a poetry reading here and got a peek inside the studio of famed conductor Skitch Henderson.

Skiing

MOHAWK MOUNTAIN
46 Great Hollow Rd.
Cornwall, CT 06753
(800) 895-5222
mohawkmtn.com

Mohawk is the largest and oldest ski area in the state, with 23 trails, 5 lifts, and state-of-the-art snowmaking equipment. There are also cross-country ski trails in the Mohawk State Forest, and some of them are very challenging, heading all the way to the top. If you're interested in snowmobiling, the park also has designated areas for your use. On the western slopes, the ski area has a retail shop, rentals, waxing and repair services, and a learning center that provides lessons for all ages and skill levels. The trails interconnect, so you can create new paths and feel like you're skiing a much larger mountain. Relax in Pine Lodge and get hot chocolate from their ski-in restaurant. Mohawk Mountain State Forest is a huge destination in summer too (see "Hiking, Biking & Walking").

WOODBURY SKI AND RACQUET
785 Washington Rd.
Woodbury, CT 06798
(203) 263-2203
woodburyskiarea.com

In winter these 14 downhill trails are great for beginning and intermediate skiers. Snowboarders come for the 2 large half-pipes and a quarter-pipe. There's tubing and sledding, as well as cross-country trails, all of which are kept in snow throughout the winter by Woodbury's snowmaking equipment. Everything is lighted, and they are open until 10 p.m. most nights. In January a week-long extravaganza called the Winter Carnival brings tourists by the busload. In the warmer months, you can come here for the skateboarding park, the tennis courts, the pond swimming, the camping, the "sorba ball" tubing, and the concerts.

SKI SUNDOWN
126 Ratlum Rd.
New Hartford, CT 06057
(860) 379-SNOW
skisundown.com

With 15 very different trails and 4 chairlifts, this mountain usually moves quickly, with fast runs and few waits. Three of the trails, including the black diamond Gunbarrel Trail, are difficult enough for more experienced skiers. You can rent skis in their extensive rental shop, and you can wolf down some food in the cafeteria or relax in the lodge. They offer after-school rates and different packages that make this the perfect place for families with children. The night skiing here during the week has a lot of fans, with lighted trails. Sundown keeps the trails well groomed, and you'll seldom find the icy conditions that can be the bane of East Coast skiing.

Spectator Sports

✳LIME ROCK PARK
60 White Hollow Rd.
Lakeville, CT 06039
(860) 435-5000
limerock.com

Racing fans need no introduction to this famous track, hidden in the Litchfield Hills since 1957. The first road track designed using scientific principles (by Cornell Aeronautical Labs), Lime Rock is a 1.5-mile curving and up-and-down track that challenges drivers to increase their speed. You'll find NASCAR stock cars here, as well as dozens of other types of racing. Two additional complexes were added in 2008, which gave the track 4 different possible configurations; this change has made it even more popular among drivers and fans alike. Paul Newman used to race here often, and did quite well. One of the world's leading driver-training organizations, the Skip Barber Racing School, also practices on this track; to sign up for a class, call (860) 435-1300. Lime Rock is an exciting place to go, even if (or because) you've never watched a car race before.

SALISBURY SKI JUMP
80 Indian Cave Rd.
Salisbury, CT 06068
(860) 435-0019
jumpfest.org

Built in 1926, the Satre Ski Hill is the site of the oldest ski-jumping program in the nation. Today the wooden 55-meter jump has been replaced with a 65-meter steel jump and tower, built with money raised by volunteers from more than 500 donors. It is the site of the United States Eastern Ski Jumping Championships, and with the snowmaking technology now available, you can see people jumping here throughout the winter, even for the Junior Olympics. At other times of the year, the Salisbury Winter Sports Association runs other events, like a pig roast, a hot chocolate social, and a golf tournament. And for those of you 6 and older who would like to learn how, they run a ski-jumping school here every winter. If that sounds like fun, you are braver than I am.

Water Sports

BURR POND
Mountain Road
Torrington, CT 06790
(860) 482-1817
ct.gov/dep [search "Burr Pond"]

This is a great swimming area, practically on top of a mountain but with a sandy beach and picnic grove. From May to Labor Day you can park for a small fee right by the beach and dive into this cool lake. The lake (really a very large pond) is small and shallow but perfect for canoeing. You can bring a motorboat here, but you're probably better off taking it to one of the big lakes. The launch is west of the entrance, or during summer you can rent a canoe or paddleboat. The lake is stuffed with largemouth bass, and you can fish from shore to catch them. In wintertime the lake freezes over, and you can ice fish for perch and pickerel.

NORTH AMERICAN WHITEWATER EXPEDITIONS
Bull's Bridge Inn
333 Kent Rd.
Kent, CT 06757
(860) 927-1000
nawhitewater.com/OutdoorAdventure/directions

If you're in the Litchfield Hills in April, you should not miss the exciting opportunity to raft the Housatonic. During spring runoff the gorge by the old covered Bull's Bridge becomes a Class V rapids. North American Whitewater Expeditions was the first company to attempt to take eager rafters down these rapids, and they are still doing it. During the rest of the year, the gorge is mostly dry, since the nearby canal takes most of the water. But for this month only, these might be the most challenging rapids to raft in all of New England. The trip is 8 miles and usually takes about 3 hours. The $90 price includes a snack and dinner at the Bull's Bridge Inn afterwards (see entry), where you'll enjoy a great meal and talk excitedly about the amazing scenery and adrenaline-pumping rapids.

✳SATAN'S KINGDOM FARMINGTON RIVER RAFTING
92 Main St.
New Hartford, CT 06057
(860) 693-6465
farmingtonrivertubing.com
170 Main St. (Route 44)
New Hartford, CT 06057
(860) 693-6791
mainstreamcanoe.com

In the 1700s this rugged country was the retreat of various criminals and other outcasts from Hartford society. Now it is a playground for mild whitewater recreation. There is a parking lot right next to the river on Route 44, where you'll see the sign that says Satan's Kingdom. Make sure you wear or bring appropriate clothing, because you're going to get wet. You can go through the Farmington River Tubing company, which will give you a life jacket and sit you in a large tube to glide downriver for 2.5 miles through some mild rapids, a great family activity. But if you prefer something more challenging, try Main Stream Canoe and Kayak, which will set you up to boat through some quick water and Class I–II rapids, a 3- to 4-hour trip.

TWIN LAKES
O'Hara's Landing Marina
254 Twin Lakes Rd.
Salisbury, CT 06068
(860) 424-3000
oharaslanding.com

Set in the far northwest corner of the state, the Twin Lakes in Salisbury is a great fishing destination, with huge brown trout hiding at the bottom of the lake. Go to O'Hara's Landing Marina, where you can launch your own boat or use one of their canoe, pontoon boat, or powerboat rentals. Fishing, waterskiing, or the now-popular water-tubing are fun options, but you can't rent that equipment, so bring it yourself or buy it at the shop. The marina also has a restaurant open in summer, serving breakfast and lunch.

SHOPPING

Antiques

COLLINSVILLE ANTIQUES COMPANY OF NEW HARTFORD
283 Main St. (Route 44)
New Hartford, CT 06057
(860) 379-2290
collinsvilleantiques.com

Although the name is Collinsville, a town in Hartford County, this huge multi-dealer antiques shop is not in that historic district but up the road on Route 44, about halfway between Canton and the "downtown" of New Hartford in Litchfield County. They moved to this huge building in 2006 and even have a restaurant inside the shop. There's outdoor seating on a 60-foot deck, wheelchair access, air-conditioning, and an enormous parking lot. They need it, because this route to the Litchfield Hills from Hartford is popular, and many browsers stop to explore the antique delights inside. About 50 dealers are represented here; you're sure to find something you like.

LYME REGIS LTD.

43 N. Main St.
Kent, CT 06757
(860) 927-3330
lymeregisltd.com

This interesting antiques store was originally in NYC's South Street Seaport before moving to Kent in 1999. They sell metalware, jewelry, books, pottery, paintings, and porcelain. But what you should really come to Lyme Regis for are the curiosities. You never know what new fascinating piece will be here, from an antique leather-and-brass dog collar to a dice game made of bone. The store is named for the beautiful seaside town of Lyme Regis in England, where in the 19th century collectors hunted for ammonites, which were plentiful there. And indeed, you'll find some of those fossils here at Lyme Regis Ltd. in Kent. Or perhaps you'll find your own special kind of curiosity to collect.

MILL HOUSE ANTIQUES AND GARDENS

1068 Main St. North
Woodbury, CT 06798
(203) 263-3446
millhouseantiquesandgardens.com

You're in for a treat when you push open the wide planked wooden door into Mill House Antiques and Gardens along Route 6 in Woodbury. Yes, their gardens are so nice they are practically an attraction themselves. Located in an 18th-century gristmill and specializing in 18th- and 19th-century pieces, this unique antiques store brings in an international clientele. Their most impressive collection is oak, walnut, yew, and mahogany furniture, including highboys, lowboys, tables, dressers, and desks. They also have a good collection of clocks, objets d'art, and chandeliers. There are 17 showrooms to explore here, as well as the beautiful gardens.

R. T. FACTS ANTIQUES

22 S. Main St.
Kent, CT 06757
(860) 927-5315
rtfacts.com

R. T. Facts Antiques carries unusual pieces of all sorts, and a search in this shop in downtown Kent will lead you in unexpected directions. Mid-20th-century craft furniture and decorative pieces abound: lamps, tables, benches, clocks, statues, sinks, paintings, and more. Facts specializes in garden and architectural pieces, and if you need a classy sculpture for your lawn, this is the place to get one. They also have great lanterns and mirrors here. R. T. Facts is open only on weekends, although you can call ahead and they'll be there for you on a weekday.

*THOMAS SCHWENKE ANTIQUES

50 Main St. North
Woodbury, CT 06798
(203) 266-0303
schwenke.com

This is one of the best places in the US to get Federal-era furniture, a reminder of the flowering of American democracy from 1785 to 1820. Thomas Schwenke himself has over 40 years of experience in the field and is an acknowledged authority on American antique furniture, routinely consulted on Federal-era pieces in particular. You'll explore the period barns with their exposed beams, and find antique dining tables, desks, chairs, sofas, mirrors, and sideboards. Look for the sense of proportion, scale, and line in these functional but decorative pieces, along with inlays and carvings. And if you can't afford the actual pieces, Schwenke has an exclusive American Federal Classics line of handmade replica furniture based on the finest originals.

Auctions & Flea Markets

ELEPHANT'S TRUNK FLEA MARKET

490 Danbury Rd.
New Milford, CT 06776
(508) 265-9911
etflea.com

Set against the backdrop of a large hill above Route 7, this flea market is big and busy, and one of the largest outdoor markets in the state since 1976. There are parking spaces for 1,000 vehicles, and you might see most of those filled on a busy day. The many dealers in the 50-acre field will bargain with you, and since it only costs $2 to get in, you're bound to make that back pretty quickly with the treasures you'll find. Dealers here have glassware, vintage and new tools, vintage clothing, coins, decoys, old and new books, antique toys, collectibles, antique furniture, Depression glass, jewelry, pewter, electronic equipment, baseball cards, and more. And best of all, they kick out vendors who deal in counterfeits or knockoffs, with much better oversight than most flea markets. During summer and fall you can find fresh vegetables and fruit, along with a variety of plants and shrubs.

LITCHFIELD COUNTY AUCTIONS

425 Bantam Rd. (Route 202)
Litchfield, CT 06759
(860) 567-4661
litchfieldcountyauctions.com

This unpretentious low warehouse building on the side of Route 202 just west of Litchfield proper doesn't seem like it would house some of the best auctions this side of Manhattan. But it does. Started in 1994, this 10,000-square-foot auction house regularly holds impressive estate sales, usually racking up over $1 million in one night. Owners Nicholas and Weston Thorn sell antique furniture, books, and fine art, and here that means names you'll recognize. They also do appraisals. If you want to see items go for thousands of dollars regularly, come for one of their major sales, which happen five times a year.

WOODBURY'S FAMOUS ANTIQUE AND FLEA MARKET

44 Sherman Hill Rd. (Route 64)
Woodbury, CT 06798
(203) 263-6217
thenewwoodburyfleamarket.com

Woodbury has a couple nice dealers of its own, but this is the weekly event that has made the town a hub of antiques frenzy on every Saturday from Apr to Dec for the last 40 years. In 2008 this event changed hands (they now refer to it as "new"), and there is space for up to 42 antiques vendors to sell their goods at once. This fun venue is a wonderful place to find a bargain among the mix of antiques and junk. Or you can work a little to make one—there are always negotiations going on here. Late in the day you'll probably have better luck when dealers get desperate and sunburned. Breakfast and lunch are served.

Books

BANK STREET BOOKSTORE

50 Bank St.
New Milford, CT 06776-2706
(860) 354-3865
bankstreetbooks.com

New Milford's little independent bookstore crams a lot onto its beautiful solid wood bookcases. By only carrying a couple copies of any given title at any time, owner Janet Olsen Ryan can fit more inside. They have a great children's section and schedule story time for kids as well. This is definitely a place for browsing; there are no chairs to sit in here, but that's all right. You're probably on your way north to the wonders of Litchfield County, and you can read the book on the porch of your bed-and-breakfast or in front of a roaring fire. They will even gift wrap your purchase for free. And apparently, though it seems difficult to believe in this day and age, the employees of Bank Street actually read the books.

BARBARA FARNSWORTH BOOKSELLER

407 Route 128
West Cornwall, CT 06796
(860) 672-6571
farnsworthbooks.com

Barbara Farnsworth was once a writer herself, and she knows books. Her charming shop is in a former Masonic hall in West Cornwall, once home to writers James Thurber and Mark Van Doren. The shop, only open on Saturday, houses 45,000 books on literature, biography, poetry, diaries and letters, art, architecture, photography, fashion and costume, and natural history, as well as cookbooks and children's books. The biggest selection is in horticulture and landscape design. Check this place out, along with Cornwall Bridge Pottery and the covered bridge, a short walk away (see entries).

HICKORY STICK BOOKSHOP

2 Green Hill Rd.
Washington, CT 06794
(860) 868-0525
hickorystickbookshop.com

This independent bookstore in a brick building at the crossroads of Washington Depot is a classic, with a fantastic selection of new books and classics you won't find in the big chains. They are famous for their frequent book signings, even on Sunday afternoons. Hickory Stick's owner, Fran Kilty, does the new book buying but takes recommendations from customers and staff. She also has a hand-picked music section, a huge children's section, cards, clothing, Vera Bradley bags, games, and puzzles. They get a lot of local support from some of the exclusive nearby private schools and partner with local libraries for events. Dense with quality books, this is a community bookstore in every sense of the word.

HOUSE OF BOOKS

10 N. Main St.
Kent, CT 06757
(860) 927-4104
hobooks.com

If you're in Kent looking for books, this bookstore in an old home is a great place to nose around. They have books on art, literature, history, and biography, as well as trail guides for Appalachian Trail hikers, a literal vault filled with children's books, and gifts and CDs. One of the draws (so to speak) is the nook of art supplies, for the many artists who visit the scenic Litchfield Hills and those who make their home here. You should also check out the famous Kent Library book sale, which spills onto the sidewalks near the town center every sunny weekend in summer.

Clothing

R. DERWIN CLOTHIERS
7 West St.
Litchfield, CT 06759
(860) 567-0100
rderwinclothiers.com

Right off the beautiful Litchfield green across from the iconic church, the dignified front of R. Derwin Clothiers has been a fixture in town for 20 years. Consistently rated one of the best men's and women's clothing stores in the state, it was founded by Richard Derwin and is run by his son, Jonathan, and his wife, Andrea. It brings sophistication to the village; stores like this are the reason that Connecticut's rural areas feel completely different than, say, Pennsylvania's. They are open weekdays from 10 a.m. to 5:30 p.m., Sat until 6 p.m., and Sun noon to 5 p.m. A number of events year-round are sponsored by or at the store; check their website.

Home & Crafts

BANTAM TILEWORKS
816 Bantam Rd. (Route 202)
Bantam, CT 06750
(860) 361-9306
bantamtileworks.com

The old World War II switch factory on the side of Route 202 by the Bantam River has been mostly converted into shops for various artists and artisans. The most significant of these is the Bantam Tileworks, where you will find co-owners Travis and Darren in their smocks, working hard on the latest job. On the bottom floor of the factory, underneath heavy wood beams, they create beautiful plates and platters, tiled tables, fronts for fireplaces, and tiles for kitchens, baths, and other floors. Just the samples scattered on the walls seem like decorative Roman mosaics, pieces of art worthy of hanging in your own house. This small workshop is the premier place in the state to find tiling.

CORNWALL BRIDGE POTTERY
415 Sharon Goshen Tpke.
West Cornwall, CT 06796
(860) 672-6545
cbpots.com

Just south of the famous covered bridge, you'll see a red barn that houses the workshop of Todd Piker, who since 1974 has made pots for well-known clients. He welcomes visitors to watch as he and his apprentices turn clay into beauty and function. You never know what you'll see here, so call ahead if you want to see the potters at the wheels or at work at the long wood-fired kiln. In the village the store selling these wonderful pots and bowls is just back through the bridge to the east. These are investments too; everyone agrees that Piker's work will be worth tons of cash by the time your grandchildren inherit it.

WOODBURY PEWTER OUTLET
860 Main St. South
Woodbury, CT 06798
(800) 648-2014
woodburypewter.com

The family-owned-and-operated Woodbury Pewter was founded in 1952, and the factory outlet store here has been selling the business's factory seconds (and firsts!) since then. These amazing pewter pieces are handcrafted using the same tools and methods that were used by our ancestors, spinning, casting, and finishing. This company is renowned for its authentic and high-quality pewter, and after you see it, you'll know why. These aren't those pieces you'll find at the corner gift shop or at the local Renaissance Faire. You can also get other pewter from around the world at the outlet, but why would you want to do that, when you're right here in Woodbury itself?

Outdoors

CLARKE OUTDOORS

163 Route 7
West Cornwall, CT 06796
(860) 672-6365
clarkeoutdoors.com

Clarke Outdoors runs rafting expeditions on the Housatonic River and gives kayak lessons as well. They also have a rental service that allows you to paddle or raft a 10-mile section of the Housatonic, with shuttle service that drops you off upriver in Falls Village. You make your way back to Housatonic Meadows State Park, perhaps stopping for a picnic lunch at the covered bridge in West Cornwall on your way. This is also a retail store with a huge selection of canoe and kayak equipment, perhaps the best you'll find. The employees are all experts and will steer you toward the right boat, guidebooks, and accessories to make your expedition a success.

HOUSATONIC RIVER OUTFITTERS

24 Kent Rd.
Cornwall Bridge, CT 06754
(860) 672-1010
dryflies.com

You might wonder that there are two outdoor stores so close to each other on Route 7, but you shouldn't. This area of the Litchfield Hills is an outdoorsperson's paradise. And the competition means that you might even get a bargain. Still, these two stores have different focuses, with Housatonic River Outfitters selling fishing equipment, outdoor clothing, and camping equipment. They also do fly tying on-site. This is a great place to stop before camping at Housatonic Meadows State Park. Buy your license and choose from among 50,000 flies. The outfitters also arrange guided float trips on the river.

Specialty Foods

*BANTAM BREAD COMPANY

853 Bantam Rd.
Bantam, CT 06759
(860) 567-2737
bantambread.com

Off the side of Route 202 just past Litchfield, by a small river park, the Bantam Bread Company maintains its humble quarters in the back of what appears to be a nicely kept house. The smell of baking bread draws you past bright pansies to a small shop with cheese and jams, donuts and cookies, pies and pastries. Olive oil waits "on tap," and chocolate, honey, and maple syrup are available. But it is the rich, multigrain loaves, the caraway ryes, and the oat breads that made this small destination in the Litchfield Hills famous. You can find these delicious breads at any local event of merit, or you can simply visit the BBC's shop on your next trip to the hills. They're considered by some to be one of the top 10 bakers in America. Their sourdough is my favorite ever.

MATTHEWS 1812 HOUSE

250 Kent Rd. South
Cornwall Bridge, CT 06754
(800) 662-1812
matthews1812house.com

Once a small home business in the kitchen of her 1812 house, Deanna Matthews's operation has grown from its origins (in 1979) into a huge gourmet production. She and her team now bake cakes, cookies, brownies, candies, and sauces, all made on the premises in small batches with natural ingredients to ensure quality. The Matthewses run a thriving online and catalog business shipping these goodies all over, with 165,000 catalogs printed each year. But if you're in the Litchfield Hills Mon through Fri from 9 a.m. to 5 p.m., you can stop at their shop (at the factory itself) 2.5 miles south of Cornwall Bridge on Route 7. Save yourself the shipping charges, and get the Cookies Deluxe Tin for your favorite travel guide writer, please.

NODINE'S SMOKEHOUSE
65 Fowler Ave.
Torrington, CT 06790
(860) 489-3213
nodinesmokehouse.com
The smell as you approach Nodine's Smokehouse in Torrington is just sinful. Your mouth will water and your stomach will rumble. And the sight inside the shop attached to the smokehouse will make any meat lover cry with joy. Along with all the hams and bacons and beefs you'd expect, they smoke pheasant, deer, and even alligator here. The venison summer sausage is particularly delicious, with a hint of rich gaminess mixed with a beefy flavor. Try the apple-smoked bacon, which has earned national recognition and fills my house with beautiful smells every Sunday. Nodine's has been making their custom-smoked meats since 1969, and they are featured in some of New York City's most respected stores. Come here and get these tasty treats right from the original store.

Toys

PLAY
49 Bank St.
New Milford, CT 06776
(860) 355-2134
iloveplaytoys.com
Growing up is overrated. That's what the owners of this charming shop on New Milford's charming main street say, and their customers agree. Of course this is a great place to shop for children's toys, but you'll find fun stuff for everyone, including retro toys we older folks will remember, books, jewelry, games, art, candy, magic tricks, and other novelties. It's a place for wide-eyed kids and cynical collectors. They'll wrap your

gifts for you, and you'll find something for everyone you know in this unique store—a tin lunch pail, a fake mustache, a USB gizmo, and more.

i The Litchfield Hills is such a popular destination that it has its own travel bureau. Go to litchfieldhills .com or call (800) 663-1273.

ACCOMMODATIONS

All lodgings have both smoking and non-smoking rooms unless otherwise noted, or have a designated smoking area, and do not accept pets unless noted. Hotels, motels, and resorts are wheelchair accessible unless otherwise noted. Bed-and-breakfasts and inns are not wheelchair accessible unless otherwise noted, since many are in historic buildings exempt from the Americans with Disabilities Act. Call to make sure if there's any question. We do not list specific credit cards in either this section or the restaurants section.

Bed-and-Breakfasts

CATHEDRAL PINES FARM $$$$
10 Valley Rd.
Cornwall, CT 06753
(860) 672-6747
cathedralpinesfarm.com
After a long drive through fenced meadows, you'll reach a house on a hillside with a view of this hanging valley on the Mohawk plateau. This 18th-century-style farmhouse with big wood beams on the ceiling of the kitchen is owned by the Calhoun family, which has lived in Litchfield County since 1740. It is also one of the oldest llama farms in New England, starting in 1977. There's a relaxing greenhouse porch and a house full of period antiques that has been featured in several magazines. But for many the attraction is watching llama babies frolic in the

pasture just outside. Two rooms, each with private bath, are available. If you're tall, make sure to ask for the room with a higher ceiling. After blueberry pancakes in the morning, walk down the road and up the blue trail into the forest, where you'll see the Cathedral Pines, an old-growth stand of high white pines. Unfortunately many were knocked down by a tornado in 1980.

CHAPIN PARK BED AND BREAKFAST $$
45 Church St.
Pine Meadow, CT 06061
(860) 379-1075
chapinparkbandb.com

This old Victorian house is located on the Chapin Park Green in the historic section of New Hartford, within walking distance of the Farmington River and 5 minutes from hiking. Built in 1871, today this B&B is chock-full of wonderful pieces, including carved black walnut relief-sculpted faces and white marble fireplaces. Four simple, unfussy rooms with private baths are available, as are cookies in the evening and a choice of breakfast according to your wishes, like potato casserole with scrambled eggs and bacon, caramel french toast with sausage links, or feta and spinach brunch bake. Apple cheddar bread, cranberry orange scones, pumpkin spice coffee cake . . . they know how to set a spread. They have a number of packages to choose from for all interest areas—skiing, golf, and even quilting.

THE HOMESTEAD INN $$–$$$$
5 Elm St.
New Milford, CT 06776
(860) 354-4080
homesteadct.com

Built in 1853, the Homestead Inn was originally a house and became an inn with a restaurant and rooms in 1928. Today the restaurant is gone, having been converted to rooms and leaving a nice bed-and-breakfast at the gateway to the Litchfield Hills. The prices for the 14 rooms vary widely, depending on the size of the room and whether it is a single or double occupancy. Famous guests have included Vladimir Horowitz and NY senator Charles Schumer. Well-behaved pets are allowed to stay here for a fee of $10 a night. During the high months of May to Oct, the Homestead Inn (like many Connecticut B&Bs) requires a 2-night minimum stay for Friday and Saturday nights.

THE MANOR HOUSE $$$$
69 Maple Ave.
Norfolk, CT 06058
(866) 542-5690
manorhouse-norfolk.com

This Bavarian Tudor–style 1898 house in Norfolk has been a bed-and-breakfast since the 1980s. With its stone walls, Adirondack chairs, and wood beam ceilings and paneling, this is a little different from the Victorian cottages you often find as B&Bs. Each guest room is unique, and each has different amenities like balconies, whirlpools, or fireplaces; ask for more details about each before making a reservation. The Victorian Room is the most striking, with a king-size sleigh bed, a gas fireplace, and a 2-person whirlpool with a skylight right in the bedroom. They now offer massage services, and if you see a show at the nearby Infinity Music Hall, they'll take 10 percent off your bill. The Tiffany windows in the dining room are among a hundred other great details that put this establishment a step above most nights in the country.

MARY STUART HOUSE BED AND BREAKFAST $$
160 Sharon Tpke.
Goshen, CT 06756
(860) 491-2260
marystuarthouse.com

With simple rooms that might remind you of childhood, or your own bedroom at home, this bed-and-breakfast echoes the great tradition of the business. In the days before super hotels, when the local inns filled up, people simply let you stay in an extra room of their home for a fee, serving you breakfast before you went on your way. The owner, Mary Stuart Orlando, continues this tradition with her 5 rooms (one has a private bath and Jacuzzi). The screened-in porch is perfect for the buggy months. There's a fireplace, to be sure, but this is more truly a place to become part of someone else's life and home, for a little while, before heading on your busy way.

MOUNTAIN VIEW INN $$$$
67 Litchfield Rd.
Norfolk, CT 06058
(860) 542-6991
mvinn.com

This award-winning Gilded Age bed-and-breakfast on a scenic road south of Norfolk has been serving guests for over 50 years. It has 7 unique rooms and a guest house with a full kitchen and living room, as well as the bedroom and bath. Located across the road from the Norfolk Chamber Music Festival, the Mountain View is the perfect place to stay in the northern hills. Inside, there's an art gallery with original paintings by Dean Johnson and other artists and a vintage boutique gift shop. On Saturday and Sunday mornings you'll find a complimentary mimosa waiting for you. Have it on the wide porch, and then stroll into one of the loveliest villages in Connecticut.

ORANGE GILD BED AND BREAKFAST $$$$
137 Nichols Hill Rd.
Washington, CT 06793
(860) 868-9636
orangegild.com

In sleepy Washington, this new B&B has taken a New England saltbox house and infused it with a modern European spa on the inside. The 2 guest rooms are huge, with king beds and all the amenities you could hope for. The unique flavor of the place comes in the breakfast, with Dutch specialties like poffertjes, spekpannenkoek, or krentenbollen. Then comes the luxury—they have a "wellness area" that includes a traditional Finnish sauna, an infrared sauna, and a Turkish sauna. I suggest you bring a swimsuit. All those "extras" are included in your stay, which makes the slightly expensive price suddenly understandable. You can pay extra, if you like, for massages or manicures from local experts, or for painting and flower-arranging workshops from the amazing owners.

ROCK HALL LUXE LODGING $$$$
19 Rock Hall Rd.
Colebrook, CT 06021
(860) 379-2230
19rockhallroad.com

This 10,000-square-foot manor house built in 1912 is a Mediterranean Revival masterpiece. They have massage services and a fitness room, tennis court, billiard room, Jacuzzi, and 75-foot pool. There are only 4 rooms here, so you basically have all that to yourself. That limited number of rooms is the only reason this is not listed as a resort, because it certainly has all the amenities of one. Your breakfast is a Mediterranean delight, and in the afternoons the staff will make you fabulous cocktails at the pool. Don't miss the trees on the property; there are some rare and wonderful specimens to delight any botanist. You can also walk through the 100-year-old apple orchard or use the private screening room.

7C HERB GARDEN BED AND BREAKFAST $$

210 Baldwin Hill Rd.
New Preston, CT 06777
(860) 868-7760
7cherbgarden.com

If you're looking a different kind of lodging experience, one that takes you back to the true origins of the bed-and-breakfast, try 7C Herb Garden. Located in New Preston off Route 202, the restored 1730s house offers 2 rooms (one is a suite), both with private entrance and bathroom. But the real draw of this small establishment is the hospitality as your hosts, Alicia and Hansel Collins, welcome you into their home. Outside is Alicia's garden, and she'll treat you to fresh chives in her breakfast omelets. Take a leisurely nap on the hammock, or take a book under the grand tree in the backyard. Wireless Internet is available, and children under 12 stay free. Hansel is an amazing wood carver, and you can admire and purchase his finely crafted spoons and kitchen utensils, cutting boards, napkin holders, and bowls.

STARBUCK INN $$–$$$

88 North Main St.
Kent, CT 06757
(860) 927-1788
starbuckinn.com

This charming house on the edge of Kent village was renovated in 2003, giving the center-hall Colonial air-conditioning and an updated decor. There are 5 rooms named for literary giants to choose from, all with private baths. Two have king beds, and all have cable TV and broadband ports. The real treat of this bed-and-breakfast is their afternoon tea, which includes homemade sandwiches, breads, pâtés, and a variety of dessert options. Breakfast is even more sumptuous. From here you can walk downtown to shop for antiques and eat dinner, all for some of the most reasonable prices you'll find in this high-traffic tourist area.

Hotels & Motels

IRON MASTERS MOTOR INN $$$$

229 Main St. (Routes 41 and 44)
PO Box 690
Lakeville, CT 06039
(860) 435-9844
innatironmasters.com

"Motor inn" no longer has the cachet it had in the 1920s, but this recently renovated lodge with 28 large rooms that open out onto the parking lot is a classic of its kind, with Ethan Allen furniture instead of the usual cheap stuff. In winter relax in the Hearth Room in front of a roaring fire, and in summer splash in the outdoor pool. Iron Masters is sufficiently set back from the road so you won't really hear the traffic, and the furniture and decor are a step above a typical motel. Dogs are permitted in 2 rooms, making this the perfect place to stop when traveling with your best friend. They serve a continental breakfast daily and in winter offer a ski package deal. Named for the iron industry that dominated these hills in early America and made cannons for Washington's army, this is a perfect spot from which to explore that amazing history.

THE LITCHFIELD INN $$

432 Bantam Rd. (Route 202)
Litchfield, CT 06759
(860) 567-4503
litchfieldinnct.com

Although at first you might think this is a Georgian manor outside Litchfield center, you will be staying at a modern hotel, albeit one with high ceilings and fairly formal furnishings. There are 30 rooms with private baths, 8 of them being "theme" rooms with king beds at a slightly higher price (don't worry, they aren't overdone). Try the Sherlock

Holmes Room and search for secret passages. Along with a daily continental breakfast, the Inn Between Tavern offers dinner daily and lunch on weekends. Unlike many older hotels, this one has wheelchair access, with 2 rooms (including a theme room) with wider doors.

THE ROCKY RIVER INN $$
236 Kent Rd.
New Milford, CT 06776
(860) 355-3208
therockyriverinn.com

Along the Housatonic River in New Milford, the Rocky River Inn has 36 rooms on 2 floors and offers a range of lodging opportunities. There is a variety of different rooms, from kings and doubles in standard, deluxe, or luxury versions, as well as several different kinds of suites. Some even have Jacuzzis. This is a modern hotel, not a colonial or Victorian one, and has great pet-friendly rooms and outdoor spaces, as well as being wheelchair accessible. The inn is near the Elephant Trunk Flea Market if you're out here for shopping, and Adrienne's award-winning restaurant is just a few steps away (see entry).

Inns

BLACKBERRY RIVER INN $$$
538 Greenwoods Rd. West (Route 44 West)
Norfolk, CT 06058
(860) 542-5100
blackberryriverinn.com

Tradition here at the Blackberry River Inn runs deep, more than two and a half centuries deep. A Georgian mansion with apple orchard, trout fishing in the Blackberry River, and hiking trails among its 27 acres, this mix of working farm and resort is the perfect place for a romantic overnight, or an entire week. They have 20 rooms, including 2 linked by a bath, perfect if you absolutely have to bring the kids along. The cottage is

a fully appointed version, with a king bed, whirlpool, and working fireplace. If your relaxation only comes after a workout, they also have tennis courts and a pool. In the daytime, relax in the hammock by the willow tree; in the evening you can sit with a glass of Cognac by the fireplaces in one of the common rooms, talking or reading, living the good life you thought only existed in movies.

FIFE 'N DRUM RESTAURANT, INN & GIFT SHOP $$$
53 N. Main St.
Kent, CT 06757
(860) 927-3509
fifendrum.com

Since 1973 this fine little yellow Victorian house with private baths has provided food and lodging in the center of downtown (such as it is) Kent. The prices are reasonable, especially in the off-season. There are 8 rooms; try the Oak Room with its huge overhead beams. The gift shop is extensive, and people stop in off the street to browse here. They also have a fine three-star restaurant that serves dishes like grilled lobster tail and butter-poached claws over forbidden black rice and a roast half-duck flambé, done tableside. The piano music in the evening is usually played by the owner himself.

HOPKINS INN $$
22 Hopkins Rd.
Warren, CT 06777
(860) 868-7295
thehopkinsinn.com

This 1847 inn serves as a central location in the Litchfield Hills, but Lake Waramaug is a destination itself. The inn has 11 rooms and 2 apartments available and features parlors and porches aplenty. The lake often features regattas and races, which you can watch from the private beach down the hill or from the chairs on the lawn. Certainly don't forget to stop in for a tasting at the winery next door. Serving breakfast, lunch, and dinner, the inn has a popular Austrian restaurant with some unique dishes, always surprisingly busy despite the rural location (see entry). Try to get a room overlooking the lake, but don't be disappointed if you don't. You'll see plenty of it while you're here.

MAYFLOWER GRACE INN $$$$
118 Woodbury Rd. (Route 47)
Washington, CT 06793
(860) 868-9466
gracehotels.com/mayflower

The Mayflower Grace Inn has been rated one of the top 35 hotels in the world by *Travel + Leisure* magazine. That's the world. Opened in 1992 on the site of one of Connecticut's countless private schools, the Mayflower and its luxury spa have become a destination for everyone who wants a little (or a lot of) pampering. The 30 guest rooms in 4 different buildings—the Mayflower House, the Speedwell cottage, the Standish cottage, and the Allerton cottage—are all uniquely appointed and provide different experiences, with touches like marble baths, feather-topped mattresses, and antique oriental rugs. The art on the walls is real. You should obviously eat at the fine restaurant while you're here (see entry), and don't forget the spa; try the eponymous Mayflower massage, which is geared to your specific needs, combining oils, Swedish and deep-tissue massage, reflexology, and more, all for the same price. The inn is not cheap, but it provides tons of amenities, including cross-country skis in winter and boots and umbrellas if it rains. When you walk wide-eyed into your room at the Mayflower, a single orchid will welcome you, signaling your choice to submit to one of the most luxurious experiences you'll have this side of heaven.

✳OLD RIVERTON INN $$$
436 East River Rd.
PO Box 6
Riverton, CT 06065
(860) 379-8678
rivertoninn.com

This Early American inn fronts the road across from the Farmington River and was a former stagecoach stop on the Boston-Albany Turnpike. It has been giving "hospitality for the hungry, thirsty, and sleepy" since 1796. The inn and the current innkeepers, Mark and Pauline Telford, are unpretentious and friendly, and a night here won't break your bank the way some in the Litchfield Hills will. The grindstone terrace is a wonderful addition, made of grindstones from Nova Scotia, once used in nearby Collinsville to grind axes. The Hobby Horse Bar is full of fly-fishing memorabilia, a tribute to the inn's most loyal customers. If you eat in the wonderful low-ceilinged restaurant, try the duck—it's the chef's specialty—and enjoy sitting in the old (and valuable) Hitchcock chairs. This has been voted the most romantic restaurant and inn in the area many times, and it is truly one of the treasures of Connecticut. My wife and I were married by the innkeeper here and enjoyed the inn's hospitality many times.

TOLLGATE HILL INN $$
571 Torrington Rd. (Route 202)
Litchfield, CT 06759
(866) 567-1233
tollgatehill.com

The 1745 Captain Bull Tavern is the centerpiece around which two other more modern buildings have been added to make a large inn. Set in a grove of white birch trees, the Tollgate has 20 rooms, with 5 suites among them that boast wood-burning fireplaces and extra sofa beds. Suite 9, located in the "schoolhouse" building, is a favorite among book lovers. The colonial furniture in the rooms might be reproductions, but the flavor of the entire place is genuine. The Mockingbird Kitchen and Bar is open for special events and parties, and lighter fare is served on the patio. Call to see if they are currently serving dinner in the historic tavern Thursday through Saturday nights, which depends on the season.

WAKE ROBIN INN $$$
106 Sharon Rd. (Route 41)
Lakeville, CT 06039
(860) 435-2000
wakerobininn.com

This inn was once the Taconic School for Girls, and you'll see little touches that remind you of that throughout the huge building on a hilltop well back from Route 41. Since 1914 Wake Robin has been welcoming guests, including the usual celebrities like Bette Davis and Douglas Fairbanks. The 23 rooms in the school building are all unique, with private baths, and were upgraded in 2002. There are also 15 less-expensive rooms in a motel-like building nearby, which is only open May through Oct. On-site is Michael Bryan's Irish Pub, where you can get a drink, and a dining room for a fine evening meal. Wake-robin is the common name for the trillium flower, which blooms every spring and heralds the arrival of all the birds. It's a great time to come to the Litchfield Hills.

Resorts

INTERLAKEN RESORT AND CONFERENCE CENTER $$$$
74 Interlaken Rd.
Lakeville, CT 06039
(800) 222-2909
interlakeninn.com

The original Interlaken Inn is in a Victorian bed-and-breakfast (with modern conveniences). But this popular destination has expanded, with duplex-style units with kitchens, 82 hotel rooms in a large building, and more. Set on 30 acres with 2 lakes, Interlaken features a restaurant, a pool, tennis, and more. Unlike most resorts in the state, dogs are allowed here. This is a popular conference site, but it's always jumping with families and couples as well. Take a canoe out onto Lake Wononscopomuc or play a round of golf on their chip-and-putt course. If you're in the mood to relax, they offer a full range of spa services, including facials, massages, and hot stone treatments. Or you might just sit in one of the ridiculously comfortable chairs by the lake and fall asleep.

✳WINVIAN $$$$
155 Alain White Rd.
Morris, CT 06763
(860) 567-9600
winvian.com

The main house of Winvian is a 1776 white clapboard that looks like others you can find throughout the state (though we shouldn't be so blasé about that fact). However, there are other lodging choices, like the Beaver Lodge cottage down by the pond, a treehouse cottage 35 feet in the air, and one called Secret Society, which is a mystery you'll have to discover for yourself. There are 17 cottages total, and you'll probably want to stay a night in each one. However, at these prices, that is unlikely. This is a resort steeped in opulence, but a simple, New England style of opulence that is comfortable rather than showy, with a stone hearth rather than a gilded fireplace. Don't miss their spa, which offers a full range of massages and skin treatments. If you want to be treated like Connecticut royalty, Winvian will make you the king or queen.

Camping

BLACK ROCK STATE PARK $
Route 6
Watertown, CT 06795
(860) 283-8088 (May through Sept)
ct.gov/dep [search "Black Rock State Park"]

This 439-acre park of pine and oak ledges, named for the dark rock around this part of the Naugatuck Valley, was once a popular haunt of Native Americans. Ninety-one open and wooded sites are open from Apr to Sept, with the sites in the 80s and 90s the most secluded, if you're looking for that. Black Rock Pond has a small beach and is always full of happy children. This is also a great place to hike, with its own trails as well as the Mattatuck Trail, which heads through the park to the northwest on its way to the White Memorial Foundation in Litchfield. Across Route 6 to the east and slightly up the road, the Mattatuck Trail heads back into the forest, and in 0.5 mile you'll reach the Leatherman Cave, one of many in Connecticut but probably the most impressive. Really not a cave at all but a collection of gigantic rocks leaning on a cliff, this spot was one of 34 that the strange character known as the Leatherman stopped at during the 365-mile circuit he made continuously through the state.

HOUSATONIC MEADOWS STATE PARK $
Route 7
Sharon, CT 06069
(860) 927-3238
ct.gov/dep [search "Housatonic Meadows State Park"]

The green sward of meadows on the west side of the Housatonic River is the setting for the 95 sites at this riverside campground. If you want to be right by the river, try to get one of the northernmost sites; if you want more privacy, the sites along the forested eastern edge of the upper section are best. This is a favorite of fly fishermen, who walk down the hill to the river to fish the Trout Management Area that extends down to Cornwall Bridge. Across the street, the Pine Knob Loop Trail heads sharply up the ridge to the Appalachian Trail for anyone who wants to burn off a few calories to make room for marshmallows. In the hotter months, this is a cool place to camp, along the river in the shadow of the Taconic Mountains. Though this is a state park and does not have the amenities of a private campground, there are several stores just south on Route 7 in Cornwall Bridge, where you can pick up all the supplies you need.

LAKE WARAMAUG STATE PARK $
30 Lake Waramaug Rd.
New Preston, CT 06777
(860) 868-0220 (seasonal)
ct.gov/dep [search "Lake Waramaug State Park"]

Staying at any of the inns or spas around the lake will cost you a few pennies, so camping here at one of the 77 sites is an inexpensive and fun way to see one of the prettiest lakes in Connecticut. Waramaug was the name of a chief from a local tribe who summered on this lake; hundreds of years later, people from New York and beyond come to do the same. Canoers and kayakers camp here and push off from the docks by the campground. There is a challenging golf course at the Lake Waramaug Country Club, and this is also a great bicycling hub, with kids and professionals making long loops around the lake. You'll actually want to get a site farther away from the water if you don't want to be disturbed by cars on this narrow but well-traveled route around the picturesque lake.

LONE OAK CAMPSITES $
360 Norfolk Rd.
East Canaan, CT 06024
(800) 422-2267
loneoakcampsites.com

This is a huge, fun, family campground with a lot of RV sites, but secluded tent sites are available from Apr 15 to Oct 15. Or you could lodge in one of their 40-foot trailers—complete with kitchen, bath, and bedroom—or the two-room cabin. There's a swimming pool for the kids, a lounge, and a camp store. With 500 sites spread over 250 acres, this is an enormous place that will take you days to explore by walking or biking around. Like most family campgrounds, Lone Oak runs scheduled activities and events; check their website for both children's and adult programs, including theater and day trips.

*MACEDONIA BROOK STATE PARK $
159 Macedonia Brook Rd.
Kent, CT 06757
(860) 927-3238
ct.gov/dep [search "Macedonia Brook State Park"]

This is my favorite place to camp in the state. The road twists up along Macedonia Brook, which descends through a "hanging valley" amid a bowl of ridges. The campsites stagger up through this high valley, shaded by large trees. Small trout splash in the book, and red-tailed hawks hover in the updrafts. It is a quiet place to camp, without traffic noise or the rowdiness you sometimes find at private campgrounds, and there are several choice tent sites by themselves along bends in the stream. They are obvious on the campground map available on the website, and you should go for them unless you are bringing a large family. The hiking here is good too, and you can do a loop around the entire park up along both eastern and western ridges, if you're so inclined. This is a great place to stay to go antiquing in Kent, but the real joy of it is the complete removal from anything even approaching civilization. You'll feel like you're in a world far away.

WHITE MEMORIAL FOUNDATION $
80 Whitehall Rd.
PO Box 368
Litchfield, CT 06759
(860) 567-0089 (May through mid-Oct)
(860) 567-0857 (mid-Oct through Apr)
whitememorialcc.org/campgrounds
.html

The White Memorial Foundation is a great place for quiet family camping in the absolute center of the Litchfield Hills. It offers 2 different areas for family camping: Point Folly and Windmill Hill. Point Folly is 47 sites on a peninsula out on Bantam Lake, a perfect place to canoe or fish from. The Windmill Hill sites are closer to the main road, but quieter and away from the hikers and birders during the day. The White Memorial Foundation also offers lodging in its large carriage shed for 60 people, but it is only used by large groups who rent it out for conferences and group activity. The foundation has a campground store and of course the nature museum and all the trails that people from around the state come here to enjoy. However, this is more like a state campground than a private one—a calm, pure camping experience.

RESTAURANTS

Please note that all Connecticut restaurants are smoke free, and all are required to be wheelchair accessible. Pets are not allowed inside most restaurants, but during the warmer months, there are plenty of restaurants with patio areas just right for your canine friend. Call ahead to make sure it's okay.

American & Modern

BOATHOUSE AT LAKEVILLE $$$
349 Main St.
Lakeville, CT 06039
(860) 435-2111
facebook.com/theboathouselakeville

With its rambling blue exterior and fire-places and dark wood inside, the Boathouse is a difficult restaurant to categorize. The main menu is American and Italian modern cuisine, with dishes like four-cheese ravioli and beer-braised baby back ribs. The half roasted crispy duck with citrus soy glaze is crunchy, fresh, and rich all at once. But if you're looking for Japanese sushi up here in the northwest corner, the Boathouse is also a great place; in fact, they have sushi rolls named for all the local private schools (it's a popular place for families to bring their kids). The locals love this place, and along with the Woodlands, it is a destination for everyone wanting a comfortable meal in a place that will soon seem like home.

BULL'S BRIDGE INN $$
333 Kent Rd. (Route 7)
Kent, CT 06757
(860) 927-1000
bullsbridge.com

This classic tavern right at Bull's Bridge in Kent is a casual, less-formal version of the New England country inn, perfect for families. Words like home-style, cozy, and friendly come to mind. It serves only dinner and Sunday brunch, with meat-and-potato meals and classic mid-20th-century entrees. However, the executive chef is a CIA (Culinary Institute of America) graduate and keeps these classic dishes from getting stale or boring. During winter, stop here for a hot (and probably alcoholic) drink by the fireplace before heading to your inn or hotel. In summer you'll find expert kayakers getting ready to head down Class V rapids in the gorge here, one of the most difficult

stretches in the state. You might also see a few bewildered-looking patrons in hiking clothes and beards. Don't worry; those are just Appalachian Trail thru-hikers poking their heads back into civilization.

*CAROLE PECK'S GOOD NEWS CAFE $$$
694 Main St. South
Woodbury, CT 06798
(203) 266-4663
good-news-cafe.com

Inconspicuous at the corner of a Woodbury shopping center, the Good News Cafe is legendary; it's always mentioned when someone asks about the best restaurants in the state. Owner Carole Peck is one of the forerunners of the local food phenomenon, and her menus feature organic, seasonal, farm-fresh food. Try the wild boar schnitzel or antelope meatballs if you're in the mood to experiment, or the grass-fed beef short ribs if you're not. Peck bakes her own loaves of country peasant bread; you should take one home with you for the next day. Outside, there are lawn sculptures; inside, a changing selection of art. But the art you're probably most interested in here is on your plate, at one of Connecticut's consistently delicious restaurants. If you're really adventurous, take a culinary tour of France with Carole.

*COMMUNITY TABLE $$$
223 Litchfield Tpke.
Washington, CT 06777
(860) 868-9354
communitytablect.com

This new restaurant based on locally grown, seasonal ingredients is already one of the state's finest. The beehive in the backyard, the communal table made from a 300-year-old black walnut tree, the building designed and built by local architects—everything shows an attention to detail that makes you know immediately that you are cared for. And food? Unbelievable stuff—simple but delicious—scallops and sprouts, duck breast and celery root, coconut milk and chicory . . . the combinations will surprise and delight you, and the presentation is perfect. The chef here worked at Noma in Copenhagen, Denmark, recently rated the world's top restaurant, and is one of our hopes that the honor may soon come to Connecticut.

MAYFLOWER GRACE INN $$$
118 Woodbury Rd. (Route 47)
Washington, CT 06793
(860) 868-9466
gracehotels.com/mayflower

The small restaurant at the luxurious Mayflower Grace Inn is as excellent as the rooms and spa. The changing menu focuses on fresh, seasonal food in traditional dishes done with a light touch of genius. The menu is kept small to focus better on the meals available, a smart move that doesn't overtax the chefs, who then put all their energy into perfecting seasonal delights. Try the game sausage and house-smoked salmon if they're still on the list. If you're there for Sunday brunch, the vanilla bean and ricotta pancakes have to be tasted to be believed. The award-winning wine cellar has plenty of choices to accompany your meal, including a few options from Connecticut wineries. You'll be eating on tables set with Limoges china, so try not to drink too much of the great wine and break something.

✳OLD RIVERTON INN $$$
436 E. River Rd.
PO Box 6
Riverton, CT 06065
(860) 379-8678
rivertoninn.com

Located along scenic Route 20 and within walking distance of the charming village center, the Old Riverton Inn is the quintessential Early American establishment. The dining room, with its rustic wood beams and pillars, is located on the downstairs floor of the historic 1796 inn. The atmosphere is intimate and charming, and dishes will give you a sample of traditional fare. Enjoy the fireplace in cooler months and the bay windows' ample light in the early evenings of summer. Favorites include duck, which is moist and rich, prepared with cherry chutney; the turkey dinner, with traditional fixings; and trout caught in the Farmington River just across the street. The chef usually prepares a pasta special, such as eggplant ravioli, and always uses fresh, local ingredients. If you're here fishing, they'll fry up your catch for dinner.

WEST STREET GRILL $$$
43 West St.
Litchfield, CT 06759
(860) 567-3885
weststreetgrill.com

The mirrored walls, wood paneling, and immaculate white tablecloths introduce you to the experience you'll have here in Litchfield's West Street Grill. Right off the green, this is by far the best choice for fine dining in the village, and the food will not disappoint. The intelligently limited menu allows the chef to focus on a handful of creative dishes. They will all look familiar on the menu, without any intimidating names, but are all done in a startling modern way, with twists and turns. Their lunch menu is a great deal for what you get here; try the pulled beef short rib sandwich with aged cheddar and espresso bean barbecue sauce, and then try not to beg for the recipe. This is a great place for celebrity watching too, especially at Sunday brunch.

*WINVIAN $$$$
155 Alain White Rd.
Morris, CT 06763
(860) 567-9600
winvian.com

Winvian's chef, Chris Eddy, worked with world-class chefs Alain Ducasse and Daniel Boulud, and you will find his New American fare right at the top of the food chain, so to speak. The menu is prix fixe, with little appetizers and in-between course tidbits that whet the appetite. The carte du jour changes here, but some of the wonders include parsnip soup, scallops in sunchoke puree, Long Island duck breast, and roast halibut. Though you will pay handsomely for the wonders that come to your plate, because the meal is prix fixe, you won't pay as much as you might otherwise. Everyone who has been there agrees that Winvian is everything it is cracked up to be.

THE WOODLAND $$$
192 Sharon Rd.
Lakeville, CT 06039
(860) 435-0578
thewoodlandrestaurant.com

This is the place people go for a fine meal after watching the races at Lime Rock Park. For years it was a local secret, off the Internet and off the culinary map, but recently the word has gotten out, thanks to some tongues loosened by the wonderful wine selection. The menu is diverse but consistent, with lots of nice fish and steak dishes, a couple Mexican choices, and a sushi menu that is always impressive (get one of the special rolls). Many locals come here for drinks and appetizers, which are creative and delicious. Try the key lime pie for dessert. This place is so good that others in the area have tried to imitate the unusual menu, with less spectacular and consistent success.

THE WOODWARD HOUSE $$$
4 The Green
Bethlehem, CT 06751
(203) 266-6902
thewoodwardhouse.com

This remote area of farmlands and forest offers some of the most pleasant driving in the state, and you couldn't have a better destination than the Woodward House. This fine-dining restaurant in a 1740 saltbox on Bethlehem Green is consistently recognized for its decor and service. Inside, the wainscoting and original handmade beams and nails will take you back to colonial times in Connecticut. Known as the Bird Tavern in the 1700s, the building itself went through various hands, having lives as a post office and an Underground Railroad stop. The dinners are traditional fare with a nice twist, like the sweet spring pea risotto or roasted baby beets in an avocado puree. Note that the Woodward only serves dinner from 5 to 9 p.m. and requires business casual attire. If you get the chance to go upstairs, check out the 12-foot barrel ceiling in the ballroom.

Austrian and German

THE ALPENHAUS RESTAURANT $$
59 Bank St.
New Milford, CT 06776
(860) 799-5557
alpenhausct.com

We usually think of German restaurants as old, but this one is nearly brand-new. The owner ran the nice little Café Europa in Brookfield but has now expanded and opened this bastion of authentic German cuisine. It has a quieter feel than East Side (Connecticut's most famous German biergarten) and is a more romantic place to take a date. The potato pancakes, the schnitzel, the spaetzle, the sauerbraten—all taste like they are straight from the Black Forest. Try stopping for lunch too; the sandwiches are amazing. German prosciutto with a fried egg on top? Bratwurst on a pretzel roll? Sign me up.

✳HOPKINS INN $$$
22 Hopkins Rd.
Warren, CT 06777
(860) 868-7295
thehopkinsinn.com

High on a hill overlooking Lake Waramaug, this beautiful old 1847 inn serves Austrian and American cuisine. A tank of live trout peeks at you from the barroom, ready for you to choose their fate as pan-fried trout meunière with demi-glace. Inside, weathered wood-plank walls and door, fireplaces, and woodstoves lend a rustic, colonial feel without being kitschy. The server comes around and offers delicious fried rösti potatoes and small fresh loaves of perfectly crusted bread. For your main course, you could try an Austrian specialty like Wiener schnitzel or, if you're in the mood for something different, veal kidneys Dijonaisse or sweetbreads Viennese. To accompany your meal, be sure to pick an Austrian Riesling or a local bottle from Hopkins Vineyard next door. If you're there in summer, sit on the wide stone porch underneath the huge iron chandelier, which gives off a glow that can be seen from across the lake.

Breakfast & Lunch

BANK STREET COFFEE HOUSE $
56 Bank St.
New Milford, CT 06776
(860) 350-8920
bankstreetcoffee.biz

Open until 6 or 7 p.m. most days, this adorable coffee shop in New Milford has a selection of places to sit: couches, booths, chairs, armchairs, and stools. You'll find the local hipsters perching on stools next to a grandmother in a lounge chair. Food selections include breakfast sandwiches and bagels, wraps and grilled cheese, along with specials like quiche. If you don't want coffee you can sample a large selection of bag and organic loose-leaf teas, hot cocoas, and smoothies. Oh, and they have one little bonus for the true coffee lover—coffee ice cubes for iced coffee. Why every serious coffee place does not offer this is a mystery.

DOTTIE'S DINER $
740 Main St. South
Woodbury, CT 06798
(203) 263-2545
dottiesdiner.com

"Got Donuts?" is Dottie's question to us, but of course if we are at Dottie's Diner, we do. It's hard to say which of the donuts are yummiest, but the cinnamon have been called the best in the country by *Gourmet* magazine. They will be so clearly superior to other donuts you've tried that you'll be hard-pressed to go back to those stale, sugary imitations in the local chain store. Dottie's other breakfast and lunch dishes are also done well, like their poached egg on toast or their Connecticut potpie stuffed with juicy pieces of chicken. The corned beef hash is spiced with thyme and cumin, and my wife claims the eggs Benedict here are the best she's ever had. This throwback diner has taken the food we all love and done it with just a bit more class, but for the same price. The kicker is the donut bread pudding, made with leftover cinnamon donuts from yesterday and topped with crème anglaise and berries. One note for donut lovers: These are the crusty, cakey kind of donut, not the light fluffy kind, just in case that is not your thing.

CHAIWALLA $
1 Main St.
Salisbury, CT 06068
(860) 435-9758
No website

Great for brunch, lunch, or just tea, Chaiwalla is an easy stop in the heart of Main

Street in Salisbury. The tearoom is cozy and beautifully decorated with signature antique pieces, providing a relaxing charm. Pastries and pies under glass domes on the sideboard invite the eye and tell the stomach to leave room for dessert. The menu is simple, and the emphasis is on homemade quality. Enjoy tomato pie and eggs Benedict for brunch. The real draw is the loose-brewed tea, and the selection is vast. Enjoy your pot of Darjeeling or chai, which simmers in its pot over a candle as you chat with friends or enjoy the newspaper or a book. You might run into a thru-hiker taking a break from the Appalachian Trail, which crosses Main Street nearby.

KELLY'S KITCHEN $
438 Main St.
Winsted, CT 06098
(860) 738-9828
kellyskitchen.net/breakfast

Kelly McCarthy's tagline is "where something good is always cooking," and she couldn't have found a better one for her little restaurant in downtown Winsted. She serves some amazing french toast and omelets, and the lunch wraps are always fresh and delicious. The bakery at Kelly's makes pastries and breads that they use for their sandwiches, as well as their own pie crusts (with new and inventive pies each day). Kelly's also serves dinner, but this is really a breakfast and lunch place. Of course, some people like breakfast food all day (available here), and who can blame them?

PASSIFLORA TEAROOM AND HERBAL APOTHECARY $
526 Main St.
PO Box 79
New Hartford, CT 06057
(860) 379-8327
passiflorateas.blogspot.com

This cafe and gourmet supply shop is a haven for locals, healthy eaters from Hartford, and tourists passing through on Route 44, right in the "downtown" of New Hartford (blink and you'll miss it). The 160 varieties of tea at Passiflora are the big draw, but try the innovative sandwiches and dishes made with local ingredients and no high-fructose corn syrup or additives. The quiche of the day is always a winner, and their organic grilled cheese melt is scrumptious. For those looking for a beverage other than tea, the smoothies are inventive and tasty. Passiflora supports other local businesses like Little Women's Kitchen and Planted Feather bakeries and gets their vegetables from Wild Carrot Farm (along with their own garden). Although not strictly vegetarian, the menu has plenty of options, and they will even make things vegan or gluten-free for you.

French

PASTORALE $$$
223 Main St.
Lakeville, CT 06039
(860) 435-1011
pastoralebistro.com

This charming French restaurant run by Karen Hamilton and Frederic Feveau (once the chef at the Birches) brought French cuisine to the far northwest of Connecticut. The colonial house it's located in has been painted sunny Provençal tones, and the food you'll get here will bring you straight to France itself. With positive reviews from the *New York Times* and *Bon Appétit,* Feveau did not get a swelled head. He maintains his steadfast devotion to great cooking, with classics like steamed mussels and steak and frites. You'll also find a few southern French dishes here, edging into Italian territory and taking it over with joie de vivre.

Ice Cream

ARETHUSA DAIRY STORE
822 Bantam Rd.
Bantam, CT 06750
(860) 361-6600
arethusafarm.com

It's tough to decide which section to put this entry in, since they have a farm, a restaurant, and the epic dairy store. You can visit the farm on Saturday from 12:30 to 2:30 p.m. (check the website), the home of 350 champion cows. The milk, cheese, yogurt, and ice cream are all for sale at the dairy store right on Route 202, once the village fire house. The ice cream is amazing. Last but not least, located in the former village general store next door at 828 Bantam Rd., Arethusa al tavolo (860-567-0043) is open Sat and Sun for lunch and Wed through Sat for dinner in summer (check website for other seasons). In addition to the great farm dairy products, you can get dishes like pan-roasted monkfish wrapped in speck (a cured meat), with lump crab, English peas, fingerling potatoes, chanterelles, and corn chowder broth.

S&S SWEET TREATS $
38 Main St.
Torrington, CT 06790
(860) 485-3935
downtowntreats.com

S&S Sweet Treats in downtown Torrington, only a few steps from the Nutmeg Ballet and the Warner Theater, is the best place in the area to get a hand-dipped Hershey's ice-cream cone, cup, or milk shake. The friendly staff will offer you 20 varieties of ice cream, along with Greek frozen yogurt, sorbet, chocolate pretzels, cake pops, and Italian ice. They even have sugar-free and gluten-free options. You can also stop in for lunch and get their delicious grilled cheese, garden salads, wraps, hot dogs, and two freshly made soups every day. Insiders' tip: Get your soup in the bread bowl.

Italian

UPPER CRUST $$
373 Litchfield Rd.
New Milford, CT 06776
(860) 350-0006
theuppercrustcucina.com

In this vintage home on a hill above US 202, they make northern Italian food, including delicious potato gnocchi with duck confit, porcini mushroom ragu, and shaved pecorino cheese, among other delights. But mostly the Upper Crust makes pizza. Unusual pizza. Pizza that might redefine your ideas about this common dish. Try the fig and prosciutto with Gorgonzola pizza, a mind-bending combination that sounds weird but makes so much sense on the plate that you'll wonder if this wasn't the original idea for pizza all those years ago, and we somehow just got sidetracked with our pepperonis and mozzarellas. The Upper Crust was once the stomping ground of Carole Peck (now the chef/owner of the Good News Cafe in Woodbury), and they have continued her high-quality traditions.

THE VENETIAN $$$
52 E. Main St.
Torrington, CT 06790
(860) 489-8952
thevenetianrestaurant.com

The finest Italian restaurant in Litchfield County for over 40 years, the Venetian is owned and operated by Michael DiLullo and his family, after he worked in restaurants in Rome and honed his craft. You'll find escarole, manicotti, spaghetti with meatballs, ravioli, roasted peppers with cheese—all classics, all done to garlicious perfection here. Pick up a bottle of their famous housemade salad dressing (for sale there), and if you're a chemist, try to figure out the ingredients at home. It's worth the trouble. There are a few dishes that are either updated, modern ones or forgotten classics from the old country, like the fire-grilled veal chop. It's hard to keep track of all that anymore. But what we shouldn't lose track of is how to appreciate great food. At the Venetian, you'll get a great lesson in that art.

THE VILLAGE RESTAURANT $$$
25 West St. (on the Green)
Litchfield, CT 06759
(860) 567-8307
village-litchfield.com

With Italian-influenced American dishes, the Village isn't breaking any new foodie ground here, but it serves excellent classic 20thcentury fare and is a great place for families in Litchfield. You'll see all the locals here. Get one of the comfortable high-backed booths and settle in for a hearty meal. The meat loaf (seriously) is excellent, and the poached mussels are a forgotten favorite. The Sunday a la carte brunch for a fixed price is a delicious bargain; you can stuff yourself with pancakes, omelets, and sausages. If you're in Litchfield in the evening, the taproom here is the place to hang out.

Mediterranean & Middle Eastern

JOHN'S CAFE $$$
693 Main St. South
Woodbury, CT 06798
(203) 263-0188
johnscafe.com

A trend in modern restaurants is not to be categorized and to offer a global mix of fascinating styles and dishes, as well as changing seasonally. With its seasonal menus and a bistro atmosphere, John's Cafe offers American food and dishes with enough Mediterranean hints to fall into this category, though some others might disagree. Expect fresh, surprising dishes like house-made gnocchi with smoked chicken or crispy soft-boiled organic Marans hen eggs with a warm spinach and bacon salad. John does an amazing job with profiteroles for both dinner (blue

crab and sweet corn in romesco sauce) and dessert (coffee ice cream with chocolate sauce and almonds). He is open to preparing the dishes with small twists, so feel free to suggest something to your server. John believes in making his food just the way you like it, in order to bring you the maximum pleasure. Fancy that.

OLIVA CAFE $$
18 E. Shore Rd.
New Preston, CT 06777
(860) 868-1787
olivacafe.com

Near the shores of Lake Waramaug, this Mediterranean cafe brings a little summer into Litchfield County. At first the white clapboard building looks like a typical country tavern, but there are touches that begin to bring you into the Straits of Gibraltar. Chef Aamar's food is, in fact, Moroccan in origin, though it often has more in common with New American, Food Network–friendly cuisine. The Moroccan eggplant with pecans, lemons, and mint is a great starter, as is the caramelized Bosc pear. There are pizzas (with twists) for the kids and traditional dishes like lamb tagine for the adults. Try the sautéed wild haddock or the sweet potato gnocchi. This is a breath of fresh Mediterranean air for tourists and locals alike.

Pubs & Taverns

GEORGE WASHINGTON TAVERN $$
20 Bee Brook Rd.
Washington Depot, CT 06794
(860) 868-6633
gwtavern.com

This beautiful, deep-red wood 1850 building by the Shepaug River greets you just north of Washington Depot's "town center" (don't blink). In summer the tavern has a flagstone patio open, and in winter there's a huge open fireplace indoors to keep everyone toasty and comfortable. The menu includes such American classics as chicken potpie, meat loaf, macaroni and cheese, fried oysters, chili, and George Washington's favorite cherry pie. Game and game birds are available in winter, soft-shell crabs in summer. After dinner, try the candy cane–infused vodka "George's Nightcap," a sweet treat. If you're there for Sunday brunch after a weekend at one of the nearby inns, try the eggs Benedict by the fireplace and read the Sunday funnies.

INFINITY BISTRO $$
20 Greenwoods Rd. West
Norfolk, CT 06058
(860) 542-5531
infinitybistro.com

Located at the historic opera house turned music hall, the polished wood floors and colorful piano-key designs on the walls make the Infinity Bistro a hip place to eat dinner in these hills full of colonial inns jam-packed with antiques. There's outdoor seating in the warmer months, and deals with the music hall if you want dinner and a show. The New American food is delicious and inventive. For an appetizer, try the lobster hush puppies, each a warm, crunchy delight, dipped in the homemade remoulade. Entrees include classics like pan-seared scallops or new dishes like basil and Parmesan crepes. Get Connecticut's Thomas Hooker beer on tap here (it goes especially well with the spice-rubbed pork chop). They use local farms for many of their products, trying to be as green as the paint on the music hall itself (you'll understand when you see it).

Road Food

COLLIN'S DINER $
100 W. Main St.
North Canaan, CT 06018
(860) 824-7040
collinsdiner.com

There is no lack of diners in Connecticut, but few of the classics remain. Not only is Collin's a genuine diner from way back (1941), it has been featured in numerous films and is on the National Register of Historic Diners. Marble counters brought from a bar in Texas, the metallic trailer shape, and the vintage sign will not disappoint those looking for an authentic experience. Since 1969 it has been owned by a Lebanese family, the Hamzys, and they have kept all the original diner dishes like Salisbury steak and spaghetti (you can even get a Fluffernutter here) and often add a few others like their Lebanese plate of hummus, loobi, tabouli, and mjedera. The latest generation, Ameen Abo-Hamzy, both a second lieutenant in the US Army and an English major from Norwich, began a poetry reading series at the diner in 1994 that has become a classic during Canaan's Railroad Days.

WHEN PIGS FLY $$
29 W. Main St.
Sharon, CT 06069
(860) 492-0000
hudsonvalleybbq.com

The tiny hamlet of Sharon, Connecticut, does not have room for too many restaurants; luckily it has a good one, perfect for a quick stop. The tiny and charming When Pigs Fly Southern BBQ serves excellent pulled pork sliders and a selection of dry-rubbed ribs. Their shoepeg corn pudding was an unusual treat in this part of the country, since our version of classic corn pudding is significantly different. Owner Bennett Chinn is from Atlanta, so it is understandable that he wants to bring us the tastes and flavors of his heritage, and of course "Southern BBQ" is a food institution. But how many great barbecue places does a state have to have before "Connecticut BBQ" is a viable label?

WOOD'S PIT BBQ & MEXICAN CAFE $$
123 Bantam Lake Rd. (Route 209)
Bantam, CT 06750
(860) 567-9869
woodspitbbq.com

The rusted pig on the old-fashioned sign will guide you to this unique eatery. Their Mexican food, especially the chimichanga, is good, and they serve chips and salsa instead of bread. But people usually come here for the blackened catfish, jerk chicken, brisket, and beef and pork ribs. The toasted rolls hold up to the pulled pork and beef, and don't be shy about adding extra barbecue sauce—a sweet and spicy version whose recipe is a secret. Owner "Woodie" traveled around the US with a motorcycle and tent to learn his craft, and he has perfected it. Decades later Woodie is still at it 7 days a week, a man who cares about authenticity. The restaurant has a surprising mix of patrons: anglers and families, motorcycles and minivans. They actually have a vegan and vegetarian page on the menu, so this is a perfect place for a family that can't agree on their feelings about meat. Beer lovers should try the local Farmington River Brown Ale on draft. Right next door is the Bantam Cinema, a red barnlike building that shows independent films. You won't believe such a place still exists.

Seafood

LITCHFIELD SALTWATER GRILLE $$$
26 Commons Dr. (Route 202)
Litchfield, CT 06759
(860) 567-4900
litchfieldsaltwatergrille.org

Litchfield County isn't exactly a seaside resort; its appeal is entirely different. But at least one restaurant up here is dedicated to bringing fresh fare from the sea to diners spending time in the hills. If you have a large (more than 2) group, get one of the seafood towers for an appetizer. The oysters here are expertly shucked, and the clams are never

rubbery and overdone. Try their pasta with meat from Nodine's Smokehouse in nearby Goshen or the surprising Shrimp Olvera, with lobster sauce and a grilled artichoke. If you're really hungry, on their lounge menu is the so-called big chowder supper with mashed potatoes, steamed clams, bacon, and sourdough toast. It's like a meal for the early settlers of this hill town, hundreds of years ago. Perhaps you won't be clearing the land of trees for your farm, but you're probably working hard enough to deserve this. Try one of their signature cocktails before or after dinner; the Saltwater Grille knows how to do them right.

DAY TRIP IN LITCHFIELD COUNTY

Driving the roads of Litchfield County is a joy unto itself. Be prepared for a longer drive today, but also be prepared to see some of the most beautiful scenery in America. Start on Route 8, the cable that brings traffic to Litchfield from the south. Take exit 42 and head west on Route 118 (East Street) to Litchfield, stopping to take photos of the iconic church and the green. If there's an event that day, you may want to stop; but you do have a lot to see, and you're probably hungry for breakfast.

If so, stop for croissants at the Bantam Bread Company at 853 Bantam Rd. west of Litchfield (860-567-2737). To get there, you will go straight through town, though the road changes to West Street and Route 202. After stopping here, continue west on Route 202 toward New Preston, taking a right on Route 341 (Woodville Road), and in a short while a left on Route 45 (Lake Road). This will take you to Lake Waramaug, where you'll turn right on North Shore Road.

If you are in the mood for a morning wine tasting and/or want a bottle for later that night, take a quick right on Bliss Road and again up Hopkins Road, where you'll

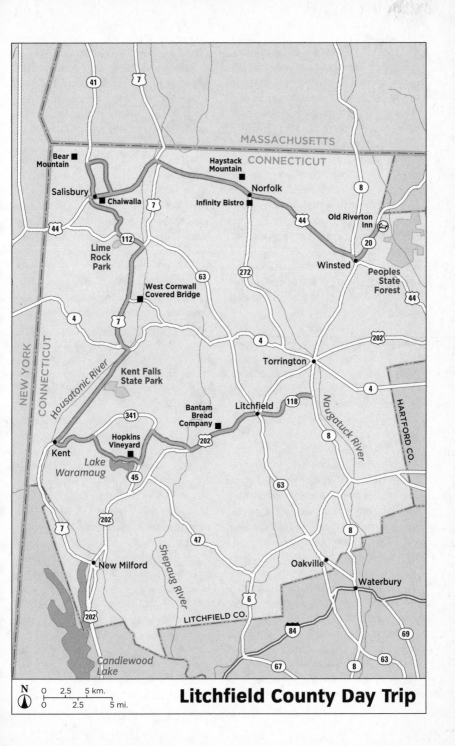

Litchfield County Day Trip

find Hopkins Vineyard, one of the best in the state (860-868-7954; hopkinsvineyard .com). They open at 10 a.m., so if you're an early riser, you might beat them to it. Be sure to take photos of the vineyards, especially if the grapes are getting ripe and full. There are also great views of the lake from up here, on the lawns in front of the Hopkins Inn.

Go back down to the lake and continue west on North Shore Road, turning right on Anderson Acres Road and right again on Kent Hollow Road, which will take you to Route 341 (Segar Mountain Road), where you'll turn left. These are some of the most isolated and charming roads in the state, through forest and farmland, and you might be sorry to leave them in a few miles when you reach Route 7. Don't worry, there are wonders to come.

Route 341 turns right on South Kent Road before hitting Route 7 in downtown Kent. If you're in the mood for shopping, check out one of the many antiques stores here (see Lyme Regis and R. T. Facts entries), or grab some chocolates for later at the Belgique Patisserie at 1 Bridge St. (860-927-3681). But your real destination is north of town along Route 7 at Kent Falls State Park.

You won't miss the falls, a few miles north of town in a large park to the right of the road. But the waterfall you can see from the road is only one of many, and if you did not have too much wine at Hopkins, you'll love hiking up the wooden staircases and path to find new falls around each corner. The top one is the largest, with a 70-foot drop, so you'll know when you've reached it. This is certainly the most dramatic series of falls in the state.

Continue north on Route 7 along the scenic Housatonic River, staying to the left at a split (Route 4 joins and then leaves here). A mile or so after Housatonic Meadows State Park, you'll reach West Cornwall, where you can turn right briefly onto Route 128 and

drive across the river on the covered West Cornwall Bridge, then turn around in town to retrace your steps, getting out to take a few photos, no doubt. Feel free to stop at the Cornwall Bridge Pottery store (see entry) while you're here to pick up some handmade pottery by one of the masters of the craft.

After this interlude, continue north on Route 7 until you reach the intersection with Route 112. Here you have a choice. If you're not sick of waterfalls, and not too hungry yet, you can turn immediately right on Dugway Road. This will turn into Housatonic River Road where Falls Mountain Road crosses it. Up a small hill, in a little over 0.25 mile past Falls Mountain, park where it says scenic overlook and head along a wide trail to the observation area, where you will see the Great Falls of the Housatonic—an impressive sight much different from the delicate Kent Falls. Incidentally, the Appalachian Trail comes through here, so you're walking a little piece of it. You might be walking more later today.

When you're done here, head back the way you came onto Dugway Road, but take a right on Brinton Hill Road, reaching Salmon Kill Road, where you'll turn right. If you've chosen not to go to the falls, head west on Route 112 from Route 7 and take a right on Salmon Kill Road. Salmon Kill will take you through more scenic farmland and forest (you can never get enough) until you reach Route 41 (Main Street) in Salisbury. Here you'll head up Main Street, and just where Route 44 comes in from the right, Chaiwalla sits on the hill to your left (860-435-9758). Have lunch here, and don't forget to try some of their excellent tea.

After lunch you have another choice: Do you want an easy climb or a tough one? How good a shape are you in? If you feel up to it, the tough (though not long) climb up Bear Mountain just north of town will take you to Connecticut's highest peak and a spectacular view of all the county you just drove through. Drive north on Route 41 (now called Undermountain Road) until you see the turnoff to the left for the Undermountain Trail. This is what you'll take up to the peak, turning right on the white blazes of the Appalachian Trail until you reach the huge stone cairn on top of Bear Mountain (see entry). Retrace your steps to come down, and retrace your short drive back to the intersection with Route 44 (Canaan Road) in Salisbury.

For an easier climb, take Route 44 east through Canaan to Norfolk. The road name will change several times here, but just stick to the number 44. When you reach Norfolk, take a left on North Street (you'll see the huge Immaculate Conception church across from you) and the entrance to Haystack Mountain State Park will be on your left just past Old Colony Road. Occasionally this paved road will be open and you can drive up. Otherwise, take the short walk up to the stone tower on this road and enjoy much easier, if perhaps less satisfying, views of northwest Connecticut than you would from Bear Mountain. If you take this option, you'll certainly have time to check out the Norfolk Historical Society, right on the town green in the historic district of this charming town.

If you're exhausted, or simply feel done for the day, eat dinner at the chic Infinity Bistro in the center of Norfolk (860-542-5531; infinitybistro.com). If not and/or if you are planning an overnight stay, then drive east along Route 44 until you reach the intersection with Route 182 (Colebrook Road). Again, this rural route will change names several times, to Old Colebrook Road, a slight left onto Old North Road, and slight right onto Smith Hill Road. This comes out at Route 8 (Colebrook River Road), and you'll cross the intersection (there's a slight jag to the right, then take a left) onto Route 20 (Riverton Road). Stay on this road into the charming village of Riverton, where you'll stay on Route 20, turning right on Main Street, passing the old Hitchcock Chair Factory, and crossing the bridge over the Farmington River, where you'll find dinner and lodging (if you like) at the Old Riverton Inn (860-379-8678; rivertoninn.com).

You've come a long way today and gotten to know the cultural and natural landscapes of northwest Connecticut. Relax with a bottle of wine at this 1796 coaching inn, and think of the travelers who have passed this way before you. Did they enjoy themselves as much as you did? Did they earn their meal and rest? You surely have, and the memories you will take from this whirlwind (though surprisingly simple) tour of Litchfield County will last a lifetime.

NEW HAVEN COUNTY

The old New Haven Colony nearly became the center of Connecticut, and it shared the capital with Hartford for many years. The colony's harboring of three rebel judges from England was probably the only thing that prevented it from becoming its own state. But New Haven became truly its own city and cultural area with the founding of Yale University, which for more than 300 years has brought the area refinement and wealth.

The center of the county in many ways, New Haven is Connecticut's second-largest city after Bridgeport, and it's chock-full of museums, theaters, and exciting annual events. Few would argue that Fairfield County as a whole might have better restaurants, but no single city has as many top-quality (and famous) eating establishments as New Haven has. This was the oldest planned city in America, and you can still walk the old green and among the towering spires of Yale, imagining the fight against the British here in the Revolutionary War.

The immediate suburbs of New Haven—Hamden, East Haven, and North Haven—all have their own characteristics. Though this is the third most populous county in the state, hiking and biking trails abound, including the Quinnipiac Trail—the oldest in the state's extensive blue-blazed system—in addition to huge parks like Sleeping Giant and the Farmington Canal Greenway.

New Haven County also contains a number of towns along the shoreline of Long Island Sound. To the west, Milford and West Haven are more-populated suburban towns with fine beaches and parks. To the east, Branford, Guilford, and Madison have quaint village centers along the Old Post Road that hearken back to times gone by.

At the north end of the county, the factory towns Meriden and Waterbury are still huge population centers. Waterbury has some fine museums, and Meriden features the wonderful vistas of Castle Craig in Hubbard Park. South of Waterbury are the old industrial towns of the Naugatuck Valley, designated an "All-American Valley" for its part in the textile and brass industries. Meriden's suburb of Wallingford is a charming town built around one of the best private schools in the country, Choate Rosemary Hall.

In between these larger towns are quiet rural communities like Oxford, Bethany, Prospect, and North Branford. But New Haven County's charms are not like Litchfield's or Windham's. This county is a healthy mixture of town and gown, seaside and mountain. With restaurants rivaling Fairfield County, and attractions rivaling New London, this area has a little of everything for all tastes and inclinations.

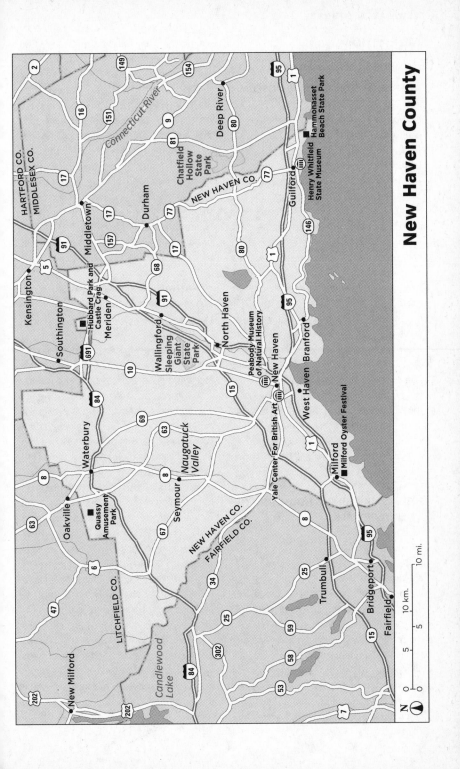

New Haven County

ATTRACTIONS

Historical Sites & Landmarks

✳HENRY WHITFIELD STATE MUSEUM
248 Old Whitfield St.
PO Box 210
Guilford, CT 06437
(203) 453-2457
cultureandtourism.org/cct

This remarkable stone manor house is the oldest building in Connecticut and the oldest stone house in colonial America, begun in 1639 by Henry Whitfield, a minister from England. Built to last, like a small castle, it doubled as the defensive structure for the town of Guilford. Inside the house are period artifacts, as well as a small museum on the top floor. You can't miss the 1726 tower clock, which resides upstairs. If you don't get enough history here, the Guilford Green a long block away is definitely worth a walk. The local historical societies keep two houses a few blocks east on Water Street. The Hyland House, with its walk-in fireplace, and the blacksmith shop at the Thomas Griswold House are both worth a look if you're here in the summertime. However, because it's run by the state, the Whitfield House is open year-round.

HITCHCOCK-PHILLIPS HOUSE AND THE HERITAGE WALK
43 Church Dr.
Cheshire, CT 06410
(203) 272-2574
cheshirehistory.org

Although busy Route 10 passes through the Cheshire town green, it remains startlingly intact. The Heritage Walk takes you around the green with its Civil War monument, past an ancient sycamore tree, and down Main Street past 10 historic buildings from the 18th and 19th centuries. The most impressive are the Abijah Beach Tavern from 1750 and the Foote House from 1767, owned by a prominent family with a governor and a Civil War hero in its ranks. The 1785 Hitchcock-Phillips House, open on Sunday in summer and by appointment, has a fine collection inside, including the traveling desk of president Millard Fillmore and a glass-topped table used by President Grant for his medals. This museum of not only Cheshire but American history contains various paintings, tools, artifacts, and photographs from the last two centuries and beyond. Don't miss the folding game table used in the White House by presidents from Abraham Lincoln to Harry Truman. You can find a walking tour map on the website.

JONATHAN DICKERMAN HOUSE
105 Mount Carmel Ave.
Hamden, CT 06518
(203) 248-6030
hamdenhistoricalsociety.wordpress.com

Built in 1792, this charming farmhouse includes period furnishings and a sweet-smelling folk medicine herb garden. The site also features a historic 1810 cider mill barn and outhouse, and Sleeping Giant State Park is literally across the street. Walk along the river path to the remains of the stone-walled Axle Works factory, a sluiceway, and an old millpond used by factories and mills here as early as the 17th century. Jonathan was a member of the storied Dickerman family of Hamden, which includes a Civil War hero, three sisters who started an early private school for girls, several writers, a famous painter, and the founder of one of the earliest commercial vineyards in Connecticut. Today Hamden has dozens of well-preserved historic homes by architects like Henry Austin and Alice Washburn, occupied by people like authors Thornton Wilder and William Linton. The historical society's handy book provides driving tours of the whole town.

MADISON MILE OF OUTDOOR ART
Main Street
Madison, CT 06443
(203) 421-3039
hollycroft.org
Madison is a charming town with a great bookstore and downtown. But another reason to come here is its outdoor sculptures. There are always about 40 pieces, and many change every 6 months, so you'll see new entries in this open-air art gallery managed by the Hollycroft Foundation. The sculptures are always unconventional, and sometimes radically experimental. While you're here, check out the Deacon John Grave House, built in 1685 and complete with original fireplace and a magnificent loom, in case you find yourself yearning for a more traditional style. You should also browse the galleries in the center of town, where you'll see amazing works, even an original Picasso or two.

NAUGATUCK HISTORICAL SOCIETY
195 Water St.
Naugatuck, CT 06770
(203) 729-9039
naugatuckhistory.com
Downtown Naugatuck around the green has a completely different look than many Connecticut cities, featuring more brick, and including strange mixes of styles like high Victorian Gothic. Visit the museum in the old Spanish Colonial Revival train station, designed by Henry Bacon (who also designed the Lincoln Memorial), in the afternoons Wed through Sat, and learn the history of the town, which includes Charles Goodyear's forays into galvanizing rubber—one of the processes that made driving around Connecticut in our cars, or walking on our sneakers, possible. One of the most active historical societies in the state, they have huge annual events like Savor Connecticut, where they bring local flavors together: Fascia's Chocolates,

Nardelli's Grinder Shoppe, Avery Soda, and more.

NEW HAVEN GREEN
250 Temple St.
New Haven, CT 06511
(203) 787-0121
newhavencenterchurch.org
This multiple attraction at the center of New Haven was the first planned green in America, completed in 1638. The city hall, courts, and Yale University group around the 16-acre space. There are 3 churches on the green itself: the 1814 United Church on the Green, the 1812 Center Church on the Green, and the 1816 Trinity Episcopal Church. The crypt under Center Church, which was built by architect Ithiel Town over a much older one, contains 1,000 remains, 137 of which are identified, the oldest from 1687. You can visit from Apr to Oct on Thurs and Sat from 11 a.m. to 1 p.m. On the east side, take the crosswalk to 165 Church St. to see the 14-foot bronze Amistad Memorial. Walk north on College Street to Grove Street Cemetery, where you'll find the graves of Eli Whitney, Noah Webster, and Charles Goodyear, among others, and where many of the graves under the green were moved in 1796. But not all—it's estimated some 5,000 to 10,000 people remain under the green. That's only a fraction of the Puritans' original intention, however. They supposedly designed it to hold the number of people they believed would be spared during the second coming of Christ: 144,000.

THOMAS DARLING HOUSE MUSEUM
1907 Litchfield Tpke.
Woodbridge, CT 06525
(203) 387-2823
visitnewhaven.com
This historic home just outside New Haven was built in 1772 by merchant Thomas Darling, a friend of both Roger Sherman and

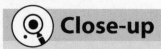 **Close-up**

Connecticut Lobster Rolls

In the past century Connecticut has not been proactive with its branding. We have been modest and retiring when it comes to our cultural accomplishments in particular. One of the areas in which we have not trumpeted our innovations is food. We all know New Haven–style apizza with its coal-fired, crispy crust and chewy center. But we might not know that clear-broth clam chowder comes from Connecticut, or that the first Italian sandwich was made in New London.

But perhaps the most surprising is the hot lobster roll—an iconic shore food we all have eaten without even the faintest hint of local pride. Of course we don't need the extra feeling of pride to enjoy one of these amazing buttery treats. Still, the fact that Harry Perry of Milford invented it in 1934 in a fish market on the Post Road should bring us some sense of satisfaction. He grilled French bakery rolls four at a time and called his place "Home of the Famous Lobster Roll." This information is a surprise to many, including the shacks and restaurants serving them to us. No more. Our local foods are parts of our culture, and just as we should brag more about Eugene O'Neill, Alexander Calder, and Meryl Streep, we should brag about our food.

For those of you who don't know, the Connecticut hot lobster roll is very different from the cold salad version popular in Maine and Massachusetts and, let's face it, far superior. I mean, mixing celery and mayonnaise with a meat as delicate and rich as lobster doesn't seem like the best approach, does it? Seriously, I enjoy cold lobster rolls too, but the proper way to eat lobster, or any fine seafood for that matter, has always been with lemon and butter. The lobster should be steamed lightly and cooled, and then the meat removed, broken up, and poached lightly in butter and the excess lobster juice, tossing it for about 4 to 5 minutes.

You can often tell a good roll by whether it has some of the white, fatty substance you find on the inside of a shell. That means the meat is fresh and not out of a can. If it has been boiled or poached too long, it will be too rubbery. Another issue is too much butter, which drowns the taste of the lobster rather than bringing it to the fore. Lemon can be spritzed on or given as an option.

The roll used is usually a New England hot dog roll, which stands straight up and can be grilled or toasted on both sides after a light brushing of butter. It is a good choice, but due to the butter used with the lobster (or if you're lucky, the large helping of meat), the roll can sometimes fall apart. The Lazy Lobster in Milford (6 Broadway; 203-283-1864) solves this problem by using French bread, which is sturdy and crunchy, but limits the amount of lobster to a smaller helping than I like (though it might be enough for you). Lobster Landing (152 Commerce St., Clinton; 860-669-2005) has what seems to be the best solution—a small grinder roll. However, both these methods require a toaster oven of some sort rather than just a flat grill, because the roll should be a little firm and crunchy all around to complement the heap of buttery lobster meat.

This is one of the best sandwiches ever developed, and we can be proud to have invented, and perfected, it here in Connecticut.

Benjamin Franklin. The house is open for tours June to Oct from 2 to 4 p.m., and you can see the vintage quilts, farm implements, and period furnishings. They also run events like "tavern night" throughout the year. For those of you with wandering feet, trails behind the museum will take you right up to West Rock Ridge, or in a huge loop around the entire town of Woodbridge past dams and house foundations, and along ancient stone-walled roads. Print out the maps from the town website (woodbridgect.org) and explore.

Museums

BARKER CHARACTER, COMIC, AND CARTOON MUSEUM
1188 Highland Ave.
Cheshire, CT 06410
(203) 699-3822
barkermuseum.com

When Herb and Gloria Barker opened this museum to the joys of memory and story, they knew they had one of the largest toy collections in the country, but they didn't know how much other people would enjoy it. This is so much more than a cartoon museum, you might think it needs a few more additions to its already long name. You will also agree that they need a larger space for the thousands of items. Classic children's lunch boxes line the walls, and huge Simpsons characters greet you. The museum has first-edition Star Wars figures still in the box, old Looney Tunes puzzles, PEZ dispensers, and other nostalgic items that might lead you to believe this museum is more for adults who never grew up than for today's children. However, the collection keeps growing and includes many current toys, such as Harry Potter items. They have everything from original California Raisins memorabilia to toys from the 19th century. You can also buy original cartoon cels in the gift shop.

BEINECKE RARE BOOK AND MANUSCRIPT LIBRARY
121 Wall St.
New Haven, CT 06511
(203) 432-2977
library.yale.edu/beinecke

This huge, marble Rubik's Cube building near the center of Yale's campus is a book lover's shrine. Marble walls filter the light to protect the rare books and give the effect of being in a cavern, if a cavern had comfortable leather chairs and low-lit cases of valuable books. The huge glass tower in the center, with 5 floors of incredibly old books, is surrounded by extensive, changing thematic exhibits with manuscripts, authors' drafts, and notes. You'll also find a Gutenberg Bible from 1455 and a huge original copy of Audubon's *Birds of America*. The real research areas of the library spread out beneath the marble edifice and courtyard. Outside, don't miss the Isamu Noguchi sculpture court or the Alexander Calder stabile sculpture across the way.

MATTATUCK MUSEUM
144 W. Main St.
Waterbury, CT 06702
(203) 753-0381
mattatuckmuseum.org

This exceptional small museum right on the green in Waterbury contains exhibits on art, history, and science. The first floor is beautifully and professionally dedicated to the history of the area, focusing on the Industrial Revolution. The second floor art galleries focus entirely on Connecticut artists and themes, including works by John Trumbull, Frederic Church, and Alexander Calder. The Mattatuck has period furniture and re-creations of house frames and brass mills. Don't just look; listen to the voices of immigrants, factory workers, and slaves. Upstairs there are 10,000 buttons, many of which come from Waterbury factories. Don't miss the courtyard garden with its Calder stabile sculpture. In Ken Burns's epic documentary *The War*, Waterbury was one of the four American towns he focused on. Come to the Mattatuck and find out why.

NEW HAVEN MUSEUM
114 Whitney Ave.
New Haven, CT 06510
(203) 562-4183
newhavenmuseum.org

This museum tells the history of the New Haven Colony, and here you get the impression that although the city became part of a larger colony and then America, it remains an autonomous entity. The building was actually built by the New Haven Historical Society to house its collections, and the professional and engaging way it has been curated inside tells the story well. Permanent exhibits focus on the inventions and industry of the city and its suburbs, with Charles Goodyear's rubber inkwell, Eli Whitney's cotton gin, and A. C. Gilbert's original Erector Set. There are numerous paintings amid the rotunda and marble staircases, and changing exhibits on the second floor. The museum hosts frequent lectures by eminent historians and other speakers, so check their schedule. If you'll be here for the day, pick up their walking tour of New Haven and take a stroll past the mansions of Hill House Avenue and through Grove Street Cemetery.

SHORELINE TROLLEY MUSEUM
17 River St.
East Haven, CT 06512
(203) 467-6927
bera.org

Perhaps this should be categorized as a wildlife attraction, because this museum is, in fact, dedicated to the preservation of an endangered species: the trolley. This is also one of Connecticut's oldest tourist attractions, as well as the oldest steadily operating trolley line in America. When you get to the end of this street near the Branford Green, you'll find yourself at a small building, while the road becomes a trolley line, heading into the forest. The museum itself contains exhibits about trolleys, while outside there are a number of other trolleys in the yard and barns. But this is a truly interactive museum; you will take a ride on the trolley line to Short Beach, which heads through the salt marsh near the sea. The museum is usually in the process of refurbishing more trolleys, so you never know what you'll see. There are theme rides at various times of year, including a haunted ride at Halloween. There is no limit to the number of rides you can take on any of the line's 6 cars; one small fee pays for the whole day. That might be the best part of all.

TIMEXPO MUSEUM
175 Union St.
Waterbury, CT 06702
(203) 755-8463
timexpo.com

You'll see the giant Easter Island moai first. The owners of Timex were friends with researcher Thor Heyerdahl and funded his famous Kon-Tiki expedition. When the museum was created, they wanted to give him a nod. Inside, as you might imagine, the gift shop has an enormous selection of outlet-priced Timex watches. Take the elevator up to the third floor and make your way down through this very professionally done museum, with exhibits and histories along with hundreds of valuable clocks and watches. Kids will love the giant Mickey Mouse watch and the interactive exhibits scattered throughout. There are exhibits on Indiglo, pagers, and other innovations, including how timekeeping helped win World War II. And you'll find a huge gallery dedicated not just to Thor Heyerdahl but to the possibilities of ancient long-distance travel, as well as a newer exhibit on the mound-building societies of the Midwest. The museum looks to both the past and the future, cleverly forcing you to think more carefully about the phenomenon of time itself.

✳YALE CENTER FOR BRITISH ART
1080 Chapel St.
New Haven, CT 06510
(203) 432-2800
britishart.yale.edu

This modern building designed by Louis Kahn, with its calming oak-and-linen interior, boasts the largest collection of British art outside Great Britain itself. After blithely strolling in at the corner of Chapel and High Streets (it's free) and heading up the elevator or winding staircase, you'll find 3 floors of paintings, decorative arts, and sculptures from the 1500s to today. Check out the wonderful seascapes of Turner, the clever drawings of Hogarth, and the crumbling ruins of Constable. Don't miss Whistler's *Nocturne in Blue and Silver,* one of the paintings that prefigured modern art. The museum runs lectures, tours, concerts, and films; they also bring in great temporary exhibits, so check their schedule. And don't forget the gift store, one of the best museum shops you'll find this side of the Met.

YALE PEABODY MUSEUM OF NATURAL HISTORY
170 Whitney Ave.
New Haven, CT 06511
(203) 432-5050
peabody.yale.edu

You'll see crowds of excited children flocking to the life-size torosaurus outside before you see the museum's sign above what looks like a church, and in a way it is: a church of science. The halls dedicated to explaining evolution are punctuated with (among other marvels) a *Homo erectus* skeleton that is 1.6 million years old. But your kids will drag you through the hall of mammals, past the Irish elk, the mastodon, and the glyptodont shell to the hall of reptiles. Of course the great apatosaurus and stegosaurus skeletons draw the most interest, but the giant Archelon turtle is just as spectacular. Upstairs is a great collection of gems and minerals, with sections focusing on Connecticut's own geology; the North American mammals and birds section does the same. This is a great opportunity to learn more about the land beneath our feet. All the way in the back of this floor you'll find the mummy, hidden in the Egypt room. Don't miss the small intermediate floor and the Discovery Room, where you can look down on the hall of reptiles and Rudolph Zallinger's amazing mural. The glass is usually fogged with the breath of wide-eyed kids. The leaf-cutter ant colony and live poison dart frogs will grab their attention as well.

✳YALE UNIVERSITY ART GALLERY
1111 Chapel St.
New Haven, CT 06520
(203) 432-0600
artgallery.yale.edu

University art galleries are often overhyped, but let's face it; this is Yale. They have one of the best collections of art—period—and what isn't at the Center for British Art is here, right across the street. If you like sculpture and craft, they have collections of ancient art, African art, Asian art, and Indo-Pacific art. If you're into European art, they have a great selection of Impressionists and Postimpressionists (including van Gogh's Night Cafe), as well as earlier Renaissance and medieval paintings. The modern art includes works by Duchamp and Liechtenstein, and you'll find works by Hopper, O'Keeffe, Cézanne, Picasso, Degas, Kandinsky, Monet . . . the list goes on. This is yet another free attraction, thanks to the generosity of Yale's benefactors. They have recently renovated the whole thing, with the top floor dedicated to large exhibits. Look for the grave of John Trumbull (painter) in the floor of the sculpture gallery.

Parks & Beaches

CASTLE CRAIG AND HUBBARD PARK
199 Notch Rd.
Meriden, CT 06451
(203) 630-4259
cityofmeriden.org

Near the entrance, Hubbard Park is a pleasant enough town park, designed by the sons of Frederick Law Olmsted (designer of Central Park in Manhattan). However, the 700-foot cliffs of the volcanic Hanging Hills that rise abruptly from the parkland are the real attraction here. On the top a stone tower was built in 1900, and the 360-degree view from the battlements is one of the top five views in the state; you can see from Long Island Sound past the northern border into Massachusetts. From Memorial Day to October the drive around the reservoir and up to the tower is open, and dozens of families make the trip up from the picnic tables to view the state. However, the hiking trails are more fun, especially when the road is closed and you can have the mountains to yourself. Look for deer and turkeys and a small colony of parrots that has made its way up here from the coast. If you want a more challenging hike, try the white trail. Last time I was here I told a couple it was an easy walk. Sorry!

CONNECTICUT AUDUBON COASTAL CENTER AND SILVER SANDS STATE PARK
1 Milford Point Rd.
Milford, CT 06460
(203) 878-7440
ctaudubon.org/
coastal-center-at-milford-point
379 Meadowside Rd.
Milford, CT 06460
(860) 424-3200
ct.gov/dep [search "Silver Sands State Park"]

The Connecticut Audubon Society's Coastal Center at Milford Point is a small nature center with a demonstration tank and salt marsh lab. It is attached to the Smith-Hubbell Wildlife Refuge and Bird Sanctuary, and on the back side of the park, in the mouth of the Housatonic River, the 840-acre Charles Wheeler Salt Marsh and Wildlife Management Area is a prime nesting area. This is a birding hot spot: An amazing 315 species have been identified here. The 70-foot covered observation tower gives panoramic vistas of the coast and the Housatonic River. If you'd rather soak up some rays, head a mile east to Silver Sands State Park, which is partially developed but has a fine beach and is one of the few in the state that doesn't require a fee. Tiny Charles Island, just across from the park, is one of the spots where Captain Kidd reportedly buried gold in 1699. Both of these places are likely to be quiet refuges from the bustle of the coast in summer, and they are absolutely lovely in autumn and early spring.

✴HAMMONASSET STATE PARK
1288 Boston Post Rd.
Madison, CT 06443
(203) 245-2785
ct.gov/dep [search "Hammonasset State Park"]

This is Connecticut's longest single stretch of public shoreline, with 2 miles of pristine beach. You can walk out a long way in waist-deep water, and the water at this end of Long Island Sound is crystal clear. Kiting is popular here, and a bicycle trail parallels the beach in the small dune area for most of the length. Surf fishing is great from the beach, but even better at the eastern end of the park from the rocky outcrops. This is also excellent birding territory; hike on the trail behind the Meig's Point Nature Center into the salt marsh with your binoculars to find herons, egrets, and oystercatchers. The nature center is a great place to take your children for an educational interlude. Stop by Hammonasset in winter (when there's no park fee) and go for a bundled-up walk on the beach. Trust me, it's a lost pleasure that the birds will gladly share with you.

ROARING BROOK FALLS

Roaring Brook Road
Cheshire, CT 06410
(203) 271-6670 (Environmental Planner)
cheshirect.org/recreation-and-leisure/
parks/

Maintained by the Environmental Commission of Cheshire, this 80-foot waterfall leaps off the plateau in Prospect and is the highest single drop in the state. The trail starts from a small paved lot on Roaring Brook Road, 0.3 mile west from Mountain Road. It's a suburban setting that hardly seems the place for a dramatic waterfall. But in just a few hundred feet, you'll reach a viewpoint (there are several to feel out and explore for the best photo) of the falls. Continuing up the orange-blazed trail, you'll reach the northern section of the Quinnipiac Trail, the oldest blue-blazed in the state. If you hike to the south a mile or so, you'll cross a road and reach Mount Sanford, an 800-foot mountain with views to the west (don't worry; you've already done most of the uphill work). Go in spring, when the falls are gushing, or in winter, when they are sometimes frozen to the cliff wall.

WEST HAVEN BEACH AND
PROMENADE

Captain Thomas Boulevard
West Haven, CT 06510
(203) 937-3651
cityofwesthaven.com

If we take too much advantage of the West Haven beaches, I'm sure someone will start charging us money, but for now this is one of the only shorefronts in Connecticut where you can park and swim without a fee. The free lots by Jimmies in the center or by Chick's Drive-In at the eastern end are always available. People are always fishing from the stone and wood jetties, and although the beaches are not as pristine as some in the eastern part of the state, let me remind you: They are free. The long bike trail and boardwalk are huge draws, and people come down from the entire New Haven area to in-line skate, ride, or walk along the long harbor. This is where the old Savin Rock Amusement Park was located, and writer Jack Kerouac swam off the seawall just down the road when his family lived in West Haven. If you're here from 9 a.m. to 2 p.m. on a weekday, check out the 17th-century Ward-Heitmann House at 277 Elm St. (203-932-9713; wardheitmann.org), where docents in colonial garb will tell you the story of the town.

WEST ROCK RIDGE STATE PARK

Wintergreen Avenue
New Haven, CT 06515
(203) 287-5658 (c/o Sleeping Giant State
Park)
ct.gov/dep [search "West Rock Ridge
State Park"]

Driving up Wintergreen Avenue, just before you cross under the Merritt Parkway where it tunnels through the cliffs, you can turn left and head up a long, winding road to great views more than 600 feet above the city of New Haven. Across the city you'll see East Rock Park, a much smaller park run by the town (cityofnewhaven.com), which you can also drive up for great views. A spur road will also take you to the Judges Cave (or you can hike there along the blue-blazed trail), where in 1661 Edward Whalley and William Goffe hid from bounty hunters searching for them for their part in the execution of England's Charles I. West Rock is actually shared by Hamden and Woodbridge; it stretches north for 7 miles, networked with hiking trails. The old asphalt Baldwin Parkway along the top, now closed to cars, is an excellent place for mountain biking. Lake Wintergreen, farther up the road in Hamden, is a great place to start hiking or to fish. Near the entrance to the park road, just by the Merritt, is the West Rock Nature Center, the oldest urban nature center in the nation and a great place to take the kids.

i New Haven is known as the "Elm City," and its streets were once lined with some of the most beautiful elm trees in the world.

Wineries & Breweries

*GOUVEIA VINEYARDS
1339 Whirlwind Hill Rd.
Wallingford, CT 06492
(203) 265-5526
gouveiavineyards.com
Established in 1999, this winery brings the Portuguese heritage of its owner, Joseph Gouveia, to the Wallingford Hills. You'll pass farm silos and fenced pastures on the way to Gouveia Vineyard, just past the Mackenzie Reservoir. With 140 acres, Gouveia is one of the largest vineyards in the state; 15 acres are planted, and there's plenty of room to expand. The tasting room is a gorgeous stone structure, and visitors flock to the site year-round. Inside, high wood beams frame the larger of two rooms, greenhouse-like windows shape the side walls, and a double-sided fireplace warms patrons in winter. In warmer months, you're likely to see picnickers on the lawn and on the patio under the pergola, sipping Stone House Red and sharing cheese, sandwiches, or possibly a birthday cake. The winery is equally beautiful in winter, as late afternoon light reflects off the snowy vines. Gouveia offers a wide range of wines, including whites like Seyval Blanc, Cayuga, and two styles of Chardonnay. For a red, try the Cabernet Franc, which is rich and earthy. Open Thurs through Sun.

NEW ENGLAND BREWING COMPANY
7 Selden St.
Woodbridge, CT 06525
(203) 387-2222
newenglandbrewing.com
The craft-brewing industry has changed drinking in America in the past 25 years, and Rob Leonard of New England Brewing has been part of the action since 1992. You can stop by for a tour of this unpretentious brewery just outside New Haven in Woodbridge, where Rob cooks up Sea Hag Ale, Atlantic Amber, Gold Stock Ale, Elm City Lager, and a number of seasonal beers and ales such as Gandhi-Bot and Alpha Weizen. These brews are available at bars and package stores throughout New Haven County, so keep your eyes open. Rob promises never to produce a beer with a dog as part of the name or label, which is something of a relief. Those are getting confusing.

PARADISE HILLS VINEYARDS
15 Wind Swept Hill Rd.
Wallingford, CT 06492
(203) 284-0123
facebook.com/paradisehillswinery
One of the newer wineries in the state, Paradise Hills sits on 65 acres in the beautiful Wallingford Hills, an easy jump from nearby Gouveia Vineyards. Paradise Hills has a small but varied selection of reds and whites. The owners have been growing grapes for over 25 years, and opened the Tuscan-style tasting room at the end of a cul-de-sac in 2011. You'll feel as though you stepped into an Italian landscape painting. The ambience, inside and out, is elegant and airy, and you're sure to admire the copper bar and patio as you relax and sip. The historic Washington Trail passes through the property, and a red and a white blend are both named for it.

Also honoring that famous trail that General Washington traveled on through Wallingford is President's Choice, a red blend made with Cabernet Sauvignon, Merlot, and estate-grown Chambourcin. The tasting room is open Thurs through Sun.

SAVINO VINEYARDS
128 Ford Rd.
Woodbridge, CT 06525
(203) 387-1573
savinovineyards.com

Framed by stone walls and located in a quiet neighborhood in Woodbridge, Savino Vineyards might go unnoticed, except for the 8 acres of vines that sprawl beside the driveway. The family-owned-and-operated winery was opened in 2009 by Jerry Savino, a native of Salerno, Italy, and his wife. He's planted Seyval Blanc, Vidal Vlanc, Merlot, St. Croix, Frontenac, and Cabernet Franc. The small red tasting room is quaint, with a bar, vintage cash register, and a few tables. Sample the Seyval Blanc, which is aromatic with citrus as well as mineral notes. The Merlot is dark plum with notes of cherry and vanilla. A plate of crackers, pepperoni, and Parmesan slices accompanies the tasting. They are open Sat and Sun from noon to 6 p.m.

STONY CREEK BREWERY
5 Indian Neck Ave.
Branford, CT 06405
(203) 684-3150
stonycreekbeer.com

Opening in January 2015, this local craft brewery's 30,000-square-foot, state-of-the-art production area and 2,500-square-foot tasting room will be one of the prime attractions in the area. The spot is perfect—close to I-95, right on the Branford River (you can dock your boat on-site), and with on open air deck that will surely become one of the prime spots for summer. A bocce court, a charging station for electric cars, air for bike tires . . . they are doing this right. These new craft breweries have been spreading like wildfire across the landscape of Connecticut, and it's one fire we don't want to put out.

ACTIVITIES & EVENTS

Amusement Parks

PEZ FACTORY VISITOR CENTER
35 Prindle Hill Rd.
Orange, CT 06477
(203) 298-0201
pez.com/visit_us

Okay, this isn't really an amusement park, but how else would you qualify this strange and wonderful place? The visitor center at the Pez Factory in Orange contains the largest collection of PEZ memorabilia on public display in the world, including a PEZ motorcycle built by Orange County Choppers. You can watch the production from a viewing area and learn about this nearly century-old brand of candy. They are usually open Mon through Sat 10 a.m. to 6 p.m., Sun noon to 5 p.m., but check first—the hours sometimes change. Admission is only $5 (cheaper for kids), and they knock $2 off any purchases in the store. And who can resist buying some of these classic candy toys? The world's largest PEZ dispenser on the premises is unfortunately not for sale.

QUASSY AMUSEMENT PARK
2132 Middlebury Rd.
Middlebury, CT 06762
(203) 758-2913
quassy.com

Named for Lake Quassapaug, on whose shores it's located, this amusement park doesn't look or feel like one of the giant parks, or even like nearby Lake Compounce. However, although it feels like an old-fashioned amusement park, it has been recently refurbished and remains a great time for all concerned. Quassy has 3 roller coasters, bumper cars, carnival rides, a carousel, a miniature railroad, a petting zoo, paddleboats, and a swimming area on the lake. There's also a huge water park jungle gym unlike anything you've probably ever seen and about 100 carnival and arcade games to play. For adults, an 18-hole golf course is on the premises. As you can tell, this is not a typical amusement park but has much more to offer than many others.

Arts Venues

NEW HAVEN SYMPHONY ORCHESTRA
105 Court St., #302
New Haven, CT 06510
(203) 865-0831
newhavensymphony.org

With its first performance in 1895, this is the fourth-oldest orchestra in the US and persists in its success even though it is located in a much smaller city than Boston, New York, or Chicago. They run two different series, the first at Woolsey Hall at Yale, currently directed by famous English conductor William Boughton. These are primarily classical concerts, such as Beethoven symphonies or new works by composers in residence. The orchestra also runs a Pops series at the Shubert Theater and at area high schools. They focus on other sorts of works, like big band, jazz, and flamenco, and are directed by Chelsea Tipton, the associate conductor. The New Haven Symphony often collaborates with soloists like Glenn Gould, Yo-Yo Ma, and Itzhak Perlman.

OAKDALE THEATRE
95 S. Turnpike Rd.
Wallingford, CT 06492
(203) 265-1501
oakdale.com

The current title of this theater is technically Toyota Presents the Oakdale in Association with Comcast, but no one actually calls it that. "The Oakdale" opened in 1957 as a tent

in an alfalfa field and in 1972 was upgraded to a 3,000-seat theater in the round with a slowly spinning stage. Rebuilt in 1996, the theater is the largest in the state of Connecticut and has gone through a variety of corporate sponsorships. The theater hosts Broadway shows, comedy performances, and (mostly) popular music concerts featuring rock, hip-hop, and country stars. The Oakdale is wheelchair accessible and non-smoking, although there is a designated smoking area. There are concessions, and beer and wine are available. The best seats by far are the "red" loge seats at the front of the balcony. Get them if you can!

✳PALACE THEATER
100 E. Main St.
Waterbury, CT 06702
(203) 346-2000
palacetheaterct.org

Part of Waterbury's cultural renaissance, the Palace Theater has been renovated at the cost of $35 million, and you can tell. With marbled panels, private boxes draped in velvet, red carpets, and gold leaf, the Palace is an architectural delight. It brings in musicians like Leonard Cohen and speakers like Anthony Bourdain, in addition to featuring musical theater and other performances throughout the Sept to May season. This not-for-profit arts center is staffed by volunteers who love the Palace and love Waterbury and will make your visit special. There is a snack bar and 3 alcoholic beverage bars with incredibly inexpensive beers and cocktails. This is a huge theater with many great places to see the show from, but try rows D through H in section 1C.

SHUBERT THEATER
247 College St.
New Haven, CT 06510
(203) 562-5666
shubert.com

Broadway musicals, legendary ballets, all-star concerts, and comedy shows all have a home at the Shubert Theater in downtown New Haven, just a block from the Green. The 1,600-seat theater opened in 1916, and the Shubert has been called the "Birthplace of the Nation's Greatest Hits." Every season classics like *South Pacific, Beauty and the Beast,* and *The Wizard of Oz* show up on the marquee. Parking is available right next door at the Crown Street Garage (entrances on both Crown and College). The glass-front lobby lights up as night falls, and comfortable seating ensures that all theatergoers have a great view of the stage. Run by CAPA, a nonprofit organization, the theater is committed to quality arts and community enrichment. Education and outreach programs help bring theater to the people of the city and the state.

Cruises

LONG WHARF PIER
60 S. Water St.
New Haven, CT 06519
(203) 865-1737
schoonerinc.org

Long Wharf Pier is the home of the reproduction schooner *Quinnipiack*. This nonprofit organization has daily public sails, charters, and camps. Walk west along the seawall through Veterans Memorial Park and get lunch at one of the excellent Mexican food trucks that park here every day. The *Quinnipiack* is usually there, but call to make sure. Definitely take the opportunity to sail on a schooner in the Sound. If you choose to do one of their sunset tours, bring a jacket, even in August.

THIMBLE ISLANDS CRUISES
Sea Mist II
Stony Creek Dock
Branford, CT 06405
(203) 488-8905
thimbleislandcruise.com

Volsunga IV
Stony Creek Dock
Branford, CT 06405
(203) 488-9978
thimbleislands.com

As early as the 1840s, the Thimbles became a summer resort for the rich, but by the 1920s they had mostly left. There are 30-some islands (plus a huge number of rocks and reefs visible at low tide), 25 of which are inhabited in summer, some with 1-room cabins and one with a 27-room mansion. These two cruises, equally good, are available to take you through these fascinating islands. The *Volsunga IV* is a 40-foot vessel that takes 49 passengers, and Captain Bob tells great stories. The *Sea Mist II* is 45 feet long and takes 46 people and also does chartered seal and bird watches in groups of 10 or more. Everyone loves these tours, and if you travel to the coast of New Haven County, you should take one.

Festivals & Annual Events

GUILFORD CRAFT EXPO
411 Church St.
Guilford, CT 06437
(203) 453-5947
guilfordartcenter.org

On the quaint Guilford Green every summer for more than 50 years, the Guilford Art Center's annual Craft Expo brings in up to 20,000 artists, collectors, and visitors from around the US. Featuring over 150 exhibitors of decorative, functional, traditional, and contemporary crafts, it lasts for 3 or 4 days every summer, making it one of the top craft shows in New England. Some years they feature other events, such as silent auctions of donated items. You might find crafts in clay, glass, leather, metal, paper, soap, or wood; every one of these works is one of a kind, and they are all for sale. There are food trucks around the green (or head to Ballou's Wine

Bar on the west side; see entry), and every night expect exciting musical performances.

INTERNATIONAL FESTIVAL OF ARTS AND IDEAS

195 Church St.
New Haven, CT 06510
(888) 278-4332
artidea.org

This huge 15-day festival in June takes place primarily on the New Haven Green and includes concerts, street performers, opera, theater, and dance performances. There are also "ideas" lectures and discussions, which focus on everything from food to international politics. Most of the events are free or cost only a pittance for materials. In addition to the lectures and performances, there are walking tours of New Haven by experts, food tours through the excellent New Haven restaurants, and more. They usually organize some of these events through multidisciplinary themes, like "freedom's journey" or "civil liberties." This fascinating festival shows all of New Haven's strengths, and there's something for everyone. Someone once tried to do everything during the 15 days of the festival, and failed miserably. Your mind and heart will never be the same.

*MILFORD OYSTER FESTIVAL

PO Box 5161
Milford, CT 06460
(203) 878-5363
milfordoysterfestival.org

This annual August event is one of the largest in New England, with over 50,000 people attending every year. Milford has been running the Oyster Festival since 1975, and it seems to get bigger every time. Lasting only 1 day, the event features dozens of food vendors and hundreds of artists and craftspeople. Yes, hundreds. There are boat races, a nationally known headlining band, amusement park rides, cruises on the Sound,

and a classic car and motorcycle show. This is also a great time to check out the historic Wharf Lane complex with its 3 18th-century houses (milfordhistoricalsociety.org). It's unclear whether the people come for all this great entertainment or the chance to consume dozens of fresh, raw, on-the-half-shell oysters. Whatever the case, this is one event not to be missed if you're on the central Connecticut shoreline on the third Saturday in August. If not, change your schedule.

NEW ENGLAND ARTS AND CRAFTS FESTIVAL

Milford Downtown Green
Milford, CT 06460
(203) 878-6647
milfordarts.org

Run by the Milford Arts Council, this 2-day festival in July features over 100 booths filled with original artwork handmade by artists and craftspeople. On Milford's expansive green, near the harbor and amid great restaurants and shops, you can wander through the amazing paintings, sculptures, pottery, weaving, and other crafts. The festival also features food vendors, dance lessons, henna tattoos, live music, and other live events. There is a sidewalk chalk contest and a festival of one-act plays, at which you can vote for your favorite. The festival is juried, so try to guess who will win. All this with free admission and parking.

NEW HAVEN JAZZ FESTIVAL

370 Amity Rd.
Bethany, CT 06524
(203) 393-3002
jazzhaven.org

For over 30 years, the Jazz Festival on New Haven Green has been one of the premier festivals in the country. Now run by the organization Jazz Haven in collaboration with the city, the festival is slightly smaller than in the past (usually just 1 day now) but still features a stellar lineup and free admission. Jazz Haven runs shows all year long, in the city and the suburbs, in collaboration with various other organizations, bringing this uniquely American art form to new generations. For the big annual festival, the city's fleet of tasty food trucks line up on Temple Street, and everyone comes out to hear the music from afternoon into the evening hours. And once again, it's free.

Gaming

WINNERS SPORTS HAVEN
600 Long Wharf Dr.
New Haven, CT 06511
(203) 946-3201
mywinners.com

You can't miss this huge round building that looks like an oversize oil tank from I-95. Inside is what can only be described as a Disneyland for off-track wagering, with veteran gamblers sitting by couples making their first bet. Four giant screens showing the current races preside over a stadium of hundreds of seats, each with an individual television. The entire interior is open, with an easy flow between different sections dedicated to jai alai, greyhound racing, and horse racing. In the center is a huge fish tank surrounded by the Shark Bar, which serves thirsty customers all day long. There is also a food court in the back serving snacks and grinders, and Friday and Saturday nights the Saratoga Grill serves more high-end food. Sports Haven has touch-screen wagering and pool tables for the downtime between races, and is certainly the best off-track betting in the state.

Golf

GREAT RIVER GOLF CLUB
130 Coram Ln.
Milford, CT 06461
(203) 878-9623
greatrivergolfclub.com

This par 72, 18-hole course in Milford lies right against the Housatonic River, and the scenic views from the links make for a delightful distraction, as well as a water challenge for 12 holes. There are 7 wooden bridges to cross and a 30-foot waterfall by the 11th hole. You can play the course from 5 sets of tees, which make it 2,000 yards longer or shorter for different play levels. Players of all levels are accommodated with 5 sets of tees stretching the course from 5,170 to 7,191 yards. However, the back 9 are definitely more challenging, with a 150 slope. The restaurant, Monty's, is open Mon through Sat for lunch and dinner and on Sun for brunch until 3 p.m. You should call ahead and make reservations if you want to play this course, and if you plan on eating at the restaurant. The list of awards and stellar ratings is too long to cite here; we'll just say they are consistently rated one of the top 10 courses in Connecticut and top 100 public courses in the nation.

HUNTER MEMORIAL GOLF CLUB
688 Westfield Rd.
Meriden, CT 06450
(203) 634-3366
huntergolfclub.com

In the shadow of Lamentation Mountain and owned by the people of Meriden, the Hunter Memorial Golf Club features 18 holes to challenge any golfer. You can golf all 18 or either the front or back 9. There's a practice green, a driving range, and a beautiful hexagonal clubhouse. Hole 11 has several fun water hazards surrounding the green, and hole 16 makes a turn to the left that leaves beginners searching the forest. On-site is Violi's Restaurant, open daily from 10 a.m. to 11 p.m., which serves Italian food ($$) and offers patio seating and views of the course. Try the twilight rates at Hunter Memorial, which are a third of the price of a day tee time.

OXFORD GREENS
99 Country Club Dr.
Oxford, CT 06478
(203) 888-1600
oxfordgreens.com

Oxford doesn't really seem like it should even be in New Haven County, wedged up between Fairfield and Litchfield Counties, far from New Haven. But it is, and its public golf course is considered one of the best in the state. Designed by Mark Mungeam, the course features bent grass cultivars that are considered the very best. The trees of Naugatuck State Forest surround the course, and it has some great views as well. Par 72, Oxford Greens has a selection of tees that allow someone to play the course a total of 2,000 yards closer than a stronger partner. This course is partnered with the Connecticut Audubon Society and contains natural preserves worth paying attention to, if you can pull your attention from your game. With fun holes like Fortress (#16), this is a championship layout course for those who want to mix up their golf game a little, as well as practice new approaches and new shots.

Hiking, Biking & Walking

FARMINGTON CANAL LINEAR PARK
940 Whitney Ave.
Hamden, CT 06517
(203) 562-6312
farmingtoncanal.org

Very soon, possibly by summer 2015, the last piece of the New Haven section of this amazing canal trail will probably be finished, and it will stretch from the shore through Hamden into Cheshire. In the 1820s this canal was the dream of businessmen and towns along the 83-mile pathway, but in 1848 the dream was killed by the introduction of the railroad. Now turned into a multiuse footpath, it is a fantastic place to bike, walk, in-line skate, and cross-country ski in winter, mostly on the towpath of the old canal (with some sections still in evidence). In the Hamden section you can stop at the restored Lockkeeper's House, where there is a small museum (and restroom facilities) and take the spur trail into Brooksvale Park, where in summer you can check out their peacocks, rabbits, goats, and chickens, as well as a large network of rough mountain-biking trails. Farther up the line in Cheshire, stop at Lock 12 Historical Park, where you can see the working locks that allowed canal boats to float up to the next elevation.

OSBORNEDALE STATE PARK
555 Roosevelt Dr.
Derby, CT 06418
(203) 735-4311
stateparks.com/osborndale.html

This beautiful park above the Housatonic River was willed to the state in 1956 by Frances Osborne Kellogg, who gradually acquired this collection of separate farms during her career as a businesswoman and investor. Numerous trails of various difficulty levels can be found here, including one that makes a loop of the entire park. There are heavily forested areas, meadows, fishing ponds, and stone walls aplenty. At the southwest corner of the park, the Kellogg Environmental Center has a nice nature center and provides educational lectures and hands-on learning experiences. The small nature trail by the center is a great starter for kids just learning to hike, and the pond across the street from the center in the park proper is absolutely stocked with turtles. Check out the nearby 1698 General David Humphreys House at 37 Elm St. if you're there on a weekday afternoon in summer (203-735-1908; derbyhistorical.org). Humphreys was a fascinating guy: part of the nation's first literary movement, an aide and friend to George Washington, and the introducer of merino sheep into America.

i Connecticut's Regional Water Supply companies offer recreational options in and around their lakes and reservoirs. The Regional Water Authority of south-central Connecticut (around New Haven) even offers a permit program, and for a minimal fee you can get access to hiking, horseback riding, and fishing opportunities that few residents take advantage of. On busy holiday weekends, when state parks are swamped with visitors, you'll have the trails and shorelines mostly to yourself. Visit rwater.com/recreation for more information.

SHORELINE SEGWAY
260 River St.
Guilford, CT 06437
(203) 453-6036
segwaytoursandrentals.com

This could actually be in New London or New Haven County, since you can take these Segway tours in Guilford, Hammonasset State Park, or Mystic (2 Roosevelt Ave.). Since 2007 they have been taking people on these unusual tours through historic towns and gorgeous natural scenery. Segways are battery-operated green machines with few moving parts, and they are surprisingly maneuverable. Maybe you've seen police officers trying them out in some of Connecticut's towns. The guides at Shoreline are patient while getting you up to speed if you never used a Segway before and will give you a new experience, great for dates or with older children. Rides are offered by appointment 7 days a week, year-round, weather permitting.

✳SLEEPING GIANT STATE PARK
200 Mount Carmel Ave.
Hamden, CT 06518
(203) 287-5658
sgpa.org

Many call this the best place to hike in Connecticut, and the claim is difficult to argue with. This large park, saved from development by citizen activists in the early 20th century, gets its name from its unique appearance. As you drive up I-91, you can see the mountain, clearly looking like an enormous sleeping man. The network of trails is extensive and offers numerous styles and levels of hiking opportunities. If you're looking for a gentle walk to the top of the mountain, the easy-graded Tower Trail is the most popular in the entire state, but of course that has drawbacks for those looking for find peace and quiet. For a challenge, hike from the parking lot down to the river, and then take the blue trail along the edge of the quarry up the "head" of the Giant. This precarious, steep trail has an amazing reward—the spectacular view from the "chin" cliff of New Haven and across the Sound to Long Island. If you can follow a trail map well, park on Chestnut Lane at the Giant's "feet" and explore less-traveled trails. In spring, walk along the purple trail and find a hidden seasonal waterfall.

WESTWOODS TRAILS
Sam Hill Road
Guilford, CT 06437
(203) 454-8068
guilfordlandtrust.org

This is one of the largest (it's hard to measure these things accurately) networks of trails in the entire state. You could walk different combinations of these 39 miles of trails for years without getting bored. There are waterfalls, salt- and freshwater marshes and swamps, rock sculptures, and several cave formations. There's also an inland tidal lake called Lost Lake that you should definitely check out along the white circle–blazed trail. In the western section on the green trail is a cave where colonial artifacts were found, and the yellow trail goes along a beautiful open cliff and then down it near a huge fallen section. On the orange trail you'll find another cave, and you will sometimes have vistas of Long Island Sound. Some of these trails are also great for experienced mountain bikers, since the entire preserve is rather flat geologically (no big hills) but the trails go up and down quite a bit.

Horseback Riding

RAP-A-PONY FARM
995 North Farms Rd.
Wallingford, CT 06492
(203) 265-3596
rapaponyfarm.com

Catering to beginner riders, Rap-A-Pony Farm has been running for over 25 years, teaching children (of all ages) English and Western riding techniques. They have school vacation and summer programs for very reasonable prices if you want to learn the care and riding all in 4 days. Otherwise, they have 1-hour group lessons, where they teach you how to tack and ride properly, or half-hour private lessons (which of course can be extended). Rap-A-Pony has indoor and outdoor arenas, so you can even go on a rainy day or in cooler weather. They provide helmets, but be sure to wear sturdy shoes and clothes.

Kidstuff

ELI WHITNEY MUSEUM
915 Whitney Ave.
Hamden, CT 06517
(203) 777-1833
eliwhitney.org

Although you'll find Eli Whitney's unique barn across the street (remarked on by two early US presidents) and Eli Whitney Jr.'s dam still holding back a huge lake, this is not really a historical museum. Rather, it is an experimental learning workshop for kids, with a number of hands-on activities, including a

Water Learning Lab. You should register in advance for the many workshops and activities, although walk-in visitors can participate. The summer camp program is legendary. If you're here for more than a week and want to explore the sights of New Haven County, but feel guilty about leaving the kids, you won't if you leave them here. If you're just here for an afternoon, check out the reconstructions of the first-ever covered bridge (invented and built right here!) and a blacksmith shop. A trail also leads from the museum east up to the top of East Rock Park (you can also drive) and spectacular views of New Haven and Long Island Sound. You can also check out the exhibits in the armory about Whitney's many inventions. Meanwhile your kids will be playing happily, unaware that they are absorbing scientific principles and ideas.

THE ONLY GAME IN TOWN
275 Valley Service Rd.
North Haven, CT 06473
(203) 239-4653
onlygamect.com

North Haven's premier family amusement center has been around for over two decades, and they seem to add something new every year. Open daily from Apr to Oct, the Only Game in Town features an arcade, a driving range with 40 tees, 8 batting cages, and 2 minigolf courses. But the most popular attraction is the go-kart track with banked curves, a tunnel, and a bridge, bringing out families to compete with one another. Somehow you never get too old for go-karts. There is a food court to refuel at, and they are open well into the evening in summer, so your family can all go after you get home from work. At Halloween they include an "only haunt in town" scarefest that makes the bravest kid tremble. This could be listed in the amusement parks section as well, and if they add a roller coaster soon, no one will be surprised.

Nightlife

BAR

254 Crown St.

New Haven, CT 06511

(203) 495-1111

barnightclub.com

BAR looks far more like a tavern than a night-club, and it actually serves some fantastic pizzas. The front room has a long bar and pool table, and there are two other rooms to dine in as well. This is a popular after-work party place for employees of the various companies in the city, and you can see them gathered around the front room's tables, eating brick-oven pizza and drinking the tavern's microbrews. The huge back room, called Bartropolis, is where the action is, on a large dance floor with a giant purple tower. DJs spin hip-hop, techno, tribal, samba, and whatever gets the crowd moving. During the week they also have acoustic nights with local musicians. BAR has been around since 1991, which is very long for a club. That is partly due to its double life as a popular tavern, partly due to its unique architecture, and partly due to the fact that it remains a great place to go to dance.

✳FIREHOUSE 12

45 Crown St.

New Haven, CT 06510

(203) 785-0468

firehouse12.com

Both recording studio and performance space, this unique venue in New Haven is, obviously, located in an old firehouse. Downstairs, the bar looks like a combination of a modern art museum and a 1920s speakeasy and serves classic cocktails along with a great selection of wine and beer. Hanging over the bar is the recording studio, which won an award for its unique design. The soundproof space seats 75 people, the band, and the recording engineers. The bands who play here are usually creative, experimental

groups, mostly jazz artists; be prepared to have your musical expectations challenged. You can buy tickets for one or both performances, and have an old-fashioned or a mint julep in between. This is a neat opportunity to be part of the recording process, and, hey, your claps and whistles might even make it into the next album.

TOAD'S PLACE

300 York St., #1

New Haven, CT 06511

(203) 562-5694

toadsplace.com

Since 1976 this music club has hosted some of the greats: Muddy Waters, the Rolling Stones, Bob Dylan, Billy Joel, Bonnie Raitt, U2, the Talking Heads, Radiohead, et cetera, et cetera. Why do they all play this relatively small club in New Haven? The official story is that even megastars want to connect with the fans, and they know this is the place to do it. The real reason (here's an insiders' secret) is that Yale is so influential that even rock-and-roll rebels know that the buzz created from here will give them cachet. The sound is great, and since they revamped the main room to allow teens to come without letting them near the bar (there used to be a giant net across the middle of the room), Toad's is once again a classic venue. If the opening band is too loud, hang out in the back room, where another full bar awaits. And don't be surprised if you run into the performers on your way to the restrooms in the basement. When you do, try not to make a fool of yourself.

Pick Your Own/Farms

DUDLEY FARM

2351 Durham Rd.

Guilford, CT 06437

(203) 457-0770

dudleyfarm.com

The Dudley Farm could just as easily be listed under historical attractions. The Dudley

Foundation has restored this 1840s farmhouse (all 17 rooms) and runs the farm as it was in the 19th century . The house is a great tour. In the Munger Barn you'll find a display of Native American artifacts; and there's a sugarhouse, an herb garden, beehives, and animal enclosures with oxen, geese, and sheep. That's probably what the kids want to see. There's also an easy, kid-friendly 2-mile loop trail through the woodlands behind the farm. You'll want to come here on Saturday mornings in summer, when the market is going on. They have Dudley Farm produce, as well as that from nearby farms, including fruits and vegetables, flowers and herbs, baked goods, jams and jellies, maple syrup, eggs, pickles, naturally raised meats, and handmade arts and crafts. You can also watch or participate in traditional farm and house chores.

Spectator Sports

CONNECTICUT OPEN
900 Chapel St., #622
New Haven, CT 06515
(203) 776-7331
ctopen.org

Once called the Pilot Pen Tournament, the Connecticut Open brings big-name tennis players every year to play at Yale's Connecticut Tennis Center. Part of a linked series of tournaments leading to the US Open, the New Haven event is broadcast on ESPN and around the world. Accompanying the open is the New Haven Food and Wine Festival, which features different events during the days of tennis, such as a barbecue contest, cocktail-making classes, wine and champagne tastings, and tastings of the city's top restaurants' top dishes. Besides these events, there is a large food court. Park on Central Avenue across from the Yale Bowl and follow the signs to the Tennis Center, where you can watch the main event or wander out to the outer courts to watch secondary play. It's

a great tournament and usually features the top female players in the world, like Wimbledon champion Petra Kvitova.

Theater

LONG WHARF THEATRE
222 Sargent Dr.
New Haven, CT 06511
(203) 787-4282
longwharf.org

This Tony Award–winning, nonprofit regional theater opened in 1965 with Connecticutian Arthur Miller's opening of *The Crucible*. Ever since it has been one of four (or more) excellent theaters in New Haven, even though it is situated in a food terminal away from the center of town. They have both traditional and experimental plays here, have won Pulitzers for their original plays, and bring in Hollywood actors like Al Pacino, Kathleen Turner, and Kevin Spacey. Long Wharf also hosts jazz concerts and other shows on "stage 2," a cement-block (and yet still somehow charming) theater next to the main stage. The main stage is surrounded on three sides by seating, so you'll have a good view of the action from wherever you sit, but try for a few rows back in section C or E.

SEVEN ANGELS THEATRE
1 Plank Rd.
Waterbury, CT 06705
(203) 757-4676
sevenangelstheatre.org

Seven Angels in Waterbury was founded 25 years ago as a not-for-profit professional regional theater. They bring in off-Broadway hits like *Nunsense* as well as original world-premiere plays. As an equity theater, they have an apprenticeship program and children's theater, and are one of the most consistent dramatic groups in the state. They also feature other events, such as comedy performances. Located in the historic Hamilton Park Pavilion near I-84, restored for the theater's use, these plays are readily accessible to more than just Waterbury residents. Even to you.

YALE CABARET
217 Park St.
New Haven, CT 06511
(203) 432-1566
yalecabaret.org

The Yale Cabaret has been making New Haven proud for over 40 years. Located a block from the Yale Rep, the Cabaret is more bohemian. The basement theater is intimate, funky, and exactly what a cabaret should be. Productions are student-run, and performances are interpretive, often edgy, and passionately performed. The theater is small, so seating is limited at round tables with high chairs. The lighting is low, and the music before the performances is jazzy and mellow. Food and drinks are served. The season runs during the academic year and shows are Thurs, Fri, and Sat at 8:30 p.m., with a second performance on Fri and Sat at 11 p.m. The Summer Cabaret is in full swing in late June and early July. Tickets are reasonable ($25, $14 for students), so it's a great way to enjoy theater on a student's budget, even if you're well past graduate school.

*YALE REPERTORY THEATRE
1120 Chapel St.
New Haven, CT 06510
(203) 432-1234
yalerep.org

The Yale Repertory Theater consistently produces world-premiere plays and interesting adaptations of classic drama. Housed at the corner of Chapel and York Streets, the theater was once the Calvary Baptist Church, and the building's Gothic Revival architecture dates from 1846. Award-winning and up-and-coming playwrights join exceptional directors, designers, and actors for dynamic performances. Plays that begin at the theater often move on to Broadway, and such productions have been nominated for more than 40 Tony Awards. The Yale Center for New Theatre, established in 2008, has worked closely with new Repertory productions and for theaters across the country. Notable past productions include *Death of a Salesman, Notes from the Underground,* and *The Piano Lesson.*

Water Sports

STONY CREEK KAYAK
327 Leetes Island Rd.
Branford, CT 06405
(203) 481-6401
No website

Stony Creek is a fascinating little fishing village that will have you thinking you stepped into a book of long ago, complete with lobstermen and oyster boats. It is also a great place to launch a kayak into Long Island Sound. Christopher Huage offers instruction to beginners and longer tours to those who already know how. You can also reserve tours of the Connecticut River and other destinations, but this is his home base. You will kayak out among the Thimble Islands, truly one of Connecticut's most fascinating areas. Some are mere tidal rocks; others sport mansions and summer homes historically owned by notables like President William Taft. You'll also see cormorants and egrets, ospreys and oystercatchers. This is an area of Connecticut you shouldn't miss, and kayaking is the best way to see it.

SHOPPING

Antiques

ANTIQUES ON WHITNEY
2285 Whitney Ave., #4
Hamden, CT 06518
(203) 287-9015
antiquesonwhitney.com

Established at the end of the 20th century, this antiques store just off the Merritt Parkway in Hamden caters to the New Haven crowd, and to those passing through on their way north to Hartford. They specialize in lamps and crystal and brass chandeliers, paintings, vintage costume and estate jewelry, linens, sterling silver, cameos, glass, china, and stunning furniture. Open every day but Monday, Antiques on Whitney offers appraisal and estate liquidation services as well. This is not a junk store, and yet, perhaps because it is not in a heavily shopped antiques district, the prices are reasonable and fair.

THE CONNECTICUT STORE

116 Bank St.
Waterbury, CT 06702
(800) 474-6728
ctstore.com

This unassuming storefront in Waterbury is in a class of its own, an unclassifiable and unique place to visit. Once the old Howland Hughes Department Store, it is now just called the Connecticut Store and is located in a smaller, more manageable area of the old building (the larger part has been turned into a gallery). When Howland Hughes, the last downtown department store in New England, turned 108 years old, they did not abandon the building but stayed as caretakers and generated income by specializing in local products. In fact, they do most of their business online but display some of the merchandise here for you to come and see. In the rambling store you'll find local jams, relishes, and honeys; Pez candy; real Christmas tree ornaments made from recycled Christmas trees; pressed flower creations; and locally made jewelry. You'll find Woodbury pewter, brass buttons from Waterbury, Liberty Candles from Bolton, and Wiffle Ball sets from Shelton, which the store ships to 52 countries plus Antarctica. Talk to the owner, Hank, who will tell you the stories of old Connecticut. Maybe you'll even come away with a little piece of future history.

FRED GIAMPIETRO FOLK ART

153½ Bradley St.
New Haven, CT 06511
(203) 787-3851
fredgiampietro.com

Fred Giampietro and his wife, Kathryn, run this antiques store in New Haven, specializing in 19th- and 20th-century folk art. Giampietro is a leading expert in the field and helps many people build private collections. The store also has a gallery with changing exhibitions of contemporary art, open Tues through Fri from 10 a.m. to 4 p.m. Call if you'd like to also browse the collection of antiques, in which you might find painted furniture, folk art portraits, decoys, weathervanes, needlework samplers, whirligigs, game boards, carousel figures, cigar store Indians, hooked rugs, and more. Giampietro has been in the business for over 25 years, and as a leader in his discipline, is a great resource for other Connecticut antiques dealers.

GRASS ISLAND MARKET

301 Boston Post Rd.
Guilford, CT 06437
(203) 689-5072
facebook.com/grassislandmarket

Once a car dealership, the Grass Island Market is now a collection of antiques and collectibles dealers run by Charles Mannix, who exchanged cars for this. Many of these dealers are amateurs rather than professional antiques dealers, and bargaining is encouraged as a fun part of the process. Think of it as a high-class tag sale that the whole street is putting on at once. The flea market is open from 9 a.m. to 3 p.m. at the old car dealership next to the water tower. Expect to find bargains here; there are solid antiques, but most is fun stuff that you will be excited to take home for only a few dollars. Everything from clocks to bottles to jewelry is available. It's also right next to the Shoreline Diner, so stop there for a bite and then browse to your heart's content.

Auctions

NEST EGG AUCTIONS
30 Research Pkwy.
Meriden, CT 06450
(203) 630-1400
nesteggauctions.com

The Brechlin family runs this auction house in Meriden, and their events often feel more like theater than auction—fun even if you don't buy anything. They have a series of estate and thematic auctions throughout the year, mostly on Saturday nights or afternoons, as well as a weekly Monday-night auction, at which local dealers and amateurs can reserve a table or just bring one item to sell. (They offer a dozen or so other fine pieces each Monday as well.) The huge, 12,000-square-foot warehouse where they hold the auctions is always packed, so get there early. You can get great bargains here, especially on those Monday nights, or at the end of Saturday night, when the serious dealers and collectors have tapped their resources. If you've never been to an auction, Nest Egg is an approachable place to start this exciting hobby, or just buy a couple of chairs to accent your living room.

Books

ATTICUS BOOKSTORE AND CAFE
1082 Chapel St.
New Haven, CT 06510
(203) 776-4040
atticusbookstorecafe.com

This independent bookstore has been serving New Haven for the almost 40 years. It actually predates the Yale Museum of British Art, below which it is located. The selection of books is top-notch, authors stop by even when they don't have an event, and it is located in the heart of the Yale shopping district. The Yale Rep is a few doors down, and the Yale University Art Gallery is across the street. The cafe has great sandwiches and salads, as well as some surprising entrees like slow-roasted chicken with crispy macaroni and cheese or barbecue pork turnovers. The coffee is perfect, and the breads and pastries from the Chabaso Bakery (run by the owners of Atticus) are to die for. Even if you're not interested in the books, grab one of their famous baguettes to enjoy as you walk up Chapel Street between museums and theaters.

BARNES & NOBLE BOOKSELLERS
Multiple Locations
barnesandnoble.com

Check the website for a location in this area. A well-known franchise, it has many locations throughout the state that offer a selection of products based on clientele preferences.

COLLECTED STORIES
12 Daniel St.
Milford, CT 06460
(203) 874-0115
collectedstoriesbookstore.com

This small but packed bookstore in the center of Milford has a great collection of used classics in fine condition. There is a large fiction section, along with carefully chosen architecture, essay, and history books, including a sizable local history section, as well as books on pirates and other seafarers. For literature lovers they have a great selection of the Beats and the modernists. Collected Stories also sponsors events like weekly tarot readings. This downtown area of Milford is definitely worth a walk, with many small shops and restaurants, a long village green, and a quaint, protected harbor and marina. Try the Bistro Basque for lunch, or head over to the classic Stonebridge Restaurant (see entry).

JOHN BALE BOOK COMPANY
158 Grand St.
Waterbury, CT 06702
(203) 591-1801
johnbalebooks.com

The natural connection between books and food comes to fruition at this bookstore and cafe in downtown Waterbury. But this is not just a cafe for book nerds; you'll find this is also a place that local businesspeople, police officers, and construction workers frequent. The old stained glass under the metal awning lets you know you're in for an unusual treat as you head under the movie-marquee entrance into this 2-story antiquarian bookstore. Try one of the stews if you're there for lunch. On Saturday you can even get breakfast, and on occasion a live pianist has been known to accompany your meal (or your search for books). They have thousands of comic books; if you're a collector, you'll be salivating at more than the food.

*R. J. JULIA BOOKSELLER
768 Boston Post Rd.
Madison, CT 06443
(203) 245-3959
rjjulia.com

Downtown Madison is home to the most famous independently owned bookstore in the state. R. J. Julia opened in 1990 and continues to be committed to the joys of the written word. The atmosphere is relaxed and inviting, and the floor-to-ceiling selection on two floors is vast and easily navigable with the help of dedicated booksellers who will point you in the direction of what you may be looking for or introduce you to hidden gems. With over 300 events each year, R. J. Julia's is the premiere establishment for author readings and signings. As you browse, scan the sizable photo collection of authors who have read here, including the likes of Martha Stewart, Toni Morrison, and Salman Rushdie. Workshops, book clubs, and kid-friendly events also fill the calendar. You may even run into chef and author Jacques Pépin, who lives nearby, coming in to autograph a book. The cafe in the back of the store, operated by La Rosticceria, offers sandwiches, salads, cupcakes, and coffee.

WHITLOCK'S BOOK BARN
20 Sperry Rd.
Bethany, CT 06524
(203) 393-1240
whitlocksbookbarn.com/shop

Whitlock's has been in the book business on a charming horse farm in Bethany since 1948, and once you see it, you'll understand why it is still going strong. The two small barns have plenty of rare and inexpensive used books for both the casual browser and the avid collector. Don't miss the upstairs of the second barn, which has an amazing collection of maps and prints for sale. Enjoy the horses in the adjacent pasture, and the groundhogs scurrying around the parking lot. When you've had your fill of books, take a drive north on picture-postcard Sperry Road, or if you're in the mood for a walk, head down the gravel extension just south of Whitlock's. It is one of the most gorgeous old stone-walled roads in the state. Go left at the turnoff to Sperry Park, on a path that leads past a foundation from Sperry Farm (where one of the three judges who ordered the execution of the British King hid from their pursuers) to a rushing waterfall with the remnants of an old mill.

YALE BOOKSTORE
77 Broadway
New Haven, CT 06511
(203) 777-8440
yale.bncollege.com

Technically run by Barnes & Noble, the Yale Bookstore bears only a slight resemblance to the well-known chain. Along with all the Yale memorabilia that you can imagine, this huge multi-level store has a larger selection of new books, magazines, art books, and literary journals than any other store in the state. Along with apparel and school supplies, you will also find small appliances, computer accessories, and backpacks. Park at the very convenient and strangely cheap lot in the center of Broadway, and spend an hour or two browsing the shelves before enjoying a sandwich at the cafe. If all college bookstores could only be this extensive and well run, students might not complain about the price of textbooks so often.

Clothing

FLIRT
3551 Whitney Ave.
Hamden, CT 06518
(203) 287-0092
flirtboutiquect.com
Near the old millpond, at the location of the old Carriage Axle Factory, Flirt is Hamden's (many say all of New Haven County's) premier boutique. The staff is incredibly helpful, and will tell you what clothes will fit your frame best. The owner, Meryl Henrici, brings in fashions from New York City once a month, and the store is always filled with new merchandise. Dresses, jewelry, belts, and handbags are all available, and Meryl and her staff will work with you to find something just for you without ever being pushy or patronizing like some boutiques unfortunately are. Flirt is everything a boutique should be: a place for women to find confidence in their appearance.

Farm Stores/Pick Your Own

*BISHOP'S ORCHARDS
1355 Boston Post Rd.
Guilford, CT 06437
(203) 453-2338
bishopsorchards.com
Bishop's has been in operation for more than 140 years, providing the finest farm products to residents up and down the shoreline for six generations. Open year-round and conveniently located on Route 1 in Guilford, the market is vast. Inside you'll find the bakery, filled with fresh pies, breads, donuts, and other goodies. Outside is the garden center. Besides fresh produce that changes with the seasons, the market offers a wide selection of local meats. Most notably, the orchards provide peaches, pears, and apples, and these along with strawberries, blueberries, and pumpkins make up the pick-your-own choices. Located in the market, the winery is open for tastings 7 days a week. Apple wines are the signature offerings, and you can try Celebration 1871, which tends toward the dry side, or Stone House White for a sweeter sip.

PINCHBECK ROSE FARM
929 Boston Post Rd.
Guilford, CT, 06437
(203) 453-2186
No website
Do you like roses? Sure you do. Well, then you couldn't find a better place than Pinchbeck's to get some of the most beautiful roses in America, beloved by clients from the late Joan Crawford to Barbara Bush. Since 1929, when William Pinchbeck Jr. founded the farm, they have used the largest iron-framed greenhouse in the world (1,200 feet long and 81 feet wide) as well as another huge greenhouse to grow 90,000 rose bushes. That's 3 million blooms a year. They heat their greenhouses with recycled wood and use steam from their boilers to produce

electricity. Pinchbeck also runs Roses for Autism (rosesforautism.com) a wonderful nonprofit organization that ships and delivers fresh roses, lilies, and gifts across America.

Home & Crafts

DOMESTIC POSSESSIONS
11 Garnet Park Rd.
Madison, CT 06443
(203) 350-0558
domesticpossessions.com

Domestic Possessions is a collective of small boutiques, all of which rent space in the larger store. This business model is catching on fast, and this Madison version is one of the most successful, melding all these different specialties into a cohesive whole. One of the boutiques is Annie Mame, the creation of local news anchor and celebrity Ann Nyberg, and is my personal favorite, filled with the nostalgia of yesteryear. Browse this beautifully arranged space and find furniture, jewelry, bath and body products, and countless items for the home.

FAIRHAVEN FURNITURE
72 Blatchley Ave.
New Haven, CT 06513
(203) 776-3099
fairhaven-furniture.com

This remarkable store in the Fair Haven section of town is the place to go if you are designing your new home, or just looking for that perfect piece. These are not antiques, but the best of modern craft furniture and accessories. For over 30 years the store has been a family-run business, located on three floors in a historic factory building, with a loyal customer base. Kerry Trifin and Elizabeth Orsini specialize in wood—cherry, walnut, maple, ash, mahogany—and scour the country's craft shows and artists' studios to get the best pieces from up to 150 suppliers. Wandering through the store is itself a calming experience; imagine having this furniture in your home.

*KEBABIAN'S ORIENTAL RUGS
73 Elm St.
New Haven, CT 06510
(203) 865-0567
kebabian.com

Kebabian's Oriental Rugs is the oldest business of its kind in America, owned and operated by the same family since 1882. John Kebabian emigrated from Turkey to attend Yale, and sold his first rug to help pay his tuition. The current owner, also named John Kebabian, has been running the store since 1992 and brings in authentic, hand-knotted rugs and carpets from all over the world. They also offer other services, like restoration and padding, and give demonstrations by hosting traveling Turkish and Tibetan weavers at the shop; these are well attended by locals and rug enthusiasts every time. Simply put, you will not find a more well-respected and durable shop to buy your next rug.

Malls

WESTFIELD CONNECTICUT POST SHOPPING MALL
1201 Boston Post Rd.
Milford, CT 06460
(203) 878-6837
westfield.com/connecticutpost

This mall right off I-95 in Milford is always a buzzing hive of activity. The large stores—Dick's Sporting Goods, Sears, Target, JCPenney, and Macy's—anchor the giant 215-store shopping center. You will find many others that will suit your needs, from Generation X to Yankee Candle. There are over 30 places to eat, including Sakura Garden and Buffalo Wild Wings, and a movie theater as well, making the mall a great place to spend the day and evening. The mall is also located along the famous Post Road, which has hundreds more shopping opportunities up and down its length, in case the hundreds of stores at the mall aren't enough to satisfy your endless shopping needs.

Music & Video

BEST VIDEO
1842 Whitney Ave.
Hamden, CT 06517
(203) 287-9286
bestvideo.com

This is the only video store in this guidebook, and there's a good reason for that. Founded by iconoclast Hank Paper in 1985, it is consistently rated the best in the state (it might be the only one left actually) and offers a unique selection of 60,000 movie titles on DVD and VHS. Many are also for sale, often for under $5, and they have everything you need for a night at the movies, like popcorn and ice cream. They also now feature a coffee shop that serves donuts from Beach Donuts and coffee from Willoughby's, a great example of independent local businesses helping one another. Best Video also has a space amid the rows of videos where lecturers speak and musicians give performances, so they are technically competing with themselves for an evening's entertainment. That's okay—Best Video is still in business despite the web-based companies because they do things better, faster, and friendlier than anyone else.

Specialty Foods

BON APPETIT
2979 Whitney Ave.
Hamden, CT 06518
(203) 248-0648
bonappetitct.com

Among the many specialty food stores in Connecticut, Bon Appetit stands out for reliable service with a smile since 1971. Not only will they work with customers to bring in whatever specialties they desire, they also carry hard-to-find cheeses, pâtés, pastas, coffees, olives, jams, scones, salsas, tarts, chocolates, cookies, olive oils, and vinegars. People drive all the way up Whitney Avenue from New Haven and down I-91 from Meriden for this store. While you're here picking up caviar or smoked salmon, grab some wine to go with it next door at Mount Carmel Wine and Spirits. We don't usually include liquor stores in these guides, but the selection of fine French wines at this amazing 1934 shop in the 19th-century James Ives general store is worth your attention.

EDDY'S BAKE SHOP
317 Main St.
Ansonia, CT 06401
(203) 735-0501
eddysbakeshop.net

This is the place to get fresh breads, rolls, pastries, donuts, Danishes, cakes, cookies, and pies in the Naugatuck Valley. They make cookie trays delivered to your door and the best rye bread for miles around. They actually serve coffee in the morning as well, and could just as easily fit into the breakfast & lunch category in the restaurants section, because so many people stop here in the morning. But their breads are also used by dozens of local businesses, especially their fine Portuguese rolls. Eddy's has been in business for almost 50 years and is a classic Italian bakery, but they also make the best Eastern European babokva around. Don't worry about that incongruity, just taste.

FILIPEK'S MARKET
262 Elm St.
Meriden, CT 06450
(203) 237-3488
No website

Drive too fast and you will miss this little store in a residential neighborhood of Meriden. It was originally owned by the Filipek brothers and has been in business for over

60 years, now in the fourth generation. They make kielbasa—the best kielbasa you might ever taste. My brother-in-law swears by the double-smoked, but you might prefer the spicy one. Sure they sell pierogi and cabbage and other Polish specialties, but their kielbasa is the reason everyone comes back time and time again. Everyone I know in the area speaks of this tiny family-run market with reverence because of their dedication to the craft. It's also like stepping back in time to go here—a time when we all got our food from little family markets like this, and they stood or fell on the strength of their friendliness and their quality. The quality here has been high enough to keep Filipek's going when so many others like it have disappeared from the American landscape.

FOXGLOVE AND MADISON CHEESE
119 Samson Rock Dr.
Madison, CT 06443
(203) 245-5168
foxgloveandmadisoncheese.com
If you're in the mood for a delicious grilled cheese, head to Madison Cheese, where they can make one from any of their dozens of delicious cheeses. Of course you can also stop in for the cheese itself, or other wonderful gourmet foods. The tomato soup was pretty good too! Order ahead for a cheese platter or gift basket. This place has the largest selection of cheese in Connecticut as far as I can tell, including some of my favorites: Drunken Goat, Cotswold, and Humbolt Fog. But it will take me a couple years to get through them all, so my favorites might change.

SUGAR CUPCAKERY AND BAKERY
422 Main St.
East Haven, CT 06512
(203) 469-0815
thesugarbakery.com

Just a minute from the old stone church on the East Haven green, this "cupcakery" is a splash of color on Main Street, both outside and inside. Round racks of candy, a jelly bean dispenser, chocolate-covered marshmallow popsicles, and "Sugar Addict" T-shirts are just the warm-up for the huge selection of cupcakes. They have unbelievably decadent flavors like chocolate butter crunch, Oreo explosion, peanut butter riot, red velvet, cookie dough, pink flamingo, icebox cake—the list goes on. The Oreo explosion tastes like an Oreo, if it was a home-baked cupcake. They also make fresh cookies and pizzelles. In the back at the "Custom Candy Buffet" they will do your wedding cake or, better yet, your wedding cupcakes. The mother-daughter team of Carol Vollono and Brenda DePonte even won an episode of Food Network's *Cupcake Wars*. It was well deserved.

ACCOMMODATIONS

All lodgings have both smoking and non-smoking rooms unless otherwise noted, or have a designated smoking area, and do not accept pets unless noted. Hotels, motels, and resorts are wheelchair accessible unless otherwise noted. Bed-and-breakfasts and inns are not wheelchair accessible unless otherwise noted, since many are in historic buildings exempt from the Americans with Disabilities Act. Call to make sure if there's any question. We do not list specific credit cards in either this section or the restaurants section.

Bed-and-Breakfasts

CORNUCOPIA AT OLDFIELD $$$
782 Main St. North
Southbury, CT 06488
(203) 267-6772
cornucopiabnb.com
Southbury doesn't seem like it should be part of New Haven County, and even the

innkeepers at the Cornucopia announce their presence in the Litchfield Hills, which geographically they certainly are. Built in 1818 by John Moseley, the house is in Southbury's historic district and on the National Register of Historic Places. It contains over 2 acres of gardens and lawn, as well as a large flagstone patio and swimming pool for you to relax in. Inside, large public rooms with original fireplaces and 5 guest rooms with private baths are full of modern amenities for modern travelers. Innkeepers Christine and Ed Edelson love to help you plan your activities, and expect a nice conversation in the Keeping Room over a plate of cheese and a few glasses of wine.

HIGH MEADOW   **$$**
1290 Whirlwind Hill Rd.
Wallingford, CT 06492
(203) 269-2351
high-meadow.com

This house is ancient, constructed in 1742, but has been moved from its original location in Branford up the road to a farm in Wallingford. Once it was known as the Jonathan Towner Half Way Tavern, a popular travelers' stop between New York and Boston. Since 1975 it has served the same purpose here among meadows in Wallingford. There are 3 rooms in the main house, one of which is decorated in a fascinating "Thai" manner and the others more traditionally. You can also stay in Brae Cottage, a small home in an open field overlooking a pond, with a fireplace, terrace, kitchen, dining room, and bathroom with whirlpool tub and shower. It even has its own washer and dryer and is the perfect place for a long stay here in central Connecticut. Your location on Whirlwind Hill puts you right between two of Connecticut's vineyards, so you should certainly stop at one (or both) on your travels from High Meadow.

TIDEWATER INN   **$$$**
949 Boston Post Rd.
Madison, CT 06443
(203) 245-8457
thetidewater.com

Off the Post Road in Madison near the tidal wetlands of Long Island Sound by the shores of Fence Creek, this charming bed-and-breakfast features an English garden for you to relax in. Of the 9 nonsmoking guest rooms available, 2 rooms on the ground floor have fireplaces. The inn also features a private cottage, with a king bed, galley kitchen, and Jacuzzi. And of course you can get breakfast, with specialties like peach soup. From the inn you can walk into downtown Madison to shop at R. J. Julia's or ride your bike down to the beach. They have an unbelievable number of package deals and special offers, from the Lobster Lover's Escape to Connecticut Eccentricities. Browse them on the website, or ask the innkeepers which one suits you best.

TUCKER HILL INN   **$$**
96 Tucker Hill Rd.
Middlebury, CT 06762
(203) 758-8334
tuckerhillinn.com

Opened first as a "tea room" in 1923, the Tucker Hill Inn has a winding staircase and is surrounded by huge oaks and maples. Located in Middlebury, the inn is literally at the center of three counties and is the perfect spot from which to journey to all of them. There are 4 guest rooms, 2 of which can be combined into a family suite. They are all named for works by Nathaniel Hawthorne (like the Scarlet Room), because owner Susan Cebelenski is related to that famous author. She is also an expert in fashion, and her husband refurbishes antiques. You'll see evidence of their crafts throughout this beautifully appointed home. Prices are radically different according to season, as might be expected. Why not make an off-season trip here to the nexus of New Haven, Litchfield, and Fairfield Counties?

WALLINGFORD VICTORIAN BED AND BREAKFAST $$$
245 N. Main St.
Wallingford, CT 06492
(877) 269-4499
bedandbreakfastwallingford.com

For the last 10 years this beautiful Victorian house in Wallingford has been welcoming guests to its large rooms. You can walk into the center of town here, or jump onto the Merritt or I-91 to reach New Haven or Hartford easily. There are 3 rooms in the house currently available, each with its own amenities. The Samuel Suite has a Jacuzzi and private entrance. The Georgianna Suite includes a sitting room and work area in the tower, as well as a private balcony. The Margaret Room can be joined to the Georgianna for a family suite. Owners Jeff and Brenda also run a furnished condo unit a mile away by the railroad station; with 2 bedrooms, it's the perfect place for a longer stay, available by the week or month.

Hotels & Motels

✴MADISON BEACH HOTEL $$$
94 W. Wharf Rd.
Madison, CT 06443
(203) 245-1404
madisonbeachhotel.com

Right on a private beach overlooking a small island, the Madison Beach Hotel has 33 nonsmoking waterfront rooms and suites, all with balconies. It was once a hotel in the 1800s, and has recently been refurbished and reconstructed into a world-class destination. There are 3 dining options right on the premises, including a traditional steak and seafood restaurant called Tides on the Sound, with a bar that's open until midnight. The Wharf is a more casual dining room with views of the Sound and a stone fireplace for chillier evenings. It's also open until midnight for late-night cocktails after a walk on the beach. Rick's Raw Bar is your third option, open only in summer until sunset and offering fresh-shucked clams and more in the great outdoors. You can rent bikes and kayaks to work off all those calories, and the hotel also features a spa with massages, facials, manicures, and pedicures. People loved this place even before it was renovated, and now it is one of the prime waterfront hotels in the state.

✴THE STUDY $$$
1157 Chapel St.
New Haven, CT 06511
(203) 503-3900
studyhotels.com

This unique boutique hotel in New Haven has set a new standard for the city. The Study offers 124 guest rooms that include 8 suites and the Presidential Suite, as well as a variety of levels of accommodation from doubles to deluxe kings. But that doesn't really tell you about the soft leather reading chairs with ottomans in every room, as well as work spaces, featherbeds, seersucker robes, glass showers, and flat-screen televisions. Many of the rooms have a separate "den" with stocked bookshelves. The lobby (or living room) features calming music and tons of reading material (including huge art books and international newspapers like *Le Monde*), and serves coffee, tea, and snacks. There is a fitness center, a number of meeting spaces, and a ballroom. The Penthouse Lounge has panoramic views of the Yale campus, and the Heirloom restaurant attached to the Study is a fantastic seasonally inspired restaurant (see entry). The thing you will study here is your own life, and how lucky you are to have reached the point where you can live in such inspired luxury.

Inns

DOLLY MADISON INN $$
73 W. Wharf Rd.
Madison, CT 06443
(203) 245-7377
cristysmadison.com

A few steps from Madison Beach, "The Dolly" is a New England country inn with a seaside flavor. It is a relatively inexpensive place to stay in New Haven County, with 6 modern rooms and 5 that have not been updated for a few decades. The main building dates back to the turn of the 20th century. The restaurant at the inn serves lunch and dinner all day, every day, and Sunday breakfast from 9 a.m. to 12:30 p.m. They have many seafood dishes, like oysters on the half shell and fisherman's platters, as well as beef, duck, and other classic American delights. The bar is popular with both locals and people summering on the shore here; it is a great place to get an evening drink.

INN AT LAFAYETTE $$$
725 Boston Post Rd.
Madison, CT 06443
(203) 245-7773
innatlafayette.com

In downtown Madison you'll see the blue sign for Cafe Allegre first, then underneath it a smaller one for the Inn at Lafayette. It's not usual to have the restaurant take first billing, but since Cafe Allegre's food is legendary (see entry), why not stay the night upstairs at their inn? There are 5 comfortable, suite-like rooms with marble baths and Egyptian linens, as well as all the amenities a business traveler might need. You are literally downtown here, right next to the Madison Cinema and across the street from R. J. Julia's. It's a great pleasure to walk upstairs after your meal, following a day of excitement in coastal New Haven County. Try the inn above Cafe Allegre, and you'll eat and rest well.

Camping

HAMMONASSET STATE PARK $
1288 Boston Post Rd.
Madison, CT 06443
(203) 245-2785
ct.gov/dep [search "Hammonasset State Park"]

There are 550 campsites here at this beautiful park, an astounding number in Connecticut, and you'll rarely not be able to get a spot without reservations, except perhaps on Memorial Day or Labor Day weekend. The park is known for having the longest public beach in the state, and you'll feel like you're in Cape Cod or Cape Hatteras. The camping is at the west end of the park, near the entrance, and some of it is only steps from the beach. Those sites on the "beach road" are windblown classics, although you will have people tramping by your tent or trailer to get to the beach. Otherwise, get a site in Area 1, the most wooded and wilderness-feeling of the many camping areas. Try camping here in autumn, when there are few rowdy children or loud radios; and though you won't want to swim, the 2-mile beach walk is lovely, and you'll have the bike trails to yourself.

RESTAURANTS

Please note that all Connecticut restaurants are smoke free, and all are required to be wheelchair accessible. Pets are not allowed inside most restaurants, but during the warmer months, there are plenty of restaurants with patio areas just right for your canine friend. Call ahead to make sure it's okay.

American & Modern

HEIRLOOM $$$
1157 Chapel St.
New Haven, CT 06511
(203) 503-3919
studyhotels.com/heirloom

The glass vestibule leads you into a restaurant that is clean and open, like a modern library for food. The chef trained with Todd English, but the menu is not Italian. Instead you'll find old favorites re-imagined, like cool buttermilk corn soup, crispy farm okra, local butter clam pan roast, and duck sausage with caramelized potato. You never know what you'll find on this seasonally changing menu, like bacon-wrapped dates and pistachios, asparagus and buffalo mozzarella, or salmon with sorrel sauce. There is a bar next to the restaurant where you can get small plates, though most of the so-called small plates at Heirloom could be meals themselves. This is one of the many cutting-edge restaurants in New Haven serving creative food that still tastes like something Mom would make. If your mom was a classically trained French chef, that is.

HOME $$
1114 Main St.
Branford, CT 06405
(203) 483-5896
homerestaurantct.com

Home is a fascinating blend of everything that shouldn't work but does. The restaurant is split into a "living room," with plush couches for lunch or drinks, and the "dining room," a slightly more formal, white-tablecloth area, though still quite casual and hip. You can get "homey" dishes like grilled cheese and tomato soup, or cutting-edge cuisine like Faroe Island salmon with sweet corn succotash. During an afternoon you'll find women relaxing with a fig Cosmo or Bloody Mary next to a group of teenagers drinking coffee and eating pork belly Reubens. They also have extensive gluten-free options. If your mother actually made food this good, we wouldn't need restaurants.

JIMMIES $$
5 Rock St.
West Haven, CT 06516
(203) 934-3212
jimmiesofsavinrock.com

Jimmies of Savin Rock has been a mainstay of the West Haven shore since 1925. Back then, Jimmie Gagliardi and his family started with a road stand, drawing customers with his split hot dogs. The restaurant continues to be family operated. Their famous hot dogs are still available and are just one reason to check out this classic eatery. Seating is ample, inside and out; umbrellas shade the sun in warmer months, and Long Island Sound is just outside, past the bike path and beach. Consistently awarded Best Waterfront Dining, Jimmies' blue vinyl booths and sunny tables fill up all year. Seafood, hand-cut steaks, and pasta dishes fill the menu, and the platters are a big draw, featuring deep-fried samplings of clams, calamari, scallops, or oysters. Portions are huge, and early birds take advantage of dinner specials.

116 CROWN $$$
116 Crown St.
New Haven, CT 06510
(203) 777-3116
116crown.com

The green onyx bar is the first thing you'll notice when you step into this old hotel on Crown Street. You can eat in a fiberglass pod constructed by a local shipbuilder (cooler than it sounds) or at more traditional tables in the back. But the food and drink is what should have your full attention here, because this fairly new restaurant is breaking ground in New Haven. They have small plates like Scotch eggs, roasted bone marrow, hush puppies, and charcuterie (including a seasonal acorn-fed Berkshire pork trio that will make you a born-again pork lover). Larger plates include small pizzas and sandwiches like the John D. Rockefeller with pork belly.

They cure their own pickles here, a sure sign that they care about the craft. 116 Crown also sports a huge selection of creative original cocktails, which you can have with dinner or drink at their ultracool bar. If you're stuffed after dinner, try their spiked hot chocolate, a beautiful and tasty concoction. And if you want to know how to make a great drink, they run cocktail classes, which are really social events where everyone learns to mix.

PARK CENTRAL TAVERN $$$
1640 Whitney Ave.
Hamden, CT 06517
(203) 287-8887
parkcentraltavern.com

In the historic Spring Glen section of Hamden, right up Whitney Avenue from New Haven, this beautiful restaurant serves great food at a better price than equivalent fine American dining in New Haven. It's a place where you can wear jeans or take your children, but with top-of-the-line food. The fried oysters are done exactly right, and if you've never tried this treat (Abraham Lincoln's favorite dish) before, this is the place to do it. Johnson's macaroni and cheese takes an American classic and instead of turning it on its head as so many modern restaurants do, just does it exactly right, with or without lobster. That's the Park Central Tavern in a nutshell—food the way you hope it used to be, and actually is today.

ZINC $$$
964 Chapel St.
New Haven, CT 06510
(203) 624-0507
zincfood.com

When Zinc first opened back in the day, I thought their prices too high and their food just okay. Unfortunately, I did not go back right away and missed a revolution in food happening right under my nose. Now they have cutting-edge farm-to-table cuisine with global flavors, plus great drinks and creative fusion dishes. For an appetizer get the smoked duck nachos, for dinner try the naturally raised hangar steak, and for dessert enjoy the caramelized corn pudding. Then relax with one of their amazing cocktails, like the Rojo Pimenton, which includes Sombra Mezcal, red bell pepper juice, fresh OJ, lime, simple syrup, and Hellfire bitters.

Asian & Indian

✳BENTARA $$
76 Orange St.
New Haven, CT 06510
(203) 562-2511
bentara.com

Chef Hasni "Jeff" Ghazaliv creates amazing Malaysian dishes at Bentara, located in the Ninth Square historic district of New Haven. The name translates as the "king's highest servant," and sampling the fascinating dishes that cull from Indian, Chinese, and other ethnic influences will make you feel like a king. The spacious 150-seat interior is decorated with dark wood, Malaysian masks, and artifacts silhouetted like shadow puppets behind screened boxes in the walls. Take some time to read the menu descriptions to get a sense of the diverse offerings. Griddle breads are a great place to start, even if you order an appetizer. The unleavened ghee breads are filled with meat, onions, and eggs or, if you prefer, plain. Wok-fried dishes and noodle soups are just part of the menu, and you won't be disappointed with the kelantanese kerutuk, with your choice of beef, chicken, or tofu simmered in rich spices. For a real Malaysian classic, try the nasi lemak (coconut milk rice stir-fried with beef and tossed with spices, eggs, peanuts, and cucumber); you'll soon add Bentara to your list of favorite restaurants.

DARBAR $$

1070 Main St.
Branford, CT 06405
(203) 481-8994
darbarindia.com

The most popular Indian restaurant in New Haven County is out here in the village of Branford. The naan bread is great, the yogurt lassi drinks are great, the biryanis, the vindaloos; everything is great. Like most Indian restaurants, Darbar has multiple selections for vegetarians, and the chef/owner is from Nepal, so the menu has a few great specialties from that mountainous land. They also experiment with dishes like *mirch pakora,* jalapeño peppers dipped in lentil batter. Get one of the dinner specialties, really a reasonably priced feast, which comes in either vegetarian or non-vegetarian options. If you get the chance, come for the Friday to Sunday lunch buffet; it's a great bargain for some of the best Indian food in the state.

MIDORI $$

3000 Whitney Ave., #4
Hamden, CT 06518
(203) 248-3322
No website

This Asian fusion restaurant right off the Route 40 connector combines the best of Korea and Japan. There are any number of fine sushi restaurants in Hamden, more than in its larger neighbor, New Haven, in fact. However, there are few Korean restaurants in the county, and this one is by far the best. It's nestled in an unassuming shopping center in the Mount Carmel section of town, and the reasonable prices often draw a full house in the relatively small, no-frills space. The lunch and dinner specials are a great, cheap introduction to high-quality sushi. The real treasures are the bibimbap hot pot and the selection of Korean noodle soups. The *duk bokki* (rice cake in red hot sauce) is also amazing. Linger over a cup of hot tea at the bar with a good book, and as the other customers leave, listen to the silence of your satisfied taste buds.

*MIYA'S SUSHI $–$$$$

68 Howe St.
New Haven, CT 06511
(203) 777-9760
miyassushi.com

Back in 1982, Miya's was the first sushi bar in New Haven, and it now boasts the first sustainable sushi in the Northeast. It is a cipher in many ways, both high end and affordable, with unassuming decor and prices ranging from cheap as the cheapest sushi joint to as expensive as they come. Like many modern sushi restaurants, they have a selection of unique rolls, some of which do not seem like they would work, but they do, like the peanut butter and jelly roll, using jellyfish. The "invasive species menu" has become famous, taking nonnative species from Long Island Sound and turning them into food. The increasingly famous chef, Bun Lai, also uses elements from global cuisines in Japanese forms to continually surprise you. There is tilapia with sea salt and a little lime, but it comes mostly frozen, "Eskimo style." So good and right, you'll wonder why everyone is not doing it. Bun Lai has unbelievable creativity and an unbelievable commitment to his craft. He has created the most unusual restaurant you'll ever eat at, for many reasons all at once.

THAI AWESOME $$

1505 Dixwell Ave.
Hamden, CT 06514
(203) 288-9888
thaiawesome.net

Located on busy Dixwell Avenue in Hamden, Thai Awesome's small storefront is easy to miss, so look for the sign just south of Treadwell Street. Parking in front is limited; try Bagley Avenue behind and walk around. It's well worth any effort. The restaurant serves traditional Thai dishes, and does them exceptionally well. Do not miss the tom yum goong soup—easily the best around—perfectly harmonized chili-lime goodness, rich and hearty. A small bowl may be enough, or you may have to indulge in the tom yum noodle dish. The menu offers a full range of appetizers (the tofu triangles with chili and ground peanuts is a good bet), salads, and meat, seafood, duck, and vegetable selections. Standouts include wild boar with basil and paradise shrimp. The service is great, and the dining room is tastefully decorated with traditional Thai images. Lunch specials are a great bargain and come with a Siam roll, soup, and salad; go for the drunken noodle.

TIKKAWAY $
135 Orange St.
New Haven, CT 06510
(203) 562 1299
tikkawaygrill.com

Every once in a while a restaurant comes along that changes the way we feel about food. That is the dream of Gopi Nair, owner of this new Indian fast-casual restaurant in New Haven. He was a managing partner in the popular Coromandel chain and is now trying to do for Indian food what Chipotle did for Mexican. And he is on to something. The mix-and-match menu of fresh ingredients makes it incredibly easy to understand and to begin to appreciate the flavors of Indian cuisine. You pick your base, your filling, and your toppings, and presto, you've got a bowl or wrap or salad tempting your taste buds with scents like masala or vindaloo. It will not be a surprise if Gopi's design and model takes this small New Haven bistro nationwide.

TOKYO SUSHI II $$
117 Washington Ave.
North Haven, CT 06473
(203) 907-4050
tokyosushi2.com

The best restaurant in North Haven is Japanese, and it should come as no surprise. There are so many excellent Japanese restaurants in the state, it is often difficult to choose which to praise. Here the quality of the fish is consistently high, and the sushi and rolls come out like culinary art, with small Zen paintings of trees and flowers, done in soy, hot mayo, and wasabi. Try the North Haven roll, with tuna, avocado, and tobiko inside and salmon outside. Or go for the fried oyster roll, a wonderful Japanese twist on this Connecticut invention. The soba and tempura are great here, but this is really a place for Japanese raw fish, done by experts in the craft.

YORK STREET NOODLE HOUSE $
166 York St., #1
New Haven, CT 06511
(203) 776-9675
yorkstnoodlehouse.com

A favorite of Yale students, York Street Noodle is affordable and yummy. The small restaurant is up the stairs from the street, across from the Yale Rep. The menu is rich with Asian fare: dim sum, salad, rice selections, and of course an ample selection of noodle and soup dishes, each under $8, many under $7. Dumplings are available steamed or fried; rice offerings include spicy basil rice with chicken, beef, or seafood. Choose your noodles from thin or thick wonton, rice, or vermicelli. The Vietnamese noodle soup and coconut curry choices are all excellent. The bowls are deep, the noodles are plenty, and the broth steams with aromatic spice. Noodles stand up on their own in dishes like Spicy Mee Yok, wonton noodles and veggies tossed with hot sesame sauce. Go for one of the 25 selections of bubble tea, most under $3.

Austrian & German

WATCH FACTORY RESTAURANT $$$$
122 Elm St.
Cheshire, CT 06410
(203) 271-1717
watchfactoryrestaurant.com

This restaurant anchors the Watch Factory Shops here in Cheshire and features an Austrian menu, which is quite rare in Connecticut. The Central European cuisine by Chef Markus Patsch is delightful, with treats like mussels in cream sauce and roasted monkfish. The duck leg is scrumptious, and be sure to split the gruyère cheese, spaetzle, and crispy onion appetizer. For those preferring a traditional Austrian meal, both the Jaeger and Wiener schnitzels are delicious. Be sure to accompany dinner with a German wine like a Lemberger or Riesling to complete the experience. Their hours can be changeable and they often host large parties, so call ahead and make a reservation. If you come early, wander around the shops and up to the old Cheshire Green to work up an appetite.

Breakfast & Lunch

CAFE ATLANTIQUE $$
33 River St.
Milford, CT 06460
(203) 882-1602
cafeatlantiquedtm.com

This is one of the state's top coffee bars but, oh, so much more. Owned by Sandy Dzialo and Tina Roberts, this corner cafe by the train station serves excellent soups, pastries, salads, crepes, and wraps. Changing art from local artists hangs on the walls, and the Atlantique features poetry and open-mike nights. There's free street parking in Milford, an unusual pleasure, and more across the street near the green. There are a few comfy couches (it is a coffee shop, after all), but if you're there in summer, definitely sit on the alley porch, which will take you immediately to another time and place.

THE CORNER $
105 River St.
Milford, CT 06460
(203) 882-1150
thecornerbrunch.com

Walking into the Corner is a little like walking into an ancient tearoom, or your grandma's sitting room, complete with hutches stacked with china. You will certainly not be expecting culinary experimentation here. But you would be wrong. You'll find things like crispy goat cheese medallions on English muffins and apricot french toast. Their most popular dish is probably an African beef hash, with lentils and spices. Their Sunday brunch is legendary, and you can find things like wild boar sausage and alligator wraps. Of course the Corner also has more traditional food, like buttermilk pancakes and eggs Benedict. But why not go for the gusto? They hand-write lists of the day's specials and only accept cash, so stop by the ATM on your way here.

FUNKY MONKEY $$
130 Elm St.
Cheshire, CT 06410
(203) 439-9161
thefunkymonkeycafe.com

At first you might think this hangout in the Watch Factory Shops of Cheshire is just a neighborhood hangout, but it is much more. With changing exhibits of local art and musical and comedy events throughout the year, this has become a destination for the locals in the surrounding towns. Unlike most coffee shop and sandwich joints, the Funky Monkey has handpicked beer and wine selections as well. Their delicious wraps and paninis are supplemented by baked goods, quiches, gourmet salads, and fruit smoothies. Try the Funky Monkey BLT, with its jalapeño bacon and avocado. Scrumptious.

KATZ'S DELI $$

1658 Litchfield Tpke.
Woodbridge, CT 06525
(203) 389-5301
katzsdeli.net

Off exit 59 of the Wilbur Cross Parkway, just shy of the West Rock Tunnel, Katz's Deli serves some of the most authentic Jewish deli food in the state. "Have a nosh," their menu says, and this family-run joint serves free pickles and coleslaw to all comers, even before you've chosen something from the extensive menu. Blintzes, chicken-in-a-pot, and potato pancakes are served alongside more "mainstream" sandwiches and wraps. Other delicacies, like chopped liver or pickled herring, are well worth the adventurous eater's time. Of course today's adventurous eater was yesterday's traditionalist, and something like hot shaved beef tongue on rye bread will please both grandparents and their foodie grandkids. It certainly melts in my mouth after a morning workout. Although primarily a sit-down, diner-style establishment, Katz's has takeout as well, so you can carry some of this authentic deli food home with you.

NARDELLI'S $

540 Plank Rd.
Waterbury, CT 06705
(203) 754-5600
nardellis.com

Are they hoagies? Submarine sandwiches? Grinders? Whatever your preference, you will find that the Nardelli family of Connecticut makes some of the best you'll ever eat. They use fresh buns and quality meat, far better than those chain stores you might run into (although Subway was, in fact, started in Bridgeport). You definitely want the Miletes bread for your grinder, and try the Italian combo—it's the classic. They have their own peppers and olive mix that they add to them, and accept the wisdom of this on

yours. There are six Nardelli's franchises open now—in Naugatuck, Southbury, Danbury, Middletown, Oxford, and another in Waterbury. Everyone agrees the Waterbury (515 Watertown Ave.) and Naugatuck (87 Maple St.) versions are the best, perhaps because the Nardelli family still oversees them more closely. Nevertheless, these days you can get their grinders all over Connecticut, and you certainly should.

i For a unique food experience, jump off I-95 at Long Wharf Drive (exit 46) and stop at one of the food trucks that gather here every day from 9 a.m. to 9 p.m. If you want real Mexican food like soft tacos with lengua or cabeza, or just a chicken enchilada, this is the place to go.

NEIL'S DONUTS $

83 N. Turnpike Rd.
Wallingford, CT 06492
(203) 269-4255
neilsdonuts.com

Connecticut loves its donuts. This is evidenced by the fact that there are at least twice as many Dunkin' Donuts as its nearest chain fast-food competitors in the state. However, there are also some great local donut shops, and Neil's is one of the best. The chocolate-covered sprinkle donuts are leagues ahead of the fast-food competition. However, it is the old-fashioned donut that is startling: It is either the way donuts used to be or some new fantastic creation. For those of us used to the little old-fashioned "rock" donuts you get at the chains, suddenly we understand their appeal. Make sure to get them warm in the morning, crunch through the outer crust into the dense and chewy layers, and dip them in your hot coffee. Neil's also bakes cookies, pies, coffee rolls, muffins, croissants, and Danishes, as well as a selection of breakfast sandwiches. But as I said, this is a donut-loving land, and Neil's is for the true connoisseur.

TOP O' THE MORNIN' $
2740 S. Main St.
Waterbury, CT 06706
(203) 754-3338
topothemornin.com

If you're looking for something other than donuts for breakfast, the Irish flag awning at Top o' the Mornin' will lead you to a great alternative. Their homemade corned beef hash is amazing; get that and the hash browns with onions and cheese. If that doesn't appeal, how about the filet mignon Benedict? For lunch, try the grilled Reuben (again, that corned beef is delicious) or one of their 100 percent Angus beef burgers. This is simple American food done right, with attention to flavor (not to calories). This is not "fast food," but they do serve you fast. And remember, breakfast is the most important meal of the day.

French

CAESUS FROMAGERIE AND BISTRO $$
93 Whitney Ave.
New Haven, CT 06510
(203) 624-3373
caseusnewhaven.com

This bistro on the corner of Whitney and Trumbull Streets is small but stylish, with a bar area and patio seating upstairs. The downstairs dining area provides the flavor of a Parisian cafe, and the menu is inspired by French cuisine. Order the cheese plate to sample four of the hundreds of artisanal cheeses, selected daily and served with honey, nuts, quince or similar fruit preserves, and breads. *Poutine*, a classic dish of french fries with cheese curds and gravy, is good as an appetizer or as a meal itself. Mac and cheese with big shells full of perfectly blended cheeses is baked and steaming. Try it with bacon, though the added richness

might send you over the edge. Omelet specials and sandwiches are additional pleasures. Visit the cheese shop after lunch and take home Gouda, Manchego, or other delectable goodies.

✴LE PETIT CAFÉ $$$
225 Montowese St.
Branford, CT 06405
(203) 483-9791
lepetitcafe.net

Right off the green in Branford is Le Petit Café, a charming French cafe–style restaurant. Chef Roy Ip creates four-course prix-fixe menus that change weekly and are always extraordinary and well worth $55.50 per person. Open Wed through Sun, reservations are recommended and weekend seatings are at 6 and 8:30 p.m. Duck leg confit (or some variation thereof) is usually one of the appetizer choices, as are the little wonders of the crustacean world and French cooking—escargot. Enjoy the second course of fresh salad with vinaigrette while you finish off fresh bread with truffle butter. Provençal-style rack of lamb, Angus steak au poivre, Chilean sea bass, or duck breast with toasted almonds and sautéed *haricots verts* (green beans) are examples of third-course entrees. Save room for crème brûlée or chocolate hazelnut fondant. The chef selects the proper wine from the wine list, so you'll be sure to have the perfect match for your meal.

UNION LEAGUE CAFE $$$$
1032 Chapel St., #A
New Haven, CT 06510
(203) 562-4299
unionleaguecafe.com

Located in an 1860 brownstone building home to, yes, the Union League, this romantic French restaurant has a rich wood interior and fireplace. They serve "country French" cuisine, which means all the favorites from *confit de canard* to escargot. However, the

Union League changed hands and chefs awhile back, and everyone agrees it is more casual and with even better-tasting food these days. They now feature polished brasserie cooking that follows the seasons, like wild mushroom ravioli and seared New England cod. There's a smaller and less expensive club menu during the week. This was once the site of the home of Roger Sherman, the only man to sign all three founding documents of the US.

Ice Cream

ASHLEY'S ICE CREAM $
280 York St.
New Haven, CT 06511
(203) 776-7744
ashleysicecream.net

Founded in 1979 and named for an amazing Frisbee-catching whippet named Ashley, this ice-cream shop in New Haven never uses artificial colors or flavors, whipping cream fresh in the store every day. Countless Yale students, celebrities, and visiting presidents have come to Ashley's to eat. Flavors vary from traditional, such as espresso bean and strawberry, to interesting creations like Nutella chip, and red, white, and blueberry. Try the Grape-Nuts ice cream, with a sweet cream base and Grape-Nuts cereal, a New England tradition. They bake their own waffle cones and make their own hot fudge as well. There are also shops in Hamden, Guilford, Branford, and Madison.

BIG DIPPER ICE CREAM FACTORY $
91 Waterbury Rd.
Prospect, CT 06712
(203) 758-3200
bigdipper.com

New Haven County (and in fact all of Connecticut) is just jammed with great ice-cream places. Here at the Big Dipper, small-batch ice cream is made from farm-fresh dairy cream, in dozens of flavors, from toasted almond to cookie crunch sundae to Grape-Nuts pudding. They are open every day in summer until 10 p.m., and many times I've satisfied a late-night craving by driving 20 minutes over the hills to this cold and lovely ice-cream parlor. They use the world's highest quality vanilla from the island of Madagascar and the best cocoa made from Holland, along with a choice selection of chocolates, nuts, berries, and the purest of flavors and extracts.

SWEET CLAUDE'S $
828 S. Main St.
Cheshire, CT 06410
(203) 272-4237
sweetclaudes.com

Sweet Claude's old Victorian house in Cheshire seems incongruous. You might notice people relaxing on the green hillside under the twisted cherry tree, or the line snaking out the door even in the off-season, and wonder what you're missing. We'll tell you. All the ice cream (and hot fudge) is made on the premises, with tempting flavors like toasted almond and cupcake. Their "only for adults" Bailey's Irish Cream and rum raisin are a delightful change for Mom and Dad. Sit on the porch above busy Route 10 and wonder why everyone else isn't stopping too.

WENTWORTH'S ICE CREAM $
3697 Whitney Ave.
Hamden, CT 06518
(203) 281-7429
No website

Located along Whitney Avenue (Route 10) between Hamden and Cheshire, Wentworth's is a great stop for old-fashioned homemade ice cream. Look for the sign outside the yellow house with black shutters, especially after a hike on nearby Sleeping Giant or a bike ride along the rail trail. A gazebo and benches are available outside, and it tends to get crowed toward evening.

Inside, a few tables are available with vintage heart-shaped wire-back chairs, checked-tile floor, and cotton candy–colored walls. Creamy classics, unique flavors (try the maple, peppermintstick, or mocha lace), and seasonally made fruit flavors are always generously scooped. Put your own spin on a sundae; try brownies, cookies, and fresh lemonade (if you need a break from the ice cream); and take home a pint. Wentworth's is open year-round, but unfortunately not on Sunday.

Italian

DIORIO $$$
231 Bank St.
Waterbury, CT 06702
(203) 754-5111
diorios.com

In the 1920s legendary Waterbury business-man Rocco Diorio opened this classic restaurant, and after a brief period of disuse in the 1980s, it was opened again after being restored to its original condition. The marble bar is original, as are the large mahogany booths, tile floors, etched back-bar mirrors, and tin ceiling. Serving modern Italian cuisine, Diorio has all the customary Italian dishes, along with some great unsung ones like gemelli with sausage, sun-dried tomatoes, and a mascarpone cream sauce. The veal Diorio is excellent, and the steaks and raw bar are consistently well done. Check out the old buzzers on the wall that used to call the waiters. And don't forget to try one of their signature martinis.

ROÌA $$$
261 College St.
New Haven, CT 06510
(203) 200-7045
roiarestaurant.com

A couple years ago Roìa moved into the old bank at the Taft Hotel/Apartments, a space previously occupied by less-successful restaurants. Named for the border area between France and Italy, its cuisine shows the influence of both (though I sensed more Italian). Try the pappardelle with hen ragu, the duck alla diavolo, the persimmon and hakurei turnips carpaccio, and specials that will have you wanting to come back again and again. The atmosphere is unlike any other restaurant in the state, dark and light at the same time—not great for Instagramming your meal photos, but perfect for a nervous first date or a romantic anniversary.

Latin American

GERONIMO $$
271 Crown St.
New Haven, CT 06511
(203) 777-7700
geronimobarandgrill.com

The steps up to Geronimo's patio on Crown Street lead you to what first looks like a typical bar and grill, perhaps one of those Southwest ones you see once in a while. And in one sense, that's exactly what Geronimo is. In another, it transcends that categorization, taking both cuisine and drinks to another level. The "Santa Fe" cuisine is a mix of Native American, Spanish, and Anglo-Saxon influences, with a variety of authentic dishes using chiles, *pasole* (hominy stew), pine nuts, squash tomatillos, Anasazi beans, fish, and wild game. The game is what really puts the cuisine here over the edge, with buffalo not just making an appearance but seeming to dominate the menu. The prickly pear gazpacho is a cool delight, and don't forget to get a basket of the Navajo fry bread with your meal. Geronimo specializes in tequila, with dozens and dozens of examples, including reserves like Don Julio 1942. Try one of their gourmet tequila flights, and that cheap stuff that you needed salt and a lemon to get through in college will be a distant memory.

PACÍFICO $$$

220 College St.
New Haven, CT 06511
(203) 772-4002
pacificorestaurants.com

This could just as easily go under seafood, but the Nuevo Latino cuisine at this 2-story restaurant at the corner of College and Crown stands out more than the oceanic origins of much of its menu. Dishes like caramelized salmon and seafood paella are always winners. They have a number of tapas (who doesn't these days?), and many people come here just for those and one of the excellent margaritas or a pitcher of sangria. Pacífico also features a prix-fixe lunch menu that is a bargain if you're in New Haven during the day. For dessert, try the Colombian chocolate cake. This is high-end Latin American dining, not a chain Mexican restaurant, so don't expect a giant plate of tacos or chimichangas for under $10. Elevate your taste and find out what everyone is raving about.

Mediterranean & Middle Eastern

ISTANBUL CAFÉ $$

245 Crown St.
New Haven, CT 06510
(203) 787-3881
istanbulcafect.com

This Turkish restaurant next to Louis' Lunch and just around the corner from the Shubert Theater is a gem, and the first and only such restaurant in New Haven. Walking inside, you are immediately in Istanbul, with the patterned design and decorations prefacing the genuine food. There is practically a whole page of kebabs to choose from, and the appetizers like *yaprak dolma* can be ordered tapas style. If you like Greek food, you'll find many similarities, with mousakka and baklava making delicious appearances. For those less adventurous in your family, there are pizzas and sandwiches on the lunch menu, although with a variety of delicious Anatolian flavors. The Turkish coffee is an absolutely, wonderfully thick version, so be careful about drinking it too late—you'll be up all night, probably thinking about the great meal you just had.

LALIBELA $$

176 Temple St.
New Haven, CT 06510
(203) 789-1232
lalibelarestaurantct.com

If you've never taken a delicious spongy piece of injera bread and used it to pick up Ethiopian food, you have missed out in life. Go to Lalibela and fix that oversight immediately, especially your relationship with this addictive fermented teff grain bread. They have vegetarian and vegan options (the *yemisir wat* lentils in a mix of spices is amazing), as well as meaty goodness like the classic *gored gored*, lean beef in red wine and rosemary. Take the piece of injera and fold it, grabbing a few pieces of spicy lamb or cabbage. As an after-dinner drink, try the Ethiopian honey wine. Lalibela is named for the small town in Ethiopia where 11 rock-hewn churches exist, and is said by some to be the resting place of the Lost Ark of the Covenant. And there is a covenant here too, between the chef and you: He promises you great food.

Pizza

*FRANK PEPE PIZZERIA NAPOLETANA $$

157 Wooster St.
New Haven, CT 06511
(203) 865-5762
pepespizzeria.com

A few years ago, Frank Pepe Pizzeria Napoletana was rated the third-best pizza in the country, with Sally's down the street coming in at number 4 and nearby Modern making it to number 12. The small metropolis of New Haven is simply the creative center of pizza in America, despite claims by the larger cities of New York and Chicago. Established in 1925, Frank Pepe's, now a statewide chain, invented the white clam pizza, something that sounds wrong but tastes so very right. Though any of its chains make fantastic, mouthwatering pizza, the ancient coal-fired ovens at the original restaurant in New Haven add a certain something to the crusts that is unrepeatable. This is a once-in-a-lifetime apizza (pronounced "ah-beets") experience. Unless of course you live here, in which case that experience will be repeated again and again. And again.

LITTLE RENDEZVOUS $$

256 Pratt St.
Meriden, CT 06450
(203) 235-0110
thelittlevous.com

This place is somehow unknown outside of Meriden, but it is the fourth great coal-fired New Haven–style pizza place in the area. The oven has been in operation since 1888, and in 1938 it began baking pizza pies. That makes it possibly the oldest operating brick oven in the state. And those coal-fired, New Haven–style, thin-crust, chewy-center pizzas. Delicious. If Frank Pepe's has the best crust and Sally's has the best sauce, the "Vous" has the best cheese. It is clearly one of the state's best pizza joints. And it is a "joint," make no mistake, with limited seating and no frills. You might be better off calling ahead and eating your pie in the car or in the park across the street. But who cares when the pizza is this darn good.

MODERN APIZZA $$

874 State St.
New Haven, CT 06511
(203) 776-5306
modernapizza.com

Yet another great pizza restaurant in New Haven? Started in 1934? You bet. No doubt feeling cursed to be in the shadow of Sally's and Frank Pepe's, when in any other midsize city they would be a clear winner, Modern Apizza struggles to maintain its identity. However, because they have to try harder, they produce pizza that some think is even better. Try the hot cherry peppers or crabmeat on yours. Some of their other dishes have been paid attention to as well. The eggplant rollatini is a hit, and their calzones are cheesily delicious. One note for those coming from out of state: If you like cheese, never order a "plain" pizza in Connecticut, especially at Modern, or you will be puzzled to get one with dough and sauce, but none of that gooey loveliness you expect on a "plain" in other areas of the country. These are "mozzarella" or "cheese" pizzas, not plain.

✳SALLY'S APIZZA $$

237 Wooster St.
New Haven, CT 06511
(203) 624-5271
sallysapizza.com

If Frank Pepe's pizza restaurant did not exist, this would be the most famous pizza in Connecticut. Many say it is the best. Waiting in line outside under the classic sign is an experience everyone in Connecticut must have, and you can peer down the block to Pepe's to see which line is longer. The prices are cheap, and the gourmet bacon or anchovy pizzas are unbelievable at any price. As a family operation run by the Consiglios, Sally's (short for Salvatore) has been in business since 1938, and stepping into their dining room is a step back in time. Sadly for pizza in America, perhaps, no one has ever improved on their formula. Frank Sinatra used to have his driver come all the way from New York to pick up a few of Sally's pizzas. Taste them and you'll find out why.

ZUPPARDI'S APIZZA $$
179 Union Ave.
West Haven, CT 06516
(203) 934-1949
zuppardisapizza.com

Hidden in a residential area of West Haven, Zuppardi's has been a well-known, not-so-hidden gem for local residents for many years. In any other metro area this would be the top dog, but in the greatest small city for pizza in the world, they have a lot of competition. Their ovens are not coal-fired like the famous ones downtown, but they do use the stiff cornmeal crusts, which are a bit sweeter than usual for New Haven style. The cheese is stringier too. Most say that their specialty is the sausage and/or meatball pizza, and I agree. However, if you like our New Haven clam pizza, then ask for the "freshly shucked" clam pie at Zuppardi's. It's worth the slightly longer wait and greater expense.

Pubs & Taverns

ARCHIE MOORE'S $
188 Willow St.
New Haven, CT 06511
(203) 773-9870
archiemoores.com

This 1898 pub on Willow Street became famous in the 1980s because of its stellar buffalo wings, and now that is what everyone knows it for. They are consistently rated the best in the state, and their sauce goes on other things as well (the buffalo calamari is a surprising delight). They also have a wide selection of wraps and sandwiches, and even a vegetarian menu. But you really should have the wings here, with baskets in multiples of 7, up to 49 (I don't know why either). They have franchised into a Connecticut chain, with locations in Fairfield (48 Sanford St.; 203-256-9295); Milford (15 Factory Ln.; 203-876-5088); Derby (17 Elizabeth St.; 203-732-3255); and Wallingford (39 N. Main St., 203-265-7100). You can also buy bottles of Archie Moore's wing sauce at the restaurants or at any local grocery, though it seems they always use it to better effect. To make sure, stop by one of these restaurants and taste the difference.

CASK REPUBLIC $$
179 Crown St.
New Haven, CT 06510
(475) 238-8335
thecaskrepublic.com

The Cask Republic is a destination for all those who love beer. The bar has 53 rotating taps. Yes, 53, including rare tap beers like America's Dogfish Head 90 Minute IPA and Belgium's Delerium Tremens. They also have a cask engine for cask-conditioned ales (if you knew such a thing existed, this is the perfect bar for you), not to mention more than 80 different bottled beers. They also barrel- and bottle-age ales at the restaurant itself. A huge selection of single-malt Scotch is available for heathens who don't like a sudsy brew. The food is classic pub fare, with mac and cheese with bacon, fish-and-chips, and a smoked sausage plate. The standout is the German pretzel sandwich with breaded pork cutlet. It goes with almost any beer, but not with soda or water. If you noticed the word *beer* a number of times in the preceding paragraph, you have certainly gotten the politics of the Cask Republic. Long live beer!

MIKRO $$
3000 Whitney Ave.
Hamden, CT 06518
(203) 553-7676
mikrobeerbar.com

The Mount Carmel section of Hamden is a foodie destination, with several solid restaurants as well as wine and specialty food shops. Mikro has taken it to the next level, with an inventive menu that changes seasonally. They have 18 rotating taps that serve all sorts of American and European craft beers, as well as a great selection of bottles. Don't expect to get a Bud here. The food here is awesome: rich and creative, with belly-satisfying poutine (fries, gravy, and cheese curds, for those who haven't been to Quebec), confit chicken wings with Indian spices, and other outrageous delights. In winter, the pork belly Reuben will make you wonder why everyone isn't making these at every deli across America. The owner has another place down the road (2323 Whitney Ave.; 203-909-6545) called Smokebox. He and the owner of Caesus (see entry) needed a place to smoke their meats . . . and it has turned into one of the best fast-casual lunch places in the area.

WHEELERS RESTAURANT AND TAPROOM $$

180 Amity Rd.
Woodbridge, CT 06525
(203) 553-9055
wheelers-newhaven.com

Wheelers is like a neighborhood place with Thursday-night jazz and wing night, but run by foodies who turn fresh, local ingredients into interesting dishes. You know immediately when you see their wing options: smoked soy-brown sugar wings, Thai green chile, honey sriracha, maple lime cilantro—these are not the flavors of the typical neighborhood bar. Get a crawfish mac and cheese if you need comfort food, a fun and tasty taco flight for variety, or steak and eggs with a side of jalapeño bacon for lunch. If you want something healthier, try the falafel wrap. They have spicy curry fries, beet salad, and charred brussels sprouts with honey almonds. Get a beer from nearby New England Brewing or Two Roads to wash it down while you enjoy live music, or get takeout from their beautiful deli-like counter.

Road Food

✳BLACKIE'S HOT DOG STAND $

2200 Waterbury Rd.
Cheshire, CT 06410
(203) 699-1819
blackieshotdogs.com

Opened in 1928, this classic road-food stand just off Route 84 has ancient signs inside that proclaim No Dancing. But you'd probably be okay if you really wanted to these days. Still, they maintain the strict Catholic tradition and don't open on Friday or holidays like Easter. But their traditions with food are far more interesting to us. Blackie's (as in Black Irish) boils their hot dogs in cottonseed oil and then grills them, creating some of the best in the state. Don't ask for fries, though; they serve only chips. The milk shakes are excellent; get the vanilla one, or a birch beer to go with your dog. The relish is the key, though—a homemade concoction that makes relish haters love the stuff. They even have jars to take home now, so make sure you grab one on your way out.

FRANKIE'S $

700 Watertown Ave.
Waterbury, CT 06708
(203) 753-2426
frankieshotdogs.com

Established in 1937 by the Caiazzo brothers, Frank and Paul, this Waterbury institution still draws huge crowds today with its amusing but truthful motto: "Come in and eat or we'll both starve." The restaurant seemingly pulls people off Route 8 with the smell of sizzling meat and onions. A sign proclaims "The secret of happiness is a good dog," and customers eagerly rest elbows on the old marble counters, peering inside. Though Frankie's might be the "hot dog king," it has a huge menu with standards like burgers and lobster rolls, as well as more unusual items like tasty fried cauliflower and rich cheddar cheese cubes. There is a pavilion at the north end of the parking lot, but this is really an old-fashioned drive-in; eat in your car and love it. For those who don't like that method, Big Frank's down the street is owned by the same family, and along with delicious barbecue they have some of Frankie's classics (572 Watertown Ave.; 203-753-7427).

LOUIS' LUNCH $

263 Crown St.
New Haven, CT 06511
(203) 562-5507
louislunch.com

You might miss this historic eatery located on Crown Street simply because it's small. Then again, the brick one-room building in the middle of a parking lot seems noticeably out of place in downtown New Haven. But Louis' is known for doing things a little differently. Heralded as the creator of the hamburger, Louis' (pronounced "Lou-ie") Lunch still uses the recipe invented by Louis Lassen in 1900, when he slapped a beef patty between two slices of bread for a customer who wanted something quick, and the burger was born. The antique grill still operates, holding burgers vertically to let the fat drip. They're still juicy, and served only on white toast. Cheddar cheese, grilled onions, and fresh tomatoes are options if you're looking to dress your burger up, but don't ask for ketchup or mustard, as condiments are strictly forbidden. You can sip Foxon Park sodas and sit in the wood booths, decoratively embossed with carved acknowledgments of past patrons.

THE PLACE $$

901 Boston Post Rd.
Guilford, CT 06437
(203) 453-9276
No website

This seasonal "restaurant" is really a permanent open-air clambake on the side of Route 1. Grilling and roasting since 1971, The Place can be found by its huge, red wooden menu sign and the smoke from its wood fires. Seat yourself on a tree-stump chair above the crushed clam shell floor, and drink the local Foxon Park soda or bring your own beer or wine to enjoy with these seafood delights. Roasted clams with a homemade barbecue sauce are their signature treat, and once you try them, you'll wonder why anyone ever thinks of steaming them. Their roasted corn on the cob complete with husk, roast lobster, and grilled steak are also excellent. This is one of the places in Connecticut to get the native bluefish, and grilled is the way to eat it. There is a large tent for rainy days, but please note that The Place is cash or check only. It's tough to swipe credit cards at a truly outdoor facility like this.

TED'S RESTAURANT $

1046 Broad St.
Meriden, CT 06450
(203) 237-6660
tedsrestaurant.com

This small, modest-looking shop has been serving Meriden since 1959, and likely will continue for another 50 years or more. Ted's world-famous cheeseburgers are steamed, and that's their unique appeal. The buns they use are thick and buttery, and the cheese melted over the burgers will immediately make you a convert to this style of hamburger. You won't find much else on the menu, except for some steamed hot dogs and a BLT sandwich. There are sides (like fries) and extras (like bacon, not steamed) as well. They have been so successful that they opened a second location in Cromwell, but come to the original here in Meriden. This is road-food history.

TWO GUYS ONE GRILL $
32 N. Turnpike Rd.
Wallingford, CT 06492
(203) 284-5998
facebook.com/pages/2-Guys-One-Grill/225274800823231

Two Guys One Grill took the place of another road-food stop in Wallingford a couple years ago, and since then the "two guys" have impressed everyone with their dynamite cuisine. Don't be put off by their gravel parking lot and shack-like appearance. These guys know how to grill a hamburger or hot dog. The chili cheese dog is a winner, and the burger with two grilled cheeses for buns is decadent. Anything they do with chicken (which is a lot) is good, especially the buffalo chicken dog—a piece of boneless fried chicken done in buffalo sauce, put in a New England hot dog roll and topped with blue cheese. It makes so much sense that I can't believe no other restaurants are doing it. Well, soon everyone will be, because this innovation has helped put this tiny road-food shack on the map for insiders like us.

UNCLE WILLIE'S $$
473 Saw Mill Rd.
West Haven, CT 06516
(203) 479-4017
unclewilliesbarbecue.com

You know when you see the pink pig smoker outside the restaurant that it has to be good. And it is. Uncle Willie's is barbecue, authentic wood-smoked pit BBQ, Southern-style goodness in New England. The restaurant is small; it seats about a dozen inside at picnic-type tables and fills up quickly. Order at the counter and hang out with a ginger beer and the salivating aromas from the kitchen until the platters are brought to the table. Try the brisket or pulled pork with Memphis classic sweet sauce (or any of the other selections). Your best bet might be to go with the rib sampler, with baby back, St. Louis pork, and

Texas beef ribs, all sweet and tender, falling off the bone and perfectly messy. Sides include jalapeño-mashed potatoes, excellent coleslaw, hand-cut fries, sweet potato fries, and mac and cheese, among others. Catfish, po'boys, fried chicken, and burgers will satisfy, but you'll come back for the ribs. Willie's is growing, with new restaurants in Seymour (225 West St., #3; 203-881-8102) and Fairfield (937 Post Rd.; 203-955-1295) and more on the way.

Seafood

LENNY'S INDIAN HEAD INN $$
205 S. Montowese St.
Branford, CT 06405
(203) 488-1500
lennysnow.com

Located in the less-traveled Indian Neck section of Branford, this shoreline favorite sports a patio with weathered tables and an outdoor bar overlooking a reedy salt marsh where egrets hunt and ospreys nest. Inside are wooden booths packed with families under the old, cracked 1950s sign. This surprisingly roomy restaurant has a huge, classic seaside shack menu that includes daily seasonal specials. Lenny's eschews the partisan bickering and offers both kinds of lobster roll: hot with butter and cold with mayo. The soft-shell crabs are tasty without even tartar sauce, and the cherrystone clams are fantastic. Suck them down like oysters. Their famous Shore Dinner includes chowder, cherrystones, sweet corn, lobster, steamers, and watermelon; and though it depends on the market price of lobsters, it is well worth your time and money. Just be sure to bring an appetite.

STONEBRIDGE RESTAURANT $$
50 Daniel St.
Milford, CT 06460
(203) 874-7947
stonebridgerestaurant.com

This classic Milford restaurant with its many rooms in a rambling building is popular with people throughout the entire county. If you're there in the warmer months, make sure to sit somewhere on the huge deck and patio, which overlook the Wepawaug River and its romantic waterfall. Many people come here just for drinks and the lighter-fare menu they offer on the decks. But if you've got an appetite, try the littleneck clams and then get the lobster grilled cheese or the fried whole-belly clams. If you're not in the mood for seafood, the steaks here are done just right. The blue crab and lobster cassoulet is a revelation: picked lobster baked under a crab crust, topped with béarnaise sauce. Wow.

Spanish

*IBIZA TAPAS $$
1832 Dixwell Ave.
Hamden, CT 06514
(203) 909-6512
ibizatapaswinebar.com

This is where internationally known chef Juan Garcia experiments with modern tapas. Of course the beautiful orange-lit Ibiza Tapas serves all the classic Spanish treats, with amazing cheeses and chorizos. But they often come in surprising presentations and deconstructions, like triangular potato and onion omelets with an original aioli sauce. And the modern tapas are a culinary delight. *Foie gras* and raw tuna on a spoon together? It melts in your mouth. Wood-fired red peppers stuffed with oxtail? Amazing. The best part of the menu is that it changes with the seasons and with the experimental whims of the chef. Their selection of Spanish wines is well chosen, picked to go with the ceviches, braised short ribs, and codfish croquettes. You can come here again and again without running out of choices, even if you get 6 or 7 tapas a night. Best of all, you won't pay an arm and a leg for these masterpieces. Bring a large party and share 20; but be warned, there are no reservations—first come, first served.

Vegetarian

CLAIRE'S CORNER COPIA $$
1000 Chapel St.
New Haven, CT 06510
(203) 562-3888
clairescornercopia.com

Opened in 1975, Claire's Corner Copia has been a favorite for locals, visitors, and downtown lunchgoers for its vegetarian, vegan, organic, and kosher offerings. Claire Criscuolo, chef and owner, is a registered nurse and focuses not just on health but also on flavor. Come in and check out the huge daily menu or browse the glass-fronted display cases. Try one of her vegetarian lasagnas, sandwiches, chilis, or quesadillas. This is not a table-service restaurant, but the quality of the food is far above the usual run of self-service order and pick up places. Don't forget to get dessert, and perhaps take home a loaf of the amazing bread or the award-winning coffee cake.

SHORELINE DINER AND VEGETARIAN ENCLAVE $$
345 Boston Post Rd.
Guilford, CT 06437
(203) 458-7380
shorelinediner.com

The Shoreline Diner was built in 1956 and restored in 2009, making sure this piece of American history is around for new generations. The name lets us know that this is not your ordinary diner, though, but a road-food place where vegetarians feel at home. Don't think that you're just going to get vegetables here, however. The diner has pancakes, challah french toast, waffles, omelets, steak and eggs, and all the lunch classics like lobster rolls and hamburgers. Like most diners, the menu often seems endless, but their menu for vegans is huge, with grilled tofu, chili, stuffed peppers, falafel, and more. My wife enjoyed the tempeh Reuben with chili (though she is far from vegetarian). They train their kitchen staff to be aware of cross-contamination and allergies, and they also serve things like gluten-free pilaf and pasta. The french fries are actually gluten free and vegan, although you'd never know it from tasting them. That makes the Shoreline Diner a great place for families who can't agree on their feelings about meat.

Wine Bars

*BALLOU'S WINE BAR $$$
51 Whitfield St., #1
Guilford, CT 06437
(203) 453-0319
ballouswinebar.com

Wine bars have made a comeback in the US, and Ballou's is at the head of the pack. The wine list looks impressive, but not outrageous, until you realize that every single wine is available by the glass. Then it is staggering. This is currently also the only place in the state where you can get an entire flight of Connecticut wines from different vineyards. The food is excellent, with wicked fondues like cheddar Merlot and "tiger cheese." They also have a large selection of salads, sandwiches, paninis, and pastas, with the brie and apricot panini and potato gnocchi as standouts. Owners Steve Kaye and Debbie Ballou choose every wine carefully, and use the latest technology to keep the many bottles fresh and new. Debbie also makes truffles, and some people come to Ballou's just for those, along with a glass of port of course. They recently opened another location in Branford (2 Sybil Ave.; 203-208-1701), which is open for tea in the afternoon.

DAY TRIP IN NEW HAVEN COUNTY

If you haven't had breakfast yet, that's good, because there will be a lot of food on the menu today, for both the stomach and the mind. You'll start just off exit 59 of I-95 on the Post Road, with breakfast at Shoreline Diner in Guilford (see entry). Get a heaping plate of pancakes if you like, but don't overdo it, because you'll be heading out to sea soon, and there's a big lunch and dinner ahead.

Right at the diner you will see the intersection of Route 146. Take this west for a bit, then turn left on Lover's Lane, noting the historic Thomas Griswold House on your left. You need to get in the mood for the Henry Whitfield House, which you'll reach after turning right on Stone House Lane. This house is the oldest stone building in colonial America, built in 1639 like a small fortress. If you're pressed for time, take pictures and move on; otherwise take the self-guided tour of this amazing place.

You'll continue on Stone House Lane and take an immediate right onto Old Whitfield Street and then a left when you reach Route 146 again (Water Street). Stay on this as it becomes Sam Hill Road and then Leetes Island Road. Finally, you'll take a left on School Street and then again on Thimble Islands Road. You are now in the charming fishing village of Stony Creek, and here you have a choice.

If you are an athletic sort who enjoys (or thinks you might enjoy) kayaking, now is the time to try a Stony Creek Kayak tour of the Thimble Islands. Otherwise you should take one of the cruises out to these amazing maritime gems (see entries under cruises and water sports). Either way, you should make a reservation, and after parking here at the marina, allow the tour guide to show you this amazing seascape.

Afterwards, you will no doubt be hungry from the salt air. Head back out Thimble

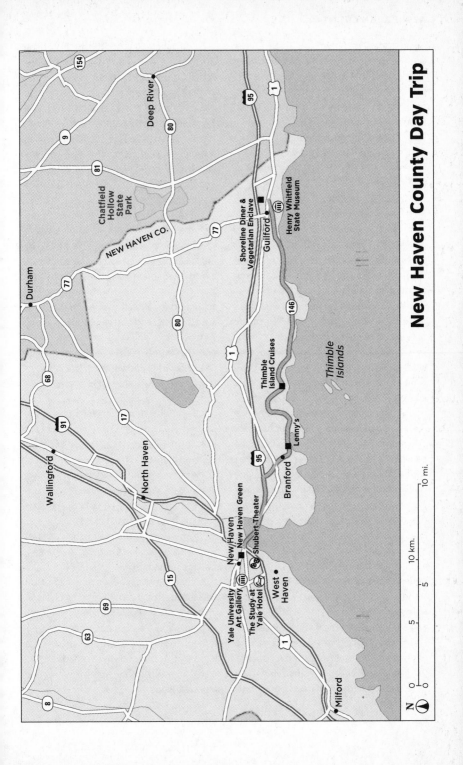

New Haven County Day Trip

Islands Road to Route 146 (Stony Creek Road) and continue west. Route 146 changes names a number of times through this section of Branford, but simply follow the route number. Your lunch stop is Lenny's Indian Head Inn along the seashore (see entry). If you've had enough air, sit inside; otherwise relax on the deck and discuss your morning's adventure over a lobster roll and some cherrystone clams.

Continue on Route 146 (now South Montowese Street) and turn left with it on Main Street in Branford. This will eventually come out at Route 1 across from a Starbucks underneath a precarious cliff. Take a left, and then the second right onto the I-95 connector road. Head west on I-95 toward New Haven. Once you've crossed the huge Quinnipiac River Bridge, take exit 47 to merge onto Route 34 toward downtown.

Turn right on Howe Street, and then another right onto Broadway. Here you'll want to do a little U-turn to the left after you pass through a light, so get in the left lane. If you reach York Street, you've gone too far. As you swing around in front of the Yale Bookstore, you'll see the entrance to the parking lot that you've been circling. Park here; it's convenient, reasonably priced, and you won't have trouble finding your car later.

From here on, this is a walking tour. Check out the Yale Bookstore if you like, then walk east on Broadway, which becomes Elm, noting the amazing Gothic architecture of Yale. Take a left into the pedestrian mall across from High Street, staring up at the fortress-like walls. On your right will be a different kind of building, the huge white cube of the Beinecke Rare Book and Manuscript Library (see entry). The entrance is on the east side of the building. Go inside and check out the Gutenberg Bible, printed in the 1450s and one of only 21 in existence.

Come back out and go east, peeking down into the sculpture garden and investigating the red Alexander Calder stabile, before heading through the corner entrance of Memorial Hall, checking out the names of Yale students who gave their lives for America. Turn right on College Street, and head to the green. Wander around here if you like, checking out the Amistad Memorial on the east side, city hall, and the three churches along Temple Street.

Turn right on Chapel Street, and head into the Yale University Art Gallery, where you should go upstairs and see Van Gogh's *Night Cafe*. If you have time, keep browsing these excellent collections, but if you're going to be seeing a show tonight, you should go for an early dinner. Your options are countless, and you might just want to window-shop and find one that seems good to you, but certainly try either Bentara (Malaysian), 116 Crown (New American), or Miya's Sushi (see entries for all these, or pick another from the guide).

If you've gotten tickets for a play at the Shubert (247 College St.), Yale Cabaret (217 Park St.), or Yale Rep (1120 Chapel St.), head there a little early after you've eaten dinner. These venues have some of the best shows in the state, with big-name actors and up-and-coming thespians, so sit back and feast your mind on some great drama.

If you want to stay overnight, definitely try the Study at 1157 Chapel St. (see entry), but go back and get your car so they can valet park it for free in an underground lot nearby. Relax in one of the plush leather chairs in your room at this boutique hotel, and reflect. Hopefully this intelligently planned journey through New Haven County has given you a lot to think about, and your stomach a lot to enjoy. After all, man (or woman) cannot live on books alone.

MIDDLESEX COUNTY

The Connecticut River was at the heart of what was once the Old Saybrook Colony, and it remains so today. Poet Wallace Stevens called it "the river of rivers" and said: "It is the third commonness with light and air, a curriculum, a vigor, a local abstraction. Call it, one more, a river, an unnamed flowing, space-filled, reflecting the seasons, the folk-lore of each of the senses; call it, again and again, the river that flows nowhere, like a sea." The mouth of the Connecticut by Old Saybrook has been named one of the 40 last great places in the Western Hemisphere by The Nature Conservancy.

The smallest Connecticut county geographically, Middlesex is also generally flatter than the others, though it contains many small rocky hollows and rises up from the river and the coast in rolling hills. Until recently, travel was primarily by boat, and today there are still only three car bridges that cross the wide river in the whole county—at Middletown, East Haddam, and the I-95 bridge at Old Saybrook.

Old Saybrook itself is a charming town that for most of the 20th century was the home of Katharine Hepburn, winner of more Academy Awards than any other actor. She started her acting career up the road at the famous Ivoryton Playhouse. The other two coastal towns of Clinton and Westbrook have become famous for their shopping outlets and their delightful resorts.

Ivoryton got its name from the business of making piano keys and today forms a nexus of charming villages with its neighbors of Essex, Deep River, and Chester. Essex is often cited as one of the prettiest towns in the nation, and that distinction is difficult to argue with. All these towns along the western side of the river have great antiquing. Across the river, Gillette Castle in East Haddam holds huge appeal for visitors to the state, and all these attractions make this part of the river a popular place to canoe and sail.

The north end of the county is anchored by Middletown, where Wesleyan University sits high on a hill, bringing culture and wealth to the area. This is where, long ago, the Connecticut River's course may have changed, from heading directly south to modern-day New Haven to its present southeasterly course. Whether or why it did so remains a mystery—one of many that you will find to intrigue you in Middlesex County.

ATTRACTIONS

Historic Sites & Landmarks

GENERAL WILLIAM HART HOUSE AND GARDENS
350 Main St.
Old Saybrook, CT 06475
(860) 395-1635
saybrookhistory.org

This historical 1767 home is the flagship of the Old Saybrook Historical Society and is on the National Register of Historic Places. The wealthy General Hart led a light horse regiment against the British in the Revolutionary War, and had his own fleet of merchant ships outfitted for privateering against the British fleet. The house looks more like a Virginian or Pennsylvanian residence than a New

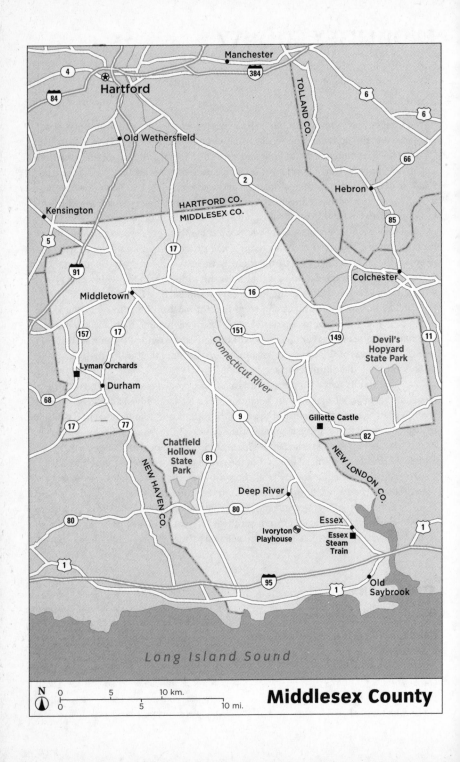

Middlesex County

England one, and has architectural features only present on the finest homes, such as eight corner fireplaces and Dutch tiles. Next door is the archives building, where you can research the deep history of the Saybrook Colony, one of the three that formed Connecticut. There is also a very nice garden area in the back. If you're already here, drive a mile south to Fort Saybrook Monument Park, 18 acres that include the site of the old fort, a tidal marsh, and tracks from the roundhouse and turntable of the old Connecticut Valley Railroad.

✳GILLETTE CASTLE
67 River Rd.
East Haddam, CT 06423
(860) 526-2336
ctrivervalley.com
This "folly" mansion is one of the greatest sights of Connecticut. High above the Connecticut River and commanding a beautiful prospect, the unusual fieldstone castle was built by actor William Gillette, famous for his portrayal of Sherlock Holmes (he was the man who wore the deerstalker hat, which never made an appearance in the books). The inside of the house is no less remarkable than its fairy-tale appearance outside. Everything is custom-built, and the tastes of Gillette are strange and wonderful. Built-in couches and bookshelves you may have seen before, but there are touches throughout that will first have you scratching your head, and later thinking how much sense they made. The light switches alone are worth an examination. You have never been in a house like this, nor ever will be again. Take a walk around the grounds on paths that cross stone-arched and wooden-trestle bridges, investigate the spooky train tunnel, and visit the pond, which is absolutely stuffed full of plate-size frogs. Who knows? Maybe one is a prince.

THANKFUL ARNOLD HOUSE AND GARDENS
14 Hayden Hill Rd.
Haddam, CT 06438
(860) 345-2400
haddamhistory.org/arnold_house.htm
This 1794 house in Haddam was home to a woman named Thankful Arnold and her family, and presents an unusual bell-shaped profile. Inside you'll find a number of interesting artifacts, including the puzzling pot shards found in the walls. Remaining in the family until the 1960s, when it was given to the Haddam Historical Society, the house has been restored and furnished as it was in the 1820s after Thankful had been widowed. The gardens were built and planted in the 1980s as they would have been in the 1820s, with over 50 herbs used for cooking, medicine, dyeing, and fragrance. It is a member of the exclusive Connecticut Historic Gardens (cthistoricgardens.org). Unlike some historical houses, this one is open year-round, Wed 9 a.m. to 3 p.m., Thurs 2 to 8 p.m., and Fri noon to 3 p.m., as well as Sun in summer from 1 to 4 p.m.

Museums

CONNECTICUT RIVER MUSEUM
67 Main St.
Essex, CT 06426
(860) 767-8269
ctrivermuseum.org
At the end of land in Essex, right by the wharves and marina, sits the 1878 Steamboat Dock, now housing the Connecticut River Museum. Inside, the old wide-plank floors support three levels of the museum of the longest waterway in New England. Starting with the Native Americans and Dutch, the museum takes you all the way up to the passage of the Clean Water Act in 1972 and its wonderful effect on the river. There are interactive "sound sticks" to listen to at many exhibits, and the third floor hosts changing

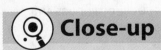

Close-up

The Quintessential Connecticut Village

One reason travelers love our state is the picture-perfect, walkable villages that speckle the landscape. These charming New England towns attract people from the West in particular, who marvel at the age of the buildings and old-world feel of the streets. There are dozens of amazing villages in Connecticut. The Litchfield Hills make it their business to preserve their postcard villages, and nearly every coastal town east of New Haven has an idyllic downtown filled with shops and restaurants. The clapboard houses from the 19th, 18th, and sometimes 17th centuries; the white, steepled Congregational churches; and the old inns and taverns are a vision of long-ago America for most visitors, even though insiders often take these wonders for granted.

Some villages deserve special mention as perfect examples. The downtown greens of small, strollable places like Madison, Salisbury, Guilford, Litchfield, Collinsville, and Putnam have restaurants and shops aplenty. But the towns of Ridgefield, Chester, and Kent stand out for their abundance of galleries, studios, and unique, independent shops, yet remain livable, places you might want to retire to run a used bookstore or a country inn, or to write your memoir.

Chester's twisted main street feels like a village in England but contains a dozen worthy shops and galleries, like EO Artlab (eoartlab.com), one of New England's most respected contemporary art galleries, and the Lori Warner Gallery (loriwarner.com), full of award-winning works. The River Tavern and the Restaurant L&E provide top-shelf dining, and you can visit shops like the Connecticut River Artisans (ctriverartisans.org) and the Norma Terris Theatre, where the Goodspeed Opera House develops new musicals and nurtures acting talent (goodspeed.org).

Every car slows down to a crawl along Route 7 in Kent, as if the occupants had never seen a charming village before. Perhaps they haven't. The antiques stores in Kent are legendary destinations for New York socialites looking to find a piece for their apartment, and you can find your own at R. T. Facts Antiques (rtfacts.com). While there you can eat and stay at the Fife 'n Drum Restaurant and Inn (fifendrum.com). Don't miss the annual Kent Memorial Library outdoor book sale, which lasts all summer from Memorial Day to Columbus Day. There are treasures to be discovered here.

Ridgefield's long main street is a marvelous blend of the old and new, with modern shopping centers filled with unique, independent stores. There are plenty of restaurants to choose from, like Luc's (lucscafe.com) or Bernard's (bernardsridgefield

displays. Stand-out exhibits include the burning of Essex by the British, the building of the warship *Oliver Cromwell,* and the strange history of the *Turtle,* a submarine built during the American Revolution. For the more adventurous, there are two daily departures on the historic *Mary E* schooner, which will take you up and down the mighty river itself.

✳ESSEX STEAM TRAIN
1 Railroad Ave.
Essex, CT 06426
(860) 767-0103
essexsteamtrain.com

Few insiders miss this two-in-one attraction on their travels in Connecticut, choosing either the Steam Train and Riverboat or the Essex Clipper Dinner Train. The first is better

.com), considered one of the top restaurants in the state. The town's Ballard Park is relaxing and ageless, with amazing trees of all sorts and free summer concerts. Stay at the West Lane Inn (westlaneinn.com), and on your walk into town, stop at the Aldrich Museum of Contemporary Art (aldrichart.org), which has changing exhibitions of cutting-edge artwork.

Of course not everyone comes to these villages for the shopping and food. The destinations of Norfolk and Stonington are not exactly havens of walkable capitalism at work. But they have something else—a photographic perfection and calming, timeless feel that draws visitors. In Norfolk, stay at the Manor House Inn (manorhouse-norfolk.com), watch a performance at Infinity Hall (infinityhall.com), and don't forget to walk up the street to Haystack Mountain State Park (ct.gov/dep; search "Haystack Mountain State Park"), where you can get a great view of the Berkshire Mountains.

Stonington Village is attractive in a different way—crowded onto a peninsula in Long Island Sound, with the narrow streets of a seafaring community. Surrounded by water, it feels like the old whaling town it is, with a sense of living history and a great smell of the sea. Stay at the Inn at Stonington (innatstonington.com) and walk the streets to the historic lighthouse while picturing the brave citizens defying the British Royal Navy and defeating them.

There is one village that transcends all these categories. On a peninsula like Stonington—though on the Connecticut River, not the Sound—Essex has the shopping and restaurants along with the timeless postcard feel of the best villages. In fact, author Norman Crampton called it the "best small town in America" in his book about the same. You can walk miles of sidewalks past dozens of colonial and 19th-century homes, or take a historic schooner out to look back at town from the river (ctrivermuseum.org). Like Ridgefield, Kent, or nearby Chester, Essex boasts dozens of galleries, antiques stores, and shops, and gives both a feel of a Connecticut long past and a wonderland for shopping and gourmands. Stay at the classic Griswold Inn (griswoldinn.com), one of the oldest continuously operated inns in America, with the best taproom in Connecticut, and experience something that you thought only existed in the imagination.

There are many more deserving villages to explore in Connecticut, and no doubt you will find a favorite of your own. These quintessential "perfect" villages are often referenced in literature and film, but so rarely exist in reality. You can find a denser concentration of them here than in any other state in America.

with children, and the second for a romantic night out. Right off Route 9 in Essex, Connecticut Valley Railroad cars greet you as you pull into the gravel parking lots. The Steam Train and Riverboat offers several different excursions, including one across the river to nearby Gillette Castle. The Clipper serves a seasonal four-course meal in its 1920s Pullman diner cars. You can see them restoring old train cars in the barn; other old cars sit idle in the yard, like the 1941 Porter Heavy Steam Locomotive. Next door is the old Dickinson Witch Hazel factory and water tower; this area once was the world center of production of this herbal tonic. These trains were used in the last Indiana Jones film, and taking a journey on them certainly feels like stepping into a movie.

Parks & Beaches

CHATFIELD HOLLOW STATE PARK
381 Route 80
Killingworth, CT 06419
(860) 345-8521
ct.gov/dep [search "Chatfield Hollow State Park"]

A hollow is a low place between the hills, and as you drive on Route 80, you will surely notice the huge dip into the lake valley at the center of this Killingworth gem. Chatfield is a popular place to swim, complete with lifeguards, and offers many opportunities for rock climbers. You can fish (with a license) in the lake as well, catching mostly bass and pickerel. There are also numerous hiking trails that loop around the center valley. Just in from the parking lot at the main entrance, a side trail leads to the left and some "Indian caves," where many artifacts were found. The Indians did not actually live in these caves, but probably stopped here often on hunting and camping expeditions. There are caves on the Chatfield Trail that starts on the south side of Route 80 as well, a few hundred yards west from the main park entrance.

DEVIL'S HOPYARD STATE PARK
366 Hopyard Rd.
East Haddam, CT 06415
(860) 873-8566
ct.gov/dep [search "Devil's Hopyard State Park"]

No one is actually sure how this park got its name, but it could be that a local man named Dibble owned a hopyard in the area, and his name changed through usage over the centuries. The Eightmile River drops 60 feet down some large steps, known at Chapman Falls, and at the bottom there are some interesting cylindrical pothole formations that could have been thought to be the Devil's hoofprints. Whatever the case, today this is one of the most popular parks in the area, featuring some great loop trails

that take hikers through groves of mountain laurel, blueberries, and witch hazel on the west side, and up to some good views of the valley from the east (on a short trail just off the orange trail). On the green trail there are some large pegmatite boulders, and the river is full of brook trout. There are also 21 open campsites here, all in a row above the falls. The falls are just off Hopyard Road near the north end of the park, in case you just want to see this natural wonder.

i Where the Salmon and Moodus Rivers meet in East Haddam is the center of mysterious minor earth tremors known as the Moodus Noises. Known to Native Americans and terrified colonial settlers, these low rumblings deep underground have become accepted and even liked by almost everyone today.

WADSWORTH FALLS STATE PARK
721 Wadsworth St.
Middletown, CT 06457
(860) 344-2950
ct.gov/dep [search "Wadsworth Falls State Park"]

If you're just looking to step off the road and see an amazing waterfall, Wadsworth is the one. Go around to the "back" of the park by taking Cherry Hill Road south from Route 157, and park in the small lot by the Coginchaug River. Barely a hundred feet away, the huge, Niagara-style 30-foot falls is also over 50 feet wide and is impressive in any season. I'm told this is also a great place to break out your fishing rod and try for trout, though I have yet to catch one here. If you park at the main entrance, where swimming is allowed in a large pond, take an easy hike through the park to find the "little falls" on the blue trail. This long cascade down exposed layers of limestone may be sparse compared to the massive flume of the main falls, but it's well worth a trip by itself. The entire network of trails is perfect for easy hikes with children or dogs, while still seeming like an unusual adventure.

Wildlife & Zoos

*CONNECTICUT RIVER EXPEDITIONS
1 Marina Park
Haddam, CT 06438
(860) 662-0577
ctriverquest.com

Connecticut River Expeditions (also called Riverquest) runs a number of cruises on the river year-round, including daytime and sunset cruises that take you past Gillette Castle. However, they also run a large number of special cruises throughout the year, with special dates and times. The most popular of these are the eagle watches, which run in February and March and take you to a few of the annual bald eagle nests along the Connecticut River, as well as viewing some other wildlife like golden eagles, loons, and harbor seals. The cabin is enclosed and heated, but wear warm clothing, because you'll want to be outside looking at the birds. They also feature other special cruises, like a geology cruise, fall foliage cruise, and a circumnavigation of Selden Island during summer, which takes you through a narrow salt meadow gap on the eastern side of the island, absolutely chock-full of wildlife.

STEWART B. MCKINNEY NATIONAL WILDLIFE REFUGE
733 Old Clinton Rd.
Westbrook, CT 06498
(860) 399-2513
fws.gov/refuge/stewart_b_mckinney

The Salt Meadow section of Connecticut's coastal national wildlife refuge is also the headquarters, donated in 1972 by Ester Lape to save some of the state's shoreline from development. From that date the local area grew to 274 acres, and more sections along

the entire coastline were added (see entry for the Milford Point section in New Haven County, under the Connecticut Audubon Coastal Center). This spot provides resting, feeding, and nesting habitat for 280 species during the fall and spring migrations. You can find brants, scoters, black ducks, woodcock, bluebirds, tree swallows, wild turkeys, egrets, ibis, kingfishers, ospreys, red-tailed hawks, and endangered roseate terns. There are trails that wind through the different habitats of barrier beach, tidal wetland, and grasslands here, and you should take them very slow, with a pair of binoculars and a quiet heart. Spring and fall are the best times here, with the most species, but during summer you can sometimes watch the permanent avian residents in the little aerial dramas of their lives.

Wineries

CHAMARD VINEYARD
115 Cow Hill Rd.
Clinton, CT 06413
(860) 664-0299
chamard.com

Ideally situated in proximity to Long Island Sound's beneficial growing effects, Chamard Vineyard in Clinton is a great stop for daytrippers. The long gravel drive, easily found off exit 63 on I-95, is decorated with vines on both sides, and the beautiful fieldstone winery lies ahead. Inside, the tasting room is grand and intimate, rustic and cosmopolitan, with wood beams and a stone fireplace. The vineyard has 30 acres planted, mostly Chardonnay. Chardonnay is in the classic style, with a touch of honey on the finish. Cabernet Franc is also excellent, with notes of smoky berry and a little butterscotch. Enjoy a glass of Merlot on the patio terrace and view the vines across a small pond with the fountain spouting in the center. A great venue for music, and open until 9 p.m. on Fri and Sat, the winery offers a prolific list of singer-songwriters, jazz, and bluegrass performers throughout the year. The vineyard is a spectacular and popular setting for weddings.

ACTIVITIES & EVENTS

Adventure Sports

EMPOWER LEADERSHIP SPORTS AND ADVENTURE

2011 S. Main St.
Middletown, CT 06457
(860) 638-4754
leadershipsports.com

Empower offers several adventures for families and individuals, the most popular of which is the zip line canopy tour, taking you through the treetops in a magical tour that seems like it should be in Disneyworld and not Middletown. There are 5 zip lines, 2 sky bridges, a vine traverse, and a cargo net obstacle. Kids enjoy the map-and-compass scavenger hunt. They also have tree climbs, which you do with the safety of a harness. It feels totally different than climbing a rock wall—perhaps because you are interacting with another living thing.

Arts Venues

KATHARINE HEPBURN CULTURAL ARTS CENTER

300 Main St.
Old Saybrook, CT 06475
(860) 570-0453
katharinehepburntheater.org

Known affectionately and officially as "The Kate," this huge, pillared 1911 former town hall on Main Street in Old Saybrook now houses a theater for dramatic and musical performances. Inside are posters of the hometown girl's films. Next to the box office, a small museum dedicated to her life includes her Emmy and a harrowing story of the 1938 hurricane that destroyed her first house in Old Saybrook. A relatively small theater, only 250 seats, The Kate gives intimate performances and plays that delight residents and tourists alike. Katharine Hepburn started her career up the road at the Ivoryton Playhouse in 1931 and was tickled by the idea that the old town hall would be named for her and repurposed in this way. Her house, only 2 miles away, has passed into new hands, but The Kate is both a memorial and move to the future. Call ahead to reserve tickets.

WESLEYAN CENTER FOR THE ARTS

Wesleyan University
283 Washington Ter.
Middletown, CT 06457
(860) 685-3355
wesleyan.edu/cfa

This 11-building complex, designed by Kevin Roche and John Dinkeloo Architects in 1973, highlights all the arts at once. The Crowell Concert Hall, the World Music Hall, the Davison Art Center, the Ezra and Cecile Zilkha Gallery, and a cinema and theater also host events and exhibits. Lectures, dances, operas, plays, rotating art exhibits, book tours, performance art, and more are available for your eyes and ears. The noontime talks and performances are free, and the evening ones are quite reasonably priced. The Davison Art Center has a nice permanent collection (check out the Rembrandt drawings). The Green Street Arts Center also offers classes to the public, such as dancing and drawing (860-685-7871; wesleyan.edu/greenstreet).

Festivals & Annual Events

BLUEFISH FESTIVAL

Clinton Andrews Memorial Town Hall
Clinton, CT 06413
(860) 669-1195
clintonbluefishfest.com

Held in July for the last four decades, this is an annual fishing tournament but so much more, with craft vendors, live music, a chowder cook-off, a pie-eating contest, and other activities. It opens on a Friday with registration and live music, and on Saturday the chowder cook-off and a variety of other events keep people interested while the fishing goes on out in Long Island Sound. For the kids there are pony rides and games. Of course the largest fish wins the prize, with the ceremony and live music that evening.

DEEP RIVER FIFE AND DRUM MUSTER
62 N. Main St.
Ivoryton, CT 06426
(860) 767-2237
companyoffifeanddrum.org

Held on the third Saturday in July, this event is the largest of its kind in the world, with close to 70 corps from all over the nation (and Europe) parading up Main Street in Deep River. Afterwards, you should head to Devitt Field at the end of the parade route to watch the evening performances and check out vendors selling fifes, drums, music, hats, and more. The event is free, though it will probably cost you to park, since the town funnels you into designated lots (though clever people have been known to get around that). The Museum of Fife and Drum features all parade music, but mostly "ancient" fife and drum corps. It is full of uniforms, performance gear, musical instruments, and photographs. Open June 30 to Labor Day on weekends, the museum offers evening performances on Tuesday nights. Check the schedule to make sure, and don't miss the ancient muster.

✳DURHAM FAIR
The Durham Agricultural Fair Association
Durham Green
Durham, CT 06422
(860) 349-9495
durhamfair.com

This is the largest agricultural fair in Connecticut, begun in 1916, and takes place on the last full weekend in September on the Durham Town Green and the adjoining fields. You'll visit the Fair Farm Museum, with antique equipment and collectibles, and a Discovery Center with seminars on food, farming, and garden care. You'll be astonished at the animal pulls, where horses, oxen, and ponies compete the way they have for thousands of years. There are also exhibits of livestock—unbelievable premium cattle, goats, llamas, poultry, rabbits, pigs, and sheep—and of products, like baked and canned goods, crafts, needlework, photography, plants, flowers, fruit, and of course giant pumpkins. Every year about 12,000 entries compete for blue ribbons and a best-in-show rosette. There's a talent show for singers, dancers, and entertainers on the last day, and for the kids there are pie-eating contests and fun things like bubble stations. If these traditional fair events are not enough, there's also a demolition derby, a truck pull, a carousel, midway rides, and more. And unlike many country fairs you might have attended in the past, they have flush toilets.

SAYBROOK TORCHLIGHT PARADE
Main Street Business Association
Old Saybrook, CT 06475
(860) 388-3266
oldsaybrookchamber.com

Have you ever been to a parade at night? In winter? If not, perhaps you're missing out on something. This unusual but historic parade has been held the second Saturday in December for the past 40 years in Old Saybrook. In colonial America the village militia would muster during early December and march to the town green carrying torches and lanterns; the rest of the townspeople followed, all joining in a carol sing. The revival today is much the same, except with the addition of floats put together by local merchants. And as the title suggests, it is still held today by torchlight (and quite a few strings of Christmas lights). Dozens of fife and drum corps march and play, filling the cold air with merriment. The parade route is not long, down Main Street past the town hall (the reviewing stand is usually set up across the street) to the muster site, where the carol sing happens. This event is a wonderful way to get into the Christmas spirit.

Fishing

CONNECTICUT RIVER
Fishin' Factory 3
238 E. Main St.
Middletown, CT 06457
(860) 344-9139
fishinfactory3.com

The Connecticut River has plenty of fishing opportunities from Middletown south to the mouth of the river. You can take a canoe, rowboat, or powerboat, or just fish from the banks and wharfs. You're likely to catch brook trout, rainbow trout, brown trout, shad, smallmouth bass, striped bass, catfish, American eel, and more. Landlocked salmon are also frequently caught in this part of the river during spring and fall spawning. They are protected, though, so after taking a photo, slip them gently back in the water. The Fishin' Factory 3 in Middletown will help you get outfitted with equipment and bait, and tell you the spots to go for the species you are interested in. If you want a charter boat, there are quite a number, and owner Andrew Nichols will give you options and advice.

SEA SPRITE
113 Harbor Pkwy.
Clinton, CT 06413
(860) 669-9613
captainpete.com

For more than two decades, Captain Pete has been running charters from Clinton out into the eastern end of Long Island Sound.

He takes groups from May 1 to Dec 1 by reservation only. The boat is a 42-foot Hatteras Sportfisherman named the *Sea Sprite* that holds up to 6 people. They have several different options for fishing trips, with half- or full-day trips out to the Race, Plum Gut, and the islands. You can fish for stripers, blackfish, porgies, fluke, and blues, as well as the occasional shark. Captain Pete provides fishing gear, life jackets, and a license. You should bring a cooler (to leave in your car) for the catch, soft-soled shoes, hat, sunglasses, and sunscreen. All ages are welcome on the *Sea Sprite*, so this is a great introduction for budding anglers of any age.

Golf

FOX HOPYARD
1 Hopyard Rd.
East Haddam, CT 06423
(860) 434-6644
golfthefox.com

The Fox Hopyard has membership options but also has public access for the rest of us, and this Roger Rulewich–designed course in East Haddam will make you glad about that. The course is par 71, at 7,000 yards from the back tees, and includes water, woods, and wetland features. The clubhouse is unique, set on a rock ledge with open decks that view some of the holes. The golf shop has everything you'll need, and there is a practice facility to get your rusty moves tuned up. The On the Rocks restaurant serves classic American dishes; try the Stonington sea scallops, either fried or sautéed. There's a dinner and golf special too. Although this is a public course in some ways, there is a dress code, so no logo T-shirts, tank tops, gym shorts, cutoffs, blue jeans, or crazy shoes. Make a reservation if you're coming here to join the huge list of celebrities and golf legends who have played Fox Hopyard.

*LYMAN ORCHARDS GOLF CLUB
70 Lyman Rd.
Middlefield, CT 06455
(888) 995-9626
lymangolf.com
This 1741 farm in Middlefield has become a destination for two reasons: its excellent farm store and its award-winning golf club. Notice that it is a golf club, not just a golf course, because there are actually two courses here. The first was designed by Robert Trent Jones and opened in 1969. Expect rolling hills and doglegs as the course lazily winds through the Connecticut landscape, seeming to never end. There are 4 sets of tees on each hole, water features on the back 9, and 44 bunkers throughout. This challenging course has even been used for the Connecticut PGA Championship. The other course was designed in 1994 by Gary Player, and both are consistently ranked in the top 10 public courses in the state. Zagat rates them both as two of the best in the US. The golf shop features custom-fitted equipment, and the Grille Room halfway through the Jones course offers breakfast and lunch. You can also rent clubs, and USGA handicap services are provided.

Health & Wellness

PARISIAN SALON AND DAY SPA
9 Berlin Rd.
Cromwell, CT 06416
(860) 632-2144
parisiandayspact.com
Right off exit 19 of I-91, the Parisian Day Spa in Cromwell features massages, body wraps, facials, and other services like Brazilian smoothing treatments for your hair. The Parisian takes care of your stomach too, with espresso, cappuccino, coffee, and herbal tea, as well as spa lunches for anyone getting a day spa package. This is the sort of place to go when you want to be pampered by professionals who make it their business to do it.

The Parisian is very involved in the town and sponsors many charity events as well, believing that a spa should fix up the community as well as the individual. That's something we can all appreciate.

*SPA OF ESSEX
63 S. Main St.
Essex, CT 06426
(860) 767-7796
thespaofessex.com
This spa is just outside the center of the charming village of Essex, and though you could walk from there, you might be so relaxed that you won't want to walk back. Drive into their spacious lot (or get dropped off under their portico) and head inside. After changing in the comfortable locker rooms, you'll relax (briefly) in the plush waiting room and then be escorted along the long, curved hall to one of 7 treatment rooms, or the manicure/pedicure room or makeup room, followed by the relaxation room for recovering from their exquisite treatments. Along with massages and the usual spa services, you can choose herbology, an aromatherapy oil wrap, a back glow treatment, or one of their "wet room" treatments, like the Dead Sea mud experience. Their treatment options and choices change much more often than most spas, with the season and with the needs of their clients. Don't forget to tip the masseuse or technician if she does a good job.

Hiking, Biking & Walking

COCKAPONSET STATE FOREST
18 Ranger Rd.
Haddam, CT 06438
(860) 345-8521
ct.gov/dep [search "Cockaponset State Forest"]
Cockaponset, named for an Indian chief who's buried in the Ponset section of Haddam, is the second-largest state forest in

Connecticut. This is a popular place for swimming in summer, at the Pattaconk Reservoir. Take Cedar Lake Road north off Route 148, and a short left will take you into the parking lot at the beach here. This is also a great place to start a hike; there are a dozen great hiking trails throughout this large forest, most of which are great for mountain biking, up and down but without any huge hills. This makes the Cockaponset perfect for cross-country skiing in winter as well. There is also another section to hike, right in the four-corner area of Killingworth, Clinton, Deep River, and Westbrook. This section, the Weber Woods Parcel, also has some nice loops and remains fairly flat.

NEW ENGLAND SCENIC TRAIL

(860) 346-2372

newenglandtrail.org

Beginning with the Menuncatuck Trail in Guilford, this national trail winds through Middlesex County south to north. In the Timberlands Reserve, stop for lunch at the glacial pond at Rock Creek; and as you head north to join the Mattabesett you'll go over Pyramid Rock and the glittering Mica Ledges. I once saw frog egg sacs in the protected streams of these highlands. You'll keep going over Totoket Mountain, a plateau with some of the loveliest meadows I've ever seen. Farther north the ridge walk at Mount Higby is one of the most rewarding in the state, even though (or because) it is right above I-91. In 1 mile you will go from the parking lot on Route 66 to Pinnacle Rock, where you can see far to the west and north all the way to Massachusetts. You can follow the basalt ridge for miles to the north, continuing to gain great views. After dipping into Preston Notch, you will see a natural bridge formation on the next ascent. If you'd like to keep going, the trail continues over I-91 and up Lamentation Mountain, one of the hardest ridge walks

in the state. By then you've left Middlesex County far behind.

SEVEN FALLS

Route 154

Middle Haddam, CT 06456

(860) 346-2372

ctwoodlands.org

This section of the Mattabesett Trail and its adjoining loops is located at Seven Falls, the state's first roadside picnic area, with a series of little cascading falls in Bible Rock Brook. Just off exit 10 of Route 9, take Route 154 south for less than a mile; you will see the small park on your left. The Mattabesett comes in from the west here, but you'll head east through a small labyrinth of picnic trails (follow the blue blazes) and go as far as you like into this woodland paradise. You can make a 3-mile loop if you head back on the blue circle trail, or cross Freeman and Aircraft Roads, where three more loops (all with blue circles to lead you back) are waiting. You'll find strange rock formations, old stagecoach roads, babbling brooks, and thickets of huckleberries along the way. In the middle of the fourth loop, Bear Hill rises up and makes for a nice end point to the hike, giving you about 8 miles if you follow the blue circles back to your car.

Horseback Riding

ALLEGRA FARM AND HORSE-DRAWN CARRIAGE AND SLEIGH MUSEUM

Route 82 and Petticoat Ln.

East Haddam, CT 06423

(860) 873-9658

allegrafarm.com

Okay, if you've never gone on a New England sleigh ride in the winter, get to it. The perfect place to do it is Allegra Farm on Lake Hayward, the largest authentic "livery stable" in Connecticut. First of all, they have a huge collection of horse-drawn carriages and sleighs, most of which have been in films or television shows, from *Amistad* to *Sex in the City*. The horses and carriages you see at Mystic Seaport are from Allegra too. They have open carriages or coaches enclosed with glass windows for warmer season rides, and open sleighs with blankets for going over the river and through the woods. Make a reservation and check the snow conditions before you go.

Kidstuff

AMY'S UDDER JOY FARM
27 North Rd.
Cromwell, CT 06416
(860) 635-3924
No website

Amy's Udder Joy Farm is full of exotic animals in a humane, fully licensed setting; this is a treat for kids on a summer day. With over 50 exotic and native animals, your kids will love to see the antelope, wallabies, ostriches, coatimundi, maras, giant hissing cockroaches, and land tortoises. There are interactive areas, like the saltwater tidal pool, and kids can feed the llamas and sheep. Guided tours are available for those who want one, along with pony rides on weekends. Don't miss the Tennessee fainting goats. Why are they called that? Go to Amy's and find out.

KIDCITY CHILDREN'S MUSEUM
119 Washington St.
Middletown, CT 06457
(860) 347-0495
kidcitymuseum.com

For kids 8 and under, this is heaven. The owner, Jennifer Alexander, wanted a place where parents and kids could play together, and she has succeeded. There are two linked buildings right in downtown Middletown, with 13,500 square feet of play space. A number of different activities are available, like a sailing ship, a diner, a post office, and even a bagel shop. Kids will hoist sails, push streetlight buttons, sell produce, or play school at a giant chalkboard. There's a video production theater and a number of instruments, a library from the classic tome *The Borrowers,* and a garden where kids can plant vegetables (really). This is intelligent play time, a place that will spur your child's creativity even as it (thankfully) drains his or her energy.

Skiing

POWDER RIDGE MOUNTAIN PARK AND RESORT
99 Powder Hill Rd.
Middlefield, CT 06455
(860) 349-3454
powderridgepark.com

Closed for several years, this classic Connecticut ski resort has been purchased by the owners of the successful Brownstone Discovery Park, who have revamped and revitalized it. You can eat at the new tavern, and enjoy the 525-foot vertical drop and 2,000 foot runs on 22 trails. There's skiing, snowboarding, tubing, and even mountain biking in the other three seasons of the year. Other off-season events include music festivals or having your wedding at the top of the mountain in a specially built gazebo with a spectacular view of the Connecticut Valley. Or you can just go in autumn and take the lift for a fall foliage tour.

Theater

*GOODSPEED OPERA HOUSE
6 Main St.
East Haddam, CT 06423
(860) 873-8668
goodspeed.org

The huge wedding cake of the Goodspeed Opera House opened in 1877, the largest wooden structure ever built along the Connecticut River. It went under in 1920 but was saved in 1963 and now houses Broadway musicals and other plays. The prices are reasonable, and you'll see families waiting for performances on the lawns overlooking the river every weekend. There are usually three musicals every Apr to Dec season at the Goodspeed, with classics like *Camelot* and *Showboat* as well as new productions. Goodspeed also runs the smaller Norma Terris Theatre in nearby Chester, where they develop new musicals and actors. You can also take tours of the opera house's workings, usually on Saturday and Monday, but call to make sure. The steel swing bridge leading across the river to the opera house is the longest such structure in the country, and on the hill above you will find one of two surviving schoolhouses that hosted state hero Nathan Hale.

*IVORYTON PLAYHOUSE
103 Main St.
Ivoryton, CT 06426
(860) 767-3718
ivorytonplayhouse.org

Built in 1911 as a recreation hall for the Comstock-Cheney factory workers, the first play was put on here in 1930 and the Ivoryton Playhouse became the first self-supporting summer theater in the nation. The actors who have graced its small stage are legion: Marlon Brando, Helen Hayes, Groucho Marx, Gloria Vanderbilt, Alan Alda, Jayne Mansfield, Myrna Loy, William Shatner, Eartha Kitt, Gene Hackman, and many more. Of course local girl Katharine Hepburn got her start here. In recent decades a complete renovation has made the Playhouse more comfortable, including new heating and air-conditioning as well as new seats and state-of-the-art sound and lighting. The Playhouse puts on a variety of different plays throughout the year, from drama and musicals to children's theater and Christmas programs. There are only 280 seats, so there aren't really any bad ones, although the front row of the balcony is particularly close and excellent

here. The intimate setting highlights how sometimes a play is much better than a film, and the connection between the actors and audience is electric.

Water Sports

*BROWNSTONE EXPLORATION AND DISCOVERY PARK
161 Brownstone Ave.
Portland, CT 06480
(860) 342-5017
brownstonepark.com

Built in a brownstone quarry in operation since 1660, Brownstone Park is one of Connecticut's newest and most creative attractions. The two quarries that make up the park are flooded (since the 1938 hurricane, in fact) and now fed by natural springs. There are so many activities here that it is difficult to even list them. You can swim, snorkel, and scuba dive in these amazing pits; there are even carefully mapped underwater scuba stations and training platforms. You can rock climb, cliff jump, wakeboard, canoe, water bike, water ball, and kayak. There is a zip-line and a challenge course, along with ample hiking and biking opportunities on well-cleared trails. This is a continually expanding attraction, and things may be more developed by the time you get there, with a museum, learning center, and other activities in the works. It's great to see this creative way of reclaiming these quarries for recreation, and Brownstone Park is sure to become one of Connecticut's most popular summer attractions in future years.

HAPPIEST PADDLER
70 N. Main St.
East Hampton, CT 06424
(860) 267-1764
happiest-paddler.com

With Happiest Paddler you can rent quality canoes and kayaks to paddle on 512-acre

Lake Pocotopaug in East Hampton, one of Connecticut's larger bodies of freshwater. They also offer fishing boats, so you can get out on the lake and catch some bass and trout. Oh, yes, they also have bright yellow paddleboats for rent, great for families. The last option is a party boat, complete with driver, for up to 14 people. For special occasions, they offer sunset cruises with appetizers and dinner. The prices at Happiest Paddler will certainly not make you sad, either. Pocotopaug is a great place to practice your skills or to relax on the water on a hot day.

INDIAN RIVER MARINA
58 Commerce St.
Clinton, CT 06413
(860) 664-3704
indrivmar.com

The Indian River Marina offers different marine services to locals, but you are probably most interested in their canoe and kayak rentals. They offer touring, recreational, and fishing kayaks and hard plastic canoes for rent by the hour, half day, or full day. You just need to bring your hat, water bottle, camera, binoculars, and bug spray. And bring your willingness to get wet of course. If you paddle 0.25 mile downriver you'll reach Clinton Harbor, and from there, the Sound. They will also drop you and a kayak in the Hammonasset River if you want to explore that area instead. Either way, you'll see egrets, herons, and cormorants, as well as osprey nests high above. If you have your own boat, this is also a great place to launch. You can arrange to have picnic lunches made by a local deli or use the marina's own picnic area and barbecue and enjoy it in their screened gazebo.

SHOPPING
Antiques
CLINTON ANTIQUES CENTER
78 E. Main St.
Clinton, CT 06413
(860) 669-3839
No website

Open every day but Wednesday, this shop facing Main Street in Clinton seems small from the front, but it's an illusion. The building goes back a long way, including 85 dealers' booths. You'll find mostly smalls in the store, with tons of porcelain, glassware, plates, vases, boxes, miniatures, pewter, jewelry, and knickknacks of all kinds. Don't forget to look up! Clinton also has some other fine antiques stores, all along East and West Main Streets, so if 85 dealers aren't enough for you, you should explore this area fully. In summer there is also a flea market at the center of town (327 E. Main) starting at 7 a.m. on Sunday.

ENGLISH ACCENTS ANTIQUES
Essex Square
4 N. Main St.
Essex, CT 06426
(860) 767-0113
englishaccents-ct.com

The owners of English Accents travel to England every year and import antiques and accessories to Essex. Most are "manor house"–style antiques, with 19th-century furniture, fine porcelain, vintage jewelry, paintings, lamps, and rugs. But they also have an interesting selection of sporting antiques; maybe you'll want a pair of ancient cross-country skis or a bamboo fishing rod for over the mantle. Get yourself a pair of leather club chairs, in which you can suitably rustle your newspaper and drink a single-malt whiskey. Open Thurs through Sun, the English Accents store is located right on the corner of the main intersection in Essex; you can hardly miss it as you drive into town.

THE ESSEX SAYBROOK ANTIQUES VILLAGE

954 Middlesex Tpke.
Old Saybrook, CT 06475
(860) 388-0689
oneofakindantiques.com/
art_antique_collectors_guide

With its blue whale sign, the Antiques Village calls you in to this nice selection of booths filled by different dealers. There are paintings, antique toys, swords and knives, jewelry, furniture, and more. Dig around. You'll find a rare book for $20 or a set of antique whiskey glasses to bring out for company. They have a selection of old Connecticut postcards, oriental rugs, fishing rods, and saddles—something for every interest. Down Route 154 South is the similarly named Old Saybrook Antiques Center, which has many fine pieces but caters to a wealthier clientele. North are a number of other antiques shops within a few hundred yards. Just over the border in Essex is Valley Farm Antiques, a standout among them, with trestle tables and decorative architectural pieces of all sorts.

SHORELINE ANTIQUES, LLC

13 Boston Post Rd.
Westbrook, CT 06498
(860) 669-3330
shorelineantiques.webs.com

Located right between seafood rivals Lenny and Joe's Fish Tale and Westbrook Lobster, Shoreline Antiques carries everything from early 18th-century furniture to 20th-century toys. They consistently change the inventory, but you are likely to find some fine art, folk art, cut glass, oriental rugs, needlework, and clocks. It's not as cluttered as some shops, with a clean and neat appearance, and the staff is very helpful. Shoreline keeps good hours, Tues through Fri from noon to 5 p.m.

and weekends 9 a.m. to 5 p.m. There are a lot of choices here, but the real question will be which restaurant's lobster rolls to go for after browsing the shop.

Clothing

ANCHOR AND COMPASS

163 Main St.
Deep River, CT 06417
(860) 322-4327
anchorandcompass.com

This men's clothing and accessories store opened in 2010 and has since become the go-to in the area for real men. The beautiful wood and maritime fixture shop carries brands like Woolrich, Carhartt, Life Is Good, Tommy Bahama, Salt Life, and Old Guys Rule, as well as belts, shaving gear, and other necessities. And we get our knickknacks too, with things like mugs, compasses, and magnetic bottle caps. Come here to be tough, or at least act like you are. You may not be able to stop a runaway train, but your shirt might.

CLINTON BOOTERY

203 East Main St.
Clinton, CT 06413
(860) 669-2747
clintonbootery.com

The one thing you never want to do is buy shoes online. How do you know if they will fit? I know someone who is addicted to this practice, and it takes up hours sending stuff back. How about a quick trip to the Clinton Bootery instead. They have awesome boots, but not just boots—this is the independent store to buy shoes in Middlesex County. Located on Route 1, they carry Keen, Frye, Uggs, Dansko, Carolina Boots, Birkenstock, Sperry, New Balance, and on and on. They often have brands that no one else does. They use Aetrex iStep foot scanning technology to measure you. That's service.

THE SILKWORM OF ESSEX VILLAGE
23 Main St.
Essex, CT 06426
(860) 767-1298
essexct.com

This is a small, independent boutique with seasonal dresses and excellent service. You'll find it right across from the lovely town park that leads down to the water, a charming back bay off the Connecticut River. Along with outfits from designers like Lilly Pulitzer, Sara Campbell, and Nicole Miller, the Silkworm also has gifts and accessories like bags, belts, and scarves. Get an Eric Javits hat to keep off the summer sun. There are dozens of great shops in Essex, so be sure to explore. But the Silkworm is a standout for their consistently reliable service and hand-picked selection.

Farm Stores/Pick Your Own

CHESTER SUNDAY MARKET
Main Street
Chester, CT 06412
(860) 790-5007
chestersundaymarket.jimdo.com

More than just a farmers' market, this is a town-wide event that happens every Sunday from June to Oct in Chester. Local vendors sell fruits and vegetables, cheese and breads, honey and pottery. The entire main street is closed off and music plays as the people of the town and surrounding communities stroll the streets, sipping coffee and perusing art. Events like this one do not just bring a town together, they create a town as a living entity, one where the people have actual neighbors, one that connects us to one another and to the land where we live.

LYMAN ORCHARDS
Routes 147 and 157
Middlefield, CT 06455
(860) 349-1793
lymanorchards.com

Since 1741 this family-owned farm has been a destination for generations of Connecticut families. There are pick-your-own apple and peach orchards, and pumpkin, raspberry, strawberry, and blueberry fields. The hugely popular farm store features not just fresh produce and milk but also baked goods, cheese, fudge, and a small deli and cafe with wraps, coffee, and sandwiches. Lyman Orchards also runs seasonal festivals, such as a Strawberry Festival in June, with horse-drawn wagon rides, pony rides, pie-eating contests, and live music. See the entry for their award-winning golf courses as well.

OLD SAYBROOK FARMERS' MARKET
210 Main St.
Old Saybrook, CT 06475
No phone
oldsaybrookfarmersmarket.com

For the past decade and more, the Old Saybrook Farmers' Market has been one of the most consistent and lauded in the state. Open from late June to the end of Oct, usually Wed and Sat, the market is held on the property of William Childress. There are usually about 30 vendors, all strictly Connecticut products. You'll get meat from Stonington, pottery from Madison, and berries from Norwich, along with fresh-baked bread, kettle corn made on-site, and a variety of handcrafted items for sale. There is usually live music or other demonstrations, anything from martial arts to craft skills.

Home & Crafts

CONNECTICUT RIVER ARTISANS
5 W. Main St.
Chester, CT 06412
(860) 526-5575
ctriverartisans.org

This shop above the old mill sluiceway in Chester is an artists' co-op, which requires a juried process to join. You'll find locally made handcrafted and painted pottery, jewelry, handbags, and more here, as well as a nice selection of fine paintings and prints. There is a changing gallery exhibit in the back. They share their building with Mystic Sisters antiques and the Belle Design Studio, both worth a look themselves. Next door is Helene Johnson's sculpture gallery in an unusual 1913 building, and the rest of the town is simply swamped with studios and galleries of all sorts. If you're here on a weekend in summer, stop at the Chester Museum at the Mill run by the local historical society. Park on Main Street and walk around the corner.

THE PINK SLEIGH
512 Essex Rd.
Westbrook, CT 06498
(860) 399-6926
No website

You'll find this little piece of Christmas magic in an old 1830s barn in Westbrook. The silver and gold of colorful displays fill two floors; you can find thousands of ornaments for your tree, as well as other decorations. They also carry Halloween and harvest decorations in early autumn and Thanksgiving wreaths and centerpieces later on. Candles, tassels, garlands, ribbons, silks, and more fill the shelves of this charming shop. It is a great place to go to on a cold November day when you just want to start thinking of the holidays. Closed Monday and Tuesday in winter.

THE SHOPPES AT WHITTEMORE CROSSING
1365 Whittemore Rd.
Middlebury, CT 06762
(203) 528-0130
middleburyconsignment.com

This consignment shop has amazing prices on amazing furniture, maybe the best I've seen outside an estate auction. They opened in September 2009 and have grown every year since. The unmistakable green building used to be a woodworking workshop but is now a huge, well-appointed showroom. The cafe (open 11:30 a.m. to 3:00 p.m.) has dishes like Mandarin beet salad and prosciutto, fig & goat cheese baguette, and the best French onion soup in the state. They also have a huge showroom kitchen, where they run special events with some of the state's best chefs. Check their kitchen web page for the prices of the upcoming cooking extravaganzas.

WESLEYAN POTTERS
350 S. Main St.
Middletown, CT 06457
(860) 344-0039
wesleyanpotters.com

With 9,000 square feet of studio and gallery space, this cooperative houses more than just pottery, with 100 artists and craftspeople exhibiting their work in weaving, basket making, and jewelry making (and, yes, pottery). Classes and workshops run here, and you'll probably see one during your visit. You can call ahead for tours as well. The time to come is November and December, when you can see all the crafts by everyone (and not just selected exhibits), and buy them at the annual sale. Call ahead to find out the exact times the Potters will be open.

Malls

CLINTON CROSSING PREMIUM OUTLETS

20A Killingworth Tpke.
Clinton, CT 06413
(860) 669-3066
premiumoutlets.com/clinton

Outlets often draw people disproportionately to the savings they imagine they are going to get. You might see buses at these outlets from Florida or Texas and wonder at savings versus the travel expense. However, if you are already here, shopping at Clinton Crossing is more than worth your time and money. Right off I-95 in Clinton, these outlets feature designer fashions, shoes, jewelry, and housewares. Unlike some outlet malls that focus solely on brand-name clothes, though, there are also little gems here like Bose speakers, Fossil watches, and Lindt chocolate. Don't miss the chance to stock up at Yankee Candle. The pleasant walkways between the shops give the sense of walking in a small village, and make this a great stop on the way to the attractions of eastern Connecticut.

TANGER FACTORY OUTLETS

314 Flat Rock Place
Westbrook, CT 06498
(860) 399-8656
tangeroutlet.com/westbrook

With almost 60 stores, this expansive set of outdoor malls is more like a small village than an outlet. There is a huge variety of stores in all categories, from Timberland to Bath and Body Works. There's even a Vanity Fair outlet here, with prices so low for jeans (with one stitch misplaced or similar minor problems), you'll be confused, until you snatch them up and happily take them home. Tanger Factory Outlets also includes a movie theater, in case you want to relax in a dark room after being dazzled by so much merchandise. Tanger rhymes with hanger, as in clothes hangers, and yours will be full after a visit to these outlets.

Specialty Foods

CHEESE SHOP OF CENTERBROOK

33 Main St.
Centerbrook, CT 06409
(860) 767-8500
cheeseshopcenterbrook.com

The cheese-loving insiders already know this place, rated one of the best cheese shops in the state, possibly the world. They have a huge selection, and the cheesemonger (Paul) knows his stuff. In fact, I'm not sure I've ever met someone who knows more about cheese. My favorites? Costwold, Stilton, Roaring 40s Blue, Beemster Aged Gouda XO, Drunken Goat . . . oh, I can't choose. You can also get bread, crackers, olives, and meats, as well as a nice espresso, way cheaper than Starbucks. Closed on Sunday, this place is heaven for those of us who love cheese.

FROMAGE FINE FOODS AND COFFEES

873 Boston Post Rd.
Old Saybrook, CT 06475
(860) 388-5750
fromagefinefoods.com

For over two decades, Christine Chesanek has run this charming store with the largest selection of cheese on the shoreline. Along with over 100 cheeses, Fromage Fine Foods has coffees, pastas, olive oils, jams, salamis, sausages, spices, wild game pâtés, caviar, cookies, and fresh breads from the Copper Beech Inn's bakery. You can get a fresh-brewed cup of gourmet coffee to drink as you browse the shop. This gourmet shop used to be located in a much smaller store, and the new counter is as big as the entire old store. That's good news for you, because Christine can fit in a lot more cheese.

SUNDIAL GARDENS
59 Hidden Lake Rd.
Higganum, CT 06441
(860) 345-4290
sundialgardens.com

The tea shop here at Sundial sells herbal tisanes, teapots, and accessories, as well as specialty foods and chocolate. However, this is not just a specialty food shop. For a small fee you can also visit the three formal architectural gardens: a Persian knot garden, a topiary, and a geometric 18th-century style. Sundial's longtime owner, Ragna Tischler Goddard, also runs a tea tasting, lecture, and demonstration about once a month, so check the website for times and sign up. She also runs baking and gardening classes. This shop has been featured in numerous magazines and on television shows, and for good reason: It is unique.

ACCOMMODATIONS

All lodgings have both smoking and non-smoking rooms unless otherwise noted, or have a designated indoor or porch smoking area, and do not accept pets unless noted. Hotels, motels, and resorts are wheelchair accessible unless otherwise noted. Bed-and-breakfasts and inns are not wheelchair accessible unless otherwise noted, since many are in historic buildings exempt from the Americans with Disabilities Act. Call to make sure if there's any question. We do not list specific credit cards in either this section or the restaurants section.

Bed-and-Breakfasts

ANGELS' WATCH INN
902 Boston Post Rd.
Westbrook, CT 06498
(860) 399-8846
angelswatchinn.com

You don't need to go to Vegas, because the Angels' Watch Inn has an elopement package. Seriously. There is a justice of the peace on-site who performs elopement wedding ceremonies, along with normal small weddings and vow renewals. All 5 rooms have fireplaces and private baths, and 4 feature 2-person pedestal soaking tubs. There are minifridges and snack baskets filled with complimentary treats, and all rooms have wireless Internet, TVs, DVD and CD players, and all the other amenities you could want. Breakfast always includes a huge selection of baked goods. Best of all, you can walk to the beach after you get hitched.

BUSHNELL HOUSE INN $$$
106 S. Main St.
Westbrook, CT 06498
(800) 342-3162
bushnellhouse.com

This yellow 1840 Greek Revival inn has a wraparound porch with wicker furniture that calls you to relax. Inside, the historic furnishings and original granite fireplaces, heart pine floors, and moldings make you immediately feel like you've stepped back in time. Of course this magical past comes with wireless DSL connections and LCD cable televisions, but that's what we expect in these fast-paced times. There are 3 guest rooms, all with private baths that include sani-jet Jacuzzis and heated porcelain floors. The beds are all kings, with fine linens, and each room is climate controlled. Your room comes with a full breakfast, beach passes, and beach bags, towels, beach chairs, and umbrellas for you to borrow. Once the Westbrook Inn, this house was restored in 2005, and you can really feel and see the difference.

CAPTAIN STANNARD HOUSE
COUNTRY INN $$$$
138 S. Main St.
Westbrook, CT 06498
(860) 399-4634
stannardhouse.com

This rambling house of 10,000 square feet was built by Captain Elbert Stannard in 1872 as his home away from home (his other being his ship of course). After Stannard died, the house became an inn, going through a number of names until the present day, when it was named (properly at last) for its original owner. There are 9 large guest rooms, 6 of which are "garden rooms" and 3 of which are larger "manor rooms." There is a larger number than usual of common areas, with a pool table, fireplace, and a huge 1,000-square-foot porch. You can also walk to the beach or the center of the village from here. No children under 16 or pets are allowed, and smoking is only permitted outside the house. The inn was restored and painted its original colors in 2006, and this is now one of the most beautiful places to stay along the coast.

DEACON TIMOTHY PRATT BED AND BREAKFAST $$$
325 Main St.
Old Saybrook, CT 06475
(860) 395-1229
pratthouse.net

The beautiful light-blue 1747 saltbox on Main Street in Old Saybrook is right next to the famous James Pharmacy and within walking distance of all the attractions. It once served as a private school in the 1790s, but now offers 2 rooms with fireplaces and private baths with Jacuzzis and one larger 2-room suite. There are four-poster beds, air-conditioning, and other modern amenities like cable television and modem lines. In winter an ice-skating pond is right down the street, and 0.5 mile away is the canoe and kayak launch. The wide-board floors, beehive oven, and hand-hewn beams of this ancient house will give you chills if you think about the history here, but don't worry—there are 12 working fireplaces to warm you up! There's a nice garden area in the back, with a tree swing and hammock for sitting on a summer eve. Cross the street and walk the sidewalks past the white clapboard Congregational church (where Timothy Pratt was deacon) into town for dinner and shopping.

NEHEMIAH BRAINERD B&B $$$–$$$$
988 Saybrook Rd.
Haddam, CT 06438
(860) 345-8605
brainerdhousebb.com

As you pull into the huge circular drive and see the large 18th-century home on a bluff over the Connecticut River, you'll instantly feel like you've come home. There are 2 guest rooms, a large suite, and a guest cottage. The cottage's stone porch with a double Adirondack chair looking out over the river valley is perfect; you won't want to retire inside to the brass bed and full kitchen, but rather stay out as the gloaming fades into night. The Nehemiah Brainerd House is not the place to stay if you have children under 13, but it's the perfect place to stay if you're going to the Goodspeed Opera House, Essex Steam Train, or Gillette Castle.

RIVERWIND INN $$$–$$$$
209 Main St.
Deep River, CT 6417
(860) 526-2014
riverwindinn.com

This 1854 house in "downtown" Deep River (it's a village) has 8 rooms, large for a bed-and-breakfast in Connecticut. There are 3 sitting areas, 1 downstairs and 2 upstairs, 1 with a fireplace and small refrigerator and a small coffee/tea maker. No pets or children under 13 are allowed at the Riverwind, which makes this the perfect place for a romantic overnight. All the rooms have private baths, hair dryers, air-conditioning, wireless Internet, ceiling fans, and period antiques. A few have fireplaces, including the wonderful

Moonlit Suite in the attic, which also has 2 beds, a living room, and Jacuzzi. The ceiling gets too low for me near the walls, but I am 6'3". Sit on the wraparound porch and sip a glass of complimentary sherry.

*WESTBROOK INN $$$$
976 Boston Post Rd.
Westbrook, CT 06498
(800) 342-3162
westbrookinn.com

Voted one of the most elegant inns in the nation, this 1876 Victorian home built by a sea captain has been restored to its original state, but with the modern conveniences of air-conditioning, color televisions, and refrigerators in all the rooms. There are 9 rooms in total, with a suite and a 2-bedroom cottage. They offer a full breakfast daily, as well as complimentary beach passes, towels, and chairs, and you can easily walk to the sandy stretch from the inn. They also rent boating, biking, and fishing gear, and since it is located right on the river, you can stroll out on the dock and fish. Or just sit on the wraparound porch or by the fireplace and read a book from their library. If you're coming in autumn, as with all Connecticut bed-and-breakfasts, make reservations well in advance.

Inns

*COPPER BEECH INN $$$$
46 Main St.
Ivoryton, CT 06426
(860) 767-0330
copperbeechinn.com

Step into New England elegance at the Copper Beech Inn, located in the picturesque village of Ivoryton, which is technically part of Essex. The historic property dates from 1889, built by Archibald Welsh Comstock, son of ivory importer Samuel Comstock. The inn began in 1972 and is named for the majestic European beech

whose limbs spread out over the front of the Victorian-style mansion. The inside lobby is attractively designed, with wood paneling and embossed wallpaper. There are 22 rooms, with options in the Main House and the adjacent Carriage House and Comstock House. Each room is exceptional, individually decorated and styled. You'll find four-poster beds, antique highboys, stylish armoires, and richly upholstered armchairs and sofas. Craft a letter or poem on a leather-top writing desk, soak in a claw-foot or hydro-massage tub, and sip a glass of wine on the deck overlooking the gardens. And don't forget to make reservations here for the Brasserie Pip (see entry).

*GRISWOLD INN $$$$
36 Main St.
Essex, CT 06426
(860) 767-1776
griswoldinn.com

The British invaded and burned ships at Essex in 1814, but they thankfully missed the white clapboard Griswold Inn. Built by Sala Griswold in 1776, it is called "The Gris" by everyone in town, and its fluttering Union flags are impossible to miss. There is a selection of rooms at different price levels, but all have private baths and climate control. If you stay over on a Saturday night, be sure to get the Hunt Breakfast on Sunday morning, started by those British invaders long ago. They recently added to the rambling old restaurant with a wine bar, which has a different menu and will appeal to a different set of guests. Maybe you're one of them. The inn also has a shop across the street in the 1799 Timothy Starkey House with "goods and curiosities," books, and maps. Don't miss a cone at Sweet P's ice-cream and candy store.

INN AT MIDDLETOWN $$$–$$$$
70 Main St.
Middletown, CT 06457
(860) 854-6300
innatmiddletown.com

This inn was actually once a National Guard armory and now features 100 guest rooms, 12 of which are 2-room junior suites with microwaves and refrigerators. There's a heated indoor pool, a fitness room, and in-room dining. Even better, their king-size beds are actually king-size, and the inn is located right on Main Street. Walk down to all the shops or up the hill to the stunning campus of Wesleyan University. The on-site restaurant, called the Tavern at the Armory, features traditional New England cuisine, like rainbow trout fillets and lobster and tarragon salad, as well as some global delights like Moroccan chicken ($$$$).

Resorts

*SAYBROOK POINT INN AND SPA $$$$
2 Bridge St.
Old Saybrook, CT 06475
(860) 395-2000
saybrook.com

This resort by the mouth of the Connecticut River is one of the state's first green hotels. They have 62 rooms in English country–style decor, all of which overlook either the river, the Sound, or the marina. There are also 7 large suites and a "lighthouse room" with a kitchenette. The Saybrook Point Inn features a steam room and fitness room, indoor and outdoor pools, and bicycles for guests to borrow. A bike trail heads out along the causeway, and a golf course is within walking distance, on the peninsula where Katharine Hepburn lived. Of course you shouldn't forget to visit the spa; try the seascape ritual, which uses basalt stones and sustainable seaweed, or the shea butter rock massage. The inn even will deliver champagne and spa robes to your room. This is a place to indulge your taste for luxury, the comfortable seaside luxury particular to this relaxing stretch of the Connecticut shore.

WATER'S EDGE RESORT AND SPA $$$$
1525 Boston Post Rd.
Westbrook, CT 06498
(860) 399-5901
watersedgeresortandspa.com

Set on a hill above the Sound, the Water's Edge has hosted famous guests from Woody Allen to Barbara Streisand. With 101 sleek rooms with private baths, the resort also includes 2 pools, a fitness center, a steam room, tennis courts, a sauna, and a whirlpool. The Water's Edge also has 68 seaside "villas," total-amenity condominiums of over 1,000 square feet perfect for long stays on the shore. The rooms are clean and modern, with attention to design and function. Along with a martini bar, an outdoor grill, and the main dining room, there is also a coffee bar, with all your favorite caffeinated beverages and pastries. You can walk down the grassy hill to the beach and watch the sailboats, or maybe swim out to the small offshore island to soak up the rays. One caveat: Call ahead to make sure they aren't hosting a big wedding or event, at least if you want a quiet night.

Camping

MARKHAM MEADOWS CAMPGROUND $
7 Markham Rd.
East Hampton, CT 06424
(860) 267-9738
markhammeadows.com

Family owned and family oriented, Markham Meadows is set in the middle of a large farm. Over 100 RV and tent sites spread out around a couple of ponds, and among woodlands and scattered trees. They just installed a huge pool and offer a general store, bingo every Friday, a rec hall, paved basketball court, playground for children, snack bar, video arcade, hot showers, laundry facilities, hayrides, bass fishing in the ponds (catch-and-release), free kayaks and paddleboats, and 2 sandy-bottom ponds for swimming. If it sounds more like an amusement park than a campground, you might be right. Except you can stay overnight at this one, roasting marshmallows over an open fire and enjoying the fellowship only camping can bring.

WOLF'S DEN FAMILY CAMPGROUND $–$$
256 Town St. (Route 82)
East Haddam, CT 06423
(860) 873-9681
wolfsdencampground.com

The Gustine family owns the Wolf's Den Family Campground, and when they say "family" they mean you, them, and everyone who stays at this charming place. They have 205 grassy tent and RV sites available from Apr to Oct, with seasonal and week-long options to save you money. They also have trailer rentals in case you don't want to stay in a tent. Nightly the trailers are $$, but if you get them by the week, they are $. Like all the best family campgrounds, the Wolf's Den includes tons of amenities: an Olympic-size pool, a camp store, firewood, ice, picnic tables, fireplaces, a laundry room, flush toilets, hot showers, a game room, miniature golf, tennis courts, a fishing pond, and a swimming pond. And, yes, they have wireless Internet access at the rec hall. Now that's camping.

RESTAURANTS

Please note that all Connecticut restaurants are smoke free, and all are required to be wheelchair accessible. Pets are not allowed inside most restaurants, but during the warmer months, there are plenty of restaurants with patio areas just right for your canine friend. Call ahead to make sure it's okay.

American & Modern

FRESH SALT $$$
2 Bridge St.
Old Saybrook CT 06475
(800) 243-0212
saybrook.com/restaurant

Opened in 2011, the new restaurant at the Saybrook Point Inn took everyone by surprise with its, well, freshness. With gorgeous views of the Sound, this is a perfect place for a date. You can get the oysters or do a crudo tasting for an appetizer, and then try the autumnal chestnut soup. Hand-dug Ipswich whole clams are a seafood treat, while the roasted duck breast is tender and juicy. This is American dining at its finest. Try to time your meal for sunset, if you really want to impress your date. Mine was (though she was already my wife).

GABRIELLE'S $$$
78 Main St.
Centerbrook, CT 06409
(860) 767-2440
gabrielles.net

This bistro set in a remodeled Victorian home is a local favorite for fine dining, with creative dishes that bring out the foodie in all of us. Try the cornmeal-crusted oysters or crispy tuna rolls, little East-West fusion delights. They also have more approachable dishes like artisanal pizzas, fish-and-chips, and burgers, albeit done with class and delicate touches you won't find just anywhere. And make sure to try one of Gabrielle's creative martinis before or after dinner. The menu quotes Anthony Bourdain: "I have long believed that good food, good eating is all about risk. Whether we're talking about unpasteurized Stilton, raw oysters or working for organized crime associates, food, for me, has always been an adventure."

Gabrielle's restaurant has taken that philosophy to heart and provided adventures for all of us.

✳GRISWOLD INN RESTAURANT AND TAP ROOM $$$
36 Main St.
Essex, CT 06426
(860) 767-1776
griswoldinn.com/food

The restaurant at the 1776 Griswold Inn is simply an experience not to be missed. The curved ceiling of the historic taproom highlights the old woodstove in the center of the room, the ancient blackened fireplace, and the Currier and Ives seafaring prints covering the walls. It has been called "the most handsome barroom in America" and consistently voted the best in Connecticut. The signature chowder is amazing, and they serve it with a Caribbean sherry pepper sauce, an authentic relic mostly forgotten. The house-made Long Island duck pâté is creamy and delicate in a generous portion. The lunch will cost you no more than a TGI Friday's, and the experience and taste are light years ahead. Although the Tap Room is the most famous, it is by no means the only room to dine in. The Gun Room features antique firearms in glass cases, and the Library tempts diners to crack open one of the old books.

✳RIVER TAVERN $$$
23 Main St.
Chester, CT 06412
(860) 526-9417
rivertavernchester.net

With its orange and blue Sol LeWitt design, the dining room, tavern bar, and outdoor cafe of the River Tavern are stylish but welcoming, with views of either the open kitchen or Pattaconk Brook. Chef Jonathan Rapp keeps the menu short, allowing seasonal changes and daily specials to take the focus. They literally change the menu with the seasons, so it is impossible to predict what you'll find. In the past, Stonington lobster crepes with leeks and lemon cream was a top choice. You might find handmade pasta dishes, spicy lamb sandwiches, or a parsnip soup. They offer a large selection of wines, with some interesting appellations and varietals. The River Tavern also participates in Dinners at the Farm programs with local farmers. This focus on farm-fresh meals is growing throughout America, and we can hope it means a greater connection to the land for all of us.

WATER'S EDGE RESTAURANT $$$
1525 Boston Post Rd.
Westbrook, CT 06498
(860) 399-5901
watersedgeresortandspa.com

The terraced lawns of the Water's Edge bring people throughout the year, and the flowering bushes from spring to fall seem to sparkle with luxury. The huge windows of the main dining room look out to one of the best views on the shore. The barbecued duck breast and veal porterhouse are both worthy entrees, and the emulsion they use with their crispy fried oysters is remarkable. The main room is not your only option here, either. The Seaview Bistro and Martini Bar offers burgers, pizzas, and sandwiches, along with great cocktails. The even more casual (and less expensive) Sunset Bar and Grill is open seasonally, and offers live music Wednesday through Sunday nights. The Water's Edge is also known for having one of the best Sunday brunches in Connecticut, which includes a Belgian waffle and French crepe bar that will have you reevaluating your relationship with breakfast. At nights there is entertainment in the lounge, and you will be taken back (or perhaps forward?) to the time of the great American resorts.

Asian & Indian

FORBIDDEN CITY BISTRO $$
335 Main St.
Middletown, CT 06457
(860) 343-8288
forbiddencitybistro.com

This fine-dining Chinese restaurant in Middletown is the brainchild of Eric Leong, and he has pushed the boundaries past what we've unfortunately come to expect from this delicious and varied cuisine. He's focusing on healthy, modern-looking dishes with a long tradition behind them. If that seems like a contradiction, it's not. It's genius. Try unusual but somehow familiar dishes like chilled Chinese eggplant, five-spice duck wrap, Silk Route lamb shank, and fruit-glazed crispy shrimp. Leong tries to bring in different styles from different regions of China, and his menu is a reminder that China is pretty much the size of all of Europe, and just as varied when it comes to its food. There are displays by contemporary Chinese artists, and if you're interested in the history of the dishes you're eating, the servers will happily tell you the tales.

Breakfast & Lunch

BEACH DONUT SHOP $
344 E. Main St.
Clinton, CT 06413
(860) 669-4241
beachdonutshop.com

For over 60 years, Beach has made their donuts by hand, and the quality they have achieved is unbelievable. This is one of the top donut shops in the state, probably the country, and yet it looks so modest in the tiny strip mall along Route 1. They have a selection of pastries, actually, all delicious and fresh, like the cinnamon crullers hot from the fryer. But the donuts! Oreo crumble donuts! Chocolate Bavarian cream! The glazed are particularly tempting, and I like the chocolate frosting

as well. In autumn try the seasonal cider donuts, and stop back for other experiments and delights time and time again. With a place like this, I'm not sure why anyone would go to . . . what's the name of that chain again?

WHISTLE STOP CAFE $
108 Main St.
Deep River, CT 06417
(860) 526-4122
whistlestopcafe.biz/index.html

Owner Hedy Watrous keeps the traditions of her grandfather, who opened this cafe in 1928. Open for breakfast and lunch, the Whistle Stop serves omelets, sandwiches, salads, and other delicious entrees. If you're a vegetarian, you'll love the options for you, including the Marasco Fiasco, a wheat sandwich with eggplant, artichokes, sun-dried tomato, leeks, and swiss cheese (take that off if you're vegan). If you're a meat eater, try the shaved steak with Gorgonzola or the excellent corned beef hash. Tell them the diet you prefer, and they will make suggestions from the menu. This cafe is literally one small room, and is always full of smiling families, locals, and very lucky tourists.

French

CAFE ROUTIER $$$
1353 Boston Post Rd.
Westbrook, CT 06498
(860) 399-8700
caferoutier.com

After moving from Old Saybrook to Westbrook, this French cafe has changed its format and focus. Along with French food, Routier has New American dishes on its menu, as well as global food influenced by a dozen different countries. The menu has three panels: one with the consistent classics, one with a different region of the world every eight weeks, and one with locally sourced seasonal ingredients. This great format has made fans of everyone in the area. You can also get small plates at the bar like mac and cheese croquettes and Portuguese shellfish stew. Cafe Routier is open for dinner only, but there's also a "mood lounge" where they have small tapas-style dishes and live music.

✳RESTAURANT L&E AND
FRENCH 75 BAR $$$
59 Main St.
Chester, CT 06412
(860) 526-5301
restaurantfrench75bar.com

For 30 years this was the Restaurant du Village, consistently rated one of the best in the state. The current owners come from Nantucket, where they ran the exclusive American Seasons restaurant, and have continued and possibly improved it. As soon as the bread comes, you know you're in for a treat. The menu is absolutely sinful, with crepes of rabbit confit and wild mushroom, truffle-dusted sweetbreads, braised Berkshire pork cheeks, fresh Wellfleet oysters—and these are just the appetizers. For dinner, the skate wings in wild ramp butter with braised pork belly and the oven-roasted quail with fig-almond bread stuffing are both unbelievable in their delicate flavors. In season they have shad from the Connecticut River, and they always have a great selection of wines. The cool tables in the courtyard are perfect for summer, and if you choose to sit inside at the clean white tables by the French doors, you can stop regretting the missed trip to Paris.

Ice Cream

JAMES PHARMACY AND SODA
FOUNTAIN $
325 Main St.
Old Saybrook, CT 06475
(860) 395-1229
pratthouse.net/jamesgallery.htm

Now part of Tissa's Le Souk du Maroc, this is surely one of the most unusual shops in Middlesex County. The building was once the Humphrey Pratt Tavern and appears on the National Register of Historic Places. The Marquis de Lafayette made a purchase here on his way to Boston in 1824, and Katharine Hepburn used to use the phone in the old oak booth after it became the pharmacy. Anna Louise James, the first African-American woman to graduate from the Brooklyn College of Pharmacy, ran it as a pharmacy and soda fountain from 1917 to 1967. Today you can still buy ice cream here, as well as wonderful North African treats and wraps. The store sells lentils, preserved lemons, tea, and Turkish delight, while still preserving the ancient floorboards, low ceiling, and charm of yesteryear. This wonderful blend of East and West, past and present, bodes well for the future of a changing America.

Italian

ALFORNO $$
1654 Boston Post Rd.
Old Saybrook, CT 06475
(860) 399-4166
alforno.net

With its billowing ceiling drapes, patio floor, and brightly decorated walls, dining inside Alforno is like being on the patio of an Italian cafe. Since 1992 owner Bob Zemmel has served up some of the best Italian food in the state. He began by focusing on the brick-oven pizzas that have made Connecticut famous and expanded to a trattoria-style menu, with risotto, pasta, and ravioli. They make everything on-site, including their stocks, breads, pastas, and sauces. They have won awards and accolades for their simple, fresh food and great service. It's refreshing to find such an inexpensive restaurant with such commitment to quality.

Pizza

OTTO PIZZA $$
69 Main St.
Chester CT 06412
(860) 526-9445
ottochester.com

Owned by the geniuses who run the nearby River Tavern, Otto Pizza is the best wood-fired in Middlesex County. They have specials like egg, bacon, thyme, ricotta, and grana padano pizza, and you should trust that they know what they are doing. However, like all good pizza places, they let you build your own pie. I would say that the difference in their pizza is that the outer crust is thicker and crisper than the usual New Haven style, though the bottom remains "thin crust." Open 5 to 9 p.m. every day except Friday and Saturday, when they are open until 10 p.m. Be warned, though, this place is almost always packed.

Road Food

CROMWELL DINER $$
135 Berlin Rd.
Cromwell, CT 06416
(860) 635-7112
cromwelldiner.com

Open 7 days a week, 24 hours a day, the Cromwell Diner is not only a classic all-night hangout but also a family-owned restaurant, a lot more spacious and cleanly designed than most diners. The macaroni and cheese topped with bacon is wonderful, and the meat loaf will make you revisit your feelings about meat loaf. Breakfast all day long, root beer floats . . . what more do you want out of a diner? If you're on I-91, get off at exit 21, or take exit 19 off Route 9 and go west. This is a thousand times better than the fast-food or chain restaurant options, or even than most of the other diners you'll run into along the highways of America.

JOHNNY AD'S $
910 Boston Post Rd.
Old Saybrook, CT 06475
(860) 388-4032
johnnyads.com

Johnny Ad's in Old Saybrook was founded in 1957 as a small weekend seafood shack but has since become a 7-day-a week, year-round phenomenon. The lobster bisque is incredibly rich and buttery—maybe too rich! The lobster roll, on the other hand, was not as buttery as some, so you could really taste the lobster. The waffle fries were absolutely delicious—some of the best I've had any-where. So good that the cheese sauce they serve on the side is unnecessary. The codfish tacos, the hot dogs, and the soft shell crabs are also good. A couple times we took some of our dinner home—there is no skimping on the portions.

i If you're on Route 66 between March 1 and November 1, Tuesday through Saturday from 10 a.m. to 3 p.m., look for a vintage Checker cab pulling a 1963 Airstream in the form of a hot dog parked along the way. Stop and grab a delicious dog (and nothing but) from Andrea Spaulding, whose husband restored this amazing Top Dog food truck.

*O'ROURKE'S DINER $
728 Main St.
Middletown, CT 06457
(860) 346-6101
orourkesmiddletown.com

At this location next to the Connecticut River bridge in Middletown, a ramshackle wooden diner served a hungry public in the early 20th century. John O'Rourke purchased it in 1941, and five years later replaced it with the more permanent metal diner that quickly became legend. Try the french toast if you're there for breakfast (or lunch, or dinner); the

Irish soda bread makes it unique. You might also want to try one of their famous omelets, or an Irish Benny. For lunch or dinner, try the steamed cheeseburger or the kielbasa sandwich. In 2006 a fire ripped through the diner, but the community united behind it and brought it back from the dead only a year later. That's a tribute to the food and camaraderie created at O'Rourke's classic restaurant.

Seafood

BILL'S SEAFOOD RESTAURANT $-$$
548 Boston Post Rd.
Westbrook, CT 06498
(860) 399-7224
billsseafood.com

Near the singing steel bridge in Westbrook (drive across and you'll understand), this restaurant on the Patchogue River is a local hangout with all the great seafood you'd expect here on the coast. There's a family-friendly indoor dining area (air-conditioned), or you can sit outside on the deck under umbrellas and watch the birds in the tidal marsh. The steamers are particular favorites, and you can get some of state's best ice cream at the small shop next door. They have live music in different genres, even old-time banjo, most nights.

THE BLUE OAR $$
16 Snyder Rd.
Haddam, CT 06438
(860) 345-2994
No website

This is one of those marina restaurant shacks designed for yachters that is still actually used by them quite often. But you can drive there instead of sailing up the Connecticut River. This is also a seasonal restaurant, open Apr to Oct, due to the fact that dining is outdoors. Try the chowder, and enjoy a casual dinner on the veranda, with bright picnic tables on the large deck. You might see Chef Jacques Pépin enjoying a lobster roll; this place is one of his favorites. Bring cash, and your own alcoholic beverages if you like.

LENNY AND JOE'S FISH TALE $$
86 Boston Post Rd.
Westbrook, CT 06498
(860) 669-0767
ljfishtale.com

Since 1979 this seafood shack that has become a restaurant has been making award-winning lobster rolls and other seafood. The two brothers who opened it wanted a place to serve fresh seafood, and have created just that. Lenny and Joe have dozens of great dishes but specialize in two things: fried seafood done just right, at a higher quality than a traditional seafood shack, and sandwiches. The lobster rolls here are famous, but the shrimp roll, clam roll, scallop roll, hot buttered crab roll, and soft-shell crab sandwich are all the best of their kinds you'll find anywhere. Their second Fish Tale restaurant opened several miles down the shore in Madison, at 1301 Boston Post Rd. (203-245-7289), and their third is in New Haven at 501 Long Wharf Dr. (203-691-6619). All are open year-round, and the Madison outpost has a small carousel for the kids too. This is family seafood dining a step above the traditional seafood shack, and many steps above in taste.

LIV'S OYSTER BAR $$$
166 Main St., #4
Old Saybrook, CT 06475
(860) 395-5577
livsoysterbar.com

The young owners of Liv's, John and Krissie Brescio, are very particular when it comes to using fresh ingredients, and their passion and sincerity have made this restaurant a success. As far as their specialty, you can get the oyster sampler and try them in different sauces and preparations, get them fried the Connecticut way, or get them clean and fresh and slurp them down. They turned me on to Saddle Rock oysters from the Sound. The fluke, the char, and the scallops are all excellent, and they'll give you extra bread if you want to soak up the amazing broths. Of course they have other options, like pork with polenta and Angus hamburgers. For dessert, the ice-cream sampler with choco-late thyme, eggnog, and gingersnap flavors is delightful. Go for happy hour, from 4 to 6 p.m. Mon through Fri, and get one-third off the price of the appetizers.

✳LOBSTER LANDING $
152 Commerce St.
Clinton, CT 06413
(860) 669-2005
facebook.com/pages/
Lobster-Landing/127777687285413

Also known as the BB&G Lobster Landing, this fascinating little shack is literally on the dock by the marina. The white building with red borders and a simple wooden sign leads you to a place to buy live lobsters, or steamed ones for a little more cash. You're getting them without the markup, so if you're willing to eat them in a slightly less (understatement) fancy setting, why not get them here? This is a place for true lobster fanatics; these lobsters are literally right off the boat, and you can see fishermen bring-ing in their traps and nets. Lobster Landing also serves lobster rolls (that many people swear are the best in the state), hot dogs, drinks, and chips. They even take credit cards now. It's only open Apr through Dec, Tues through Sat from 9 a.m. to 5 p.m. and Sun until 3 p.m., but it's worth the trip to try this fascinating experience.

WESTBROOK LOBSTER $$–$$$
346 E. Main St. (Route 1)
Clinton, CT 06413
(860) 664-9464
westbrooklobster.com

Since 1957 Westbrook Lobster has been a lobster and fish market, but when Larry Larivere bought it in 1989, he turned it into one of the most popular seafood restaurants in the state. Westbrook is known for their fresh tank lobsters (obviously) and their clam chowder, but also for their signature dessert: s'mores that you roast for yourself at the table. The lobster bake and the fried whole-belly clams are also worth your attention and respect. During happy hour they have oysters on the half shell for only $1.75 each in the bar area (called the Captain's Lounge). There is a second location in a historic mill in Wallingford (New Haven County) at 300 Church St. (203-265-5071). Either one has the great seafood you are craving, but the Clin-ton location is the original, and somehow its location on the coast makes it seem, well, more authentic.

Vegetarian

IT'S ONLY NATURAL $$
386 Main St., #106
Middletown, CT 06457
(860) 346-9210
ionrestaurant.com

Known as "ION," this is one of the most popu-lar vegetarian restaurants in the state, just off exit 15 of Route 9 in Middletown. It's been around for over 30 years, and since 1992 has consistently won accolades for its vegetarian menu. Inside you'll find an art gallery display-ing the work of local artists, and tables with chalk so you can draw while you're waiting for your noodles or mushroom pizza. The sweet potato enchilada and the potato-spinach pierogis will have everyone wanting to go vegetarian. Try one of their wonderful juices, like the Bee Green (cucumber, celery, parsley, and agave), or choose from the large selection of organic beers and wines. This is a hangout for Wesleyan students, but vegetar-ians come from all over the state for a meal at this classic restaurant.

DAY TRIP IN MIDDLESEX COUNTY

This trip through Middlesex County is all about the Connecticut River, of which Pulitzer Prize–winning poet and Yale student Stephen Vincent Benet said, "Its blades of water call and enclose the temper of its skies." You will start high above the river on the hill of Middletown at O'Rourke's Diner for a breakfast of french toast or one of their famous omelets (see entry). Then you will turn east on Hartford Avenue (Route 17) and go south on Route 9 along the river.

Continue on Route 9, taking exit 10 (Aircraft Road). As you come off the exit, take a right onto Route 154 (Saybrook Road). This is a more pleasant drive than the highway, and will take you down to the river again. Continue until you reach the intersection where Route 82 (Bridge Road) heads east; turn left. You will drive across the country's longest steel swing bridge and pass the huge wedding cake of the Goodspeed Opera House. Route 82 becomes Norwich Road and turns right to become Town Street. Follow it and just at the Wolf's Den Family Campground, you will turn right onto Route 431, also called River Road. Turn right when you reach the sign for Gillette Castle State Park.

Drive to the parking lot and take a tour of this fascinating house, unlike any other you have ever seen, or probably will ever see again. Along with its unusual exterior appearance, note the fascinating touches inside, like the carved wooden light switches. There is a variety of nice walking paths here at the castle, but you have a lot to do today. So make sure to take pictures of the winding river far below, and get back in your car.

If the seasonal Chester-Hadlyme ferry is open, take a right out of the park and continue south on River Road, which shortly becomes Geer Hill Road and Ferry Road, leading right to the wharf. If the ferry is not open, retrace your steps back to the intersection of Routes 154 and 82 by turning left out of the park, then left again when you reach Town Street (Route 82), and then following the numbers back past the opera house and across the river.

Continue south on Route 154, where you will soon reach the intersection with Ferry Road (which you will also be on after you take the ferry). Continue south on Route 154, which changes road names several times, taking you into the village of Deep River. Turn left here onto Essex Street, a charming back road that will change to Book Hill Road as it heads into Essex, your destination. You will reach a T intersection, where you should turn right. This is another River Road, but quickly becomes North Main Street and brings you right into the center intersection of Essex.

Turn left here onto Main Street and park somewhere on the street, preferably near the Griswold Inn, because that is where you'll be having lunch (see entry). Go into the Tap Room, which has been called the most handsome barroom in America. Afterwards, you can walk around the charming streets of Essex if you like, but don't take too long, because you've got more to do. Take your car and turn left, then left again, coming back up Pratt Street to the center of town, and head across to West Avenue. This will take you up to the intersection with Route 154 again. Here you will have a choice of activities, depending on the time.

Your afternoon attraction is the Essex Steam Train (see entry). It leaves at 2 or 3:30 p.m. If you are going to take the longer riverboat and steam train combination, you will need to leave at 2 p.m. and should go straight there, turning right under Route 9 and immediately finding the parking lot on your left. If you are taking the 3:30 p.m. steam train only, you might have time to turn left and head south down Route 154 to browse

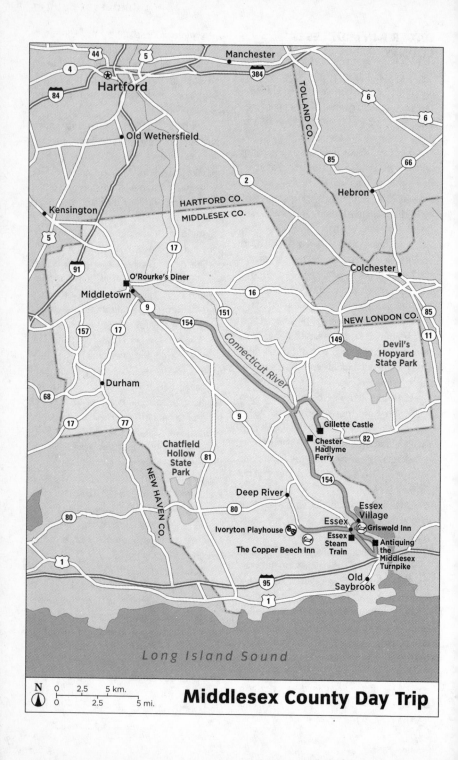

Middlesex County Day Trip

the antiques shops along the Old Saybrook border. Keep your eyes on your watch.

Beyond the Essex Saybrook Antiques Village, you will reach Route 9. Head north one exit and get off. You'll be back at the Middlesex Turnpike, where you'll turn left. Passing back under Route 9 again, you will immediately find the Essex Steam Train parking lot to your left. Enjoy this ride on one of America's historic steam locomotives.

On your return, turn left and head west on Route 154 again. It will quickly merge onto Main Street. Take this until you reach the Copper Beech Inn, on your left. The inn's restaurant, Pip's, is a fine place for a romantic dinner, with exquisitely prepared food amid dark wood, marble, and leather seats, or you could drive up the road into Chester to the River Tavern or Restaurant L&E (see entries).

If there is a performance tonight at the Ivoryton Playhouse, you should have made reservations already. Continue west on Main Street and you'll reach it in a half mile. This classic venue kicked off the career of local girl Katharine Hepburn (among others), and a play here is the perfect end to a perfect day in Middlesex County. If you'd like to stay overnight, head back to the Copper Beech, where their luxurious monogrammed robes and beds will help you get ready for the next day. Who knows what it will bring?

HARTFORD COUNTY

Mark Twain said once of Hartford, "Of all the beautiful towns it has been my fortune to see, this is the chief. . . . You do not know what beauty is if you have not been here." Sure, he might have been talking about the city when it had the highest per capita income in the US. But there are beauties to be found here still, and the surrounding suburbs and villages have some of the most interesting attractions in the state. Hartford County surprisingly includes the most remote area of the state, on the Tunxis Trail, while the tobacco farms that fill the rich, flat floodplains around the Connecticut River seem out of place in central New England.

The history is long and rich here, and in general, more relics and houses have been preserved, possibly because this is the state capital. Hartford is widely known as the insurance capital of America, though it was once known for its revolvers. Like the best cities, Hartford rings a large public park, Bushnell, the oldest in the nation. The *Hartford Courant* is the nation's oldest and longest-running newspaper, and the city also contains the oldest art museum, the Wadsworth Atheneum.

The county also boasts the oldest continuously operating ferry in the US, crossing from Glastonbury to Rocky Hill; the state's oldest settlement from 1633, Windsor; and its oldest gravestone, Rev. Ephraim Huit's, 1644. Old Wethersfield is only a year younger than Windsor, and its collection of 17th- and 18th-century houses is unrivalled. But Hartford County also looks to the future, and Windsor Locks has the state's only international airport, Bradley.

The larger suburbs are really cities themselves, including Manchester and West Hartford, both great places to shop and eat. At the south end of the county, Bristol and New Britain are old industrial cities that now contain art and history museums, as well as large companies like ESPN. The New England National Scenic Trail heads along the traprock ridges that form the spine of this county, and you can step out of these cities into a seeming wilderness in minutes.

To the west are the charming towns of Simsbury, Burlington, Canton, and Granby, retreats and homes for the city's elite. The Farmington is the best-stocked trout river in the state, and its long, tumbling length is haunted by anglers, as well as kayaks, canoes, and rafts in summer.

You'll find very quickly that Hartford is more than just the state capital. Take your children to the country's longest-running amusement park, or take yourselves to a romantic dinner on the breezy porch of a country inn. Whatever you do, take your time to explore the diverse attractions of this county on your travels through Connecticut.

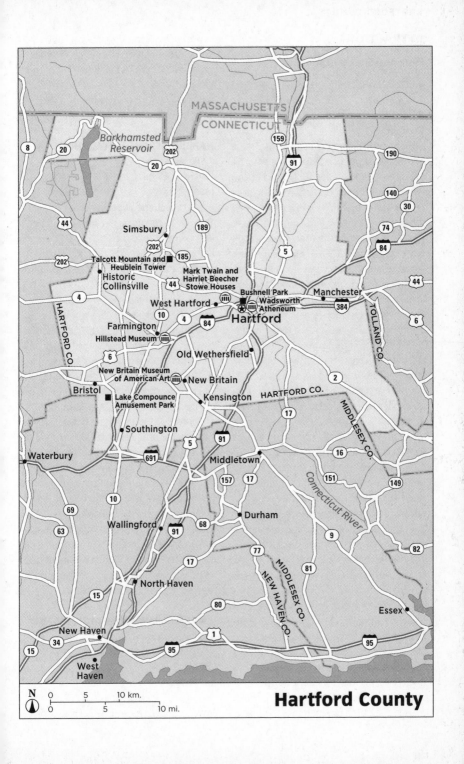

Hartford County

ATTRACTIONS

Historical Sites & Landmarks

✳COLLINSVILLE
104 Main St.
Collinsville, CT 06019
No phone
visitcollinsville.com

The Collinsville section of Canton is a factory town built around the Collins Company, which for 140 years dominated this corner of Connecticut, making axes sold around the world. Today you'll find Collins tools and more in the Canton Historical Museum at 11 Front St. (860-693-2793). There are antiques stores, restaurants, and galleries in this small section of town, and the Farmington Valley Greenway heads south along the river from here, a spectacular bike ride or walk alongside one of the prettiest rivers in New England. Many of the state's historical towns are from an earlier era and are not factory based. Collinsville provides you with a different perspective on the local industrial revolution that made Connecticut a powerhouse of America.

ENFIELD HISTORICAL SOCIETY
1294 Enfield St.
Enfield, CT 06083
(860) 745-1729
enfieldhistoricalsociety.org

The Enfield Historical Society operates 3 museums, all open to the public for free. The Old Town Hall Museum at 1294 Enfield St. was built as the third meeting house of the First Ecclesiastical Society of Enfield in 1774, and became the town hall. Today it is a museum of Enfield history, where you'll learn all about the Thompsonville carpet industry, the Hazardville gunpowder industry, and the Enfield Shaker Community, on Sun from 2 to 4:30 p.m., May through Oct. The 1782 Martha A. Parsons House at 1387 Enfield St. houses one of the best and most complete

family collections in the state, also open Sun 2 to 4:30 p.m., May through Oct. The Wallop School at 250 Abbe Rd. was built in 1800 and remained in service for almost 150 years. You can visit one Sunday a month, June through Sept, 2 to 4 p.m.

HARRIET BEECHER STOWE HOUSE
77 Forest St.
Hartford, CT 06105
(860) 522-9258
harrietbeecherstowecenter.org

This Gothic cottage at the west end of Hartford was the residence of Harriet Beecher Stowe after she wrote one of the most popular and certainly one of the most influential books of the 19th century, *Uncle Tom's Cabin*. When Abraham Lincoln met Stowe, he said, "So, you're the little woman whose book started this great war." He was only exaggerating slightly. Inside the house you'll find an impressive collection of memorabilia and original furnishings. The Stowe House was at the center of Nook Farm, a large community of buildings that housed some of Hartford's most important figures, including international celebrity Mark Twain. A number of other authors, abolitionists, and suffragists lived here as well, and you'll learn all about their triumphs and struggles at the Harriet Beecher Stowe Center. When asked about her part in the struggle for equality, Stowe said, "I wrote what I did because as a woman, as a mother, I was oppressed and broken-hearted with the sorrows and injustice I saw." We should all take a page from her book.

✳MARK TWAIN HOUSE AND MUSEUM
351 Farmington Ave.
Hartford, CT 06105
(860) 247-0998
marktwainhouse.org

This is a can't-miss attraction in Connecticut. Mark Twain, whose real name was Samuel

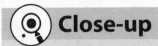

Close-up

The Remarkable Cemeteries of Connecticut

A great way to get to know Connecticut is by exploring its cemeteries. Yes, you read that correctly. Some of the oldest graves in America are scattered around the state, and exploring these fascinating landscapes with their beautifully carved stones gives us insight into history, genealogy, and perhaps even our own souls. Nearly every town has an "ancient" or "old" burying ground that dates back to the 18th or even 17th century. Wethersfield's has some unmarked graves that are probably the oldest European ones in the state, and Hartford's includes the grave of Thomas Hooker, founder of the Connecticut Colony (theancientburyingground.org).

During the 19th century, cemeteries were a common place to walk, to meet people, and to contemplate eternity. Huge gray beech trees and sweet-smelling cedars often line the rows of internments. There are some great examples of these beautifully sculptured "grave gardens" in the state. At Mystic, check out beautiful Elm Grove Cemetery, which abuts the Mystic River (elmgrovecemetery.org). Look for the stones of actress Katharine Hepburn, inventor Samuel Colt, and poet Wallace Stevens at the 1864 Cedar Hill Cemetery in Hartford, with its gently forested hills and meandering paths (cedarhillcemetery.org). Or walk through the strange Egyptian Revival gates designed by architect Henry Austin that lead you from the campus of Yale into New Haven's Grove Street Cemetery (grovestreetcemetery.org). There among rows of famous graves, you will find Eli Whitney and Noah Webster. Finally, at Mountain Grove Cemetery in Bridgeport, commissioned by P. T. Barnum himself in 1849, wander around ponds through Civil War graves to the tall monument of Tom Thumb, complete with a life-size statue of the diminutive entertainer (mountaingrovecemeteryassociation.org).

If you're looking for a particular famous grave, or perhaps an ancestor, try checking findagrave.com before heading out. But your favorite cemetery will probably be the one where you stop for a picnic lunch on a summer outing. Perhaps hidden behind a stone wall, perhaps on a steep hillside overlooking the winding country road, you'll find an entire rich history in its grassy hummocks and tilting stones. My favorite cemetery perches on the ridge of a mountain, has only 10 marked graves, and is guarded by a family of raccoons in a hollow tree. Which will yours be?

Clemens, was America's most beloved writer for decades, and his novels are still required reading for elementary school children and college students alike. You start the tour in a brand-new museum facility behind the house, full of artifacts and gifts. The red-brick building of Twain's actual home is an architectural marvel, presiding over Farmington Avenue like a Yankee suddenly become monarch. Among the many startling details in the house, don't miss Twain's ornate bed, which he claimed so intrigued him that he slept with his head at the foot, to better examine the carvings. The amazing billiard room at the top of the house is where Twain smoked his famous cigars while he wrote *A Connecticut Yankee in King Arthur's Court* and *Huckleberry Finn*. The museum's Murasaki cafe serves a cut above the usual museum food (I enjoyed their Chicken Katsu Don). Although Mark Twain lived all over the country (and world), he always thought of this as his only true home.

NOAH WEBSTER HOUSE

227 S. Main St.
West Hartford, CT 06107
(860) 521-5362
noahwebsterhouse.org

In 1828 New Haven and West Hartford resident Noah Webster published his dictionary, expanding and defining the new American English language and inspiring people like Frederick Douglass and Emily Dickinson. His popular blue-backed "speller" went through 385 editions in his lifetime alone, and it was used by five generations of American children. Today his house in West Hartford is restored, and tour guides in colonial garb will take you through the history of America. This is also the home of the West Hartford Historical Society, and there is an exhibit detailing the remarkable record of the town. There are many historical societies in the state, but few are lucky enough to have their base also be the home of one of the most important men in American history.

OLD STATE HOUSE AND ANCIENT BURYING GROUND

800 Main St.
Hartford, CT 06103
(860) 522-6766
ctoldstatehouse.org
60 Gold St.
Hartford, CT 06103
(860) 561-2585
theancientburyingground.org

This two-in-one attraction is at the heart of the old capitol of the Connecticut Colony. Start at the 1797 Greek Revival State House, often called "the people's house," one of the oldest in the country. This brick building contains historical exhibits and a re-creation of Joseph Stewards Museum of Oddities and Curiosities, which resided in the building in 1798. You can do this as a self-guided tour, but should probably take the guided one through the old legislative, judicial, and executive areas of this remarkable building. They'll tell you about events like the Amistad trial, which took place here. When you're done, walk a block to the Ancient Burying Ground, which has some of the oldest graves in the state, including (most likely) the unmarked grave of the colony founder, Rev. Thomas Hooker. The Center Church next door is worth your time too, an 1807 structure that replaced the original 1636 one that accompanied the cemetery.

OLIVER ELLSWORTH HOUSE

778 Palisado Ave.
Windsor, CT 06095
(860) 688-8717
ellsworthhomesteaddar.org

Oliver Ellsworth was one of five men who drafted the US Constitution, and he served at George Washington's request as the third chief justice of the Supreme Court. He was also Connecticut's first senator and the author of the Judiciary Act, which forms the basis of our current federal justice system. In other words, he was one of the founders of this country, and the fact that his homestead still exists here above the Connecticut River is a gift to us in this present day. Managed by the Connecticut DAR, the museum focuses on the early years of America, and how the everyday life of people at that time impacted law, and vice versa. It's open Wed, Thurs, and Sat from noon to 4 p.m. and on the last Sunday of each month from 1 to 4 p.m. In the words of Ellsworth himself, "I have visited several countries, and I like my own the best. I have been in all the States of the Union, and Connecticut is the best State; Windsor is the pleasantest town in the State of Connecticut and I have the pleasantest place in Windsor. I am content, perfectly content, to die on the banks of the Connecticut."

SALMON BROOK HISTORICAL SOCIETY
208 Salmon Brook St.
Granby, CT 06035
(860) 653-9713

facebook.com/sbhsct The Granby historical society of Salmon Brook has one of the better collections in the state, of both buildings and artifacts. All sit at 208 Salmon Brook St., though all but one were moved there. The Abijah Rowe House is original; it's the oldest structure left from the settlement, built about 1732 as the house of blacksmiths, who may have made some of the hardware still in the house. The Moses Weed saltbox is from 1790, and was located up the road at what is today Enders State Forest (drive up Route 20 and find the excellent waterfall just off the parking lot there). Inside today you'll find a Victorian parlor, complete with Edison phonograph, and a gift shop. The Cooley School is a one-room schoolhouse from 1870 that still has the teacher's writing on the chalkboard from when it closed in 1948. The last building is a large 1914 tobacco barn,which houses the society's main collection of farming, quilting, spinning, and weaving tools, Civil War memorabilia, a small "meeting house" re-creation (from original pieces), a dressmaker's shop, a shoemaker's shop, a creamery, a voting booth, and a "village store." Visit on Sunday from 2 to 4 p.m., June through Sept.

WEBB, DEANE, AND STEVENS HOUSES
211 Main St.
Wethersfield, CT 06109
(860) 529-0612
webb-deane-stevens.org

Washington and Rochambeau met here to formulate plans for the last campaign of the Revolutionary War, staying at the 1752 Webb House. Silas Deane was a member of the first Continental Congress, and one of the most tragic figures of the Revolution. The 1788 Isaac Stevens House is full of period antiques. Behind these three houses a nice herb garden lies in a large open space. They are open 10 a.m. to 4 p.m. daily except Tuesday from May to Oct. A number of other restored homes are within walking distance, including the Captain James Francis House (120 Hartford Ave.), the Buttolph-Williams House (corner of Marsh and Broad), and the Hurlbut-Dunham House (212 Main St.). Take a walk to see these, and don't forget to stop across the street at the Old Academy Museum to check out its changing exhibits. There are a number of 18th- and 19th-century homes, a 17th-century graveyard, and the large brick Meetinghouse (250 Main St.) from 1761. This section of Old Wethersfield is one of the oldest towns in America, and it is surprising how much is left.

Museums

AMERICAN CLOCK AND WATCH MUSEUM
100 Maple St.
Bristol, CT 06010
(860) 583-6070
clockandwatchmuseum.org

The oldest in America dedicated to clocks, this strange and wonderful museum sits in an 1801 house donated by Edward Ingraham, great-grandson of the founder of the Ingraham Clock Factory. It is simply chock-full of clocks and watches of every sort, from a giant tower clock with a heavy pendulum to the most delicate pocket watch. After your ears adjust, the overwhelming ticking forms a sort of pleasant cicada-like hum. Interactive recordings tell visitors about Connecticut clock making and the Industrial Revolution. One room features the role of women in the industry, including the nationwide radium-poisoning tragedy of dial painters. There's a re-creation of a Plymouth clock store, sandglasses, sundials, astrolabes, "dock clocks," experimental devices, and the 1830 desk of Connecticut's premier clock maker,

Eli Terry. Try to get there at the noon hour, when all the clocks strike.

CONNECTICUT VALLEY TOBACCO MUSEUM AND NORTHWEST PARK

135 Lang Rd.
Windsor, CT 06095
(860) 285-1888
tobaccohistsoc.org

The tobacco here in the Connecticut valley is primarily used as cigar wrappers, and it has been used to wrap the world's finest. The Luddy/Taylor Connecticut Valley Tobacco Museum includes a restored tobacco-curing barn, where authentic equipment shows the process of harvest and curing. Historical displays in the museum next door show the industry's contribution to the region's economy and culture. There are live animal exhibits in the Animal Barn and Nature Center, and a concert series is held from Sept to May. The 475 acres surrounding the museum, called Northwest Park, include 12 miles of trails through a variety of habitats that are great for mountain biking or for cross-country ski in winter (northwestpark.org). They also have an annual cigar barbecue for all those smokers out there.

✳HILL-STEAD MUSEUM

35 Mountain Rd.
Farmington, CT 06032
(860) 677-4787
hillstead.org

This is one of the most beautiful attractions in the state, a rambling 1901 house with one of the best personal collections of art in the country. It was originally home to Alfred Atmore Pope, an iron baron from Cleveland who was persuaded by his daughter, Theodate, to move here (she attended Miss Porter's school down the road). The house was designed by architect Stanford White and Theodate, who became the first licensed female architect in the US. The

Popes assembled an eclectic collection of art, furniture, porcelain, and sculpture. But the Impressionist paintings on the walls, including three Monets, are what draw most people. The gardens (including the famous Sunken Garden) are a wonderful place to ramble as well, and the trails teem with bird-life, extending up to the blue-blazed Metacomet Trail, now part of the New England National Scenic Trail. Sit on the porch of the Hill-Stead before you leave, and meditate on the beauty that wealth can bring and wish that everyone left a legacy for the public like Theodate Pope did.

MUSEUM OF CONNECTICUT HISTORY

231 Capitol Ave.
Hartford, CT 06106
(860) 757-6535
museumofcthistory.org

Located across from the capitol building, the Museum of Connecticut History is in the same building as the state library, also open to the public. The museum is open weekdays and on Saturday from 9 a.m. to 2 p.m. It consists of 3 large rooms and features portraits of all the governors since the 1600s, items from the state's political history, sections about the wars, and memorabilia of all sorts. The most intriguing item is the original charter from Charles II of England, the one famously hidden in the oak tree to protect it. Today it is housed in a fireproof safe in the museum. Gun enthusiasts will spend an hour just in one room, which houses every type of gun manufactured at the Samuel Colt plant in Hartford, as well as a few from Eli Whitney's Hamden factory. Saturday is the best day to go, since no one is working in the government buildings and you have free parking and admission, but be sure to enter the building through the rear entrance right off the parking lot.

*NEW BRITAIN MUSEUM OF AMERICAN ART
56 Lexington St.
New Britain, CT 06052
(860) 229-0257
nbmaa.org

This 1903 museum is the oldest in the country dedicated to our national art. Paintings by Mary Cassatt, Georgia O'Keeffe, Andrew Wyeth, Albert Bierstadt, George Bellows, Isamu Noguchi, and John Singer Sargent are the backbone of this muscular collection. There are some nationally famous Connecticut artists like Childe Hassam and Sol LeWitt as well. The Arts of Life in America murals by Thomas Hart Benton are spectacular, with details that you have to really pay attention to. Sometimes people ignore this museum in favor of Hartford's Wadsworth Atheneum, and it is baffling why. Perhaps American art is not taken seriously enough by Americans. Don't forget to stroll the park behind the museum; it was designed by Central Park architect and Hartford native Frederick Law Olmsted. They've been running free admission on Saturday mornings from 10 a.m. to noon, so check their website and sneak in before lunch.

NEW ENGLAND AIR MUSEUM
Bradley International Airport
36 Perimeter Rd.
Windsor Locks, CT 06096
(860) 623-3305
neam.org

There are only four museums of any size in the US dedicated to aviation, and this is one of them. They have a Bleriot monoplane from 1909, a huge collection of World War II fighters and bombers, and modern jet fighters. Fifty airplanes are housed inside the facility, and there are many more outside, some of which are being restored. They have more than airplanes too, like the control car of the Goodyear blimp and an 1870 balloon basket, the oldest surviving one in the US.

The smaller items owned by the museum are even more spectacular, since Connecticut was and is a center for US aviation; local companies like Pratt and Whitney and Sikorsky have donated some amazing stuff. In spring and summer they have open-cockpit days and car shows here too, a huge treat for kids of all ages.

NEW ENGLAND CAROUSEL MUSEUM
95 Riverside Ave. (Route 72)
Bristol, CT 06010
(860) 585-5411
thecarouselmuseum.org

This is billed as three museums in one, set in an old brick 1836 factory that once made silk underwear for Civil War soldiers. You'll find a museum of Greek culture, one showcasing fire history, and the headliner, the Carousel Museum. Dozens of carousel animals hide around every corner: river monsters, tigers, herons, deer with real antlers, and even a UConn Husky dog. Kids love the museum of fire history upstairs, ringing the old fire bells and inspecting the old round-bottomed buckets. Helmets, nozzles, and spanners from around the world are featured, as well as code signal transmitters, antique fire truck toys, and historical photos. For the parents, a history of the carousel as entertainment is detailed, from the Byzantine age to the height of the phenomenon in the early 20th century. The museum also maintains the Bushnell Park carousel in Hartford and does restoration on-site of horses from around the world. Don't miss the gift shop, which sells some really amazing museum-quality pieces, usually donated to help the museum.

*WADSWORTH ATHENEUM
600 Main St.
Hartford, CT 06103
(860) 278-2670
thewadsworth.org

This is the nation's oldest continuously operating art museum, and certainly among the best of its size. The permanent collection of 19th-century American and French Impressionists and Postimpressionists is inspiring, with delights like the saint-like self-portrait of Vincent van Gogh. There are modern and contemporary paintings, old masters, Hudson River School paintings, and a great collection of American furniture and decorative arts. You'll see works by Georgia O'Keeffe, Andrew Wyeth, Winslow Homer, Salvador Dali, Andy Warhol, Piet Mondrian, Thomas Cole, Albert Bierstadt, Max Ernst, Claude Monet, Joan Miró, and Auguste Renoir, as well as Connecticut artists like Sol LeWitt, Alexander Calder, William Metcalf, and Jonathan Trumbull. The Wadsworth brings in excellent temporary exhibits as well and features free admission the last Saturday of the month. Don't miss Calder's *Stegosaurus* stabile sculpture, around the side of the museum in a small park.

Parks & Beaches

BUSHNELL PARK
1 Jewell St.
Hartford, CT 06103
(860) 232-6710
bushnellpark.org

This is actually the first park in America taken by eminent domain for that use. It was designed by Frederick Law Olmsted, who designed Central Park in Manhattan and Prospect Park in Brooklyn, as well as many others in Connecticut. There are monuments throughout the park, but the most impressive is the Soldiers and Sailors Monument Arch, which used to span the Park River (since routed underneath the city). The 1914 Bushnell Carousel still revolves here, and you can still try to spear the brass ring, like the knights of old. It only operates from May to Sept, but the park

is open year-round. Don't miss the *Stone Field Structure* along Gold Street between Main and Lewis, an arrangement of 36 boulders installed in 1977 by artist Carl Andre. Bushnell Park is a great central location in Hartford from which to walk to all the downtown sights and activities, but is certainly a destination itself.

DINOSAUR STATE PARK
400 West St.
Rocky Hill, CT 06067
(860) 529-8423
dinosaurstatepark.org

It's not often you get to see 500 dinosaur tracks in their original excavated setting, but that is what this unique state park offers. Including a nice boardwalk and nature trail through the wetlands where kids can pretend to search for dinosaurs, the park centers on a geodesic dome that protects the collection of tracks (open every day but Monday). What's even better is that you can make your own plaster casts of the 16-inch-long tracks to take home. Although this is a quick stop off I-91 for most families, definitely make the time to complete this amazing project. Both kids and kids that never grew up will never tire of showing them off to the neighbors.

WICKHAM PARK
1329 Middle Tpke. West
Manchester, CT 06040
(860) 528-0856
wickhampark.org

This private, nonprofit park donated by Clarence and Edith Wickham will cost you to park your car, but it's well worth the few dollars. The park contains 250 acres of gardens, open fields, woodlands, ponds, picnic areas, sports facilities, and other attractions. It is really just a great place to spend an afternoon, with attractions like an aviary, a nature center, and a sensory garden. You can play disc golf or picnic or take the fun hiking trail with your kids. It's only open Apr through Oct, though it seems like a great place for cross-country skiing or snowshoeing to me. If you're there on a nice day, you'll probably see a wedding, a business group playing baseball, or hipsters playing volleyball. But don't worry; there is plenty of space for all at this beautiful "active" park.

WINDSOR LOCKS CANAL
Windsor Locks/Suffield, CT 06096
(860) 242-1158
ct.gov/dep [search "Windsor Locks Canal State Park"]
Built in the 1800s, this canal is really a bypass of the Enfield Rapids that is still used occasionally for boats today and for water power. But the old towpath that follows it is the marvel for visitors and locals. The path hovers between the canal and the river, seemingly magical in its continued existence. As you walk, skate, or bike the length, trees give an illusion of solidity, and then the view opens and the water on either side makes you feel like you're heading off the edge of the earth. This trail along the towpath is almost 5 miles long, and you can park at either end. At the northern end you can take a spur and head up to the Route 190 bridge across the Connecticut River, with great views south and north. Across the bridge is historic Enfield, which you can explore, or bike down Enfield Street paralleling the river.

Wineries & Breweries

LOST ACRES VINEYARD
80 Lost Acres Rd.
North Granby, CT 06060
(860) 324-9481
lostacresvineyard.com
This is one of the newest Connecticut vineyards, and along with making good wine (I like the un-oaked Chardonnay), they got

absolutely everything else right about creating a space for people to enjoy it. There is a nice lawn to picnic on, a deck off the tasting room, an art gallery inside, a fireplace for cold-season tastings, lots of live music events, and a cheap tasting with free wine glass. What's more, they have yoga at the vineyard and a pen with pigs and horses. You and your sweetheart can even take a horseback ride of the vineyard, with a private picnic lunch and bottle of wine for $150. But that is so popular that they sell out months in advance, so be sure to make reservations if you plan to surprise someone for an anniversary.

ROSEDALE FARM
25 E. Weatogue St.
Simsbury, CT 06070
(860) 651-3926
rosedale1920.com
Down the road from the mighty Pinchot Sycamore, Rosedale Farm is committed to providing Simsbury and the region with fresh fruits, vegetables, flowers, and even wine. Established in 1920, the farm is now in its fifth generation. With four varieties of sweet corn and at least that many kinds of tomatoes, the farm market is stocked with beautiful, healthy produce—from beets to broccoli, carrots to cabbage, potatoes, peppers, and parsnips, just to name a few. Nine species of flowers are grown for summer bouquets, and you'll also find local cheeses, breads, jams, and cakes in the market. Diversification is one of the keys to the family-owned operation, and in 2005 they opened a winery. Award winners include Three Sisters, an Alsatian-style white made from estate-grown Cayuga white blended with Niagara grapes. Chef-to-Farm dinners are a summer staple on the farm, and corn mazes and hayrides will delight young and old in autumn.

*THOMAS HOOKER BREWERY

16 Tobey Rd.

Bloomfield, CT 06002

(860) 242-3111

hookerbeer.com

Named for the ministerial founder of the Connecticut Colony, Thomas Hooker brews beer that is distributed throughout the Northeast, and you'll probably find it at the pubs and restaurants you visit here. However, why not head to Bloomfield to see where it is made? Every Saturday from noon to 5 p.m. you can visit the brewery for tastings, and every other Friday they have open houses from 5 to 8 p.m. (more like parties than open houses). The beers range up and down the scale, from American Pale Ale to Liberator Doppelbock. The Imperial Porter is dark, sweet, and lovely; the Munich Style Lager is refreshing and malty. Talk to them about the brilliant Connecticut Beer Trail (ctbeertrail.net), and pick up a growler full of Irish Red on your way out. You'll be the hero of the next party.

ACTIVITIES & EVENTS

Amusement Parks

LAKE COMPOUNCE

186 Enterprise Dr.

Bristol, CT 06010

(860) 583-3300

lakecompounce.com

In 1846 Lake Compounce was the site of a series of electrical experiments, and the huge crowds made the owner consider the monetary possibilities of the property, setting up picnic tables for concerts. In later years rides and other entertainments were added. Today the country's oldest continuously running amusement park includes an old-fashioned carousel with original carved horses and a Wurlitzer organ. In addition to the roller coasters and rides, Compounce has a water park called Crocodile Cove. If you haven't run off the kids' energy in the park, there is a nice section of the Tunxis Trail right behind the park, including part of an old, stone-walled road that George Washington rode on. Try to go on Halloween, when the haunted house scares the heck out of all those brave enough to enter.

SONNY'S PLACE

349 Main St.

Somers, CT 06071

(860) 763-5454

sonnysplace.com

Sonny's Place is a family fun experience, with go-karts, batting cages, a bounce house, zip-lining, and a rock wall to climb. The minigolf is quite challenging, with sloping greens that baffle experienced putters and delight the kids. It's actually the perfect place for a birthday party, whether the kid is 5 or 25. But along with families and groups of teenagers, you'll also find corporate groups and volleyball leagues here. There's a restaurant that serves alcohol and an ice-cream parlor as well. You'll never have trouble parking in the huge lot, even though Sonny's is hugely popular. My nieces and nephew love this place, and they make their parents drive down from Massachusetts just to go here.

Arts Venues

*THE BUSHNELL

166 Capitol Ave.

Hartford, CT 06106

(860) 987-6000

bushnell.org

This 2,800-seat center was built in 1930 as a memorial to Rev. Dr. Horace Bushnell, a leading public voice in Hartford during the 19th century. The Georgian Revival exterior is matched by an Art Deco interior. In 2001 an addition was put onto it in which the gift shop, cafe, and a smaller 907-seat theater are located. Broadway shows and other dramatic productions form the backbone of the event season, but this is not only a theater for drama. The Hartford Symphony Orchestra performs here regularly, and the Connecticut Forum regularly uses the Bushnell to host their conversations, discussions, lectures, and idea exchanges between today's top leaders, authors, and creative minds. Get there early to park across the street in the free lot, chat with the city's elite, and have a cocktail. The best seats are (where else?) up front.

XFINITY THEATRE
61 Savitt Way
Hartford, CT 06120
(203) 204-8892
xfinitytheatre.net
Once called the Meadows, this is the largest outdoor concert venue in Connecticut. You can sit "indoors" up front in the large barn, or behind on the general seating lawns with a blanket and picnic. Along with bringing rock and roll, country, alternative, hip-hop, pop, and more to Hartford, they are usually the spot for larger, all-day music festivals as well. The Xfinity also hosts a few other events throughout the year, like the DayGlow World's Largest Paint Party. Go early and park near the exit so you can get out of the tight squeeze of the free lot more quickly.

Ballooning

BERKSHIRE BALLOONS
190 Tomlinson Avenue #12H
Plainville, CT 06062
(203) 250-8441
berkshireballoons.blogspot.com
The Berkshire Balloons company launches their amazing flights from Southington, Plainville, Farmington, and New Hartford just after sunrise. You'll spend at least an hour in the air, with the entire trip taking 2.5 to 3 hours, flying gently over the western hills of Connecticut. You might go up in the air

as much as a few thousand feet, depending on conditions, from where you can see the Catskills in New York, Long Island, and the mountains of Vermont and New Hampshire. Wear waterproof shoes (the launch fields are often squishy), and don't wear high heels or sandals. Bring sunglasses and of course your camera. Make a reservation 2 weeks ahead, maybe more in autumn, though it's possible to get last-minute flights. The prices run about $275 a person, or $1,000 for a private couples flight. It's well worth it.

Festivals & Annual Events

APPLE HARVEST FESTIVAL
PO Box 907
Southington, CT 06489
(860) 276-8461
southington.org
Every October since 1968, 100,000 people have descended on Southington for this annual festival. It lasts a week, beginning with a parade and proceeding through arts and crafts shows, a carnival, a road race, a talent show, fireworks, music, and dancing. Of course the mighty apple is featured heavily, with all sorts of apple-based foods to eat (as well as other delicacies like fried dough and lobster pies). You can try your luck at apple pie–eating contests, bed races, and singing competitions. The nearby orchards get into the fun, with wagon rides and apple picking. Parking and admission are free, and so is the live music and entertainment.

CELEBRATION OF CONNECTICUT FARMS
Connecticut Farmland Trust
77 Buckingham St.
Hartford, CT 06106
(860) 247-0202
ctfarmland.org
Since 2002 the private Connecticut Farmland Trust has worked toward preserving the state's working farmland. Every year for one

day in September, they hold their award-winning Celebration of Connecticut Farms, with celebrity guests like Jacques Pépin, to highlight the food and drink produced by these farms. Called the "hottest food event in the state" by *Connecticut Magazine,* it is held in a different location every year, so you might not find it strictly in Hartford County. Enjoy a feast of local food prepared by local chefs and wine, dance to live music, bid at a silent auction, and tour the farm.

HARTFORD MARATHON
41 Sequin Dr.
Glastonbury, CT 06033
(860) 652-8866
hartfordmarathon.com

The Hartford Marathon Foundation actually sponsors a couple dozen running events throughout the year. The NU Marathon and Half Marathon is the big one, with the serious runners coming from around the region to compete in this autumn urban run. But they have so many others—from 5k runs to riverfront scrambles to the Litchfield Hills triathlon. If you are doing a serious run of any sort, you are probably doing it through the HMF. Of course this is an "event," but it could just as easily be listed in Spectator Sports or Adventure Sports, depending on whether you are participating or cheering someone on. My brother-in-law has done many of these, and if he keeps it up, he will shame me into doing one or two soon.

NUTMEG STATE GAMES
Connecticut Sports Management
Group Inc.
50 Flounders Plaza, Ste. 301
East Hartford, CT 06108
(860) 528-4588
nutmegstategames.org

The ShopRite Nutmeg State Games sponsors around 500 different team and individual matches every year in about 25 different sports. That's right, 500 matches. You'll find kids competing in baseball, cycling, basketball, fencing, fast-pitch softball, figure skating, field hockey, golf, ice hockey, gymnastics, jai alai, lacrosse, judo, shooting, swimming, rugby, wrestling, soccer, and track and field events. Done in tandem with the US Olympic Committee, the Nutmeg Games are essentially the trials, where you can see the athletes of tomorrow training to compete against the world. If you're my age, go to watch. But if you're a young Connecticut resident, forget about watching the games. Instead, why not enter an event and show us what you're made of?

i Try the calendar aggregate social hartford.com if you want to find all the upcoming events in the area.

RAILS TO THE DARKSIDE AT THE CONNECTICUT TROLLEY MUSEUM
58 North Rd.
East Windsor, CT 06088
(860) 627-6540
ct-trolley.org

There are countless labyrinths, corn mazes, haunted houses, and the like throughout the state in the weeks leading up to Halloween. But the most original scare fest has to be at the Connecticut Trolley Museum on Friday and Saturday from Columbus Day to Oct 31. Head to the museum from 7 to 9:30 p.m. and hop a ride on this deliciously frightening express. There are more than 30 trolley cars on display here at this museum (with more being restored in the barns), which began in 1940 as the only one dedicated to the preservation of the trolley. At other times of the year you can visit the museum (and the Fire Museum next door) from 10 a.m. to 4 p.m. Mon, Wed, Thurs, and Fri, and noon to 4 p.m. on Sun. On those days, cars run every 20 minutes. They run other events throughout the year like Winterfest, the Easter Bunny fun

day, and BBQ on the Line. Check their schedule, because these fun events are the best
way to see this unique attraction.

RIVERFEST
50 Columbus Blvd.
Hartford, CT 06106
(860) 713-3131
riverfront.org/events/festivals
Hartford poet and insurance salesman
Wallace Stevens said of the rivers around
Hartford: "It is not to be seen beneath the
appearances / that tell of it. The steeple at
Farmington / Stands glistening and Haddam
shines and sways." Celebrating this amazing
area, Riverfest has become an Independence
Day tradition in Connecticut, with free live
entertainment, fireworks, food, clowns, and
more. It takes place in two parks across the
river, the Mortensen Riverfront in Hartford
and Great River Park in East Hartford. You
can actually take the Founders Bridge Promenade and walk between the two parks if
you'd like to see both attractions, about 1.5
miles either direction. The event ends with
spectacular fireworks, shot into the air from
pyrotechnic firing barges on the Connecticut River. Don't miss it, or any of the other
events throughout the year (check their
website).

SUNKEN GARDEN POETRY FESTIVAL
Hill-Stead Museum
35 Mountain Rd.
Farmington, CT 06032
(860) 677-4787
hillstead.org
One of the country's premier poetry venues,
the Sunken Garden Poetry Festival takes
place Wednesday evenings every summer
on the grounds of the Hill-Stead Museum
in Farmington. Since 1992 the gardens
have drawn nationally acclaimed poets and
upwards of 5,000 visitors annually. Lawn
chairs and picnic blankets spread out in front
of the majestic pillars of Hill Stead's white
mansion, and the sunken gardens' topiary
bushes and manicured hedges frame the
gazebo where the artists perform. The festival sponsors competitions for adults and
high school student writers. Winners are
featured along with top poets. In past years
readers have included Billy Collins, Maxine
Kumin, Yusef Komunyakaa, Mark Doty, and
Dick Allen. Musicians and bands like Ol'
Skool, an 11-piece horn ensemble, begin
the evening's affair. The event is free, though
parking fees apply. Doors open at 4:30 p.m.
Pack a picnic dinner, get there early, enjoy
the summer green of the gardens, and
appreciate poetry as twilight descends.

TALCOTT MOUNTAIN SUMMER
CONCERT SERIES
Performing Arts Center at Simsbury
Meadows
22 Iron Horse Blvd.
Simsbury, CT 06070
(860) 244-2999
hartfordsymphony.org
Of course you can go to the Hartford Symphony year-round, but by far the best way
to see them is at the outdoor venue of Simsbury Meadows. On the west side of Talcott
Mountain, the sunlight lingers in the summer months, and from the end of June to
the end of July you can bring your blankets
and enjoy an evening of music as the sunset
moves up the mountain wall. Parking is in a
number of lots along Iron Horse Boulevard;
you'll have to walk from there to the venue
(although there is a handicapped entrance
on the east side of the road that goes closer).
Guest musicians show up every summer,
and the Fourth of July concert includes a
fantastic fireworks show. For more money
you can sit up front at tables, but really
you just need to be in the big field to hear
the music well. When you choose where
to sit, I suggest the side closest to the food

and beer trucks, but not too close to the port-a-potties.

Fishing

FARMINGTON RIVER

Farmington River Watershed Association
749 Hopmeadow St.
Simsbury, CT 06070
(860) 658-4442
frwa.org

When I think about fishing in Connecticut I think of the Farmington. With shady banks and large rocks and boulders along its length, the temperature doesn't get much more perfect for rainbows. What's even better is that the access to this river is easy along almost its entire length, with Route 44 paralleling huge sections, while the Farmington Valley Greenway allows easy walking along much the route. The river splits in New Hartford, and the section of the West Branch that flows past Riverton is a favorite for anglers. Though you'll compete with rafters and kayakers in the summer, this is well worth the occasional armada passing by. Start in Collinsville and work your way downstream, or try the river at its confluence with any of the feeder streams: the Nepaug River, Salmon Brook, or the Still River. This is the only river in Connecticut that currently holds a national reputation, and though others should probably be added to that list, the Farmington deserves its accolades.

SHAD DERBY FESTIVAL

261 Broad St.
Windsor, CT 06095
(860) 688-5165
windsorshadderby.org

Derby Day in Windsor is the high point of 2 weeks of festivities celebrating the arrival of this unusual fish. The shad is a bony (though plump) relation of the herring. They migrate north along the Connecticut River to spawn, and Windsor is one of their destinations.

Sign up to fish the river, or just come for the shad and festivities. There is a prize for the largest shad caught, and other events that vary, like a road race or a golf tournament. This is a town-wide festival, and Windsor's Broad Street is usually packed with people and booths. If you get a chance to try these seasonal treats for dinner, don't miss it; for the more adventurous, shad roe fried with bacon is a delicacy.

Golf

EAST HARTFORD GOLF CENTER AND DRIVING RANGE

55 Hillside St.
East Hartford, CT 06108
(860) 282-7809
easthartfordgolfcenter.com

Just minutes from downtown Hartford, in-between Burnside Avenue and Silver Lane, this driving range is a great place to stop after work to hit balls in the 300-yard range and improve your game. You can take group and individual lessons with a professional, practice in a sand trap area, and try your luck on artificial or real grass. And while you're there, buy a few of the thousands of used balls they have sorted and packaged for you. Or sell your own back! This is where my father goes to sharpen his game when he doesn't want to embarrass himself playing against more experienced opponents.

WINTONBURY HILLS

206 Terry Plains Rd.
Bloomfield, CT 06002
(860) 242-1401
wintonburyhills.com

Golf Week magazine called this the best municipal golf course in New England, and once you play it, you'll probably agree. Set above the Tunxis Reservoir, the course was designed by Pete Dye and opened in 2005 with a 6,711-yard, par 70 layout, with 4 sets of tees. There are 125 bunkers framing this course, with some holes open and some surrounded by trees. The greens use bent grass. The challenging hole 9 is set among bunkers like a patch of uneaten grass amid a beautifully manicured rabbit warren. There's a driving range, a putting green, and chipping areas to brush up your skills. The Tap Inn restaurant at the clubhouse is a great place to get a burger after a tough morning on the links, and the pro shop offers all the apparel and equipment you'll need.

Health & Wellness

CONNECTICUT CENTER FOR MASSAGE
75 Kitts Ln.
Newington, CT 06111
(860) 667-1886
ccmt.edu

Everyone loves to get a massage, but no one likes to pay for it. Usually I pay $75 plus a $20 tip. And many places charge more. For a far less expensive option, head over to the Connecticut Center for Massage. Currently it is $32 for an hour (maybe 50 minutes in reality) massage. The employees here are professional and polite, and the students are eager to do a good job—unlike the masseuse I had last year at an expensive spa (which did not make it into this guide of course). CCM also has public clinics in Groton (1154 Poquonnock Rd.; 860-446-2299) and Westport (25 Sylvan Rd. South; 203-221-7325), where the price is slightly higher.

CONTOURS SPA & WELLNESS
2 Bestor Ln.
Bloomfield, CT 06002
(860) 243-0340
contourswellness.com

Winner of the Best of Hartford 2014, this salon and spa combination has a full menu of options for pampering. One thing that distinguishes the spa is its huge selection of facials, including the Rose Quartz and the Liftosome. The massage menu has all the greats, and the body treatments will make you feel like you have shed your skin and are born anew. Try the Chinese herbology treatment, which involves exfoliation, a coating of alpha hydroxy oil and herbs, and a blanket wrap to promote deep penetration, leaving your skin soft, repaired, and well nourished. For those of you who want to learn the trade, Contours also runs a school for cosmetology.

Hiking, Biking & Walking

FARMINGTON VALLEY GREENWAY
PO Box 576
Tariffville, CT 06081
(860) 202-3928
fvgreenway.org

Not to be confused with the Farmington Canal Rail Trail in New Haven County, although it is the dream of many bicyclists and walkers that one day soon they will connect. Only the area from northern Cheshire to Southington remains unpaved, and the Valley Greenway follows both the old canal line north and the river upstream to the northwest, making it one of the longest completed greenways in the state. It provides access to great fishing and rafting; it is also a dream for in-line skaters, walkers, and bikers who want to get out of the cities for a day. Along the route you'll find the charming village of Collinsville at one end; at the other end the trail heads into Massachusetts in Suffield. Unlike some other greenways, this one passes through many villages and provides eating and resting opportunities at comfortable intervals.

i The impressive oak tree on Day Street in Granby is more than 450 years old, with a spread of over 130 feet. Nearby, at the river crossing of Route 185 in Simsbury, the Pinchot Sycamore is the largest tree in the state, with a trunk over 26 feet around.

RAGGED MOUNTAIN
West Lane
New Britain, CT 06489
No phone
raggedmtn.org

At the confluence of Southington, Hartford, New Britain, and Meriden, Ragged Mountain is still wild partly because of the reservoirs below it and partly through the work of various groups interested in its preservation. More of a cliff-sided plateau than a mountain, it has a number of trails, including a figure eight of loops that takes you along the border of the plateau (about 10 miles). This is also one of Connecticut's premier rock-climbing sites (perhaps the best), and you will always find climbers roped up on the south- and west-facing crags along the Metacomet Trail. You'll want to park at the intersection of Sheldon and Moore Hill Roads for that activity, rather than walk all the way in. For an interesting short hike, instead of taking the blue-blazed trail, take the old dirt road straight up the hill from the parking lot at West Lane. Along this you'll find some rusted old cars and trucks, abandoned here decades ago, like the remnants of some lost age.

TALCOTT MOUNTAIN AND HEUBLEIN TOWER
240 Montevideo Rd.
Avon, CT 06001
(860) 677-0662
friendsofheubleintower.org

The Talcott Mountain ridge separates the charming towns to the west from the tobacco farms to the east. Hiking opportunities abound here, north into Penwood Park and south along the New England National Scenic Trail toward Farmington. But the most popular hike on Talcott Mountain is the one up to the massive tower. It's about 1.25 miles to the tower from the parking lot at Route 185, and there are a lot of steps after that, but the climb is well worth it. There have been towers on this spot since 1810, but this 1914 one was actually the family home of the Heubleins, a 165-foot-tall building from which you can see four states. Few will argue that this is not the best view in Connecticut, and just the view of Hartford and Springfield, Massachusetts, seemingly both within spitting distance, is worth the effort. If you continue west on Route 185, right at the river you will find the Pinchot Sycamore—the state's largest, and possibly oldest, tree. You can't miss it.

TUNXIS TRAIL
Bristol/Burlington/Hartland, CT
(860) 485-0226
ct.gov/dep

The Tunxis Trail (or trails) comes in three sections. The southernmost portion is behind Lake Compounce Amusement Park in Bristol and provides some challenging slopes up to a plateau, where you can find, virtually untouched, one of the roads George Washington rode on through Connecticut. The middle section in Burlington has a network of trails throughout pine forests, swamps, and limestone ridges. Start at the Barnes Nature Center at 175 Shrub Rd. in Bristol, and plan a full day of exploration here. This section connects to the northern one by old logging trails that swing close to (though high above) the Farmington River near Satan's Kingdom. The northern section in Hartland is the most remote in the state, a former hunting ground of the Tunxis Indians, it feels like a forest far north in Canada. There are in fact moose here, so be alert during their rutting season in late fall. I was charged by a large male while simply taking photos, and it was not a pleasant experience.

WEST HARTFORD RESERVOIRS

1420 Farmington Ave. (Route 4)
West Hartford, CT 06107
(860) 278-7850
themdc.com/recreation-areas/reservoirs

This is a great little mountain-biking area just off Route 4 (Farmington Avenue), minutes away from Hartford center. Park at the MDC water treatment plant and start exploring. There are dikes over meadows in between the reservoirs, and wooded trails along the base of the Metacomet Ridge, making for fun and variable riding. The area contains over 30 miles of trails, mostly wooded roads. Make sure to download a trail map from the website, although there are large detailed maps posted along the trails here and there. You can hike here too, and just north of Route 9 at Reservoir 6, the trails around the water become walking only. You can hike up to Heublein Tower on Talcott Mountain here, the long way, if you like.

WINDING TRAILS

50 Winding Trails Dr.
Farmington, CT 06032
(860) 674-4227, ext. 25
windingtrails.org

This is a hidden gem for cross-country skiing and bicycling. This extensive 12-mile network of trails, which began as a cross-country center, is now open to mountain bikers in summer. The trails are tightly interconnected, with turnarounds and small connecting paths that make the network seem endless. It can get confusing, though, so make sure to bring a trail map along. There is a small fee to use it for mountain biking, but Winding Trails is worth it. They run the Fat Tire Classic here every spring for those of you who are more than enthusiasts. If you're coming here in winter for cross-country skiing, be sure to call ahead to confirm the condition of the trails.

Kidstuff

THE NEW CHILDREN'S MUSEUM

950 Trout Brook Dr.
West Hartford, CT 06119
(860) 231-2824
thechildrensmuseumct.org

The whale out front will welcome you to this children's museum, and the full-scale model inside is still fun to walk through. This long-running kid's attraction reopened in 2014 and now includes a pre-school. There are changing and permanent exhibits, all interactive, from the Kid's Corner, where you learn about sound, light, and touch, to the Excavation Station, where you "study" earth science. The Travelers Science Dome has a digital projection system, where you can learn about the galaxy or just watch laser light shows. There's a toddler area and a LEGO racetrack. Outside the museum is a wildlife sanctuary, where you can see birds, mammals, and reptiles from around the world—mostly confiscated illegal pets, injured animals, and unwanted pets, from alligators to bobcats.

PUTTER'S PARADISE MINI-GOLF

1801 Berlin Tpke.
Berlin, CT 06037
(860) 828-7518
berlinbattingcages.com

This is one of the great family fun places in the Hartford area, with two minigolf courses, one of which is a bit more difficult (easily decoded by their names: the "fun" course and the "challenge" course). They also have batting cages, which you can rent by the hour or by 12-ball increments. The go-kart raceway is good as long as you're 54 inches tall, but the bumper boats are the most fun, in my opinion. A single ticket combines the karts, boats, and minigolf—a serious bargain. There are a number of family fun places on the Berlin Turnpike, but this one is the best.

SCIENCE CENTER OF CONNECTICUT
250 Columbus Blvd.
Hartford, CT 06103
(860) SCIENCE
ctsciencecenter.org

This interactive museum at the Hartford waterfront dedicated to science is really for both adults and children. On 5 levels, a variety of labs and interactive galleries demonstrate the power and wonder of science. Physics, chemistry, and biology are all explored from a variety of angles. The Sports Lab is a favorite, where you can analyze your performance at games scientifically. You can also learn about levitating trains and new helicopter designs. You'll get to explore space, learn about DNA, and solve puzzles. Or you can just walk into the giant kaleidoscope or watch a film in the 3-D theater. There's a "kidspace" for children 2 and under and a roof garden you can visit in the warmer months. Oh, and in case you're wondering, the Science Center has dinosaurs too.

Nightlife

BLACK-EYED SALLY'S
350 Asylum St.
Hartford, CT 06103
(860) 278-7427
blackeyedsallys.com

Watching a blues or jazz band jamming out in front of the gritty brick wall of Black-Eyed Sally's "juke joint" is a pleasure not to be missed. But the other pleasure is their award-winning barbecue ribs and Southern specialties like fried okra, catfish fingers, and gumbo. Get the Sally's Pig Out, which is pork ribs, pulled pork, and local Nodine's Smokehouse sausage with smoked cheddar cheese grits. This is one of the best blues bars in the nation, and you'll see the greats here, as well as up-and-coming masters in this American art form. They're closed on Sunday, except when there's a UConn event. Every other day you can come to eat and boogie at Black-Eyed Sally's. The bar really starts hopping after 8 or 9 p.m. each night, when the live music starts.

CADILLAC RANCH
45 Jude Ln.
Southington, CT 06489
(860) 621-8805
caddyranch.com

Got a little country in you? Then you probably want to come to the Cadillac Ranch for line dancing or to ride the mechanical bull. Don't know how to line dance? They have lessons some nights for a very small fee, or free with cover charge, to try a little East Coast swing. The restaurant serves classic American food with a few country specialties. Sun, Wed, and Thurs the Ranch has karaoke, so you can put your pipes up against the best country stars. This is a great place to meet and greet other country music fans. In fact, my brother-in-law met his future wife here. Maybe true love is waiting for you at Cadillac Ranch as well.

CITY STEAM
942 Main St.
Hartford, CT 06103
(860) 525-1600
citysteambrewerycafe.com

In the historic 1877 Richardson Building downtown, City Steam fits in many categories. First and foremost they are a brewpub, with handcrafted beers from Black Silk Stout to Colt Lager. They also have a restaurant with classic American sandwiches and pasta, as well as homemade ice cream. And third, the reason they fit so neatly into nightlife, is the Brew Ha Ha Comedy Club, which is Hartford's only live comedy club, bringing in laugh meisters from around the country. There's live music in the bar, and pool tables to pretend you're a shark at. There's even a cigar bar. Oh, and one more thing: The place is actually heated and powered by steam, brought in courtesy of the Hartford Steam Company.

Skiing

SKI MOUNT SOUTHINGTON

396 Mt. Vernon Rd.
Plantsville, CT 06479
(860) 628-0954
mountsouthington.com

Mount Southington has 14 downhill trails with 5 surface lifts and 2 chairlifts, along with a full ski shop and rental shop. Night skiing is popular here, and the after-work crowd in the winter is fun and raucous. The Mountain Room Restaurant becomes quite popular at this time as well. Snowboarders also love Mount Southington, with its terrain park that includes tabletops, spines, and rails. You can get private lessons and group instruction, as well as participate in the electronically timed courses if you want to learn to race. Snowmaking begins in December, so get your skis waxed and get ready to shred those moguls.

Spectator Sports

NEW BRITAIN ROCK CATS

230 John Karbonic Way
New Britain, CT 06051
(860) 224-8383
rockcats.com

This AA affiliate of the Colorado Rockies competes in the Eastern League. The stadium has a covered concourse from which stairs come up into the split-level seating areas. There are skyboxes and general seating, along with a picnic area along the right field line. On the left field line, a kids' play area is installed for those too young to sit through an entire baseball game. There's an outdoor grill and bar near the third base seating area, with an open patio, and vendors downstairs. Don't worry, if you run down to get a hot dog, you won't miss a play, since there are closed-circuit televisions at every concession stand. And be sure to bring a glove. Balls always end up flying into the stands. Note that a controversial deal has been struck to move them to Hartford, so if you're reading this after 2015, make sure.

RENTSCHLER FIELD

615 Silver Ln.
East Hartford, CT 06118
(860) 610-4700
rentschlerfield.com

Rentschler Field was originally the name of the Pratt and Whitney airfield where the stadium is now located. Owned by the State of Connecticut and managed by Bushnell Management Services, this 40,000-seat stadium is primarily the home of the University of Connecticut Huskies football team. However, it is now also the home field for the Hartford Colonials, part of the United Football League, and also hosts big concerts, like Bruce Springsteen and the Rolling Stones. There are about 16 concession stands and 3 ATMs, and the club level includes 2 bars. You can come 4 hours early and tailgate if you like, and you should, especially if you're coming to see the Huskies.

XL CENTER

1 Civic Center Plaza
Hartford, CT 06103
(860) 249-6333
xlcenter.com

Once called the Hartford Civic Center Veterans Memorial Coliseum, the venue was home to sports and entertainment, from the Hartford Whalers to Luciano Pavarotti. Today the XL Center hosts mostly sports events, though a few concerts come here instead of to the Comcast Theater or Rentschler Field. In 1997 the Hartford Wolf Pack began playing here; in 2010 they were renamed the Connecticut Whale and began wearing the colors of that long-ago professional team.

There's a restaurant and bar, which can seat up to 180 gourmet dinner buffet guests before and during events, and a dozen vending stands for those of us who prefer a hot dog and nachos with cheese sauce. The XL Center hosts the Boston and New York basketball teams, as well as the frequent national-champion Connecticut Huskies, both men's and women's teams. Definitely get tickets for the Big East Championship held here every spring, and come to cheer on the Whale, named for Connecticut's state animal of course.

Theater

CHENEY HALL
177 Hartford Rd.
Manchester, CT 06040
(860) 647-9824
cheneyhall.org

The Little Theatre of Manchester company produces three or more plays a year at Cheney Hall. The hall itself is a National Historic Landmark, the oldest operating theater in the state. It was built by silk industrialists in 1866 and dedicated a year later by famous journalist Horace Greeley; plays here have been attended by Presidents Cleveland and Taft, Susan B. Anthony, and other luminaries. In 1925 it became a fabric salesroom, and then was renovated in the late 20th century to reflect its former glory. Along with plays and musical revues, you'll find special events like "folk on Fridays" and silent cinema at Cheney Hall. Head into this historic district of town for a night of laughs or drama.

HARTFORD STAGE
50 Church St.
Hartford, CT 06103
(860) 527-5151
hartfordstage.org

With its unmistakable brown, black, and red Robert Venturi–designed building in downtown Hartford, this is one of the leading resident theaters in the country and winner of some of the nation's most distinguished awards. It was founded in 1963 by Jacques Cartier, opening with a production of *Othello*, and moved in 1968 to the present 498-seat Huntington Theatre. You can come here to see works by Molière, Tennessee Williams, Edward Albee, Beth Henley, and more. The theater participates in an oral history project with the city of Hartford, as well as the Break-dancing Shakespeare project. The stage itself is sometimes set in thrust configuration and sometimes proscenium, depending on the production. You can park in the MAT garage right next door, and plenty of Hartford's restaurants are within walking distance. Many famous movie and television actors come here to perform, or you might see the next future star before he or she becomes famous. But that's not the reason to go to the Hartford Stage: It's a place you can feel transformed through the power of theater.

NATIONAL THEATRE OF THE DEAF
139 N. Main St.
West Hartford, CT 06107
(860) 236-4193
(860) 607-1334 (videophone)
ntd.org

The National Theatre of the Deaf is a touring company whose home base is in West Hartford. They play across the country, from Boston to Las Vegas, but often right here in Connecticut, sometimes at the Old State House in Hartford or at various other venues that offer them space. Their first performance was in 1967 (when 6 people attended), and they have lasted almost 50 years and won a Tony Award for their work, as well as the respect and admiration of both the deaf and hearing public. The performances are in American Sign Language, and even if you don't understand it, it is beautiful to behold. There are 40 theaters of the deaf around the world today, inspired and founded from this original one, here in West Hartford. They have done almost a hundred tours and visited all 50 states, making them the oldest continually producing touring theater company in the nation.

THEATERWORKS
233 Pearl St.
Hartford, CT 06103
(860) 527-7838
theatreworkshartford.org
Walking down Pearl Street you'll see banners depicting a lion with a mouse in his jaws. This is the symbol of Theaterworks, a symbol of the courage to do the thing most frightening. The group has restored the Moorish Revival Art Deco building at 233 Pearl and turned it into City Arts on Pearl, a collection of nonprofit arts organizations that includes a gallery and the dramatic performance space. The plays they put on are more cutting edge than the Hartford Stage or other larger productions. Go to City Arts on Pearl and see drama the way it was meant to be done, by a community theater for the benefit of the community's spirit.

Water Sports

HUCK FINN ADVENTURES
21 Waterville Rd.
Avon, CT 06001
(860) 693-0385
huckfinnadventures.com
Since 1983 John Kulik's outfit in Avon has offered canoe and kayak adventures on the Farmington River. Bring your snacks and drinking water, and let them set you up with canoes, paddles, and life vests. There are 3-, 5-, and 9-mile adventures to take down this easy section of flat water, taking about 1, 2, or 3 hours. You'll pass under the Talcott Mountain ridges and by the enormous Pinchot Sycamore. Huck Finn used to run headlamp underground trips (seriously) in the tunnels of the Park River under Hartford, but

they are currently unable to. Let's hope that this fascinating canoe adventure is allowed to continue. Meanwhile, they do run moonlight, firefly, and wine-tasting trips, and you should check them out.

SHOPPING

Antiques

ANTIQUES ON THE FARMINGTON
10 Depot St. (at Route 179)
Collinsville, CT 06022
(860) 693-0615
antiquesonfarmington.com
This multidealer shop has 70 dealer spaces on 2 floors, right in the heart of historic Collinsville. You'll find furniture, lamps, linens, silver, china, glassware, clocks, paintings, jewelry, books, toys, Civil War memorabilia, and decorating accessories and collectibles. It's open from 10 a.m. to 5 p.m. daily and has a number of small rooms in this old Collinsville ax factory building to make browsing through the huge collection easier. Look for the white sign (above the old Collins Company sign) on the brick building off the street, right by the train station, and take home a piece of history from this amazing historical village. I declined to buy some great antique fishing rods there last time—you better pick them up before I change my mind.

CONNECTICUT SPRING ANTIQUES SHOW
Connecticut Expo Center
265 Reverend Moody Overpass
Hartford, CT 06102
(860) 493-1300
ctspringantiquesshow.com
For more than 4 decades, the Connecticut Spring Antiques Show has brought over 70 dealers from around the state and the country to the Expo Center in Hartford. It was founded by Frances Walker Phipps, who wrote for the *Hartford Courant* and *New York*

Times about antiques and mandated that all the furniture at the show must be from before 1840, the year when mass production changed it forever. It is held on a Saturday and Sunday, usually in March. You can get sandwiches, soups, and desserts in the Tea Room and then browse the endless stalls for the prize of a lifetime.

DICK'S ANTIQUES
670 Lake Ave.
Bristol, CT 06010
(860) 584-2566
dicksantiques.com

With over 40 years of experience in the antiques business, Dick Blaschke not only rules the roost in Bristol but also is consulted on many of the appraisals in Connecticut. The store on Lake Avenue has a fine collection of furniture, lighting, glass, and pottery. You'll find different styles here too, from Art Deco to Art Nouveau. Dick loves oak, and you'll find some great furniture from this sturdy wood. He's open Mon through Fri 10 a.m. to 5 p.m. and Sat noon to 5 p.m., except in summer, when he is often only open 1 day a week. Call ahead to make sure. If you get him in a good mood, he'll regale you with antiquing stories that sound straight out of *Lovejoy Mysteries*.

OLD VILLAGE ANTIQUES
21 E. Main St.
Avon, CT 06001
(860) 674-8621
oldvillageantiques.com

In the historic village of Avon, this antiques shop is co-owned by Stephen Gero, one of the state's leading dealers. He and his business partner, Daniel Hackbarth, seem to have an unerring sense of style and value. You'll walk into a 19th-century saltbox and find a surprising amount of display space on both floors, tastefully arranged. Most of what you'll find here is furniture and home

goods, like lamps, paintings, and accessories, and most of the pieces have been expertly restored and are ready to take home and use without any work of your own. Old Village Antiques is open Mon through Sat 10 a.m. to 5 p.m. and Sun noon to 5 p.m.

Books

BARNES & NOBLE BOOKSELLERS
Multiple Locations
barnesandnoble.com

The Barnes & Noble franchise is a convenient place to find a wide variety of books, leather-bound or eclectically designed journals, music, and more. If the location near you is out of stock on a particular item, it can either be ordered from the strategically placed kiosks or a friendly associate at the information desk can place the order for you.

Clothing

KIMBERLY BOUTIQUE
968 Farmington Ave.
West Hartford, CT 06107
(860) 523-4894
shopkimberly.com

After years of experience in the fashion industry, Kimberly Mattson has created a clothing boutique for women that caters to their needs rather than their desires, and everyone raves about it. More a haven for advice about what works best for you rather than the pushy, snotty boutiques you often find in New York, Kimberly has made its fans through its customer service. The clothes are sophisticated, trendy, and classic, with lines such as Alexis Bittar, BCBG, Beth Bowley, ECRU, French Connection, Frye, James Jeans, Jeffrey, Lilla P, Sondra Roberts, and Citizens of Humanity. Kimberly also has a satellite store at 71 Whitfield St. in Guilford, New Haven County (203-453-2554). Want to get noticed for your sense of style? Kimberly will help you out.

MICKEY FINN'S
874 Berlin Tpke.
Berlin, CT 06037
(860) 828-6547
mickeyfinnstores.com

Right off Route 9 on the Berlin Turnpike, this double store is famous for its reasonable prices. The larger building has a huge selection of athletic shoes and cowboy boots and clothing for families, with hundreds of styles and choices not found even in large department stores. But the reason Mickey Finn's stands out is the smaller store next door, with an unbeatable selection of work pants, jeans, jackets, work boots, and gloves, including brands like Carhartt and Dickies. On any day it is full of police officers, factory workers, and construction foremen picking through the racks for their work clothes. Don't be put off by the rugged exterior—it's how they keep prices so low. This is the way an independent clothing store used to be, and should be again.

OVER THE MOON
38 W. Main St.
Avon, CT 06001
(860) 676-9599
overthemoonkids.com

Children's clothes are available everywhere, so buying them from a family-run, local store is not most people's priority. However, since you bought this book, you have already proven that you do care about that. You can find a wide range of children's clothes, outerwear, footwear, hats, and accessories for infants up to size 12, in brands from Chloe to Chicken, Pink to Tea. Over the Moon concentrates on high-quality, durable products and even have eco-friendly bamboo and cotton clothes. The owners are parents themselves, which is a good sign.

STACKPOLE MOORE TRYON
242 Trumbull St.
Hartford, CT 06103
(860) 522-0181
stackpolemooretryon.com

Consistently ranked the best clothier in Hartford, Stackpole Moore Tryon has been around for over a century. That should probably be enough to tell you how respected this place is. This is the place to get a custom-tailored suit, designer dress shirts, and luxury pants and trousers. They have a wide selection of designers, including Donald Pilner, Hickey Freeman, Allen Edmonds, Frank Lyman, Lou Myles, and Arnold Roberti. I honestly have no idea who any of those people are. But they do. The staff at the store knows their stuff and gives personal attention the way an old-fashioned tailor used to.

Farm Stores/Pick Your Own

BELLTOWN HILL ORCHARDS
483 Matson Hill Rd.
South Glastonbury, CT 06073
(860) 633-2789
belltownhillorchards.com

Donald and Mike Prelli are the third generation of the family to own the farm on Belltown Hill, begun by their immigrant grandparents in 1910. You can pick your own peaches, pears, cherries, apples, pumpkins, and tomatoes here at Belltown, or buy the finished products in one of their great pies at the bakery. You'll also find apple cider donuts, caramel apples, jams, jellies, and more. The Prellis' farm is open every day June through Oct, and Mon through Sat in Nov and Dec, when you can pick out a Christmas tree. You can also catch them in Jan on weekends only. Belltown makes a secret-recipe applesauce that has become famous in the region; get some and try to figure out what they put in it to make it so darn good.

COMSTOCK FERRE AND COMPANY
263 Main St.
Wethersfield, CT 06109
(860) 571-6590
comstockferre.com

During the 19th century Wethersfield made its reputation by selling seeds. Since 1811 seeds have been sold from this spot on Main Street, and since 1838 the business has operated under the name Comstock Ferre and Company, the longest continually operating company of its kind in the US. You can find open-pollinated, pure, non-GMO seeds of the highest quality, heirlooms that you won't find anywhere else. These are herbs, vegetables, and flowers in primal forms—healthier and with different nutrients—that you can grow at home. You can also get all sorts of plants, natural food products, handcrafts, and antiques. It's a fun store and a living museum all in one.

LAMOTHE'S SUGAR HOUSE
89 Stone Rd.
Burlington, CT 06013
(860) 675-5043
lamothesugarhouse.com

The Lamothe farm is not old by Connecticut standards, starting in 1971. However, they quickly expanded to have 4,400 tapped maple trees, 15 miles of tubing, and a state-of-the-art sugarhouse, which you can tour seasonally from mid-Feb through Mar, weekends from 1 to 5 p.m. Their country gift store, open year-round, is the premier place in Connecticut to get maple syrup and other maple products (other Connecticut-made items, even farm-raised pigs, can be ordered). My favorites are the maple sugar–coated nuts, but others swear by the maple saltwater taffy. "Grade A Dark Amber or nothing" is what hard-core maple lovers say. If you take your coffee with sugar, try it with a little of Lamothe's maple syrup instead. You'll never go back.

THE PICKIN' PATCH
Nod Road
Avon, CT 06001
(860) 677-9552
thepickinpatch.com

Since 1666 this land has been a family farm, and the current descendants, Janet and Don Carville, preside over one of the most popular pick-your-own farms in the state. The strawberry patch is particularly large and famous, though you can also come here for blueberries, Christmas trees, vegetables, and a variety of other things. From Apr until Dec, you can come from 8:30 a.m. to 5:30 p.m. October weekends they have hayrides with the Pumpkin Lady to the patch. Buying directly from a farm is half the cost of retail, and it's a head scratcher why more people don't take advantage of it.

TULMEADOW FARM STORE AND ICE CREAM
255 Farms Village Rd.
West Simsbury, CT 06092
(860) 658-1430
tulmeadowfarmstore.com

The Tuller family has been farming in West Simsbury since 1768, and like many farms in Connecticut, this one has diversified extensively. They have cattle, vegetables, and an ice-cream store, which they began in 1994. From mid-Apr through Oct, you can stop by from noon until sunset. You can shop at their farm store for their own produce, like lettuce, arugula, chard, tatsoi, basil, tomatoes, cucumbers, peppers, scallions, broccoli, cabbage, bok choy, sweet corn, squashes, zucchini, cucumbers, green beans, and eggplant, as well as their grass-fed beef. They also carry the products of other local farms, like milk, honey, maple syrup, bread, salsa, chips, pesto, goat's cheese, fudge, tomato sauce, bruschetta, and Nodine's Smokehouse meat. And of course you can try one of their 50 flavors of award-winning 16 percent butterfat ice cream, the most popular of which is red raspberry with chocolate chips.

Home & Crafts

FOR THE KITCHEN
36 Main St.
East Hartford, CT 06033
(860) 206-7101
forthekitchen.com

After a fire, For the Kitchen dropped the "Everything" from its name and moved to Glastonbury, and now to East Hartford. Their stellar reputation followed them, especially that of former employee and now owner Vickie Griffeth, who simply knows everything about cooking and baking and, more importantly for you, everything about the proper tools. Knives, cookware, baking implements, teapots—all come at different price points, so you can find the best quality at a price you can pay. Vickie and her crew wrap gifts and give advice freely. This is the premier place to get your cooking gear in Hartford County, maybe in the state. Don't expect to come into a crowded store overflowing with 400 different kinds of knives. For the Kitchen has done the weeding out for you, leaving choices among only the best.

TRADING POST
Route 44
Canton, CT 06019
(800) 530-5124
tradingpostct.com

In 1983 this store was opened as a new and used bookstore, but over the years they have added more and more, evolving into a full-service music store, with not only CDs and DVDs but also clothing, posters, tapestries, incense, jewelry, and more. The Trading Post also owns Eastern Accents, farther west on Route 44, just after you cross the Farmington River in New Hartford. There they sell wood and stone carvings, primitive art, furniture, and clothing from Thailand, Nepal, and Bali.

The Trading Post itself is a unique shop of the sort you've probably only seen in movies set in California, right here in Canton. And they still have a small collection of used and new books. Maybe you'll find one about the importance of diversification to stay in business in a changing world.

Malls

THE PROMENADE SHOPS AT EVERGREEN WALK
501 Evergreen Way
South Windsor, CT 06074
(860) 432-3398
thepromenadeshopsatevergreenwalk.com

Some people say that malls are doomed by the Internet, but that is hard to believe. People like to walk around in nicely designed spaces, and to browse the shelves in a way that they can't online. Malls replaced downtowns in the 20th century, and as long as we have sprawling suburbs, they will remain centers of capitalism and family life. The Promenade in South Windsor is one of the nicest malls in the state, with high-end clothing stores, specialty food stores, a hair salon, L.L.Bean, an Apple store, home goods stores, and many restaurants. Along with the usual eateries, they have local food places like Munson's Chocolates and Sakura Garden. And if you're tired out from all that shopping, you can relax at the Green Tangerine Spa and Salon.

RIVERDALE FARMS
124 Simsbury Rd.
Avon, CT 06001
(860) 677-6437
riverdalefarmsshopping.com

This collection of specialty shops is built in an old dairy farm, with 11 original barn structures. Back in the 1600s it was Case Farm, and it grew to over 600 acres in the 1900s. More recently, the remaining 26 acres were bought by Silvio and Theresa Brighenti, who transformed it into this collection of shops. There are some very specialized stores here, like All That Jazz, which sells dance, skating, and gymnastic supplies, and the Equestrian Centre, which sells horse-related items. For lamps and clocks, go to Avon Clock and Lighting; for children's clothing, My New Wardrobe. Stop for breakfast or lunch at the Avon Country Deli.

WESTFARMS MALL
1500 New Britain Ave.
West Hartford, CT 06110
(860) 561-3024
shopwestfarms.com

This large upscale mall off I-84 on the border of West Hartford and Farmington has over 160 shops, anchored by Nordstrom, Macy's, Lord & Taylor, and JCPenney. With 1.3 million square feet of shopping, this is a mall-walker's paradise. Stores include Coach, Free People, Restoration Hardware, Tiffany and Co., 77kids, and J. Crew. There are a number of retailers only found here in northern Connecticut and southwestern Massachusetts, making this mall a destination. There's no food court, but a number of restaurants and fast-food joints are scattered throughout the mall, including the signature restaurants P.F. Chang's China Bistro and Brio Tuscan Grille. There's plenty of free parking, and the mall is close to all the sights and tastes of Hartford County.

Outdoors

CABELA'S SPORTING GOODS
475 E. Hartford Blvd. North
East Hartford, CT 06118
(860) 290-6200
cabelas.com

Sure, Cabela's is a chain store, but it is a destination for any outdoorsman or woman in the state. Kids (including 60-year-old ones) love the animal dioramas throughout the store, the trout in tanks, and the nearly carnival atmosphere that pervades it. You can find everything and anything you are looking for to camp, boat, fish, hunt, hike, climb, and live outdoors. One note: GPS navigation to this place (hidden in an office park) is way off, and you won't see a sign until you get close. Get off at the Silver Lane exit at Pratt and Whitney and head in on Airport Avenue, bearing left onto East Hartford Boulevard North. Something so large shouldn't be so hard to find, but it is. Nevertheless, you'll be glad you made the effort, because the selection here is the best in Connecticut.

COLLINSVILLE CANOE AND KAYAK
41 Bridge St. (Route 179)
Collinsville, CT 06022
(860) 693-6977
cckstore.com

This family-owned business has been in the old Miner Lumber Company building in historic Collinsville since 1990. Starting small, they have expanded to 10,000 square feet. It is simply the best place to come for canoes or kayaks in the state, with a large selection and knowledgeable staff. If you buy a canoe or kayak, the accessories come at a substantial discount. The store also offers self-guided and guided canoe and kayak trips on the Farmington River, as well as the Connecticut shoreline. Oh, and you can try out the equipment in the river right behind the store. How's that for customer service?

Specialty Foods

AVERY'S SODA
520 Corbin Ave.
New Britain, CT 06052
(860) 224-0830
averysoda.com

Since 1904 this company has been making soda for connoisseurs, handcrafting low-volume flavors—sort of a microbrewed soda. They use pure cane sugar, and the effect on, say, their sarsaparilla is extraordinary. You can stop by the factory to buy the sodas and more in their little shop, and the machine is right there in the store to watch. The place doesn't really look like a retail shop at first, but just head in through the center door. They also have interesting "sodagusting flavors" like Kitty Piddle (actually very tasty pineapple and orange). The kids, especially overgrown teenage ones, love them. Avery's also makes special batches for other Connecticut businesses, like Sunset Meadow Vineyards.

MODERN PASTRY SHOP
422 Franklin Ave.
Hartford, CT 06114
(860) 296-7628
modernpastryshop.com

With its brick building and vintage sign, Modern Pastry may not look "modern" to some eyes. But the glass-and-chrome cases, long coffee counter, and swivel stools give this place an air of authenticity, compared by many to the north end of Boston—except, you know, better. Family owned since 1958, Modern will fill the thin crusts of your cannolis to order while you wait with filling that must be (or should be) illegal. They also have homemade pastries, lemon ice, mocha cakes, whipped cream cakes, gelato, and imported Italian candies and chocolates. You can sit at the long counter with an espresso or cappuccino from 6 a.m. every day but Monday, or take some of these delicious pastries to work, where you will be the hero of the office.

PODLASIE MEAT MARKET
188 High St.
New Britain, CT 06051
(860) 224-8467
No website

A deli and market has to be pretty special to make it into this guide, and this one fits the bill. Podlasie is for all your Polish yearnings, from drinks to chocolates. Don't miss the dense black bread and the selection of meats that you simply won't find in a regular supermarket. Expect to do some pointing and nodding at items behind the counter; often the workers and the patrons do not speak English. And make sure to stop at the other stores and markets in this wonderful little section of town. Once, these enclaves were the rule, not the exception; and though we all know that certain ethnicities live in certain sections of towns, it is not often brought home with this clarity.

SIXPENCE PIE COMPANY
26 North Main St.
Southington, CT 06489
(860) 681-6118
sixpencepiecompany.com

Sixpence started out as one of those little businesses that people set up at local farmers' markets, but it became so much more. They had a good idea: Bring the savory pies that are beloved in the British Commonwealth countries to Connecticut. And now I can get the handheld pasty pies that I enjoyed in Scotland and Canada here at home. Except, maybe even better! Their rich, custardy quiche, their flaky crusted pastries, their Little Piggy stuffed with pulled pork and onion dipped in barbecue sauce—I couldn't pick a favorite. You can get their pies at a number of markets and retail stores in the state, but you can also get them at their home store in downtown Southington. Oh, they also have sweet dessert pies.

ACCOMMODATIONS

With the recent closing of the Goodwin Hotel, there are no independent lodgings in the downtown area of Hartford at all. However, there are literally dozens of hotels in the Hartford area, all large reliable chains, which we have not focused on. All lodgings have both smoking and nonsmoking unless otherwise noted, or have a designated smoking area, and do not accept pets unless noted. Hotels, motels, and resorts are wheelchair accessible unless otherwise noted. Bed-and-breakfasts and inns are not wheelchair accessible unless otherwise noted, since many are in historic buildings exempt from the Americans with Disabilities Act. Call to make sure if there's any question. We do not list specific credit cards in either this section or the restaurants section.

Bed-and-Breakfasts

CAPTAIN JOSIAH COWLES PLACE $$
184 Marion Ave.
Plantsville, CT 06479
(860) 276-0227
southingtonbedandbreakfast.com

This charming bed-and-breakfast is in the 1740 house of Captain Josiah Cowles, who supplied the American army with wheat during the Revolution. Today the owners, Mary and David Potter, offer their hospitality just off exit 30 on I-84, in a relaxing setting. There are 2 reasonably priced rooms, both with private baths and some original details from the restored home. The owners will regale you with tales of the Captain, and point out the amazing architecture of this seemingly simple home. You'll enjoy pancakes in the morning, complete with maple syrup tapped from trees on the property.

CHESTER BULKLEY HOUSE $$$
184 Main St.
Wethersfield, CT 06109
(860) 563-4236
chesterbulkleyhouse.com

This 1830 house right at the center of Old Wethersfield is a Greek Revival with wide pine floors and working fireplaces. The 5 rooms are furnished with antiques and decorative objects. Three of the rooms have private baths; this is a truly restored historic home, so it's amazing they have private baths at all. The innkeeper, Thomas Aufiero, serves a great breakfast; his specialty is french toast. You are literally across from the Webb-Deane-Stevens Museum here, and within walking distance of all the sights of the old town. There is no television in your room, but that's not why you get a room at a bed-and-breakfast, is it? Besides, they have them in the sitting areas, or you could, you know, open a book.

✳CHIMNEY CREST MANOR $$-$$$
5 Founders Dr.
Bristol, CT 06010
(860) 582-4219
chimneycrest.com

At the top of a steep hill in Bristol is this Tudor Revival mansion, with a huge, 40-foot "grand room" with stone fireplaces at either end, a vaulted ceiling arcade, a paneled library, a sunroom, oak paneling, plaster ornament ceilings, and framed artwork. It's really more than a "manor," it's a castle. However, there are only 5 rooms here, 3 of which are suites, 1 with a fireplace and 1 with a thermal spa. So, you will be treated like visiting aristocracy by Cynthia and Dante Cimadamore with pillow chocolates, fresh fruit, homemade cookies, and a large breakfast. Sit on the back terrace for tea and enjoy views of the Farmington Ridge to the west. If you get up early enough, you can watch the sunrise here, although with the plush feather king beds, you'll be lucky to get up before noon.

THE CONNECTICUT RIVER
VALLEY INN $$$-$$$$
2195 Main St.
Glastonbury, CT 06033
(860) 633-7374
ctrivervalleyinn.com

This large, rambling Colonial has been restored and updated into one of the most luxurious bed-and-breakfasts in the state by Patricia and Wayne Brubaker. Patricia is an artist, and she designed the inn with an eye on the past and the future. This is modern luxury, with tastefully decorated rooms, each unique, complete with small touches like a copper sink or a body spray shower. There are 5 rooms in all, each with gas fireplaces and sinfully comfortable beds. Depending on the room, you'll find flat-screen televisions, drop-down writing desks, balconies, and more. Breakfasts included homemade delights like quiche. Though you're close to the center of Glastonbury, you'll feel like you're miles away from anything at the Connecticut River Valley Inn.

LILY HOUSE BED AND BREAKFAST $$-$$$
13 Bridge St.
Suffield, CT 06078
(860) 668-7931
thelilyhouse.com
This beautiful but modest guest house in downtown Suffield is the perfect base for exploring northern Connecticut. Bring your bikes and head down to the river to join up with the Windsor Locks Canal trail. Lorraine's homemade brownies will welcome you back from your excursions. For those who want to stay at "home," there is a common room downstairs with puzzles, books, a microwave, and a refrigerator stocked with complimentary drinks and snacks. All rooms have a private bath and are located on the second floor. Each has a CD player, and you can borrow the innkeeper's wireless laptop. You might prefer the Stargazer Suite, which is the largest and includes a fireplace and private balcony. But since I have a fireplace at home, I like the Octagon Room with its soaking tub. To each his own!

SILAS ROBBINS HOUSE $$$$
185 Broad St.
Wethersfield, CT 06109
(860) 571-8733
silaswrobbins.com
Right on the beautiful Broad Street Green, this unusual and elaborate Victorian mansion sports 5 rooms with private baths for anyone looking for the splendor of a bygone age. You can also enjoy things that the Victorians never did, like flat-screen cable televisions and wireless Internet. Note that no pets or children under 14 are allowed. You are right in the middle of the largest historic district in the state at the Silas Robbins House, and you can walk to attractions like the Webb-Deane-Stevens House (see entry) or enjoy the farmers' market on the green.

TRUMAN GILLET HOUSE BED AND BREAKFAST $$
151 North Granby Rd.
Granby, CT 06035
(860) 844-1212
trumangillethousebb.com
This one-and-a-half story saltbox-style bed-and-breakfast is only 8 miles west of Bradley International Airport but feels worlds away. In fact, Granby is one of the most isolated villages in the state and seems to be a hundred years in the past—at least. There are only 2 rooms at this quaint little B&B, both of which are inexpensive for what you get. The Connecticut Room has a private whirlpool bath and a queen-size canopy bed, perfect for a romantic getaway. In the morning stuff yourself with cranberry bread and blueberry pancakes and head off for a day of hiking or antiquing.

Hotels and Motels

AVON OLD FARMS HOTEL **$$$$**
1 Nod Rd.
Avon, CT 06001
(860) 677-2818
avonoldfarmshotel.com

This 160-room luxury hotel, situated on 20 acres of manicured grounds, includes an outdoor pool, sauna, fitness room, complimentary high-speed Internet, daily newspaper delivery, continental breakfast, and more. But these facts don't really describe the wonder of this luxury hotel, with its curved staircases and plush bedrooms. The rooms are dark wood and clean white, with options of king, queen, and double canopy beds. The on-site restaurant, Ferme, is one of the best in the state, with a farm-to-table ethos that appeals to all (see entry). They also have a taproom, where you can get lighter fare, beer, and wine. Pets are welcome; call for information about their policies. There are even iPhone chargers in the rooms. That's luxury.

SIMSBURY INN **$$$**
397 Hopmeadow St.
Weatogue, CT 06089
(860) 651-5700
simsburyinn.com

The Simsbury Inn's splendid lobby gives you an idea of what you're in for here. The 100 guest rooms and suites are in yellow-and-blue French country decor, with four-poster or sleigh beds. Amenities include saunas, a health club, and an indoor heated pool. You'll find bowls of fresh fruit, hot cocoa, and popcorn set out for you. All the rooms have high-speed Internet access, goose down comforters, refrigerators, and Frette linens. You can also arrange in-room spa services. The on-site restaurant, Evergreens (see entry), has your breakfast and dinner if you like, or choose the lighter fare of the Twigs Lounge or the Nutmeg Cafe. Pets are accepted for a small fee. This is luxurious living in the country, beneath the cliffs of Talcott Mountain and within walking distance of the Pinchot Sycamore but barely a 10-minute drive from downtown Hartford.

RESTAURANTS

Please note that all Connecticut restaurants are smoke free, and all are required to be wheelchair accessible. Pets are not allowed inside most restaurants, but during the warmer months, there are plenty of restaurants with patio areas just right for your canine friend. Call ahead to make sure it's okay.

American & Modern

ANN HOWARD'S APRICOTS **$$**
1593 Farmington Ave.
Farmington, CT 06032
(860) 673-5405
apricotsrestaurant.com

Apricots mixes seasonal country cuisine with nouvelle French-American techniques for a wonderful result. Downstairs, a pub serves a lower-priced menu in a more boisterous atmosphere. Upstairs, the linen tablecloths are spread with finery, and the food that comes out of the kitchen is some of the best in the state. The menu changes, because Ann Howard and the chefs are always searching for the next flavor. But the apricot dessert sampler is a staple here, with gelato and truffles made with this underused flavor. Sit in one of the rambling rooms overlooking the river in summer and watch fly fishermen and barn swallows catching their own treats. At night the river is floodlit, and the experience is even better.

✳COTTAGE RESTAURANT AND CAFÉ $$
427 Farmington Ave.
Plainville, CT 06062
(860) 793-8888
cottagerestaurantandcafe.com

Headed by Patty Queen, who worked at some of the best restaurants in the country, the Cottage Restaurant in Plainville is a wonderland of contemporary American dishes, with touches from global cuisines like Creole and Japanese. The crispy, frizzled onions side that comes with the meals is amazing, and the cornmeal oyster appetizer is delicious. But the entrees are where Cottage shines, with the pork meat loaf and brick chicken as the standouts. They also have an a la carte menu where you can mix and match, or eat tapas style; many patrons swear by this unorthodox method, sampling the pickled beets and truffle fries. Try the bread pudding for dessert or one of their daily items, fresh from local sources.

THE ELBOW ROOM $$
986 Farmington Ave.
West Hartford, CT 06107
(860) 236-6195
theelbowroomct.com

The best macaroni and cheese in Connecticut? In the country? Well, the Elbow Room is not making such claims, but some of its loyal patrons are. Of course their secret "many cheese" macaroni is not the only great dish here. The bison burger, the fried oyster salad, and the chicken potpie (seriously) are great. You can choose from different flatbread pizzas, small plates, and a huge selection of salads. The Sunday brunch is also popular, with a spotlight on eggs. Many people come here just for the excellent martinis in the crowded bar area (no elbow room, get it?). In summer months the roof is open for dining, a unique experience that makes West Hartford Center really seem like the place to be.

EVERGREENS $$$
397 Hopmeadow St.
Simsbury, CT 06070
(860) 651-5700
simsburyinn.com

Evergreens, the restaurant at the Simsbury Inn, is always mentioned when someone asks about the most romantic or most reliable restaurant. That's a good combination to have. For appetizers, try the crispy goat cheese with roasted garlic, red pepper, and sautéed baby spinach, or the maple-glazed pork belly with acorn squash mousseline. The lobster potpie with creamy leek béchamel, the venison tenderloin with parsnip puree, or the butternut squash ravioli make for great entrees. The Sunday brunch is also excellent here. The inn has two other places to eat: the Twigs Lounge, which is a much more casual tavern setting with a summer terrace that has views of Talcott Mountain, and the Nutmeg Cafe, their breakfast joint, with pancakes, coffee, and freshly baked pastries.

✳FIREBOX $$$
539 Broad St.
Hartford, CT 06106
(860) 246-1222
fireboxrestaurant.com

In a vintage brick factory complex within walking distance of downtown, Firebox has made a big impression on the local food scene. Little touches like the Amish farm tables in the back dining room make this a haven for the trendy, but the celebrity chefs who stop here when in Hartford all come for the food. The restaurant focuses on farm-to-table, local, sustainable, and organic products, like the wild ramps I had last time I was there. You can get Connecticut ingredients in delicious preparations, like the Four Mile River Farm rib eye with confit Red Bliss potatoes, roasted cippolinis, *haricots verts,* and sage butter, or the Stonington fluke with fingerling coins, pancetta, hen-of-the-woods mushrooms, and English pea coulis. On Thursday and Friday you can get a prix-fixe menu that ends up being much cheaper. Serving lunch on weekdays and dinner Mon through Sat, Firebox also runs a farmers' market in the small green next to the restaurant on Thursday in summer.

GRANT'S $$$
977 Farmington Ave.
West Hartford, CT 06107
(860) 236-1930
billygrant.com

This is chef Billy Grant's flagship restaurant, and just walking into its dark wood interior you know you're going to be served great food. It's probably not as creatively strange as some of the other fine-dining choices in the city and environs, but for many of you, that's a good thing. The steaks are done properly. The pasta is handmade. The Connecticut Blue Point oysters are fresh. The menu is full of dishes you know and love already, but Grant does them just a little better, with a twist on preparation and a pairing that at first seems strange but then makes total sense. Grant's is known for desserts; in fact, you can just come and have some cake or an éclair at one of the small tables in front by the dessert case. But I'm not sure why someone would do that. You have access to amazing food here, so by all means, take advantage of it.

MAX DOWNTOWN $$$$
185 Asylum St.
Hartford, CT 06103
(860) 522-2530
maxrestaurantgroup.com/downtown

Across from the civic center, this downtown place for the elite to meet brings global cuisine to a fine point. In the tasteful and classy restaurant, you'll be offered wild coho salmon and Max's "world-famous" strip steak.

You can get table tastings, like one for mozzarella that will have everyone salivating for the main course. If you don't want one of their red meat specialties, get the pork chop on the bone, and don't forget to try one of their creative (and very strong) martinis. Your biggest choice may come between the truffled french fries and the blue cheese cottage fries. Always on the cutting edge, they offer a gluten-free menu as well. There are 7 Max restaurants in the Hartford area, all owned by Richard Rosenthal, but they are not a chain. Each has its own character and menu. Max Downtown is the flagship, and it is sailing on smooth seas.

*THE MILL AT 2T $$$
2 Tunxis Rd., Ste. 101
Tariffville, CT 06081
(860) 658-7890
themillat2t.com

Owners Kellyanne and Ryan Jones have created a surprising restaurant on the cutting edge of fine dining. The menu literally changes daily, so you are never quite sure what to expect. However, they do consistently serve popovers instead of bread, and their flaky, puffy wonderfulness will give you a hint of what's to come. You might have choices of foie gras sliders, beet salad, cider-infused pork belly, pan-roasted duck breast, lemon-scented gnocchi, and more. For dessert, the brioche donuts with caramel are a revelation. The Mill at 2T is only open Wed through Sat between 5 and 10 p.m., and seating is limited, so make a reservation. Try to get a seat near the open kitchen so you can watch the geniuses behind one of Connecticut's best new restaurants at work.

MILL ON THE RIVER $$$
989 Ellington Rd.
South Windsor, CT 06074
(860) 289-7929
themillontheriver.net

A huge old gristmill on the Podunk River is now a romantic favorite in northern Connecticut, with its riverside deck, gazebo, and covered bridge. The interior just oozes class and sensible design, without the kitsch that sometimes accompanies historic restaurants. In fact, if it wasn't in a 200-year-old mill, you might think it was out of some perfect restaurant dream. The menu shows influences of both French and Mediterranean cooking, with chilled gazpacho and Escargot Chablisienne. Try the crispy Blue Point oysters, the blackened redfish nouvelle, or one of their great steaks, complete with creamed spinach and truffled fries. This is a place to impress a date, or maybe even ask someone to marry you.

POLYTECHNICON20 $$$
1 State St.
Hartford, CT 06103
(860) 722-5161
ontwenty.com

On the 20th floor of the Hartford Steam Boiler Building, PolytechnicON20 is a place for the adventurous eater, who can be adventurous not just once but time and time again. Called the Polytechnic Club for many years, PolytechnicON20 was a genteel experience, but just for a select few. Now you can enter this classical retreat to see the view, be treated like aristocracy, and try the amazing food. The menu looks surprisingly normal, with chicken and grilled salmon, shrimp and Wagyu steaks. But the preparations are elaborate, and the ingredients are all the highest quality. When the "bacon and eggs" comes to your table, you might be scratching your head. However, don't be intimidated by the molecular gastronomy; this is one of the premier dining experiences in the state. Just don't wear jeans—this is fine dining the way it used to be, even if the food is somewhere in the future.

i For a great view, you can go to the top floor of the Travelers Insurance Company tower (1 Tower Square) in Hartford, open year-round. Take the elevator and then 70 stairs to the top.

POND HOUSE CAFE $$$
1555 Asylum Ave.
West Hartford, CT 06117
(860) 231-8823
pondhousecafe.com

In the often ignored section of Hartford north of the Mark Twain House, you'll find the Pond House Cafe hidden in beautiful Elizabeth Park. The high-ceilinged room is always bustling with professors from the nearby University of Hartford and St. Josephs College, and with a seasonal, creative menu, it gets a lot of return business. You might find short rib sliders on brioche buns or nut-encrusted tempeh with roasted parsnips and carrots as appetizers. For entrees you could choose smoked bacon–wrapped pheasant breast with wild mushroom risotto or lobster mac and cheese with tomatoes and green onion. But save a small corner for the chocolate bread pudding. The Pond House is open for lunch and dinner Tues through Sat and for Sunday brunch. In the summer you can sit on the terrace by the 1904 rose garden, which is on the National Register of Historic Places.

Asian & Indian

ASIAN BISTRO $$$
396 Cromwell Ave.
Rocky Hill, CT 06067
(860) 269-3276
asianbistrorockyhill.com

With such an uninspiring name, you might be a little wary of this place, but you will be pleasantly surprised by the quality of its food and the fun of its hibachi grill service, with all the tricks you've come to expect from this art. What? You've never watched a real hibachi chef go wild and flip shrimp into your mouth? Try it here. This is an upscale Chinese/Japanese combination restaurant with very good sushi and elaborate presentations. But it's really the hibachi that brings me back here. Lobster tail? Chilean sea bass? Yes, please.

BLUE ELEPHANT $$
75 Main St.
West Hartford, CT 06107
(860) 233-4405
blueelephanttrail.com

Chef Soden Tek arrived from a Thai refugee camp with his family as a young boy and spent his childhood in the West Hartford schools. When he came home he watched his mother and grandmother cook Thai and Cambodian dishes. Now he gets to share his passion for Southeast Asian cuisine with his new homeland. The classics are on display here, with great summer and spring rolls, pad thai, sticky rice, and lettuce wraps. On your second trip to the Blue Elephant, try one of the more interesting dishes like Thai pumpkin curry or loc lac (cubed beef tenderloin lightly caramelized in black pepper, garlic, and mushroom soy). And raise a glass of Thai coffee to another story of an immigrant who helped make America great.

BUTTERFLY RESTAURANT $$
831 Farmington Ave.
West Hartford, CT 06105
(860) 236-2816
butterflyrestaurantct.com

Often ranked among the best Chinese restaurants in the state, the Butterfly is not "fine dining" but rather a fun restaurant with live piano music, a karaoke lounge, and casual elegant design. In other words, this is a restaurant for most of us. They have all the delights you hope to find, from fried dumpling to moo shu pork, from crab Rangoon to scallops with garlic sauce. You'll also find

rarer delights, like hot and sour mussels. In fact, they have 100 items on their menu, along with 30 changing chef's specials. This is the best that family Chinese dining gets, affordable and creative food in a fun setting. Perhaps you'll even get up to sing Journey's "Don't Stop Believin'" after your meal.

CHAR KOON $$
882 Main St.
South Glastonbury, CT 06073
(860) 657-3656
charkoon.com

The small dining room and the line of people at the little aquarium waiting for takeout at Char Koon might lead you to believe that this is just another typical Asian restaurant. Nothing could be further from the truth. All sorts of creative Asian fusion comes into play here, from India to Japan, with Thai and Malay and Vietnamese in between. If anyone has any complaints, it's that the chefs at Char Koon are too creative with dishes like Orchid Crispy Shrimp with melon balls, and that's a great problem to have. This is cutting-edge fusion cuisine that will leave you wondering what new delights are coming to Connecticut from the Pacific Rim. I'll take the mee laut, please.

GREAT TASTE $$
597 W. Main St.
New Britain, CT 06051
(860) 827-8988
greattaste.com

Great Taste is one of the highest-ranked Chinese restaurants in the state, with multiregional food and a classy dining room. For over 20 years owner Kam Kwok has been working to please his customers, and has done so time and time again. The main menu is fairly typical of a Chinese restaurant, with all your favorites, from crispy spring rolls to beef chow mein. But the specials menu is where Great Taste really shines. You can choose from creative items like nutty sea bass, tangerine prawns, and sizzling Mongolian lamb. And their Peking duck. Oh, their Peking duck. It's like meat candy, the perfect dish to share with loved ones who love Chinese food—or just love food, period.

Breakfast & Lunch

BOB'S COFFEE SHOP $
33 New Britain Ave.
Rocky Hill, CT 06067
(860) 529-2540
No website

This small, 24-table joint is popular with locals. Once even smaller, it expanded a couple of years ago because of such good business. They are open for breakfast and lunch every day but Sunday (with specials and homemade soups), and on Thurs through Sat for dinner specials. For breakfast try the fluffy waffle or the three-egg omelet stuffed with extras. The crispy bacon is usually done just right. Check out the local advertising on the coffee mugs. And the prices will make you feel like you stepped back in time.

KEN'S CORNER $
30 Hebron Ave.
Glastonbury, CT 06033
(860) 657-9811
No website

This mom-and-pop breakfast joint in Glastonbury always has a line for seating, but it's definitely worth a few extra minutes for the quality "big eater" meals. The biscuits and gravy and the banana-walnut pancakes are the same price as chain diners or restaurants, but light years ahead in taste. Try the french toast stuffed with cream cheese and strawberries; it is as decadent as it comes. The sides shine here, with corned beef hash and potatoes as standouts. You can always find specials on the board, and if Ken is there, he's always willing to tweak your meal. This is a hole-in-the-wall off the street, nothing

fancy, just great breakfast food done by chefs who care.

LASALLE MARKET AND DELI $
104 Main St.
Collinsville, CT 06029
(860) 693-8010
lasallemarket.com

Primarily a breakfast and lunch spot, the LaSalle Market in the quaint village of Collinsville has become an institution. There has been a market or deli on this spot for over a century, and the current incarnation lives up to the reputation of its forebears. They serve sandwiches, breakfast dishes (try the pancakes), salads, wraps, and wonderful daily soups. But then they go beyond the usual breakfast/lunch joint and serve a delicious selection of pizzas, including a flank steak pizza that was just as yummy as it sounds. They are open until 6 p.m. during the week, and many locals order their pizza and rush there after work to grab it take-out. They are open until 10:30 Friday night, though, and that is when a variety of fun events happens. One is an open-mike night that they've had for 10 years now, and downtown Collinsville jams with the tunes of up-and-coming musicians. You'll feel immediately at home in the eclectic interior, with games for kids (or adults) and an art gallery.

QUAKER DINER $
319 Park Rd.
West Hartford, CT 06119
(860) 232-5523
No website

Harry Bassilakis's grandfather built the Quaker Diner in 1931, and he continues the traditions of this local legend today. It's been restored to its original state: high wooden booths, stools, and Harry's collection of antiques. The chef works the open grill like a madman just a few feet away from the long lunch counter. Open from 6 a.m. to

2:30 p.m., they serve lunch (try the meat loaf) but are most famous for their breakfasts. The three-cheese omelet, the french toast with a poached egg inside, and the egg sandwich on a Portuguese roll are all fluffy and delightful. If the Belgian waffles are available (usually a daily special), get them, with blueberry topping and whipped cream. If you've been up all night, you can get a milk shake for breakfast if you like. And if you order french toast, get the jumbo bread instead of the regular. Trust me.

French

CAVEY'S $$$
45 E. Center St.
Manchester, CT 06040
(860) 643-2751
caveysrestaurant.com

This unique place is really two restaurants—one Italian, one French—side by side in one building. They have separate kitchens, separate waitstaff, and separate menus. However, they are both called Cavey's. The villa-like Italian side of the restaurant makes homemade pasta, fresh figs wrapped in prosciutto and Gorgonzola, and ravioli in brown butter. On the French side, which looks straight out of a Toulouse-Lautrec painting of the Belle Epoque, you can get all the classics, from *foie gras* to duck confit. They are open for dinner only, and closed Sunday and Monday. Wear a jacket; this is formal dining. A double restaurant seems like a *Kitchen Nightmare* in the making, but Cavey's has been around since 1933. So they are doing something right, and that "something" is probably the amazing food.

METRO BIS $$$
928 Hopmeadow St.
Simsbury, CT 06070
(860) 651-1908
metrobis.com

This French-style bistro has all the trappings, from a wall of mirrors to the doors of a Paris metro. However, the food is not just French but Asian, or American, or something new altogether. The products are as local as possible, and chef-owner Christopher Prosperi presides over a constantly changing, creative kitchen. For an appetizer, the crispy goat cheese and potato tart is just French enough, but you can also get Thai spring rolls or tandoori chicken. Rainbow trout with a sweet potato apple bacon hash or the slow-roasted Niman Ranch pork with steamed baby bok choy are favorites, but since the menu changes often, you'll have to see for yourself what Chef Prosperi has cooked up for you. The chef's daily tasting menu is a great way to do that as you put yourself in his hands, with four courses of wine and food pairings. This seasonal menu thing can be scary to some people, but don't let yourself be one of them. It heralds a great new age of American cooking.

German

EAST SIDE RESTAURANT $$–$$$
131 Dwight St.
New Britain, CT 06051
(860) 223-1188
eastsiderestaurant.com

If you haven't seen the giant billboards advertising East Side, you haven't been in Connecticut long. It's been around for more than 70 years, serving authentic German cuisine. Sure, the waitresses in their Bavarian beer maid outfits are fun, and you might get sick of hearing the "ticky-tocky-ticky-tocky-hoy-hoy-hoy" song that at first made you grin, but guess what? The East Side hasn't lasted this long because of great lederhosen, they've done it by serving great food. The crazy biergarten atmosphere is just a bonus (sit on the actual rooftop biergarten in summer). Bratwurst, sauerkraut, potato pancakes, paprika schnitzel, red cabbage, smoked pork loin, applesauce, roasted potatoes, goulash, corn fritters . . . all the food is great and should be washed down with frosty mugs of German beer, which is plentiful. The restaurant is hidden in a residential area away from the main drags, so follow your GPS carefully.

Ice Cream

A. C. PETERSON FARMS
RESTAURANT $$
240 Park Place
West Hartford, CT 06119
(860) 233-8483
acpetersenfarms.com

This West Hartford staple is best known for their many flavors of homemade ice cream, including Grape Nuts, and their own ice-cream sauces. The hot fudge is the best. They also serve breakfast, lunch, and dinner—or breakfast for dinner if that is what you prefer. Around since 1940, they are constantly adding new classics, like their "build your own sliders." One warning: They are often packed. If you're in Old Lyme in the warmer months, you can stop by their drive-in at 113 Shore Rd. (860-598-9880).

COLLINS CREAMERY $
9 Powder Hill Rd.
Enfield, CT 06082
(860) 749-8663
thecollinscreamery.com

Standing outside the Collins Creamery, someone remarked, "Why is all the best ice cream made at farms?" Let's hope it was a rhetorical question. Farms are so clearly the best place to get ice cream, for five reasons at once, but we'll answer it in the way it was at the time: freshness. The Collins Creamery makes over 20 flavors at their small dairy store at Powder Hill Farm, and you can get them in waffle cones, sundaes, and milk shakes, along with a variety of other vehicles. But of course what you want is the delicious, creamy substance that has made gluttons of us all. They also have yogurt, sorbet, and

fat-free and soft-serve ice cream. In Connecticut, many dairy farms were not able to compete with giant corporate farms out west that are as big as our entire state. Many, like Collins, have turned to gourmet ice cream, and we can all be glad they did.

PRALINE'S ICE CREAM $
1179 Farmington Ave.
Berlin, CT 06037
(860) 828-3626
pralinesct.com

With flavors like Graham Cracker Smacker, Espresso Ripple Bean, and White Russian, Praline's Ice Cream, just off the Berlin Turnpike, is a fantastic stop for your family. It's near the junctions of Routes 9, 84, and 91, and easily accessible from all three. Perhaps a hike on Ragged Mountain followed by a caramel sundae? Praline's also makes ice-cream cakes for parties and ice-cream pies to take home. The black bottom pie is so good that you won't want to share (even though it feeds 8). Unlike some ice-cream shops, they are open year-round. This is decadent ice cream done right. Chocolate-dipped waffle cone, anyone? You know you want it.

Italian

BRICCO $$
78 Lasalle Rd.
West Hartford, CT 06107
(860) 233-0220
billygrant.com/bricco

Although Billy Grant's restaurant Bricco has Italian and Mediterranean influences, this is contemporary American cuisine at its best, with seasonal menus and creative twists on old favorites. The Tuscan pot roast is a perfect example, with truffled potato puree, glazed parsnip, and hen-of-the-woods mushrooms. For an appetizer, you have difficult choices between the tasty golden beets and winter citrus, the buffalo mozzarella, and the braised baby artichokes. Bricco has artisanal pizzas like "fig jam," with fresh mozzarella, Gorgonzola, rosemary, prosciutto, and arugula salad. They do have regular pizzas too, and spaghetti with fava beans for those of you who want a more traditional meal. Try a Connecticut Chardonnay with your meal or, for nondrinkers, one of the local Hosmer Mountain sodas. Billy Grant has two other restaurants in Hartford County (Grant's and Trattoria), but Bricco is the most casual and, dare we say, the most Italian.

CARBONE'S RISTORANTE $$$
588 Franklin Ave.
Hartford, CT 06114
(860) 296-9646
carboneshartford.com

An icon on Franklin Avenue since 1938, this is an Italian restaurant that makes all the others look like imitators. Three generations of Carbones have run it right in the heart of Hartford's Little Italy. The dining room is large, and you'll find happy families dining on linguini with clam sauce, veal Bergamo, and ravioli in pomodoro sauce. Along with the families you'll find the politicos of Hartford chowing down here on a regular basis, maybe on one of the specials, which are always good bargains. Get a flambé for dessert and they'll do it right at your table, the way they used to in the movies, right? Carbone's was actually started as a fried chicken joint back in the 1930s, but they've been doing classic Italian American recipes since the 1960s. Let's all raise a glass of Chianti in celebration of that change.

FIRST AND LAST TAVERN $$
939 Maple Ave.
Hartford, CT 06114
(860) 956-6000
firstandlasttavern.com

For nearly eight decades this tavern has been a neighborhood staple, serving Italian food, seafood, and brick-oven pizzas in a casual setting. Sit in a booth or at the long wooden bar and eat spaghetti, meatball grinders, or shells with marinara. Make sure to get the homemade bread. They also have a number of other locations (and a bakery), including 26 W. Main St. in Avon (860-676-2000), 220 Main St. in Middletown (860-347-2220), and 32 Cooke St. in Plainville (860-747-9100). They also sell their own popular line of pasta sauces, all made and bottled on the premises. The wall of the dining room in the original restaurant in Hartford is covered with photos of celebrities who have eaten here. Maybe you'll have your picture up there someday.

JOEY GARLIC'S $$
150 Kitts Ln.
Newington, CT 06111
(860) 372-4620
joeygarlic.com

Italian and proud of it, Joey Garlic's Newington location features grinders, salads, and a great selection of appetizers (some people come just for the anchovy pizzette, crispy fried ribs, or fried dough). But it's the old-fashioned burgers and milk shakes that have made Joey's reputation. The thick shakes come in a number of flavors, from cinnamon caramel to creamsicle, and the hamburgers are ground fresh twice daily. Joey Garlic's has two other locations. At the 372 Scott Swamp Rd. (Route 6) location in Farmington (860-678-7231), in addition to the delights of the Newington location, you can get New Haven–style brick-oven pizza and more pasta dishes. The other, newer location is a smaller pizza shop at 353 Park Rd. in West Hartford. All serve huge portions at reasonable prices, and all fill up quickly on a weekend night.

TREVA RESTAURANT $$$
980 Farmington Ave.
West Hartford, CT 06107
(860) 232-0407
trevact.com

Treva is yet another owner/chef success, this time with classic northern Italian cuisine in a high-end restaurant in West Hartford. They have fresh homemade pastas, imported buffalo mozzarella from Italy, and a large selection of cured sliced meats and Italian cheeses. A standout is the cheese trio al forno, a wonderful mix of melted goat cheese, mozzarella, and Parmesan served in an earthenware crock. Squid-ink pasta, gnocchi, and porchetta . . . all the dishes you want in an Italian restaurant, done perfectly. The service here is top-notch, and don't be surprised if the chef visits your table to see how you are faring.

Latin American

AGAVE GRILL $$
100 Allyn St.
Hartford, CT 06103
(860) 882-1557
agavehartford.com

This downtown grill has a Mexican-Caribbean menu and a flair for experimentation. Simply decorated and presenting occasional live music, they have improved the Latin American food in Hartford tenfold. Sure, you can get chili con queso and an enchilada, but why not try one of the more interesting dishes, like the lobster, black bean, and corn tostada; the shrimp on sugarcane skewers and glazed with passion fruit and chipotle; or the mango-rubbed ribs. They make the guacamole right at your table, as fresh as the moment. For dessert, the banana chimichanga is almost too rich and good to really exist. Try one of the 30 tequilas, especially the 9 "supremas," the best tequilas in the world. Don Julio 1942 never fails to surprise, and neither will Agave Grill.

Pizza

CAPA DI ROMA $$
358 Burnside Ave.
East Hartford, CT 06108
(860) 282-0298
capadiroma.com

Since 1982 the Capaccios have been serving Italian food at this family restaurant, but they made their reputation with some of the best pizza in Hartford County. Sure you can try one of their Italian dishes here, and the homemade red sauce gets rave reviews, but the hand-tossed, brick-oven pizzas are fabulous. They put cornmeal on the bottom when they bake them so they don't stick, and it adds something indefinable to this already great pizza. If you have a large party, get the 30-inch size (yes, you read that right), which has 40 pieces. Grab some of their sauce to take home; it's also available at many local grocery stores.

HARRY'S PIZZA $$
39 South Main St.
West Hartford, CT 06107
(860) 231-7166
harryspizza.net

For lunch and dinner, there is nothing else to eat at Harry's but thin-crust pizza. Don't expect to order buffalo wings or a steak grinder here. Some might think this is a problem, but the small shop has nothing to distract them from making great pies. If you like seafood, try either the shrimp or clam pizza, but their traditional tomato and mozzarella is excellent. They also have some versions not seen elsewhere, like the Godmother, with fresh mozzarella, asparagus, crispy pancetta, fresh oregano, and Pecorino Romano, and the West Hartford Center, with fresh basil, ricotta, artichokes, sun-dried tomatoes, and light fresh garlic. This family-run shop with high-backed wooden booths does take a break from baking pizza to serve breakfast, though, with great waffles and pancakes. Harry's is a local place that you might pass by without insiders' knowledge; don't make that mistake. They now have another location in Glastonbury (363 New London Tpke.; 860-633-7338).

Polish

BALTIC RESTAURANT   **$$**
237 New Britain Rd.
Berlin, CT 06037
(860) 828-9967
thebalticrestaurant.com

Although the Baltic Restaurant seems to be primarily a banquet facility, its restaurant has what might be the best high-end Polish food in the state. Though my wife is Polish-American, I had never tried a pyzy before I ate here—potato dumplings stuffed with meat with bacon and onions, but created in a new way that was absolutely delicious. I will be back for that, and for the rest of their quality dishes, from hunter's stew to beef roulades. Of course they have all the classics: pierogi, stuffed cabbage, potato pancakes, and more. The food is not only authentic, it is consistently delicious, and has a stamp of approval from my very picky Polish wife.

CRACOVIA   **$**
60 Broad St.
New Britain, CT 06053
(860) 223-4443
cracoviarestaurant.com

If you weren't clued in by the Polish signs on the adjoining stores, you can tell this is a genuine Polish neighborhood restaurant as soon as you walk in and spot the Polish-language newspapers and hear the words from its patrons. However, the menu and waitresses speak perfect English and can explain some of the more interesting menu items. They have the great Polish food that is part of the American lexicon too, like onion-and-potato pierogis and cabbage rolls

stuffed full with beef and rice. The soups (like borscht and dill pickle) are huge, and the kielbasas are delicious. Don't expect the decor to amaze you, but expect it from the food. This is genuine fare in the heart of Polish New Britain.

POLISH NATIONAL HOME   **$$**
60 Charter Oak Ave.
Hartford, CT 06106
(860) 247-1784
polishhomect.org

Hailed by *Gourmet* magazine and the *New York Times* as a treasure, this secret restaurant hidden in a nondescript brick building is an insiders' treat. Once you find your way inside, through a door around back by the parking lot, you'll find some of the best Polish food in the state. The potato pancakes, stuffed cabbage, and pierogi dumplings are perfection itself. Try the "Polish plate" that includes all of the above, as well as some delicious sauerkraut (called *bios*). If you're in the mood to dance a polka, come on Saturday night. Don't expect to be impressed by the decor—this looks like a heavy, utilitarian Eastern European hall. But the food, although certainly heavy, is anything but utilitarian.

Pubs & Taverns

COREY'S CATSUP AND MUSTARD   **$$**
623 Main St.
Manchester, CT 06040
(860) 432-7755
catsupandmustard.com

This burger bar in Manchester has very limited seating, and because it is very popular, you will almost always have to wait. I recommend the barbecue brisket; waffle fries for an appetizer; the horseradish roast beef on Texas Toast sandwich; and any of the very large burgers, especially the Potato Crunch (with local Deep River Snacks chips). Root beer floats, chicken n' waffles . . . you'll want to come back and try all their specialties. They also have a well-stocked bar, with 17 drafts and local Hosmer soda. The owner (Corey, obviously) is a Manchester boy who made good, so this is about as local as you can get.

J. TIMOTHY'S TAVERNE $$
143 New Britain Ave.
Plainville, CT 06062
(860) 747-6813
jtimothys.com
The menu at J. Timothy's Taverne seems like a classic pub restaurant, with solid entries like shepherd's pie and pomegranate pork medallions. They also have a huge selection of draft and bottle beer, including some Connecticut classics. But what makes them famous is their wings, recently rated the second best in America. They make them "dirt style," which is a terrible name, but essentially they are sauced, fried, and sauced again. I am a huge wings snob, and these are probably the best I've had in the state, although a few times I've had "confit" wings that might have been better (but those were expensive). The decor of this large, rambling place is a combination of colonial and English pub, plenty of wood and quotes by Benjamin Franklin on the lintels. The oldest part of the building is 225 years old, so that is appropriate. But this is not a stuffy old inn; it pops and buzzes. I was there recently on a Tuesday night and it was jam-packed.

PLAN B BURGER BAR $$
138 Park Rd.
West Hartford, CT 06119
(860) 231-1199
planbburger.com
The great thing about this "burger bar" is its commitment to local, organic, and sustainable food. Their beef is certified 100 percent humane and is ground in-house, never frozen, and hormone free. Of course you might not care about that, in which case the 100 American craft beers and 50 boutique Bourbons and ryes might appeal to you. The huge list of beers changes weekly, so you need to read the current list. The menu is full of comfort food done with better ingredients than Mom used. Try the blue cheese burger; it's particularly yummy. Though Plan B has a bar atmosphere, kids are welcome. And make sure to get there early to get a spot. They now have several other locations throughout the state (and beyond), including one at 120 Hebron Ave., # 6, in Glastonbury (860-430-9737).

TISANE EURO-ASIAN CAFE $$
537 Farmington Ave.
Hartford, CT 06105
(860) 523-5417
mytisane.com
We all loved Starbucks back in the 1990s, but Tisane does everything so much better. For breakfast and lunch this is a coffeehouse, but at night it is a martini bar. Try 100 different kinds of tea or 80 different kinds of coffee. The menu is global, with little touches from here or there. The moo shoo pancakes or the Far East nachos make great appetizers, and no one can turn down a brie fondue. Sandwiches and noodle bowls for entrees seem to make this more of a lunch place than anything else, but instead you'll find Tisane a hip hangout all day long, from the morning coffee addicts to the after-work cocktail sippers. It's a good thing this is out on Farmington Avenue rather than in the center of the city (or in the center of West Hartford, for that matter), or seats would be impossible to get. As it stands, travelers with a car, like yourself, can reach this delightful cafe best. Tisane is only closed for 6 hours a night, and you might wonder why they bother.

Road Food

BART'S DRIVE-IN $
55 Palisado Ave. (Route 159)
Windsor, CT 06095
(860) 688-9035
bartsdrivein.com

Begun as a hot dog stand 65 years ago, this classic joint that looks like an old brick gas station now includes a grill and a counter that serves cold sandwiches. They have hamburgers, ice cream, chicken, and all the other dishes that are so often done poorly by chain restaurants, and so often done right by places like Bart's. The milk shakes are excellent, and the whole-belly clam roll is something that should be served in every restaurant in Connecticut. They have special events during summer that include Family Nights, where you can compete in games like hula-hooping. Bart's is famous for its service, so when you stop by, expect to be treated like family.

CAPITOL LUNCH $
510 Main St.
New Britain, CT 06051
(860) 229-8237
capitollunch.com

Operating since 1929, this place has served hungry Hartford lunchtime diners for generations. The menu is not large, with cheeseburgers, onion rings, fries, and the Cappie Dogs. These hot dogs are good, but what made this place famous was, appropriately, the Cappie's Famous Sauce, an unidentifiable brown sauce they coat them with. It's a meat-based sauce, surely, with a hint of clove, but other than that, it is a secret. However, you can get it to go by the pint. If you have the tools, why not break it down and try to figure it out? Or just enjoy it on all your hot dogs (and everything else) at home.

HEN HOUSE BAR-B-Q $$
192 Main St.
Southington, CT 06489
(860) 276-0798
henhousebbq.com

Founded in 1988 by Ronald Amorando, this Southington restaurant started out with just a few items, but as they quickly became popular, they began to offer more and more. Today you can get everything from a bison burger to fried flounder. The Philly cheesesteaks are quite good here, a rarity in Connecticut, so if you're from Pennsylvania and long for home, this is a great place to stop. However, what keeps people coming back is the barbecue, both ribs and wings. The moist and delicious barbecue chicken is what you should order here, for a ridiculously cheap price. There are other places to get great ribs in Connecticut, but few do chicken so well. If you have lived your life on just dry white breast meat, try a whole barbecued chicken for less than $10 (!), and understand at last the appeal of a perfectly cooked bird.

OLYMPIA DINER $
3413 Berlin Tpke.
Newington, CT 06111
(860) 666-9948
olympiadiner.net

With its huge neon sign atop a classic metallic diner, the Olympia has been the Berlin Turnpike's great road-food destination for over 50 years. Where else can you get a ham steak with a side of mashed potatoes and gravy? This could just as easily be listed under breakfast and lunch, with grilled English muffins and hot, fluffy omelets. But the shiny metal everywhere! It must be road food. Unlike some diners, though, they serve beer and wine. Play the individual jukebox at your table, perhaps the classic Fats Domino tune "Blueberry Hill." And you're sure to find your thrill here at the Olympia Diner, right in the strip mall heart of Connecticut.

SAINT'S $

1248 Queen St.
Southington, CT 06489
(860) 747-0566
saintsct.com

Don't mess with success. Since 1967 this hot dog joint in Southington has produced some of the tastiest dogs in the state. More particularly, they specialize in chili dogs, and since they opened they have used the same mustard, relish, and chili sauce (a sweet but not meaty version). All three are excellent, so why change? It's really the chili sauce that has put Saint's on the map, though. What, you've never had a chili dog? Well, then perhaps you don't want to get one here, because every other version of these delicious creations will taste less impressive compared to Saint's. To drink, get one of their extra-thick milk shakes. This is a local hangout and a road-food destination, and under the red sign with its tilting halo you'll find everyone behaving, if not like saints, at least like friends.

SHADY GLEN DAIRY STORE $

840 Middle Tpke. East
Manchester, CT 06042
(860) 649-4245
No website

This 1948 family-run restaurant got its start as a dairy store for the owners' farm. Today it's a throwback to another time, complete with an old-fashioned soda fountain, retro outfits, and a mural of hungry elves chowing down on ice cream in a magical forest. Their cheeseburgers are famous; on top of the burger is a chunk of fried cheese. Once you try it, you'll wonder why every cheeseburger doesn't include this instead of the boring melted kind. You can also get it on the side. For dessert they have a rotating selection of two dozen ice-cream flavors, including mince and Grape-Nuts. This place is a Manchester institution, and waiting for a table is worth it. There is a second store

in the Manchester Shopping Parkade with the same wonderful burgers, if not the same authentic atmosphere.

Seafood

CITY FISH MARKET $$

884 Silas Deane Hwy.
Wethersfield, CT 06109
(860) 257-6465
cfishct.com

For over 80 years this market has been the place to come in the Hartford area for fresh fish. With over 100,000 cubic feet devoted to -10 degrees of frozen storage, 70,000 cubic feet of 34-degree cold storage, and a 5,000-gallon lobster pound, the City Fish Market services many of the county's restaurants. However, it is also a restaurant itself, with a stylish dining room (not a "lobster shack"). Enjoy a cold draft beer, a glass of wine, or a soda with fresh, beautifully cooked seafood. The fish-and-chips is the classic dish here, although the daily specials are probably what to go for. The lobster is their biggest seller to other restaurants, so you should probably get a hot Connecticut lobster roll. Unlike some evil restaurants (not featured in this guide) where the specials are what they want to get rid of, the specials here are what has just come in the door. Try them out.

✳MAX'S OYSTER BAR $$$

964 Farmington Ave.
West Hartford, CT 06107
(860) 236-6299
maxrestaurantgroup.com/oyster

This is another of Max's excellent restaurants, which they bill as a big-city fish house. However, we like to think of it as a Connecticut fish house, and one of the best in the state. Some people come just for the high-rise tower of scallops, mussels, and oysters on a skyscraper of ice. Get the local cherrystone and littleneck clams from Branford, or the Rosedale Farms sweet corn bisque from Simsbury, or the

Broad Brook Beef burger from East Windsor. They know how to prepare and present a fish to you too, so consider the market catch with their amazing citrus relish. In summer, sit on the sidewalk tables and watch the people come and go in the hip, hopping West Hartford Center. The presence of Max's Oyster Bar was one of the things that have made it such a popular destination.

DAY TRIP IN HARTFORD COUNTY

You're going to start in Hartford County off I-84 at a classic breakfast spot, the Quaker Diner (see entry). To get there, get off at exit 43 (or 42 coming east), which takes you up to the intersection with Park Road, where you'll take a right. After you have the french toast with poached egg, you can get back on the highway by heading west on Park and then taking a left onto the Trout Brook Connector to I-84 West. Take this to exit 39 toward Route 4/Farmington. You will merge onto Route 508, which becomes Farmington Avenue. Take a left on High Street and then your first left on Mountain Road. The entrance to the Hill-Stead Museum (see entry) will be directly on your left.

Enjoy your time here among beautiful Impressionist art in a stylish mansion. If you think you'll have time, stroll the grounds or sit in the sunken garden and read a poem out loud. Then get in your car and retrace your steps, taking a right on Mountain Road, then a right on High Street, and heading right again onto Farmington Avenue. However, you are not getting on the highway again; you will be staying on this road, so keep to the right, which will take you to a swinging exit for Route 4/Farmington Avenue.

This will take you into West Hartford Center. You'll know it when you see it, because the mostly residential area will suddenly become all restaurants. If you reach Main Street, you've gone too far. Parking is behind the restaurants, on either side of the road. You have a number of choices here, but for a casual lunch try the Elbow Room for its macaroni or Harry's Pizza for the best pizza in the county (see entries).

If you aren't hungry yet, you could go to your next destination, the Mark Twain House, first and then come back here. However, it's probably good to break up these two attractions, so why not walk around West Hartford Center and shop until you get hungry? When you're done, head east on Farmington Avenue (Route 4) again, and in about 2 miles you'll reach the sign for the Mark Twain House on your right. This attraction is right next to the Harriet Beecher Stowe House too, so you could make it a two-for-one (see entries). Both authors were hugely influential in American literature and history, and their houses are quite remarkable, set in this little area of town formerly known as Nook Farm.

When you're done, you can simply continue down Farmington Avenue to the east. This will eventually merge with Asylum Avenue as you head under I-84. Turn right onto Jewell Street (you can't go straight). The Hilton parking lot is on your left here. Park there or at one of the other garages on the couple of blocks heading left up Pearl Street, left again at Main, and left again to come back to Asylum.

From here until night, this is a walking tour. You should head across Bushnell Park, checking out the Soldiers and Sailors Arch, the Capitol Building, and more. If you'd like to see the Old State House and Ancient Burying Ground (see entry), head left (east) across the park and up 1 block to Main Street; they are a couple blocks on your left. However, if you've spent a lot of time at the Twain House, you might just want to have dinner. Walk up (south) on Trinity Street past the Capitol Building and turn right on Capitol Avenue. Take this 3 blocks to Broad Street and turn

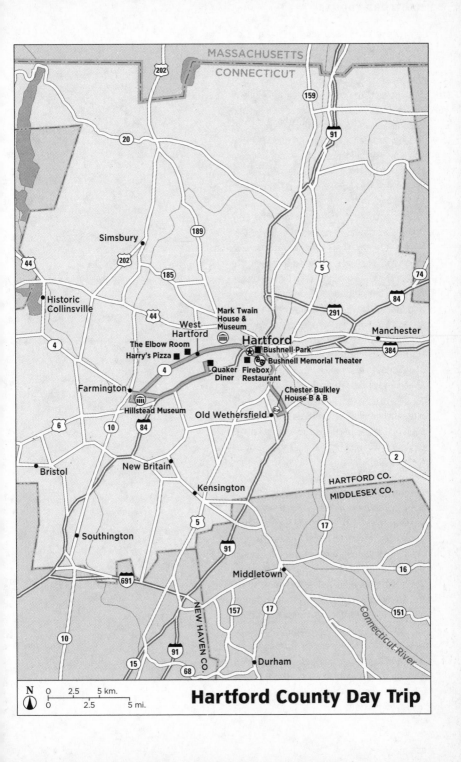

Hartford County Day Trip

left, where you'll see Firebox restaurant on your right (see entry).

Eat a fresh, organic, delicious meal here at this creative restaurant, and then retrace your steps toward the park on Capitol Avenue. If you've made reservations for a show at the Bushnell Theatre tonight (which you should!), it is on your left just past the park. Perhaps you'll be watching a play, the symphony, or a discussion hosted by the Connecticut Forum. When you're done, walk back up Trinity Street to your car.

If you'd like to stay overnight, the only options in central Hartford are chain hotels. However, if that suits you, you don't have to go far, since you parked right near the Hilton. There are five others in the few blocks north of the park, along Trumbull and Asylum Streets. However, if you're in the mood for something a little more historic, there is a bed-and-breakfast, the Chester Bulkley House (see entry), not far away, though it only has a few rooms, so be sure to call ahead and make reservations.

Get in your car and head south on Trinity Street, where you've just been walking. Take a left on Elm, which takes you around Pulaski Circle and straight onto the connector road to I-91 South. Take the highway south from here, along the river, past Wethersfield Cove, to exit 26 toward Old Wethersfield. Turn right onto Great Meadow Road and then immediately left on Marsh Street. This will curve around to the right; stay on it until you hit Main Street. Turn left and the Chester Bulkley House will be on your left, just past the Webb-Deane-Stevens Museum.

Enjoy your night in this historic house and get ready for the next morning, which you can start by walking around Wethersfield, the oldest (or perhaps second-oldest, next to Windsor) community in the state. Though you saw a lot, you only drove a mere 23 miles today, so you should have plenty of energy for tomorrow.

TOLLAND COUNTY

Tolland County takes great pride in being the home to Nathan Hale—American patriot, spy, and martyr of the Revolutionary War. In the sleepy town of Coventry you can find his homestead and memorial, engraved with those immortal words, "I only regret that I have but one life to lose for my country."

The county's social life revolves around Storrs, home of the former agricultural land grant college that became the University of Connecticut. UConn causes the county's population to jump by over 20,000 every September, and stay that way until May. Famous for their championship Huskies basketball teams and for being the top public university in New England, UConn is beloved by people throughout the state who haven't even gone there for school. Storrs itself is a classic college town, simply crawling with Husky fever.

North of I-84 is Stafford Springs, home to one of Connecticut's premier car-racing venues, Stafford Motor Speedway. Otherwise, the north half of the county is full of sleepy towns that are excellent places to find a little peace and quiet. Tolland itself has been rated one of the best towns in the country to live in.

Tolland may be the smallest Connecticut county, but it is full of both national and local pride. Visiting here will surely instill you with it too.

ATTRACTIONS

Historical Sites & Landmarks

BENTON HOMESTEAD AND OLD TOLLAND COUNTY JAIL
160 Metcalf Rd. and 52 Tolland Green
Tolland, CT 06084
(860) 870-9599
tollandhistorical.org

Run by the Tolland Historical Society, these two buildings are different windows into the history of what has been called one of the best places to live in America. The Cape-style Benton Homestead was built in 1720 and was occupied by descendants of Daniel Benton until 1932. Just to put that in perspective, Daniel's sons fought in the French and Indian War; his grandsons fought in the Revolution.

The jail is a low stone building built in 1856. It operated until 1968 and includes an attached 1893 jailer's home. The historical society also keeps its museum in the jail, including items depicting life in the 18th and 19th centuries that were donated by people in the town. You should also check out the third building owned by the society, the Tolland County Courthouse, built in 1822, across the green from the jail.

NATHAN HALE HOMESTEAD AND MEMORIAL
2299 South St.
Coventry, CT 06238
(860) 742-6917
ctlandmarks.org

Built in 1776, the Hale homestead is virtually intact, with family furniture and period antiques based on accurate inventories. Six of the eight sons of Richard Hale served in the Continental Army, and three paid the

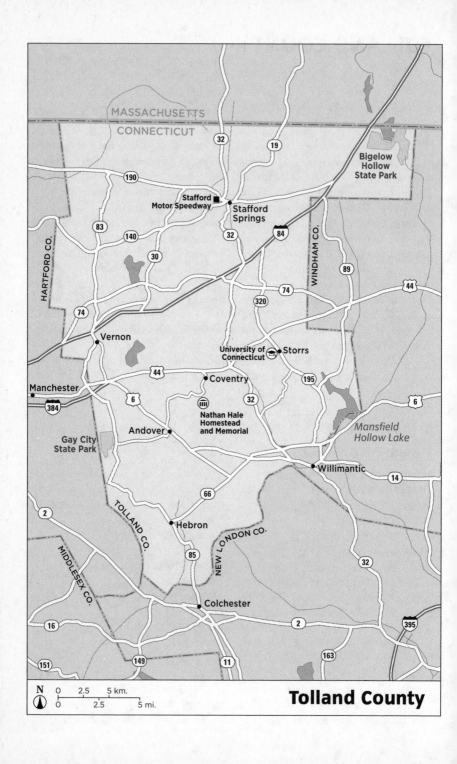

Tolland County

ultimate price. The most famous, Nathan, served as one of America's first spies and was hanged by the British, uttering the last words, "I only regret that I have but one life to lose for my country." Many family artifacts are on display, including Nathan's powder horn and hunting rifle. On the back of one door, you'll also see a drawing of Hale's head by his sister. There is a grove of maples in front of the house planted in 1812 called the Holy Grove. The trails behind the homestead leading into the state forest are the very trails young Nathan Hale walked centuries ago. The memorial at Nathan Hale Cemetery, on the shores of Wamgumbaug Lake at the center of town, is worth a stop as well. But Nathan Hale is not buried here. Thrown in a grave somewhere on the island of Manhattan by the British, he rests somewhere far beneath the concrete today.

Museums

BALLARD INSTITUTE AND MUSEUM OF PUPPETRY
6 Bourne Place
University of Connecticut
Storrs, CT 06269
(860) 486-0339
bimp.uconn.edu
This fascinating small museum at UConn was created in 1987 to house the puppets of professor Frank Ballard, and it has expanded since then. Today there are 2,500 puppets from around the world, as well as an impressive archive on the history of puppetry, the largest collection of its kind in the US. As well as putting on exhibitions at the museum and elsewhere, the Ballard Institute runs workshops in toy theater, mask making, and shadow puppetry. Both children and teachers love these instructional activities; if you like puppets, you will too. You can visit the museum itself on Fri through Sun from noon to 5 p.m.

CONNECTICUT STATE MUSEUM OF NATURAL HISTORY AND CONNECTICUT ARCHAEOLOGY CENTER
2019 Hillside Rd., Unit 1023
University of Connecticut
Storrs, CT 06269
(860) 486-4460
cac.uconn.edu
This partnership between the state and UConn is leading toward an even larger museum in the next decade. Begun as an exhibit of a small part of UConn's extensive natural history collections, the new Archaeology Center has added to that, and in the future a larger space will no doubt be needed. Right now the growing Archaeology Center has a permanent exhibit on humans and our environment, and there are also exhibits in the fields of geology, ethnobotany, and climatology here. The museum is the largest repository (meaning not everything is on display) of Connecticut Native American, colonial, and industrial artifacts, spanning 11,000 years of history. Located at the center of UConn's campus, the museum is open weekdays from 10 a.m. to 4 p.m.

WILLIAM BENTON MUSEUM OF ART
245 Glenbrook Rd., Unit 2140
University of Connecticut
Storrs, CT 06269
(860) 486-4520
thebenton.org
UConn has a 5,500-piece permanent art collection, some of which (it changes often) is displayed in the Benton Museum. Artists include Childe Hassam, Mary Cassatt, Thomas Hart Benton, George Bellows, Georges Braque, Gustav Klimt, and Kiki Smith. The Benton also features changing exhibitions, bringing in everything from Dr. Seuss to Japanese woodcuts of the 19th century. Closed on Monday, this excellent university museum is two and a half floors and has

recently been refurbished. The building itself is on the National Register of Historic Places, and there is a small cafe called the Beanery where you can grab a bite to eat. Don't miss the sculpture gardens outside.

Parks & Beaches

BIGELOW HOLLOW STATE PARK
Route 171
Union, CT 06076
(860) 684-3430
ct.gov/dep [search "Bigelow Hollow State Park"]
Right on the state line is a remarkable state park, with 3 large ponds and a series of interesting ridges. There are 17 miles of blue-blazed trails, as well as others (yellow and white) around the ponds and connecting the larger paths. If you want an easy walk with a great result, take the connector trail (more of a woods road) from the parking area at the north end of Bigelow Pond and head up to Breakneck Pond. This thin glacial valley with hills on both sides is like nothing else in Connecticut. You can launch your boat on Bigelow Pond or the much larger Mashapaug Pond in the northwest corner of the park. Beavers live here, and you can hear the slap of their tails in the ponds. You can fish in the ponds, inhabited by huge pike, an exciting struggle for any angler.

MANSFIELD HOLLOW STATE PARK
Bassett Bridge Road
Mansfield, CT 06259
(860) 928-6121
ct.gov/dep [search "Mansfield Hollow State Park"]
This 2,300-acre park surrounds the 550-acre reservoir created by the damming of the Natchaug River in 1952. You can find sports fields, picnic areas, fire pits, horseshoe pits, and more open daily year-round. No swimming is allowed, although powerboats are—at a slower speed than you might be used to, though. (There's a boat launch on Bassett Bridge Road near where it crosses the lake.) There is good bass fishing here, and you might also catch brown trout or large northern pike. As far as hiking, this is where the blue-blazed Nipmuck Trail begins its northward track toward the border. The yellow and red trails are multiuse, so you can bicycle them with impunity. The dam itself is certainly worth a look as well.

Wineries

CASSIDY HILL VINEYARD
454 Cassidy Hill Rd.
Coventry, CT 06238
(860) 498-1126
cassidyhillvineyard.com
The lovely town of Coventry in the Last Green Valley National Heritage Corridor provides the backdrop for Cassidy Hill Vineyard. The picturesque landscape spreads out over 150 acres, ample room to stroll and enjoy the vines, which are planted on only a tenth of that. The winery's logo was inspired by a lone maple called the Thinking Tree, located just a short walk from the log cabin tasting room. Balanced between whites and reds, the tasting menu includes an off-dry Riesling and Chardonnay, both on its own and blended with Viognier for a wine called Winding Brook. Coventry Spice blends Merlot and estate-grown St. Croix. And as they expand I hope they'll add even more AVA and Connecticut label wines. The tasting room is open 11 a.m. to 8 p.m. on Fri and 11 a.m. to 5 p.m. Sat and Sun. Use your GPS, because Cassidy Hill is not easy to find.

ACTIVITIES & EVENTS

Adventure Sports

✳**THE ADVENTURE PARK AT STORRS**
2007 Storrs Rd.
Storrs, Connecticut 06268
(860) 946-0606
storrsadventurepark.com

What? You've never been in an "aerial forest"? Well, these new zip-line, rope, tree-platform, aerial bridge adventures are the latest in family fun. At Storrs the Adventure Park has 5 different trails to try, all at different levels of difficulty, for a total of 60 different challenges throughout the park. You wear a harness and two clips attached onto different ropes and cables and never feel like you're going to fall (unless you have really bad acrophobia). Of course kids 7 and up love it, but this is actually a great place to come on a date. Open Apr to Nov, Frid through Sun, and during the week for groups.

Arts Venues

JORGENSEN CENTER FOR THE PERFORMING ARTS
2132 Hillside Rd., Unit 3104
University of Connecticut
Storrs, CT 06269
(860) 486-4226
jorgensen.uconn.edu

Since 1955 the Jorgensen Center has been the largest college-based presenting program in New England. With 2,630 seats and 25 to 30 different performances annually, this is an impressive venue. They host musicals, comedies, dance, opera, and plays, with appearances by professional touring acting companies, symphonies, and soloists. There is pop music, jazz, classical, country, world music, and electronica. Musicians from Itzhak Perlman to Duke Ellington have played here in the past, along with groups like the Royal Shakespeare Company and the Moscow Ballet. Jorgensen also houses the Jorgensen Gallery and Harriet S. Jorgensen Theatre, which is the home of the Connecticut Repertory Theater. More than 70,000 people watch events at this center every year. Will you be one of them?

✴MANSFIELD DRIVE-IN THEATRE
228 Stafford Rd.
Mansfield, CT 06250
(860) 423-4441
mansfielddrivein.com

One of two drive-ins remaining in the state (the other is in Litchfield County), the Mansfield offers double features, with the first usually a family film and the second perhaps a comedy or action-adventure. These are first-run movies, out at the same time as "normal" theaters, so you can see the latest gems from Hollywood. Unlike most other drive-ins, though, this one has 3 big screens to watch films on. There's a full-service snack bar, much better than most indoor movie theater options—an excellent idea, since you're sitting through 2 late films. On Sunday from Mar to Nov a flea market runs here, the largest one in eastern Connecticut, with 200 or more dealers selling hundreds of thousands of items.

Festivals & Annual Events

ANNUAL ICE FISHING DERBY DAY
Coventry Lake
5 Crystal St.
Ellington, CT 06029
(860) 424-FISH
ct.gov/dep/fishing

If you've never tried ice fishing, the annual derby on Coventry Lake (also called Lake Wangumbaug) is the perfect place to learn. The Department of Energy & Environmental Protection provides gear and bait for a modest entry fee, and has made sure the lake is well stocked in advance. This is great family fun on a winter's day in February every year. Go to the Rockville Fish & Game Crystal Lake Club House, located at the south end of Crystal Lake in Ellington, and arrive as early as 5:30 a.m. Dress warmly (especially gloves and waterproof boots) and pack a lunch, although they do provide a warm-up lodge with coffee, hot chocolate, and donuts. There are prizes of up to $500 for kids 15 and under.

HEBRON MAPLE FESTIVAL
Main Street
Hebron, CT 06248
hebronmaplefest.com

This festival takes place throughout the town of Hebron on the second weekend in March every year, from 10 a.m. to 4 p.m. both days. All the local sugarhouses give tours, but that is only the tip of the maple leaf. There is a craft fair, blacksmiths, candle making, woodworking, face painting, an antique tractor parade, an ice-cream eating contest, pancake breakfasts, and more. You can eat icy maple milk, hot dogs, homemade soup, glazed donuts, kettle corn, fried dough, and maple pudding cake. There is nothing else going on this time of year, so why not head out to Hebron and enjoy the end of the maple sugaring season in style.

PODUNK BLUEGRASS MUSIC FESTIVAL
Hebron Lions Fairgrounds
347 Gilead St. (Route 85)
Hebron, CT 06248
podunkbluegrass.com

This annual music festival brings the best of bluegrass to Connecticut every summer. Along with enjoying a lineup of the top bluegrass musicians in America, you can attend free workshops, make traditional crafts, listen to storytelling, and eat a variety of food for breakfast, lunch, and dinner. They also offer children's entertainment and a children's activity area. Bring your instrument—some say the best parts of this festival are the pickup jam sessions in the fields. You can also bring umbrellas and even tents, but you'll have to set up in the back of the concert area. One warning: If you let your kids or dog run wild, you will be asked to leave.

Fishing

WILLIMANTIC RIVER
Route 32
Stafford/Willington/Mansfield, CT
willimanticriver.org

This is the most ignored of the great trout streams in Connecticut, and if you're willing and able to put in a little work, it will be the most rewarding. The Trout Management Area in West Willington does get a lot of action, but upstream from that all the way to Stafford Springs, this river has fine water and great, fat trout. That section is easily accessed from the side of Route 32. However, if you go south from West Willington toward Mansfield Depot, you'll find even more-ignored water. The only explanation for this is that small amounts of walking are needed to access good areas (which may change with the proposed Willimantic Greenway). Some people drive across a bridge, peer at overhanging banks and deep-looking water, and give up. Don't make that mistake; there are great, easy-flowing areas to fish here.

Hiking, Biking & Walking

HOP RIVER STATE PARK TRAIL
DEP Eastern District Headquarters
Bolton, CT 06043
(860) 295-9523
ct.gov/dot [search "Hop River State Park Trail"]

The Hop River State Park Trail that begins on Colonial Drive in Manchester and ends in Windham is one of Connecticut's many rail trails, and part of the proposed East Coast Greenway. It is over 20 miles long and runs along a former railroad line to just west of the town of Willimantic (Windham County), where it will eventually be linked to the Air Line Trail (if you're riding the whole way today, you can just take the road east and you'll hit the Air Line in downtown Willimantic). The other side will eventually connect to the Charter Oak Greenway in Manchester and Hartford. A spur trail heads off into Vernon. The trail is mostly gravel and dirt, with two short detours around downed bridges. All in all, it makes for an exciting day out on your mountain bike (avoid trying a street bike on it) or for a very long walk (you can just take small sections at a time). In winter, you will love to cross-country ski here. At any time of year, you might come across someone riding a horse, especially in the eastern section. I biked over Bolton Notch on the Hop River Trail recently. With over 300 feet of elevation gain each way, it made for a fascinating, and calorie-burning, experience.

GAY CITY STATE PARK
Route 85
Hebron, CT 06447
(860) 295-9523
ct.gov/dep [search "Gay City State Park"]
This is one of the ghost towns of Connecticut, also known as Factory Hollow, and is filled with stone foundations covered in grapevines and creepers. It was settled in 1796 by a religious sect and named for the second leader, John Gay. They built a town of 25 families, a sawmill, 2 gristmills, and a woolen mill. The ruin of one of those mills is along the Blackledge River, straight up the main path from the parking lot. On the way you'll pass an old cemetery filled with some of the abandoned village's residents. Any of the several loop trails you can make in Gay City are easy and pleasant walking, but bring bug spray during the summer months. There is swimming available at a large pond, and in winter this is the perfect place to cross-country ski, with the stone walls blanketed gently with snow.

NIPMUCK TRAIL
Route 171
Union, CT 06076
(860) 684-3430
ctwoodlands.org

This fairly remote trail connects Mansfield Hollow to Bigelow Hollow, running south to north in Tolland County. There is also another southern branch that starts at Puddin' Lane, 0.5 mile west of Route 195. The main Nipmuck is mostly along the Fenton River, under canopies of lofty pines, with the most interesting section near Gurleyville. Many people have seen flying squirrels here. Almost 2 miles south of Gurleyville Road you'll find the ruin of the Old Gurleyville Gristmill, built in the 1700s and one of only three in New England. It's open on Sunday in summer from 1 to 5 p.m. In the Yale Forest section, the trail crosses the dirt Boston Hollow Road in a fascinating narrow notch (worth biking along for sure). The section of the Nipmuck between Iron Mine Lane and Eastford Road, close to where it connects to the Natchaug Trail, is part of the original Great Trail that connected Boston and Hartford, the route Thomas Hooker used when he founded the Connecticut Colony in 1636.

Horseback Riding

SHALLOWBROOK EQUESTRIAN CENTER
247 Hall Hill Rd.
Somers, CT 06071
(860) 749-0749
shallowbrook.com
This 50-acre farm is the largest family-owned horse complex in America, and one of its top riding schools. Shallowbrook has a hunt course, indoor and outdoor rings, an outdoor polo course, and the largest indoor polo arena in the country. They offer riding lessons for all levels and ages during all seasons of the year, and their special birthday party events are hugely popular. Check their events, because rodeo, carriage shows, and more happen here, and Shallowbrook becomes not just a place for you to be active but also a venue for spectator sports like polo and championship horse shows.

Spectator Sports

STAFFORD MOTOR SPEEDWAY
55 West St.
Stafford Springs, CT 06076
(860) 684-2783
staffordspeedway.com

When you find that Stafford Motor Speedway has been in existence since 1870, you might scratch your head and think, Have there been cars for that long? But it began as a cutting-edge agricultural park, with people from Hartford taking trolleys right to the gate to watch horse racing. Until the end of World War II, Stafford Springs hosted these nonmechanized races, and then adapted to a new age with motor racing. Today, under a new lighting and sound system, you can watch the newly resurfaced 0.5-mile speedway heat up under the tires of cars. The speedway hosts NASCAR's Whelen All-American Series, Whelen Modified Tour, a Modified Racing Series, ISMA Supermodifieds, NEMA Midgets, and other events like monster truck rallies. Do you feel the need for power and speed? Scratch your itch in Tolland County at Stafford Motor Speedway.

UNIVERSITY OF CONNECTICUT BASKETBALL AT GAMPEL PAVILION
Stadium Road
Storrs, CT 06269
(860) 486-4712
uconnhuskies.com

Sure, Connecticut doesn't have an NBA team, but some say that watching the UConn Husky men's and women's basketball teams is even better. Plus, both are contenders for the national championship practically every year, and the huge domed Harry A. Gampel Pavilion is a hub of activity at the Storrs campus. It's the largest on-campus basketball arena in the Northeast, with over 10,000 seats, which usually sell out to capacity. The teams also use the XL center in

Hartford for "home" games and playoffs as well. Why? Those extra 6,000 seats fill up pretty quick too. So get yours early, and cheer these national champion teams on to victory. UConn has a number of other fine teams, and you should check out the soccer teams at the Joseph J. Morrone Stadium (rated one of the best fields in the nation), the swimming and diving teams at the 39,000-square-foot natatorium, the field hockey and track-and-field teams at the George J. Sherman Family-Sports Complex, and men's and women's ice hockey at the Mark Edward Freitas Ice Forum.

SHOPPING

Antiques

MEMORY LANES COUNTRY-SIDE ANTIQUES
2224 Boston Tpke.
Coventry, CT 06238
(860) 742-0346
No website

These 3 buildings (2 barns and a house) at the junction of Routes 44 and 31 contain a total of 50 dealers, who sell every kind of antique you could possibly want. Lamp shades, garden furniture, sculpture, textiles, pottery, silver, Depression glass, and more await you at this charming multidealer shop. Search the shelves for bargains, because you're not along the shore or in the Litchfield Hills, where the more expensive antiques are found. You'll be coming this way anyway to go to the Nathan Hale homestead, so why not take home a little piece of history too? Open 10 a.m. to 5 p.m. Wed through Sun.

TOLLAND ANTIQUES SHOW
Tolland Historical Society
52 Tolland Green
Tolland, CT 06084
(860) 870-9599
tollandhistorical.org

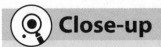

Close-up

UConn Basketball

While Connecticut sports fans might be torn between teams from nearby states, there's one game that most everyone in the state can support wholeheartedly: UConn basketball. The University of Connecticut men's and women's teams have consistently proven themselves as NCAA Division I teams, and with 13 national championships between them since 1995, their prestige ranges far past the state's borders. Twice the men's and women's teams have shared the national championship in the same year, an unprecedented feat in Division I basketball.

With their 2014 win over Kentucky in the NCAA finals, the UConn men won their fourth national championship, spurred on by the play of Shabazz Napier and guided by novice coach Kevin Ollie. Coming after a season-long suspension for academic violations, the retirement of Jim Calhoun, the departure of top players, and the breakup of the Big East, the team's victory reestablished the men's team as a top college contender and put to rest talks about the team's commitment and the new coach's abilities. But for fans, it was no real surprise. When Calhoun arrived on the scene in 1986, the team began to earn regional prestige and success in the National Invitational Tournament (NIT). Big East Tournament wins and showings in the NCAA tournament culminated in their first championship in 1999, when "Rip" Hamilton brought victory to the 7-point underdog Huskies against Duke. With Ben Gordon and Emeka Okafor, the team again won national honors in 2004, sharing the top spot for the first time with the women. A third victory came in 2011, when Kemba Walker earned MVP in the finals against Butler. In 2014 the men again shared the spotlight with the women's team. Thirty-five UConn Huskies men have gone on to play in the NBA. This consistency and status ensures fan support not only among college students and alumni; UConn is truly the whole state's team, and pride is widespread.

But it is really the women who put UConn on the map in terms of college basketball and sports history. Under the coaching of Geno Auriemma, the women have won 9 NCAA National Championships, held the Conference title 30 times, and have been to the Final Four 15 times. Moreover, 4 of those championships came at the end of undefeated seasons. The 1995 team, featuring Rebecca Lobo and Jennifer Rizzotti (who now coaches the University of Hartford), ushered in the era of UConn basketball. The 2000 team beat rivals Tennessee for a second championship. The three titles of 2002, 2003, and 2004 were won during the reign of Diana Taurasi. Back-to-back wins again came in 2009 and 2010 and again in 2013 and 2014. In the middle of all of this, the team posted not one but two 70-plus-game winning streaks, the second streak billowing to 90 games—the longest in NCAA history—before a December 2010 loss to Stanford. *Sports Illustrated* put the UConn women at the number 3 spot on their list of to 25 sports franchises of the decade (2000–09). Names like Lobo, Rizzotti, Taurasi, not to mention Maya Moore and Kaleena Mosqueda-Lewis, might be relatively unknown outside the world of college sports, but these names have celebrity status across the state. It might not be an exaggeration to say that the success of UConn women's basketball led to the formation of the WNBA. The state's professional team, the Connecticut Sun, moved to the state in 2003 and play their games at Mohegan Sun Arena.

Many historical societies in the state pair with antiques dealers to support their mutual interest in history. Tolland runs one of the best of these. For close to 50 years, the Tolland Historical Society has run this antiques show in the snowbound winter of north-central Connecticut. Dealers come from all over New England and the Atlantic coast to participate. The pieces you'll find are mostly 18th- and 19th-century American furniture, tools, textiles, decorations, iron, pottery, and folk art. It is run at one of the venues in town, usually the Middle School, and in the past over 65 exhibitors have come to show and sell their wares.

Bookstores

UCONN CO-OP
2075 Hillside Rd., Unit 1019
Storrs, CT 06269
(860) 486-3537
bookstore.uconn.edu
Although this is technically a separate, not-for-profit business unaffiliated with the school, the UConn Co-op serves as the official bookstore. It is "owned" by 30,000 members, and the board of directors has a majority of students on it. Here you can find textbooks and course materials of course but, more importantly, a selection of literature, computers, software, art and engineering supplies, cards, gifts, health and beauty products, and Husky apparel and memorabilia. There is a cafe located inside with a view of the Gampel Pavilion, where you can get breakfast or lunch, including desserts from the UConn bakery. The co-op also operates the much smaller stores at the satellite campuses throughout Connecticut. This is one of the largest and most lauded college bookstores in the nation; stop in and you'll see why.

Farmers' Markets

*COVENTRY REGIONAL FARMERS' MARKET
Nathan Hale Homestead
2299 South St.
Coventry, CT 06238
(860) 742-1419
coventryfarmersmarket.com
Coventry boasts the largest farmers' market in the state from June to Oct every Sunday from 11 a.m. to 2 p.m. The setting at the Nathan Hale Homestead is a gorgeous and historic backdrop for what is really more a small fair than a farmers' market, with horse and wagon rides, demonstrations, sheep shearing—you never know! Fiddlers are there every weekend providing music, and dozens of vendors show up selling everything from traditional jams and preserves to smoked bacon to chocolate fudge. You'll also find local artists and artisans selling handmade wares, from soap to candles to beadwork. And if you're in the mood for a market from Dec to Mar, Coventry runs one of those too, at the same time of week and day but at Coventry High School (78 Ripley Hill Rd.), with about 30 farmers and vendors taking part. After all, we don't stop eating in winter.

Home & Crafts

BAKERS COUNTRY FURNITURE
42 W. Main St. (Route 190)
Stafford Springs, CT 06076
(860) 684-2256
bakersfurniture.com
This is one of the oldest furniture stores in the nation, founded in 1808 and now occupying a Victorian home in Stafford Springs, less than a mile from the original store. Sixteen thousand square feet of furniture and accessories awaits you, set up in beautiful rooms. Bakers brings in quality merchandise from high-level craftspeople, but they also

happen to be a manufacturer of top-of-the-line reproductions of 18th-century American furniture, dedicated to handcrafted work of skilled artisans. But you can also find other things here for your home, from candles to linens. There is a full curtain shop and a bargain basement, where you can always find a deal.

KLOTER FARMS
216 West Rd.
Ellington, CT 06029
(860) 871-1048
kloterfarms.com

When Kloter Farms burned down, I thought I would have to cut it from the second edition of this guide. But amazingly they rebuilt and are going strong again. At the corner of Routes 83 and 286, this unique shop builds and sells sheds, gazebos, and a variety of other storage buildings, as well as various items for the interior of your home. They are family owned and operated, created in 1980 by the Kloter family, and have a printed catalog that includes all the product specifications (yes, some businesses still do that). They will custom build a building suited to your needs, or you can (and should) come browse their stock. Kloter Farms also has a huge selection of handcrafted wood furniture, from benches to sideboards to blanket chests—all beautiful examples of skilled work. Find a reclaimed kitchen table or a carved jewelry box to make part of your home.

Specialty Foods

*MUNSON'S CHOCOLATES
174 Hop River Rd. (Route 6)
Bolton, CT 06043
(860) 649-4332
munsonschocolates.com

Begun in 1946 in Manchester as the Dandy Candy Company, Munson's is now a huge business, with chocolates spinning around the earth on the international space station. By far the largest retail chocolate manufacturer in Connecticut, it is still a family business run by the second and third generations. They have 10 stores throughout the state, with the original here in Bolton. You will find chocolate truffles, nut bark, and cordial cherries here, as well as more snackable candy bars, fudge, peanut brittle, chocolate-covered pretzels, and turtles. The store is open every day; if you want great Connecticut-made chocolate, get it here.

ACCOMMODATIONS

All lodgings have both smoking and non-smoking rooms unless otherwise noted, or have a designated smoking area, and do not accept pets unless noted. Hotels, motels, and resorts are wheelchair accessible unless otherwise noted. Bed-and-breakfasts and inns are not wheelchair accessible unless otherwise noted, since many are in historic buildings exempt from the Americans with Disabilities Act. Call to make sure if there's any question. We do not list specific credit cards in either this section or the restaurants section.

Bed-and-Breakfasts

DANIEL RUST HOUSE $$–$$$
2011 Main St.
Coventry, CT 06238
(860) 742-0032
thedanielrusthouse.com

The Daniel Rust House was built in 1731, and from 1800 to 1832 it served as a tavern. Today it serves much the same purpose, a rest for weary travelers. There are 4 rooms available, all with private baths. One has a Jacuzzi and working fireplace; another has a working fireplace and a secret closet thought to have been part of the Underground Railroad. The Maybell Cottage has a full kitchen and is great for a longer stay. Note that they cannot accommodate children under 13, but dogs are allowed for a small fee (see the website for full policy). Relax by the historic fireplace and read a book on a cold winter's night, or stroll the landscape of fruit trees and gardens during the summer. If you're at the Connecticut Historical Society Museum in Hartford, look for the original sign of this ancient tavern (when it was called the Bird in Hand).

AN INN KEEPER'S PLACE $$–$$$
111 Stafford St.
Stafford, CT 06075
(860) 458-9047
innkeepersplace.com

This 18th-century house, part 1732 saltbox and part 1778 Federal brick style, is a great place to spend a night. Once it was a tavern and meetinghouse, and you can see the history in the wide plank floors, hand-carved molding, and barreled ceilings. There are 2 guest rooms and a larger suite to stay in. Next door is a 200-acre wildlife refuge that you can walk into from the backyard. In the morning, Angelina Fleury will make you a hearty country breakfast with gourmet butters and breads, cinnamon french toast, eggs Benedict, or Finnish pancakes. In winter expect hot mulled cider and gourmet cocoa to relax with in the evening or to get you ready for a day exploring northeastern Connecticut.

TOLLAND INN $$–$$$$
63 Tolland Green
Tolland, CT 06084
(860) 872-0800
tollandinn.com

Right on Tolland Green, this was an inn called the Steele House in the early 20th century and now has returned after renovation and updates. Relax in front of the huge fireplace, read one of the hundreds of books, or stroll the flowering gardens. They have 7 rooms with private baths, 1 with a fireplace and

hot tub, and 3 suites, 2 of which include a hot tub and fireplace. Susan and Steven Beeching will make you feel like part of their home, and you'll soon be part of the charming community of Tolland too. Perhaps you'll even decide to stay.

Inns

NATHAN HALE INN $$$$
855 Bolton Rd.
Storrs, CT 06268
(860) 427-7888
nathanhaleinn.com

For UConn games, graduations, and parents' weekends, the Nathan Hale Inn and Conference Center on the UConn campus is packed. But its incredible facilities are available pretty much all the other nights of the year, so why not take advantage of this great hotel and restaurant to explore eastern Connecticut? There are 100 guest rooms and 18 suites, along with access to a fitness room, passes to UConn athletic facilities, and an indoor heated pool and spa. There are 2 restaurants on-site, including the Blue Oak Cafe (see entry), and you are within walking distance of all the attractions in Storrs. This is a perfect base for exploring Hartford or Windham County, as well as south into New London and Middlesex Counties.

Camping

WILDERNESS LAKE CAMPGROUND
& RESORT $
150 Village Hill
Willington, CT 06279
(860) 684-6352
wilderness-lake.com

This family campground set on Wilderness Lake in Willington has everything you want, from picnic tables and fire rings to a full-service general store. And the bathrooms! Heated, flush toilets, warm showers . . . it's almost like you're not camping at all. The

RV and camper sites are located around the game room and dining hall area; the tent sites are at the north end of the lake, nicely secluded in a forest. Sites 1, 2, and 3 are all the way on the other side of the lake, and hiking trails leave the campground directly from them. If you like peace and quiet, that's the place to reserve. On the other hand, if you want all the joys of family camping, then stay on the west side. There is swimming in the lake, volleyball, and a playground, and there's even a 9-hole miniature golf course. How's that for roughing it?

RESTAURANTS

Please note that all Connecticut restaurants are smoke free, and all are required to be wheelchair accessible. Pets are not allowed inside most restaurants, but during the warmer months, there are plenty of restaurants with patio areas just right for your canine friend. Call ahead to make sure it's okay.

American & Modern

✳ALTNAVEIGH INN **$$$$**
957 Storrs Rd. (Route 195)
Storrs, CT 06268
(860) 429-4490
altnaveighinn.com
This 1734 clapboard house in Storrs was named Altnaveigh, Gaelic for "hilltop," in 1951. It has been an inn and restaurant for decades, and the new owners have set about restoring it. Inside you will find 3 dining rooms full of hungry UConn students and their indulgent parents. They serve mostly classic American dinner fare, with small deviations like the *foie gras* and wild mushroom tart appetizers. In summer, dine on the patio. And if you eat too much, you can stay overnight in one of the two recently renovated rooms upstairs, which are air-conditioned and have private baths.

Considering the price of dinner downstairs, the rooms are a bargain ($–$$).

THE BLUE OAK CAFE **$$$**
Nathan Hale Inn
855 Bolton Rd.
Storrs, CT 06268
(860) 427-7888
nathanhaleinn.com/dining-en.html
The Blue Oak Cafe at the Nathan Hale Inn and Conference Center serves up classic New England cuisine. The tavern steak and the lobster and shrimp ravioli are highlights, and the Big Blue burger is a delicious patty topped with Gorgonzola and bacon. When staying at the inn, this is a fine end to the day—or a start to the next (they serve a hearty breakfast). If the white tablecloths of the Blue Oak intimidate you, next door is the True Blue Tavern ($$), the inn's more casual option, decorated in the spirit of UConn athletics. They serve burgers, nachos, and a few entrees, as well as a selection of beers to celebrate the game. For either of these places, you should make a reservation if you're going to be there on the night of a game or other big UConn event.

Asian & Indian

UTSAV INDIAN CUISINE **$–$$**
575 Talcottville Rd.
Vernon Rockville, CT 06066
(860) 871-8714
This small Indian restaurant in Vernon consistently gets great reviews for both its inexpensive, tasty food and its friendly service and tasteful, colorful decor. They seem to pile on the food as soon as you come through the door, with papadums and chutneys, and the meals are varied and delicious. Classics like tikka masala and less frequently seen dishes like prawn balchao are all done with attention to detail and given a cleaner presentation than some other restaurants give. The

fish curry is juicy and perfectly spiced, and the mulligatawny, well, it's divine. The lunch buffet during the week is less than $10 and on the weekends is only $5 more. This is an unbelievable bargain for food of this quality. And if you go five times, your sixth is free. Utsav doesn't need that kind of promotional gimmick, but it's just one of many things they do to make fans out of everyone in the area. *Utsav* means "festival" in Sanskrit, and you will feel like celebrating every time you go to this hidden gem.

Breakfast & Lunch

MIDDLE GROUND CAFÉ $
42 Main St.
Stafford Springs, CT 06076
(860) 851-8900
middlegroundcafe.com
Located in a refurbished factory building with other shops in the center of town, the Middle Ground serves breakfast and lunch, with a variety of breakfast sandwiches, paninis, and salads. They also feature daily specials including soup and specialize in many different flavored teas (both hot and cold). Of course they have coffees and lattes, bagels and scones, muffins and cookies. The area to eat in is small but has local art displayed and for sale. There is wireless Internet and reading materials for your enjoyment. The Middle Ground focuses on organic and local foods and has fun events like open-mike nights. Hopefully they are bringing some life to this often-ignored area of Connecticut.

REIN'S DELI $$
435 Hartford Tpke.
Vernon, CT 06066
(860) 875-1344
reinsdeli.com
Bringing the flavors of one place to another is always a chancy business, but some have done it so well that they compete with or surpass the original. In 1972 Bob Rein wanted to bring authentic New York Jewish deli food to New England, and everyone agrees he has succeeded. Using the best corned beef and pastrami, they re-created the classic sandwiches of New York and then branched out, making unbelievable dishes of franks and beans, sour cream and bananas, and breakfasts that bring people out from Hartford and Storrs every day to eat. The Reubens and Rachaels are stuffed and dripping with flavor. The lox is amazing, the tongue and eggs is amazing, and the sheet cakes are better than Mom's. Though steeped in tradition, Rein's is also experimental, with interesting dishes like the mac and cheese island surrounded by chili, or the piña colada bread pudding. It is called a deli, but it is more of a restaurant with a take-out option. If you're on I-84 and you're hungry, don't stop at McDonalds. Go to Rein's.

SOMETHING SIMPLE CAFÉ $
12 Main St.
Hebron, CT 06248
(860) 228-2266
somethingsimplecafe.com
The first thing you will notice is the building that Something Simple is located in—built in 1750 and transformed into a store sometime between 1816 and 1829. Inside, it is full of local pottery, paintings, and jewelry. The menu is painted on the wall, and you'll find something for every taste, with breakfast specials like french toast, bagels, and sandwiches piled with scrambled eggs. For lunch, there are crispy paninis filled with Boar's Head products. The coffee is amazing, with flavors like honey lavender latte, and they use local dairy and eggs for all their dishes. They are open Mon through Thurs 7 a.m. to 6p.m., Sat 8 a.m. to 6 p.m., and Sun 8 a.m. to 3 p.m. Let me say it again: some of the best coffee in the state.

TRAVELER RESTAURANT $
1257 Buckley Hwy.
Union, CT 06706
(860) 684-4920
No website

Ever want a free book with your meal? If so, the Traveler Restaurant on the border of Massachusetts is your dream store. Started in 1970 by Marty Doyle, a voracious reader himself who loved to give his guests books, this restaurant with a simple pine-walled dining room and porch is unique. Doyle's habit of giving each guest a book snowballed, and new owners kept it going. Check out the walls, where letters from authors hang, lauding the experiment. You can choose three books from the upstairs bookshelves free with your meal, and buy more downstairs in a surprisingly well-stocked used bookstore. The food? Oh, yes. Try the turkey; it's their specialty, unless you count the books.

Ice Cream

FISH FAMILY FARM $
20 Dimock Ln.
Bolton, CT 06043
(860) 646-9745
fishfamilyfarm.com

This 211-acre dairy farm in Bolton has its own bottling plant for milk, which you can buy in their store at the farm. Munson's also uses their milk for its wonderful chocolate (see entry). However, you are probably more interested in the ice cream here, sold year-round by the quart in their freezer: vanilla, maple walnut, coffee, peanut butter, cherry vanilla, chocolate chip, and more. During the summertime you can get this ice cream on a cone, from 8 a.m. to 8 p.m. every day but Sunday, which is why this farm made it from specialty food into the restaurant section of the guide. This is some of the absolute freshest ice cream you'll find, made from Jersey milk that you can watch being pumped out every day at 3:30 p.m.

UCONN DAIRY BAR $
3636 Horsebarn Hill Rd. Ext.
Storrs, CT 06269
(860) 486-2634
dairybar.uconn.edu

The UConn Dairy Bar has been in business since 1954, and its ice cream is made from the ground up, with 24 flavors at any one time, all mixed by the students. The ice cream has 14 percent butterfat, which is probably why it is so popular. The most popular flavor (perhaps due to sentimentality rather than taste) is Jonathan Supreme, named for the school's mascot, Jonathan the Husky Dog. It contains vanilla ice cream swirled with peanut butter and chocolate-covered peanuts. Other flavors include Husky Tracks, Cake Batter, and Chocolate Chip Cookie Dough. The store itself is without frills, like a classroom with stools and napkins, but it brings in 200,000 customers a year. Unlike some ice-cream shops, this one is open year-round.

Mediterranean & Middle Eastern

SARA'S POCKETS $
125 N. Eagleville Rd.
Storrs, CT 06268
(860) 429-2900
saraspockets.com

For vegetarians attending UConn, this is a welcome haven, offering a large number of options that are no doubt a welcome change from "salad" or whatever they are usually offered. However, meat eaters can also get nice kebabs, and a hamburger pizza that is absolutely delicious. The mix of Mediterranean and Middle Eastern food is classic, with spinach pies, falafel, tabouleh, grape leaves, and baba ghanouj. This is not a fancy restaurant, but rather a solid lunch or casual dinner place, popular with students and locals alike. The Lebanese owners, Sara and Samir Saad, focus on authentic ingredients and making fresh food each day. But what makes them famous in town is their friendly, accommodating attitude and welcoming nature.

Pizza

RANDY'S WOOSTER STREET PIZZA $$
1232 Storrs Rd.
Storrs, CT 06268
(860) 487-9662
woosterstpizza.com

It takes a lot of guts to name your pizza restaurant for the holy land of Wooster Street, home to both Sally's and Frank Pepe's nationally famous pizzas, especially if you're located nowhere near New Haven. But Randy has done it, and done it well, creating a popular restaurant that caters to college kids looking for a second childhood, and those who are old enough to bring their own beer. That is also an indication that this is a BYOB restaurant, although their root beer is excellent. There's another location at 1000 Tolland Tpke. in Manchester (860-649-1166), in case you're in that area. They are both great places to take a family, with a Hot Wheels–themed, kid-friendly atmosphere. Is the pizza as good as the ones on the actual Wooster Street? You decide.

WILLINGTON PIZZA $$
25 River Rd. (Route 32)
Willington, CT 06279
(860) 429-7433
willingtonpizza.com

If you're headed up to UConn or Stafford Springs for a sporting event, someone will suggest a stop at Willington Pizza. It is inevitable, and it is a good idea. The red potato pizza is their most famous creation, although their taco and cheeseburger pizzas are also classics. They also have hot oven grinders, sandwiches, Italian dishes, and a variety of cheese-dripping appetizers. There's a good selection of beers, including local Ten Penny Ale, and the milk shakes are excellent. This place is a huge favorite among UConn

students and families, as well as Stafford Motor Speedway drivers and crews, but also brings in pizza lovers from across the nation.

Pubs & Taverns

BIDWELL TAVERN $$
1260 Main St.
Coventry, CT 06238
(860) 742-6978
No website

There aren't many 1822 taverns famous for chicken wings, but that's the Bidwell. Housed in a former water mill, the building and the decor are a fascinating mix of family restaurant and ancient tavern, comfortable and not intimidating. The wings come in about 30 different flavors, from Green Mountain to Mustard Horseradish to Mexican. These sauced and dry-rubbed (yes, both) fried wings are a little crunchier than some others you may have had, but they remain juicy and tender inside. If you come with a group, get the tavern-size platter of 24 wings in 3 different flavors. Of course you can get other things to eat, like Yankee pot roast and a blackened burger, but don't miss the wings. Wash them down with one of the locally made Hosmer Mountain sodas or a microbrew.

Seafood

ELMO'S DOCKSIDE RESTAURANT AND PUB $$
48 Hartford Tpke.
Vernon, CT 06066
(860) 646-3474
elmosdockside.com

Real seaside dining away from the seashore? That's what Elmo's Dockside promises, and that's what you'll get, with all the seafood platters you love in a family-friendly restaurant in operation for over 40 years. They pay attention to the clams on the half shell and raw oysters, and you can expect them to always be fresh. The lobster bisque is full of lobster chunks, a welcome change from watery lobster-flavored salt broths. The fried oysters, that Connecticut classic, are done perfectly. The pub is open straight through the day, so if you get hungry at a strange hour, Elmo's can accommodate you.

DAY TRIP IN TOLLAND COUNTY

Tolland County is small, so you'll be driving less than 40 miles today. But in that short space, you'll see most of the county. If you're on I-84, get off at exit 65 and head north on the Hartford Turnpike (Route 30) to Rein's Deli in Vernon (see entry). Have the lox, eggs, and onions, or maybe just a bagel. Make sure you have enough, though, because the morning will be long.

Drive back to where the turnpike crosses Dobson Road, at which you'll take a left, actually becoming Washington Street and then Lake Street in a very short time. This will veer to the right, becoming Route 533, Cider Mill Road, and finally Route 85 after you cross Route 44. You're still going straight, mind you.

Take a right from Route 85 on Clark Road, which becomes West Street, and then North Street before you hit Gay City State Park, your first destination. Park and take a leisurely walk through this ghost town with its foundation holes and crumbling stone walls. Make your walk as long or short as you want, but leave some time for one more thing this morning before lunch.

Get back in your car and continue south past the Gay Cemetery, making an almost immediate left onto London Road (also Route 603). This merges into a larger road and continues straight, becoming Boston Hill Road. Confused yet? It's much easier than it sounds.

Turn left at the T intersection at Hebron Road (Route 316), and take another quick left on Route 6 in the tiny village of Andover.

Then make an immediate right onto Long Hill Road. This will end at Skinner Hill Road, where you'll take another right. A second right at a T intersection will put you on South Street, where you'll find the Nathan Hale Homestead in Coventry (see entry). If it's a Sunday in summer, you will find Connecticut's largest farmers' market here; otherwise, tour the house and relax in the Holy Grove out front before heading on.

You'll continue on Long Hill before taking the first left on Daly Road. This will end at Main Street in Coventry, where you'll take a left. Then make a right onto Sam Green Road, which merges and becomes Richmond Road, which again merges and becomes Route 44, which you'll continue east on. Your second left will be Stafford Road (Route 32), which will lead you to your lunch stop at Willington Pizza (see entry), on the banks of the Willimantic River. Try the red potato pizza, which they are known for.

Turning around, take Route 32 back south, turning left onto Storrs Road (Route 195). This will take you right into the center of the University of Connecticut campus. You have several options here, so find parking and, using the handy campus maps, go to either the William Benton Museum of Art, the Museum of Natural History, or the Ballard Museum of Puppetry. Or, if you like, just walk around the beautiful campus of the top public university in New England.

You now have two options. If there's a UConn basketball game or a performance at the Jorgensen Center, buy a ticket and stay on campus to eat at the Blue Oak Restaurant at the Nathan Hale Inn (see entries). If you're staying overnight at the inn (the best place to stay on campus), check in now and eat dinner there before or after the game or concert. If you're staying there, it's a great place to park and check in before even heading to the museums.

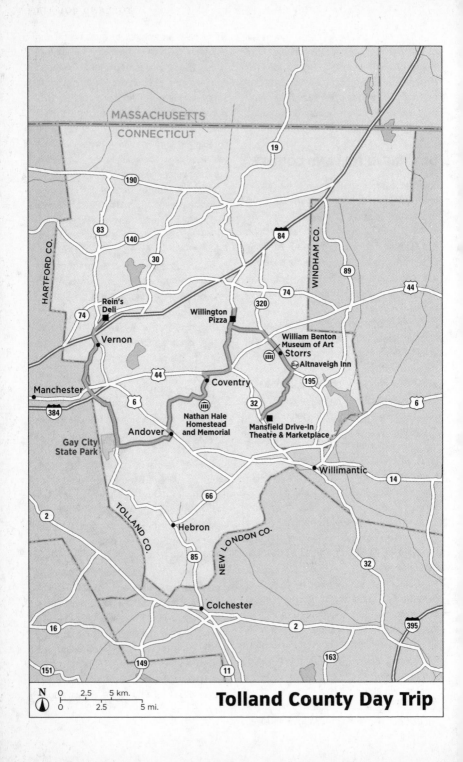

Tolland County Day Trip

MASSACHUSETTS
CONNECTICUT

HARTFORD CO.

WINDHAM CO.

Rein's Deli

Willington Pizza

William Benton Museum of Art

Storrs

Altnaveigh Inn

Vernon

Coventry

Manchester

Nathan Hale Homestead and Memorial

Mansfield Drive-In Theatre & Marketplace

Andover

Gay City State Park

Willimantic

TOLLAND CO.

NEW LONDON CO.

Hebron

Colchester

N

0   2.5   5 km.

0   2.5   5 mi.

If you're heading on to the classic Mansfield Drive-in (see entry), keep going down Route 195. The Altnaveigh Inn (see entry) is located on your right on this road barely a mile away (I bet you're happy there aren't more turns), and you can eat an early dinner there. Then it's on to the theater back on Stafford Road (Route 32), where you can catch a double feature, or head back into Storrs if you want to stay overnight.

To get to the theater from the Altnaveigh, continue south on Route 195, but take the first right past the church on Spring Hill Road. Spring Hill will make a hard left at an intersection, then a hard right, so stay alert. It will finally end at a T on Mansfield City Road. Take a right, and then your first right onto Browns Road. This will take you back out to Stafford Road (Route 32), where you'll turn left and find the theater barely a mile away on your left. If you're going back to the Nathan Hale for the night, just take Route 32 North until you hit Route 275 East, where you'll take a right. Then take a left on Route 195 and you're back, having seen most of this small but fascinating slice of Connecticut.

NEW LONDON COUNTY

Often called the playground of Connecticut, New London County's population is a third that of New Haven, Hartford, or Fairfield County, but it brings in over a third of the state's tourism. The two Native American gaming casinos, Foxwoods and Mohegan Sun, have become two of the biggest destinations in New England. And with the maritime activities, the wineries, and the well-preserved historical attractions, this area of the state is simply too good for you to pass up. You could easily spend a week seeing everything here without venturing into any other part of Connecticut (not that you should).

Mystic was a destination long before Humphrey Bogart and Lauren Bacall honeymooned here. The historic seaport and the aquarium anchor a tourist town steeped in maritime history, and nearby Stonington has a beautifully preserved village for those who aren't as interested in shopping and restaurants. The harbor of New London is a home of American sea power, with Fort Trumbull, the Coast Guard Academy, and the *Nautilus* submarine all big draws, and charming 19th-century streets hide around every corner. At the west end of the coast, the towns of Lyme and Old Lyme have maintained their rural charm, and the Florence Griswold House was the center of American Impressionism.

The entire seashore surrounding these towns is dotted with parks like Rocky Neck, Harkness Memorial, and Bluff Point, giving the visitor an opportunity to explore wooded beaches that the Native Americans used centuries ago. You can charter cruises on the Sound from almost any of these seaside ports to fish, learn, or party.

Inland, the city of Norwich and its environs boast the two casinos that bring thousands of people from New York and Boston every day. They are not just coming for the gaming; these are two of the largest and most beautiful casinos in the entire world, featuring shopping, restaurants, and events like concerts. The nearby Mashantucket Pequot Museum has been called the best museum of Native American history in the country, competing only with the Smithsonian. Walking through a completely reconstructed Pequot village makes you almost not mind losing at the Foxwoods gaming tables that evening.

And though it seems so far north that it should be part of a different county, Lebanon is a must-see for anyone interested in American history. The town green and surrounding houses are among the most important sites of the Revolutionary War.

In short, New London County is the place to be. Although most of these attractions are geared toward the summer visitor, you will find something to do here in any season. And whatever you do, don't forget to bring your appetite for the local Noank oysters and littleneck clams. They are as delicious as they were when the Pequots treasured them centuries ago.

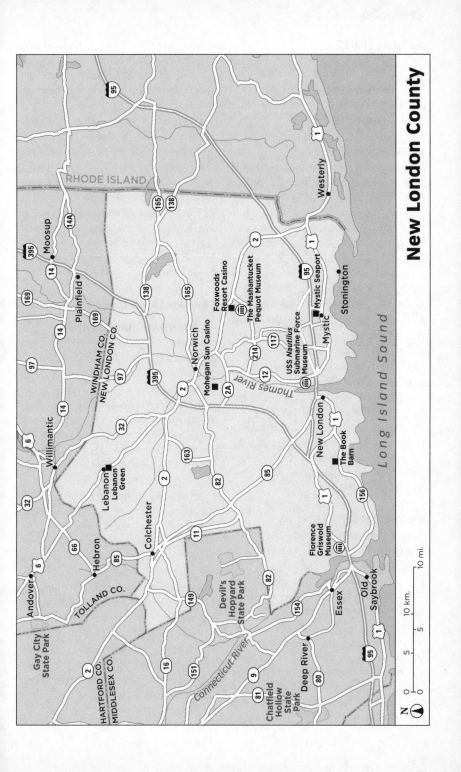

New London County

ATTRACTIONS

Casinos

*FOXWOODS RESORT & CASINO
350 Trolley Line Blvd.
Mashantucket, CT 06338
(800) 369-9663
foxwoods.com

The largest casino in the US, Foxwoods is a destination for people from around the world. There are over 380 gaming tables, including baccarat, blackjack, craps, keno, money wheel, pai gow, roulette, and a variety of poker games, all calling people to eastern Connecticut. There is also a sports betting facility, bingo, and the most slot machines of any casino in the world. It qualifies as a mall too, with dozens of shops and restaurants. In 2008 the MGM Grand opened, adding 53 gaming tables, 1,400 slot machines, a 4,000-seat theater, and 825 hotel rooms to the complex. There are, in fact, hotel accommodations here (see entry), a spa (see entry for G Spa), and a golf course (see entry for Lake of Isles). This is, quite simply, the centerpiece of the tourist industry that makes New London County thrive. Try not to get lost wandering the countless halls and rooms. You could spend a week here, and many people do.

*MOHEGAN SUN CASINO
1 Mohegan Sun Blvd.
Uncasville, CT 06382
(888) 226-7711
mohegansun.com

On the banks of the Thames River sits one of the most beautifully designed casinos in the world, and one of the largest in America, the Mohegan Sun. It is more than a casino; it is an arts venue, a sports arena, a mall, a hotel, and an architectural marvel. The 12,000-seat arena is home to the WNBA Connecticut Sun. There are 2 theaters, the Northeast's largest ballroom, and dozens of retail shops, making Mohegan a prime shopping and nightlife destination in New London County too. You can play slots, poker, blackjack, roulette, craps, Caribbean stud poker, baccarat, and keno. You can also bet on jai alai and live horse and greyhound racing. The Casino of the Sky area has a planetarium, a 3-story-high alabaster rock wall, and a 55-foot-high indoor waterfall. They have a day spa, a 10,000-square-foot pool, a convention center, and a family entertainment facility called KidsQuest. Above is the 34-story, 1,200-room luxury hotel, and there are 40 restaurants and bars throughout the 3 connected casinos. After you come here, the casinos in Vegas seem much less impressive.

Historical Sites & Landmarks

CAPTAIN NATHANIEL B. PALMER HOUSE
40 Palmer St.
Stonington, CT 06378
(860) 535-8445
stoningtonhistory.org

At the age of 20, Captain Nathaniel Palmer was the Yankee skipper who discovered Antarctica, and "Palmer Land" on modern maps of the southern continent stands as a monument to his 15,000-mile voyage in 1820. He also designed some of the fastest and largest clippers ever, and when he retired to his home of Stonington, he built this 1853 villa, now a National Historic Landmark. From its octagonal cupola, you can see the sea in all directions. You can take tours of the house and view the exhibits of the Stonington Historical Society inside. The gardens out back are well kept, and you should walk down to the salt marsh for encounters with birds and blackberries. Your admission fee lets you see the Old Lighthouse Museum (see entry) in the village, and you should certainly stop by.

FORT GRISWOLD
Park Avenue
Groton, CT 06320
(860) 449-6877 (seasonal)
ct.gov/dep [search "Fort Griswold"]

At this spot on September 6, 1781, Benedict Arnold and his British forces massacred 88 of the fort's defenders during his treacherous assault on New London Harbor. Walk around the battlefield site and check out the old ramparts, battlements, and historical displays in the Revolutionary War museum. The 1750 Ebenezer Avery House, which sheltered the wounded, has been restored in the park (it was originally on Thames Street), and you can tour it. During Sept, Fort Griswold is the site of reenactments of the battle. Many come here for the 134-foot granite tower that affords amazing views of the entire coast. But we shouldn't forget that this is the site of a massacre. The fact that Arnold could come back to his home turf and burn 150 homes and slaughter men who surrendered (including the heroic Col. William Ledyard) is why his name is synonymous with "traitor" today.

FORT TRUMBULL
90 Walbach St.
New London, CT 06320
(860) 444-7591
fortfriends.org

Built in the 1840s to replace the Revolutionary War fort that Benedict Arnold had attacked, this is a masterpiece of stonework and masonry, with a sweeping view of New London Harbor from its walls. Along with the huge walls, cannons, and living quarters, you can view a multimedia presentation in the visitor center and check out their exhibits focusing on the 1781 attack, the U-boat menace during World War II, and the Cold War antisubmarine efforts. This is actually a great place to come and fish—the 500-foot fishing pier sticks out into the harbor at a

particularly vital spot for bass, bluefish, and tautog. You can also see the vintage Thames Base Ball Club (organized by the New London County Historical Society) play their home matches here according to the rules of 1861. The fort is open Wed through Sun from 9 a.m. to 5 p.m. from May 21 through Columbus Day. Mark Twain actually set one of his short stories here at Fort Trumbull during the Civil War. It's almost as exciting as coming to the place itself.

i **The Connecticut Freedom Trail leads you to sites that embody the struggle toward freedom and human dignity and celebrate the accomplishments of the state's African-American community. Currently there are more than 130 sites in more than 50 towns. Check them out at ctfreedomtrail.org.**

HISTORIC NEW LONDON AND WHALE OIL ROW
Huntington Street
New London, CT 06320
(860) 444-2489
newlondonmainstreet.org

The restored row of 1832 Greek Revival houses on Huntington Street was once owned by whaling investors, and now they are a great place to start a walking tour of New London. There is a Heritage Trail with 30 bronze plaques leading you around to many of the fascinating sites in this storied town. From Huntington Street you should walk down State Street and then stroll along Bank Street to the Custom House Maritime Museum (150 Bank St.), whose front doors are made from oak planks of USS *Constitution*, the world's oldest commissioned warship. This is also where the ship *Amistad* was escorted in 1839, and where the controversy over its "slaves" began. It is now a small museum of New London's long and storied maritime history. If you're there mid-May to mid-Oct,

Thurs through Sun from noon to 4 p.m., you should also check out the Hempsted Houses at 11 Hempstead St. (860-443-7949). They both survived the burning of the town, and one dates from 1678, making it one of the oldest frame buildings left in New England. The other, from 1759, has 2-foot-thick walls, no doubt how it survived the burning so well.

✳LEBANON GREEN AND HISTORICAL SOCIETY
856 Trumbull Hwy.
Lebanon, CT 06249
(860) 642-6579
historyoflebanon.org

This is a must-see for anyone interested in the history of America or just being human. The remarkable mile-long green was the center of provisioning for the Revolutionary War and is surrounded by 68 historical homes. Yes, 68. One of them is the home of Governor Jonathan Trumbull (who Washington said really won the war), and his red clapboard store was the War Office where people like Trumbull, Rochambeau, and Washington planned their moves in over 1,000 meetings during those few years. Trumbull's son's paintings are the ones you see in the Capitol Rotunda in Washington, DC. Other homes include that of William Williams, a signer of the Declaration of Independence; Dr. William Beaumont, father of physiology; and William Buckingham, friend of Abraham Lincoln and governor of Connecticut during the Civil War. Most of the buildings on the green are still private homes today, but you can visit the Trumbull houses and the War Office and walk this long green, where America planned its path to freedom.

LEFFINGWELL HOUSE
348 Washington St.
Norwich, CT 06360
(860) 889-9440
leffingwellhousemuseum.org

The 1675 Leffingwell House in Norwich is one of the best examples of New England colonial architecture. The house served as an inn until it passed to Christopher Leffingwell, a rich merchant and industrialist who became an ardent patriot during the American Revolution. He used his business connections and skills to supply Washington's army. Today the house is run by the Norwich Historical Society and is open on Saturday from noon to 4 p.m., Apr through Oct. While you're here, make sure to stop at the Indian Burial Grounds on Sachem Street, the last resting place of Uncas, the Mohegan chief who gave the colonists land for the settlement of Norwich.

MONTE CRISTO COTTAGE
325 Pequot Ave.
New London, CT 06320
(860) 443-5378
theoneill.org

This gingerbread house overlooking New London Harbor was where America's greatest playwright spent many childhood days. But if you've watched Eugene O'Neill's often disturbing plays (such as *Long Day's Journey into Night*), you'll know that childhood was not exactly pleasant. In fact, the cottage is said to be haunted by Ella, his mother. The house has wraparound verandas, and the first floor is completely restored and furnished, including the living room featured in several of his plays. O'Neill's father was an actor, and the cottage was named for his most famous role, the Count of Monte Cristo. The author's statue stands on a rock overlooking the harbor, off the renamed Eugene O'Neill Drive, north of the house about a mile near the center of town. Walk around the streets of New London and muse on how this small, unhappy boy became the only American to win the Nobel Prize for drama.

✳MYSTIC SEAPORT
75 Greenmanville Ave.
Mystic, CT 06355
(860) 572-5302
mysticseaport.org

This is one of Connecticut's premier attractions, a re-creation of a whaling village that is pure recreation for all. Although you'll probably just walk around staring at life in another century, don't miss the educational reenactments throughout the day; they are what makes this place special. You can learn skills like rope making, printing, and oystering from experts dressed in period costume. Horse and buggy rides, sea chantey sing-alongs, tours of the tall ships, and the permanent *Amistad* exhibit are all ways to immerse yourself in the culture of the sea. There are lectures, concerts, and excursions; there's even a planetarium. The museum shop is huge, and full of treasures. If you're here in New London County for a while, go to one of the living-history workshops or send your kids to the Mystic summer camps. In Oct and Dec the lamplight tours of the village are magical, and there are fun events throughout the year, like the marathon reading of Melville's *Moby Dick*. The Seaport's restaurant, the Spouter Tavern, is a great place to grab lunch while you're walking around and taking it all in. Maybe it's an obvious choice, but try the chowder. It tastes of history.

SHAW-PERKINS MANSION
11 Blinman St.
New London, CT 06320
(860) 443-1209
nlhistory.org

Built in 1756 for a wealthy sea captain named Nathaniel Shaw, this house was used as the state's naval office during the American Revolution. It's one of the few houses in town that survived the attack by Benedict Arnold. The house was modified in 1845, and a summerhouse from 1792 sits on a granite ledge behind the mansion in the gardens. It is open Wed through Fri 1 to 4 p.m.; Sat 10 a.m. to 4 p.m. Park in the lot on the corner and head around to the mansion's stone facade and porch, and don't miss the gardens in the back. This is a great stop before getting onto the Fisher's Island Ferry right down the street or in tandem with Fort Trumbull, a few blocks in the other direction. There's so much right here in the New London Harbor area that this mansion often gets missed. Don't make that mistake.

SMITH-HARRIS HOUSE
33 Society Rd.
Niantic, CT 06357
(860) 739-0761
smithharris.org

This white clapboard Greek Revival house was built in 1845 and was home to Herman Smith and his nephew Francis Harris, who interestingly married two sisters. For 60 years the two couples lived in the house. This unusual family's personal effects are scattered throughout the home, along with pottery, utensils, and many original furnishings. It is open Apr through June and Sept through Dec on weekends from 1 to 4 p.m. In July and Aug, the house is open Thurs through Sun, noon to 4 p.m. If you really want to see it from Jan through Mar, you can make an appointment. Stop here along with visits to Rocky Neck State Park and The Book Barn (see entries) to complete your tour of the charming village of Niantic.

UNITED STATES COAST GUARD ACADEMY
31 Mohegan Ave.
New London, CT 06320
(800) 883-8724
cga.edu

Founded in 1876 as a training ground for the US Coast Guard, the 100-acre campus above the Thames River has a museum and visitor center for us to visit. The tours are free and self-guided, and there's a multimedia show on cadet life. The training barque *Eagle* is often in port as well, and is usually available Fri through Sun from noon to 5 p.m. In the fall, full dress reviews take place on Fri at 4 p.m., also a sight to behold. The Coast Guard has fought in all the American wars since they were founded, and operated the landing craft at Normandy beaches during World War II. Though this branch of the armed forces mostly responds to search-and-rescue calls and keeps our waters free of drug smugglers, they are a vital part of the nation's security.

Museums

*FLORENCE GRISWOLD MUSEUM
96 Lyme St.
Old Lyme, CT 06371
(860) 434-5542
florencegriswoldmuseum.org

On the Lieutenant River in Old Lyme is a beautiful mansion filled with the works of American Impressionists. In the back is an interestingly designed modern building containing changing exhibits. But this is not just a museum. This house was the boardinghouse and artist colony of Florence Griswold, the patron saint of American Impressionism, and the artists whose work you'll see here actually stayed here, painted here, and even painted parts of the house. The restored studio of William Chadwick is also on the grounds. In July an annual 2-day art show is held along the streets of town and, other than parking, is a great time to visit, although the museum itself is open year-round. While you're here, check out the lovely First Congregational Church in the center of Old Lyme, built in 1816 and painted by many of the American Impressionists, including Childe Hassam. But the jewel here is the dining room, one of the most amazing rooms in America. In fact, with permanent panels painted by a dozen famous artists, there is probably not a room like this in the world.

LYMAN ALLYN ART MUSEUM
625 Williams St.
New London, CT 06320
(860) 443-2545
lymanallyn.org

Part of the Connecticut Art Trail, but somehow ignored by many travelers, the Lyman Allyn is next to the Coast Guard Academy. Along with Indian artifacts, dollhouses, toys, and classical European artifacts, it has a great collection of American art. You can follow the development of American silver, glass, porcelain, furniture, and paintings as the museum takes you through the various art forms using their impressive collection. You can also see the 19th-century mansion, home to whaling captain Lyman Allyn, and tour the first floor. The display of dollhouses in the house is only a small portion of the museum's impressive collection. Your children will enjoy climbing on the sculptures (apparently allowed) out in front of the museum.

*MASHANTUCKET PEQUOT MUSEUM
110 Pequot Trail
Mashantucket, CT 06338
(800) 411-9671
pequotmuseum.org

For over 10,000 years native peoples occupied southeastern Connecticut, and just before the Europeans landed, the Pequots were a tribe of 8,000 people. The Pequot War and the slaughter of 700 men, women, and children by the colonial forces devastated the tribe, leading to centuries of wandering and reservation life. Then, in 1992 the remaining descendants of the Pequots opened the Foxwoods Resort Casino. With the money available to them, they have created this amazing museum honoring their ancestors. At first you make your way through large, life-size dioramas like *A World of Ice* and *Changing Lifeways,* thinking this is a great, professionally built museum, almost as good as the Smithsonian's Native American museum. Then you step out into the full-size re-creation of the Pequot village and realize that it is actually better than the Smithsonian. This remarkable attraction is open Wed through Sat, 9 a.m. to 5 p.m., with the last admission at 4 p.m. If you're going to have fun at the casino, stop here first, and be amazed at the best museum on Native American life in the US.

OLD LIGHTHOUSE MUSEUM
7 Water St.
Stonington, CT 06378
(860) 535-1440
stoningtonhistory.org

In some ways, all of Stonington is a museum, and walking the streets once trod by whalers and sailors from around the world has its own reward. However, the lighthouse at the end of the peninsular island, built in 1823, deserves special mention. Since 1927 this lighthouse has been the museum for the town's historical society. There are 6 rooms of exhibits, all of which explore the rich history of the town and region. One of the exhibits is a display of Stonington pottery from 1780 to 1834, all fired from a specific type of grayish clay. However, the most popular activity is climbing the iron steps to the top, where you can see views in all directions. The museum is open daily May through Oct, and on weekends in Apr and Nov. Your admission fee lets you see the Captain Nathaniel Palmer House just outside the village, and you should certainly stop there too.

SLATER MUSEUM
108 Crescent St.
Norwich, CT 06360
(860) 887-2506
slatermuseum.org

This beautiful brick Romanesque Revival building with its high pointed tower is located on the Norwich Free Academy campus, a combination private and public school in operation since 1854. The museum was dedicated in 1888 and contains not only Norwich history but also that of a wider world. You will find artwork from the 18th to 20th centuries, 17th- to 19th-century European paintings, Native American objects, African and Pacific sculptures, and a stunning plaster-cast collection of the world's greatest sculptures. The Vanderpoel Collection of Oriental Art, presented to the museum in 1935, contains many fine pieces from the Tokugawa period of Japanese art. This museum will surprise you with its breadth and scope, especially since many "insiders" don't even know it exists.

USS *NAUTILUS* SUBMARINE FORCE MUSEUM
1 Crystal Lake Rd.
Groton, CT 06340
(800) 343-0079
ussnautilus.org

Just off I-95 in Groton you can see the first nuclear-powered submarine in the world, which was also the first to reach the North Pole. The submarine was named for the boat in the 1850 book by Jules Verne, *20,000 Leagues Under the Sea,* which predicted this invention over a hundred years earlier. That boat, in turn, was named for American inventor Robert Fulton's submersible vessel. But it is not only the *Nautilus* that is the attraction here. Inside the museum there are large and small models of submarines, theaters, and a World War II attack center from the Sturgeon-class vessels. They are only closed on Tuesday, and admission and parking are free. But it could cost a bundle and still be worth it; whether you are a submarine fanatic or not, this is a great attraction for everyone and highlights the importance of the submarine industry to Connecticut. Check out the nearby memorial to the 3,600 seamen who lost their lives in World War II, set at the place most of those men last touched dry land.

Parks & Beaches

BLUFF POINT STATE PARK
1 Depot Rd.
Groton, CT 06340
(860) 444-7591
ct.gov/dep [search "Bluff Point State Park"]

This peninsula between Groton and Noank is one of the few wild areas left on the Connecticut shoreline. Hiking out to the cliffs from the parking lot takes about half an hour, and the reward is views out to Watch Hill, the New London Ledge Lighthouse, and Fishers Island. You can also walk down from the bluffs to Bushy Point Beach, a sliver of sand out in the mouth of the Poquonnock River. There is great fishing, shellfishing, snorkeling, and scuba diving here as well, but there are no lifeguards, so be careful when heading out to (or into) the water. The ruins of the historic home of former governor John Winthrop are just by the park road as you walk in. You can also bicycle or horseback ride the 4-mile loop of old horse-cart paths; in winter these are popular among cross-country skiers as well. This is a real insiders' place to come—you might have Bushy Point Beach all to yourself on a summer weekday.

GUNGYWAMP STONE SITES
Denison Pequotsepos Nature Center
109 Pequotsepos Rd.
Mystic, CT 06355
(860) 536-1216
dpnc.org

On about 20 acres near Groton sits a collection of unusual stone sites that puzzle researchers enough so that various conspiracy-type theories have sprung up about them. Most think the location is merely a Native American site that was later used by colonial farmers for sheep rearing. This is supported by archaeological research. However, the area is fascinating nevertheless, with an "Indian cave," a huge three-sided colonial foundation, the remains of a number of underground chambers (possibly for icehouses or sheep tanning), stone bridges, and the row of small standing stones that caused all the controversy in the first place. Access is limited and you'll need a guide, so call the Denison Pequotsepos Nature Center for their schedule of tours. But it's worth the trouble—this is a mystery begging to be solved. Although maybe it's better that some mysteries are left as they are. It's more fun that way.

HARKNESS MEMORIAL STATE PARK
275 Great Neck Rd.
Waterford, CT 06385
(860) 443-5725
ct.gov/dep [search "Harkness Memorial State Park"]

Once the summer home of Edward and Mary Harkness, today this 234-acre former estate on the shores of Long Island Sound is the best place to fly a kite in Connecticut. You'll see many people attempting to keep their multicolored kites in the air along the slopes down to the beach, while others picnic on the grounds. Tour the house on free guided tours. The gardens by the mansion are some of the loveliest in the state, making this a hugely popular place for weddings. Be careful of swimming here, though: There are no lifeguards, and the tidal inlet has a powerful current. Don't miss the huge old beech trees around the property, with their smooth gray bark and green or copper leaves. The one (or is it many?) you'll see in front of the house on the way in is one of the most impressive specimens in America.

ROCKY NECK STATE PARK
244 W. Main St. (Route 156)
East Lyme, CT 06357
(860) 739-5471
ct.gov/dep [search "Rocky Neck State Park"]

The crescent-shaped beach at Rocky Neck is not huge, but it is picturesque, with clean, finely ground sand. If you're interested in fishing, this is a good spot to catch flounder and striped bass, usually from a stone jetty by the beach. The impressive pavilion was constructed by the Works Project Administration back in the 1930s. There is wheelchair access to a deck across Bride Brook and an observation deck overlooking the salt marsh. Rocky Neck is also great in winter. Just pull off I-95 and park, walking under the railroad and coming out onto an empty beach, with crashing winter waves. In summer, if you're just coming to the park to sit on the beach awhile, here's an insider's tip: Park on Route 156 just east of the I-95 connector road and hike to the beach on the trails, which skirt the salt marsh and put you right on the bluff after crossing the railroad on a bridge. You'll save your fee in summer, if you don't mind a mile of pleasant woodland walking, that is.

Wildlife & Zoos

MYSTIC AQUARIUM
55 Coogan Blvd.
Mystic, CT 06355
(860) 572-5955
mysticaquarium.org

Recently redesigned and expanded, the Mystic Aquarium is transforming from a solid marine-life attraction to the best aquarium in New England. You will explore the estuaries, coral reefs, and upwelling zones of the world's oceans as you walk around this extensive, living museum. There are also exhibits on the *Titanic* and other shipwrecks in the Institute for Exploration, created by oceanographer and explorer Robert Ballard. Budding explorers can also try the climbing wall, in case they need to rappel down a cliff to examine a gannet or reach a hidden cove. For the more sedentary among us, there is a 3-D motion theater and a marine theater starring trained sea lions. There's also a neat little spot where you can watch the veterinary care lab, where you'll often get the chance to view scientists and doctors at work. You can even touch the rays and watch them gather around and make noise in anticipation of their feeding (a decidedly strange experience). You'll see seals, sharks, penguins, and beluga whales. What more could you want?

Wineries & Breweries

COTTRELL BREWING CO.
100 Mechanic St.
Pawcatuck, CT 06379
(860) 599-8213
cottrellbrewing.com

Nicholas Cottrell was one of the early settlers who founded Westerly, Rhode Island, in 1666, and his descendant Calvert Cottrell formed a manufacturing company across the river in Pawcatuck, making printing presses that soon dominated the world market. The great-great-grandson of Calvert, Charles, and his wife, Ann, began the Cottrell Brewing Co. in 1996, brewing and bottling Old Yankee Ale in the old factory walls. They formed the company 330 years after Charles's ancestor helped found Westerly, a staggering number that really shows how old this area of the country—and the long tradition of Yankee ingenuity—is. One of the country's best water supplies provides the crisp, clean taste, and the dry finish is a classic. You can take tours Thurs at 3 p.m., Fri on every half hour from 3 to 6 p.m., and Sat from 1 to 5 p.m. And, of course, taste the excellent beer.

JONATHAN EDWARDS WINERY
74 Chester Maine Rd.
North Stonington, CT 06359
(860) 535-0202
jedwardswinery.com

Owner and winemaker Jonathan Edwards developed his winery on 48 acres of land that had been farmed for centuries. The majestic white barn that sits atop the slope and overlooks the vines is the picturesque snapshot of what we picture when we think of a winery. It's a distinctive destination for events and weddings, and the winery provides tasters with a unique opportunity. Edwards travels across the country each season to harvest grapes and make wine in the Napa Valley, and then ships the product back to Connecticut for customers to enjoy. These wines show the Napa Valley appellation and are everything you'd expect from California wines. But the flavor of Connecticut is only a glass away. Chardonnay, Pinot Gris, Gewürztraminer, and Cabernet Franc are all grown on-site. The Napa reds are big and bold, made with grapes like Petite Sirah that just aren't suited to Connecticut's growing season. But Cabernet Franc is a standout among the Connecticut reds, and the estate-bottled Chardonnay may just beat out the Napa version in your taste test. Open year-round Wed through Sun.

MAUGLE SIERRA VINEYARDS
825 Colonel Ledyard Hwy.
Ledyard, CT 06339
(860) 464-2987
mauglesierravineyards.com

Just south of Foxwoods Casino in Ledyard is a small winery run by physicist Paul Maugle. Built in the 1740 Ledyard House, the brand-new tasting room and performance space is a popular stop. Less than 5 miles from the sea on a 100-foot hill, Maugle makes wine mostly from his prize St. Croix grapes. He uses methods like removing the acidic seeds to reduce the tannins and make the wines easier to drink. He cold ferments small batches, using St. Croix to make rosé as well. The vineyard hosts festivals and wine dinners, so check the schedule. Maugle is a perfectionist, and he will probably tell you all about his methods when you stop by. "You want to taste the fruit, not the barrel," he says. At Maugle Sierra, you will.

PRESTON RIDGE VINEYARD
100 Miller Rd.
Preston, CT 06365
(860) 383-4278
prestonridgevineyard.com

One of the newer vineyards in Connecticut, Preston Ridge is beginning to expand its plantings on the 60 acres they own, with Chardonnay, Riesling, Vidal Blanc, and more. My favorite is the estate bottled Cabernet Franc, which has the added benefit of being made completely from grapes grown on their land. Open Fri through Sun. In the evenings stop by for music in the tasting room. Or sit on their porch and enjoy the view across southeastern Connecticut, which is quickly becoming the most important wine destination in New England.

✳PRIAM VINEYARDS
11 Shailor Hill Rd.
Colchester, CT 06415
(860) 267-8520
priamvineyards.com

Priam is New England's only solar-powered winery, and you'll see the panels and the grapes soaking up sun here in Colchester. It has also been certified as a natural bird and wildlife habitat. Gary Crump and Gloria Priam named this winery for her Hungarian grandfather, who worked a vineyard near Budapest. On Friday in summer and fall you'll find a farmers' market here; they also team up with a local chef and pair food and

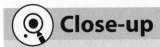 **Close-up**

Traveling the Wine Trail

Wine in Connecticut? You bet. Ever since the first European colonists found wild grapes growing in their new backyards, wine has been produced here. In the late 1800s and early 1900s, commercial wineries began to spring up around the state, with heavy concentrations in the Hartford-to-Meriden corridor. The 1897 state flag even consists of three grapevines on a silver shield, symbolizing the three colonies that became one. Under the shield appears the state motto, "Qui transtulit sustinet," meaning "What is transplanted, sustains."

However, Prohibition put a stop to this growing industry in Connecticut, as it did throughout much of the nation. It wasn't until 1978, with the passage of the Farm Winery Act, that commercial winemaking again became possible in the state. After a few pioneers like Sherman Haight and Bill Hopkins proved that our climate was great for growing not only native grapes but also many European varietals, others joined in.

The two greatest concentrations of wineries today are found in Litchfield and New London Counties. To grow great grapes here, you must either be near the moderating influence of Long Island Sound or be situated on a hillside to allow the cold air to sink away from the vines in the Connecticut winters. However, yearlong hot weather is not necessary for most grapes (except a few like Pinot Noir or Cabernet Sauvignon), and the state's climate is similar to northeastern France, where some of the best wines in the world are made.

Today you can find over 30 farm wineries across the state, as well as other vineyards and winemaking operations. Tastings usually include a signature wine glass to take home; you'll impress friends at the next dinner party with personally selected wines in their own glasses.

The state of Connecticut sponsors a "passport" program, in which you can visit wineries and acquire stamps in order to enter a drawing for free vacations abroad and at home. These passports are available at any winery from May to October. In recent years a winter passport has also been available in the Litchfield Hills area. Many of the wineries have also joined in a convenient "wine trail" that provides maps, hours, and other information, as well as providing road signs and guidance in your travels from vineyard to vineyard. Along with sponsoring frequent festivals of their own, they also get together for the annual Connecticut Wine Festival at the Goshen Fairgrounds. Find them on the web at ctwine.com.

The wine you will taste here will surprise you with its complexity and accessibility. If you like reds, try the vanilla and earthy Cabernet Francs or a floral, spicy St. Croix. For white drinkers, sample the crisp and refreshing Chardonnays or a citrusy Vidal Blanc. Many wineries also make rosés, sparkling bubblies, and sweet dessert wines. There is a wine here for every palate, and visiting a winery for a tasting flight is the best way to find yours. See you on the trail.

wine in a farm-to-table event. Like most Connecticut wineries, Priam creates original flavors that fit the climate and terroir. Their Riesling and Gewürztraminer bring German and Austrian winemakers here to buy cases for themselves. As Gary says, it "shouldn't taste like it comes from California. It comes from Connecticut." What does that taste like? Head to Priam and find out the flavors you've been missing.

✳SALTWATER FARM VINEYARD
349 Elm St.
Stonington, CT 06378
(860) 415-9072
saltwaterfarmvineyard.com

Set on a peninsula in a bay next to Ston-ington Village (a minute by car), Saltwater Farm Vineyard used to be an airport, and if you'd like to land your plane there, you still can (but no drinking and flying, please). The tasting room is in the old airplane hangar, beautifully remodeled into one of the most stunning banquet facilities in the state. Wed-dings are booked years in advance here. Sit on the porch overlooking the Sound and sip the appley Sauvignon Blanc or rich, smoky Cabernet Franc. This is also a great spot for birding when the tasting room is open from Apr to Nov; don't miss the osprey nests to your right as you drive in. Stroll the vineyard and watch kayakers paddle these secluded coves and salt marshes, or better yet, paddle them yourselves.

STONINGTON VINEYARDS
523 Taugwonk Rd.
Stonington, CT 06378
(860) 535-1222
stoningtonvineyards.com

With the ocean and its moderating breezes just miles away, Stonington Vineyards' 58 acres are ideal for grape growing. Add expert winemaker Mike McAndrew, and the result is some of the best wines in the state. The vine-yard has been in operation since the mid-1980s and specializes in Burgundian-style wines. Try two versions of Chardonnay—one fermented and barreled in oak, the other in steel—to experience why this grape is so versatile. The latter, Sheer Chardonnay, is comparable to the best versions of French Chablis, with mineral notes characteristic of the limestone terroir. Seaport White and Triad Rose are two delightful blends, and Stonington's version of Cabernet Franc

shows why the coast's cooler temperatures, long growing season, and moderate winters suit this grape. The tasting room and facilities are housed in a long white structure, and the grounds are a popular choice for weddings. The winery is open year-round and easily accessible off I-95. Daily winery tours offer a glimpse of the state-of-the-art machinery and introduce visitors to the techniques behind their great wines.

ACTIVITIES & EVENTS

Amusement Parks

OCEAN BEACH PARK
98 Neptune Ave.
New London, CT 06320
(800) 510-7263
ocean-beach-park.com

From Memorial Day to Labor Day this family fun park offers several ways to beat the heat. You can take the triple-run waterslide, one of the only remaining amusement park rides from when this was more of a carnival than a park. A mere $16 will get you unlimited runs down the slide throughout the day, and this is a great way to tire out your kids while you relax on the beach. There is also a beautiful Olympic-size swimming pool right by the beach, for those who want a warmer, freshwater swim. The beach itself is beautiful, and a wide wooden boardwalk spans its length. There are fast-food vendors, an arcade, a playground for smaller children, volleyball courts, and an 18-hole miniature golf course. You can actually come to the beach free of charge in the off-season and walk the length of the boardwalk, dream-ing of next summer, or enjoy the cooler temperatures while reading a book on the immaculate beach, or walk with your sweet-heart into the twilight.

Arts Venues

EUGENE O'NEILL THEATER CENTER
305 Great Neck Rd.
Waterford, CT 06385
(860) 443-5378
theoneill.org

The O'Neill Theater overlooks the Sound and provides you with another unique experience. The center is really the home for intensive workshops between master and student writers, actors, directors, musicians, and designers. The reasonably priced public performances by the National Theater Institute allow you the opportunity to see the openings of new plays, with minimal stage production, before the rest of the world. Staff and alumni of the O'Neill have won every major award in the theater world, and the plays and musicals developed here include John Guare's *House of Blue Leaves,* August Wilson's *Fences,* and Wendy Wasserstein's *Uncommon Women and Others.* Eugene O'Neill was the only American playwright to ever win the Nobel Prize; he racked up four Pulitzers too, for good measure. Come here and watch performances that keep his high standards alive.

FLOCK THEATRE
10 Prospect St.
New London, CT 06320
(860) 443-3119
flocktheatre.org

This theater troupe actually does shows throughout New London—at St. Mary's Star of the Sea Church, the Garde Arts Center, the Connecticut College Arboretum, the Custom House Pier, the Shaw Mansion, and the Hempsted Houses. Since 1994 they have put on everything from Shakespeare to puppetry. They have acting classes in the Garde for ages 9 and up—something everyone should try once. The Flock troupe will show up at the most unexpected places in New London, in the best tradition of street theater. The most exciting thing they've done recently is to reinaugurate the annual burning in effigy of Benedict Arnold, who burned down the town in 1781. It comes complete with a parade through town and, yes, an actual burning of a two-faced puppet of the traitor.

GARDE ARTS CENTER
325 State St.
New London, CT 06320
(860) 444-7373
gardearts.org

This was once a 1926 movie palace. Yes, palace, because theater is too small a word for the impressive, gilded luxuriousness that has been restored (at the price of $19 million) to both reflect this glorious past and also allow for modern performing arts of all sorts. As you walk through the grand entrance, you'll find three floors of Moroccan-style lobbies. Sit in the plush seats and enjoy Broadway plays, comedy shows, popular musical performers, classical concerts, and dance exhibitions. Along with live performances, you can also watch classic films on the big screen here, and be taken back to the golden age of Hollywood, right in one of the movie palaces where it flourished almost a century ago.

SPIRIT OF BROADWAY
24 Chestnut St.
Norwich, CT 06360
(860) 886-2378
spiritofbroadway.org

In an old firehouse in the Rose City of Norwich, the Spirit of Broadway produces musicals for all tastes and seasons, always full professional productions, for all 12 months of the year. In its 17th year, this little 74-seat theater brings in actors and staff from New York. Catch one of the original plays or first-run events, and be part of the proud tradition of Connecticut drama that produced four of the five great playwrights of the 20th century (Arthur Miller, Thornton Wilder, Edward Albee, Eugene O'Neill) and some of its best actors (such as Meryl Streep and Katherine Hepburn). Look for the slide pole of the old firehouse, which is still in place!

Cruises

PROJECT OCEANOLOGY
1084 Shennecossett Rd.
Groton, CT 06340
(860) 445-9007
oceanology.org

This cruise leaves from the Institute of Marine Science at the UConn Avery Point campus, but unlike some, it is an active cruise. You will sail off Groton and spend 2.5 hours measuring and recording geological and biological data, as well as learning how nautical charts and navigation works. You can collect and test water and mud, or pull in the large trawl nets to examine the sea life. The vessel is staffed by marine research scientists and teachers. Depending on the day, you might catch lobsters—to study, not to eat. Project Oceanology runs from the middle of June to Labor Day, with two cruises a day for ages 6 and up. They also run seal observation cruises in Feb and Mar, and a trip out to the wonderful New London Ledge Lighthouse. Of course, like any cruise, this has nice views and the snap of salt air, but what makes this one special is your opportunity to become part of the grand march of science.

*MYSTIC WHALER
35 Water St.
New London, CT 06320
(860) 447-1249
mysticwhalercruises.com

This 110-foot schooner with huge sails takes cruises from New London that are among the best in Connecticut. The *Whaler* crew offers many different options, and seems to create new ones every year. Checking out their schedule, you might find a lobster dinner cruise, a day sail in Fishers Island Sound, treasure hunts, moonlit sails, and overnight and multiday sails to Block Island, Mystic, Martha's Vineyard, New York, and more. They have a kitchen on the ship and boil your lobsters or grill your burgers so you can eat right on the deck of this magnificent vessel. Musicians are often on board, entertaining you while you sail the sea. You can hoist the sails and take a turn at the wheel if you like. The multiday journeys are truly experiences that you will not forget, making you feel a part of the great age of sail.

SABINO MYSTIC RIVER CRUISES
75 Greenmanville Ave.
Mystic, CT 06355
(860) 572-5302
mysticseaport.org

Take a ride on the last coal-fired passenger steamboat in America (possibly the world). It was built in 1908 in East Boothbay, Maine, to ferry passengers on the Damariscotta River. Now a working exhibit at the Mystic Seaport, the double decks of the *Sabino* are a fascinating experience, cruising on the Mystic River out into the Sound for day or evening journeys. The longer trip lasts about an hour and a half, with shorter half-hour cruises from 10:30 a.m. to 3:30 p.m. each day. There are several other recreational cruises out of Mystic Seaport as well, but this is certainly the most interesting vessel to ride on.

SUNBEAM EXPRESS NATURE CRUISE CENTER
15 1st St.
Waterford, CT 06358
(860) 442-2710
sunbeamfleet.com

Leaving from Captain John's Sport Fishing Center, technically called the Nature Cruise Center, the Sunbeam Express Fleet offers private whale watching, yes, but also a number of other interesting options, from seal-watching trips in Mar, Apr, and May to bald eagle cruises in Feb and Mar. In summer you can take the famous lighthouse cruises on Wed, Sat, and Sun; this twice-a-day trip lasts 5 hours and crosses the Sound, passing 11 lighthouses. Whatever you do, don't forget the binoculars and camera. The small fleet of boats owned by Sunbeam can also be chartered for deep-sea fishing, daily from June to Labor Day. Try the night bass-fishing excursion, an exciting ride out onto dark waters, when the struggle of the fighting fish is illuminated only by the stars.

Festivals & Annual Events

CONNECTICUT RENAISSANCE FAIRE

14 Stott Ave.
Norwich, CT 06360
(860) 478-5954
ctfaire.com

If you've never been to a Renaissance Faire, get rid of any preconceptions. These are enjoyable days out for the whole family, or a fantastic place for a date. You don't even have to dress up in costume (though that can be a lot of fun). Connecticut runs two, the Robin Hood Springtime Festival on Lovers Lane in Guilford and the King Arthur Fall Harvest Faire, which runs on Sept and Oct weekends at the fairgrounds in Hebron. You'll see jousting, yes, but also comedy shows, musicians, acrobats, fire eaters, puppets, parades, and general good fun. There are numerous shops full of handcrafted items: leather, costumes, jewelry, metalwork, woodwork, toys, and games. You can go to a psychic or get a massage. And the food? Have you ever munched a turkey leg while watching two knights collide on the field of sport? C'mon! It's a rare pleasure these days, and one you'll only find at the Renaissance Faire.

✸SCHEMITZUN

Foxwoods Resort Casino
350 Trolley Line Blvd.
Mashantucket, CT 06338-3777
(800) 369-9663

This annual powwow event on the Mashantucket Reservation is held on a weekend in late Aug, and is one of the best of its kind in the country. The dance contest is the big attraction, and Native American dancers come from around the country to participate. You can also watch wampum making, flint knapping, storytelling, net and bead making, cooking over an open fire, and more. Enjoy clam chowder and Native tacos while shopping for certified baskets, paintings, weavings, leathers, feathers, carvings, sage bundles, silver, regalia, and books. Note: Unless you are a participant, you'll have to get the shuttle from the casino or Two Trees Inn.

SEA MUSIC FESTIVAL

Mystic Seaport
75 Greenmanville Ave.
Mystic, CT 06355
(860) 572-5302
mysticseaport.org

Mystic Seaport has a number of events throughout the summer and fall, and each one is special. There's Lobster Days, 3 days of live music and lobster at picnic tables in the large boat shed on the Mystic River. There's the Antique and Classic Boat Rendezvous, when you get to see dozens of restored beauties gather at the seaport for the weekend. There's the Rum Runner's Rendezvous, River Jazz, the *Moby Dick* Marathon Reading, and more. But arguably the biggest and most important is the Sea Music Festival, which for over 30 years has brought together sea chantey performers to carry on classic musical traditions of the golden age of sail. They feature music from maritime cultures around the world, including the United Kingdom, Italy, the Netherlands, France, Canada, and Africa. The performers take turns throughout the day, and any visitor can listen; the evening performances are extra (usually Thurs, Fri, and Sat) but well worth it. There is a concurrent symposium that delves into the art form, usually held in tandem with the Coast Guard Academy in New London.

SAILFEST
124 State St.
New London, CT 06320
(860) 444-1879
sailfest.org

Every year in July, this 3-day festival brings 300,000 people into downtown New London. There's a road race, fireworks, a lobster dinner, fine arts and crafts vendors, cruises in the harbor, a beer tent, food vendors, and a temporary amusement park for the kids, and all the local historical houses and museums are open. There are also 3 stages set up in different areas of town, with different performances at each—oh, and of course the sails that give the festival its name, a tall ship or two to tour on the docks downtown. This is a great way to celebrate Connecticut's (and especially its most important port's) relationship with the sea.

Fishing

BLACK HAWK II
PO Box 46
Niantic, CT 06357
(860) 448-3662
blackhawksportfishing.com

The crew of the *Black Hawk* has a new approach to fishing trips on the Sound. They supply the bait and setup, and you can rent rods and reels if you don't have your own. You can bring your own food, or get burgers and dogs at their small snack bar. If you're a beginner, the crew of the *Black Hawk* will give free instruction. The trips last 5 or 6 hours, but unlike chartered fishing boats, this is first come, first served. Show up early at the dock in Niantic Beach Marina, and get on board. The price is less than most chartered boats, at less than $65 a person, children

under 12 are half price. It's up to you to decide whether junior is old enough to haul in a large bluefish. If so, it is the experience of a lifetime.

HEL-CAT II
181 Thames St.
Groton, CT 06340
(860) 535-2066
helcat.com

Captain Brad Class takes fishing trips for striped bass and bluefish from May to Oct, and cod, mackerel, and other fish the rest of the year. This 114-foot party boat leaves at 9 a.m. and comes back around 3 p.m.—what they call the banker's hours special—and is not a charter, but rather a one-person, one-price daily trip. If you're not fishing you can pay half fare, but that just seems silly. Even if you've never fished before, this is an exciting introduction, with a substantial indoor area to get out of the sun, beers on draft, food, and a huge deck with plenty of space for everyone to fish. You can also charter this boat for parties or night-fishing expeditions.

✳SALMON RIVER
Route 16
Colchester, CT 06415
(860) 295-9523
ct.gov/dep [search "Salmon River"]

This beautiful little river begins in Colchester, which is in New London County, but heads into Middlesex as well. The section in the Salmon River State Forest is the favorite, though, and the area right off of Route 16 near the Comstock Covered Bridge is usually swamped with fishermen. It's a beautiful setting to fish in. However, walk on the convenient trail a little upstream, or drive down Gulf or Stockburger Road to the south, and you'll find many areas untouched by the bridge anglers. It all depends on whether you want to catch trout or want a nice picture to show your friends of you fishing by a charming New England covered bridge. Be careful mistakenly catching sea-run salmon, however, since they come up this river often and look very much like trout. Of course the chance to catch salmon is not exactly a deterrent, but make sure to put these endangered creatures back. I caught a fat 20-inch trout here on the south side of the Route 16 bridge without even trying.

Golf

ELMRIDGE GOLF COURSE
229 Elmridge Rd.
Pawcatuck, CT 06379
(860) 599-2248
elmridgegolf.com

On a hilltop at the Rhode Island border, the Elmridge Golf Course is a challenging par 71 course that opened in 1966. Designed and built by Joseph and Charles Rustici, there are actually 27 holes to choose from here, all set on a former dairy farm (note the large grain silo behind the first tee on the white course). The fields have extensive views to the west, and the breezes off the ocean make for a pleasant game. At the 19th hole is a modern clubhouse, and the Restaurant at Elmridge is full service for breakfast, lunch, and dinner. Check the pro shop for discounted supplies, and relax on the covered deck that overlooks the course. They also offer lessons by a PGA professional, because no matter how good we think we are, we can always use some great advice.

✳LAKE OF ISLES
1 Clubhouse Dr.
North Stonington, CT 06359
(888) 475-3746
lakeofisles.com

The Lake of Isles is Foxwoods Resort Casino's award-winning 36-hole course, right across the street from the casino. The grand ball-room in the 50,000-square-foot clubhouse

seats 300 people, just to give you an idea of the scope of the place. Designed by Rees Jones, the course is divided in two parts, the north course and the south course, both with rolling terrain and wooded borders. Across from the pro shop in the clubhouse set into the hill, the Matches Tavern overlooks a large lake. Lake of Isles also has a year-round golf academy and offers packages with lodging at the Foxwoods hotels. But the most amazing things about this course are the island greens and tees, and walking across the quiet bridges under the red and gold colors of autumn.

PEQUOT GOLF CLUB
127 Wheeler Rd.
Stonington, CT 06378
(860) 535-1898
pequotgolf.com

Designed in 1958 by Wendell Ross, this classic semiprivate Connecticut course offers 5,903 yards from the longest tees and has a slope rating of 118. The course seems "traditional" today, but that doesn't make its deceptively straight holes and "simple" greens any less fun. They offer packages with local hotels like the Whaler's Inn, and eat-and-golf packages with the restaurant, and they have a pro shop and rental clubs. The Pequot's golf course also has undulating greens that will challenge your short game for sure. Jack Nicklaus set the official club record here in 1966, at 65 strokes. See if you can beat him.

Health & Wellness

ELEMIS SPA
Mohegan Sun
1 Mohegan Sun Blvd.
Uncasville, CT 06382
(888) 226-7711
mohegansun.com/spa

The Elemis Spa at Mohegan Sun offers a huge line of treatments in the 22,000-square-foot facility. There are 15 spa therapy rooms, 2 exotic suites, and 1 couples room. The Elemis also has a full-service hair and nail salon. They have 7 different kinds of facials, 8 kinds of massages, and 5 stress-relief and detox treatments. The spa also offers "exotic rituals and ceremonies" inspired by the Native American ethos, such as the Ceremony of the Strawberry Moon, and a couples massage lesson and exotic jasmine flower bath for two with a bottle of champagne and chocolate-covered strawberries. You can also get personal training and body composition analysis at the spa's full gymnasium and fitness center, or just swim in the huge pool in the 10,000-square-foot solarium. The sun is a rejuvenator, and the casino has harnessed its power for your well-deserved leisure.

G SPA AT MGM GRAND
Foxwoods Resort Casino
350 Trolley Line Blvd.
Mashantucket, CT 06338
(800) 369-9663
foxwoods.com/gspa.aspx

The 21,000-square-foot G Spa was designed by Gretta Monahan to be an oasis amid the flashing lights and jingling slots of America's largest casino. You can find facials, body treatments in Vichy shower rooms, hair and nail treatments, and an entire menu of relaxing massages. Try the "vino therapy," which uses grape-seed extract for its treatments. The spa also includes a fitness center, indoor lap pool, and coed Jacuzzi. You can also use the raindrop massaging jet showers, waterfall Jacuzzis, eucalyptus steam rooms, and saunas in the locker rooms. You must be 21 and over to use the spa. Foxwoods also includes a satellite of the Norwich Spa (see below), because, you know, there are a lot of stressed people coming to these casinos, and relaxation is a full-time job.

*NORWICH INN AND SPA
607 W. Thames St.
Norwich, CT 06360
(800) ASK-4-SPA
thespaatnorwichinn.com

Amid oak trees and a reflecting pool, this full-service spa at the Norwich Inn has an astonishing 32 treatment rooms, as well as a health club that includes indoor and outdoor pools. They offer facials, waxing, body wraps, body polishing, and of course massages. The milk and honey masque gets rave reviews. You can get the spa accessories, lotions, and herbal remedies in the boutique attached to the spa. There is also a full-service hair salon attached to the spa, and you can stay overnight at the luxurious inn. The Norwich has been called the best day spa in Connecticut for 10 consecutive years by *Connecticut Magazine* and the "Best Destination Spa in New England" by Yankee magazine. You should visit and find out why.

Hiking, Biking & Walking

HARTMAN PARK
Gungy Road
Lyme, CT 06371
No phone
lymelandtrust.org

In the Hamburg section of Lyme is a small park that contains some of the most interesting ruins in the state. The entrance is on Gungy Road, about a mile from where you turn off Beaverbook Road. Trails are marked with painted metal disks, and you should study the map to find where you want to go. The orange-blazed Heritage Trail is probably the one you want to stick to, with barn and house foundations, piles of stones from various farm buildings, and the most impressive feature—the Three Chimneys "fort" on a ridge. It may be one of the original Puritan forts that Lyonel Gardiner was commissioned to build in 1634, but archaeologists are not sure. It fits the layout of one of these lost forts, though it may be a very unusual site of some other sort. You'll have to see it for yourself. There are also charcoal kiln remnants, a mill site, and an ancient cemetery—if you can find it—just past a nice cascade in the power line clearing. Take a right off the orange trail onto a yellow connector trail; it will be on your right at the top of a small hillock.

PACHAUG STATE FOREST
219 Ekonk Hill Rd.
Voluntown, CT 06384
(860) 376-4075
ct.gov/dep [search "Pachaug State Forest"]
The first patent for a complete bicycle was issued to Connecticut inventor Pierre Lallement in 1866, and in 1878 Albert Pope produced the first high-wheeled Columbia bicycles here. Many people who could not afford horses, and women especially, found new freedom with this ingenious machine. Connecticut's largest state forest is the perfect place to find that freedom again, on a network of dirt roads made for horse and buggies, or perhaps made for you and your bike. You'll see old cellar holes and endless stone walls among the oaks and pines, as well a giant rhododendron sanctuary, a coniferous swamp full of these rare shrubs. In winter you can snowmobile here, and there are plenty of hiking trails too, including one up Mount Misery, with a great panoramic view across eastern Connecticut and Rhode Island. Camping is also available in three different sites at the park (see entry under camping).

Kidstuff

CHILDREN'S MUSEUM OF SOUTHEASTERN CONNECTICUT
409 Main St.
Niantic, CT 06357
(860) 691-1111
childrensmuseumsect.org

This building in downtown Niantic is called a museum, but it is really nothing of the kind. It is a hands-on experience for children: learning disguised as play. They can learn about health, literature (the sort of adventure stories that appeal to children), other cultures, and marine life. There's a crawl-in planetarium (seriously) and a re-creation of Anne Frank's attic. Like any museum, they also have changing exhibits, so things are always new for the children who come to this fun place regularly. There are two outside play areas as well. If this is the future of the playground, it is a very bright future indeed.

NATURE'S ART VILLAGE
1650 Hartford–New London Tpke.
Oakdale, CT 06370
(860) 443-4367
naturesartvillage.com
The main attraction at Nature's Art Village is a trail around a pond (called Raptor Bay) with life-size dinosaur replicas. They never fail to astonish children, though the erupting volcano will probably wow them as well. In summer the 10,000-square-foot water-spray park is probably where your kids will spend most of their time, with countless dinosaur-themed water features. So bring the swimsuits (they have changing rooms outside). Inside, the Fossil and Mineral Gallery has a collection of real artifacts, like petrified wood, real dinosaur eggs, and fluorescent minerals. The life-size dinosaur skeleton casts are impressive to kids of all ages as well. There are other activity areas too, like Thunder Creek, where you can pan for gold, and the Gateway Museum, showcasing innovation. For adults they now feature an antiques market. You can buy ice cream in the Cobalt Cafe and buy hundreds of stuffed dinosaurs in the gift shop. Or rather, you can buy one stuffed dinosaur from among the hundreds to choose from. Your kids, on the other hand, might want them all.

Nightlife

MOHEGAN SUN CASINO

1 Mohegan Sun Blvd.
Uncasville, CT 06382
(888) 226-7711
mohegansun.com

Although both casinos could obviously be considered nightlife, Mohegan deserves special mention. While Foxwoods has focused on fine-dining options, Mohegan has focused on a younger crowd, with a large selection of bars and nightclubs to choose from. Pubs like the Dubliner, Geno's Pub, Bow and Arrow, and Lucky's are more traditional sports taverns, for those of you who don't want to miss the game. For cocktails, head to Leffingwells Martini Bar by the glowing onyx mountain or the Sunset Bar on the sky level. If you like tequila, go to the SolToro Tequila Grill, and if you want freshly brewed beer, go to the Brew Pub. The Harvest Moon Bar, the Star Bar, the Lodge, the Taughannick Falls Bar . . . the options seem endless. If you're in the mood to dance, head to the Ultra 88 Night Club, with personalized bottle service, dancing, and VIP seating. Just like any good nightclub, they have a dress code, so don't wear flip-flops or ripped jeans and expect to get in on Friday night.

Spectator Sports

CONNECTICUT TIGERS AT DODD STADIUM

14 Stott Ave.
Norwich, CT 06360
(860) 887-7962
cttigers.com

This minor-league affiliate of the Detroit Tigers plays at the 6,000-seat Senator Dodd Stadium, and players that have passed through the organization include Bernie Williams, Jorge Posada, Andy Pettitte, and Don Mattingly. There are fun promotional giveaways and special events at every game. You can also buy snack bar meal and ticket combos. And best of all, you can arrange for messages to be announced or posted on the scoreboard, from "Happy Birthday" to "Will you marry me?" Check out the Yard Bar and Grill on the suite level, or the Hole in the Wall Bar on the right field line, both of which provide a unique way to see the game.

WATERFORD SPEED BOWL

1080 Hartford Tpke.
Waterford, CT 06385
(860) 442-1585
speedbowl.com

Not every place to go in New London County has to do with boats. One very important one has to do with cars: the Waterford Speed Bowl. Opened in 1951 as the New London Speedway, the short oval track is a third of a mile long, and you can watch stock cars, late models, minis, and modifieds tear it up every Saturday night. They also feature legend cars and wacky race series. There are 7,500 seats up for grabs, with general admission seating, so get there early to make sure you get your favorite spot. There's a midway with burgers, Italian sausages, and fried dough, as well as all sorts of NASCAR gear. Bring sunglasses, since the grandstand faces southwest, and early in the evening you might have some glare. You're also allowed to bring a cushion for the wooden bleachers: a good idea, since you'll be glued to your seat.

Water Sports

GARDNER LAKE

Route 354
Salem, CT 06420
(860) 526-2336
ct.gov/dep [search "Gardner Lake"]

Named for the local Gardner family, this natural lake on the border of Salem and Montville has been raised 4 feet by a 168-foot earthen dam, bringing the surface area to 528 acres. With an average depth of 14 feet, it is perfect for all sorts of boating activities. If you're there between sunset and 8 a.m., don't go over 6 mph, but otherwise you can water-ski to your heart's delight. The lake is stocked with a nice population of walleye, bullhead, and catfish if you'd like to fish. The best fishing is around Minnie Island, where the water is deepest. Incidentally, this heavily wooded island is technically a state park, Connecticut's smallest. Gardner Lake State Park is on the southern end and has a nice beach, though not much else. To get to the boat launch, take the turn off Route 354, and continue past the park entrance to a large turnaround and ramp at the lake. There's enough room for 54 vehicles here.

SHOPPING

Antiques

GRAND AND WATER ANTIQUES
145 Water St.
Stonington, CT 06378
(860) 535-2249
grandandwater.com

Billing itself as "antiques with a modern twist," Grand and Water is a pleasant shop full of reasonably priced items. One thing you'll find in abundance is formal mahogany furniture and accessories from the 19th and early 20th centuries, but you will also see china, silverware, and lithographs. Some of the antique furniture has been given new upholstery, and owner Deborah Norman also sells modern lamps and other accessories that match the decor, thus the "modern twist." Unlike some antiques stores, this is a place to actually shop to decorate and furnish your home. Also unlike some other antiques stores, Grand and Water is open year-round, Mon through Sat 10 a.m. to 5 p.m. and Sun noon to 4 p.m.

NEW LONDON ANTIQUES CENTER
123 Bank St.
New London, CT 06320
(860) 444-7598
newlondonmainstreet.org

With more than 100 dealers on 3 floors in the heart of downtown New London, this antiques center is one of the most interesting in the state, and the exact opposite of Grand and Water (above)—a hodgepodge of crazy stalls that you have to dig through like an archaeologist. The dealers obviously have almost everything, but you can expect to find books, clothing, furniture, paintings, vases, lamps, and thousands of knickknacks of all sorts. They have an especially impressive collection of sheet music and record albums, for those of you who love vintage music. They are open every day but Tuesday from 10 a.m. to 5 p.m. Park on the street, walk the waterfront, and check out the historical downtown sights like Whale Oil Row. Then take a piece of history home with you.

Books

BANK SQUARE BOOKS
53 W. Main St.
Mystic, CT 06355
(860) 536-3795
banksquarebooks.com

On the corner across from Mystic Pizza is one of Connecticut's great independent book stores. In fact, owner Annie Philbreck calls it "fiercely independent" and handpicks many of the selections. The painted whale out front has become a mascot of sorts, heralding the great selection of boating and local books. The children's section is the biggest, and there are also games and crosswords, maps and cards. The staff picks are legendary, and everyone who works there is knowledgeable and helpful. If you love books, walk up the hill past Mystic Pizza and the huge Baptist church, turning right on Library Street to see the gorgeous brick masterpiece of a library, built in the 1800s. There are other good shops to visit here, like the Company of Craftsmen (with American-made arts and crafts) and Peppergrass and Tulip (a women's clothing boutique). But Bank Square is the core of the town, and clearly people know it, because they recently expanded to twice their size. An independent bookstore expanding in this day and age? Yes indeed.

✳THE BOOK BARN
41 W. Main St.
Niantic, CT 06357
(860) 739-5715
bookbarnniantic.com

Scouring the used book stores of the world, you will not find one better than this. First of all, though it is called a book barn, it is actually not one barn, but five. And, with over 350,000 books and growing, they have expanded in the past decade, opening two smaller stores farther down Main Street toward the center of Niantic. The Book Barn "Downtown" has transportation, performing arts, movies, religion, philosophy, classical literature, humor, fashion, cookbooks, hard science, and genre fiction. The Book Barn "Midtown" has romances, fiction, mysteries, children's books, westerns, crafts, antiques, and education. The five barns at the original site have everything else. Kids can pet the goats or play with the barn cats. There is free coffee and donuts while you browse. This is an amusement park for book fanatics, and all who have been there speak of their selection, friendliness, and dedication to the printed word with reverence and love.

Farm Stores/Pick Your Own

HOLMBERG ORCHARDS
12 Orchard Ln.
Gales Ferry, CT 06335
(860) 464-7305
holmbergorchards.com

Established in 1896, Holmberg's farm and orchards grow fruits and vegetables for the greater Groton area. Seasonally available pick-your-own fruits include strawberries, blueberries, and raspberries, and the orchard trees bear apples, peaches, nectarines, and pears. Don't miss pumpkins in autumn. The farm market is located just below the farm on Route 12. Fresh pies, muffins, and pastries are the main draw, as well as a colorful array of farm-fresh fruits and vegetables. Other locally produced products are available, such as honey products from Full Bloom Apiary in Preston, goat milk soap from Old Lyme, and Boxed Goodes' signature rice, lentil, and bean packaged mixes and spices. You'll also find wine from local wineries, as well as Holmberg's own fruit wines and ciders. Fourth-generation son Russell guides the winery and cider press. Hard cider uses russet apples and tastes full-bodied and tart. Tour the orchards and newly planted grape vines, and look out for curiously placed glass bottles hanging from pear branches. These are placed around blossoms as they bud, and the pears grow in the glass. Holmberg partners with Connecticut's Westford Hill Distillery, which fills the pear-trapped bottles with its distilled *eau-de-vie*.

SANKOW BEAVER BROOK FARM
139 Beaver Brook Rd.
Lyme, CT 06371
(860) 434-2843
beaverbrookfarm.com

Stanley and Suzanne Sankow have a flock of over 700 Romney sheep that live on the farm and donate their wool, and the Sankows make blankets, hats, scarves, sweaters, and mittens, sold in a small shop on the farm. However, the farm also has cows and East Friesian sheep, which they milk to make cheeses, like Nehantic Abbey and a nice feta. They also have a thick farmstead yogurt that will completely change your ideas about this too often mass-produced breakfast food. You can also buy chops and sausages, vegetables, shepherd's pie, and ice cream here at the shop. Sankow's cheese is considered some of the best in the US and is at the forefront of the new movement that will hopefully put America back on par with the great cheese makers of Europe. Like many Connecticut farmers, they wear many hats. Theirs happen to be wool.

Home Goods and Crafts

THE BOWERBIRD
46 Halls Rd.
Old Lyme Marketplace
Old Lyme, CT 06371
(860) 434-3562
thebowerbird.com/about.htm

Established in 1989, The Bowerbird in Old Lyme is named for the family of Australian birds that create nests full of bright and sparkly things. Just like us. So if you want home goods, this is, as they say, "the quint-essential family shopping experience." They have everything from baby gifts to gourmet food, from jewelry to garden accessories. They have a fine collection of local goods too, which is always nice to see—all hand-picked from over 2,000 vendors. I picked up a couple kitchen gadgets and a joke gift last time I was there. Like most businesses, you can buy from their website. But that defeats the purpose of going to their charming store and browsing . . . you never know what you will find here.

Malls & Outlets

CRYSTAL MALL
850 Hartford Tpke.
Waterford, CT 06385
(860) 442-8501
simon.com [search "Crystal Mall"]

The Crystal Mall in Waterford is anchored by JCPenney, Macy's, and Sears. They also have 125 specialty stores in a clean, white indoor mall with such favorites as Forever 21, Victoria's Secret, Bed Bath & Beyond, and a Christmas Tree Shop. You'll find plenty of parking here without having to squeeze into spots a mile from the mall. A Target and Best Buy are also nearby. The food court has been recently improved, and other changes are afoot. And though most mall walkers don't notice it, this is the home of the world's largest Waterford crystal chandelier, made in Waterford's sister city in Ireland. Look up.

OLDE MISTICK VILLAGE
27 Coogan Blvd.
Mystic, CT 06355
(860) 536-4941
oldemistickvillage.com

Right off I-95, this re-creation of a 1720 village should not be confused with the Mystic Seaport. That is a little more authentic. How-ever, Olde Mistick Village provides a very pleasant shopping experience, with its cin-ema and shops that look more like houses and its stone walls, waterwheels, and ponds. There are 60 stores and restaurants here, including tea shops, clothing boutiques, and toy stores, as well as free concerts and events in summer and the Christmas season. Check out the Franklin's General Store and Eliza-beth and Harriet's Fine Handicrafts for sure. If you're hungry and don't feel like driving downtown, try the Steak Loft (steakloftct .com). There are shops and fine restaurants downtown by the harbor too; don't miss those and get stuck on this strip of road between the seaport and the aquarium.

Specialty Foods

B. F. CLYDE'S CIDER MILL
129 N. Stonington Rd.
Old Mystic, CT 06355
(860) 536-3354
bfclydescidermill.com

The oldest steam-powered cider mill in the US, established in 1881, is a National Historic Mechanical Engineering Landmark operated by the sixth generation of the Clyde family.

Open 7 days a week Sept until late Dec from 9 a.m. to 5 p.m., the cider mill also features cider making demonstrations on Saturday and Sunday. But you can come any day in season to get their hard or sweet ciders and apple wines, pies, jams, and jellies, along with local honey, maple syrup, fudge, pumpkin bread, gourds, Indian corn, pumpkins, candy apples, and kettle corn. Their apple cider donuts are the best I've ever tasted. But it's a treat just to be there, watching steam rising from the roof of the mill, hearing apples tumbling off the trucks, and smelling that sweet smell of fermentation.

BRIE AND BLEU
84 Bank St.
New London, CT 06320
(860) 437-2474
thamesriver.com

This cheese shop plus bistro in the center of downtown New London is a popular place in a blossoming district by the Thames River. Inside you'll find a restored 19th-century shop with wooden floors and a deck. You can come here just to pick out a creamy, delicious cheese, or you can have a meal in the little bistro in the back. The eatery offers a small but tasty menu of fondue, bruschetta, and of course cheese plates. They also have larger dishes like short ribs and roast chicken. Next door is Thames River Wine & Spirits, owned by the same company and featuring an outstanding brick cellar. You can even check it out while you're waiting for the food through the shared door. Combining wine and cheese makes so much sense that it makes you wonder why more of these shops and bistros aren't around.

CATO CORNER FARM
178 Cato Corner Rd.
Colchester, CT 06415
(860) 537-3884
catocornerfarm.com

Elizabeth MacAlister's amazing artisanal cheeses have won fans from across the country, and across the ocean in France. The cows are subjected to no hormones, herbicides, or chemical fertilizers—one reason their milk is so pure. But the other reasons are legion. The underground cave that Elizabeth built to keep the raw milk cheeses at the proper temperature might be one reason. The use of local Willimantic Brewing Company beer and Priam Vineyards wine in some of their cheeses might be another. Their creamy Brigid's Abbey cheese and the popular Bloomsday are two not to miss here. Also try the Black Ledge Blue or the aged Jeremy River cheddar, spectacular examples of their kinds. The farm shop is open Sat and Sun from 10 a.m. to 3 p.m.

ACCOMMODATIONS

All lodgings have both smoking and non-smoking rooms unless otherwise noted, or have a designated smoking area, and do not accept pets unless noted. Hotels, motels, and resorts are wheelchair accessible unless otherwise noted. Bed-and-breakfasts and inns are not wheelchair accessible unless otherwise noted, since many are in historic buildings exempt from the Americans with Disabilities Act. Call to make sure if there's any question. We do not list specific credit cards in either this section or the restaurants section.

Bed-and-Breakfasts

ABBEY'S LANTERN HILL INN $$$
780 Lantern Hill Rd.
Ledyard, CT 06339
(860) 572-0483
abbeyslanternhill.com

If you're more interested in a contemporary bed-and-breakfast than a colonial mansion with wide planked floors, Abbey's provides a nice alternative. There are 7 rooms, 2 of which have Jacuzzis and 2 with fireplaces. The location is perfect for exploring Mystic Country, with the casinos within walking distance in one direction and the seashore 20 minutes in the other. All this is under the backdrop of the quartz cliffs of Lantern Hill, which you can hike up on the Narragansett Trail off Wintechog Hill Road on the opposite side (look for the blue blazes). The view of the Foxwoods Casino from the top is well worth it.

FITCHCLAREMONT VINEYARD BED AND BREAKFAST $$$
83 Fitchville Rd.
Bozrah, CT 06334
(877) 889-0266
fitchclaremonthouse.com

This 1790 restored post-and-beam farmhouse sits on 4 acres of vineyard and contains 4 guest rooms, all with private bath, air-conditioning, and fireplaces. The breakfast is substantial and delicious, and the inn itself is within striking distance of all the major attractions of southeast Connecticut. Although they are not part of the Connecticut Wine Trail, they do make their own wine, which you will get to sample as one of their guests, including the Sweet William breakfast wine. The kindly retired couple, Nora and Warren, who own the B&B will do their best to make you comfortable. And if you're in the mood to get married, Warren is a justice of the peace.

FOURTEEN LINCOLN STREET $$$$
14 Lincoln St.
Niantic, CT 06357
(860) 739-6327
14lincolnstreet.com

Fourteen Lincoln Street has been restored by owners Susan and Benji Hahn and provides you with a unique experience: original tin pressed ceilings, wide pine floors, and leaded glass windows in a 19th-century Congregational church. This exceptional bed-and-breakfast is within walking distance of Niantic's pristine beaches (you get a pass if you're staying in town), seaside boardwalk, and quaint downtown center. Choose from 4 elegant guest rooms, and find nooks and quiet corners throughout the house. In the morning you'll enjoy cinnamon coffee cake, fresh fruit, and fresh-brewed coffee. Fourteen Lincoln Street also offers culinary classes at the bed-and-breakfast, with Chef Sherry Swanson, for between 8 and 12 people.

HIGH ACRES BED AND BREAKFAST $$$
222 NW Corner Rd.
North Stonington, CT 06359
(860) 887-4355
highacresbb.com

This 1743 farmhouse was added onto into the 1840s, but somehow that doesn't seem to stop purists from admiring it. You can choose from 5 guest rooms with private baths and full breakfast. But the most spectacular part of this accommodation might be the 150 acres of walking trails and views. You're in the middle of farm country here, with friendly horses living in stables right on the property. On the way through North Stonington at 1 Wyassup Rd., you should stop at the Stephen Main Homestead, maintained by the historical society (nostonhistoricalsociety.homestead.com). The annual Dye Day, held in June, features dyeing, spinning, and weaving.

HOUSE OF 1833 BED AND BREAKFAST $$$–$$$$
72 N. Stonington Rd.
Mystic, CT 06355
(860) 536-6325
houseof1833.com

This B&B was once a banker's mansion, now beautifully restored by owners Carol and Matt Nolan. The tall columns and a high cupola signal the sort of night you'll have here. There are 5 guest rooms, 2 with whirlpools, all with fireplaces. The house is full of antiques, and outside there is a swimming pool, croquet, and even a tennis court. You can borrow bicycles to ride around town. Innkeepers Robert Bankel and Evan Nickles also have a downtown location, a 3-room suite in the 1853 Captain Spicer mansion 2 blocks from the Mystic River drawbridge. At both locations, you'll enjoy custom details, unusual antique pieces, and good old-fashioned Connecticut hospitality.

LATHROP MANOR BED AND BREAKFAST $$$–$$$$
380 Washington St.
Norwich, CT 06360
(860) 204-9448
lathropmanor.com

Did you say you wanted to stay in a house that George Washington slept in? How about Benedict Arnold instead? This was the house of Dr. Daniel Lathrop, a pharmacist who apprenticed a local boy named Benedict Arnold, who of course went on to become a great general and even greater traitor. This was also briefly the home of Lydia Sigourney, the most popular poet of the early 1800s. Today you can enjoy an 18th-century fairy tale along with wireless Internet, showers, and a delicious breakfast. Though their number of available guest rooms has changed in the past, as of this writing you can stay in one of two 2 with private baths. Relax in one of the leather chairs by the fireplace in the Tavern Room and discuss how the young apprentice who worked for Dr. Lathrop could have gone so wrong.

✳OLD MYSTIC INN $$$
52 Main St.
Old Mystic, CT 06372
(860) 572-9422
oldmysticinn.com

In this old house and carriage house, you'll find 8 rooms named for New England

authors, including Connecticut's Mark Twain and Harriet Beecher Stowe. That's appropriate, because at one time this was a large bookstore. All the rooms have baths and queen-size beds; a few have working fireplaces and whirlpools. There's also a package deal with a local spa. Have your breakfast in a lamp-lit dining room and stroll the gardens. Or you might want to fall asleep in the hammock in the backyard. If the bugs aren't too bad, why not stay there all night? However, make sure you wake up for the gourmet breakfast made by owner and Culinary Institute of America graduate Michael Cardillo.

ROSELEDGE FARM BED AND BREAKFAST $$–$$$
418 Route 164
Preston, CT 06365
(860) 892-4739
roseledge.com

This 1720 farmhouse has fireplaces in each of its 3 guest rooms. Innkeepers Gail and Sandy Beecher will invite you to help with the morning chores, and you should take this opportunity to feed the goats and sheep or collect the morning's eggs. There's even a beehive on the property, but don't worry, you won't have to smoke it to check the honey. Instead, you'll be treated to feather beds, fresh flowers, wood-burning fireplaces, homemade soaps, and evening wine. In addition to selling plants, garden products, and books, Roseledge is also open to the public for tea and baked goods. You'll enjoy those in the morning of course, only one of many reasons to regret ever having to leave this wonderful place.

Hotels & Motels

✳BELLISSIMO GRANDE $$
411A and 411B Norwich Westerly Rd.
North Stonington, CT 06359
(860) 535-9924
bellissimogrande.com

This 164-room hotel benefits from its location only 3 miles from Foxwoods Casino, and smartly offers a complimentary limousine service in a stretch SUV for all the guests going to and from the casino. This makes it a slightly cheaper alternative to staying at the resorts themselves, and yet the spacious and amenity-filled rooms are just as nice. There's a heated indoor pool, a Starbucks coffee bar where you can get breakfast, Jacuzzis in many rooms, plasma televisions, and more. They have "quiet hours" to make sure the drunks don't come back and whoop it up while the rest of us are trying to sleep. (I wish every place had this rule, which is how I can tell I'm getting older.) The Bistro is open on Friday and Saturday nights, and they also have a spa at the hotel if you'd like to relax after a tough day at the gaming tables. All this, and they rate as an eco-friendly "green lodging" establishment too.

Inns

BEE AND THISTLE INN $$$
100 Lyme St.
Old Lyme, CT 06371
(860) 434-1667
beeandthistleinn.com

In this 1756 homestead on the Lieutenant River are 11 guest rooms, only 1 of which does not have a private bath. There are also 6 fireplaces and gardens around the house. The inn also has a cottage with a full kitchen, and a deck to look out over the landscape. In winter you can get afternoon tea on Wednesday through Saturday afternoons, and the on-site spa room offers scrubs, facials, and a variety of massages. But these facts don't really seem to do the Bee and Thistle justice, nor does describing its stenciled walls, wooden floors, harpist on Saturday evening, and the most romantic dining room in the state ($$$$; reservations required). Instead, think on this: If you choose their "fall in love" package for couples, you may fall in love, but

not with each other. You'll fall for the Bee and Thistle, and perhaps for Connecticut.

INN AT LOWER FARM $$–$$$
119 Mystic Rd.
North Stonington, CT 06359
(866) 535-9075
lowerfarm.com

Walking in and seeing the open-hearth fireplace in the Keeping Room is a great introduction to this 260-year-old colonial farmhouse. There are 6 other working fireplaces in the house too, along with wide floorboards and original wood paneling. The inn has 4 large guest rooms with private baths, 2 of which have working fireplaces and 1 of which features a whirlpool. The homemade scones at breakfast or for afternoon tea are a treat, and the prices are very reasonable for Mystic Country. The 5 acres the inn sits on are a wildlife habitat and invite you to explore the stone walls and fields. Or sit on the porch swing or lie in the hammock and get ready for your next adventure.

STEAMBOAT INN $$$$
73 Steamboat Wharf
Mystic, CT 06355
(860) 536-8300
steamboatinnmystic.com

Right on the Mystic River by the drawbridge, this collection of decorator-designed suites overlooking the water is a great place to stay in downtown Mystic. There's docking for guests coming by boat (at $1.50 per foot), a full hot breakfast at their little coffee bar, and wood-burning fireplaces in 6 of the 11 rooms. The other 5 have kitchenettes and whirlpools. Every room is differently shaped and decorated, mostly because of the unusual building, which overhangs and follows the arc of the river. The inn is non-smoking, and the fireplaces are in operation Oct through Apr. They serve a full breakfast from 8:30 to 10 a.m. Stay here and you'll have yachts and sailboats gliding right by your window all day, perhaps 20 yards away.

STONECROFT COUNTRY INN $$$
515 Pumpkin Hill Rd.
Ledyard, CT 06339
(800) 772-0774
stonecroft.com

The Stonecroft Country Inn is really 2 inns and a restaurant. There are 4 rooms in the 1807 Georgian Colonial house and 6 in the renovated post-and-beam barn. Called the Grange, the barn's uniquely decorated rooms all feature whirlpool tubs, heated towel racks, wide-screen televisions, and gas fireplaces. The rooms .in the main house have wood-burning fireplaces and writing desks. Several of the rooms in both buildings have outdoor patios or decks, and there is a wheelchair-accessible room. The 75-seat Mystic restaurant serves you a fine breakfast of Russian potatoes, quiche, and french toast. You can also eat dinner there. Whatever you do, definitely sit outside by the pond and waterfall and enjoy a nightcap by the roaring fire pit.

✳WHALER'S INN $$$–$$$$
20 E. Main St.
Mystic, CT 06355
(800) 243-2588
whalersinnmystic.com

This old-style seaport inn sits right in the heart of town, with the drawbridge, the old white churches, and the awesome stone library on the hill. It's across from the Mystic flagpole, which looks suspiciously like a ship's mast. You can see the tall masts of the seaport too, and the walk around to the museum is about half a mile (though you could more easily swim or sail across). The inn has 45 rooms in a traditional downtown atmosphere, very different from the usual bed-and-breakfast or inn. This is the place the sailors would have gone to rest after their long service on board a ship,

though of course the decor and amenities are much fancier than they would have expected. The Whaler's Inn also offers 8 rooms in the Hoxie House next door, which is a re-creation of a 19th-century hotel. The best part for families is that children are free.

Resorts

FOXWOODS RESORT $$$–$$$$
350 Trolley Line Blvd.
Mashantucket, CT 06338
(800) 369-9663
foxwoods.com

Foxwoods Resort actually has 4 different lodging options, all of which are expensive, but some less so. If you're looking for a cheaper option, stay in one of the 280 rooms or suites at the Two Trees Inn, which is a long walk or quick shuttle ride from the casino. The 312-room Great Cedar Hotel is the next cheapest, and the 800-room Grand Pequot Tower and the 825-room MGM Grand hotels are the most expensive. They also have the best rooms, and the best views—far out over the woodlands of eastern Connecticut. There are "director suites" and "producer suites" at the MGM that truly give new meaning to "high roller" living. There's a 5,500-square-foot pool (with poolside cabanas and bar) for guests too. You can get discounts on the rooms as a member of the Wampum Club, and the resort is wheelchair accessible. See the entries under casinos, golf courses, and health & wellness for the many, many reasons this "hotel" qualifies as a resort, too many to list again.

✳INN AT MYSTIC $$–$$$$
3 Williams Ave.
Mystic, CT 06355
(860) 536-9604
innatmystic.com

On the National Register of Historic Places, this newly renovated resort overlooking the Sound and downtown Mystic is a former estate. There are 47 rooms, 5 suites, and 4 efficiencies. The fireplace and whirl-pool rooms in the gatehouse are the best, although there are balcony rooms in the east wing that other people swear by. The 5 suites in the central Georgian Colonial mansion include one used by Humphrey Bogart and Lauren Bacall on their honeymoon. Indoor and outdoor pools, tennis courts, boating, a fitness center, and the on-site restaurant, the Flood Tide, make this more of a resort than an inn. Go for the duckling or rack of lamb. You can even get afternoon tea here. Come for the holiday season and see the Mystic Tree Lighting and Boat Parade and partici-pate in the Community Carol Sing.

MOHEGAN SUN RESORT $$$$
1 Mohegan Sun Blvd.
Uncasville, CT 06382
(888) 226-7711
mohegansun.com

With more than 1,300 guest rooms, the Mohegan Sun hotel is a mirrored wonder, best seen from the surrounding hills (like the one at Holmberg Orchards). With luxu-rious 450-square-foot-or-more rooms that include marble bathrooms, you wouldn't think Mohegan would need "luxury suites," but they have them. There is a pool and fitness center available only to guests, and the resort is wheelchair accessible. The Sun also has an enormous guests-only sun ter-race for the summer months, and the hotel staff will get you pretty much anything you want. Along with 130,000 square feet of retail shopping, see the entry under casinos and health & wellness for the dozens of reasons this "hotel" qualifies as a resort. Stay here and complete your high stakes adventure.

✳NORWICH INN AND SPA $$$$
607 W. Thames St.
Norwich, CT 06360
(800) ASK-4-SPA
thespaatnorwichinn.com

Built in 1929 by the city, this Georgian-style inn had fallen into disrepair when it was rescued by spa developer Edward Safdie; it is now one of the best resorts in the state. The inn has 65 rooms and 60 villas. What is a villa? Well, they have studio or duplex condo-minium units with full baths, galley kitchens, dining areas, and fireplaces. If you're going to be staying here for a long time, using the inn as a base to explore New London County, these are great options. Along with the extensive spa (see entry), the inn has tennis courts, indoor and outdoor pools, hik-ing trails, and golf packages. The restaurant, Kensington's (see entry), and the Ascot Pub ($$) serve delicious modern American fare. This is luxury living for those of us who might not want to stay in the casinos or along the shoreline.

Camping

HOPEVILLE POND STATE PARK $
193 Roode Rd.
Jewett City, CT 06351
(860) 376-2920
ct.gov/dep [search "Hopeville Pond State Forest"]

Once the site of corn mills and sawmills, this small community went up in flames dur-ing the turn of the 20th century. Later, the Pachaug River was dammed to create Hope-ville Pond, managed by the Civilian Conser-vation Corps. Today campers, anglers, and hikers come to Jewett City for recreation, and the ruins of the thriving community lie under the 137-acre lake and crumbling in the surrounding woodlands. The camp-ground offers 80 sites in a wooded setting right on an ax-head-shaped peninsula on the lake. Sites E-9, E-11, E-13, and E-15 are probably the best, although they are the farthest from the bathrooms and the beach. The lake has a launch and is a great place to catch lake trout, either from a boat or from the shore. The blue-blazed Nehantic Trail also crosses the park. You can camp here from Apr to the end of Sept, when the gate closes until the next spring.

PACHAUG STATE FOREST $
219 Ekonk Hill Rd.
Voluntown, CT 06384
(860) 376-4075
ct.gov/dep [search "Pachaug State Forest"]

There are 3 wooded campgrounds in this huge state forest on the edge of Rhode Island. Green Falls campground is 3 miles east of town, with 18 forested sites next to a pond for fishing and swimming. Mount Misery's campground has 22 sites and a stream for fishing. You can bring a motor home to these campgrounds as well, but there are no hookups or dumping stations. You can also bring your pets. The third campground is for equestrians only; Frog Hollow Horse Camp has 18 sites in a lightly wooded area. The 30 miles of trails and the boat launch onto Pachaug Pond make this state forest a great place to camp.

*ROCKY NECK STATE PARK $
244 W. Main St. (Route 156)
East Lyme, CT 06357
(860) 739-5471
ct.gov/dep [search "Rocky Neck State Park"]

Rocky Neck has 150 campsites from which you can walk under the train trestle (which is cooler than it sounds) and onto the beach. There are bathhouses (not always a feature at state park campgrounds), play areas, dressing rooms, picnic tables, and of course the beach. Although it is "beach camping," most of the sites are wooded, unlike Hammonasset's huge campground down the coast. The campground is open Apr to Sept, though the park is open year-round. Junior naturalist activities and nature lectures, walks, and shows are offered

throughout the summer season. This is one of the few places in southern New England where bluffs meet the sea, and the views from the top are excellent. Don't miss the Book Barn (see entry), only a mile down the road—the best used book store in New England (possibly in America).

WATER'S EDGE CAMPGROUND $
271 Leonard Bridge Rd.
Lebanon, CT 06249
(860) 642-7470
watersedgecampground.com

This quiet family campground in northern Lebanon is set around a small lake (thus the name), where you can swim or fish. There's also a swimming pool, basketball courts, horseshoe pits, a sand volleyball court, 2 playgrounds, paddleboats, and an arcade. They have a camp store with all you'll need, and laundry facilities. Throughout the season they offer different activities, from pizza parties to horseshoe tournaments. If you'd rather not sleep on the ground, there are 5 rental units available (cabins and trailers); otherwise, there are about 150 sites to choose from, many right around the lake and some back in the woods, if that's what you'd prefer. The Air Line State Park Trail (see entry in Windham County) is only a few steps from the entrance, so bring your mountain bike or boots and set off toward Willimantic.

RESTAURANTS

Please note that all Connecticut restaurants are smoke free, and all are required to be wheelchair accessible. Pets are not allowed inside most restaurants, but during the warmer months, there are plenty of restaurants with patio areas just right for your canine friend. Call ahead to make sure it's okay.

American & Modern

BOBBY FLAY'S BAR AMERICAIN $$$$
Mohegan Sun
1 Mohegan Sun Blvd.
Uncasville, CT 06382
(888) 226-7711
mohegansun.com/dining/bar-americain
.html

Chef Bobby Flay brings interesting dishes from around the country to Mohegan, from Hawaiian yellowtail poke to soft-shell crab in New Orleans gumbo sauce. From spoon-bread to red cabbage slaw, he seems to pick and choose the most beloved American staples, and then puts his own Flay twist on them. The burger and the pizza are two classics that he has made his own here. For sides, get the creamed kale and hot potato chips with blue cheese sauce. For dessert, the red velvet brownie sundae is delicious. This isn't "American" food like you'd expect at the local chain restaurant. Sure, you've seen this guy on a dozen shows on the Food Network, and that might make you pay more attention to the celebrity than the meals he's making. But he got there in the first place by making really great food. Pay attention to it.

DAVID BURKE PRIME $$$$
Foxwoods Resort Casino
350 Trolley Line Blvd.
Mashantucket, CT 06338
(860) 312-8753
davidburkeprime.com

Prime tries to "fill that steak-shaped hole in your life" with the best cuts from Creekstone Farms in Kentucky, which are then dry-aged for 28 to 75 days in the restaurant's in-house dry-aging room. The double-cut maple-pepper bacon strips, surf and turf dumplings, and Parmesan meatballs are all great appetizers. Or if you like seafood, get the Pequot Tower raw bar. However, David Burke made his reputation with his invention of the crackling pork shank, and there's

a good reason for that. It is one of the largest, tastiest pieces of meat you will ever (try to) eat. They also have an enormous wine selection, and if you see a giant glass-walled tower of wine as you walk around the casino shops and wonder what it is, that's Prime's wine cellar. Or rather, wine tower, and you can just follow it down to the hotel level for one of the best meals of your life.

KENSINGTON'S $$$
Norwich Inn and Spa
607 W. Thames St.
Norwich, CT 06360
(860) 425-3630
thespaatnorwichinn.com/dining_
kensingtons.aspx

This restaurant at the Norwich Inn and Spa has a fantastic reputation for simple American food, done in a gourmet manner. In its impressive wine cellar full of choice vintages, Kensington's also has a huge selection of Connecticut offerings from wineries like Priam, Taylor Brooke, Jonathan Edwards, and Stonington. They also try to use as many Connecticut-grown products in their meals as possible, and that loyalty to the local farmers ends up being a huge bonus to your palate. The gazpacho is made from Holmberg Orchards tomatoes, and the lemon baked cod is caught right off the Connecticut coast. Of course they have other great stuff on their menu too, like mushroom dumplings and four-grain polenta cake. For dessert, the brie cheesecake or the chocolate ginseng decadence are delicious endings to your meal.

NOAH'S $$
113 Water St.
Stonington, CT 06378
(860) 535-3925
noahsfinefood.com

Noah's has been around for 35 years, serving "scratch cooking"—basic, fresh, and often made from local ingredients. Recently it was made extra-famous in the movie *Hope Springs* with Tommy Lee Jones and Connecticut's own Meryl Streep. If you're there for breakfast, try the challah french toast. For lunch or dinner appetizers, the Korean green onion pancakes are a nice surprise, and the oyster stew is a classic Connecticut dish. At dinner, the chicken and dumplings is a nice surprise—a classic that Noah's has brought back from the culinary graveyard and into wonderful life. They change their lobster dish daily; ask your server for what the chef is doing that day. Noah's is closed on Monday but otherwise open for breakfast through dinner every day. And don't forget their Sunday brunch! Every time I stop here the food is great—a perfect place for lunch, and my old/new go-to place in Stonington.

*OYSTER CLUB $$$
13 Water St.
Mystic, CT 06355
(860) 415-9266
oysterclubct.com

This "farm and sea to table" restaurant in a purple clapboard in historic Mystic showcases local specialties and seasonal treats. Find a seat in the vaulted exposed-beam dining room, at the bar, or outside on the porch in summer. There isn't a lot of seating compared to the nearby S&P Oyster—this is a casual bistro rather than a restaurant. But it is packed on weekends in summer, like all Mystic. When we were there on a Friday in summer, it was jam-packed, but the waitstaff was incredibly nice, and we enjoyed drinks and oysters from the raw bar while we waited for a table to open. Unfortunately I can't tell you what to order, because like most of these locally sourced restaurants, the menu is constantly changing. Some of the dishes from the past include roasted tomatoes with ricotta, lardo, and fresh basil; hot lobster rolls with lemon, parsley, and crispy shallots; and handmade pappardelle

with braised rabbit, Riesling, flame tomatoes, fresh mint, and Parmesan. The homemade bread is unbelievable, and you can end your meal with some eau-de-vie from Westford Hill Distillery.

STONECROFT COUNTRY INN $$$
515 Pumpkin Hill Rd.
Ledyard, CT 06339
(800) 772-0774
stonecroft.com

This elegant dining room in the 1807 Stonecroft Country Inn is a great place for a romantic candlelight dinner by the fireplace. For an appetizer, try the crispy lump crab, salmon, and lobster beignets with chipotle pepper, mint, and orange dipping sauce; and then get the spicy slow-braised chicken breast with beer, fennel, onion, smoked paprika, and tomato ragout. For dessert ask if they have the peanut butter pie; if they do, relish every morsel. They have a great Sunday brunch too; make sure you try the maple pecan waffles with fresh berries and cream. In summer you can sit on the terrace among the flower gardens, for breakfast or dinner.

Asian & Indian

DEV'S ON BANK STREET $$
357 Bank St.
New London, CT 06320
(860) 442-3387
devsonbank.com

Surely this is the only place in Connecticut that mixes Spanish tapas and Asian dim sum into one fantastic mélange of small plates. If not, it is the best. They get some of their ingredients from local farmers, which is always nice, but their combinations are what make this place a new classic. The Asian side features such goodies as Mongolian barbecue, Red Dragon Noodle Bowl, and Chairman Chow's Dumplings. The Mediterranean menu is slightly more extensive, with dishes like patatas bravas, painted grapes, and paella. The prices for these little treats are reasonable, especially compared to some of the high-end "tapas" joints. Along with their tapas they have a good selection of regular entrees. This has become one of the places to go during happy hour downtown.

✳SHRINE $$$
Foxwoods Resort Casino
350 Trolley Line Blvd.
Mashantucket, CT 06338
(800) 369-9663
shrinemgmfoxwoods.com
Located in the newer MGM section of America's largest and most elaborate casino complex, Shrine is the best pan-Asian food you'll find in the county, with Japanese pork katsu, grilled Mongolian skirt steak, and a General Tso chicken that will certainly not taste like the stuff you got for Chinese takeout. The menu has a fantastic selection of sashimi and rolls, along with better-than-you've-ever-had lobster Rangoon, duck buns, and red miso five-spice wings. The martinis and other cocktails are great accompaniments to the meal, or just as a nightcap after winning at the tables. The restaurant itself is huge, but believe it or not, it fills up. Get there early and get the fried rice wok dishes to share.

Breakfast & Lunch

✳ASHLAWN FARM COFFEE $
78 Bill Hill Rd.
Lyme, CT 06371
(860) 434-3636
farmcoffee.com
I first heard of Ashlawn from a connoisseur friend of ours, not a Connecticut partisan, who declared it the best coffee he's ever tasted. Well, I ordered some online, and it was fantastic. I looked up the farm in Lyme and discovered that all the roasting is done on-site, in an old workshop next to a dairy barn, using state-of-the-art equipment. Then they opened a cafe on-site, and I thought

this must be a gift from the coffee gods to me and all lovers of our state and the holy bean. Closed on Sunday and Monday, they are open until 4 p.m. on weekdays and 2 p.m. on Saturday. On Saturday in season, they have the Lyme farmers' market at Ashlawn too. They have a second cafe at the Old Saybrook Train Station (455 Boston Post Rd.; 860-339-5663), open 7 days a week.

KITCHEN LITTLE $$
Mystic River Marina
36 Quarry Rd.
Mystic, CT 06355
(860) 536-2122
kitchenlittle.org
For over 30 years Flo Klewin has served the finest and most interesting breakfasts in Mystic. In this long red building by the Mystic River you can find great, atypical breakfast options like the Portuguese Fisherman—spicy chourico and linguica scrambled with eggs, peppers, onions, and jalapeño cheese in a special sauce, on a Portuguese roll. Flo uses cage-free eggs from the best sources, and the difference to your omelets is obvious. Kitchen Little is open for breakfast daily at 6:30 a.m., and also has lunch options Mon through Fri, like lobster rolls and other sandwiches. But they are known for their breakfasts, and with options like the pancake sandwich (seriously), you can't go wrong. Since their move to the marina, they also serve beer, wine, and champagne, as well as dinner in season.

MORNING GLORY CAFE $$
11 Halls Rd.
Old Lyme, CT 06371
(860) 434-0480
morningglorycafeoldlyme.com
The owners of the Morning Glory arrived in Old Lyme as refugees from war-torn Laos in 1980, after stowing away on a convoy and sneaking into Thailand. Once they had

learned English and become part of Connecticut, they opened this lovely restaurant on the Lieutenant River, serving breakfast and lunch to the people who had welcomed them into the community. They serve all the American classics you could want—from bacon and eggs to buttermilk pancakes at breakfast, and from cheeseburgers to fish-and-chips for lunch. But they also have some delicious specialties from their home cuisine, with egg rolls, pho, and pad thai. It is hard to tell which they do better, though. After lunch take a cup of coffee and sit by the river on the Adirondack chairs, and think of your own American journey.

WASHINGTON STREET COFFEE $
13 Washington St.
New London, CT 06320
(860) 437-0664
washingtonstreetcoffeehouse.com

I first found this place when I needed a coffee fix doing research in New London. And the coffee was good. But Washington Street is so much more than coffee. They have delicious breakfast options, as you might expect (try the huevos rancheros). But when lunch rolls around, suddenly there are options from all over the world, like Thai green curry with onion, mushrooms, and carrots over jasmine rice, or spicy miso noodle soup with roast pork and bok choy. They also have banh mi and Cuban sandwiches. It's amazing. For those of you who don't like a trip around the world with your coffee, have the grilled cheese or beet salad. Sit at their beautiful wood tables and dream of a New London renaissance.

WHEN PIGS FLY CAFE $
97 Rope Ferry Rd.
Waterford, CT 06385
(860) 444-1110
whenpigsflycafe.com

Owners Sarina and Gwen McGugan swore they would never open a second restaurant, or only "when pigs fly," but we should be glad that they reneged on that promise. This cafe has become a favorite among tourists and locals. You will probably notice the many pictures and statues of pigs. The menu is much more creative than most breakfast and lunch places, and they take customer suggestions and experiment with combinations regularly. They make everything on the spot, with no precooked items, not even the soups. Some things are seasonal, like pumpkin pancakes in autumn and french toast made with eggnog in winter. They have a number of whole-grain, vegetarian, and gluten-free options as well. Note that they only take cash but do have an ATM on site.

French

*PARAGON $$$$
Foxwoods Resort Casino
350 Trolley Line Blvd.
Mashantucket, CT 06338
(800) 369-9663
foxwoods.com/paragon.aspx

Paragon considers itself "French" dining, and that's why it is in this category. But it's hard to put a label on the seriousness of this food. Featuring changing, seasonal menus and daily market specials, the menu is hard to quantify. The "taste of Paragon" appetizer perfectly sums that up, with a chef's daily selection of tasty tidbits to try. Last time I was there I had the crispy salmon belly with spicy mayo, a Peking duck sandwich in lotus roll with cucumbers and 7-UP hoison sauce, peekytoe crab salad with chilled greens, avocado, and grapefruit, mero sea bass with sticky rice, and Wagyu "eye of the rib eye" with truffle mousse. As far as lobster, Paragon has a number of different preparations, like wood grilled and Cantonese, and you can pick the sauce. Located on the 24th floor of the Grand Pequot Tower, Paragon's live piano lounge is also the place among those in the know to get some champagne and sushi appetizers while waiting for a show. The sun set over the trees of western Connecticut as we ate and listened to jazz classics, enclosed by dark wood and silver, underneath bison cave paintings on the ceiling. It was one of my finest dining experiences.

Ice Cream

BUTTONWOOD FARM ICE CREAM $
473 Shetucket Tpke.
Griswold, CT 06351
(860) 376-4081
buttonwoodfarmicecream.com

Let's face it, most people come to Buttonwood Farm for the ice cream. There are dozens of flavors, and the portions are huge. I mean, Frozen Pudding flavor, with rum, raisins, peaches, pineapple, maraschino cherries, and apples? That's insane. Call me old-fashioned, but I prefer the traditional flavor of Coffee Mocha Crunch. You can also visit Buttonwood in autumn for their corn maze, or just to enjoy meeting the cows and watching their sunflower field turn as the day goes by. Dairy farming has become a specialty business in Connecticut, and Buttonwood has figured out the formula for success.

✳MYSTIC DRAWBRIDGE ICE CREAM $
2 W. Main St.
Mystic, CT 06355
(860) 572-7978
mysticdrawbridgeicecream.com

Ice cream has been sold in this store in Mystic right across from the drawbridge's giant counterweight since the 1800s. The current owners continue this tradition, making dense ice cream without the usual air content of store-bought and homemade ice creams. They are made one batch at a time, hand mixing it with fresh fruits, nuts, and candy. Flavors like Mystic Mud and Sticky Fractured Finger are delightful twists, and their traditional flavors, like Vermont Maple

Nut, are worth a lick. They also have salads, sandwiches, and wraps, as well as fresh-baked pastries and gourmet coffees. The red velvet cake and Dirty Hippie drink (chai latte with espresso) are keepers. But of course this is a place for ice cream, and if you're seeing the attractions in Mystic Country, it's the place to take your sweetheart or your kids for a cone.

Italian

BRAVO BRAVO $$$
20 E. Main St.
Mystic, CT 06355
(860) 536-3228
bravobravoct.com

Looking for a romantic night out in Mystic after a day seeing the aquarium and seaport? Check out Bravo Bravo's small restaurant near the bridge. A wall of large windows overlooks the main street in Mystic—allowing diners to watch the hustle of the world pass by while sipping on oversize martinis or exceptional wines and feasting on creative pastas, fresh fish, and homemade desserts. Black-and-white photographs fill the walls of the bar, which flows into a dining room adorned with flickering white candles reflecting in mirrors placed throughout. The company that opened Bravo Bravo also opened the more casual Azu down the street, if you're in the mood for a more crowded and gregarious dining experience.

TODD ENGLISH'S TUSCANY $$$
Mohegan Sun
1 Mohegan Sun Blvd.
Uncasville, CT 06382
(888) 226-7711
mohegansun.com/poi/dining/todd
-english-s-tuscany.html

Celebrity chefs seem to be taking over the dining landscape, and that is not a bad thing. Todd English is an expert in Italian cuisine, and he serves both classic favorites and interesting twists. The Tuscany restaurant has a terrace right by the Taughannick waterfall, and a rustic dining room where you can enjoy handcrafted potato gnocchi, osso buco, and seafood spaghetti. Get the fresh antipasti, and save room for the Venetian dessert table. The breakfasts here are also amazing; try the Tuscan smoked pork with apple pierogis. English offers a four-course chef's tasting, and he has brought high-end Italian here to eastern Connecticut. Even if you don't like to gamble, you should come here just for the food.

Pizza

MYSTIC PIZZA $$
56 W. Main St.
Mystic, CT 06355
(860) 536-3700
mysticpizza.com

As the hill rises to the west from the Mystic River, you will find the sign for one of the most famous restaurants in the state, Mystic Pizza. Don't expect the interior to look like the one in the Julia Roberts film; those scenes were filmed in nearby Stonington. But that's a good thing, because after a 1996 expansion, the restaurant has a lot more space for you and your family. The pizza itself lies somewhere between thin and thick crust, and defies most categorizations in other ways as well. The unique location and name of the eatery inspired the writing of the film, and the film has inspired the continued success of the eatery (and its new line of grocery store pies). But guess what? The "slice of heaven" pizza is really good too.

Road Food

HARRY'S PLACE $
104 Broadway
Colchester, CT 06415
(860) 537-2410
harrysplace.biz

Since the distant date of 1918, Harry's roadside stand has been serving their juicy burgers on Route 85 near the center of Colchester seasonally from Apr to Oct each year. The hamburgers are the standout famous food here, and they are done in a slightly different, possibly revolutionary, way. The griddle is kept very hot and oiled, and the burger is cooked in a round, almost spherical manner before being squashed down with a spatula so it can be put on your roll (baked in Windsor by some sort of genius). This keeps them incredibly juicy, and it's a wonder more places don't take Harry's amazing success with it (almost 100 years!) and run. The plump chili dogs and fried clams are good alternatives if you don't like burgers (?). I am a fan of the cream cheese bites too. For dessert, they have a great homemade ice-cream selection. Dip your side of onion rings in their melted cheese sauce. I know it sounds wrong, but it is oh so right.

NORM'S DINER $
171 Bridge St.
Groton, CT 06340
(860) 445-5026
No website

This is a 1954 vintage metal-sided diner with a barreled roof, a neon sign, and Formica tables inside. Simply put, stepping inside Norm's is stepping into the past. And that past was once full of greasy spoon diners like this, a vanishing breed on the American landscape. This is still the real deal, a 24-hour hangout with cramped booths and huge portions. For breakfast, try the biscuits and gravy, considered by many to be the best in the state. For lunch or dinner, try the locally famous beef stew, and cheesecake for dessert. If you're still awake at 3 in the morning, this is the place to go for pancakes and coffee. My favorite is the "Norm's Pick," a rib-eye steak on a hard roll, tender and hearty.

*PHILLY'S CHEESESTEAKS $

33 Sherman St.
Norwich, CT 06360
(860) 886-9449
phillysct.com

You might be wondering why a Philadelphia sandwich is making its appearance in a Connecticut guide, especially from a partisan like me. However, the fact that Philly's sandwich was recently rated as the best sandwich in America makes this little Norwich gem impossible to ignore. Not the best cheesesteak, mind you, the best sandwich overall. Owner Shem Adams moved from Philadelphia, just as I did, and has found the secret formula for success that so many cheesesteak joints attempt and so often lack. In my youth I'd had them at all the classic places in Pennsylvania, and these match up or exceed the originals. Their cheesesteak truly is sublime, with that meaty, Cheez Whiz goodness balanced with just enough spice. Of course it's not just cheesesteaks at Philly's; they have hoagies (better known around here as subs or grinders) and inventive dishes like Kobe beef fries and "phried" bread. Open every day but Sunday.

Seafood

*ABBOTT'S LOBSTER IN THE
   ROUGH $$

117 Pearl St.
Noank, CT 06340
(860) 536-7719
abbotts-lobster.com

This large seafood shack in the charming seaside village of Noank is a perennial favorite among lobster-loving tourists and locals. Walk up to the array of windows and stand in line; they will call out your order. Pack a tablecloth, glasses, and a bottle of wine, perhaps a nice Connecticut Chardonnay, to have with your lobster, and sit on the decks overlooking the Sound. If you're hungry, try the Seafood Feast—a complete shore dinner with chowder, shrimp, steamers, mussels, potato chips, coleslaw, and a full steamed lobster, which is what they do best. For dessert, don't miss their strawberry shortcake. One note of caution: Abbott's heretically uses hamburger rolls for their lobster roll sandwich. Somehow no one seems to mind.

S&P OYSTER COMPANY $$$

1 Holmes St.
Mystic, CT 06355
(860) 536-2674
sp-oyster.com

The popular S&P Oyster is busy all the time in season, so make a reservation; or go for a drink upstairs in the Captain's Room, with its own bar and a view over the houses of Captain's Row along the Mystic River. In fact, always try to get seating here in the cooler months. In the warmer months, sit out in the gardens of zinnias and begonias by the drawbridge for the ultimate Mystic experience. There is plenty of seating in general compared to other Mystic restaurants. If you're here for lunch, the oyster grinder is something you're not likely to find elsewhere, although that's too bad! Their fish-and-chips comes with jicama, carrot, and roasted poblano pepper slaw, a twist on the traditional. S&P somehow combines classy with a shore restaurant vibe, and it works. They serve local barrel wine from Jonathan Edwards Vineyard by the glass. You can also catch the *Mystic Express* for a harbor tour on the dock right outside S&P.

SEA SWIRL $$

30 Williams Ave.
Mystic, CT 06355
(860) 536-3452
seaswirlofmystic.com

Sea Swirl of Mystic could be categorized under road food or seafood, but although their hot dogs, ice cream, and hamburgers are excellent, their seafood is what brings people back time and time again. Owned by the Blaney family, the Swirl has been around for three decades, serving amazing fried whole-belly clams and excellent clam fritters. Taking no sides, they serve both kinds of clam chowder—the southern New England broth chowder (which they unfortunately call Rhode Island—it's Connecticut clam chowder, guys) and the milk chowder more commonly called New England. Their specialty is fried seafood, and items like fried oysters and fried scallops are done in a secret way that makes them better than the typical shack. Sit at a picnic table on the deck by the shack and watch the sun set over Mystic.

SKIPPERS SEAFOOD $$
167 Main St.
Niantic, CT 06357
(860) 739-3230
skippersseafood.com

Skippers Seafood is a great lunch stop in between browsing at the fabled Book Barn in Niantic. This is a seafood "shack," but one that serves a solid meal of New England seafood. The clam fritters were particularly yummy, but the scallop roll, milk shakes, and fried chicken are all a step above most other shacks. Better yet, the prices were quite reasonable. Last time I checked, the hot lobster roll was only $13.99, which is about right for one served in a New England hot dog roll. I've seen them at $17.99, and if they are served in a large sub roll that is fine, but for this amount of lobster the lower price is correct. Get to Skippers and satisfy your shore food cravings.

Vegetarian

MANGETOUT $
140 State St.
New London, CT 06320
(860) 444-2066
mangetoutorganic.com

This small cafe with its chalkboard on the sidewalk in downtown New London is the place for breakfast or lunch while working or visiting the city. They focus on seasonal ingredients and organic foods, offering plenty of vegetarian, vegan, and gluten-free options. For breakfast, their frittatas are excellent, and their lunchtime selection of salads and wraps is delightful. Try the falafel wrap or the curry tuna and apple salad, a surprisingly smart combination. They also have great organic soups and baked goods. Mangetout opens for breakfast and lunch Tues through Fri at 8 a.m., Sat at 10 a.m., and Sun at 11 a.m. (for brunch), and closes at 4 p.m.

DAY TRIP IN NEW LONDON COUNTY

New London County really has too many attractions to boil down to one day trip, but we'll try. Start with breakfast at When Pigs Fly Cafe (see entry) in Waterford. If you're coming from I-95 north, get off at exit 81 and take the small parkway until your first right turn on Cross Road. If you're coming from the south, take exit 81, going left at the bottom of the short ramp onto Waterford Parkway North, and then take another left at Cross Road, going underneath the highway. Cross Road will turn into Spithead Road, which you should take until you turn left on Route 156 (Rope Ferry Road). When Pigs Fly Cafe will be on your left in less than 0.5 mile. Try the pumpkin pancakes if they are in season.

When you've eaten a hearty breakfast, continue on Route 156 East, merging with Route 1, the Boston Post Road. This will take you right through historic downtown New London, changing names to Bank Street, which you will stay on rather than continuing left on Route 1. This slight side trip will take you into historic New London, where if you like you can stop briefly and take a small walking tour of the old town (see entry in historic sites & landmarks).

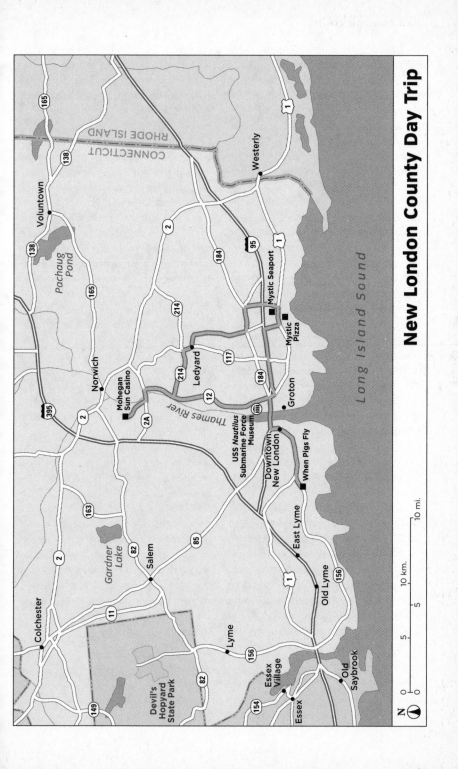

New London County Day Trip

Continue on Bank until it reaches a T intersection at State Street and take a right. Then take an immediate left on Water Street, with great views of the docks and harbor. This curves around and you'll see an entrance to I-95 North on your right. Take it, and cross the harbor on the Gold Star Memorial Bridge. On the other side, take exit 86 to Route 12 North, a left exit. At the bottom of the ramp take a right onto 12. When you reach Crystal Lake Road, take a left, which brings you right to the USS *Nautilus* Submarine Force Museum (see entry), where you can see this amazing vessel and learn the story of America's submarines.

When you're done, retrace your steps out Crystal Lake Road and south on Route 12. The entrance to I-95 North is more complicated. Head under the highway and you will quickly reach Route 349, another divided road, where you will go east, and then merge onto I-95 in the direction of Stonington/Providence. Take this to exit 89, and at the bottom of the ramp, turn right on Allyn Street. Take a left when you reach Library Street, pausing to admire Mystic's amazing library, and then turn left onto Route 1 (West Main Street). Mystic Pizza (see entry) is directly on your left, and you should stop here for lunch.

After a "slice of heaven" and a stop at Bank Square Books across the street, get back in your car and continue on West Main, turning left on Holmes Street just past the drawbridge. Enjoy the views of the tall ships to your left, but don't worry if you don't get a good look; that's your next destination. Turn left on Greenmanville Avenue (Route 27) and park in the huge lot a few blocks up on your

right. Head into Mystic Seaport (see entry), the museum of America and the sea, and enjoy an afternoon watching demonstrations, touring the tall ships, and generally enjoying yourself in one of Connecticut's biggest attractions.

When you've absorbed enough history, and after raiding the impressive gift shop, get in your car and continue north on Route 27 (Greenmanville Avenue), which will become Whitehall Avenue on the other side of I-95. Continue north into the village of Old Mystic, staying on Route 27 through town to the left. You'll reach Route 184 (Gold Star Highway) and take that west. But not for long. When you reach the Colonel Ledyard Highway, take this north to the right.

Enjoy these charming country roads in the twilight. Turn right when you hit Route 117 (Center Groton Road), then take the first left on Route 214 (Stoddard Wharf Road). Take this until you reach your old friend, Route 12, and turn right. Cross the cove and take Route 2A left, taking the immediate right after the second bridge onto Mohegan Sun Boulevard.

Mohegan Sun has a number of options for dinner, but if you'd like a fine-dining experience, check out Todd English's Tuscany. After dinner there are numerous nightlife options, or perhaps you can check out a show at the arena (of course you should probably have checked their schedule and bought tickets beforehand). If you're as exhausted as you should be after this busy day, get a room in one of the beautiful towers here and get some rest (see Mohegan Sun entries). There's a lot more to see in New London County tomorrow.

WINDHAM COUNTY

Windham County is sometimes known as the "Quiet Corner" of Connecticut, and it certainly is quieter than most, with the lowest population and position farthest away from the major cities of the surrounding states. It also forms the center of a National Heritage Corridor, the Last Green Valley, a natural and cultural area more than 78 percent forest and farmland with thousands of historic buildings.

Windham is anchored at two ends by the slightly larger settlements of Putnam, a former mill town, and Willimantic, the "Thread City." The rest of the county is made up of small villages like Woodstock, Pomfret, Brooklyn, and Scotland, where beautiful country roads take you to antiques shops, historic homes, and bed-and-breakfasts. Camping, hiking, and fishing opportunities are plentiful out here, and the numerous farms offer agricultural tourism and tasty rest stops.

When flying at night from Washington, DC, to Boston, you can look out the plane window and see an unbroken stretch of light from the megalopolis of cities and suburbs. All except right here, in Windham County, the heart of the last green valley.

ATTRACTIONS

Historic Sites & Landmarks

PRUDENCE CRANDALL MUSEUM
1 S. Canterbury Rd.
Canterbury, CT 06331
(860) 546-7800
ct.gov [search "Prudence Crandall"]
Connecticut's official state heroine, Prudence Crandall, was a schoolteacher who took a stand for racial equality when she admitted a girl named Sarah Harris into her private academy. When some local residents yanked their children out, she admitted more African-American girls as boarding students. A law was passed, then struck down, but meanwhile a mob attacked the academy. Today this historic 1805 house includes period rooms to tour, changing exhibits, and a gift shop. Ninety-five percent of this National Historic Landmark had been unaltered since Crandall took her stand here. The town green here is a National Historic District, with 32 architecturally or historically significant buildings. Stop at the First Parsonage, the oldest of them, where Connecticut's disgraceful native son Benedict Arnold was a student as a lad.

RIVER MILLS HERITAGE TRAIL
Kennedy Drive
Putnam, CT 06260
(860) 963-6811
putnamct.us
Downtown Putnam's collection of mills is not only historic but also located on the scenic Quinebaug River, creating a nice loop walk suitable for all, complete with markers along the way. There are a number of municipal parking lots; try the one at the corner of Kennedy Drive and Pomfret Street at the center of town by the 1868 Monohansett Mill, where 2.75 million yards of cotton sheetings and shirtings were produced annually. Cross

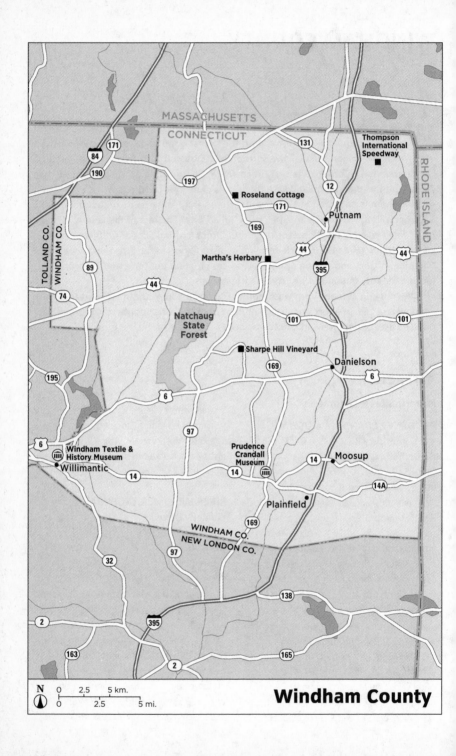

Windham County

N

0   2.5   5 km.

0   2.5   5 mi.

the river on the Pomfret Street bridge, enjoying Cargill Falls. Turning right onto Church Street, you will pass the 1868 Morse Mansion, a brick Victorian Italianate villa, and the 1874 Old Putnam High School, now the town hall. The path will turn right off Church Street into a riverside park. Here you'll find the 1861 Morse Mill, another textile manufacturing plant. Turn right onto Providence Street and cross the river again near the upper falls. The Belding and Powhatan Mill is on this side of the street, incidentally where the office of the Last Green Valley National Heritage Corridor is located today. You will also see two more mills, the 1842 Rhodes and 1861 Nightingale. After seeing these fascinating buildings, you can continue back along the river to your car. Or keep walking south along the River Trail; you can cross the river again on a 200-foot pedestrian stone railroad trestle.

ROSELAND COTTAGE
556 Route 169
Woodstock, CT 06281
(860) 928-4074
historicnewengland.org [search "Roseland Cottage"]

This pink candy Gothic Revival cottage in Woodstock was built in1846 as the summer home of Henry Bowen, a rich merchant who spent the rest of his wealth founding churches and supporting the Union cause in the Civil War. The lawn was landscaped in the 1850s and has been lovingly restored, a picturesque landscape that includes original boxwood-edged parterre gardens. The estate also includes an icehouse, an aviary, and a carriage barn. Inside, you will find the cottage to be just as colorful; along with patterned carpet and stained glass, you'll find the nation's oldest surviving indoor bowling alley. Luminaries like Oliver Wendell Holmes and Ulysses S. Grant walked these halls, and now you can too. There are festival days

throughout the year, including a spectacular Fourth of July extravaganza, similar to the ones the Bowens held centuries ago, and a Civil War encampment in August. On ordinary days you'll be served pink lemonade and can participate in the games of a summer season long ago.

Museums

WINDHAM TEXTILE & HISTORY MUSEUM
411 Main St.
Willimantic, CT 06226
(860) 456-2178
millmuseum.org

In the former Willimantic Linen Company, this small museum by the rushing river recreates the life of mill workers in turn-of-the-20th-century Connecticut. The Dugan Mill building has a variety of exhibits, including an 1880s mill shop floor, carding machine, spinning frame, loom, and textile printer. The other building has a re-creation of the company store, a laborers' tenement, a mill agent's mansion, and the 1877 Dunham Hall Library. You can visit Fri through Sun from 10 a.m. to 4 p.m. This collection of unique and unusual exhibits is creative and stirring, and will take you back to another time. But not another place. Having the museum set in the actual factory brings us right into the kiln of authenticity.

Parks & Beaches

MASHAMOQUET BROOK STATE PARK AND THE WOLF DEN
147 Wolf Den Dr.
Pomfret, CT 06259
(860) 928-6121
ct.gov/dep [search "Mashamoquet Brook State Park"]

Along Route 44 between Willimantic and Putnam, you'll find this 1,000-acre park with 7 miles of hiking trails. Unusual formations called the Indian Chair and Table Rock are only warm-ups for the Wolf Den—a narrow cave among large glacial erratic boulders. This cave is where Israel Putnam ("Old Put" to his friends) supposedly killed the last wolf in the state. The park also offers fishing and swimming in the Mashamoquet section. Near the entrance you can find the 4-story Brayton Grist Mill and Marcy Blacksmith's Shop Museum. The gristmill is the best example of an 1890s one-man operation in the state, and maybe anywhere. There's also an exhibit of 19th-century Marcy family blacksmithing tools and the water-powered shop. The museum and mill are open on weekends May to Sept from 2 to 5 p.m.

TRAIL WOOD AND BAFFLIN SANCTUARIES

93 Kenyon Rd.
Hampton, CT 06247
(860) 928-4948
ctaudubon.org/sanctuaries/trail-wood

Open daily sunrise to sunset, the 168-acre Trail Wood Sanctuary was once the home of Pulitzer Prize–winning Edwin Way Teale, author of books about the natural world, including Connecticut. Many think of him as our Thoreau. Today there is a network of well-developed trails and a small natural history museum with Teale memorabilia, as well as programs for adults, families, and children. Down the road at 189 Pomfret St. you will find the Connecticut Audubon Society's Grassland Bird Conservation Center and 700-acre Bafflin Sanctuary, a former dairy farm that is now habitat for 200 bird species. There is a network of pleasant trails here, and they connect to the Air Line State Park Trail. In fact, if you are ambitious, you can walk or bike between the two sanctuaries using the Air Line, though the distance is about 7 to 8 miles. At the center the Audubon Society runs environmental education programs, birding walks, and more.

Wildlife & Zoos

CREAMERY BROOK BISON FARM

19 Purvis Rd.
Brooklyn, CT 06234
(860) 779-0837
creamerybrookbison.net

More than 70 buffalo roam this 100-acre farm, and that alone makes it an attraction. Kids and adults in Connecticut are simply not used to seeing these magnificent animals, and you will probably spot them in the early evening any night of the year. However, July to Sept you can take a wagon ride out into the woods to see them and their new calves, as well as the bewildered second-fiddle cows that roam the property. You can even pet one of these shaggy giants. Other people come just for the farm store, where you can get bison meat as well as their delicious ice cream. No, it's made with cow's milk, not bison, though that would be an interesting experiment. You probably don't want to be the one doing the milking, however.

Wineries

✳SHARPE HILL VINEYARD

108 Wade Rd.
Pomfret, CT 06259
(860) 974-3549
sharpehill.com

Hidden in the hills of Pomfret, past forests and meadows, you'll see a western rail fence and the huge red barn of one of Connecticut's largest and most award-winning wineries. Owners Steven and Catherine Vollweiler and the winemaker, Howard Bursen, have created an institution here in this barn, which contains the winery itself, the barrel room, the tasting room, and their unique restaurant, the Fireside Tavern (see entry). They produce the best-selling wine in New England, Ballet of Angels—a semisweet summer pleaser, cool and refreshing. But their other wines are even more worthy of attention, such as the *Wine Spectator*–rated Chardonnay and the St. Croix, which tastes like spiced roses. Sit on the stone terrace behind the tasting room and enjoy a glass, but you should certainly take a walk up the hill through the rows of grapevines. At the top you'll have a view of Windham County and beyond into Massachusetts and Rhode Island.

TAYLOR BROOKE WINERY
848 Route 171
Woodstock, CT 06281
(860) 974-1263
taylorbrookewinery.com

Owners Dick and Linda Auger want visitors to feel at home when they arrive at Taylor Brooke Winery. The winery and tasting room are found in the beautiful landscape of the Quiet Corner, and a pleasant drive through Woodstock will take you there. A wide variety is offered, including intriguing blends featuring fruit infusions. Try Riesling on its own, then sample the wines that blend Riesling with concentrated essences—Green Apple Riesling, Summer Peach, Autumn Raspberry, and Cranberry Riesling are all surprising and fun. Don't miss Chocolate Essence, a Merlot port infused with chocolate: "dessert in a glass." Taylor Brooke pioneered the use of the Traminette grape, and the wine made from these hybrid grapes is delightfully floral and smooth with just the right touch of sweetness. Their version of Cabernet Franc is aged in Hungarian oak and has hints of mocha on the finish. Bring lawn chairs and set up a blanket between the rows of vines. Vineyard dogs Zima and Georgia will make sure you don't stray too far.

ACTIVITIES & EVENTS

Adventure Sports

SKYDIVE DANIELSON
41 Airport Rd.
Danielson, CT 06239
(860) 774-5867
skydivedanielson.com

Since 1996 Skydive Danielson has been the safest and most satisfying chance to fulfill your bucket list in New England. When you go for your first jump, you will be taken on a tandem skydive as a safety measure. Make a reservation, arrive early, and attend training before leaping out of a small plane 2 miles above Connecticut. Be prepared for possible weather delays—you don't want to be jumping out of a plane when the wind is gusting at 30 miles an hour. The next time you go, you can go by yourself, and the feeling of being alone in the air far above the earth is one that you should have at least once in this lifetime.

Festivals & Annual Events

BROOKLYN FAIR
15 Fairgrounds Rd.
Brooklyn, CT 06234
(860) 779-0012
brooklynfair.org

This is the oldest agricultural fair in the US. For 4 days the weekend before Labor Day, people from all over New England come to Brooklyn to see oxen pulls, draft horse demonstrations, skillet tossing, dog shows, cattle parades, and more. The circus and midway games bring in the kids, while the bingo and barbecue bring in the older folks. Everyone enjoys the country dancing, art shows, and beekeeping exhibits. There are craft vendors to bargain with and food vendors to gobble from. The fair is free, but of course the rides, games, crafts, and food are not.

Fishing

NATCHAUG RIVER
Route 198
Eastford, CT 06242
(860) 295-9523
ct.gov/dep

The deep pools of the Natchaug hold legendarily large trout, witnessed by record after record here. Many sections will remind you of a stream in northern New Hampshire or Vermont, with plunge pools and endless runs and riffles. Much of it follows state forest lands, and it is never far from an access road. In spring, stay at one of the private campgrounds along Route 198 south of Eastford and you'll find fish that have used this section to hide in all winter long. If you don't mind hiking a little, try Bigelow Brook, the feeder stream that comes down from Bigelow Hollow State Park as well, accessed by sections of the blue-blazed Natchaug Trail. I caught two trout here in 20 minutes during the middle of a hot summer day.

Golf

CONNECTICUT NATIONAL GOLF CLUB
136 Chase Rd.
Putnam, CT 06260
(860) 928-7748
ctnationalgolf.com

Once the Putnam Country Club, the new Connecticut National Golf Club is an 18-hole, par 71 golf course now open to the public. Designed by Mark Mungeam, this 6,169-yard course is full of small hillocks and presents fun challenges for medium-level players especially. Holes 4 and 9 are hilly and challenging. The course includes 2 practice greens, a driving range, a short game area, and a restaurant that serves lunch and beer, wine, and spirits. The course is considered one of the best in New England, and has recently been renovated to great acclaim.

Hiking, Biking & Walking

AIR LINE STATE PARK TRAIL
(860) 295-9523
ct.gov/dep [search "Air Line State Park Trail"]

Called the Air Line because of its straight path, this railway was completed in the 1870s, 20 years after it was expected to be. In the 1880s fancy train cars with white-suited porters ran the line to Boston until 1902, when freights took over until the 1960s. Today you can hike or ride a 50-mile section of this wonderful path all the way from East Hampton to Putnam, though some sections remain gravel and difficult to bike. The section south of Willimantic (technically in New London County) often rises up above the surrounding swamps and woodlands on a causeway, while the northern section cuts through the surrounding rock. Rudyard Kipling rode this railroad often, and wrote, "Without a jar, or roll, or antic / Without a stop to Willimantic / Rain nor snow ne'er stops its flight / It makes New York at nine each night." You can no longer take that train, but you can still ride the rails, and this is one of the best places to do it in Connecticut.

NATCHAUG STATE FOREST
Pilfershire Road
Eastford, CT 06242
(860) 928-6121
ct.gov/dep [search "Natchaug State Forest"]

There are remnants of old foundations throughout the forests, and stone walls and old roads abound in these 13,000 acres. The nearby horse farms all bring expeditions through here, and it is one of the only places in the state that you can actually horseback camp, with 15 free sites at Silvermine Horse Camp. The network of trails attaches to the Natchaug Trail, which meets the Nipmuck in Tolland County, as well as the Air Line State Park Trail, making this the hub of an endless hiking and biking network. The south end of the Natchaug meets Goodwin State Forest, which has even more trails and some of the absolutely loveliest stone-walled roads you'll find in the entire state. In winter these state forests are a popular place for snowmobiling and cross-country skiing. This is also a water-sports destination, with easy canoeing from the junction of Routes 198 and 44 south to the England Road Bridge, and more difficult rapids south all the way to Mansfield Hollow State Park.

Horseback Riding

VALLEY VIEW RIDING STABLES
91 Lake Rd.
Dayville, CT 06241
(860) 617-4425
valleyviewridingstables.com
This full-service equestrian center in Dayville was once a dairy farm but is now occupied by owner Amy Lyons and more than 30 horses. She has installed a large indoor riding arena and a huge outdoor arena that includes a 12-fence hunter course, a 30-obstacle cross-country course, and a 60-foot round pen. A variety of trails snake through the 250 acres of woods and pastureland, and you can go on guided trail rides on these after a 30-minute lesson. For younger children there are pony rides and birthday parties. Just be sure to wear jeans and tough shoes, but otherwise they provide all the equipment. The prices are very reasonable, and you'll be amazed at how an hour on a horse will change your entire outlook on life.

Pick Your Own/Farms

BUELL'S ORCHARD
108 Crystal Pond Rd.
Eastford, CT 06242
(860) 974-1150
buellsorchard.com
Off Route 198 in Eastford, this 100-acre farm has pick-your-own fruit beginning with strawberries in June and then moving through blueberries, peaches, apples, and pumpkins. The small store also sells the produce, as well as cheeses, preserves, candles, maple syrup, and cider. Buell's has become famous for its caramel apples, available after Labor Day. From Aug to Oct, watch the apples enter the machine and become candied. Check the website for updated seasonal hours and the day of their annual fall festival, with hayrides, apple pie, hot dogs, hamburgers, cider, and donuts. This is the most popular farm in the area, and everyone speaks fondly of their food and their fun.

Spectator Sports

THOMPSON SPEEDWAY
205 E. Thompson Rd.
Thompson, CT 06277
(860) 923-2280
thompsonspeedway.com
In 1938 after the great hurricane, John Hoenig cleared land and created America's first asphalt-paved oval racetrack. The ⅝-mile high-banked track was huge by the standards of the day, called a "super speedway," and Thompson became known as the Indianapolis of the East. Today it is still an amazing short track, hosting NASCAR Whelen All American Series events. There is a variety of races, including the NASCAR Modifieds, as well as late models and mini stocks. Fast Track Concessions provides the hot dogs, kettle popcorn, and beer. The speedway also has an 18-hole golf course and a driving range (racewaygolf.com), along with the Raceway Restaurant.

Water Sports

QUADDICK STATE PARK
818 Town Farm Rd.
Thompson, CT 06277
(860) 928-6121
ct.gov/dep [search "Quaddick State Park"]

This area was once the summer camp of the Nipmuck Indians; today it is a haven for boating, fishing, swimming, and more. The reservoir is 466 acres, with a sandy beach by the swimming area. The facility includes changing houses, restrooms, a picnic pavilion, ball fields, horseshoe pits, and food concessions, and so makes for a full day out with the family. For those who want to use personal watercraft or take the boat out, there's a launch located north of the beach. Some red-blazed trails snake through the woodlands as well, making a small, 1.5-mile loop. This park is open year-round, and only on summer weekends will you have to pay.

SHOPPING

Antiques

*ANTIQUES MARKETPLACE
109 Main St.
Putnam, CT 06260
(860) 928-0442
antiquesmarketplace.com

At the corner of Main and Putnam Streets in an old mill is central New England's largest antiques and collectibles mall, with an astonishing 350 dealers in 22,000 square feet. As you might imagine from those numbers, you can find anything here: books, prints, fine art, crafts, clocks, coins, embroidery, linens, furniture, glass, china, gold, jewelry, ornaments, lamps, metalwork, musical instruments, records, pottery, quilts, rugs, silver, toys, and vintage clothing. The store is quite organized, and you can spend hours just looking over the huge inventory. In fact, there are so many floors and rooms, you could get lost, so be careful. Luckily, they are open 7 days a week from 10 a.m. to 5 p.m., so eventually you'll find your way out.

Farm Stores/Pick Your Own

EKONK HILL TURKEY FARM STORE
227 Ekonk Hill Rd.
Moosup, CT 06354
(860) 564-0248
ekonkhillturkeyfarm.com

The Brown Cow Cafe at Ekonk Hill has become famous for its ice cream, but that's not the only reason people come to this turkey farm. The Milkhouse Bakery on the farm is also open year-round, with muffins, pies, cookies, donuts, and breads, along with the Goose and Gobbler shop, with eggs, poultry, potpies, honey, maple syrup, and more. Of course there are also hundreds of free-range birds to see roaming the fields. The corn maze is open in Sept and Oct, and you can also see the barnyard animals, explore the pumpkin patch, and take a hayride. At the Brown Cow, try the maple milk shake, which makes total sense and will become your new favorite.

SAFE HAVEN ALPACA FARM
39 Drain St.
Hampton, CT 06247
(860) 455-0054
safehavenalpaca.com

Did you know that alpaca wool is five times warmer than sheep wool? Well, now you do. So that is a great reason to get over to Safe Haven Farm from Thurs to Sat, where you can see and pet these amazing South American animals without trekking high into the Andes. The gift shop features yarn and clothing, the largest selection of these unique products in New England. Get a stylish sweater for Mom or a hat for the coming winter. Safe Haven also breeds and sells alpacas to farms throughout the Northeast, so if you're in the market for one, well, this is the place.

Home & Crafts

CELEBRATIONS GALLERY AND SHOPPES

330 Pomfret St.
Pomfret, CT 06259
(860) 928-5492
celebrationsshoppes.com

In a spacious Victorian home, Celebrations has a large gallery with crafts, paintings, and other original art. From watercolors to woodworking, you can find the best of the Quiet Corner here. However, Celebrations is much more. They have begun a new program that makes this the perfect place to experience afternoon tea. They have special days (one during the week and one Saturday each month) when you can reserve a place for afternoon tea from 2 to 5 p.m., at which you'll enjoy freshly brewed pots with unlimited refills, a soup course, and a classic three-tiered selection of sandwiches, savories, and scones. They also have other things for sale at the shop, like adult and children's tea sets, jewelry, and other knickknacks. Open Wed through Sun.

MARTHA'S HERBARY

589 Pomfret St.
Pomfret, CT 06259
(860) 928-0009
marthasherbary.com

This is a wonderful store to find a unique gift for someone who has everything, a small shop that makes use of all its space. Martha's not only has herbs to buy for your garden, but inside the shop they carry natural-fiber clothes, bags, jewelry, art, homemade potpourri and soaps, special teas, and unusual knickknacks. You can also walk through the English herb garden outside, with raised beds and arbors, and a sunken medicinal garden. In spring the smells that come from Martha's are divine: basil, tarragon, sorrel, and cilantro. Stop by in winter, though, and the friendly staff will treat you to mulled cider. They also run classes on gardening, and if you see their garden just once, you'll know you could probably use their expertise.

SAWMILL POTTERY

112 Main St., #14
Putnam, CT 06260
(860) 963-7807
sawmillpottery.com

Located in an old mill, this shop sells pottery made by some of northeastern Connecticut's most talented potters. Founded in 2003 by potter Dot Burnworth, Sawmill's dedication to community is part of each piece, as she donates 10 percent of her online sales to nonprofit organizations. There are unique pieces for sale, including jewelry and buttons, mugs and plates. They hold classes for all ages and abilities, as well as private lessons that include all materials and firing fees. Sawmill also has a line of bisqueware that you can paint. Check out Burnworth's Stone Soup Pottery collection; it's one of the best.

ACCOMMODATIONS

All lodgings have both smoking and non-smoking rooms unless otherwise noted, or have a designated smoking area, and do not accept pets unless noted. Hotels, motels, and resorts are wheelchair accessible unless otherwise noted. Bed-and-breakfasts and inns are not wheelchair accessible unless otherwise noted, since many are in historic buildings exempt from the Americans with Disabilities Act. Call to make sure if there's any question. We do not list specific credit cards in either this section or the restaurants section.

Bed-and-Breakfasts

BED AND BREAKFAST AT TAYLOR'S CORNER $$$
880 Route 171
Woodstock, CT 06281-2930
(860) 974-0490

When you arrive at Taylor's Corner and see the 18th-century house surrounded by lush gardens and an old stone wall, you know you're in vintage Connecticut. Inside, antique furniture and wide-board floors are exactly what you expect and want from a B&B experience in the Quiet Corner. All 3 guest rooms are air-conditioned, have working fireplaces, and private baths. The sunsets viewed from the Jules Van Damme Room are special. Each of the 3 common rooms (!) has its own fireplace too. You can munch on complimentary snacks and drinks, including homemade granola, cookies and breads. Owners Kevin and Brenda collect air-cooled Volkswagens. See if they'll show you some of their collection.

FEATHER HILL BED AND BREAKFAST $$-$$$$
151 Mashamoquet Rd.
Pomfret, CT 06259
(866) 963-0522
featherhillbedandbreakfast.com

This home was built in 1936, not 1736, but is charming in a different way, with 5 bright, airy rooms, all with private baths and recently renovated with all the amenities modern travelers want. There is also a separate 900-square-foot cottage with fireplace, kitchen, and dining room. Breakfast is included; let them know if you would like something for a special diet. Owners Fred and Angela will make you feel like part of their family, and that is what staying at a bed-and-breakfast should be all about. The rooms at Feather Hill are named for birds, and after a night here you will feel the freedom of these winged creatures as you fly to your next nest in the Quiet Corner of Connecticut.

GWYN CAREG INN $$-$$$
68 Wolf Den Rd.
Pomfret, CT 06259
(860) 928-5018
gwyncareginn.com

Built in 1760 by the Osgood family of Pomfret, this National Historic Register house was developed into a mansion in 1899 and named Gwyn Careg, which means "pure stone" in Welsh. The land around was turned into a landscaped estate, with a stone-walled Spanish garden and a scenic 3-acre pond, rich with rustic stone walks and flowering trees. In 1980 the mansion was refurbished and became an inn, run by the Bove family. There are 5 guest rooms here, 2 with fireplaces and all with antique charm. You are within walking distance of Mashamoquet Brook State Park, and the Air Line State Park Trail runs right behind the property, offering 50 miles of uninterrupted bicycling. Sharpe Hill Vineyard is 3 miles away on a country road, and you should make reservations for dinner at the Fireside Tavern there (see entries).

NATHAN FULLER HOUSE $
147 Plains Rd.
Scotland, CT 06280
(860) 456-0687
nathanfullerhouse.com

Georgia and Bruce Stauffer have taken this dairy farm and turned it into one of the quietest (and most reasonably priced) bed-and-breakfasts you'll find. Surrounded by maple trees, the house is an 1820 half Colonial wedded to a 1790 Cape, built by Nathan Fuller for his sisters. There are an astonishing 10 fireplaces, a bake oven, and a built-in cauldron in the oldest part of the house. The 3 rooms share 2 baths, but that includes a claw-foot tub to soak in. Along with breakfast, you will get afternoon tea; the owners will even arrange a snack or simple dinner for you if you decide to stay in.

Hotels & Motels

KING'S INN AND SUITES $–$$
5 Heritage Rd.
Putnam, CT 06260
(877) 784-6835
kingsinnputnam.com

This classic hotel/motel just off exit 96 of I-395 in Putnam is a great alternative to both camping and luxurious inns. There are 40 rooms and a king-size suite with a full kitchen and living room, as well as 2 conference rooms. Out back next to the highway there is a pond with a charming little bridge, and 7 acres to roam. You can also take a dip in their outdoor pool or grab a bite in the small Casa Mariachi Mexican restaurant and bar attached to the main building. The inn has free wireless Internet, and staying here will allow you to spend that much more on the antiques down the street in the center of Putnam.

Inns

✳INN AT WOODSTOCK HILL $$$$
94 Plaine Hill Rd.
Woodstock, CT 06281
(860) 928-0528
woodstockhill.net

On 14 acres in rural Woodstock, this 1816 inn was built by William Bowen, the grandfather of the man who built Roseland Cottage, and now has 18 rooms with private baths for your pleasure. There is also a cottage with 3 more rooms. Six of the rooms are furnished with four-poster beds, and 8 have working gas fireplaces. They offer seasonal packages and wedding packages, and host corporate meetings throughout the year in this rambling mansion. The attached fine-dining restaurant serves breakfast for guests, and lunch and dinner for everyone ($$$). You'll find classics like rack of lamb and interesting twists like Madagascar green peppercorn sauce. The nearby fields and forests still belong to the storied Bowen family, though the inn was sold in 1981.

✳MANSION AT BALD HILL $$$–$$$$
29 Plaine Hill Rd.
Woodstock, CT 06281
(860) 974-3456
mansionatbaldhill.com

The 4-story-high Mansion at Bald Hill is enormous, with over 13,000 square feet, surrounded by formal English gardens and stone walls. However, there are only 6 guest rooms, elegantly appointed and furnished. You will feel like a guest of the Bowen family, perhaps like one of the many US presidents who lodged and dined with them. You will be treated to a gourmet breakfast in the dining room or on the sunlit terrace by the gardens. The Mansion serves dinners every night (except Monday) and uses local organic ingredients whenever possible. For an appetizer, try the white cheddar tater tots, and for an entree, the grilled barramundi. Their Sunday brunch is famous; try the banana-pecan french toast or the lobster mac and cheese.

Camping

BEAVER PINES CAMPGROUND $
1728 Route 198
Woodstock, CT 06281
(860) 974-0110
beaverpinescampground.com

At the very north edge of the state on Route 198, Beaver Pines Campground is a relaxed and quiet family campground with 60 large forested sites that give a lot of privacy. There are even a few secluded sites off the main tracks deep in the woods. They have hot showers, a laundry room, and a camp store, as well as a field for horseshoes, volleyball, and Wiffle Ball. There is a small pond for canoeing, fishing, and kayaking as well. Red squirrels play throughout the pines and chatter excitedly. Best of all, Beaver Pines

Campground borders the Nipmuck State Forest, and you can hike or mountain bike on a path that leads out the back of the campground into 25 miles of trails. Now that's true relaxation.

CHARLIE BROWN CAMPGROUND $
98 Chaplin Rd. (Route 198)
Eastford, CT 06242
(877) 974-0142
charliebrowncampground.com

Nestled in the crook of the Natchaug River and adjoining the huge state forest, the Charlie Brown Campground has 123 open sites for tents and RVs, a laundry room, restrooms, hot showers, flush toilets, pavilions, a camp store, and a recreation hall. It does have the "amusement park" atmosphere of some other family campgrounds, so if you're looking for the amenities without the crowds of children splashing in a pool or miniature golf, this is it. The Natchaug River is one of the best places to catch trout in the county, and you can throw in a line right from sites 41 to 70. The Natchaug Trail crosses the road just north of the property, making this a great stopover on a multiday hike. It is also the perfect place to launch a kayak or canoe to head down this exciting river toward Willimantic.

MASHAMOQUET BROOK STATE PARK $
147 Wolf Den Dr.
Pomfret, CT 06259
(860) 928-6121
ct.gov/dep [search "Mashamoquet Brook State Park"]

The Wolf Den section of Mashamoquet Brook State Park offers 35 open campsites with flush toilets and drinking water from Apr 15 to Oct 15. The lower-numbered sites are on the outside of the ring and are therefore more desirable, especially sites 4 to 16. A nature trail leaves right from the campground to a wildlife-viewing platform. The

Mashamoquet Brook section is more rustic, with 20 wooded sites, composting toilets, and pump water. Its entrance is just west of the main park entrance on Route 44. You can make reservations, and vacancies are filled first come, first served. This is a great place to hike, fish, and swim, but also a great central location from which to explore Windham County.

RIVER BEND CAMPGROUND AND
MINING COMPANY $
Route 14A, Box 23
Oneco, CT 06377
(860) 564-3440
riverbendcamp.com

More than a campground, River Bend is a treasure. The 160 campsites bring overnight guests here, but many come just for the day to pan for minerals and gems in the outdoor sluice. There are trailer, camper, and cabin rentals in addition to the sites, for those who don't like sleeping on the ground. The amenities include hot showers and laundry facilities, though perhaps you'll just want to jump in one of 2 heated pools. They also have canoe rentals, a kiddie train, basketball, volleyball, a moon bounce (seriously), miniature golf, paddleboats, and aquacycles, all for peanuts. Like many family campgrounds, they have activities like bingo, outdoor movies, and other special events. For those who want privacy, site 101 is the most secluded, but now that it's in this guide, it's probably going to fill up quickly.

RESTAURANTS

Please note that all Connecticut restaurants are smoke free, and all are required to be wheelchair accessible. Pets are not allowed inside most restaurants, but during the warmer months, there are plenty of restaurants with patio areas just right for your canine friend. Call ahead to make sure it's okay.

American & Modern

✳CAFEMANTIC **$$**
948 Main St.
Willimantic, CT 06226
(860) 423-4243
cafemantic.com

The small-plate culture has merged with the farm-to-table movement to birth Cafemantic, which has grown from a baby coffee shop into the best full-service restaurant in the area. Stop in for lunch and get a meatball sub with a fancy name or five-cheese mac and cheese. For dinner try the hand-rolled russet potato gnocchi. The genius of Cafemantic, though, is the small plates, with delicious items like "tiger-striped" figs with speck, warm goat cheese, almond, and a fennel-citrus vinaigrette. Global ingredients like yuzu mix with local farm-sourced meats and vegetables. Cafemantic has proven that even in the wilds of eastern Connecticut, people want locally sourced good food.

CORIANDER CAFE **$$**
192 Eastford Rd.
Eastford, CT 06242
(860) 315-7691
coriandercafeeastford.com

Where do these chefs keep coming from? You know, the ones who graduate from culinary school or make their way through the restaurants and then, instead of dreaming of working at some fancy New York establishment, open their own restaurant in the middle of nowhere. That is the new dream, shared by Chef Brett Laffert of Coriander. He finds the best, freshest ingredients of the moment and creates new dinners every week, events from Wed through Sun that are quickly becoming legend. Coriander also serves breakfast and lunch—try one of their specialties, like the homemade meat loaf, caramelized onions, melted cheddar, and spicy ketchup on a grilled kaiser roll. I now love meat loaf in way I never did as a child.

FIRESIDE TAVERN AT SHARPE HILL **$$$**
108 Wade Rd.
Pomfret, CT 06259
(860) 974-3549
sharpehill.com

Up an ancient staircase in the loft of Sharpe Hill Vineyard's huge red barn is the Fireside Tavern, with its hand-hewn beams and high-backed colonial chairs. The location is traditional New England, but the food is far-ranging and global, with dishes like jerk chicken, Creole shrimp, and sea bass. Some of the herbs and flowers are local, however, grown right in the garden outside, and the produce is locally sourced. Let the waitstaff suggest which of Sharpe Hill's wines go with the dishes, although you might have your own ideas after tasting them downstairs. (Show up early and visit the charming tasting bar for sure.) For dessert, the Moon Mountain torte is sinful. The exclusive restaurant is only open Fri through Sun and is not wheelchair accessible; reservations are required for specific timed seatings.

✳GOLDEN LAMB BUTTERY **$$$**
499 Wolf Den Rd.
Brooklyn, CT 06234
(860) 774-4423
thegoldenlamb.com

This place is legend. Period. The romance of the Golden Lamb at Hillandale Farm is not just in the food; cocktails are served on a tractor-drawn hay wagon that takes you to the eclectic restaurant in a barn while you are serenaded by guitar. There are fresh herbs, locally sourced meat, and fresh vegetables and fruits. No preservatives, no salt, and no-holds-barred food that will have you crying for more. The menu changes, but expect to be amazed. The service is family style and the dinner is prix fixe, beginning at 7 p.m. Fri and Sat from May to Dec. You must make a reservation and dinner here is literally booked months in advance; all the foodies in the state seem to converge on the Golden Lamb regularly, as they have since 1963. They have good reason. This is food done correctly by a family who cares about making you happy.

✳STILL RIVER CAFE　　　　　**$$$**
134 Union Rd.
Eastford, CT 06242
(860) 974-9988
stillrivercafe.com

The Zagat guide selected the Still River Cafe as one of America's top restaurants, and when you eat there, you'll see why. The repurposed barn is 150 years old, and is simply and beautifully appointed. The cafe is only open Fri and Sat for dinner and lunch on Sun, so make reservations. The rabbit is marvelous—small medallions along with a stuffed and roasted leg with farm onions and a leek crepe. The butternut squash soup will make you want to start a new religion around it. Save room for dessert, like the crème brûlée trio of lavender, vanilla bean, and lemon thyme. Much of the food is really locally grown, as in right there, on the 27-acre North Ashford farm the cafe sits on. This is one of the top 10 dining experiences in the state, and everyone, diners and chefs alike, speaks reverently about the work they are doing. Open in spring and summer only, they feature wine dinners and guest celebrity chefs.

Asian & Indian

THAI PLACE　　　　　**$-$$**
214 Kennedy Dr.
Putnam, CT 06260
(860) 963-7770
thaiplacerestaurant.net

This surprisingly little restaurant in Putnam has given the locals and tourists a little variety in the Quiet Corner. Classics like pad thai and *tom yum goong* are done very well, but try something different here and expand your taste buds. The Panaang curry chicken and the Thai Place duck are both big hits, and in season the soft-shell crab curry is a fusion delight. Wash it down with a Singha beer or one of those delicious Thai iced teas. There are a number of options for the vegetarians in your family, like basil tofu and vegetarian pad thai. They also have takeout, but the fairly large dining room is bright and tastefully decorated, so why not stay a while? Save room for dessert; the ice cream here is reputed to be delicious.

Breakfast & Lunch

BILL'S BREAD AND BREAKFAST　　**$$**
149 Providence St.
Putnam, CT 06260
(860) 928-9777
billsbreadandbreakfast.com

Bill's is a little storefront breakfast place with exposed brick walls that give it a homey feeling. At 9 a.m. on a weekday morning, expect it to be packed with locals ordering the daily specials. If the specials do not appeal, try the homemade hash or the wheat pancake with blueberries, a meal in itself the size of a dinner plate. The homemade sausage patties are the size of saucers, and the omelet is also huge, filled with sizable chunks of ham and cheese. The large homemade muffins come in many different flavors, and the black bottom muffin with cream cheese filling is a fan favorite. And in case you didn't get it from the preceding description, the portions are, shall we say, large.

JESSICA TUESDAY'S　　　　　**$**
35 Main St.
Putnam, CT 06260
(860) 928-5118
jessicatuesdays.com

This used to be just a market deli in Putnam, but it has grown into one of the food destinations in town and beyond. I mean, how many delis serve a banh mi sandwich with house-cured pork-belly bacon? A local Pomfret farm, Unbound Glory, sources 90 percent of their vegetables. In the warmer months sit out on their deck and enjoy a break from work, or a stop by on your explorations of the Quiet Corner. There may be fewer quality dinner options out here in the eastern wilderness, but they seem to have made up for it with some of the best lunches and breakfasts in the state. Don't forget to try Jessica's "Forever Changing Cheesecakes," which, as you might expect, are forever changing. Closed on Sunday.

MRS. BRIDGES PANTRY $
292 Route 169
Woodstock, CT 06281
(860) 963-7040
mrsbridgespantry.com

Across from the Woodstock Fairgrounds, you'll find a charming wood-paneled barn house, with a British flag, that serves all the traditional delicacies of an English tea, from tea and cocoa to scones and clotted cream. Meat pies, salmon cakes, Cornish pasties, Scotch eggs, and tea sandwiches make this the perfect place to stop for lunch in Windham County. If you don't want the hot tea, the ginger-lemon iced tea is refreshing. You can also find gifts in the gift shop from the British Isles, from lemon curd to biscuits to china. Tea is best when it is shared, so let Mrs. Bridges share hers with you.

SWEET EVALINA'S $
688 Route 169
Woodstock, CT 06281
(860) 928-4029
No website

Known as "Evy's" to insiders, this local independent store (once a smaller roadside stand) serves seasonally grown, locally sourced food as much as possible. It's a lunch and breakfast place, but they also have become famous for their Thursday to

Saturday night pizzas. They also make what some call the best meatball sandwiches in Connecticut. You'll see both locals and tourists enjoying the fried clams or the deli sandwiches. For those of you with a sense of humor, the "play dough"–flavored ice cream is a classic—yellow colored with small morsels of what is probably cookie dough. Best not to ask; just enjoy.

THE VANILLA BEAN CAFE $$
450 Deerfield Rd.
Pomfret, CT 06259
(860) 928-1562
thevanillabeancafe.com

Across the street from Martha's Herbary at the corner of Routes 169 and 44, this busy cafe serves three meals a day in their stained glass–lit, clean, comfortable dining room. Order at the counter and they'll bring you your quiche or chili, burger or Cajun sausage hot dog. They have large sandwiches packed full of meat, served with pickle and chips, just like a good deli should. You can create your own with their interactive menu. If you're there for breakfast, try the chili omelet or the cinnamon-vanilla french toast. Though this is primarily a lunch place, Friday and Saturday nights The Vanilla Bean features entertainment and a small dinner menu. The cafe also offers gluten-free foods, like their chili.

THE WOODEN SPOON $
217 Pompey Hollow Rd.
Ashford, CT 06278
(860) 429-3825
No website

In this age of fresh, boutique restaurants, the idea of a "family restaurant" perhaps brings up images of greasy plates, small portions, and soggy potatoes. That is absolutely not what you will find at The Wooden Spoon. If you're coming here for breakfast, bring your appetite, with thick sausages just off the griddle, crisp toast, homemade maple syrup, and delicious eggs. The home fries are amazing, and the biscuits are flaky and rich. For lunch they have thick, juicy hamburgers and fries. The food comes out fast, in less than 10 minutes, and they refill your coffee mug constantly. The portions are huge. And the price? You will pay just a couple dollars more than at a fast-food restaurant, just as you will wait a couple minutes longer. That's all. It's hard to believe that we as a society would sacrifice this kind of food to save a minute or 50 cents. Take your family to The Wooden Spoon instead of the local fast-food joint; you'll never regret it.

Ice Cream

WE-LIK-IT ICE CREAM $
728 Hampton Rd. (Route 97)
Pomfret, CT 06259
(860) 974-1095
welikit.com

This 120-acre farm's herd of Holsteins is milked twice daily, and they make the ice cream fresh. If you stop by and they are "out" of a flavor, it's because they literally just made a batch and it sold out. They have interesting flavors; try the Guernsey Cookie if they have it—a coffee ice cream with Oreos. Road Kill is another favorite— vanilla with cherry swirl, white chocolate chips, and walnuts. The ice cream is rich and creamy, and the portions are huge. Some say to get the ice cream in a dish because the cones can't stand the amount. But the waffle cones are made fresh while you wait. Let me repeat: They make the waffle cones fresh on the spot. Open Apr through Oct, the farm also has hay and sleigh rides, as well as a greenhouse with seeds, flowers, and greens to buy. They also sponsor clam chowder bakes!

Pubs & Taverns

HARP ON CHURCH $$
69 Church St.
Willimantic CT 06226
(860) 423-8525
harponchurch.com

Harp on Church is part of the upsurge of foodie havens in Windham County. As one resident of the Quiet Corner put it, "You know if Willimantic has great food that something big is going on." And it is, as Connecticut continues to lead the nation in small-town restaurants. Harp on Church seems like a traditional Irish pub, but somehow they let interesting things onto the menu. Try the Asian chicken poppers or the onion soup gratinée for an appetizer, and the banh mi or tuna sandwich with sliced apples for a main course. Or get the traditional shepherd's pie and Irish stew. Wash them down with one of the 17 American craft beers or Traditional Irish pub beers on tap, changed daily.

✳WILLIMANTIC BREWING COMPANY $$
967 Main St.
Willimantic, CT 06226
(860) 423-6777
willibrew.com

Located in the 1909 post office building downtown, this brewery restaurant serves up more than just sudsy cold beers and ales. Brewer David Wollner is dedicated to making high-quality microbrews, but the chefs are just as dedicated to serving your stomach. Go for the wings, sliders, planked maple salmon, jambalaya, and the flatbread pizzas, including one with Beer-B-Q sauce pulled pork, red onions, cheddar jack cheese, and lime-cilantro sour cream. Or you could just go for a pint of the Rail Mail Rye or Amberlicious on tap at the 60-foot mahogany bar. Check their schedule for a variety of beer-and-food-themed events and specials that happen many times a week. Go for the amazing beer; stay for the gastropub food.

Road Food

AERO DINER $

361 Boston Post Rd.
North Windham, CT 06256
(860) 450-1959
aerodiner.com

The Aero is a unique 1958 "Bramson," for those of you who are diner fanatics and know what that means, since the company that built it usually made hospital equipment. For the rest of you, just know that it is a really neat-looking old diner that looks straight out of a retro film about the 1950s. They are open for breakfast and lunch every day, but also dinner Wed through Sun. Their breakfasts are top-notch—try the corn beef hash or sausage-gravy biscuits. Their fries and hot dogs are totally solid, and you can wash it down with a local Hosmer Mountain soda or a thick milk shake. Check their website for upcoming "cruise nights," where people come in their classic cars to gather at the Aero and reminisce about an age long gone.

ZIP'S DINER $–$$

Routes 101 and 12
Dayville, CT 06241
(860) 774-6335
zipsdiner.com

Zip's is one of those classic diners that remind everyone of childhood, even if you are still a child. This one is a 1954 O'Mahoney diner, and nothing has changed in its appearance or its food. Stainless steel, spinning counter stools, and a neon sign says EAT. Try the roast turkey with trimmings or the Zip Burger. However, don't forget to save room for dessert, especially the puddings, custards, and strawberry shortcake on which they use real whipped cream. The Grape-Nuts pudding is also a classic. This place is a favorite for

truckers on I-395, but also with foodies looking for an authentic experience. They surely find it at Zip's.

Seafood

85 MAIN $$

85 Main St.
Putnam, CT 06260
(860) 928-1660
85main.com

Set in the old Union Station in Putnam, 85 Main offers American fusion cuisine with fresh ingredients and organic products. The casual fine-dining atmosphere is a great place to enjoy any of the wonderful entrees and appetizers, from the pulled pork to the maple-glazed scallops. They also have a number of daily specials, including sushi rolls. Try the raw bar too, the best place to get fresh seafood this far from the sea. If you like mussels, the saffron broth they use is outstanding. Get the Ballet of Angels from nearby Sharpe Hill Vineyard with your seafood. A stop at 85 Main is a great end to a day spent walking the heritage trail and browsing the antiques shops of Putnam.

DAY TRIP IN WINDHAM COUNTY

Today's day trip immerses you deeply in the history of the Last Green Valley. You'll start the journey with breakfast in Putnam at Bill's Bread and Breakfast (see entry). You've got a lot to see today, so start early, and load up on pancakes or eggs. From here you can walk leisurely south along the Quinebaug River into town if you like, taking the River Mills Heritage Trail (see entry) past waterfalls and the old mills and mansions. In the center of town, if you're interested in antiques, you should stop at the wonderful Antiques Marketplace on Main Street, although if you buy something large, you should probably get your car. Putnam has become a charming

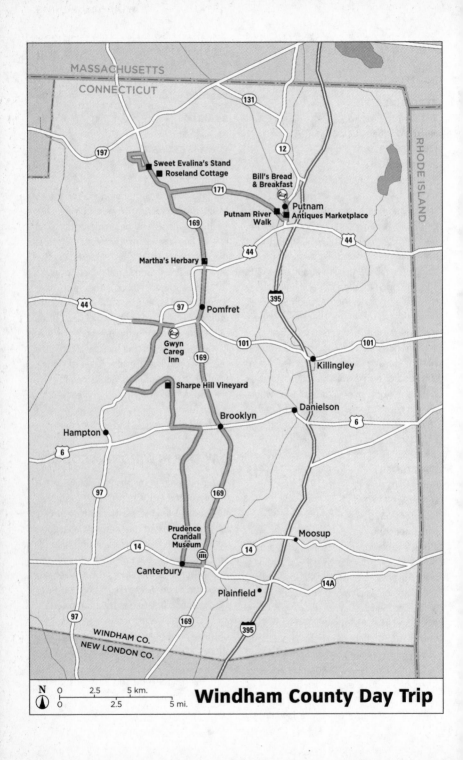

town in the past decade, and it is tourist friendly with many fine shops.

If your car is still at Bill's, on the corner of Church and Providence Streets, you'll head west on Providence, which is also Route 171. If you're in the center of town on Main Street, take this north until the T intersection at Massicote Circle. Turn left, and then take the right onto Kennedy Drive. This will take you back to a T intersection on Providence Street. Turn left to head west.

Providence Street merges and becomes the Somers Turnpike and Woodstock Avenue, but just follow the Route 171 signs. This merges briefly with Route 169, and when the two roads split again in the center of Woodstock village, take 169 North. About a mile on your left is the pink wonder of Roseland Cottage (see entry), your next stop this morning. Take the tour of this unique house and have some pink lemonade.

For lunch, continue north for less than half a mile to Sweet Evalina's (see entry). Try the meatball grinder, fried clams, or a juicy burger. They also have lighter options if you filled up too much at breakfast. When you're done, turn around and head back down Route 169, continuing on this road through Woodstock as it becomes the Norwich Worcester Turnpike. At the corner of Putnam Road where 169 intersects Route 44, stop at Martha's Herbary and shop (see entry).

Continuing south on Route 169, you'll pass the Rectory School and the Pomfret School, along one of the most scenic roads in the state. You'll take this beautiful road for 14 miles, until you reach the crossroads with Route 14 (Lovell Lane to the east and Westminster Road to the west) in Canterbury. Right across the road by the small Canterbury Green is the Prudence Crandall Museum (see entry), where you will learn the history of this brave woman, Connecticut's state heroine.

When you're done, take Route 14 West and take your first right onto Kitt Road. This will take you north, parallel to Route 169 on a less-traveled, charming rural road. It merges right into Windham Road. Take this until a T intersection at Route 6 (Hartford Road), where you'll turn left. Take the first major right at Cherry Hill Road and follow this north, taking the right fork at the second intersection to stay on this road.

At the intersection with Wade Road, take a left, bringing you to Sharpe Hill Vineyard (see entry). Taste their wines out on the stone patio, and get ready for dinner at the Fireside Tavern restaurant (you'll need to make reservations; see entry). Enjoy the historic ambience of the dining room set in the loft of the barn, full of antiques. Enjoy a glass of the winery's Riesling or Chardonnay with your dinner and talk about the sights of the day.

If you want to stay overnight, try the Gwyn Careg Inn in Pomfret, just up the road (see entry). Go back east on Wade, and at a triangular intersection, take a left onto the road you came in on, now Brooklyn Road. Then take the first right onto Jericho Road. At a split, stay left on Jericho, which becomes Wolf Den Road. Gwyn Careg will be on your left, just before you reach Route 44. Sleep in front of a roaring fireplace, full of memories and good food; hopefully you'll wake ready to do it all again the next day.

Appendix

LIVING HERE

In this section we feature specific information for residents or those planning to relocate here. Topics include real estate, education, health care, and much more.

As Hartford poet Wallace Stevens once said, "There are no foreigners in Connecticut. Once you are here you are or you are on your way to become a Yankee." For those of you relocating and living here in Connecticut, you have different concerns than the tourist or occasional visitor to these hills and shores. Among other things, you no doubt want to know about real estate, education, and health care.

The first question is where to live. Places that are not heavily featured in the attractions or activities sections of the book can often be some of the best places to live, especially if you want quiet. Would you like to live in what is essentially a postcolonial village untouched by time, but without the tourists? Try Colebrook in Litchfield County. Want to live in a land of wooded lakes away from the cities but close enough to drive in for dinner? Try Weston or Easton in Fairfield County. Want to live in a shoreline town, but not pay outrageous prices? Try Milford or West Haven in New Haven County.

Of course most of our decisions are guided more by necessity than by our fantasies. This section of the book will help you make those choices a little more wisely.

RELOCATION

Real estate prices in Connecticut are not cheap. Coming from the Midwest, for example, some stunned emigrants look at 30 or 40 houses or condominiums before realizing they are not going to get magically closer to the prices they are used to. One reason for this is the small size of the state, causing space to be at a premium. Another is the high per capita income of the state's residents (median household income is $69,519, according to the 2012 American Community Survey), including the rich bankers, traders, and celebrities that live here. Whatever the cause, you have been given fair warning that relocating to these green hills and sandy shores requires a strong stomach, and a strong wallet.

You will find that the prices of homes and local real estate taxes get steadily cheaper as you move northeast from Greenwich, with some obvious exceptions in the hearts of cities, or in particularly desirable village centers. The coastline of the state is more expensive in general as well, with a rising and falling set of prices depending on the towns, getting generally cheaper the farther east you go, but rising in certain posh

shoreline communities. The northeast corner is by far the most inexpensive area to live.

Is there hope? You bet. If you're moving here, your salary is likely to be higher as well, and many people spend a few years gaining capital before buying a residence. And if you bite the bullet and blow your savings on a house here, you are far less likely to lose huge money on that investment than in more economically unstable areas of the country. Living here for 20 years, a working middle-class couple can gain the income to retire to a huge mansion with 10 acres in Arizona, or to buy a winter home in the Caribbean, where your dollars will go far.

POPULATION MAKEUP & DIVERSITY

The state's population grew by nearly 6 percent between 2000 and 2013, and percentage-wise, more people are under 18 than over 65; the average age of the population is 37. The state's racial makeup is similar to what is found nationwide, but these numbers do not necessarily uncover the richness of ethnic diversity around the state. We see this town by town, city by city, from the variety of restaurants to colorful and pride-filled parades and festivals. Indian, Jamaican, Peruvian, and Polish markets are frequent additions to a downtown jaunt. Italian, French, or Albanian neighborhoods can be found in any city. Almost 14 percent of residents are foreign born, and over 20 percent speak a language other than English at home.

WHERE TO LIVE

Finding a home in Connecticut means more than simply searching for a house or deciding whether to buy or rent. Often those decisions are based on necessity, proximity to work, school, or family. Though it's impossible to pinpoint the qualities of the various municipalities in a comprehensive manner, this guide hopes to make some of those decisions easier. The median value of a home in the state is $285,900, and statewide nearly 70 percent of residents own homes. Only 10 percent fall below the poverty level. But to speak only of relative material comfort is to lose the individual characteristics of Connecticut's towns and cities; its urban, suburban, and rural qualities; the coastal and forested landscapes. County by county, we outline general real estate information to aid in relocation. In addition to the guide, websites like realtor.com, zillow.com, and apartmentfinder.com will get you started. There are many national brokerage companies, like Re/Max, Coldwell Banker, and Century 21, that serve Connecticut. This section highlights independent real estate agencies for each county.

Fairfield County

Fairfield County is the most densely populated of the state's counties, with 1,440 people per square mile. More than half the 940,000 residents live in the metropolitan areas of Stamford, Norwalk, Bridgeport, and Danbury, and the county's population has grown 2.5 percent in the last three years. On the other hand, a large part of the land area is left for less-populated towns, which have historic charm and manicured beauty. There's much diversity in the landscape. Nearly every town has excellent public schools. Cultural events, entertainment, business activity, and shopping, as well as privacy, are close by. Twenty percent of Fairfield County residents are foreign born, and 28 percent speak a language other than English at home.

As you might guess in one of the nation's highest-income counties, home values and real estate prices are higher than the state average. Between 2008 and 2012, the median value of owner-occupied housing units was $447,500, a decrease of 7.6 percent from the previous 5-year period, due in no small part to the economic recession of 2008. Still, homeownership in the county remains high, at about 70 percent, and recovery continues in flux, with sales falling in 2012 but rising slightly in 2013. Despite the recession, median income has risen. The average Fairfield County homeowner pays $6,500 in property taxes, and property taxes are about 6.6 percent of one's income. Apartment rentals can be found throughout the county but are more likely to be in the cities, with variance in terms of price. Rentals in Bridgeport can be found for under $1,000 per month, but in cities like Norwalk and Stamford, you're more likely to find ranges from $1,500 and onwards toward $4,000 a month. The average resident commutes 28 minutes to work, and while major highways bypass the county, I-95 in particular is heavily traveled and congestion often adds time to daily commutes. Sixty-one percent of the residents work for private firms, and many major companies call Fairfield County home, including General Electric, Xerox, Pitney

Bowes, and Sikorsky Aircraft. Locally owned and operated companies, like Stew Leonard's grocery, thrive here too.

HIGGINS GROUP REAL ESTATE

12 offices in Fairfield County,
including Stamford East Side Commons
850 E. Main St.
Stamford, CT 06902
(203) 402-0300
higginsgroup.com

FAIRFIELD COUNTY REAL ESTATE

200 Mill Plain Rd.
Fairfield, CT 06824
(203) 259-9999
fcre.com

Litchfield County

If you're looking for space, beauty, and a more rural landscape, seek out the Litchfield Hills. With the greatest area and least population density of all the counties (206 people per square mile), Litchfield feels spread out but also close-knit. Residents hold on to a rural mindset, but development and growth bring in a cosmopolitan attitude as well. While population increased nearly 5 percent from 2000 to 2010, it has fallen slightly since then (about 1.5 percent) to about 187,000. Diversity may be less and cost of living more than the national average, but people of all types find themselves at home in hills of Litchfield County. The Torrington region, which includes much of the northwest corner, is tagged a micropolitan area, centered around the core city Torrington, which has a population of 35,000, while surrounding towns draw from and contribute to population and economic growth or the area.

About 78 percent of residents own homes, with the median value of a home being $272,000. The median income is close to the state's average, at $71,000. Median property taxes paid on a home are $4,200, and taxes in Litchfield County amount to about 5.4 percent of income. The average commute time is 26 minutes, but about 54 percent commute in under 20 minutes to their place of work. Industries where employment is highest include sales and office work, retail trade, health care and social assistance, educational services, accommodation and food service, and manufacturing. Future job growth is predicted to be strong over the next 10 years, making Litchfield County a good bet for relocation.

DOOLEY REAL ESTATE

23 South Main St.
Kent, CT 06757
(860) 927-2585
dooleyre.com

KLEMM REAL ESTATE, INC.

6 Titus Rd.
Washington Depot, CT 06794
(860) 868-7313
klemmrealestate.com

Klemm serves all 26 towns with additional offices in Litchfield, Lakeview, Roxbury, Sharon, and Woodbury.

New Haven County

New Haven County offers a lot of diversity in terms of landscapes and housing options. The county has a population of 862,000 people in 862.1 square miles (although 258 square miles include water, and the city of New Haven, in particular, is an important port.) It's two major cities—New Haven and Waterbury—each draw workers and provide access to resources. The county has an interesting mix of Naugatuck Valley towns—those in the middle of the county, where both suburbs and wooded countryside share space, and coastal towns with ocean appeal. The population is up almost 4.7 percent in the past 12 years and has held steady since 2012. More than 60 percent of the county's residents were born in the state, and 48 percent of the households consist of families. Almost 12 percent are foreign born, and nearly 21 percent speak a language other than English at home. Of those, 43 percent speak Spanish. New Haven County residents like to stay put; 87 percent lived in the same place for more than a year.

The median price of homes is $263,900, and the median income is $62,234, though it varies widely among the towns, with Woodbury topping the list and the city of New Haven at the bottom. About 64 percent of those living in the county own a home, and about 40 percent live in a multiunit structure. Rental prices vary. The average rental within 10 miles of New Haven is $1,100, and the Waterbury area isn't far off that average. Depending on amenities, rentals in the county, especially along the coast, can reach the $2,500 range. Property taxes average $4,863, which amounts to 6 percent of one's income. County residents are largely employed in the civilian labor force. And with Yale University and Yale–New Haven Hospital in the area, 28 percent of the workforce is employed in educational services and health care and social assistance industries. About 13 percent work for the government. The average commute time is about 24 minutes.

CT REAL ESTATE PROS RE/MAX
55 Old Gate Ln.
Milford, CT 06460
(203) 988-7418
ctrealestatepros.com

SHOWCASE REALTY, INC.
1177 Wolcott St.
Waterbury, CT 06705
(203) 574-2500
1152 New Haven Rd.
Naugatuck, CT 06770
(203) 720-0069
showcasect.com

Showcase serves New Haven, Litchfield, and Hartford Counties, with additional offices in Southington, Oakville, and Thomaston.

Middlesex County

Almost 166,000 people live in Middlesex County, the smallest of the state's eight counties in terms of area. It covers 369.26 square miles and has a population density of 449 people per square mile. The rate of population growth since 2000 is almost 7 percent, though population has held steady in the past few years. The median age of Middlesex County residents is 39, and almost 30 percent of residents are under 18. There's not much diversity as far as racial makeup, but almost 11 percent of residents speak a language other than English at home. The 15 towns that are bisected by the Connecticut River are popular choices for their natural beauty and varied landscapes, quality of life, high standard of living, and proximity to resources and amenities. Though Middlesex County has the shortest coastline of any Connecticut county, water seekers have easy access to beaches, riverfronts, and small lakes.

Following the trend around the state, median income is up recently, while median house value is down. Median house value is slightly higher than the state average, at $299,600, and 76 percent of residents own houses, whereas about 24 percent of homes are renter-occupied structures. Median income in the county is $76,659, which is also higher than the state's average. Median amount for property taxes is $4,684, which is about 1.5 percent of a home's value. Leading industries include those in the educational, health care, and social assistance fields, with over 24 percent of the total workforce. Middlesex County workers are employed mostly in management and professional positions (43 percent) as well as in sales and other office jobs (25 percent). Fourteen percent worked for the government, and 7 percent are self-employed. On average, workers travel 24 minutes to work.

RACHEL THOMAS GROUP AT PAGE TAFT
5 Essex Sq.
Essex, CT 06426
(860) 227-7843
mogrady.pagetaft.com

STERLING REALTORS
27 Pleasant St.
Middletown, CT 06457
(860) 343-3820
sterling-realtors.com

Hartford County

The Hartford Metropolitan Area is the 45th largest in the country, and Hartford County is the second most populated county in the state. Population density is 1,215 people per square mile, and the county encompasses 735.44 square miles. Nearly 900,000 people in the county as a whole enjoy the perks of having a major city nearby. In addition to Hartford, Bristol and New Britain are also incorporated cities among the 26 other towns. Countywide, 77 percent of the people are white, 15 percent are black, and 16.6 percent are Hispanic. About 24 percent speak a language other than English at home, and 14 percent are foreign born.

Sixty-six percent of the county's residents own homes, and the median house value is $246,400. Median income is almost $64,700, and 11.5 percent of the county is below the poverty level. Property taxes average $4,464 for home owners; expect to pay about 5.5 percent of your income toward them. Median price for rental properties is about $1,100, though there is price variance throughout the county, depending on size and location of the property. About 43 percent of businesses in the area are in

the service industry, with education and health services jobs at the top of the list. Management-level and professional occupations make up a good percentage of employment, as do sales-related jobs. Trade, utility, and transportation jobs employ about 88,000 people. Financial services, leisure and hospitality industries are also high on the list of employers. Major companies in the county include Northeast Utilities and Pratt and Whitney. The city of Harford continues to be home to major insurance companies. In 2013 Amazon announced it would open a warehouse in Windsor.

SENTRY REAL ESTATE
71 East Center St.
Manchester, CT 06040
(860) 643-4060
sentrycountry.com
There are additional offices in Vernon and Windsor.

EXECUTIVE REAL ESTATE CT OFFICE
17 School St.
Glastonbury, CT 06033
(860) 633-8800
executiverealestatellc.com
Executive has an additional office in Clinton, serving Middlesex County.

Tolland County

Often called the "Gateway to the Quiet Corner," Tolland County is a peaceful mix of residential and rural space. The 13 towns that make up the county together have a population of about 151,000 people spread out over 410 square miles, so there are about 372 people per square mile. Technically included as part of the Hartford Metropolitan Area and bordering Massachusetts, the county may seem tucked away and offers respite for those looking for natural beauty and space. Seventy percent of households are made up of families, and 21 percent of the population is under 21. More than 50 percent of the population is between ages 25 and 64. Sixty-two percent of those living in Tolland County were born in the state, and 83 percent have been living there for more than a year.

The rate of home ownership is about 76 percent, and the median value for a house is $261,300. Twenty-four percent of residents rent their properties. The average monthly cost for a mortgage is $1,900, and the average rent is $925. Property taxes average $4,499, 4.8 percent of income. Median income for the county's residents is $80,887, above the state's average. The main industries fall under the categories of educational services, health care, and social assistance. Among the biggest employers are correctional facilities, hospitals, and the University of Connecticut, which employs about 8,600 people. There are more than 570 farms in the county working over 47,000 acres. The average farm is about 83 acres. Employment opportunities come from construction, retail trade, manufacturing, and agriculture.

R. F. CROSSEN GROUP
174 Merrow Rd.
Tolland, CT 06084
(860) 870-0175
crossenhomes.com

New London County

Bordered by the ocean to the south and Rhode Island to the east, New London County has a land area of 664 miles. Since 2000 the county has grown in population by 5.8 percent and now has about 274,000 residents, with a population density of about 412 people per square mile. Families make up 67 percent of the population, and 24 percent of individuals are under 18. About 40 percent of the population is between 18 and 45; 13 percent of the population is between 45 and 64, about equal to the percentage of people older than 65. Sixteen percent of

New Londoners moved there within the past year—11 percent from within Connecticut, 4 percent from other places in the country, and 1 percent from abroad. Eight percent of residents are foreign born.

Median household income is $68,310, and the median value for a house is $260,600. Sixty-seven percent of houses are owner-occupied, single-unit structures, and 33 percent are rentals. The average monthly mortgage payment is about $1,850, and the average rent is under $1,000. Property taxes average about $3,677, about 4.6 percent of income. New London County workers commute an average of 22 minutes to work. The two casinos, Foxwoods Resort and Mohegan Sun, are among the biggest employers, though out-of-state competition and fallout from the recession has hurt the casinos. The Naval Submarine Base is equally big, with 10,500 workers. The area's two hospitals and the pharmaceutical company Pfizer, as well as other health-care companies, make up 22 percent of the industries, along with educational services and social assistance professions. Retail trade, education, and health care industries have seen recent employment growth.

MARKET REALTY, LLC
28 Cottrell St.
Mystic, CT 06355
(860) 572-1155
marketrealtyllc.com

LOMBARDI REALTY LLC
18 Sachatello Industrial Dr.
Oakdale, CT 06370
(860) 443-9200
lombardire.com

Windham County

There is plenty of space in Windham County, as it is the least populated, with about 117,000 people, and the second least densely populated after Litchfield County, with about 230 people per square mile. The county covers 512 square miles over hills and forests, rivers, reservoirs, and lakes. The median age of the population is about 38, with 23 percent of those living there under the age of 18. Of the 43,000 households, 68 percent are families. The population has decreased slightly in the past few years (by 0.7 percent since 2010). The county truly exhibits the characteristics you'd expect from a place colloquially known as "The Quiet Corner," or more officially, part of the Quinebaug and Shetucket Rivers Valley National Heritage Corridor. The principal municipality is Willimantic, population 15,800, where Eastern Connecticut State University is located.

Housing is less expensive compared to the other counties. Median house value is about $219,300. Single-unit housing structures make up 67 percent of all dwellings; 69 percent of structures are owned, while 32 percent are rented. A monthly mortgage payment is about $1,600 on average, and rent averages $770 per month. Property taxes are roughly $3,137, 4.3 percent of income. Median household income is also lower in Windham County than the state average—at about $58,489. A breakdown of employment shows that 29 percent of workers in the county hold jobs in management and professional positions, and 20 percent are in general service industries. Government workers make up 17 percent of the workforce; 11 percent work in construction and repair; 17 percent work in production, transportation, and material moving; and 6 percent are self-employed. Some of the biggest employers include Crabtree & Evelyn in Woodstock, General Cable (fiber-optics equipment and systems) in Windham, and Frito-Lay in Killingly. The average commute time is about 26 minutes.

FERRIGNO-REALTORS LLC
1734 Storrs Rd.
Storrs, CT 06268
(860) 429-9351
ferrignorealtors.com
A second office is in Willimantic.

LOOMIS REAL ESTATE
25 Providence St.
Putnam, CT 06260
(860) 928-7991
loomisre.com

THE BUSINESS OF MOVING TO CONNECTICUT

VEHICLE REGISTRATION AND DRIVER'S LICENSES
Department of Motor Vehicles
60 State St.
Wethersfield, CT 06161
(860) 263-5700
ct.gov/dmv

You will have to register your vehicle if relocating to Connecticut; of course if you're purchasing a new car or changing ownership of a car, registration is needed. Out-of-state vehicles should be registered within 60 days; until then, obtain a temporary registration, which can be attained from a DMV office. Emissions testing and vehicle identification number verification are required. Many garages and service stations now perform emissions testing. Out-of-state certificate of title and motor vehicle registration are needed, as well as proof of insurance and acceptable forms of identification. There are 10 full-service DMV stations and 7 others with photo licensing or limited hours. Every county except Tolland has at least one DMV office (the Enfield, Wethersfield, or Willimantic centers would be the closest).

New residents have 30 days after moving to the state to transfer out-of-state licenses. New or transferring teen drivers (16 and 17 years old) may get a learner's permit first, but any teen driver needs 30 hours of driver training from either a commercial or high school program or home instruction. Additionally, 40 hours of road training are required. Restrictions are in place for teen drivers until their 18th birthday. For those 18 and older, an applicant needs a Social Security card or proof of legal presence in the US, identification forms, and proof of driver's education. A written test, road test, and vision test are required as well.

For those who need to apply for a license or renew, one option is to apply for the Real ID, identity-verification program. Your license will be marked with yellow star in the upper right-hand corner, and the card shows that the DMV has verified your identity according to federal regulation. The program also aims to help curb identity theft. In short, renewing applicants need to supply additional identity verification documents (such as a birth certificate or passport) and two pieces of recent mail to prove residence. The Real ID license is used in the same way a regular license would be when boarding airplanes, entering federal buildings, or proceeding through checkpoints. The program was started in 2011 so that all licenses will be compliant by 2017. Currently you can still renew your regular license without applying for a Real ID. For more information visit ct.gov/dmv/RealID.

In all cases, fees apply: application ($40) and license ($72 or $84, depending on how long the renewal is for). License renewal, including Real ID, is also available at many AAA-affiliate offices.

VOTER REGISTRATION
Office of the Secretary of State
30 Trinity St.
PO Box 150470
Hartford, CT 06115
(860) 509-6100
ct.gov/sots

Voter registration and elections are handled by the Legislation and Elections Administration Division (LEAD), which, together with local town clerks and the registrar of voters, administers and executes voting activities. Election authority falls under the secretary of state, and the state complies with the 2002 Help America Vote Act, which implemented requirements for voting machines or provisional ballots. Voter registration forms are available on the website for mail-in, and in-person registration should be done through the registrar of voters located in town government offices. Forms are also available at the Department of Motor Vehicles. Eligible voters must be residents, citizens at least 17 years old (turning 18 by election time), and have voting rights restored if previously imprisoned or on parole. General election information, calendars, and results are also easily accessible on the website. First-time voters or those transferring registration need to present identification, including photo identification and proof of address. Polls open at 6 a.m. and close at 8 p.m. on

i No longer are customized license plates only for showing off that alliterative nickname or catchy pun. A number of causes can be helped when you opt for a personalized plate. For example, Preserve the Sound plates help protect the waters of the coastline, as a portion of the fees goes to projects benefiting the Long Island Sound. Show off your love for the vanishing bobcat or the bald eagle and support their protection with Conserve Wildlife plates. Hikers and bikers may opt for the Greenway plates. Alums can show off their pride and help their alma mater, and we can show our support for police officers, firefighters, and those lost in the line of duty with purchase of these special license plates. See ct.gov/dmv for further information.

voting days, generally the first Tuesday of November.

EDUCATION

Connecticut ranks at the top of the nation at all levels of education, and the state benefits from the high levels of education among its residents. The second-lowest divorce rate in the country contributes to kids staying in school. Statewide, 88.6 percent of those 25 and older hold high school diplomas. Connecticut ranks fourth in the number of people over 25 who have bachelor's or advanced degrees; we are second in the country in issued patents per capita.

Child Care

With 70 percent of children in Connecticut under the age of 6 having both parents in the workforce, the need for child care is intense. Fortunately, child-care options in Connecticut are varied and numerous. Eighteen percent of 3 year olds and 24 percent of 4 year olds are enrolled in pre-K, Head Start, or special education programs. For private care, parents have availability through child-care centers (licensed by the State Department of Public Health for care of 13 or more children), small family care (up to 6 children in the home of an individual approved by the Department of Public Health), and large group home care (where students are grouped by age into centers or in homes, also licensed by the Department of Public Health). Unlicensed care may be given by relatives or by nannies or au pairs in the home. Comprehensive listings of licensed and accredited child-care facilities are available through publications like *Connecticut Parent Magazine* (ctparent.com) and through the 2-1-1 info line (211child care.org).

The average cost for private care for infants is about $240 a week; for preschoolers, about $200 a week; and for school-aged children, about $100 a week.

Around 8,500 children 3 and 4 years old are in state-funded pre-K programs; the Child Care Development Fund and Head Start, federally funded programs, help an additional 9,900 children. The Connecticut School Readiness Program works to establish strong pre-K programs for 3 and 4 year olds, particularly in high-priority school districts. The state Department of Social Services sponsors the CT Care for Kids program, which helps low- to moderate-income families find affordable child care.

Primary & Secondary Education

PUBLIC SCHOOLS
Connecticut State Department of Education
165 Capitol Ave.
Hartford, CT 06106
(860) 713-6543
The state ranks second, according to the US Department of Education, in elementary school performance. Such rankings are based on average scores for fourth-graders in reading and math. Middle school rankings put Connecticut in the 10th spot (based on eighth-grade average in math and reading). *U.S News and World Report* ranks Connecticut's high schools at the very top as the best in the nation. The state ranks fourth in per pupil expenditures.

Average class size for kindergarten through high school is around 20. About 98 percent of schools had high-speed Internet access on computers. In addition to strong graduation rates, public school graduates move onto two- or four-year colleges at high rates. In general, suburban schools with greater tax bases fare better. Seven of the top 10 schools in terms of student performance are in Fairfield County. However, while overall graduation rates in Connecticut are high, the state still has one of the largest achievement gaps, with Hispanic and black students falling short of their white counterparts. In the state's largest districts, Bridgeport and Hartford, only two-thirds of the students graduate on time. Even with the general affluence of the state, almost 33 percent of students are eligible for free or reduced lunch.

Charter & Magnet Schools

Two additional categories of public schools are charter and magnet schools. Both types of schools are funded by either local or regional boards of education or by the state. They are authorized by the state board of education and were set up in part to improve economic segregation of public schools and to offer parents and students a wide array of programs and choices. About 50 percent of all school districts, in urban, suburban, and rural areas, have students enrolled in charter schools. Similarly, magnet schools provide additional choices for families by offering innovative and quality multicultural curricula, especially in the realms of performing arts, science, math, and technology. Magnet schools are open to all students in the district in which the school operates.

Private Schools

Connecticut's private schools are historic, prestigious, and diverse. With over 350 across the state, private schools educate around 73,000 of the state's children. With day and boarding options, single-sex and coed choices, religious and nonaffiliated focuses, and a wide range of tuitions and enrollment selectivity, the state's private schools provide yet another choice for all levels of primary and secondary education. Standouts include internationally recognized schools like Choate Rosemary Hall in Wallingford, the Hotchkiss School in Lakeville, and Loomis Chaffee School in Windsor. But Connecticut's private schools do more than prepare the elite

for future success. Top-notch facilities, small student-to-faculty ratios, engaging curricula, and high percentages of students moving on to top colleges are some of the reasons private school education is prized by a diverse array of families. For many, a school's religious affiliation or central philosophy may be the primary draw. Many schools specifically serve students with special needs.

Higher Education

Connecticut's 43 colleges and universities have recently seen record enrollments. The state's institutions of higher learning draw candidates from around the country and from all regions of the globe. And largely, they stick around. The high level of educational facilities helps improve quality of life. The correlations are impressive, providing "cutting edge research in a number of fields, issue oriented debate and analysis, challenging architecture, cool fashion, alternative media, and the light cast into their communities by the bright, sometimes brilliant, faculty members," according to *Connecticut Magazine*.

Public Universities & Colleges
UNITED STATES COAST GUARD ACADEMY
31 Mohegan Ave.
New London, CT 06320
(800) 883-8724
uscga.edu

The United States Coast Guard Academy in New London is the smallest of the federal military academies. Admission is based solely on merit and does not require congressional recommendation, but competition is intense and only a select few are admitted. Character development, leadership, and physical fitness are all paramount in the educational philosophy of the academy. After graduation, the new officers give five years of service or more.

UNIVERSITY OF CONNECTICUT

Storrs, CT 06269
(860) 486-2000
uconn.edu

More than 30,000 undergraduate and graduate students attend the University of Connecticut, the state's major public university. The main campus in Storrs began as the Storrs Agricultural School, becoming the university in 1939. A major research university, with 15 major schools awarding bachelor's, master's, and doctorate degrees, UConn is the only public university in New England to have its own law school and medical school, as well as a school of social work and dental medicine. Besides Storrs, which is about 28 miles east of Hartford, there are regional campuses at Avery Point (Groton), Stamford, Torrington, Waterbury, and Greater Hartford.

CONNECTICUT STATE UNIVERSITY SYSTEM

The Connecticut State University System is not only an affordable way for Connecticut residents to achieve college degrees, but it also promotes the state's economic well-being and quality of life, as 93 percent of its students are in-state residents, and over 85 percent remain in the state upon graduation to work and live. Tuition averages about $9,000 a semester, and about 75 percent of students receive financial aid. Offering bachelor's, master's, and professional degrees in over 160 subject areas, the four universities in the system are especially focused on meeting the needs of the state and its people.

CENTRAL CONNECTICUT STATE UNIVERSITY

1615 Stanley St.
New Britain, CT 06050
(860) 832-CCSU (2278)
ccsu.edu

EASTERN CONNECTICUT STATE UNIVERSITY

83 Windham St.
Willimantic, CT 06226
(860) 465-5000
easternct.edu

SOUTHERN CONNECTICUT STATE UNIVERSITY

501 Crescent St.
New Haven, CT 06515
(203) 392-5200
southernct.edu

WESTERN CONNECTICUT STATE UNIVERSITY

181 White St.
Danbury, CT 06810
(877) 837-WCSU (9278)
wcsu.edu

Community College System

Accessibility and affordability are the aims of the state's system of 12 community colleges. The incentives for higher education are well known. Graduates of community colleges earn on average $16,000 more in annual income within the first six months of completion, and over their lifetimes associate's degree holders earn more than a half million dollars more than high school graduates. Couple these numbers with the fact that many go on to earn bachelor's degrees at a savings of over $30,000 a year compared to private universities, and the benefits of community college are easy to see. With campuses across the state, flexible class schedules, and over 100 programs, any student can find education within reach. Community colleges offer dynamic campuses, small class size, media-rich classrooms, tutoring, career planning, and financial aid advising.

CONNECTICUT STATE COLLEGES AND UNIVERSITIES
39 Woodland St.
Hartford, CT 06105
(860) 723-0000
ct.edu

ASNUNTUCK COMMUNITY COLLEGE
170 Elm St.
Enfield, CT 06082
(860) 253-3000
asnuntuck.edu

CAPITAL COMMUNITY COLLEGE
950 Main St.
Hartford, CT 06103
(860) 906-5077
ccc.commnet.edu

CHARTER OAK STATE COLLEGE
55 Paul J. Manaford Dr.
New Britain, CT 06053
(860) 515-3800
charteroak.edu

GATEWAY COMMUNITY COLLEGE
20 Church St.
New Haven, CT 06511
(203) 285-2000

GATEWAYCT.EDU HOUSATONIC COMMUNITY COLLEGE
900 Lafayette Blvd.
Bridgeport, CT 06604
(203) 332-5000

HOUSATONIC.EDU MANCHESTER COMMUNITY COLLEGE
Great Path
PO Box 1046
Manchester, CT 06045
(860) 512-3000

MANCHESTERCC.EDU MIDDLESEX COMMUNITY COLLEGE
100 Training Hill Rd.
Middletown, CT 06457
(860) 343-5800
mxcc.edu

NAUGATUCK VALLEY COMMUNITY COLLEGE
750 Chase Pkwy.
Waterbury, CT 06708
(203) 575-8040
nv.edu

NORTHWESTERN COMMUNITY COLLEGE
Park Place East
Winsted, CT 06098
(860) 738-6300
nwcc.edu

NORWALK COMMUNITY COLLEGE
188 Richards Ave.
Norwalk, CT 06854
(203) 857-7000
ncc.commnet.edu/default.asp

QUINEBAUG VALLEY COMMUNITY COLLEGE
742 Upper Maple St.
Danielson, CT 06239
(860) 412-7200
729 Main St.
Willimantic, CT 06226
(860) 336-0900

QVCC.EDU THREE RIVERS COMMUNITY COLLEGE
574 New London Tpke.
Norwich, CT 06360
(860) 215-9000
trcc.commnet.edu

TUNXIS COMMUNITY COLLEGE
271 Scott Swamp Rd.
Farmington, CT 06032
(860) 733-1300
tunxis.edu

Private Universities & Colleges
ALBERTUS MAGNUS COLLEGE
700 Prospect St.
New Haven, CT 06511
(800) 578-9160
albertus.edu

Established in 1925, Albertus Magnus College is a four-year liberal arts college offering 23 undergraduate degree programs with both associate's and bachelor's degrees. The School of Evening & Graduate Programs and the School of New Dimensions offer accelerated and distance learning. In addition to six other master's degree programs, AMC offers the state's only Master of Arts in Art Therapy. The campus is about 3 miles from downtown and incorporates a number of 19th-century mansions for housing and administration.

CONNECTICUT COLLEGE
270 Mohegan Ave.
New London, CT 06320
(860) 447-1911
conncoll.edu

Enrolling 1,800 students, Connecticut College is a four-year liberal arts institution offering bachelor's and master's degrees in 43 majors, many with a global focus. About 55 percent of students study abroad at some point. There are pre-professional programs, several interdisciplinary courses, and student-designed courses. The college campus includes an arboretum, which acts as an outdoor laboratory. Students come from 45 states and 72 countries, and admission is selective.

GOODWIN COLLEGE
1 Riverside Dr.
East Hartford, CT 06118
(860) 528-4111
goodwin.edu

With recently renovated facilities next to the Connecticut River in East Hartford, Goodwin College enrolls about 2,800 students, both recent high school graduates and adult learners, with enrollment rising sharply since 1994. The nursing program is the second largest in Connecticut. Goodwin's system of three semesters per year is popular with working adults, and their 2+2 degree system allows students working toward a bachelor's degree to also earn an associate's degree in their first two years. Bachelor's degrees are awarded in child study, health science, organizational study, and nursing. There are 13 associate's degree programs and 16 certificate programs. Goodwin operates a magnet high school, the Connecticut River Academy, and is planning another.

FAIRFIELD UNIVERSITY
1073 N. Benson Rd.
Fairfield, CT 06824
(203) 254-4000
fairfield.edu

Founded by the Jesuits in 1942, Fairfield University offers a liberal arts education to 5,000 students at the graduate and undergraduate levels. With a holistic approach to education, Fairfield offers 41 majors and 16 interdisciplinary minors housed in 6 colleges. According to *Business Week*, the university ranks second in students' return on investment. The Regina A. Quick Center for the Arts, called the "cultural epicenter of Fairfield County," and the Bellarmine Museum of Art operate on the campus.

MITCHELL COLLEGE
437 Pequot Ave.
New London, CT 06320
(860) 701-5000
mitchell.edu

Located on the waterfront right next to the Thames River, Mitchell College offers bachelor's and associate's degrees. Enrollment is small, but so is class size, and Mitchell emphasizes holistic student development. Disciplines include behavioral sciences; communication arts and humanities; computer science and engineering; hospitality and tourism; law and justice polices; science, technology, environmental studies, and mathematics; and sports and fitness management.

QUINNIPIAC UNIVERSITY
Mt. Carmel Avenue
Hamden, CT 06518
(203) 582-8200
quinnipiac.edu
The foot of Sleeping Giant State Park provides the backdrop for Quinnipiac University's main campus. With 52 undergraduate majors and 20 graduate programs, Quinnipiac offers core general education along with intense faculty support. The university has ranked among the best colleges in the Northeast, and the school of business and school of law are nationally ranked. The journalism and physical therapy programs are also top-notch. Quinnipiac's Polling Institute is nationally recognized. Their North Haven campus houses the school of education, school of health sciences, and the school of law.

SACRED HEART UNIVERSITY
5151 Park Ave.
Fairfield, CT 06825
(203) 371-7999
sacredheart.edu
Sacred Heart is the second-largest Catholic university in New England. Focusing on liberal arts and the Catholic intellectual tradition of active learning, SHU combines academic support and technology for 6,000 students in 40 programs at the bachelor's, master's, and doctoral levels. The Jack Welsh School of Business opened in 2006, and it has since been ranked among the top business schools in the nation. Community service is a vital part of the student experience. Students, faculty, and staff volunteer over 31,000 hours a year.

TRINITY COLLEGE
300 Summit St.
Hartford, CT 06106
(860) 297-2000
trincoll.edu
Trinity College promotes a traditional liberal arts education as it incorporates innovative new fields and interdisciplinary studies. It is the second oldest college in the state (after Yale), founded in 1823. It has been coeducational since 1969 and has 38 majors. Graduate courses lead to a master of arts. The 100-acre campus is located in the heart of the capital city. Three buildings dating from the 1870s make up the "Long Walk" and display the Victorian collegiate Gothic style.

UNIVERSITY OF BRIDGEPORT
126 Park Ave.
Bridgeport, CT 06604
(800) EXC-ELUB
bridgeport.edu
The discipline of dental hygiene was started at the University of Bridgeport, and the Fones School of Dental Hygiene is one of the premier programs in the nation. Founded in 1927 as a junior college, the university, located near Seaside Park in Bridgeport, enrolls about 2,200 undergraduates and has distinguished graduate programs in acupuncture, naturopathic medicine, chiropractic, business, education, design, and engineering. UB offers a rare doctorate in computer science and engineering. Satellite campuses in Waterbury and Stamford offer additional flexibility and distance-learning options. *U.S. News & World Report* ranks UB 10th among the most racially diverse college campuses in the nation, and it is one of the most affordable private universities in the state.

UNIVERSITY OF HARTFORD
200 Bloomfield Ave.
West Hartford, CT 06117
(860) 768-4100
hartford.edu

Spanning 350 acres in West Hartford, the University of Hartford is home to more than 7,000 students and offers over 120 degree programs at the associate's, bachelor's, and graduate levels, with 7 certificate or diploma offerings. Seven schools make up the university, including the Barney School of Business; the College of Engineering, Technology, and Architecture; and the Hartt School, a performing arts conservatory. The university began with the joining of three schools, including the Hartford Art School, which was founded in 1877 by prominent Hartford women such as Olivia Landon Clemens (wife of Mark Twain) and Harriet Beecher Stowe. It was first housed in the Wadsworth Atheneum.

UNIVERSITY OF NEW HAVEN
300 Boston Post Rd.
West Haven, CT 06516
(203) 932-7000
newhaven.edu

With a focus on experiential learning, the University of New Haven offers almost 100 degree programs. Undergraduates and graduates combine for about 6,500 total students. About 65 percent of students reside on the West Haven campus, which is located on 82 acres, conveniently near New Haven with access to the coast and beyond. Their Orange campus opened in 2014. Five colleges make up the university: the College of Arts & Sciences, the Tagliatela College of Engineering, the College of Business, University College, and the Henry C. Lee College of Criminal Justice and Forensic Sciences, which opened in 2010. Here the Institute of Forensic Science and the National Crime Scene Training Center are housed.

UNIVERSITY OF SAINT JOSEPH
1678 Asylum Ave.
West Hartford, CT 06117
(860) 232-4571
usj.edu

A four-year Roman Catholic women's college with coeducational graduate programs, Saint Joseph enrolls about 1,900 students. Undergraduate programs in the liberal arts are housed in the schools of health and natural sciences, humanities and social sciences, education, and pharmacy. Four graduate-degree programs are available, including social work, Latino community practice, and a school of pharmacy; a continuing education curriculum includes such programs as interdisciplinary certificates in autism spectrum disorders.

WESLEYAN UNIVERSITY
45 Wyllys Ave.
Middletown, CT 06459
(860) 685-2000
wesleyan.edu

Established in 1831, Wesleyan University is a four-year liberal arts college located on 360 acres on a hill above Middletown. Wesleyan's individualized approach to education produces the second most undergraduates in the nation who move on to achieve PhDs, especially in the sciences. With the van Vleck Observatory on campus, Wesleyan graduates more astronomy and astrophysics majors than any other liberal arts college in the nation. Music and film studies are among the other excellent majors: There are 44 fields of study in all, and about 29 percent of students double major, some triple major. Eighty percent move on to graduate school.

YALE UNIVERSITY
500 College St.
New Haven, CT 06520
(203) 432-1333
yale.edu

Yale University's history and prestige make it one of the most selective and sought-after educational experience in the world. The 11,250 students that attend each year as well as faculty and staff make Yale's presence in New Haven a significant social and economic factor. Founded in 1701, it is the third-oldest university in the country, and second-oldest Ivy League university. It is composed of Yale College, where undergraduates school; the Graduate School of Arts and Sciences; and 13 professional schools. The library holds 12.5 million volumes, the second-largest university library in the world; the Beinecke Rare Book and Manuscript Library houses, among other things, a copy of the Gutenberg Bible. Yale supports three museums—the Yale University Art Gallery, the Center for British Art, and the Peabody Museum of Natural History—as well as a collection of musical instruments.

Other Colleges

HARTFORD SEMINARY
77 Sherman St.
Hartford, CT 06105
(860) 509-9500
hartsem.edu

HOLY APOSTLES COLLEGE AND SEMINARY
33 Prospect Hill Rd.
Cromwell, CT 06416
(860) 632-3010
holyapostles.edu

LYME ACADEMY COLLEGE OF FINE ARTS
84 Lyme St.
Old Lyme, CT 06371
(860) 434-5232
lymeacademy.edu

PAIER COLLEGE OF ART
20 Gorham Ave.
Hamden, CT 06514
(203) 287-3031
paiercollegeofart.edu

POST UNIVERSITY
800 Country Club Rd.
Waterbury, CT 06723
(800) 345-2562
post.edu

RENSSELAER AT HARTFORD
275 Windsor St.
Hartford, CT 06120
(860) 548-2400
ewp.rpi.edu

ST. BASIL COLLEGE AND SEMINARY
195 Glenbrook Rd.
Stamford, CT 06902
(203) 324-4578
stbasilseminary.com

Technical Schools & Institutes

Individuals seeking job training, career advancement, and greater technical knowledge have a long list of technical schools and institutes to choose from. Some offer four-year degrees, others associate's degrees and certificates. Many have multiple locations, and a handful have on-campus housing. These types of schools have a wide variety of offerings, including electrical, automotive, computer instruction, health administration, medical care and technology training, and massage therapy. Some are operated by national institutes with Connecticut branches. For example, the Lincoln Group of Schools (lincolnedu.com) runs the Lincoln College of New England, Lincoln Technical Institute, and Lincoln Culinary Institute. Porter Chester Institute (porterchester.com) is another example of a conglomerate of schools that offer hands-on training and certification in a number of convenient locations. A growing number of students enjoy the flexibility offered by online learning and continuing education programs, which are available through many of these technical schools and institutes as well as many private and public universities.

Continuing Education & Distance Learning

The increasing popularity of online learning is apparent in the fact that most colleges and universities in the state offer this option in some capacity. Many universities and colleges have entire coursework online. There are a number of fully online colleges, as well as local campuses for national online programs like the University of Phoenix.

Continuing education and accelerated learning programs allow adults 25 and older, usually those who have previous college credit, to finish degrees and increase their career marketability. Many institutes have separate continuing education divisions.

HEALTH CARE

Connecticut residents are healthy overall, and the state ranks fourth in matters of health, according to the United Health Foundation's America's Health Rankings, with high percentages of doctors per capita and number of insured individuals. Eighty-nine percent of Connecticut residents are insured, 75 percent of those through private insurance consisting of both employee-based and direct-purchase insurance plans. Twenty-six percent of insured receive government insurance, including Medicare, Medicaid, and Military Health Insurance. Of those who are uninsured, half are employed.

Connecticut has the lowest rate of children living in poverty; low rates in incidences of obesity, occupational deaths, and premature deaths; and high immunization rates. Smoking rates have been in decline, as have deaths from cardiovascular disease and cancer. With the implementation of the federal Affordable Care Act (ACA), the proposed $16 billion over the next 10 years will help to incorporate key consumer protections and savings, prevention initiatives, greater benefits for seniors, and access to health care for those with preexisting conditions.

Top-rated health-care facilities and treatment centers contribute to the state's overall health. There are 29 not-for-profit acute-care hospitals in the state, with more than 9,000 beds, helping over 430,000 patients every year. More than 1.6 million people are treated annually in the emergency rooms, and an additional 7.2 million are treated as outpatients. Hospitals contribute nearly $18 million to state and local economies, maintaining a significant workforce and supply network. More than 51,000 individuals are employed by the hospital system. In addition to the acute-care facilities, there are 20 specialty hospitals and over 130 community treatment and rehabilitation facilities in the state.

> **i** The United Way of Connecticut (ctunitedway.org) sponsors 2-1-1, a dial-in service to help residents find services and programs in their area. Information and free referrals are available for most health-care or human-service issues. More than 450,000 people seek information about everything from utilities and housing to legal assistance and crisis prevention. Additional toll-free numbers provide referrals and information about child care (800-505-1000); Care 4 Kids (877-868-0871); Child Development Infoline (800-505-7000); and HUSKY, the State of Connecticut's health care for uninsured children up to age 19 (877-284-8759). Connecticut was the first state to implement the 2-1-1 structure statewide.

Major Hospitals & Health-Care Centers

BACKUS HOSPITAL
326 Washington St.
Norwich, CT 06360
(860) 889-8331
backushospital.org

Founded in 1893, the 213-bed William W. Backus Hospital, in alliance with the Backus Health Centers, which provide services in Colchester, Ledyard, Montville, Plainfield, and North Stonington, serves nearly a quarter million people in the eastern part of the state. The facility offers the only trauma center east of the Connecticut River, and it is the only hospital in the area with access to Hartford Hospital's medical-transport LIFE STAR helicopters.

BRIDGEPORT HOSPITAL
267 Grant St.
Bridgeport, CT 06610
(203) 384-3000
bridgeporthospital.org

Part of the Yale New Haven Health System, the private, not-for-profit facility serves 20,000 inpatients and nearly 230,000 outpatients a year from Bridgeport and the greater Fairfield County region and has 425 beds. The Dr. Andrew J. & Henrietta Panettieri Burn Center is the only burn center in Connecticut. Bridgeport's famous resident and philanthropist P. T. Barnum was one of the founding members when the hospital incorporated in 1871.

BRISTOL HOSPITAL
41 Brewster Rd.
Bristol, CT 06011
(860) 585-3000
bristolhospital.org

This full-service, 134-bed facility serves the greater Bristol area, caring for 40,000 patients a year. The Connecticut Gastroenterology Institute at Bristol Hospital and the Comprehensive Spine and Pain Center are two of the specialized care facilities.

CHARLOTTE HUNGERFORD HOSPITAL
540 Litchfield St.
Torrington, CT 06790
(860) 496-6666
charlottehungerford.org

A 109-bed facility, Charlotte Hungerford Hospital provides care for 30 towns in northwest Connecticut. Uri T. Hungerford, an industrialist, founded the hospital in 1916 in honor of his mother, Charlotte. Her inspiration for quality, affordable, and passionate care remains the mission of the hospital. A full range of patient-care services is available, including acute care, cardiology, pulmonary services, orthopedics, rehabilitation, and behavioral health, among others.

CONNECTICUT CHILDREN'S MEDICAL CENTER
282 Washington St.
Hartford, CT 06106
(860) 545-9000
connecticutchildrens.org

The largest pediatric-care facility between New York and Boston, the Connecticut Children's Medical Center provides medical care for about 15,000 children in the Hartford area. The nationally recognized center is a teaching hospital and also provides emergency room services, a surgical unit, intensive care, and neonatal care.

DANBURY HOSPITAL
24 Hospital Ave.
Danbury, CT 06810
(203) 739-7000
danburyhospital.org

Part of the Western Connecticut Health Network, Danbury Hospital has 371 beds and employs 4,000 staff and 750 physicians. As a university teaching hospital, it is associated with three major universities: the schools of medicine at Yale University and UConn, as well as the University of Vermont. Comprehensive care is available in cardiovascular services, cancer, weight-loss surgery, orthopedic and spine care, digestive disorders, and radiology. Danbury Hospital is the first in the state to be a member of the Connecticut Green Building Council.

DAY KIMBALL HOSPITAL
320 Pomfret St.
Putnam, CT 06260
(860) 928-6541
daykimball.org

Day Kimball Hospital is part of the Day Kimball Healthcare system, which serves Windham County, with additional facilities in Danielson, Dayville, Plainville, and Thompson. Services include primary care, home-care help, hospice and palliative care, physician services, and patient and family support services.

EASTERN CONNECTICUT HEALTH NETWORK (ECHN)
echn.org
Manchester Memorial Hospital
71 Haynes St.
Manchester, CT 06040
(860) 646-1222

Rockville General Hospital
31 Union St.
Vernon, CT 06066
(860) 872-0501

The Eastern Connecticut Health Network was established in 1995, bringing together Manchester Memorial and Rockville General Hospitals and helping increase services for the eastern part of the state. Manchester offers a full range of inpatient and outpatient surgery, including robotic surgery, maternity and neonatal care, cancer care, and cardiac care. Specialty centers include the Sleep Disorder Center and the Center for Wound Healing. At Rockville General, a 102-bed facility, patients have access to emergency care; surgery; medical imaging; physical, occupational, and speech therapy; laboratory services; maternity care; hospice; and cardiac and pulmonary retaliation. The network has additional facilities Manchester (John A. DeQuattro Community Cancer Center and CorpCare Occupational Health), Glastonbury (Glastonbury Wellness Center), Vernon (Women's Center for Wellness), South Windsor (Buckland Hills Imaging, Walden Behavioral Care, and Evergreen Imaging Center), and Tolland (Woodlake at Tolland). Urgent care centers in Somers and South Windsor treat nonemergency conditions. Both offer extended hours.

GREENWICH HOSPITAL
5 Perryridge Rd.
Greenwich, CT 06830
(203) 863-3000
greenhosp.org

One of the facilities under the umbrella of the Yale New Haven Health System, Greenwich Hospital serves the greater Fairfield County area. The partnership with Yale ensures continued advancements in technology and research. The hospital offers 45 inpatient and outpatient specialty services. The Bendheim Cancer Center received an award for Outstanding Achievement in Patient Care from the American College of Surgeons' Commission on Cancer.

GRIFFIN HOSPITAL
30 Division St.
Derby, CT 06418
(203) 735-7421
griffinhealth.org

With 160 beds and 280 physicians, Griffin Hospital serves the Lower Naugatuck Valley region. It is affiliated with Yale–New Haven Hospital. In addition to inpatient services, Griffin provides community outreach, mobile health, and school-based health resources. *Fortune magazine* cited Griffin as one of the 100 Best Companies to Work For.

HARTFORD HOSPITAL
80 Seymour St.
Hartford, CT 06102
(860) 545-5000
harthosp.org

Hartford Hospital's excellence and innovation began in 1854, when it was Hartford's first hospital. It is a teaching hospital affiliated with the University of Connecticut's School of Medicine. The hospital was the first in the state to perform a successful heart transplant, and they have pioneered the use of surgical robotics. Connecticut's only air ambulance system is operated from the hospital, the state's only Level 1 trauma center. The Stroke Center, the Spine and Joint Center, and the Surgical Weight Loss Center receive award recognition, and the hospital as a whole is recognized by *U.S. News & World Report* as the best regional hospital.

HOSPITAL OF CENTRAL CONNECTICUT
100 Grand St.
New Britain, CT 06052
(860) 224-5011
thocc.org
With campuses in New Britain and at the Bradley Memorial Hospital in Southington (860-276-5000), the Hospital of Central Connecticut employs 3,500 people and benefits the community with quality facilities and a commitment to education and research. Among the 13 specialty centers at HCC you'll find ones for endocrine and bone health, vascular health, joint and spine health, wound care, and sleep disorders. The All Heart Cardiac Rehabilitation program was the first such program in Connecticut.

JOHNSON MEMORIAL HOSPITAL
201 Chestnut Hill Rd.
Stafford Springs, CT 06076
(860) 684-4251
jmmc.com
Johnson Memorial Hospital is part of the larger Johnson Memorial Medical Center, with facilities in both Stafford Springs and Enfield. The hospital partners with other local centers, like the Tolland Imaging Center, to bring a full range of services to Tolland and Hartford Counties. More than 250 physicians and over 1,000 staff members work in the main hospital and its tertiary centers. The Evergreen Health Care Center, located on the Johnson main campus, is a 180-bed skilled nursing facility providing long-term and short-term care for patients in a home-like setting.

LAWRENCE & MEMORIAL HOSPITAL
365 Montauk Ave.
New London, CT 06320
(860) 442-0711
lmhospital.org
Since it began in 1912, Lawrence & Memorial has brought health-care services to New London County. The facility has 280 beds and staffs 2,300 people. It has the region's only inpatient rehabilitation and neonatal intensive-care units. In addition to other diagnostic and therapeutic specialties, Lawrence & Memorial Hospital has a center for sleep disorders and a nationally recognized cardiac rehabilitation program. Affiliated centers like the Joslin Diabetes Center, with locations in New London, Mystic, and Old Saybrook; the Pequot Health Center in Groton; and the Dialysis Clinic in New London provide additional locations and services for the area.

MIDDLESEX HOSPITAL AND HEALTH SYSTEM
28 Crescent St.
Middletown, CT 06457
(860) 358-6000
middlesexhealth.org
Middlesex Hospital is part of the Middlesex Health System, which aims to strengthen community health in a personalized setting where patients have access to the best advancements in research and technology. Middlesex has been named one of the 100 Best Hospitals in the nation by Thomson Reuters, and it is the only facility in the state

to win the Magna Award for nursing excellence. Hospital services are extensive and include a primary-care network, the Center for Advanced Surgery, chronic-care management, occupational and environmental medicine, and nephrology department, as well as many others. Affiliates Marlborough Medical Center and Shoreline Medical Center in Essex both offer emergency care and other services, giving patients in Middlesex County additional health-care options.

MIDSTATE MEDICAL CENTER
435 Lewis Ave.
Meriden, CT 06451
(203) 694-8200
midstatemedical.org
MidState Medical Center puts patient care above all else and is committed to bringing the most advanced procedures to the midstate region. With 144 beds, MidState Medical is the only hospital in the state with all private rooms. Among the 19 clinical services, the hospital is home to the Palladino Family Cancer Center, the Family Birthing Center, the Diabetes and Nutrition Center, and the Balance and Hearing Institute. The MediQuick Urgent Care Center helps alleviate the number of emergency room cases by treating mild injuries and illnesses quickly.

MILFORD HOSPITAL
300 Seaside Ave.
Milford, CT 06460
(203) 876-4000
milfordhospital.org
Milford Hospital is a 106-bed facility that employs over 300 physicians. It provides a full range of services to New Haven and Fairfield County residents. A recent $28 million renovation ensures patients are treated in modern facilities with the most advanced technological innovations. The emergency and urgent-care center sees upward of 12,000 people a year. Other award-winning centers include the Connecticut Joint Center, the Family Childbirth Center, and the Advanced Wound Care Center. The hospital was the first in the state to invest in 3-D and 4-D imaging for radiology screening.

NEW MILFORD HOSPITAL
21 Elm St.
New Milford, CT 06776
(860) 585-7198
newmilfordhospital.org
New Milford Hospital is part of the Western Connecticut Health Network and is affiliated with Danbury Hospital. The facility has 85 beds and offers acute and outpatient care to more than 100 communities in Litchfield and Fairfield Counties. The hospital has one of the highest nurse-to-patient ratios in the state, and the Regional Cancer Center is one of the best oncology programs in Connecticut. Other services include emergency and one-day surgery, sleep medicine, orthopedics, the Family Birth Center, and the Regional Heart Center. The hospital also ranks high in patient satisfaction.

NORWALK HOSPITAL
34 Maple St.
Norwalk, CT 06850
(203) 852-2000
norwalkhospital.org
Norwalk Hospital, with 328 beds, 500 doctors, and a staff of over 2,000, serves more than a quarter million people in lower Fairfield County. The hospital has earned awards for clinical excellence as well as in the fields of surgery and heart attack care. In addition to other clinical services, Norwalk excels in the programs for cancer, cardiovascular care, digestive diseases, emergency care, orthopedics and neurospine, and women's and children's care. It serves as one of the teaching hospitals of the Yale University School of Medicine.

ST. FRANCIS HOSPITAL AND MEDICAL CENTER
114 Woodland St.
Hartford, CT 06105
(860) 714-4000
stfranciscare.org

The 617-bed St. Francis Hospital is the largest Catholic hospital in New England. In 1990 St. Francis became affiliated with Mt. Sinai Hospital, making it the first time a Catholic and Jewish hospital merged. Among the many centers for excellence are the Connecticut Joint Replacement Institute and the Hoffman Heart and Vascular Institute of Connecticut, the first comprehensive heart institute in southern New England, as well as the Mandell Center for Multiple Sclerosis Care and Neuroscience Research located at 490 Blue Hills Ave. in Hartford. The hospital was founded in 1897 and recently completed a 318,000-square-foot addition.

i With the passage of the Affordable Care Act, Connecticut opened Access Health, the state's Official Health Insurance Marketplace. For information and enrollment options, call (855) 805-4325 or visit AccessHealthCT.com.

ST. MARY'S HOSPITAL
56 Franklin St.
Waterbury, CT 06706
(203) 709-6000
stmh.org

St. Mary's Hospital and the St. Mary's Health System provide services to the residents of Waterbury and the Central Naugatuck Valley. Founded in 1907, St. Mary's is a vital part of the greater Waterbury community, employing 1,800 people and providing services through the hospital and affiliate programs. In addition to a full range of other services, St. Mary's offers emergency and Level II trauma care; wound healing, medical imaging, and sleep disorder centers; behavioral health care; and pulmonary rehabilitation. Walk-in wellness centers are located in Wolcott and Naugatuck.

ST. VINCENT'S MEDICAL CENTER
2800 Main St.
Bridgeport, CT 06606
(203) 576-6000
stvincents.org

St. Vincent's Medical Center is part of St. Vincent's Health Services, which has many facets, including Behavioral Health Services in Westport and St. Vincent's College. The 473-bed facility is a teaching hospital affiliated with the University of Connecticut School of Medicine and New York Medical College. It has been ranked as one of the top 100 hospitals in the nation, and key services include treatment for cardiovascular diseases and cancer at the SWIM Center for Cancer Care. Other services include orthopedic and weight-loss surgery; geriatric, women's, and family services; and behavioral health services.

SHARON HOSPITAL
50 Hospital Hill Rd.
Sharon, CT 06069
(860) 364-4000
sharonhospital.com

In 2015 Sharon Hospital will celebrate 105 years of service. Combining the personal touch of a community hospital with the technological know-how needed for 21st-century health care, Sharon Hospital serves Northwest Connecticut, working with larger regional facilities to provide a full range of services. Among the specialty centers are the Center for Women's Health, the Center for Vein Therapy, and the Stroke Center. The Center for Wound Care & Hyperbaric Medicine opened in 2011.

STAMFORD HOSPITAL

30 Shelburne Rd.
Stamford, CT 06904
(203) 276-1000
stamfordhospital.org

Stamford Hospital, with 305 beds, serves lower Fairfield County and is affiliated with the New York Presbyterian Health System and Columbia University's College of Physicians and Surgeons. With superior programs in cancer care, orthopedics, and women's health, Stamford Hospital also has 13 specialty centers, including the Cyberknife Center, Infectious Disease Division, Children's Specialty Center, and Center for Integrative Health and Wellness. The Bennett Cancer Center earned the 2013 outstanding achievement award from the Commission on Cancer.

UNIVERSITY OF CONNECTICUT HEALTH CENTER (UCONN HEALTH)

263 Farmington Ave.
Farmington, CT 06030
(860) 679-2000
uchc.edu

The UConn Health Center is the teaching hospital of the University of Connecticut, and the Farmington facility includes the School of Medicine, the Dental School, and the John Dempsey Hospital, as well as the Academic Research, Medical Arts and Research, and the Cell and Genome Sciences Buildings. The John Dempsey Hospital has emergency care facilities and is noted for maternal fetal medicine, cardiology, orthopedics, and cancer care programs. The UConn Health Center employs over 5,000 people, providing a vibrant and important economic participant in the region. Continued growth and expansion is planned for the health center, funded in part by Bioscience Connecticut—an initiative started in 2011 by the General Assembly that aims to boost economic growth in the fields of bioscience research and technology.

VA CONNECTICUT HEALTHCARE SYSTEM

Newington Campus
555 Willard Ave.
Newington, CT 06111
(860) 666-6951
West Haven Campus
950 Campbell Ave.
West Haven, CT 06514
(203) 932-5711
connecticut.va.gov

The United States Department of Veterans Affairs funds two Connecticut hospitals, in Newington and West Haven. Inpatient and ambulatory care are available in the West Haven Center, and Newington also provides ambulatory care. The VA is affiliated with the Yale University School of Medicine and the University of Connecticut Schools of Medicine and Dentistry. There are six outpatient clinics, located in Danbury, New London, Stamford, Waterbury, Windham, and Winsted.

WATERBURY HOSPITAL

64 Robbins St.
Waterbury, CT 06708
(203) 573-6000
waterburyhospital.org

Waterbury Hospital is part of the Greater Waterbury Health Network and offers a full range of inpatient and outpatient services. The network has the largest outpatient center for physical, occupational, and speech therapy in the region. Waterbury Hospital offers services in emergency and advanced care, orthopedics, behavioral health, cardiology, and surgery. The gynecological services provided through the Family Birthing Center make Waterbury Hospital the only hospital in the region to offer a full range of reproductive services. It is the second-largest employer in the city.

WINDHAM HOSPITAL
112 Mansfield Ave.
Willimantic, CT 06226
(860) 456-9116
windhamhospital.org

A partner of Hartford Health, Windham Hospital began in 1908 as St. Joseph's Hospital. Since then the nonsectarian hospital has expanded and now serves 19 communities in the eastern part of the state. Services include cancer and cardiology care, diabetes education, and sleep health and pain management services. Windham Hospital's Integrative Health Services offerings include acupuncture and Chinese medicine, meditation, and yoga. Med-East Medical Walk-in centers are in Willimantic and Tolland.

YALE–NEW HAVEN HOSPITAL AND HEALTH SYSTEM MAIN HOSPITAL
20 York St.
New Haven, CT 06510
(203) 688-4242
ynhh.org

With over 8,500 employees, including nearly 4,000 community and resident physicians and 1,200 registered nurses, Yale–New Haven Hospital is the second-largest employer in New Haven. It is the main teaching facility of the Yale School of Medicine, and over 100 specialties are practiced. Founded in 1826, the hospital has 966 beds. In addition to the hospital being recognized for its clinical research, the Smilow Cancer Center, the Psychiatric Hospital, and the Children's Hospital routinely rank among the nation's best specialty facilities. Yale–New Haven Hospital is part of the Yale New Haven Health System, which includes Bridgeport Hospital, Greenwich Hospital, and the Northeast Medical Group, a physician group that includes hospital and community doctors.

SAINT RAPHAEL CAMPUS
1450 Chapel St.
New Haven, CT 06511

In 2012 Yale–New Haven Hospital merged with Saint Raphael's Hospital, making it one of the largest hospitals in the country. The Saint Raphael campus incorporates more than 500 additional beds and increased services. Saint Raphael's maintains its list of services and programs, including robotic surgery, the Bone and Joint Center, and the TakeHeart Cardiovascular Health Center, as well as rehabilitation services, physical therapy, and diagnostic testing.

MEDIA

Television Stations

Each of the major networks (NBC, CBS, ABC, FOX, and PBS) is represented by a Connecticut station. Other network affiliates, including Univision (UNI—Spanish language television), ION television (formerly PAX TV), and MyNetworkTV (MNT), all have licenses in Connecticut cities. An all-news local cable channel, News Channel 12, is sponsored by Cablevision and based out of Norwalk. Depending on your cable system, actual channels will vary, and in many parts of the state, you may pick up New York, Rhode Island, or Massachusetts local news stations. Local-affiliate stations broadcast local and breaking news, weather, sports, community information, health reports, and entertainment and style news. All have active online websites and HD offerings. ESPN, the cable sports network owned by the Walt Disney Company, has its headquarters in Bristol.

CONNECTICUT PUBLIC TELEVISION (CPTV)
Connecticut Public Broadcasting
1049 Asylum Ave.
Hartford, CT 06105
(860) 275-7550
cpbn.org

PBS-affiliate stations are under the umbrella of Connecticut Public Television, owned by the Connecticut Public Broadcasting Company, which also runs Connecticut Public Radio. Local stations are WEDN, licensed in New Haven; WEDY, out of Norwich; WEDH, from Hartford; and WEDW, in Bridgeport. Connecticut Public Broadcasting produces noncommercial, educational radio, print, and web programs, the only locally owned media group to generate all three. Many popular children's programs as well as shows like *Scientific American Frontiers* have been produced by CPTV. CPTV also has live streaming of UConn women's basketball games. CPTV also sponsors four cable networks, including CPTV Kids and CPTV Sports.

ESPN

935 Middle St.
Bristol, CT 06010
(860) 766-2000
espn.com

The leading sports broadcaster on cable, ESPN transmits from its Connecticut headquarters in Bristol. It has been called one of the most innovative companies by Fast Company rankings, and its 116-acre facility employs over 4,000 people.

WFSB TV-3

333 Capital Blvd.
Rocky Hill, CT 06067
(860) 728-3333
wfsb.com

WFSB Channel 3 is the CBS affiliate out of Hartford, with studios in Rocky Hill and a transmitter on Talcott Mountain in Avon. WFSB's show *Better Connecticut* airs weekdays at 3 p.m. *Eyewitness News* airs from 4:30 to 7 a.m., and also at 5, 5:30, 6, and 11 p.m.

WTIC-TV—FOX CT

285 Broad St.
Hartford, CT 06511
(860) 527-6161
ctnow.com

WTIC began in 1984 as an independent entertainment station; then, under the ownership of the Tribune Company, which also owns the *Hartford Courant,* it became the affiliate for the Fox Broadcasting Company. News, traffic, weather, and local features are presented during morning broadcasts from 4:30 to 9 a.m., 11 a.m., 10 p.m., and 11 p.m.

WTNH TV-8

8 Elm St.
New Haven, CT 06510
(203) 784-8888
wtnh.com

WTNH TV-8 is the ABC affiliate out of New Haven and has additional newsrooms in Hartford and New London. The station teams with WCTX, a syndicated MyNetworkTV (formerly the UPN then the CW) station, for MY TV 9 and airs primetime news at 10 p.m. WTNH is the state's oldest television station and second only to WBZ in Boston as the earliest New England station. Anchor Ann Nyberg sponsors Network Connecticut, an interactive website that features events, recommendations, and local businesses (networkconnecticut.com).

WVIT NBC CONNECTICUT

1422 New Britain Ave.
West Hartford, CT 06110
(860) 521-3030
nbcconnecticut.com

Tagged as NBC Connecticut News or NBC Connecticut HD, the station is licensed in New Britain and also has studios in Hartford and its transmitter in Farmington. It is the second-oldest station in the state, beginning in 1953. The Troubleshooters investigate local problems and bring issues to the public's attention.

Cable Service

Four companies provide service to Connecticut residents. Depending on your region, your cable provider may be Cablevision (cablevision.com), Charter Communications (charter.com), Comcast (comcast.com), or Cox Communications (cox.com). Try cablemovers.com to input your zip code and find the cable service company in your area. Most offer packages for Internet, phone, and cable service, as do many of the major phone companies, like Frontier, Sprint, and Verizon. Dish Network and Direct TV provide satellite dish service.

Print Media

Magazines
COASTAL CONNECTICUT
91 Riverview Rd.
Suite 4B
Niantic, CT 06475
(203) 767-7342
coastalctmag.com
With its inaugural issue in the fall of 2013, *Coastal Connecticut magazine* is a beautiful addition to the state's magazines. The content focuses on the 21 beach towns along the coast, and there's plenty of insightful and enthusiastic writing about the region's values, people, and events. While an online version is available, Coastal Connecticut deserves to be seen in print. It's available at local establishments from New Haven to Niantic and by subscription.

THE CONNECTICUT BRIDE
100 Gando Dr.
New Haven, CT 06513
(203) 789-5300
theconnecticutbride.com
Everything a bride needs is found in The *Connecticut Bride* magazine. Published by Connecticut Magazine Media, you'll find planning resources, reception ideas, fashion and beauty tips, cake and flower advice, and honeymoon suggestions. Prospective brides can find the magazine at bridal expos, bookstores, newsstands, bridal shops, and salons. The magazine distributes 25,000 copies each edition.

CONNECTICUT BUILDER
1078 Main St., Unit 4
Branford, CT 06405
(203) 453-5420
connecticutbuilder.com
Connecticut Builder is the official magazine of the Home Builders and Remodelers Association of Connecticut. It's geared as a trade magazine for builders, remodelers, and developers.

CONNECTICUT COTTAGES AND GARDENS
Cottages & Gardens Publications
142 East Ave.
North Building, 2nd Floor
Norwalk, CT 06851
(203) 227-1400
cottages-gardens.com/
Connecticut-Cottages-Gardens
Circulating 35,000 copies per edition, *Connecticut Cottages and Gardens* includes features about design and style, real estate, shopping, and events.

CONNECTICUT MAGAZINE
100 Gando Dr.
New Haven, CT 06513
(203) 789-5300
connecticutmag.com
The state's leading magazine, *Connecticut Magazine* has more than 340,000 readers and is distributed statewide. The monthly magazine contains articles and features, a thorough listing of events and activities, shopping and home and garden resources, reviews of restaurants, and readers' choice and best-of awards. It also regularly

highlights top Connecticut doctors, dentists, high schools, towns, and places to retire.

CONNECTICUT PARENT MAGAZINE
420 E. Main St., Ste. 18
Branford, CT 06405
(203) 483-1700
ctparent.com

Connecticut Parent is distributed to more than 1,250 locations, including libraries, public schools, doctors' offices, and child-care centers. It contains a directory of child-care facilities, including preschool and Montessori schools as well as independent schools. Resources include articles about pertinent educational topics, activity calendars, and a travel, health, and enrichment directory that lists dance, sports, language, theater, and special needs programs.

EVENTS QUARTERLY MAGAZINES
18 Industrial Park Rd.
PO Box 386
Centerbrook, CT 06409
(860) 767-9087
essexprinting.com

The Essex Printing Company publishes quarterly magazines for the towns of Branford, Chester, Clinton, East Haddam, East Lyme, Essex, Guilford, Haddam, Madison, Montville, Old Lyme, Old Saybrook, Westbrook, and Woodbridge. The full-color magazines feature town news and information, and in total reach about 83,000 people in the Connecticut River Valley and shoreline areas.

FAIRFIELD COUNTY MAGAZINES
Fairfield County alone has over 20 magazines devoted to lifestyle, leisure, and events. For example, Moffly Media publishes a number of magazines that highlight lifestyle, the social scene, dining, home and garden, travel, health, and weddings for the towns of Fairfield County. Town-centered magazines are *Fairfield, Greenwich, New Canaan, Darien,* *Stamford,* and *Westport.* They also publish *At Home in Fairfield County.*

LITCHFIELD COUNTY MAGAZINES

LITCHFIELD MAGAZINE
Morris Media Group
386 Main Street
Ridgefield, CT 06877
(203) 431-1708
townvibe.com/litchfield

Morris Media publishes magazines about Litchfield, Fairfield, Wilton, Ridgefield, Berkshire, and Bedford, NY. They focus on lifestyle issues, animals, gardens, food, and everything you'd want to know about living well. They also run blogs for Litchfield and other towns.

HARTFORD COUNTY MAGAZINES

HARTFORD MAGAZINE
106 South St.
West Hartford, CT 06110
(860) 953-0444
hartfordmag.com

Published by the Hartford *Courant,* *Hartford Magazine* features coverage of lifestyle, arts, sports, politics, health and fitness, and restaurants for the capital city.

NEW HAVEN & MIDDLESEX COUNTY MAGAZINES

NEW HAVEN MAGAZINE
Second Wind Media Ltd.
20 Grand Ave.
New Haven, CT 06513
(203) 781-3480
newhavenmagazine.com

New Haven Magazine features community information and resources for the city. Business news, health-care issues, and arts and culture news join feature articles.

NATURAL NEW HAVEN/NATURAL AWAKENINGS MAGAZINE
PO Box 525
North Branford, CT 06471
(203) 988-1808
naturalnewhaven.com
Natural New Haven is published by Natural Awakenings and provides health and wellness information for New Haven and Middlesex Counties. Available in print as a free monthly magazine and online, you'll find local news and events, as well as health, fitness, and nutrition information.

MAJOR CONNECTICUT NEWSPAPERS
As print media struggles, online news and general interest sites help keep Connecticut residents informed and up to date, minute by minute. All the major newspapers provide online content and updates, and a number of news outlets are exclusively online. Often content that doesn't make it to the print version, like entertainment, events, and community news, can be accessed online.

CONNECTICUT POST
410 Lafayette Blvd.
Bridgeport, CT 06604
(203) 333-0161
ctpost.com
Southwestern Connecticut's largest newspaper, the *Connecticut Post* began 1908 when it was called the *Bridgeport Post*. It has a weekly circulation of 53,000 readers, the third largest in the state.

DANBURY NEWS-TIMES
333 Main St.
Danbury, CT 06810
(203) 744-5100
newstimes.com
The *News-Times* covers Fairfield County and the southwestern part of the state, including the towns of Brookfield, New Fairfield, Newtown, Bethel, Ridgefield, Redding, Roxbury, New Milford, Sherman, and Kent. It has a circulation of about 30,000.

HARTFORD COURANT
285 Broad St.
Hartford, CT 06115
(860) 241-6200
courant.com
Started as a weekly paper in 1747, the *Courant* is the country's oldest continuously published newspaper. Daily publication began in 1837, and today the paper has a circulation of over 200,000. Most of its readers are located north of New Haven and east of Waterbury. Register online for Digital Plus, which provides additional content and photos.

MERIDEN RECORD-JOURNAL
11 Crown St.
Meriden, CT 06450
(203) 235-1661
myrecordjournal.com
The *Record-Journal* dates back to 1867 and covers central Connecticut, including the towns of Meriden, Wallingford, Southington, Cheshire, and Berlin. The website receives 700,000 visits per month.

NEW HAVEN REGISTER
100 Gando Dr.
New Haven, CT 06513
(203) 789-5200
nhregister.com
As the second-largest newspaper in the state in terms of circulation (about 89,000), the *New Haven Register* covers 19 towns in New Haven and Middlesex Counties.

THE DAY (NEW LONDON)
The Day Publishing Company
47 Eugene O'Neill Dr.
PO Box 1231
New London, CT 06320
(800) 542-3354
theday.com

The Day serves 20 towns in eastern Connecticut, and has won the Newspaper of the Year and Best Daily Newspaper awards. It was established in 1881 and has a weekly and Sunday circulation of nearly 100,000. The Day Publishing Company also publishes *Mystic County Magazine* and other tourism-market and community weekly magazines.

WATERBURY REPUBLICAN-AMERICAN
389 Meadow St.
PO Box 2090
Waterbury, CT 06722
(800) 992-3232
rep-am.com

Serving the 108,000 people of Waterbury and its surrounding towns, as well as the Naugatuck Valley and Litchfield County, the *Republican-American* has a circulation of 61,000.

OTHER REGIONAL NEWSPAPERS

BRISTOL PRESS
188 Main St.
Bristol, CT 06110
(860) 584-0501
bristolpress.com

This paper provides local news for Bristol, Plymouth, Plainville, Terryville, Thomaston, and Burlington. The Bristol Press also publishes the *Newington Town Crier*, the *Wethersfield Post*, and the *New Britain Herald*. The *Herald* offers *Polska Edyca,* the Polish edition of the paper in print and online.

JOURNAL INQUIRER
306 Progress Dr.
PO Box 510
Manchester, CT 06045
(860) 646-0500
journalinquirer.com

The *Journal Inquirer* is the hometown newspaper for north-central Connecticut, including the towns of Coventry, East Hartford, Enfield, Manchester, South Winsor, Tolland, Vernon, and Windsor.

NORWICH BULLETIN
66 Franklin St.
Norwich, CT 06360
(860) 887-9211
norwichbulletin.com

The *Bulletin* serves Norwich, Colchester, Hebron, and the surrounding towns in Windham and New London Counties. They also publish *Norwich Magazine*.

REGISTER CITIZEN
59 Field St.
PO Box 58
Torrington, CT 06790
(860) 489-3121
registercitizen.com

The *Register Citizen* is the local paper for Torrington, Winsted, and the other towns of Litchfield County.

STAMFORD ADVOCATE
9A Riverbend Dr. South
PO Box 9307
Stamford, CT 06907
(203) 964-2200
stamfordadvocate.com

A daily newspaper, the *Advocate* and its sister paper, the *Greenwich Time,* are published by the Hearst Corporation, which also publishes the *Connecticut Post* and the *Danbury News-Times. The Advocate*'s daily circulation is about 15,000; on Sunday it is nearly 25,000.

Radio

There are 106 stations that broadcast within Connecticut, with 40 of these on the AM dial. Whatever your tastes—classical, adult contemporary, variety, country, news and talk, educational, urban contemporary, alternative, classic hits, popular hits, or oldies—there's a radio station for you. Most stations are funded by media conglomerates.

However, many of the more unusual formats are found on local stations with limited reach. Some are supported by educational institutes like the Monroe, Westport, and Berlin boards of education.

Free-form high school radio is available from Pomfret High School (91.1 FM), Somers High School (89.7 FM), and Choate Rosemary Hall (89.9 FM). University stations are operated or licensed by Asnuntuck Community College (WACC-LP 107.7 FM), Central Connecticut University (WFCS 107.7 FM), Connecticut College (WCNI 90.9 FM), Eastern Connecticut State University (WECS 90.1 FM), Fairfield University (WVOF 88.5 FM), Quinnipiac University (WQAQ 98.1 FM and WQUN 1200 AM), Sacred Heart University (WSHU 91.1 FM and 1260 AM), Trinity College (WRTC-FM 89.3 FM), University of Hartford (WWUH 91.3 FM), University of New Haven (WNHU 88.7 FM), University of Connecticut Storrs (WHUS 91.7 FM—the nation's oldest campus station), Wesleyan University (WESU 88.1 FM), Western Connecticut State University (WXCI 91.7 FM), and Yale University (WYBC 94.3 FM and 1340 AM).

Avoid some of the predictable playlists of mainstream stations and seek out the more assorted options of independent ones. WPKN 89.5 FM, which broadcasts from Bridgeport, is one of the few truly independent stations in the nation. WPKN is 100 percent commercial free and listener funded. Programming is eclectic, and you're likely to hear everything from the blues to reggae to progressive talk. Connecticut Public Broadcasting sponsors four radio stations: WPKT, servicing Meriden, Hartford, and New Haven (90.5 FM); WNPR in Norwich and New London (89.1 FM); WEDW out of Stamford and Greenwich (88.5 FM); and WRLI-FM, which is actually broadcast from Southampton, New York (91.3 FM). These are affiliated with National Public Radio and are listener supported.

INDEX

INDEX